MANUAL OF THE GRASSES OF THE WEST INDIES

BY

A. S. HITCHCOCK
Principal Botanist Division of Plant Exploration and Introduction
Bureau of Plant Industry

Miscellaneous Publication No. 243
United States Department of Agriculture

GYAN

Published by

GYAN

Gyan Publishing House
5, Ansari Road
Daryaganj, New Delhi-110002
Phone: 011-47034999, 9811692060
E-mail: books@gyanbooks.com

Distribution Network
gyanbooks.com
India, USA, Canada, UK, Australia, France

ISBN : 978-81-212-2251-8 (HB)
First Published, 1936

2nd Impression 2021

Printed at: Gyan Press, Delhi.

Manual of the Grasses of the West Indies
Author: A. S. Hitchcock

Manual of the Grasses of the West Indies

By A. S. HITCHCOCK
Principal Botanist
Division of Plant Exploration and Introduction
Bureau of Plant Industry

Miscellaneous Publication No. 243
United States Department of Agriculture

UNITED STATES
GOVERNMENT PRINTING OFFICE
WASHINGTON : 1936

For sale by the Superintendent of Documents, Washington, D. C. . . . . Price $1.25 (Buckram)

UNITED STATES DEPARTMENT OF AGRICULTURE
MISCELLANEOUS PUBLICATION No. 243

Washington, D. C. November 1936

MANUAL OF THE GRASSES OF THE WEST INDIES

By A. S. Hitchcock,[1] *principal botanist, Division of Plant Exploration and Introduction, Bureau of Plant Industry*

CONTENTS

	Page
Introduction	1
Economic grasses	2
Gramineae (Poaceae), the grass family	3
Descriptions of the subfamilies and keys to the tribes	5
Descriptions of the tribes and keys to the genera	6
Descriptions of genera and species	14
List of new genera and species, and new names	427
Index	429

INTRODUCTION

More than 15 years ago the author and his associate, Agnes Chase, published a synoptical account of the grasses of the West Indies.[2] Since the publication of that work a large amount of material has been added to the grass collection of the National Herbarium. The additions are from various sources, but consist chiefly of grasses collected in Cuba and Hispaniola by the late Erik L. Ekman, in Haiti by Emery C. Leonard, of the United States National Herbarium, and in Cuba by Brother Léon, of the Colegio de la Salle, Habana.

The present publication is more than a revision of the earlier work. In the first work the descriptions of genera and species were abbreviated for the most part to diagnoses and, although the known ranges of the species were given, there was no citation of specimens. The present work gives fuller descriptions, with at least one species of each genus illustrated,[3] and cites specimens under each species, except for the few very common ones that are found throughout the region covered. The ranges of the species can now be indicated with much more exactness than was possible at the earlier date.

Considering the amount of attention given to the flora of the West Indies in earlier years the number of new species discovered and now described for the first time is unexpectedly large. However, the new species come for the most part from Hispaniola, the interior of which, until recently, has not been accessible, and from the larger island of

[1] Died Dec. 16, 1935.
[2] Contrib. U. S. Natl. Herb. 18: 261–471. 1917.
[3] The habit drawings were mostly made by the late Mary Wright Gill and by Edna May Whitehorn. However, B. Y. Morrison, Mrs. George M. Mullett, and Agnes Chase each contributed a few. The spikelet drawings are by Agnes Chase.

Cuba, which, though fairly well known to botanists, had many out-of-the-way places that have yielded species of local distribution.

There are a few changes in names due to an increased knowledge of the taxonomy of the grass family, and several other changes have been made because the earlier work followed the American code whereas the present work is in accord with the International Rules of Botanical Nomenclature.

As in the earlier work, the term "West Indies" as here used includes not only the West Indies proper but also Bermuda, the Bahamas, Trinidad, and Tobago, but excludes the Dutch islands off the coast of Venezuela.

ECONOMIC GRASSES

The principal economic grasses of the West Indies are sugarcane and rice. Corn (*Zea mays*) is also widely grown, and grasses furnish the greater part of the forage for domestic animals.

FORAGE GRASSES

Only a few grasses are grown for forage. Hay is seldom produced because green forage is usually available throughout the year. Much of the fodder is cut and fed while fresh. Many native species are utilized for pasture. Among them are Bermuda grass and several species of *Paspalum* and of *Axonopus*. The cultivated species are the following:

Guinea grass (*Panicum maximum*). An erect rather robust perennial, propagated usually by division of the clump. Widespread at low altitudes as an escape from cultivation, Guinea grass is used for pasture and is cut and fed green. It is a native of Africa but is now distributed throughout the Tropics of both hemispheres. In Cuba it is called hierba Guinea.

Pará grass (*Panicum purpurascens*). A straggling perennial forming a tangled mass along the banks of streams and ditches. Pará grass is easily propagated from cuttings of the stems or from the long runners. It is used for pasture on wet land and is cut and fed green. It is widespread in the lowland Tropics of America and to a less extent in the Tropics of the Old World. Other common names are: Paraná, Dutch grass, Scotch grass, hierba Paral, hierba bruja, and malojilla, though the latter name applies more properly to *Eriochloa polystachya*.

Malojilla (mal-o-héya) (*Eriochloa polystachya*). This grass resembles Pará grass but differs in the spikelet characters. It grows in the same kind of habitat as does Pará grass and is not infrequently found growing with it. Malojilla is found rather commonly in Puerto Rico and infrequently in a few other islands. It appears to have the same forage value as Pará grass. In the United States this grass has been called Carib grass.

Sudan grass (*Sorghum vulgare* var. *sudanense*). An annual commonly grown in the southern United States and now rather frequently cultivated for green forage on the larger estates in the West Indies, especially in Cuba. Other sorghums, such as sorgo (sweet sorghum), kafir, and durra, are occasionally grown for green forage.

Napier grass (*Pennisetum purpureum*). This common tropical African forage grass was introduced rather recently into the semitropical parts of the United States and has been tried at several experiment stations in tropical America. It is now coming into favor for green feed on the larger estates. This grass is often known as elephant grass. It is a robust perennial growing to the height of 2 to 4 m.

Pearl millet (*Pennisetum glaucum; P. typhoideum*). This robust annual is grown extensively by the natives of tropical Africa, and is used rather sparingly in the southern United States. It is occasionally grown in the West Indies.

Paspalum (*Paspalum dilatatum*). This grass comes from Argentina. It is a perennial, 30 to 100 cm tall (1 to 3 feet), growing in moderately dry to moist soil. It was introduced several years ago into the southern United States, where it is used for pasture and hay. It seems well adapted to conditions in the West Indies and its culture will probably increase there. It can be propagated by seed or by division of the tufts. In the United States this grass is called Dallis grass (after Mr. Dallis who was active in its introduction). Other common names are paspalum grass, water-grass, and water paspalum. Paspalum has proved valuable in Australia, South Africa, and especially in the Hawaiian Islands.

Vasey grass (*Paspalum urvillei; P. vaseyanum*). An erect perennial related to the preceding species but with a longer panicle. It has been grown occasionally in the West Indies on moderately dry ground and can be used for pasture. Vasey grass was introduced some years ago from Argentina, and is now commonly escaped into fields and waste places in the southern United States.

Bahia grass (*Paspalum notatum*). A low perennial with knotty rhizomes that soon form a firm sod. It is a native of Brazil and other parts of tropical America, where it is a constituent of native pasture land. It is now being cultivated for pasture in Central America and the subtropical United States. It gives much promise in the West Indies, especially in Cuba.

Carpet grass (*Axonopus compressus*). This is a common grass in open land at low altitudes throughout tropical America. In the United States it extends along the Coastal Plain from North Carolina to Texas. Carpet grass is one of the chief constituents of native pasture land in moist or mucky soil throughout the West Indies. It is propagated by division of the roots. It is a very satisfactory lawngrass in the Tropics where there is sufficient moisture.

Bermuda grass (*Cynodon dactylon*). This well-known species is widespread throughout the warm regions of the earth. It thrives on drier soil than is suitable for carpet grass. Bermuda grass may become a troublesome weed in cultivated soil because of its vigorous rhizomes and stolons, but as a pasture grass in open moderately dry soil it is without a competitor. It is also commonly used for lawns. In the English islands it is usually called Bahama grass. In the Spanish islands it is called grama, hierba fina, hierba del prado, pata de gallina, and several other names. A common French name is chiendent, and throughout the world it has a great variety of names.

Rhodes grass (*Chloris gayana*). This African grass was introduced into the United States several years ago and proved of value for hay and pasture in the irrigated sections of the Southwest. It is also used on the ranches of Hawaii. Rhodes grass has been tried in the West Indies and gives promise in drier regions.

Molasses grass (*Melinis minutiflora*). This African grass was early introduced into Brazil and has been used there extensively as a pasture grass. More recently it has spread northward and is now rather frequently seen in the West Indies. It escapes readily into brushland and soon furnishes much forage in such situations. Other names for this grass are catingueiro, yaragua, gordura, honey grass, Wynne grass, and Brazilian grass. The grass has a strong rather pleasant odor when fresh.

Natal grass (*Tricholaena repens; T. rosea*). A native of Africa, now widely introduced in tropical and subtropical regions of North America. It is very common in Florida where it furnishes forage on sandy lands that will grow little else. It is becoming common in the West Indies, and will be useful on light sandy lands. It is called Natal redtop in the Hawaiian Islands and wine grass in Cuba. The pink inflorescence in a mass is an attractive sight.

Jaraguá (*Hyparrhenia rufa*). An Old World grass early introduced into Brazil (there called capim jaraguá) where it is useful as a forage grass. In recent years it has been tried in the southern United States and is occasionally cultivated in the West Indies.

GRASSES FOR OTHER PURPOSES THAN FOR FORAGE

Sugarcane (*Saccharum officinarum*) and rice (*Oryza sativa*) are the important standard agricultural crops.

Indian corn or maize, and the small grains, wheat, oats, rye, and barley, are grown more or less, the small grains only at upper elevations.

Certain oil grasses are met with here and there but are not grown on a commercial scale. These are citronella grass (*Cymbopogon nardus*) and lemon grass (*C. citratus*), found around dwellings, and vetiver (*Vetiveria zizanioides*), more commonly grown as a hedge plant. The aromatic roots of the latter are used in perfumery.

Wild cane (*Gynerium sagittatum*). A giant grass native in swampy places throughout the West Indies. The stems are used by the natives for lattices and light building purposes. In Cuba it is called caña de Castillo.

Giant reed (*Arundo donax*). A native of the Mediterranean region introduced in the warmer parts of North America, and now frequent in the West Indies along river banks and in moist soil. The stems are used for lattices and minor construction work. In Cuba it is called "güín."

The large bamboo (*Bambusa vulgaris*) is commonly cultivated around dwellings. The hollow stems with cross partitions are used for a great many purposes. The large species of bamboos are known in Cuba as caña brava. The bamboos are a promising source for paper. *Dendrocalamus strictus*, with nearly solid stems, is sometimes cultivated.

GRAMINEAE (POACEAE), THE GRASS FAMILY

Flowers perfect (rarely unisexual), small, with no distinct perianth, arranged in spikelets consisting of a shortened axis (rachilla) and 2 to many 2-ranked bracts, the lowest two being empty (the glumes, rarely one or both obsolete), the one or more succeeding ones (lemmas) bearing in their axils a single flower, and, between the flower and the rachilla a second 2-nerved bract (the palea), the lemma, palea, and flower together constituting the floret; stamens 1 to 6, usually 3, with very delicate filaments and 2-celled anthers; pistil 1, with a 1-celled 1-ovuled ovary, 2 (rarely 1 or 3) styles, and usually plumose stigmas; fruit a caryopsis with starchy endosperm and a small embryo at the base on the side opposite the hilum.

Herbs, or rarely woody plants, with hollow or solid stems (culms) closed at the nodes, and 2-ranked usually parallel-veined leaves, these consisting of two parts, the sheath, enveloping the culm, its margins overlapping or sometimes grown together, and the blade, usually flat; between the two on the inside, a membranaceous hyaline or hairy appendage (the ligule).

The spikelets are almost always aggregated in spikes or panicles at the ends of the main culms or branches. The perianth is usually represented by 2 (rarely 3) small hyaline scales (the lodicules) at the base of the flower inside the lemma and palea. The grain or caryopsis (the single seed and the adherent pericarp) may be free, as in wheat, or permanently enclosed in the lemma and palea, as in the oat. Rarely the seed is free from the pericarp, as in species of *Sporobolus* and *Eleusine*. The culms of bamboos are woody, as are also those of a few genera, such as *Olyra* and *Lasiacis*, belonging to other tribes. The culms are solid in the tribes Tripsaceae and Andropogoneae and in several other groups.

The parts of the spikelet may be modified in various ways. The first glume, and more rarely also the second, may be wanting. The lemmas may contain no flower, or even no palea, or may be reduced or rudimentary.

The division of the family into two subfamilies is somewhat artificial. The tribes Zoysieae, Oryzeae, Zizanieae, and especially Phalarideae, do not fall definitely into either of the recognized subfamilies. They are placed as indicated largely for convenience. The anomalous genus *Streptochaeta* cannot as yet be assigned to any established tribe.

DESCRIPTIONS OF THE SUBFAMILIES AND KEYS TO THE TRIBES

SUBFAMILY 1. FESTUCOIDEAE

Spikelets, 1- to many-flowered, the reduced florets, if any, above the perfect florets (except in Phalarideae; sterile lemmas below as well as above in Bambuseae and *Uniola*); articulation usually above the glumes; spikelets usually more or less laterally compressed.

Key to the Tribes of Festucoideae

Plants woody (scarcely so in *Neurolepis*), the culms perennial.
1. BAMBUSEAE (p. 6).

Plants herbaceous (except in *Arundo*), the culms annual.
- Stigmas 3 .... STREPTOCHAETA (p. 23).
- Stigmas 2
  - Spikelets with 2 sterile lemmas unlike and below the fertile lemma; no sterile or rudimentary floret above .... 8. PHALARIDEAE (p. 9).
  - Spikelets without sterile lemmas below the fertile floret (or these rarely present and like the fertile ones).
    - Spikelets unisexual, falling entire, 1-flowered, terete or nearly so. 10. ZIZANIEAE (p. 10).

Spikelets perfect (rarely unisexual but then not as above), usually articulate above the glumes.
  Spikelets articulate below the glumes, 1-flowered, very flat, the lemma and palea about equal, both keeled. Glumes small or wanting. 9. ORYZEAE (p. 9).
  Spikelets articulate above the glumes (rarely below, but the glumes, at least one, well developed).
    Spikelets, 1-flowered (or the staminate 2-flowered), in groups (short spikes) of 2 to 5 (single in *Zoysia*), the groups racemose along a main axis, falling entire; lemma and palea thinner than the glumes .... 6. ZOYSIEAE (p. 8).
    Spikelets not as above.
      Spikelets sessile on a usually continuous rachis (short-pedicellate in *Leptochloa;* the rachis disarticulating in *Hordeum*).
        Spikelets on opposite sides of the rachis; spike terminal, solitary. 3. HORDEAE (p. 8).
        Spikelets on one side of the rachis; spikes usually more than one, digitate or racemose .... 7. CHLORIDEAE (p. 9).
      Spikelets pediceled in open or contracted, sometimes spikelike, panicles, rarely racemes.
        Spikelets 1-flowered .... 5. AGROSTIDEAE (p. 8).
        Spikelets 2- to many-flowered.
          Glumes as long as the lowest floret, usually as long as the spikelet (sometimes shorter in *Sphenopholis*); lemmas awned from the back (awnless in *Sphenopholis*). 4. AVENEAE (p. 8).
          Glumes shorter than the first floret .... 2. FESTUCEAE (p. 7).

SUBFAMILY 2. PANICOIDEAE

Spikelets with one perfect terminal floret (disregarding those of the few monoecious genera and the staminate and neuter spikelets) and a sterile or staminate floret below, usually represented by a sterile lemma only, one glume sometimes (rarely both glumes) wanting; articulation below the spikelets, either in the pedicel, in the rachis, or at the base of a cluster of spikelets, the spikelets falling entire, singly, in groups, or together with joints of the rachis; spikelets, or at least the fruits, more or less dorsally compressed.

Key to the Tribes of Panicoideae

Glumes membranaceous, the sterile lemma like the glumes in texture.
  Fertile lemma and palea scarcely firmer than the glumes. 11. MELINIDEAE (p. 155).
  Fertile lemma and palea indurate or at least firmer than the glumes. 12. PANICEAE (p. 161).
Glumes indurate; fertile lemma and palea, hyaline or membranaceous, the sterile lemma like the fertile one in texture.
  Spikelets unisexual, the pistillate below, the staminate above, in the same inflorescence or in separate inflorescences .... 14. TRIPSACEAE (p. 423).
  Spikelets in pairs, one sessile and perfect, the other pediceled and usually staminate or neuter (the pediceled one sometimes obsolete, rarely both pediceled) .... 13. ANDROPOGONEAE (p. 376).

DESCRIPTIONS OF THE TRIBES AND KEYS TO THE GENERA

TRIBE 1. BAMBUSEAE

Culms woody, perennial, usually hollow; spikelets, 2- to several-flowered, in panicles or racemes, or in close heads or fascicles; often 1 or more sterile lemmas at base of spikelet; lemmas usually awnless; blades usually articulated with the sheath.

Culms climbing or clambering.
  Spikelets 2- to several-flowered, racemose .... 3. ARTHROSTYLIDIUM (p. 15).
  Spikelets 1-flowered, in small panicles .... 4. CHUSQUEA (p. 22).

Culms erect.
  Spikelets 1-flowered, in a long dense terminal panicle; culm herbaceous. 5. NEUROLEPIS (p. 23).
  Spikelets several- to many-flowered, sessile in clusters, these somewhat remote on a common axis; culms woody.
    Keels of palea projecting but not winged............1. BAMBUSA (p. 14).
    Keels of palea winged............2. GUADUA (p. 14).

TRIBE 2. FESTUCEAE

Spikelets, more than 1-flowered, usually several-flowered, in open, narrow, or sometimes spikelike panicles (rarely in racemes); lemmas awnless or awned from the tip, rarely from between the teeth of a bifid apex; rachilla usually disarticulating above the glumes and between the florets.

Lemmas cleft at the summit into numerous awns; panicle contracted, elongate. 24. PAPPOPHORUM (p. 59).
Lemmas with a single awn or awnless.
  Spikelets (at least the pistillate) with copious long silky hairs on the lemmas or the rachilla; tall reeds with large plumy panicles.
    Spikelets unisexual; pistillate spikelets hairy, the staminate glabrous; plants dioecious............17. GYNERIUM (p. 49).
    Spikelets perfect.
      Lemmas hairy; rachilla glabrous............18. ARUNDO (p. 50).
      Lemmas glabrous; rachilla hairy............19. PHRAGMITES (p. 50).
  Spikelets not long-hairy, the hairs if present much shorter than the lemma.
    Glumes leaflike; spikelets concealed in the upper sheaths; plants dioecious. 13. MONANTHOCHLOË (p. 45).
    Glumes not leaflike; spikelets exposed.
      Stigmas elongate, wiry, coiled, tendrillike; spikelets in a long 1-sided raceme............21. STREPTOGYNE (p. 55).
      Stigmas not elongate nor wiry.
        Blades broad, ovate to elliptic, showing transverse veins between the nerves.
          Spikelets 3- to 5-flowered; glumes broad, truncate; panicles small. 23. ZEUGITES (p. 58).
          Spikelets 1- or 2-flowered, the second floret commonly obsolete, the elongate rachilla only present; glumes acuminate; panicles large, diffuse............22. ORTHOCLADA (p. 55).
        Blades linear, no transverse veins showing.
          Spikelets in 1-sided dense clusters, these at the ends of the few stiff panicle branches............16. DACTYLIS (p. 49).
          Spikelets not in 1-sided clusters.
            Lemmas 3-nerved.
              Nerves pubescent............20. TRIODIA (p. 53).
              Nerves glabrous............12. ERAGROSTIS (p. 33).
            Lemmas 5 or more nerved.
              Lowest 1 to 4 lemmas empty; spikelets firm, strongly compressed.
                Plants hermaphrodite, usually more than 50 cm tall. 15. UNIOLA (p. 48).
                Plants dioecious, usually less than 30 cm tall. 14. DISTICHLIS (p. 47).
              Lowest lemmas fertile.
                Florets horizontally spreading; lemmas cordate at base. 11. BRIZA (p. 30).
                Florets ascending; lemmas not cordate.
                  Lemmas awnless; spikelets small.
                    Spikelets ovate or elliptic, few-flowered; lemmas keeled. 10. POA (p. 29).
                    Spikelets linear, many-flowered; lemmas rounded on the back............9. SCLEROPOA (p. 28).
                  Lemmas awned or mucronate (if awnless the spikelets large).
                    Awn from the tip............8. FESTUCA (p. 26).
                    Awn from a bifid apex or wanting............7. BROMUS (p. 24).

TRIBE 3. HORDEAE

Spikelets 1- to several-flowered, sessile on opposite sides of a jointed or continuous axis forming symmetrical spikes.

Spikelets solitary at each node of the continuous rachis ---- 26. LOLIUM (p. 61).
Spikelets in threes at each node of the articulate rachis -- 25. HORDEUM (p. 61).

TRIBE 4. AVENEAE

Spikelets 2- to several-flowered in open or contracted panicles, or rarely in racemes; glumes usually as long as or longer than the first lemma, commonly longer than all the florets; lemmas usually awned from the back or from between the teeth of a bifid apex, the awn usually bent, often twisted, the callus and rachilla joints usually villous.

Articulation below the spikelet.
  Second glume narrowed above; lemma of second floret awned on the back, the awn hooked ---- 32. HOLCUS (p. 68).
  Second glume broadened above; lemmas awnless -- 28. SPHENOPHOLIS (p. 62).
Articulation above the glumes and between the florets.
  Plants annual.
    Spikelets more than 1 cm long ---- 31. AVENA (p. 68).
    Spikelets less than 5 mm long ---- 27. KOELERIA (p. 62).
  Plants perennial.
    Awn from between the teeth of the lemma, flat, twisted below. 33. DANTHONIA (p. 70).
    Awn dorsal, terete, straight or twisted.
      Panicle dense, spikelike; lemma acute ---- 29. TRISETUM (p. 64).
      Panicle open, lemmas truncate, erose-dentate - 30. DESCHAMPSIA (p. 64).

TRIBE 5. AGROSTIDEAE

Spikelets 1-flowered, usually perfect, in open, contracted, or spikelike panicles, but not in true spikes nor in one-sided racemes.

Lemmas awned.
  Awn trifid (lateral awns rarely minute) ---- 40. ARISTIDA (p. 87).
  Awn simple.
    Glumes awned; panicle contracted ---- 36. POLYPOGON (p. 75).
    Glumes awnless; panicle open or narrow, not contracted.
      Awn from the tip of lemma; rachilla not prolonged. 38. MUHLENBERGIA (p. 77).
      Awn from back of lemma; rachilla prolonged. 34. CALAMAGROSTIS (p. 71).
Lemmas awnless.
  Inflorescence a cylindric spikelike panicle; glumes abruptly mucronate. 37. PHLEUM (p. 77).
  Inflorescence an open or contracted panicle; glumes not abruptly mucronate.
    Glumes not longer than the floret, usually much shorter. 39. SPOROBOLUS (p. 80).
    Glumes longer than the floret ---- 35. AGROSTIS (p. 72).

TRIBE 6. ZOYSIEAE

Spikelets subsessile in short spikes of 2 to 5 (single in *Leptothrium*), each spike falling entire from the continuous axis, usually 1-flowered, all perfect, or perfect and staminate together in the same spike; glumes usually firmer than the lemma and palea, sometimes awned, the lemma awnless.

Spikelets solitary, finally reflexed; glumes subulate, awnless. 41. LEPTOTHRIUM (p. 98)

Spikelets 2 or more in a cluster, falling together.
Glumes smooth, connate at base, forming a pitcher-shaped false involucre. 42. ANTHEPHORA (p. 98).
Glumes covered with hooked spines, forming little burs, not connate. 43. TRAGUS (p. 101).

TRIBE 7. CHLORIDEAE

Spikelets 1- to several-flowered, in two rows on one side of a continuous rachis, forming one-sided spikes or spikelike racemes, these solitary, digitate, or racemose along the main axis.

Plants monoecious or dioecious; pistillate spikelets many-awned; staminate spikelets awnless; plant stoloniferous ---------------57. OPIZIA (p. 140).
Plants with perfect spikelets.
Spike solitary (rarely 2 or 3 in *Saugetia*) terminating the culm.
Spikelets with 1 perfect long-awned floret---------53. SAUGETIA (p. 121).
Spikelets with several perfect short-awned florets--46. TRIPOGON (p 110).
Spikelets awnless-----------------------------47. LEPTURIDIUM (p. 111).
Spikes 2 or more on each culm.
Spikes racemosely arranged.
Spikelets articulate below the glumes, 1-flowered; maritime grasses with stout rhizomes-------------------------------51. SPARTINA (p. 116).
Spikelets articulate above the glumes, 2-to several-flowered (the second floret rudimentary in *Bouteloua*).
Spikes short and relatively broad; upper floret often reduced to the awns. 56. BOUTELOUA (p. 137).
Spikes long and slender; perfect florets 2 or more.
Lemmas awnless or with minute awns, the upper floret reduced to an awnless small lemma---------------44. LEPTOCHLOA (p. 102).
Lemmas with awns as long as the body, the upper floret reduced to a slender awn--------------------------45. GOUINIA (p. 108).
Spikes digitate or nearly so.
Spikelets with 2 or more perfect florets.
Rachis not extending beyond the spikelets----48. ELEUSINE (p. 113).
Rachis extending beyond the spikelets-49. DACTYLOCTENIUM (p. 113).
Spikelets with 1 perfect floret only.
Sterile floret wanting; lemma obtuse---------50. CYNODON (p. 116).
Sterile floret present; lemma awned or mucronate.
Fertile floret raised on a long stipe; sterile florets reduced to long awns. 52. GYMNOPOGON (p. 118).
Fertile floret not raised on a stipe; sterile florets consisting of evident lemmas.
Fertile lemma 1-awned or awnless---------54. CHLORIS (p. 124).
Fertile lemma 3-awned----------------55. TRICHLORIS (p. 134).

TRIBE 8. PHALARIDEAE

Spikelets with one perfect terminal floret and, below this, a pair of staminate or neuter florets (one sometimes obsolete in *Phalaris*).

Spikelets not compressed; sterile florets exceeding the fertile floret, awned. 58. ANTHOXANTHUM (p. 142).
Spikelets strongly compressed, the glumes keeled; sterile florets reduced to small scales adnate to the fertile floret------------59. PHALARIS (p. 142).

TRIBE 9. ORYZEAE

Spikelets 1-flowered, perfect, strongly laterally compressed, paniculate; glumes reduced or wanting; palea apparently 1-nerved; stamens 6.

Glumes present; lemmas usually awned------------------60. ORYZA (p. 144).
Glumes wanting; lemmas awnless----------------------61. LEERSIA (p. 147).

TRIBE 10. ZIZANIEAE

Spikelets unisexual, the pistillate terete or nearly so; glumes shorter than the lemma, usually one or both obsolete, the pedicel disarticulating below the spikelet. Glumes well developed in *Pharus*, placed in this tribe provisionally.

Pistillate spikelet subglobose; glumes wanting; blades narrowly linear.
62. LUZIOLA (p. 149).
Pistillate spikelet cylindric, beaked; glumes present; blades broad, elliptic or oblanceolate-oblong ---- 63. PHARUS (p. 151).

TRIBE 11. MELINIDEAE

Spikelets disarticulating below the glumes, these very unequal, the first minute, the second and the sterile lemma equal, membranaceous, strongly nerved, the latter bearing a slender awn from the notched summit; fertile lemma and palea thinner in texture, awnless.

Awn (of lemma) bent or twisted ---- 64. ARUNDINELLA (p. 155).
Awns straight.
  Glumes awned; lemma awnless.
    Spikelets with a long pointed callus below ---- 65. ACHLAENA (p. 157).
    Spikelets without a callus below ---- 66. REYNAUDIA (p. 159).
  Glumes awnless; sterile lemma awned ---- 67. MELINIS (p. 160).

TRIBE 12. PANICEAE

Spikelets with one perfect terminal floret, and below this a sterile floret and two glumes; fertile lemma and palea indurate or at least firmer than the glumes and sterile lemma, a lunate line of thinner texture at the back just above the base, the rootlet protruding through this at germination; articulation below the spikelet.

Spikelets unisexual; plants monoecious.
  Inflorescence of 2 digitate spikelike racemes, one pistillate, the other staminate.
    Fertile floret obtuse ---- 99. MNIOCHLOA (p. 374).
    Fertile floret narrowed into a slender awn ---- 100. EKMANOCHLOA (p. 374).
  Inflorescence paniculate, the panicle often much reduced.
    Panicles large, terminal on the culms or leafy branches, the pistillate spikelets above, the staminate below in the same panicle.
96. OLYRA (p. 366).
    Panicles all axillary or axillary and terminal, the terminal when present wholly staminate.
      Fruit laterally compressed, conspicuously gibbous on the upper dorsum.
97. LITHACHNE (p. 368).
      Fruit dorsally compressed, lanceolate ---- 98. RADDIA (p. 372).
Spikelets perfect.
  Axis thickened and corky, the spikelets sunken in cavities in its joints, these disarticulating at maturity ---- 72. STENOTAPHRUM (p. 177).
  Axis not thickened, the spikelets not sunken in it.
    Spikelets subtended (only the terminal one in some species of *Setaria*) or surrounded by 1 to many bristles or spines (sterile branchlets), these distinct or more or less connate at base, forming a false involucre.
      Bristles persistent.
        Sterile palea at maturity becoming cartilaginous and winged, much exceeding the spikelet in width; spikelets secund along the branches of a simple panicle, each subtended by a single viscid bristle.
92. IXOPHORUS (p. 352).
        Sterile palea not enlarged at maturity ---- 91. SETARIA (p. 332).
      Bristles falling with the spikelets at maturity.
        Bristles solitary, much exceeding the appressed spikelet.
93. PARATHERIA (p. 352).

Bristles numerous below each spikelet or cluster of spikelets.
Bristles not united at base, usually slender, often plumose.
94. PENNISETUM (p. 355).
Bristles more or less united at the base, forming a bur.
95. CENCHRUS (p. 360).

Spikelets not subtended nor surrounded by bristles.
Fruit cartilaginous-indurate or (*Triscenia*) merely somewhat chartaceous, not rigid, papillose, usually dark colored, the lemma with white hyaline margins, these not inrolled.
Fruit open at the hyaline summit; inflorescence a narrow grayish silky panicle ---------- 69. LEPTOCORYPHIUM (p. 163).
Fruit not open at the summit; inflorescence a narrow panicle or usually of slender racemes.
Inflorescence a narrow few-flowered panicle; first glume half as long as the spikelet, acute ---------- 68. TRISCENIA (p. 161).
Inflorescence 1 to many spikelike racemes.
Spikelets conspicuously long-silky; fruit lanceolate-acuminate; racemes in a flabellate panicle ----- 70. TRICHACHNE (p. 163).
Spikelets with short pubescence or glabrous; fruit elliptic; racemes digitate or subdigitate ---------- 71. DIGITARIA (p. 167).
Fruit indurate, rigid (or if thin not hyaline-margined).
Sterile lemma splitting down the middle, the halves inrolled, appearing like two glumes side by side; raceme solitary, the rachis broad-winged ---------- 73. THRASYA (p. 177).
Sterile lemma not splitting.
Spikelets solitary, subsessile, placed with the back of the fruit turned away from the rachis.
Inflorescence a solitary erect spikelike raceme, the spikelets swollen on the side toward the rachis and fitting into alternate hollows ---------- 74. MESOSETUM (p. 180).
Inflorescence of 2 to many racemes or paniculate.
Rachilla joint and first glume forming a swollen ringlike callus at the base of the spikelet; inflorescence paniculate.
75. ERIOCHLOA (p. 182).
Rachilla joint and first glume not forming a callus at the base of the spikelet; inflorescence racemose.
Racemes racemose along the main axis; first glume present.
76. BRACHIARIA (p. 185).
Racemes aggregated at the summit of the culm; first glume wanting ---------- 77. AXONOPUS (p. 187).
Spikelets in twos or threes or solitary, placed with the back of the fruit turned toward the rachis or pedicellate in panicles.
Fruit long-acuminate, scarcely indurate, both glumes wanting; spikelet sessile, solitary, the stiff racemes horizontal or reflexed at maturity ---------- 78. REIMAROCHLOA (p. 191).
Fruit not long-acuminate, indurate (if but slightly indurate both glumes present).
First glume typically wanting; spikelets planoconvex, subsessile in spikelike racemes ---------- 79. PASPALUM (p. 193).
First glume present; spikelets usually in panicles, biconvex to globose.
Glumes or lemmas or both awned or, if short-pointed only, the summit of the fertile palea not enclosed and the spikelets crowded in short racemes.
Inflorescence of 1-sided racemes along a common axis; glumes 2-lobed (rarely entire), awned from between the lobes; fruit indurate, the palea enclosed at the summit ---------- 87. OPLISMENUS (p. 320).
Inflorescence paniculate.
Spikelets long-silky; first glume minute, remote.
90. TRICHOLAENA (p. 331)
Spikelets not silky, often scabrous or hispid.
Spikelets with a long-pointed callus at the base.
89. CHAETIUM (p. 331).
Spikelets without a callus - 88. ECHINOCHLOA (p. 325).

Glumes and lemmas awnless (fruit pointed in *Scutachne*).
  Lower floret of the spikelet perfect, usually fruitful; spikelets small, turgid, obtuse_______86. ISACHNE (p. 315).
  Lower floret staminate or neuter.
    Second glume and sterile lemma leathery-indurate; fruit mucronate_______________85. SCUTACHNE (p. 313).
    Second glume and sterile lemma membranaceous; fruit not mucronate.
      Inflorescence a cylindric or interrupted spikelike panicle; fruit either scarcely indurate, the palea not enclosed at the summit, or stipitate and the spikelets with a saccate second glume; aquatics or subaquatics.
        Second glume inflated-saccate; fruit stipitate. 83. SACCIOLEPIS (p.310).
        Second glume not inflated-saccate; fruit scarcely indurate, open at the summit, not stipitate. 84. HYMENACHNE (p. 312).
      Inflorescence an open or contracted panicle or, if somewhat spikelike, the fruit not stipitate nor the second glume saccate; fertile lemma chartaceous-indurate.
        Culms woody, bamboolike; spikelets globose, large; fertile lemma and palea bony-indurate, a downy tuft at the apex_________82. LASIACIS (p. 302).
        Culms not woody nor bamboolike.
          Fertile lemma with either lateral appendages or excavations at the base, the margins usually not inrolled_______81. ICHNANTHUS (p. 296).
          Fertile lemma with neither lateral appendages nor excavations at base, the inrolled margins clasping the palea____80. PANICUM (p. 242).

TRIBE 13. ANDROPOGONEAE

Spikelets in pairs along a rachis, the usual arrangement being one of the pair sessile and fertile, the other pedicellate and staminate or neuter, rarely wanting, only the pedicel present; fertile spikelet consisting of one perfect terminal floret and, below this, a staminate or neuter floret, the lemmas thin or hyaline, and two awnless glumes, one or usually both firm or indurate.

Spikelets all perfect.
  Inflorescence of 2 to several digitate racemes______116. ISCHAEMUM (p. 416).
  Inflorescence a densely flowered hairy panicle.
    Spikelets awned______________________________104. ERIANTHUS (p. 380).
    Spikelets awnless.
      Rachis continuous___________________________101. IMPERATA (p. 376).
      Rachis disjointing__________________________102. SACCHARUM (p. 379).
Spikelets not all perfect, the sessile usually perfect, the pedicellate usually staminate or rudimentary (pistillate in *Eriochrysis*).
  Fertile spikelet with hairy-pointed callus formed of the attached supporting rachis joint or pedicel or of the upper part of the peduncle; awns usually long.
    Racemes reduced to a single joint, long-peduncled in a simple open panicle 113. RHAPHIS (p. 410).
    Racemes of few or many joints, not in an open panicle.
      Rachis continuous; perfect spikelets pedicellate, disarticulating at the base of the pedicel; awns plumose_115. TRACHYPOGON). (p. 415).
      Rachis disarticulating, the joints attached to perfect spikelets next above, forming a callus to them.
        Racemes solitary, not subtended by leaflike spathes; perfect spikelets several to many above; staminate spikelets several to many below______________________114. HETEROPOGON (p. 412).
        Racemes several in a flabellate cluster, subtended by leaflike spathes; perfect spikelet 1 in each raceme______120. THEMEDA (p. 420).

Fertile spikelet without a callus, the rachis disarticulating immediately below the spikelet.
- Inflorescence a dense golden-brown silky panicle; spikelets awnless, the pedicellate one pistillate.................103. ERIOCHRYSIS (p. 380).
- Inflorescence not a dense golden-brown silky panicle; pedicellate spikelet staminate or rudimentary.
  - Pedicel of the sterile spikelet thickened, appressed to the thickened rachis joint or adnate to it; spikelets awnless, appressed to the joint.
    - Rachis joint and pedicel adnate. Annuals.
      - Perfect spikelet globose; sterile spikelet conspicuous. 119. HACKELOCHLOA (p. 420).
      - Perfect spikelet oblong; sterile spikelet minute. 117. ROTTBOELLIA (p. 418).
    - Rachis joint and pedicel distinct, the sessile spikelet appressed to them, its first glume lanceolate.................118. MANISURIS (p. 418).
  - Pedicel of the sterile spikelet distinct, this and the rachis joint usually slender.
    - Spikelets in reduced racemes of 1 to 5 (rarely 7) joints, these peduncled in open panicles; awns, if present, commonly deciduous.
      - Pedicellate spikelets staminate..............111. SORGHUM (p. 407).
      - Pedicellate spikelets wanting, the pedicel only present. 112. SORGHASTRUM (p. 409).
    - Spikelets in evident racemes of several to many joints.
      - Blades cordate, thin; pedicellate spikelets obsolete or present only in the lower part of the delicate subdigitate racemes. 105. ARTHRAXON (p. 382).
      - Blades linear, not cordate; pedicellate spikelets present, at least as rudiments.
        - Inflorescence an elongate panicle of whorled long-peduncled slender glabrous racemes; spikelets muricate, awnless. 110. VETIVERIA (p. 406).
        - Inflorescence not a panicle of long-peduncled racemes; spikelets not muricate; racemes commonly conspicuously woolly.
          - Margins of the first glume of the sterile spikelet involute, the sides rounded instead of sharply keeled. Racemes in pairs, reddish brown, 2 cm long, crowded in a large inflorescence. 109. HYPARRHENIA (p. 404).
          - Margins of the first glume of the sessile spikelet inflexed, the glume sharply 2-keeled, the back flat or grooved between the keels.
            - Pedicellate spikelets much larger than the sessile, almost concealing them, the first glume large and flat; racemes solitary on the branches................107. DIECTOMIS (p. 402).
            - Pedicellate spikelets sometimes as large as the sessile, usually smaller, the first glume not large and flat.
              - Racemes single, in pairs, digitate, or numerous, sometimes supported by spathes; lowest pairs of spikelets like the upper, one fertile and sessile, the other pedicellate, staminate or reduced..........106. ANDROPOGON (p. 385).
              - Racemes in pairs subtended or enclosed by a broad spathe, aggregate in large compound panicles, the lowest pair of spikelets of one of the racemes alike, staminate or neuter. Aromatic grasses..........108. CYMBOPOGON (p. 403).

TRIBE 14. TRIPSACEAE

Spikelets unisexual, the staminate in pairs, or sometimes in threes, 2-flowered, the pistillate usually single, 2-flowered, the lower floret sterile, embedded in hollows of the thickened articulate axis and falling attached to the joints, or enclosed in a thickened involucre or sheath; glumes membranaceous or thick and rigid, awnless; lemmas and palea hyaline, awnless. Plants monoecious.

- Pistillate spikelets sunken in recesses in the thickened joints of the rachis; inflorescence of solitary or digitate racemes...........121. TRIPSACUM (p. 423).
- Pistillate spikelets enclosed in a bony beadlike involucre...122. COIX (p. 423).

DESCRIPTIONS OF GENERA AND SPECIES

TRIBE 1. BAMBUSEAE

1. BAMBUSA Retz., Obs. Bot. 5: 24. 1789. [As Bambos]

Spikelets, several- to many-flowered, sessile, solitary or in clusters on an elongate axis or the branches of a panicle, the glumes and sterile lemmas persistent after the fall of the florets; glumes small; lemmas firm, sharp-pointed or awn-tipped; keels of palea projecting but not winged; stamens 6. Large usually erect bamboos of the Old World.

1. Bambusa vulgaris Schrad.; Wendl., Coll. Pl. 2: 26. pl. 47. 1810.
COMMON BAMBOO.

Bambusa sieberi Griseb., Fl. Brit. W. Ind. 528. 1864. Martinique.

Arborescent, as much as 10 m tall, freely branching; flowering branches fascicled, elongate, leafless, the sessile spikelets radiate in clusters.

Cultivated in the Tropics of both hemispheres, the native country doubtful but not American. Often planted around dwellings. Called in Cuba "caña brava." The hollow stems are used for various purposes.

CUBA: Herradura, *Léon*[4] 16091, 16094. Habana, *Léon* 16095. San Blas, *Jack* 6923, 8727. El Cristo, *Ekman* in 1922.

JAMAICA: Gordon Town, *Hart* 350a, 566. Castleton, *Harris* 11709.

HAITI: St. Michel de l'Atalaye, *Leonard* 7515.

DOMINICAN REPUBLIC: Santiago, *Ekman* H 16267.

LEEWARD ISLANDS: Guadeloupe, *Duss* 4122.

WINDWARD ISLANDS: Martinique, *Duss* 1285. Grenada, *Broadway* 1728.

TRINIDAD: Port of Spain, *Hitchcock* 9986. Four Roads, *Broadway* 2246.

TOBAGO: *Broadway* 3412.

BAMBUSA NANA Roxb. (Fl. Ind. 2: 199. 1832), 2 to 3 m tall, has spread from cultivation at Cinchona, Jamaica.

2. GUADUA Kunth, Syn. Pl. Aequin. 1: 252. 1822

Spikelets several-flowered, subterete, mostly elongate, sessile or nearly so; stamens 6; palea winged. Large erect bamboos, our species spiny.

1. Guadua latifolia (Humb. and Bonpl.) Kunth, Syn. Pl. Aequin. 1: 254. 1822.

Bambusa latifolia Humb. and Bonpl., Pl. Aequin. 1: 68. pl. 21. 1808. Venezuela.

Arborescent, as much as 8 m tall, the summit nodding; spikelets cylindric, more or less falcate.

Damp forests, Trinidad and northern South America.

TRINIDAD: Botanic Gardens, "Planted, said to be native." *Broadway* 7174 (fertile).

---

[4] On some of Brother Léon's collections a second name is associated with his, that of Brother Charles, Brother Clémente, Brother Hioram, or Brother Sergius, Father Roca, F. R. Cazañas, and others. Brother Léon has explained in a letter that these collections form a single series with his individual numbers; hence they are here listed under his name.

3. ARTHROSTYLIDIUM Rupr., Mém. Acad. St. Pétersb. VI. Sci. Nat. 3[1]: 117. 1839

Spikelets few-flowered, in racemes, the lower 1 or 2 lemmas empty, the rachilla disarticulating between the florets (rarely below the glumes); stamens 3. Mostly climbing or trailing shrubs, the short fertile branches in fascicles on the main cane. In Cuba the species are called "tibisi", as are those of *Lasiacis*.

Blades subcapillary, in dense fascicles, 1 to 3 mm wide, as much as 30 cm long, drying involute ---------- 1. A. CAPILLIFOLIUM.
Blades not subcapillary, flat.
 Tips of culms and branches retrorse-scabrous.
  Florets about 10 mm long. Blades 7 to 9 mm wide ---------- 2. A. EKMANII.
  Florets about 7 mm long.
   Blades 3 to 6 mm wide ---------- 3. A. HAITIENSE.
   Blades 10 to 12 mm wide, or those of the sterile branches as much as 3 cm ---------- 4. A. MULTISPICATUM.
 Tips of culms and branches not retrorse-scabrous.
  Blades not more than 5 cm long (rarely 6 cm long in young shoots).
   Sheaths not bristly; inflorescence racemose ---------- 5. A. SARMENTOSUM.
   Sheaths conspicuously squarrose-bristly at summit; inflorescence elongate, consisting of distant groups of spikelets ---------- 6. A. DISTICHUM.
  Blades or some of them at least 8 cm long.
   Bristles at summit of sheath very slender, 1 to 5 cm long.
    Spikelets erect, appressed; bristles 1 to 2 cm long ---------- 7. A. FIMBRIATUM.
    Spikelets reflexed by a bend in the lower part; bristles 4 to 5 cm long. 8. A. REFLEXUM.
   Bristles at summit of sheath wanting or less than 1 cm long.
    Blades 3 to 4 mm wide, as much as 25 cm long ---------- 9. A. ANGUSTIFOLIUM.
    Blades not so long and narrow.
     Spikelets in dense mostly 1-sided racemes ---------- 10. A. PRESTOEI.
     Spikelets not in dense racemes.
      Main culms strigose. Blades linear-lanceolate, up to 15 mm wide; spikelets distant, appressed ---------- 11. A. PUBESCENS.
      Main culms not strigose.
       Blades puberulent, at least beneath, stiff, 5 to 10 cm long, 3 to 5 mm wide ---------- 12. A. URBANII.
       Blades glabrous.
        Rachis of short raceme strongly zigzag. Blades oblong-lanceolate, as much as 15 mm wide ---------- 13. A. EXCELSUM.
        Rachis straight.
         Racemes elongate, as much as 15 cm long; blades linear-lanceolate, as much as 1 cm wide ---------- 14. A. CUBENSE.
         Racemes short; blades as much as 8 cm long and 12 mm wide ---------- 15. A. OBTUSATUM.

1. Arthrostylidium capillifolium Griseb., Mem. Amer. Acad. (n. s.) 8: 531. 1862. Eastern Cuba, *Wright* 738.

Arundinaria capillifolia Hack., Oesterr. Bot. Ztschr. 53: 69. 1903.

Climbing to a height of 15 m or more, repeatedly branching, swinging down from the trees in great curtains, or festooning lower growth, the linear or filiform blades crowded on short sterile branchlets, these arranged in dense whorls like great pompons at the distant nodes; inflorescence of numerous slender wiry, not zigzag racemes borne in the whorls of branchlets, the appressed rather distant spikelets about 1 cm long.

Dryish thickets and wooded slopes, northern West Indies.

BAHAMAS: New Providence, *Eggers* 4242; *Brace and Britton* 537; *Geogr. Soc. Baltimore* 46; *Curtiss* 94; *Hitchcock* in 1890; *Field* 319.

Andros Island, *Small and Carter* 8917. Great Exuma, *Britton and Millspaugh* 2997.

CUBA: Guane, *Britton and Cowell* 9774. Cajálbana, *Léon* 4853, 4854. Paso Real, *Van Hermann* 780. Habana, *Léon* 900, 901, 2031; *Ekman* 13160. Jucaral, *Britton and Wilson* 5743. Banao Mountains, *Léon* 8074. Dumañuecos, *Léon* 15742. Buenos Aires, *Bailey* 12444. La Gloria, *Shafer* 560. Nuevitas, *Shafer* 831. Holguín, *Shafer* 1244, 1398a. Sierra de Nipe, *Ekman* 2285, 6389. Guara, *Hitchcock* 23391. Isla de Pinos, *Britton and Wilson* 15755.

HAITI: Gros-Morne, *Leonard* 9734. Ennery, *Leonard* 8907. St. Michel de l'Atalaye, *Leonard* 7462. Port-de-Pai, *Ekman* H 4560. L'Arcahaie, *Ekman* H 9286.

DOMINICAN REPUBLIC: Loma Bagita, *Valeur* 101. San José de Ocoa, *Ekman* H 11667.

PUERTO RICO: Maricao, *Chase* 6248; *Hess* in 1913. Sabana Grande, *Sintenis* 3891. Arecibo, *Cowles* 1166. Vieques Island, *Shafer* 2625.

VIRGIN ISLANDS: St. Thomas, *Shafer and Fitch* 1467; *Eggers* in 1881.

2. Arthrostylidium ekmanii Hitchc., sp. nov.[5]

Culms climbing, slender (the main cane 2 mm thick), at first scabrous, becoming glabrous, the branches in fascicles at the distant nodes (25 cm apart), drooping, 20 to 30 cm long, these branching, bearing several appressed branchlets; sheaths glabrous, striate, the summit bearing several flexuous implicate bristles 5 to 7 mm long; blades (only those of the fertile branches seen) ascending, linear-lanceolate, glabrous except the pubescent tip, 3 to 6 cm long, 4 to 8 mm wide, the petiole about 1 mm long; spikelets single or 2 or 3 in a raceme at the ends of the branchlets, 3 to 5 cm long, the usually 4 or 5 fertile florets loosely arranged on a glabrous slightly zigzag rachilla (this not hidden by the florets); glumes narrow, somewhat unequal, the first 3 to 7 mm long, the second a little longer; lower lemma empty, longer than the glumes; fertile lemmas brownish (exposing the pale rachilla joints), 9 to 12 mm long, widest (about 1.5 mm) about one-third above the base, gradually narrowed to an obtusish somewhat boat-shaped tip; palea from a little shorter to a little longer than the lemma, bowed out about the middle of the floret, flat and puberulent between the strongly compressed keels, the margins overlapping toward the tip; upper floret narrow, reduced.

Type in the United States National Herbarium, no. 1410884, collected on Massif de la Selle, Marigot, at Riviére Chotard, altitude 1,750 m, Haiti, April 10, 1927, by E. L. Ekman (no. H 7982).

The only other specimen seen is:

DOMINICAN REPUBLIC: Cordillera Central, Loma la Campana, high ridge, altitude 1,000 m, *Ekman* H 11520.

3. Arthrostylidium haitiense (Pilger) Hitchc. and Chase, Contrib. U. S. Natl. Herb. 18: 399. 1917.

Arundinaria haitiensis Pilger, in Urban, Symb. Antill. 5: 288. 1907. Haiti, *Buch* 929.

Culms slender, climbing, the young internodes very scabrous; branches numerous, about 20 cm long, in distant fascicles; blades

[5] Culmi scandentes, internodiis junioribus asperis, ramis ad nodos fasciculatis 20–30 cm longis ramulosis; vaginae glabrae fimbriatae, fimbriis 5–7 mm longis; laminae lineari lanceolatae glabrae, apice pubescentes, 3–6 cm longae 4–8 mm latae, petiolo 1 mm longo; spiculae 3–5 cm longae, floribus fertilibus 3–5; lemmata 9–12 mm longa.

5 to 7 cm long, about 6 mm wide, with a petiole about 2 mm long; spikelets narrow, closely appressed to the axis, few in short racemes terminating the branches; lemmas about 7 mm long. The narrow but obtuse tip of the blades is minutely pubescent.

Mountain thickets, Hispaniola.

HAITI: Torbeek, *Ekman* H 5295, H 7460. Badeau, *Ekman* H 7779. La Selle Mountains, *Pilkington* in 1920, "grows in tangled masses over the jungle (8,000 ft.) and is so tough and strong as entirely to prevent progress." Furcy, *Buch* 929. Sierra de Ocoa, *Ekman* H 11750.

DOMINICAN REPUBLIC: Bejucal, *Ekman* H 11750.

FIGURE 1.—*Arthrostylidium multispicatum*, × ½ (Chase 6201, 6470).

4. Arthrostylidium multispicatum Pilger, in Urban, Symb. Antill. 2: 341. 1901. Puerto Rico, *Sintenis* 209.

Arundinaria multispicata Hack., Oesterr. Bot. Ztschr. 53: 69. 1903.

Climbing high, the slender growing ends of the culms and branches beset with very short retrorse prickles, these ends, often 4 m long, swinging in the breeze like whiplashes until a support is found, the radiating short, sharp scale-covered branch buds then developing, these long grappling branches freely produced, forming a dense tangled mass; prickles deciduous, the old culms smooth; sterile branchlets whorled, 15 to 30 cm long, the spreading blades 6 to 8 cm long, 10 to 12 mm wide (on vigorous shoots sometimes larger), the floriferous branches rather shorter, bearing 1 to 3 leaves and slender terminal and axillary racemes, the spikelets appressed to the straight axis; spikelets 2 to 3 cm long; fertile florets usually 3 to 5. Blades on sterile shoots are wider, rather broadly lanceolate, as much as 11 cm long and 3 cm wide, unevenly cuneate at base (fig. 1).

Mountain woods and thickets, Cuba to Puerto Rico; Trinidad.

CUBA: Banao Mountains, *Léon* 4026 (sterile); Daiguirí, *Ekman* 1570 (fertile); Lomade Gato, *Léon* 10294, 10294b, 10612 (all sterile).

HAITI: Ganthier, *Ekman* H 7752. Petit Goave, *Ekman* H 6596. Mission, *Leonard* 3691, 3817, 3857, 3951. Morne Cabaio, *Ekman* H 1696. Ma Blanche, *Ekman* H 508. Furcy, *Leonard* 4641, 4783. Morne de la Selle, *Buch* 1139.

DOMINICAN REPUBLIC: Constanza, *Ekman* H 14109.

PUERTO RICO: Maricao, *Chase* 6201; *Sintenis* 209; *Britton and Cowell* 4222. Cayey, *Chase* 6751; *Britton and Brown* 6542. Adjuntas, *Chase* 6470; *Sintenis* 4106. Joyuya, *Britton and Cowell* 953. San Narciso, *Britton* 7300.

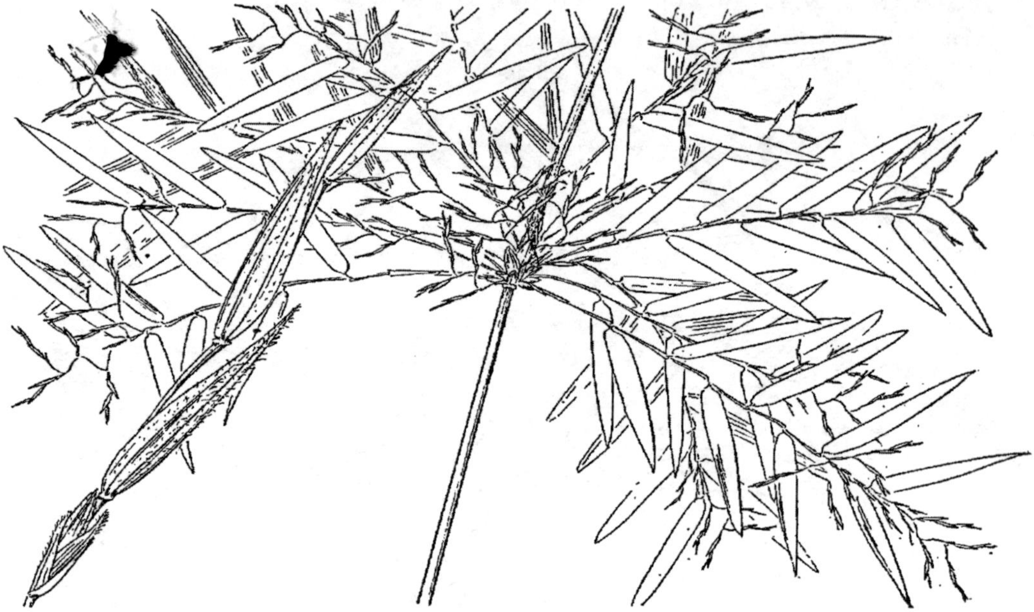

FIGURE 2.—*Arthrostylidium sarmentosum.* Plant, × ½; spikelet, × 5 (Chase 6730).

5. **Arthrostylidium sarmentosum** Pilger, in Urban, Symb. Antill. 4: 108. 1903. Puerto Rico, *Heller* 1089; *Sintenis* 354, 4046; all sterile specimens.

Culms apparently herbaceous, not more than 3 mm thick, high-climbing and pendent from trees, as in *A. capillifolium*; branchlets commonly 10 to 15 cm long, leafy, in distant usually dense whorls, the foliage pale green, drying glaucous, the divergent blades 3.5 to 5 cm long, 3 to 5 mm wide, rather thin; inflorescence of numerous short-exserted terminal and axillary zigzag racemes of 2 to 5 narrow pubescent spikelets (fig. 2).

Along streams and trails, wet mountain forests, at higher altitudes, Cuba, Hispaniola, Puerto Rico, and Trinidad. Nearly all the specimens are sterile.

CUBA: South of Sierras de Moa, *Shafer* 8047. Guantánamo, *Ekman* 10253. Monte Verde, *Léon* 3825. Yateras, *Maxon* 4487a.

HAITI: Ennery, *Leonard* 9080a; *Ekman* H 2517. Marmelade, *Leonard* 8358. Morne Brigaut, *Ekman* H 2660. St. Louis du Nord,

Leonard 14494. Jean Rabel, *Leonard* 13658. Port-de-Pai, *Leonard* 12246.

Dominican Republic: Tousaint, *Ekman* H 5709. San Francisco de Macoris, *Abbott* 2129. Laguna, *Abbott* 281. Loma Quita-Espuela, *Ekman* H 12275 (fertile). Samaná, *Ekman* H 15137. Lagunas de Cenobí, *Valeur* 52.

Puerto Rico: Maricao, *Britton and Cowell* 4209; *Sintenis* 354; *Hess* 116½; *Chase* 6190, 6223. El Yunque, *Chase* 6730 (fertile), 6731. Alta de la Piedra, *Britton and Earle* 6096. Rio Icaco, *Shafer* 3490. San Narciso, *Britton* 7283. Cayey, *Chase* 6738, 6749. Adjuntas, *Chase* 6468; *Sintenis* 4046; *Britton and Shafer* 2042. Joyuya, *Britton, Cowell, and Brown* 5236. Utuado, *Britton and Cowell* 493. Barrio de Maizales, *Britton and Cowell* 2180. Monte Torrecilla, *Britton, Cowell, and Brown* 5600.

Trinidad: Mount Tocuche, *Britton, Hazen, and Mendelson* 1289; *Broadway* 7140.

6. **Arthrostylidium distichum** Pilger, in Urban, Symb. Antill. 2: 342. 1901.

Branches solitary or in small fascicles; culms slender, a line of pubescence on one side, the nodes pubescent; sheaths bearing at summit several stiff bristles 5 to 15 mm long; blades approximate, regularly spaced, dorsiventral, lanceolate-acuminate, glabrous, scabrous on the margins, 1.5 to 3 cm long, 4 to 6 mm wide; spikelets 8 to 15, 1 to 2 cm apart.

The type collection, *Wright* 3808, bears imperfectly developed spikelets. The only other collection with spikelets is *Ekman* 10946 and this also bears abortive spikelets. All the spikelets are reflexed above the base. A few spikelets of the Wright collection have two florets about 5 mm long above the empty glumes.

Rocky banks, Cuba and Hispaniola.

Cuba: Rangel (Pinar del Río), *Wright* 3808. Gorge of Rio Taco Taco, *Léon* 16165. San Diego de Tapias, *Ekman* 10646. Lomas de Siguanéa, *Ekman* 18493. San Blas, *Jack* 6773; *Léon* 13926.

Haiti: Miragoane, *Eyerdam* 535.

7. **Arthrostylidium fimbriatum** Griseb., Mem. Amer. Acad. (n. s.) 8: 531. 1862. Eastern Cuba, *Wright* 1554.

Branches solitary, appressed or slightly spreading; blades often reflexed, rather rigid, 5 to 10 cm long, 4 to 6 mm wide; racemes 15 to 30 cm long, the spikelets appressed, more or less imbricate or somewhat distant, the axis straight; spikelets usually with two perfect florets and a terminal narrow imperfect one; lemmas short-awned. At upper altitudes plants not more than 30 to 100 cm tall.

Rocky places in the higher mountains, Eastern Cuba.

Cuba: Sierra del Cristal, *Ekman* 6817, 15964. South of Sierra de Moa, *Shafer* 8137. Loma Menqura, *Shafer* 3771. Eastern Cuba, *Wright* 1554.

8. **Arthrostylidium reflexum** Hitchc. and Ekman, sp. nov.[6]

Climbing vine; culms slender, glabrous, the branches solitary or few, appressed, the floriferous ones 25 to 35 cm long, bearing several leaves on the lower 15 cm; sheaths glabrous, somewhat cross-veined

[6] Culmi graciles, ramis solitariis vel paucis appressis; vaginae glabrae, apice setas paucas 3–5 cm longas ferentes; laminae glabrae lineari-lanceolatae 5–15 cm longae 7–10 mm latae; panicula angusta gracilis elongata 10–20 cm longa; spiculae circa 6 mm longae reflexae.

or tessellate, the summit bearing several slender bristles as much as 5 cm long; blades ascending, linear-lanceolate, rounded at base, acuminate, glabrous, scabrous on the margins, 5 to 15 cm long, 7 to 10 mm wide; panicles very slender, 10 to 20 cm long, the spikelets few to several on short distant appressed branches, the axis glabrous; spikelets terete, about 6 mm long, reflexed by a bend in the lower part; first glume 0.5 mm long; second glume a little longer than the first; first lemma sterile. The spikelets appear to be undeveloped or abortive, much as in *A. distichum*.

Type in the United States National Herbarium, no. 1502075, collected in dense thickets on the top of Sierra de Sitio Santo Tomás, Viñales, prov. Pinar del Río, Cuba, altitude 700 m, November 10, 1923, by E. L. Ekman (no. 18020).

Other specimens, both from Viñales are: Sitio Santo Tomás, steep cliffs, 500 m, *Ekman* 16627 and Loma de la Bandera, jurassic limestone, *Ekman* 16570 (sterile).

The spikelets of no. 16627 are better developed. There appears to be but one fertile floret above two sterile lemmas and a reduced floret above the fertile one. The spikelets are about 7 mm long; fertile lemma slightly inflated, about 5 mm long.

9. Arthrostylidium angustifolium Nash, Torreya 3: 172. 1903. Cuba, *Underwood and Earle* 941.

Culms 2 to 3 m long, freely branching, clambering over shrubs; ultimate branches leafy, with short overlapping compressed sheaths; blades erect, somewhat scabrous, elongate, as much as 25 cm long, 3 to 4 mm wide; panicles strict, 20 to 30 cm long, the branches erect; spikelets narrow, 1 to 2 cm long, the rachilla straight; fertile lemmas 6 to 7 mm long.

Wooded mountain slopes, Cuba. Known only from the type collection, El Yunque, Baracoa, Cuba, *Underwood and Earle* 941.

10. Arthrostylidium prestoei Munro, Kew Bull. Misc. Inf. 1895: 186. 1895; Pilger, in Urban, Symb. Antill. 2: 338. 1901. Trinidad.

Culms rather robust, bearing at the distant nodes dense whorls of slender branches about 30 cm long, these bearing one or two rather thin elongate-lanceolate blades toward their summits and terminating in a densely flowered, mostly one-sided raceme; spikelets pale, about 15 mm long; lemmas about 8 mm long, short-awned.

Forests, Trinidad and Colombia. Described from specimens collected by Prestoe in Trinidad and from plants cultivated at Kew.

TRINIDAD: *Bot. Gard. Herb.* 1675. Caparo Forests, *Broadway* 4922.

11. Arthrostylidium pubescens Rupr., Mém. Acad. St. Pétersb. VI. Sci. Nat. 3^1: 119. 1839. Trinidad.

Arundinaria pubescens Hack., Oesterr. Bot. Ztschr. 53: 69. 1903.

Culm 60 to 80 cm tall (fide Broadway), slender, roughish, the leafy sterile branches 8 to 10 cm long, rather rigid, divergent, in remote fascicles, the rough blades 8 to 15 cm long, 6 to 10 mm wide; racemes in dense fascicles, the spikelets appressed to the stiff axis; lemmas about 1 cm long.

Mountain tops, Trinidad, Tobago, and Venezuela.

TRINIDAD: Blanchisseuse Road, *Broadway* 5544. Heights of Aripo, *Broadway* 9927, 9928. Morne Bleu, *Freeman* in 1921. Without locality, *Bailey* T 3.

TOBAGO: Road to Roxborough, *Broadway* 4894.

12. Arthrostylidium urbanii Pilger, in Urban, Symb. Antill. 2: 339. 1901. Cuba, *Wright* 3810.

Arundinaria urbanii Hack., Oesterr. Bot. Ztschr. 53: 69. 1903.

Rather robust, as much as 7 m long, bearing stiff wiry branches in whorls at the distant nodes, the rather rigid sublinear blades often reflexed, readily falling from the crowded overlapping sheaths; branches terminating in slender racemes, the spikelets appressed to the straight axis; sheaths puberulent, the summit bearing several tangled yellow early deciduous bristles 3 to 5 mm long; blades puberulent beneath, sometimes on both surfaces, 5 to 13 cm long, 3 to 5 mm wide; racemes 5 to 15 cm long.

Banks of streams, bushy savannas, and low thickets, Cuba.

CUBA: Sabana de Monasterio (prov. Santa Clara) *Léon* 9228. Arroyo del Guanel, Banao Mountains, *Léon* 8043. La Cumbre, *Ekman* 13945. Savanna de Motembo, *Léon* 8230. Sancti Spíritus, *Léon* 7833. La Lanza, Manajanabo (prov. Santa Clara) *Léon* 5275. Cienfuegos, *Léon* 14738. Sierra de Nipe, *Ekman* 10016. Without locality, *Wright* 3810.

13. Arthrostylidium excelsum Griseb., Fl. Brit. W. Ind. 529. 1864. Trinidad, *Purdie*, *Crueger*.

Arundinaria excelsa Hack., Oesterr. Bot. Ztschr. 53: 69. 1903.

High-climbing; branchlets whorled, 20 to 50 cm long, the blades commonly 8 to 12 cm long, 12 to 15 mm wide; racemes terminal and axillary, the axis strongly zigzag, the spikelets divergent, 7 to 15 mm long.

Mountain woods, Guadeloupe and Trinidad.

LEEWARD ISLANDS: Guadeloupe, *Duss* 3978.

TRINIDAD: *Crueger* 82 and *Rugel*, both fragments.

14. Arthrostylidium cubense Rupr., Mém. Acad. St. Pétersb. VI. Sci. Nat. 3^1: 118. pl. 4. f. 13. 1839. Cuba, *Sagra*.

Arundinaria cubensis Hack., Oesterr. Bot. Ztschr. 53: 69. 1903.

Culms slender; blades of primary branches 10 to 15 cm long, 8 to 10 mm wide, those of the ultimate flowering branchlets elongate, linear, 3 to 4 mm wide; flowering branches very slender, 20 to 30 cm long, naked or with one or two narrow blades at base, bearing a few distant appressed spikelets toward their ends.

Pendent on cliffs, Cuba.

CUBA: San Diego de Tapias, *Ekman* 12649. San Diego de los Baños, *Léon* 4446, 16214. Campo Florido, *Léon* 591. San Sebastián, *Wright* 3811. Viñales, *Léon* 14327. Without locality, *Wright* 3809.

15. Arthrostylidium obtusatum Pilger, in Urban, Symb. Antill. 2: 340. 1901. Martinique, *Duss* 563, 1310.

Arundinaria obtusata Hack., Oesterr. Bot. Ztschr. 53: 69. 1903.

Habit unknown; fertile branches slender, the branchlets appressed; blades glabrous, rather rigid, the larger as much as 8 cm long and 12 mm wide, those on the branchlets smaller, tapering from base to apex, the tip obtuse; spikelets 12 to 20 mm long, the fertile florets 4 or 5, the rachilla straight or slightly zigzag; fertile lemmas 8 to 9 mm long, glabrous, rather strongly several-nerved, obtusish. Known only from Martinique.

WINDWARD ISLANDS: Martinique, summit of Morne d'Amour, *Duss* 563, 1310.

4. CHUSQUEA Kunth, Syn. Pl. Aequin. 1: 254. 1822

Spikelets terete or nearly so, with 2 small or minute (sometimes obsolete) glumes, and 2 sterile lemmas usually shorter than the single fertile floret. Erect or climbing shrubs, the fertile shoots often in fascicles on the usually slender main culm; the panicles usually condensed, sometimes spikelike, rarely open.

1. **Chusquea abietifolia** Griseb., Fl. Brit. W. Ind. 529. 1864. Jamaica.

Arundinaria? microclada Pilger, in Urban, Symb. Antill. 5: 289. 1907. Haiti, *Picarda* 270, *Buch* 930.

Crawling and climbing to a height of 7 m or more, the slender culms festooning and forming an entanglement across mountain trails;

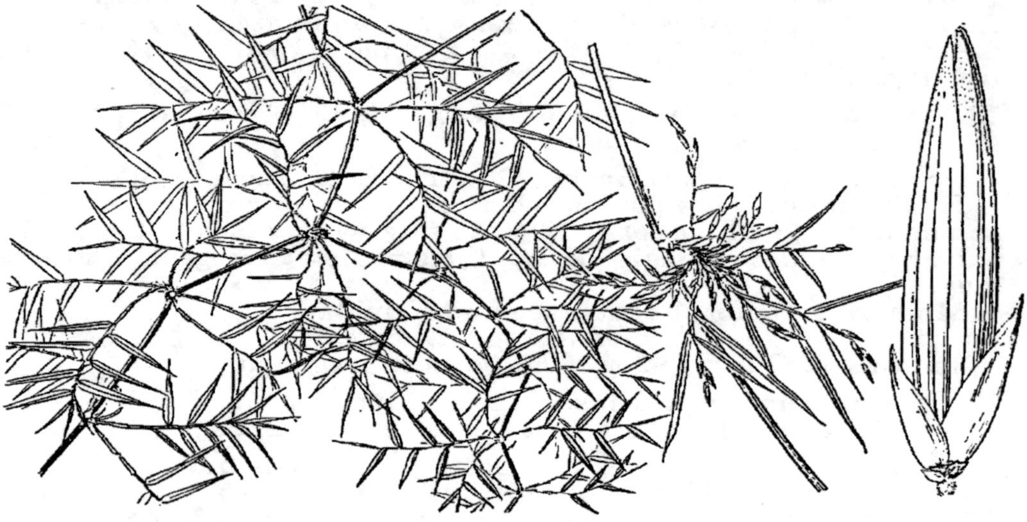

FIGURE 3.—*Chusquea abietifolia.* Plant, × ½; spikelet, × 10 (sterile plant, Ekman 5718; flowering culm, Ekman 8009).

branchlets about 10 cm long, in whorls, the numerous rigid, spine-tipped, scabrous-margined blades 2 to 3 cm long, drying glaucous; flowering branches leafy at base, terminating in a small few-flowered, nearly simple panicle, the spikelets short-pediceled; very rarely flowering (fig. 3).

Wet woods, mostly above 1,000 m, Greater Antilles.

CUBA: Pico Potrerillo (prov. Santa Clara), *Ekman* 18969. Pico Tarquino, *Bucher* 84. Sierra de Imías, *Léon* 12319. Gato Mountain, *Léon* 10077. Loma de San Juan, *Léon* 10391. Campo San Benito, *Shafer* 4056. Alto de Iberia, *Ekman* 8319. Sierra del Cristal, *Ekman* 15945.

JAMAICA: Cinchona, *Nichols* 168; *Harris* 12454 (fertile); *Hitchcock* 9715. Catherines Peak, *Hitchcock* 9734 (fertile); *Harris* 11355 (fertile). Blue Mountain Peak, *Harris* 12496 (fertile); *Hitchcock* 9375; *Maxon and Killip* 1122. Abbey Green, *Hitchcock* 9365. Cold Spring Gap, *Harris* in 1912 (*Amer. Gr. Nat. Herb.* 400). Trafalgar Gap, *Maxon* 8734. Morces Gap, *Maxon and Killip* 1064, 1291a. St. Helens Gap, *Maxon and Killip* 892. Vinegar Hill, *Perkins* 1088. Hardware Gap, *Maxon and Killip* 1265a.

HAITI: Furcy, *Leonard* 4266; *Buch* 1384. Pétionville, *Ekman* H 1188, H 1696, H 8001 (fertile). Hinche, *Ekman* H 6157. Port-au-Prince, *Ekman* H 5426, H 5887 (fertile). Morne Calumette, *Ekman* H 7310. Grand Bois, *Ekman* H 5718. Marigot, *Ekman* H 5985, H 8009 (fertile).

DOMINICAN REPUBLIC: Bejucal, *Ekman* H 11751. Loma Nalga de Maco, *Ekman* H 6306.

PUERTO RICO: Monte Alegrillo, *Hess* 116; *Stevens* 4755.

5. NEUROLEPIS Meisn., Pl. Vas. Gen. 1: 426. 1836–1843; 2: 325. 1836–1843.

(*Platonia* Kunth, Rév. Gram. 1: 139, 327, pl. 76. 1830. Not *Platonia* Mart., 1829. *Planotia* Munro, Linn. Soc. Trans. 26: 70. 1868.)

Spikelets with 2 glumes, 2 sterile lemmas and a terminal perfect floret, in elongate panicles; stamens 3. Culms erect, herbaceous or somewhat woody at base, the blades elongate, mostly more than 50 cm long and 6 cm wide.

1. Neurolepis virgata (Griseb.) Pilger, in Engl. and Prantl, Pflanzenfam. Ergänz. 2: 21. 1906.

Platonia virgata Griseb., Fl. Brit. W. Ind. 530. 1864. Trinidad, Mount Tocuche, *Crueger*.

Planotia virgata Munro, Linn. Soc. Trans. 26: 71. 1868.

Culms herbaceous, tall, robust, leafy below, the thickish blades commonly more than 1 m long, about 5 cm wide, long-attenuate, the margins serrulate; panicle much exceeding the leaves, about 75 cm long and 2 cm thick, compact, tawny, the small spikelets densely crowded.

Dense forests, mountains of Trinidad.

TRINIDAD: Without locality, *Bot. Gard. Herb.* 3371.

---

6. STREPTOCHAETA Schrad.; Nees, Agrost. Bras. 536. 1829

Spikelets, 1-flowered, terete, disarticulating below the glumes; empty bractlets (probably glumes and sterile lemmas) 4, much shorter than the spikelet, more or less toothed; lemma coriaceous, gradually narrowed into a long much contorted awn; palea shorter than the lemma, bifid nearly to the base, coriaceous; inner bracts (lodicules) 3, less coriaceous than the lemma, longer than the palea, imbricate; stamens 6, monadelphous, the tube about as long as the lemma; style 1, as long as the stamen tube, the slender stigmas 3. Broad-leaved perennials with the spikelets in elongate spikes.

1. Streptochaeta spicata Schrad.; Nees, Agrost. Bras. 537. 1829. Brazil.

Lepideilema lancifolium Trin., Mém. Acad. St. Pétersb. VI. Math. Phys. Nat. 1: 93. 1830. Brazil.

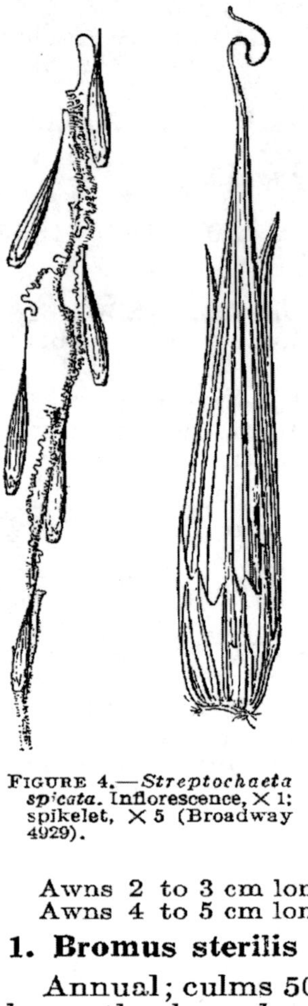

FIGURE 4.—*Streptochaeta spicata*. Inflorescence, × 1; spikelet, × 5 (Broadway 4929).

Perennial; culms erect or ascending at base in small tufts about 1 m tall; blades flat, lanceolate or elliptic, rather thin, scabrous or glabrous, veins connected by transverse veinlets on under side, hispidulous on the collar, 6 to 15 cm long, 1.5 to 6 cm wide; spike erect, 7 to 20 cm long, the rachis angled, flexuous or zigzag at the insertion of the spikelets; spikelets 6 to 20, solitary at each node, appressed to the rachis, overlapping about half their length, 2 to 3 cm long, about 2 mm thick at the base, gradually narrowed upward (fig. 4).

Wet forests at low altitudes, Trinidad and Panama to Brazil.

TRINIDAD: Caparo Forests, *Broadway* 4929.

TRIBE 2. FESTUCEAE

7. BROMUS L., Sp. Pl. 76. 1753. BROMEGRASS

Spikelets several- to many-flowered, the rachilla disarticulating above the glumes and between the florets; glumes unequal, acute, the first 1- to 3-nerved, the second usually 3- to 5-nerved; lemmas convex on the back or keeled, 5- to 9-nerved, 2-toothed at the apex, awnless or usually awned from between the teeth; palea usually shorter than the lemma, ciliate on the keels. Annuals or perennials with closed sheaths, flat blades, and open or contracted panicles of large spikelets.

Awn of lemma short or none ...... 3. B. CATHARTICUS.
Awn of lemma longer than the body.
  Awns 2 to 3 cm long; panicle branches drooping .... 1. B. STERILIS.
  Awns 4 to 5 cm long; panicle branches ascending .... 2. B. RIGIDUS.

1. Bromus sterilis L., Sp. Pl. 77. 1753. Europe.

Annual; culms 50 to 100 cm tall; sheaths pilose; panicle 10 to 20 cm long, the branches drooping; spikelets 2.5 to 3.5 cm long; lemmas about 2 cm long, the awns 2 to 3 cm long (fig. 5).

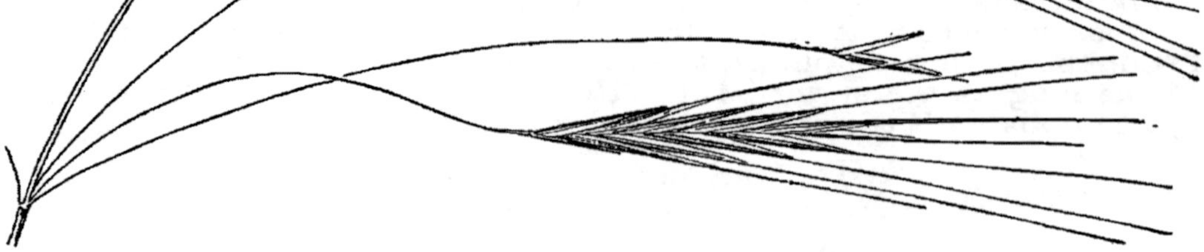

FIGURE 5.—*Bromus sterilis*, × 1 (Boettcher 2423).

A weedy grass introduced into America from Europe. Mountains of Haiti.

HAITI: Badeau, *Ekman* H 7616.

2. Bromus rigidus Roth, Mag. Bot. Roem. et Ust. 10: 21. 1790. Europe. RIPGUT GRASS.

Bromus villosus Forsk. Fl. Aegypt, Arab. 23. 1775. Not *B. villosus* Scop., 1772.

Bromus maximus Desf., Fl. Atlant. 1: 95. pl. 26. 1798. Not *B. maximus* Gilib., 1792.

Annual; culms 40 to 70 cm tall; sheaths and blades pilose; panicle open, nodding, rather few-flowered, 7 to 15 cm long; the lower branches 1 to 2 cm long; lemmas 2.5 to 3 cm long, the awn 4 to 5 cm long (fig. 6).

Open ground and waste places, introduced into America from Europe. Mountains of Jamaica.

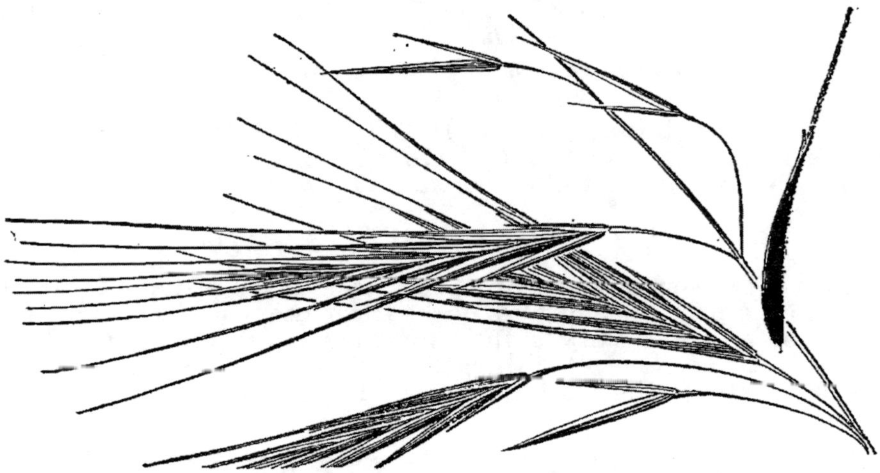

FIGURE 6.—*Bromus rigidus*, × 1 (Tracy 4702).

JAMAICA: Cinchona, *Perkins* 1075; *Hitchcock* 9714; *Harris* 10916, 11275, 12482a; *Orcutt* 5480. Arntully, *Orcutt* 5760. Strawberry Hill, *Harris* 11489. Gordon Town, *Hart* 738. Without locality, *Wilson* 486.

3. Bromus catharticus Vahl, Symb. Bot. 2: 22. 1791. Peru. RESCUE GRASS.

Bromus unioloides H. B. K., Nov. Gen. et Sp. 1: 151. 1815. Ecuador.

Annual or biennial; culms as much as 1 m tall; sheaths glabrous or pubescent; panicle open, as much as 20 cm long; spikelets 2 to 3 cm long, 6- to 12-flowered; lemmas glabrous or scabrous, acuminate, about 1 cm long, awnless or with an awn 1 to 3 mm long (fig. 7).

Cultivated occasionally. Southern and western United States; Bermuda, Jamaica, and Haiti; introduced from Europe.

BERMUDA: *Collins* 339; *Brown, Britton, and Bisset* 1911.

FIGURE 7.—*Bromus catharticus*, × 1 (Peebles, Harrison, and Kearney 1271).

JAMAICA: Cinchona, *Harris* 10919, 11455, 12482; *Hitchcock* 9699. Hope Grounds, *Harris* 11250. Gordon Town, *Hart* 741.

HAITI: Massif de la Selle, *Ekman* H 7740.

8. FESTUCA L., Sp. Pl. 73. 1753. FESCUE

Spikelets few- to several-flowered, the rachilla disarticulating above the glumes and between the florets; glumes narrow, acute, unequal, the first sometimes very small; lemmas rounded on the back, membranaceous or somewhat indurate, 5-nerved, the nerves often obscure, acute or rarely obtuse, awned from the tip or rarely from a minutely bifid apex.

First glume two-thirds to three-fourths as long as the second... 1. F. DERTONENSIS.
First glume much shorter than the second, 1 to 2 mm long........ 2. F. MYUROS.

1. Festuca dertonensis (All.) Aschers. and Graebn., Syn. Mitteleur. Fl. 2: 558. 1900.

Bromus dertonensis All., Fl. Pedem. 2: 249. 1785. Europe.

Slender tufted annual; culms 30 to 50 cm tall; blades narrow; panicles narrow, nodding, nearly simple; spikelets 4- to 6-flowered, short-pediceled; first glume about 4 mm long, the second 6 to 7 mm long; lemma lanceolate, scabrous on the back toward the apex, 7 to 8 mm long; awn slender, 10 to 13 mm long (fig. 8, *B*).

Open and waste places in the United States, especially on the Pacific coast; uplands of Jamaica; introduced

This species was referred to *F. bromoides* L. in the Grasses of the West Indies.[7]

JAMAICA: Cinchona, *Harris* 9504, 10917, 11276, 11509, 11700, 12456; *Hitchcock* 9701. Morces Gap, *Harris* 12526. Abbey Green, *Hitchcock* 9353. Gordon Town, *Hart* 681, 750.

2. Festuca myuros L., Sp. Pl. 74. 1753. Europe.

Similar to *F. dertonensis;* culms weaker; panicle longer and narrower; spikelets 2- to 3-flowered; first glume 1 to 1.5 mm long, the second 4 to 4.5 mm long (fig. 8, *A*).

[7] Contrib. U. S. Natl. Herb. 18: 395. 1917.

FIGURE 8.—*A, Festuca myuros*, spikelet, × 5 (Chase 2393). *B, F. dertonensis*. Plant, × ½; spikelet, × 5 (Palmer 2041).

Waste places and open ground in the United States; Blue Mountains of Jamaica and in Haiti; introduced.

JAMAICA: Abbey Green, *Orcutt* 5295. Farm Hill Gap, *Harris* 11564; *Orcutt* 5208. St. Helens Gap, *Harris* 11591. Salt Hill Pond, *Harris* 11604. Clifton, *Harris* 11391.

HAITI: Furcy *Leonard* 4303, 4369, 4446, 4506, 4514, 4515; *Buch* 1675, 1463. Pétionville, *Ekman* H 1114. Badeau, *Ekman* H 7615.

FESTUCA ELATIOR L., Sp. Pl. 75. 1753. MEADOW FESCUE. An erect perennial with awnless spikelets, frequently cultivated in the

FIGURE 9.—*Scleropoa rigida.* Plant, × 1; two views of floret, × 10 (Cocks).

United States as a meadow grass; represented from Jamaica by a specimen without locality (*Hart* 743).

9. SCLEROPOA Griseb., Spic. Fl. Rum. 2: 431. 1844

Spikelets small, loosely several-flowered, turned to one side, short pediceled; glumes and lemmas firm, with scarious tips. Low decumbent or ascending annuals.

1. Scleropoa rigida (L.) Griseb., Spic. Fl. Rum. 2: 431. 1844.

Poa rigida L., Cent. Pl. 1: 5. 1755. Europe.

Glabrous, usually not more than 10 or 15 cm tall, with soft linear blades and stiff spikelike few-flowered panicles (fig. 9).

Introduced in Bermuda.

BERMUDA: *Brown, Britton, and Bisset* 1955; *Brown* 521, 601, 614.

10. POA L., Sp. Pl. 67. 1753. BLUEGRASS

Spikelets 2- to several-flowered, the rachilla disarticulating above the glumes and between the florets, the uppermost floret reduced or rudimentary; glumes acute, keeled, somewhat unequal, the first 1-nerved, the second usually 3-nerved; lemmas somewhat keeled, acute or acutish, awnless, membranaceous, often somewhat scarious at the tip, 5-nerved, the nerves sometimes pubescent. Annual, or usually perennial, species of low or rather tall grasses, with spikelets in open or contracted panicles, the narrow blades flat or folded, ending in a navicular point.

Plants annual, tufted.................................... 1. P. ANNUA.
Plants perennial from creeping rhizomes.
  Culms distinctly flattened.................................... 2. P. COMPRESSA.
  Culms not flattened.................................... 3. P. PRATENSIS.

1. Poa annua L., Sp. Pl. 68. 1753. Europe. ANNUAL BLUEGRASS.

Low tufted soft smooth annual; culms decumbent at base; panicles commonly about 5 cm long, pale, open; spikelets crowded, 3- to 6-flowered, about 4 mm long; lemmas not webbed at base, distinctly 5-nerved, the nerves pilose on the lower half (fig. 10).

Open ground and grassland throughout the temperate regions of North America and extending southward in the mountains; introduced from Europe.

BERMUDA: *Collins* 158; *Brown* 474, 478.

CUBA: Habana, *Léon* 760.

JAMAICA: Cinchona, *Hitchcock* 9712; *Harris* 10920, 11266, 11496. Blue Mountain Peak, *Orcutt* 5347, 5382. Abbey Green, *Maxon* 1448; *Hitchcock* 9357. Morces Gap, *Harris* 11323. Hardware Gap, *Harris* 10112, 10906, 11438. Catherines Peak, *Harris* 11553; *Hitchcock* 9740. Wallingford, *Perkins* 1480. Gordon Town, *Hart* 749.

HAITI: Furcy, *Leonard* 4763; *Buch* 1547; *Cook, Scofield, and Doyle* 33a, 34, 41. Mission, *Leonard* 3734, 3848. Pétionville, *Ekman* H 1751. Chapelle St. Michel, *Ekman* H 6586. Morne Brouet, *Ekman* H 1116.

FIGURE 10.—*Poa annua*. Panicle, × 1; floret, × 10 (Hitchcock).

2. Poa compressa L., Sp. Pl. 69. 1753. Europe. CANADA BLUEGRASS.

Wiry perennial with extensively creeping rhizomes; culms slender, compressed; panicle narrow, rather densely flowered.

Open ground and grassland; throughout the United States, probably introduced from Europe; Jamaica, Haiti.

JAMAICA: Blue Mountain Peak, *Harris* 12663; *Hitchcock* 9371.
HAITI: Massif de la Selle, *Ekman* H 6875. Mission, *Leonard* 3848. Morne Tranchant, *Picarda* 1019.

POA TRIVIALIS L., Sp. Pl. 67. 1753. A specimen from Bermuda (*Collins* 340) may be this species.

3. Poa pratensis L., Sp. Pl. 67. 1753. Europe.

KENTUCKY BLUEGRASS.

Erect perennial, with creeping rhizomes; culms 30 to 50 cm tall; panicles open, 4 to 10 cm long, the lower branches 3 to 5, spreading; spikelets 3- to 5-flowered, 4 to 5 mm long; lemmas 3 mm long, copiously webbed at base, silky-pubescent on keel and marginal nerves, the intermediate nerves prominent (fig. 11).

Pastures and open ground in temperate regions; introduced from Europe. A standard grass for pastures and lawns in the cooler parts of the United States, but not suited to the West Indies.

BERMUDA: *Brown* 670.

JAMAICA: Blue Mountain Peak, *Orcutt* 5311.

HAITI: Massif de la Selle, *Ekman* H 1156, H 7821; *Buch* 1354, 1414. Mission, *Leonard* 3850. Furcy, *Leonard* 4371; *Cook, Scofield, and Doyle* 33.

11. BRIZA L., Sp. Pl. 70. 1753. QUAKING GRASS

Spikelets, several-flowered, broad, often cordate, the florets crowded and spreading horizontally, the rachilla disarticulating above the glumes and between the florets, the uppermost floret reduced; glumes about equal, broad, papery-chartaceous, with scarious margins; lemmas papery, broad, with scarious, spreading margins, cordate at base, several-nerved, the nerves often obscure, the apex, in the species below, obtuse or acutish; palea much shorter than the lemma. Annuals or perennials, with erect culms, flat blades, and usually open, showy panicles.

Spikelets few, 1 cm wide------------------------------------1. B. MAXIMA.
Spikelets numerous, 0.5 cm wide-------------------------------2. B. MINOR.

1. Briza maxima L., Sp. Pl. 70. 1753. Europe.

BIG QUAKING GRASS.

Slender annuals 30 to 60 cm tall with flat roughish blades and few-flowered panicles, the large handsome spikelets nodding on long capillary pedicels (fig. 12, *B*).

Open ground and grassland, introduced occasionally in America.

BERMUDA: *Brown* 679.

JAMAICA: Cinchona, *Orcutt* 5477; *Harris* 11274, 11621; *Hitchcock* 9713. Hardware Gap, *Harris* 10909.

2. Briza minor L., Sp. Pl. 70. 1753. Europe. LITTLE QUAKING GRASS.

A weak-stemmed annual 30 to 50 cm tall with thin flat scabrous blades and loosely flowered panicles, the branchlets subcapillary but stiffly spreading, the spikelets triangular-ovate, nodding (fig. 12, *A*).

Open ground, sparingly introduced in America.

JAMAICA: Cinchona, *Hitchcock* 9710; *Harris* 11414, 11603. Abbey Green, *Maxon* 1459; *Orcutt* 3242; *Hitchcock* 9356 (*Amer. Gr. Nat.*

FIGURE 11.—*Poa pratensis.* Plant, × ½; spikelet, × 5; floret, × 10 (Williams).

FIGURE 12.—*A*, *Briza minor*. Plant, × ½; spikelet and floret, × 5 (Hitchcock 2597). *B*, *B. maxima*, × ½ (Baenitz).

Herb. 699). Catherines Peak, *Hitchcock* 9739. Morces Gap, *Nichols* 40; *Harris* 11527. Hardware Gap, *Harris* 10907. New Haven Gap, *Maxon* 2652. Gordon Town, *Hart* 751.

12. ERAGROSTIS Host, Icon. Gram. Austr. 4: 14. pl. 24. 1809.
Lovegrass

Spikelets few- to many-flowered, the florets usually closely imbricate, the rachilla disarticulating above the glumes and between the florets, or continuous, the lemmas deciduous, the paleas persistent; glumes somewhat unequal, acute or acuminate, 1-nerved, or the second rarely 3-nerved; lemmas acute or acuminate, keeled or rounded on the back, 3-nerved, the nerves usually prominent; palea 2-nerved, the keels sometimes ciliate. Annuals or perennials with open or contracted panicles.

Palea ciliate on the keels, the cilia conspicuous, usually as long as the width of the lemma.
- Plants perennial, more or less viscid ---------- 3. E. GLUTINOSA.
- Plants annual, not viscid.
  - Pedicels as long as the spikelets or longer; panicle open, oblong. 1. E. AMABILIS.
  - Pedicels very short; panicle spikelike, more or less interrupted.
    - Spikelets mostly 7- to 9-flowered ---------- 2. E. CILIARIS.
    - Spikelets mostly 12- to 15-flowered ---------- 4. E. URBANIANA.

Palea scaberulous on the keels but not prominently ciliate.
- Plants annual.
  - Plants creeping, forming mats ---------- 5. E. HYPNOIDES.
  - Plants not creeping.
    - Lemmas glandular on the keel ---------- 6. E. CILIANENSIS.
    - Lemmas not glandular.
      - Panicle elongate, contracted, the minute spikelets crowded or glomerate. 7. E. GLOMERATA.
      - Panicle not elongate.
        - Spikelets 1.5 mm wide ---------- 8. E. PILOSA
        - Spikelets 2 mm wide.
          - Sheaths and blades, at least the lower, sparsely pilose. 9. E. BERTERONIANA.
          - Sheaths and blades glabrous.
            - Spikelets ovate-lanceolate, mostly less than 5 mm long; panicle rather lax ---------- 10. E. TEPHROSANTHOS.
            - Spikelets linear, mostly 8 to 10 mm long; panicle rather firm, the branches and branchlets stiffly and divaricately spreading. 11. E. BARRELIERI.
- Plants perennial.
  - Culms low, stiff and wiry, usually not more than 20 cm tall.
    - Inflorescence a strict raceme, the spikelets subsessile, rather remote. 12. E. BAHAMENSIS.
    - Inflorescence a few-flowered, narrow panicle 2 to 8 cm long. 13. E. CUBENSIS.
  - Culms taller, often robust, mostly more than 30 cm tall.
    - Branchlets of panicle elongate, capillary, stiffly spreading, bearing mostly single terminal spikelets ---------- 14. E. ELLIOTTII.
    - Branchlets of panicle bearing several mostly short-pedicellate spikelets.
      - Lemmas acuminate; axils of panicle with a tuft of long hairs. 15. E. ACUTIFLORA.
      - Lemmas acute or obtusish, axils of panicle naked or rarely sparsely pilose.
        - Panicle narrow, consisting of several more or less distant clusters of spikelets along a stiff elongate axis ---------- 16. E. EKMANII.
        - Panicle open.
          - Spikelets somewhat terete, purple, long-pedicellate; lateral nerves of the lemma faint ---------- 17. E. PURPURASCENS.
          - Spikelets compressed, mostly pale or green; lateral nerves of the lemma distinct.
            - Blades flat, pilose on the upper surface near the base. 18. E. EXCELSA.

Blades glabrous.
Spikelets falcate; panicle oblong, rather dense, 8 to 12 cm long. 19. E. SALZMANNII.
Spikelets straight; panicle usually much more than 15 cm, open.
Blades involute ---------------------- 20. E. PROLIFERA.
Blades flat, 2 to 5 mm wide, becoming involute. 21. E. DOMINGENSIS.

1. Eragrostis amabilis (L.) Wight and Arn.; Hook. and Arn., Bot. Beechey Voy. 251. 1841.

Poa amabilis L., Sp. Pl. 68. 1753. India.
Poa plumosa Retz., Obs. Bot. 4: 20. 1786. East Indies.
Eragrostis plumosa Link, Hort. Berol. 1: 192. 1827.

Annual; culms branching, slender, ascending or spreading; mostly 10 to 20 cm tall; blades flat or involute, 1 to 2 mm wide, sometimes wider; panicles oblong, somewhat open, mostly 4 to 8 cm long; spikelets about 2 mm long, 4- to 8-flowered; lemmas ovate, obtuse, 1 mm long; keels of palea long-ciliate, the hairs about 0.3 mm long (fig. 13).

Open ground and waste places, warmer regions of both hemispheres. A native of the Old World. Originally described from India. Throughout the West Indies.

FIGURE 13.—*Eragrostis amabilis*. Panicle, × ½; spikelet, × 10 (Meislahn 10).

2. Eragrostis ciliaris (L.) Link, Hort. Berol. 1: 192. 1827.

Poa ciliaris L., Syst. Nat. ed. 10. 2: 875. 1759. Jamaica.
Poa elegans Poir., in Lam., Encycl. 5: 87. 1804. Puerto Rico, *Ledru*.

Erect or spreading annual; culms slender, 15 to 40 cm tall; blades flat, 1 to 3 mm wide; panicles condensed, usually interrupted, sometimes rather loose, 5 to 15 cm long; spikelets subsessile, crowded, about 2 mm long, mostly 6- to 8-flowered, the palea prominently ciliate (fig. 14).

Open ground and waste places, warmer regions of both hemispheres. Apparently introduced in America. A common weed around towns. Probably to be found on all the West Indian islands.

Differs from the preceding in the dense narrow panicles, interrupted below, and in the larger crowded subsessile spikelets. The inflorescence of this species varies from the rather dense cylindrical panicle with short branches flowered to the base (the typical form) to one with stiffly ascending branches naked at the base (such as *Curtiss* 76, Nassau, Bahamas) and to that with a lax panicle (*E. ciliaris* var. *laxa*).

2a. Eragrostis ciliaris var. laxa Kuntze, Rev. Gen. Pl. 2: 774. 1891. St. Thomas, Barbados, and Trinidad.

Panicle branches sometimes 3 cm long, the spikelets scarcely crowded. In the specimens from the Lesser Antilles the cilia on the keels are short.

Habitat the same as for the species. Apparently confined to the West Indies.

BAHAMAS: Turks Island, *Nash and Taylor* 3846. Caicos Islands, *Wilson* 7665.

CUBA: Cayo Paredon Grande, *Shafer* 2751. Cárdenas, *Ekman* in 1923. Sierra Guane, *Shafer* 10456. Santiago de Cuba, *Léon* 880.
JAMAICA: Hope Grounds, *Harris* 11242, 11243 (in part). Castleton, *Harris* 11384.

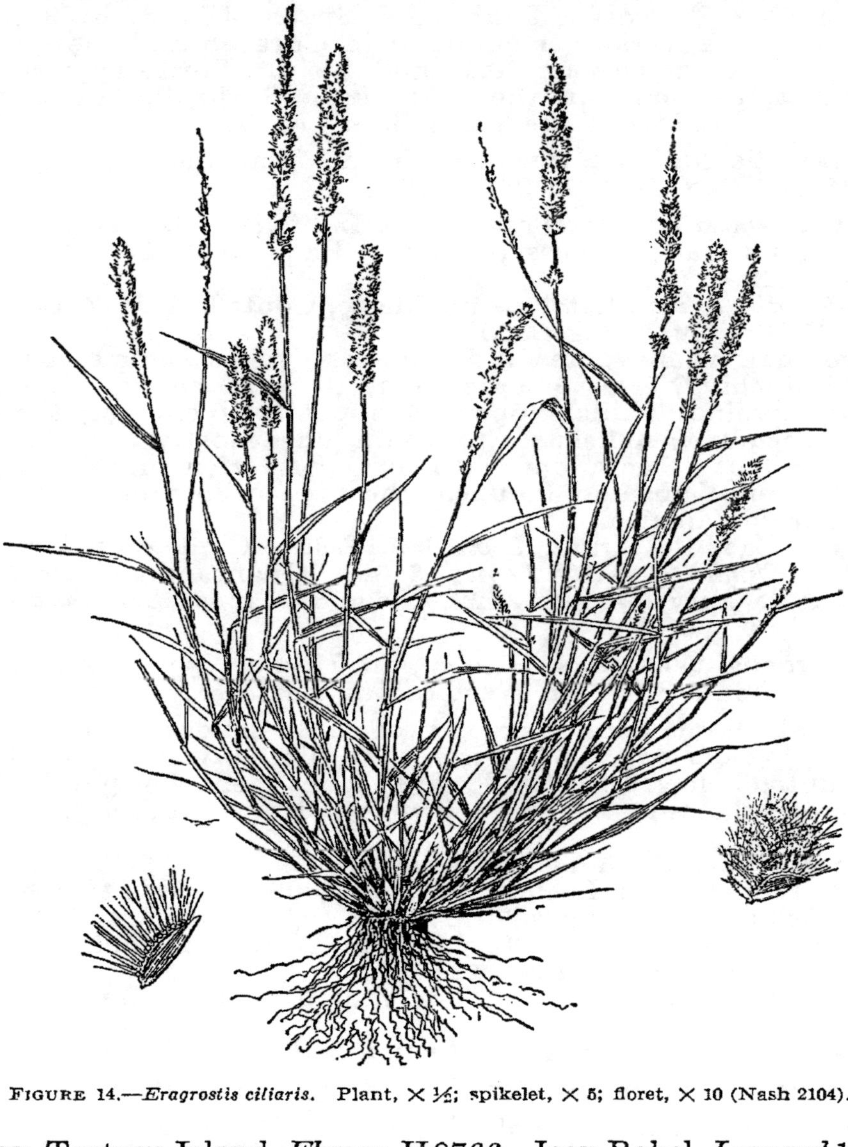

FIGURE 14.—*Eragrostis ciliaris.* Plant, × ½; spikelet, × 5; floret, × 10 (Nash 2104).

HAITI: Tortuga Island, *Ekman* H 9766. Jean Rabel, *Leonard* 12879a.
LEEWARD ISLANDS: Dominica, *Duss.*
WINDWARD ISLANDS: Martinique, *Duss* 740, 1305, 1307, 4023.
The above specimens are somewhat diverse. Many, such as the Jamaica specimens, differ only in the looser panicle. Shafer's 2751, Ekman's H 9766, and a few others differ in having stiffly spreading,

few-flowered panicle branches. The Martinique specimens have loose panicles with ascending branches, but the cilia on the keels of the palea are short and scarcely conspicuous.

ERAGROSTIS CILIARIS var. BRACHYSTACHYA Boiss., Fl. Orient. 5: 582. 1884. *E. arabica* Jaub. and Spach, Illustr. 4: 31, pl. 322. 1850–53. This variety is common in Curaçao and the neighboring islands. The panicles are dense and ovoid. Forms approaching this are sometimes found in the West Indies (Morillos de Cabo Rojo, Puerto Rico, *Britton, Cowell, and Brown* 4713).

3. Eragrostis glutinosa (Swartz) Trin., Mém. Acad. St. Pétersb. VI. Math. Phys. Nat. 1: 397. 1830.

Poa glutinosa Swartz, Prodr. Veg. Ind. Occ. 26. 1788. Jamaica.

Eragrostis sudans Griseb., Cat. Pl. Cub. 227. 1866. Cuba, *Wright* 3422.

Eragrostis leonina Hitchc. and Chase, Contrib. U. S. Natl. Herb. 18: 388. 1917. Cuba, *Léon* 885.

Perennial, whole plant more or less viscid; culms many-noded, wiry, branching, erect or ascending, 10 to 30 cm tall; blades short, slender, involute; panicles open, oblong, 5 to 10 cm long, the branches stiffly ascending; spikelets 4 to 6 mm long, mostly 7- to 11-flowered; lemmas about 1.3 mm long; keels of palea rather prominently ciliate.

Sandy soil, Cuba and Jamaica; the type collection is the only one known from Jamaica.

CUBA: Zaza de Tunas, *Léon* 885, 6732. Camagüey, *Britton* 2374. Sábalo, *Ekman* 11413; *Léon* 15100. Guantanamo, *Britton* 2123. Without locality, *Wright* 3422. Isla de Pinos, *Britton and Wilson* 15612.

4. Eragrostis urbaniana Hitchc., in Urban, Symb. Antill. 7: 167. 1912. Bonaire, Dutch West Indies, *Suringar*.

Annual; culms spreading or prostrate, slender, 5 to 25 cm long; blades 1 to 4 cm long, 0.5 to 2 mm wide, often involute; panicle narrow, interrupted below, 2 to 5 cm long; spikelets yellow or purple, fascicled, sessile or subsessile, 10- to 15-flowered, 3 to 6 mm long; palea ciliate on the keels.

Sandy plains, Bahamas to Curaçao.

BAHAMAS: Caicos Islands, *Wilson* 7608, 7628; *Millspaugh* 9234. Turks Island, *Millspaugh* 9012, 9268, 9339 (in part), 9341. Great Ragged Island, *Wilson* 7828. Inagua, *Nash and Taylor* 1372.

HAITI: Jean Rabel, *Ekman* H4007.

PUERTO RICO: Laguna de Tortuguero, *Britton, Cowell, and Brown* 3854.

VIRGIN ISLANDS: Anegada, *Britton and Fishlock* 957.

5. Eragrostis hypnoides (Lam.) B. S. P., Prel. Cat. N. Y. 69. 1888.

Poa hypnoides Lam. Tabl. Encycl. 1: 185. 1791.

Poa carinata Poir., in Lam., Encycl. 5: 86. 1804. Puerto Rico, *Ledru*.

Stoloniferous, forming mats, the flowering culms mostly 5 to 10 cm tall; blades 1.5 to 2 cm long, spreading; panicles small, more or less capitate, the pale, many-flowered spikelets commonly 1 cm long (fig. 15).

Moist, open ground along streams throughout the United States, in the West Indies, and southward to Brazil.

CUBA: Galafre, *Britton and Cowell* 9830. Cabañas, *Ekman* 10934. Santa Cruz, *Roig* 3223. Anafe, *Ekman* 222; *Léon* 4268, 4269. Laguna Castellano, *Baker and Abarca* 4328. Santa Lucea, *Shafer* 961a. Río Cauto, *Shafer* 1666. Isla de Pinos, *Britton and Wilson* 15523, 15803; *Curtiss* 391. Without locality, *Wright* 3826.

HAITI: Miragoane, *Ekman* H 7912. L'Abaillon, *Ekman* H 843.

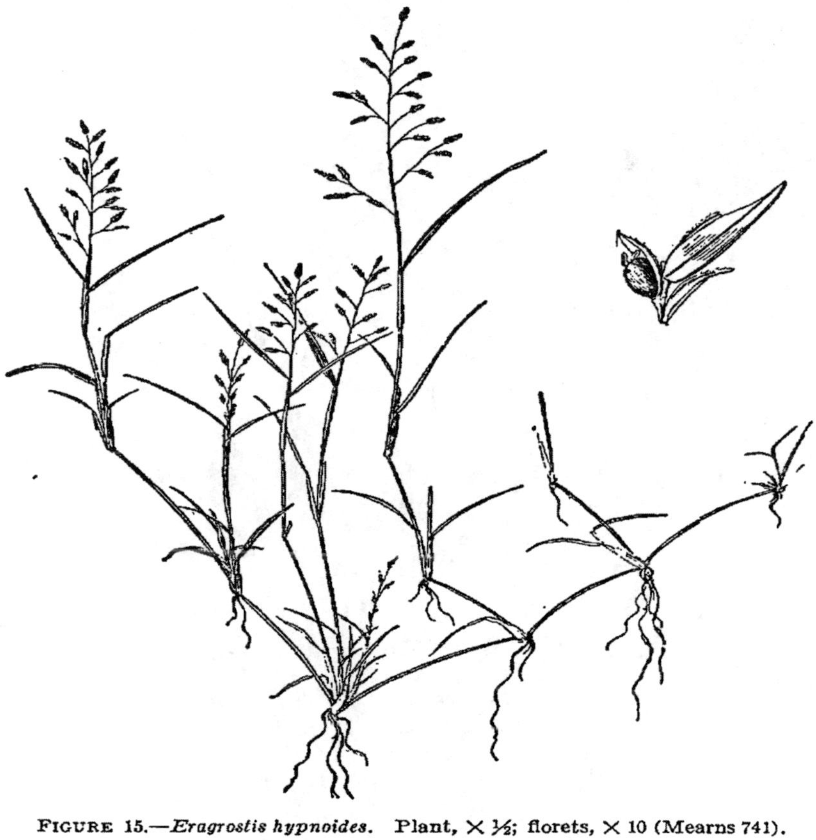

FIGURE 15.—*Eragrostis hypnoides.* Plant, × ½; florets, × 10 (Mearns 741).

DOMINICAN REPUBLIC: Samaná, *Abbott* 1327, 1420. Pimentel, *Abbott* 639, 640. Samaná Peninsula, *Abbott* 2380. Sánchez, *Rose* 4328. San Pedro de Macorís, *Rose* 4228. Santo Domingo, *Ekman* H 11172. Río San Juan, *Miller* 1169. Río Muñoz, *Eggers* 2566.

PUERTO RICO: Mayaguez, *Britton and Marble* 520. Fajardo, *Britton and Shafer* 1665. San Juan, *Chase* 6398. Rio Grande, *Chase* 6711 (*Amer. Gr. Nat. Herb.* 689). Los Mamayes, *Eggers* 1207. Vega Baja, *Heller* 649. Bayamon, *Sintenis* 1225. Cabo Rojo, *Sintenis* 674.

TRINIDAD: *Bot. Gard. Herb.* 3035; *Crueger.*

FIGURE 16.—*Eragrostis cilianensis*. Plant, × ½; spikelet, × 5; floret, × 10 (Schuette 155).

6. **Eragrostis cilianensis** (All.) Link; Vign., Lut. Malpighia 18: 386. 1904. STINKGRASS.

Poa cilianensis All., Fl. Pedem. 2: 246. 1785. Europe.

Eragrostis major Host, Icon. Gram. Austr. 4: 14. pl. 24. 1809. Europe.

Eragrostis megastachya Link, Hort. Berol. 1: 187. 1827. Europe.

Culms erect or spreading; panicles rather compact, 2 to 10 cm long, greenish or whitish, the spikelets many-flowered, larger than in the other annual species; spikelets 5 to 15 mm long, 3 mm wide, 10- to 40-flowered, the florets closely imbricate; pedicels and keels of the acute glumes and lemmas sparingly glandular; lemmas thin, the lateral nerves prominent (fig. 16).

A common weed in the United States; rare in the West Indies.

BERMUDA: *Collins* 149.

CUBA: Habana, *Léon* 8826.

7. **Eragrostis glomerata** (Walt.) L. H. Dewey, Contrib. U. S. Natl. Herb. 2: 543. 1894.

Poa glomerata Walt., Fl. Carol. 80. 1788. South Carolina.

Poa conferta Ell., Bot. S. C. and Ga. 1: 158. 1816. South Carolina.

Eragrostis conferta Trin., Mém. Acad. St. Pétersb. VI. Math. Phys. Nat. 1: 409. 1830.

Robust annual, sometimes as much as 2 m tall and appearing like a perennial, freely branching, the branches sometimes fascicled; blades elongate; panicles as much as 40 cm long, narrowly contracted, densely flowered, the spikelets about 2 mm long, 4- to 6-flowered, the lemmas scarcely 1 mm long (fig. 17).

Moist low ground, southeastern United States to Uruguay. In the West Indies known only from Trinidad.

TRINIDAD: O'Meara Savanna, *Britton* 2492. La Brea, *Broadway* 4979. Point-à-Pierre, *Broadway* 4940, 4941. San Fernando, *Hitchcock* 10110 (*Amer. Gr. Nat. Herb.* 690). Port-of-Spain, *Hitchcock* 10319. St. Joseph, *Hitchcock* 10024. Without locality, *Bot. Gard. Herb.* 3366.

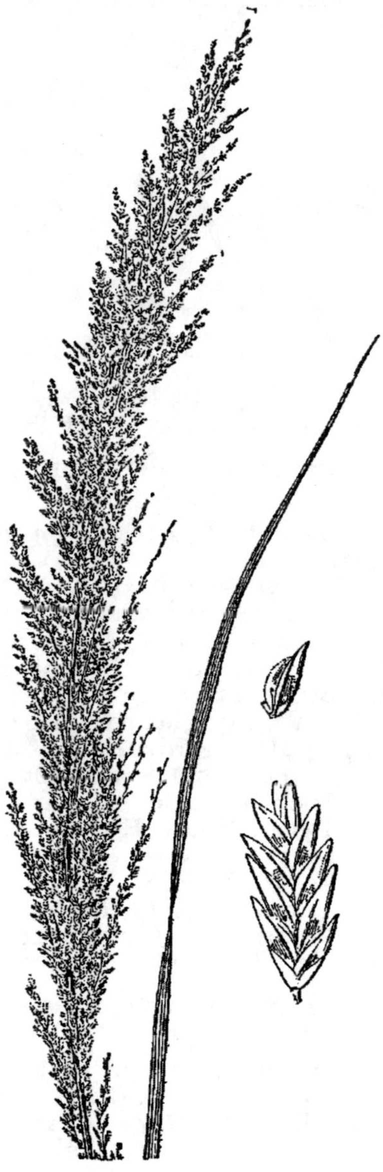

FIGURE 17.—*Eragrostis glomerata.* Panicle, × ½; spikelet and floret, × 10 (Eggert).

8. **Eragrostis pilosa** (L.) Beauv., Ess Agrost. 162. 1812. INDIA LOVEGRASS.

Poa pilosa L., Sp. Pl. 68. 1753. Europe

Weedy annual; culms slender, erect or ascending from a decumbent base, 10 to 50 cm tall; blades flat, 1 to 3 mm wide; panicle delicate, open, becoming somewhat diffuse, 5 to 20 cm long, the branches capillary, flexuous, ascending or spreading, finally somewhat implicate, the lower fascicled, sparsely long-pilose in the axils; spikelets gray to nearly black, linear, scarcely compressed, 3- to 9-flowered, 3 to 5 mm long, about 1 mm wide, the pedicels spreading, mostly longer than the spikelets; glumes acute, the first a little less than, the second a little more than, 1 mm long; lemmas loosely imbricate, the rachilla more or less exposed, rounded on the back, acute, 1.2 to 1.5 mm long, 0.5 mm wide from keel to margin, the nerves obscure; grain 0.6 mm long (fig. 18).

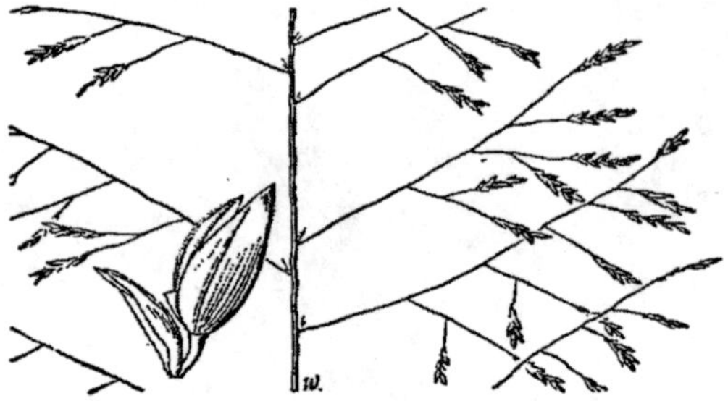

FIGURE 18.—*Eragrostis pilosa*. Panicle, × 1; floret and palea, × 10 (Ruth 514).

Open grounds, fields, and waste places, warm and temperate regions of both hemispheres. The West Indian specimens referred to this species are the form with more delicate, slender, flexuous panicle branches, apparently commoner in Asia and Africa than in Europe. Nash [8] doubtfully refers these specimens to *Eragrostis purshii* Schrad. Throughout the West Indies at low altitudes.

9. **Eragrostis berteroniana** (Schult.) Steud., Nom. Bot. ed. 2. 1: 562. 1840.

Megastachya berteroniana Schult., Mant. 2: 330. 1824. Santo Domingo.

Poa berteroniana Kunth, Rév. Gram. 1: 112. 1829.

Annual; culms erect or usually decumbent at base, 10 to 20 cm tall or even as much as 30 cm; sheaths, at least the lower, sparsely papillose-pilose, densely pilose at the summit; blades narrow, mostly involute, sparsely pilose; panicles oblong, somewhat condensed, 5 to 10 cm long, glabrous in the axils; spikelets short-pedicellate, ascending, pale or purplish, 7 to 13 mm long, 15- to 30-flowered; lemmas ovate, 1.5 to 1.8 mm long.

Open or rocky soil and dry thickets, Hispaniola.

HAITI: Jean Rabel, *Leonard* 12879, 12972, 13686; *Ekman* H 3617. Étang, *Leonard* 3560. Cabaret, *Leonard* 11832, 11835, 11867. Môle-St. Nicolas, *Ekman* H 4491. Fond Parisien, *Leonard* 4214. Morne-á-Cabrits, *Ekman* H 978. Plaine du Cul de Sac, *Buch* 2039.

DOMINICAN REPUBLIC: Villa Vásquez, *Ekman* H 13129. Valverde, *Ekman* H 13097.

10. **Eragrostis tephrosanthos** Schult., Mant. 2: 316. 1824. Martinique.

Annuals, rather soft and lax; culms branching at base, erect or decumbent-spreading, 5 to 20 cm tall, sometimes taller; blades flat, usually 5 to 10 cm long, 1 to 2 mm wide; panicles open, mostly 4 to 10 cm long, about half as wide, the branches ascending or spreading, naked below, the spikelets appressed or ascending along the upper

---

[8] Bull. Torrey Bot. Club 30: 388. 1903.

part, the lower axils pilose; spikelets, 6- to 12-flowered, 4 to 7 mm long, about 1.5 mm wide (fig. 19).

Open ground, fields, and waste places, West Indies to Brazil. Common in the Greater Antilles and Trinidad; less common in the Lesser Antilles. In Cuba called "ilusión."

Grisebach [9] refers this species to *E. poaeoides* Beauv.

FIGURE 19.—*Eragrostis tephrosanthos*. Panicle, × 1; floret, × 10 (Curtiss 5930).

11. Eragrostis barrelieri Daveau, in Morot., Jour. Bot. 8: 289. 1894. Europe.

Annual; culms erect or decumbent, 20 to 50 cm tall; blades flat, rather short, 2 to 4 mm wide; panicle erect, open but narrow, 8 to 15 cm long, the branches ascending or stiffly spreading, few-flowered, spikelet-bearing nearly to base, the axils glabrous; spikelets linear, usually 12- to 15-flowered, mostly about 1 cm long and 1.5 mm wide; lemmas 2 mm long or slightly longer (fig. 20).

Waste places. Texas to California; Hispaniola and St. Croix; introduced from Europe.

HAITI: Anse-à-Pitre, *Ekman* H 6696. Cape St. Marc, *Ekman* H 6639.

DOMINICAN REPUBLIC: Guayubín, *Abbott* 877.

VIRGIN ISLANDS: St. Croix, *Thompson* 5,302,996; *Eggers* in 1876; *Ricksecker* 221.

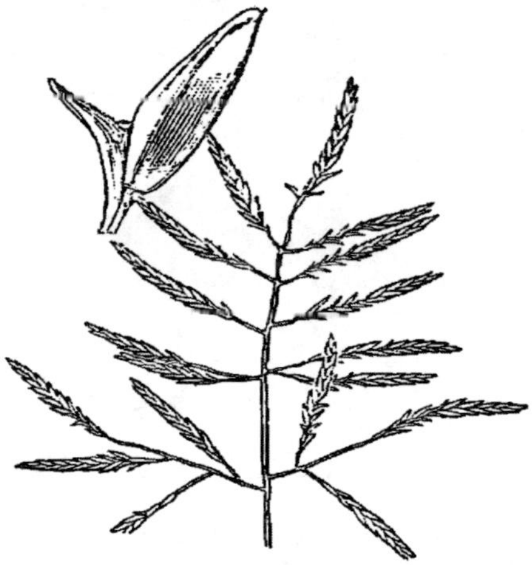

FIGURE 20.—*Eragrostis barrelieri*. Panicle, × 1; floret, × 10 (Hitchcock 5280).

12. Eragrostis bahamensis Hitchc., Mo. Bot. Gard. Rept. 4: 149. 1893. Inagua, *Hitchcock*.

Perennial; culms tufted, simple, spreading, wiry, usually about 15 cm tall; blades slender, firm, involute, a woolly tuft of hairs at the summit of the sheath; spikelets mostly in a raceme on the upper half of the culm, appressed, rather distant, short-pedicellate, 6 to 8 mm long, firm and hard, 10- to 20-flowered.

Rocky soil, Bahamas.

BAHAMAS: Rum Cay, *Brace* 3993. Little Inagua, *Nash and Taylor* 1217. Inagua, *Hitchcock* in 1890. The species has been collected on other islands of the group.

13. Eragrostis cubensis Hitchc., Contrib. U. S. Natl. Herb. 12: 243. 1909. Isla de Pinos, *Curtiss* 420.

Perennial, culms slender, wiry, erect or spreading, tufted from a hard knotty base, mostly 10 to 20 cm, sometimes 30 cm, tall; blades narrow or filiform, mostly involute, erect; panicles few-flowered, 2 to 8 cm long, the few branches erect or ascending, the lower sometimes as much as 2 cm long, usually short and appressed; spikelets short

[9] Fl. Brit. W. Ind. 532. 1864.

pedicellate, the lateral pedicels often less than 1 mm, linear, mostly 7 to 12 mm, rarely as much as 25 mm, long, 10 to 20-flowered, the florets closely imbricate; lemmas firm, acute, about 1.8 mm long.

Sandy or rocky soil, Cuba and Jamaica. Grisebach [10] refers this species to *E. bahiensis* Schrad.

CUBA: Herradura, *Ekman* 10696; *Earle* 650; *Hitchcock* 261; *Tracy* 9097. San Diego de los Baños, *Léon* 4559. Sumidero, *Léon* 3471. Sierra de Cabra, *Britton and Gager* 7271. Madruga, *Shafer* 68. Laguna Jovero, *Shafer* 10731. Pinar del Río, *Hitchcock* 23285. Baraguá, *Hitchcock* 23359, 23376. Zaza de Tunas, *Léon* 886. Without locality, *Wright* 3424, 3825. Isla de Pinos, *Britton and Wilson* 14194, 15382. Sábalo, *Léon* 15099.

JAMAICA: New Forest, *Hitchcock* 9852 (*Amer. Gr. Nat. Herb.* 691). Lititz Savanna, *Harris* 11664, 11734, 12441, 12678.

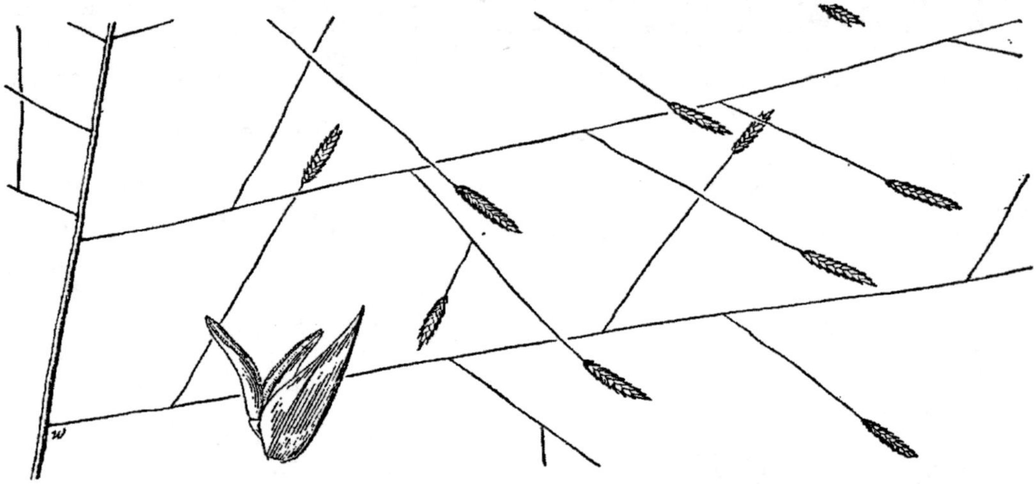

FIGURE 21.—*Eragrostis elliottii.* Panicle, × 1; floret, × 10 (Tracy 7384).

14. Eragrostis elliottii S. Wats., Amer. Acad. Proc. 25: 140. 1890.

Poa nitida Ell., Bot. S. C. and Ga. 1: 162. 1816. South Carolina. Not *Poa nitida* Lam. 1791, nor *Eragrostis nitida* Link, 1827.

Eragrostis macropoda Pilger, in Urban, Symb. Antill. 4: 106. 1903. Puerto Rico, *Sintenis* 1233.

Perennial; culms tufted, about 50 cm tall, the rather stiff leaves mostly clustered toward the base, the very diffuse few-flowered panicle more than half the entire height of the plant, the panicle axis and the capillary branches fragile; spikelets on long, rather stiff, slender pedicels, mostly 8- to 15-flowered, 5 to 12 mm long; lemmas closely imbricate, acute, about 2 mm long (fig. 21).

Sandy savannas and sterile hills, southeastern United States on the Coastal Plain and in the West Indies.[11]

CUBA: Herradura, *Tracy* 9096; *Hitchcock* 260. Guane, *Léon* 7310. Pinar del Río, *Hitchcock* 23289; *Palmer and Riley* 441; *Baker and*

[10] Fl. Brit. W. Ind. 532. 1864.
[11] The species occurs frequently in the Bahamas (Britt. and Millsp. Fl. Baham. 40. 1926).

Abarca 3735. Camagüey, *Britton* 2373. Placetas del Sur, *Léon* 6425. Cojimar, *Baker* 5332. Madruga, *Léon* 8951. Baraguá, *Hitchcock* 23386. Manacas, *Léon* 5884. Isla de Pinos, *Taylor* 25; *Palmer and Riley* 948; *Ekman* 11657; *Britton and Wilson* 14708, 14944. Without locality, *Wright* 3423.

JAMAICA: New Forest, *Hitchcock* 9854 (*Amer. Gr. Nat. Herb.* 692). Lititz Savanna, *Harris* 11661, 12435, 12680.

HAITI: Acul-Samedi, *Ekman* H 9920.

DOMINICAN REPUBLIC: Cuenca, *Ekman* H 13298. Monción, *Valeur* 145. Cotuy, *Abbott* 795.

PUERTO RICO: Bayamon, *Sintenis* 1233. Santurce, *Heller* 584. Campo Alegre, *Chase* 6798 (*Amer. Gr. Nat. Herb.* 693). Sabana Abajo, *Britton and Brown* 5719. Joyuda, *Britton, Stevens, and Hess* 2396. San Juan, *Chase* 6634.

15. Eragrostis acutiflora (H. B. K.) Nees, Agrost. Bras. 501. 1829.

Poa acutiflora H.B.K., Nov. Gen. et Sp. 1: 161. 1816. Colombia.

Perennial; culms tufted, rather rigid, sparingly branching, 20 to 40 cm tall, blades erect, flat or involute, 1 to 2 mm wide; panicles 10 to 20 cm long, the spikelets short-pedicellate, somewhat crowded along the stiffly ascending primary branches; spikelets 4 to 5 mm long, 6- to 10-flowered; lemmas acuminate, 2 mm long.

Ditches and open moist soil, Trinidad and northern South America.

TRINIDAD: Piarco Savanna, *Freeman* 7533; *Britton and Hazen* 721; *Hitchcock* 10344. Aripo Road, *Broadway* 5827. Without locality, *Broadway* 7750.

16. Eragrostis ekmanii Hitchc., sp. nov.[12]

Perennial; culms erect, firm, wiry, 50 to 60 cm tall; sheaths glabrous, the summit glabrous or very sparsely pilose; blades erect, firm, flat, folded or involute, 5 to 15 cm long, 1 to 2 mm wide, sparsely long-pilose on the upper surface near the base, otherwise glabrous; panicle erect, stiff, consisting of several clusters of spikelets along an axis 9 to 14 cm long, the lower clusters 10 to 15 mm long, distant, the upper shorter, somewhat confluent; spikelets pale or slightly tinged with purple, about 5 mm long, mostly 9- to 13-flowered; florets closely imbricate, acute, firm, minutely roughened (under a lens) about 1.5 mm long, the lateral nerves distinct; nerves of palea scaberulous (fig. 22).

FIGURE 22.—*Eragrostis ekmanii*. Panicle, × 1; floret, × 10 (type).

Type in the United States National Herbarium, no. 1387320, collected in sandy pinelands, Los Indios, Isla de Pinos, November 8,

[12] Planta perennis; culmi erecti caespitosi, 50–60 cm alti; vaginae glabrae, faucibus glabris; laminae erectae planae vel involutae 5–15 cm longae 1–2 mm latae, supra pilosae ad basen panicula erecta 7–14 cm longa, spiculis fasciculatis, fasciculis inferioribus distantibus, superioribus confluentibus; spiculae 5 mm longae 9–13-florae; lemmata acuta arcte imbricata firma minute scaberula 1.5 mm longa, nervis distinctis.

1920, by E. L. Ekman (no. 12143). This is the only specimen examined.

17. Eragrostis purpurascens (Spreng.) Schult., Mant. 2: 317. 1824.

Poa purpurascens Spreng., Nov. Prov. Hal. 33. 1819. [Uruguay.]

Culms ascending or spreading, sparingly branching below; panicles commonly about one-third the entire height of the plant, about two-thirds as wide as long, the slender flexuous branches, branchlets, and pedicels divergent; spikelets about 8 mm long, dark-colored, the lemmas thin, the lateral nerves obscure.

Open ground and rocky hills, Brazil to Argentina; also in Antigua (*Duss* 3; *Box* 17, 20; *Wullschlaegel* 644). This is the species described by Grisebach [13] as *Eragrostis prolifera*. The plants from Antigua agree with Nees's description of *Eragrostis purpurascens* [14] and with the Sello specimen cited by him, but they may not be *Poa purpurascens* of Sprengel.

18. Eragrostis excelsa Griseb., Cat. Pl. Cub. 227. 1866. Cuba, *Wright* 3425.

Perennial; culms erect, robust, 1 to 2 m tall; blades elongate, flat, becoming loosely involute in drying, as much as 7 mm wide, the base somewhat clasping, the summit of the sheaths and the upper surface of the blades at the base densely long-pilose; panicles large, somewhat open, as much as 50 cm long, the long branches ascending; spikelets 5 to 7 mm long, 4- to 8-flowered.

Thickets near the coast, Bahamas and Cuba.

BAHAMAS: Berry Islands, *Britton and Millspaugh* 2186.

CUBA: Vicinity of Habana, *Léon* 962, 963, 3444, 3678, 5270, 5651, 7485, 8420, 8421; *Ekman* 1206. Boca de Canasí, *Léon* 13690. Mariel, *Britton and Gager* 7561. Toscano, *Wright* 3425.

19. Eragrostis salzmannii Steud., Syn. Pl. Glum. 1: 277. 1854. Bahia, Brazil.

Perennial; culms in large clumps, erect or ascending, 60 to 100 cm tall, branching above, the branches fascicled; sheaths glabrous at the summit or with a few long hairs; blades flat, becoming involute, 1 to 2 mm wide, tapering to a fine point; panicles oblong, rather dense, mostly 8 to 12 cm long, 2 to 3 cm wide, the branches short, spreading or ascending, densely many-flowered, the spikelets often spreading in all directions; spikelets 6 to 10 mm long, 10- to 20-flowered, often falcate; lemmas oblong, obtuse, imbricate, 1.5 mm long.

Sandy seacoasts and saline meadows, Cuba, Colombia, and Brazil.

CUBA: Río Tayabo, *Britton and Wilson* 5566; Casilda, *Britton and Wilson* 5510. Trinidad, *Ekman* 18913.

20. Eragrostis prolifera (Swartz) Steud., Syn. Pl. Glum. 1: 278. 1854.

Poa prolifera Swartz, Prodr. Veg. Ind. Occ. 27. 1788. St. Lucia, Guadeloupe.

Perennial; culms firm and hard, tufted, erect at base, leaning, branching above, about 1.5 m tall and 3 mm in diameter near the base, the branches more or less fascicled; summit of sheaths glabrous or sparsely pilose; blades elongate, slender, more or less involute, 0.5 to 2 mm wide when flat, attenuate to a fine point; panicle rather

[13] Fl. Brit. W. Ind. 532. 1864.
[14] Agrost. Bras. 506. 1829.

narrow, 15 to 45 cm long, the long branches more or less appressed; spikelets 5 to 8 mm long, 7- to 15-flowered; lemmas 1.5 to 1.8 mm long.

Ditches and marshes near the coast, Guadeloupe. Swartz, in the original description, gives the locality "Insulae caribaeae." In a later work [15] he gives "Lucia, Guadeloupe."

LEEWARD ISLANDS: Guadeloupe, *Duss* 3142; *Hitchcock* 16414, "Erect at base but branched above and more or less leaning. Panicles all slender and narrow. In ditches along road through brackish swamp."

21. Eragrostis domingensis (Pers.) Steud., Syn. Pl. Glum. 1: 278. 1854.

Poa domingensis Pers., Syn. Pl. 1: 88. 1805. Santo Domingo.

Eragrostis gigantea Trin., Mém. Acad. St. Pétersb. VI. Math. Phys. Nat. 1: 403. 1830. Santo Domingo.

Perennial; culms rather stout, erect, 0.5 to 1.5 m tall; sheaths glabrous or sparsely pilose at the summit; blades flat becoming more or less involute in drying, elongate, 2 to 5 mm wide; panicles 25 to 50 cm long, the branches ascending or appressed, usually rather closely flowered to the base, the lower sometimes distant; spikelets mostly short-pedicellate, 5 to 10 mm long, 10- to 25-flowered; lemmas 1.5 to 1.8 mm long.

Beaches and rocky soil near the coast, Cuba, Jamaica, Hispaniola, and a few other localities.

CUBA: Bahía Honda, *Wilson* 9257; *Ekman* 12696. Habana, *Léon* 5620, 5650. Santa Fé, *Léon* 15868. Yayales, *Ekman* 11192. Carabela Grande, *Roig* 3200.

JAMAICA: St. Anns Bay, *Ridley* 87. Bushy Park, *Harris* 12518. Healthshire Hills, *Harris* 11618. Mouth of Cockpit River, *Harris* 12466. Portland, *Britton* 1923. Port Henderson, *Ridley* in 1916. Grand Cayman, *Hitchcock* in 1890; *Millspaugh* 1240.

HAITI: Bayeux, *Ekman* H 2604. Cocoa Point, *Nash* 1780. Tortuga Island, *Leonard* 11426, 12380, 12486, 13918; *Ekman* H 4211.

LEEWARD ISLANDS: Guadeloupe, *Duss* 3422.

WINDWARD ISLANDS: Martinique, *Duss* 565.

13. MONANTHOCHLOË Engelm., Acad. Sci. St. Louis, Trans. 1: 436. 1859

Plants dioecious; spikelets, 2- or 3-flowered, usually sessile in pairs, concealed in the upper sheaths; glumes leaflike, rigid, with membranaceous sheaths and short, strongly veined spreading blades, the first about equaling the uppermost floret; lemmas rather rigid, the palea with winged keels. Creeping wiry perennial, with clustered short subulate blades, the spikelets inconspicuous at the ends of the short branches, only a little exceeding the leaves.

1. Monanthochloë littoralis Engelm., Acad. Sci. St. Louis, Trans. 1: 437. pl. 13. 1859. Texas.

Culms tufted, the short branches erect; blades falcate, mostly less than 1 cm long (fig. 23).

Muddy seashores and tidal flats, in the warmer parts of America.

CUBA: Cayo Cruz, *Shafer* 2773.

[15] Fl. Ind. Occ. 1: 216. 1797.

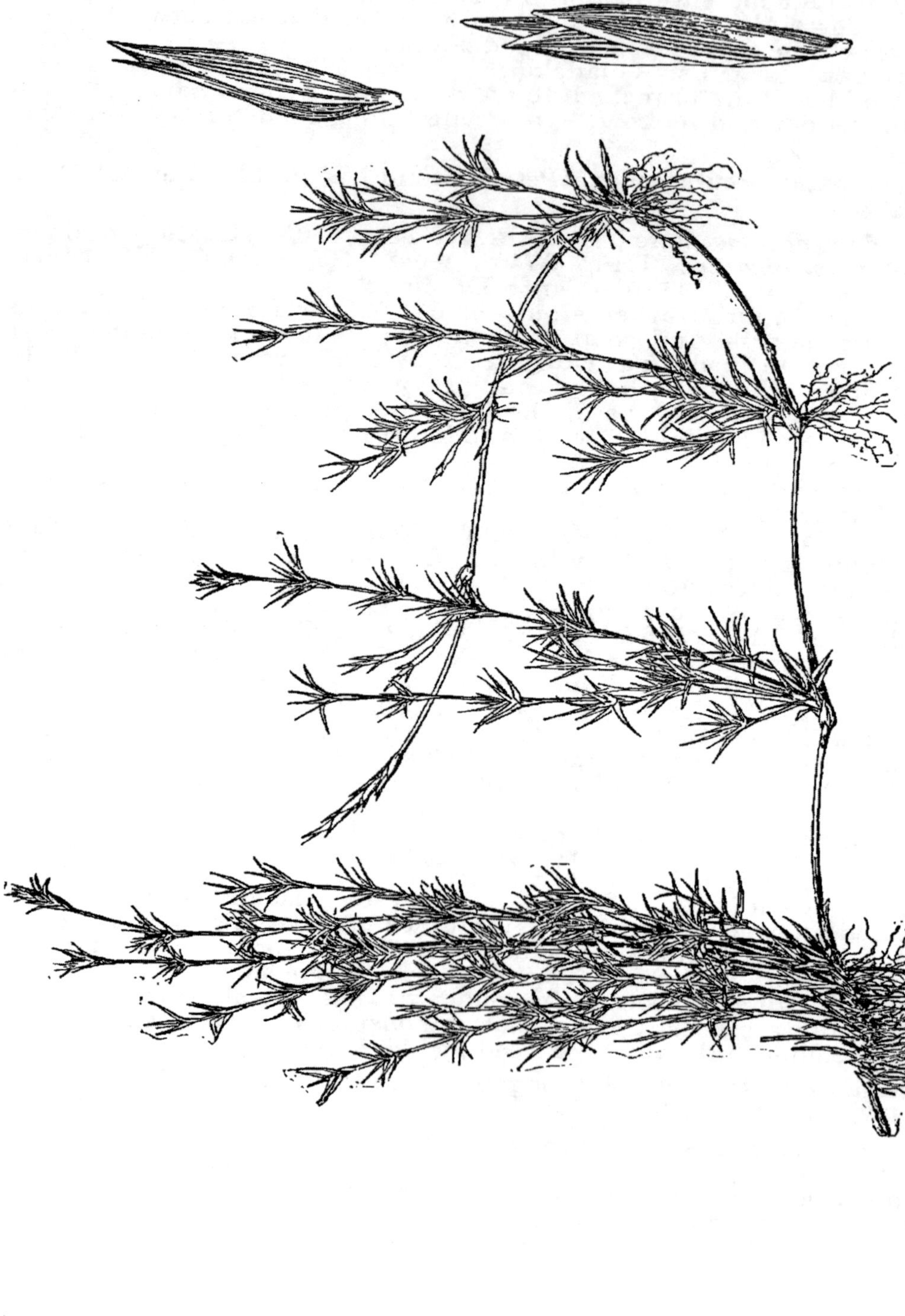

FIGURE 23.—*Monanthochloë littoralis.* Plant, × ½; pistillate spikelet and floret, × 5 (Hitchcock 623).

14. DISTICHLIS Raf., Jour. Phys. Chim. 89: 104. 1819. SALTGRASS

Plants dioecious; spikelets several- to many-flowered, the rachilla of the pistillate spikelets disarticulating above the glumes and between the florets; glumes unequal, broad, acute, keeled, mostly 3-nerved, the lateral nerves sometimes faint or obscured by striations and intermediate nerves; lemmas closely imbricate, firm, the pistillate coriaceous, the margins bowed out near the base, acute or acutish, 3-nerved, with several intermediate nerves or striations; palea as long as the lemma or shorter, the pistillate coriaceous, enclosing the grain. Low perennials, with extensively creeping scaly rhizomes, erect, rather rigid culms, and short, dense, rather few-flowered panicles.

1. **Distichlis spicata** (L.) Greene, Calif. Acad. Sci. Bull. 2: 415. 1887. SEASHORE SALTGRASS.

Uniola spicata L., Sp. Pl. 71. 1753. Atlantic coast of North America.

Low, erect, smooth perennial, with long running rhizomes, slender culms, spreading firm involute blades, and small compact panicles, the spikelets about 1 cm long. Extensive colonies of sterile plants may be recognized by the overlapping sheaths and conspicuously closely distichous stiff blades (fig. 24).

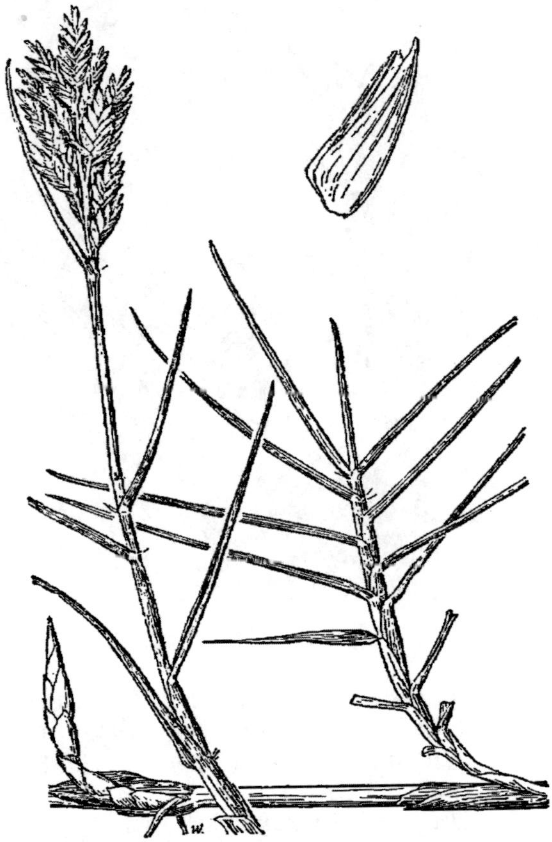

FIGURE 24.—*Distichlis spicata*. Plant, × 1; floret, × 5 (Hitchcock 2826).

Salt marshes and alkaline meadows near the coast, United States, Mexico, and northern West Indies.

BAHAMAS: New Providence, *Britton and Brace* 417; *Geogr. Soc. Baltimore* 4. Watlings Island, *Geogr. Soc. Baltimore* 491. Inagua, *Hitchcock* in 1890.

CUBA: Colonia, *Britton and Cowell* 9853. Habana, *Léon* 3476. Batabanó, *Léon* 5757; *Hitchcock* 262; *Baker and Wilson* 2293, 2348; *Ekman* 892. Baraguá, *Hitchcock* 23344. Cayo Sabinal, *Ekman* 15485. Guantanamo Bay, *Britton* 2264. Isla de Pinos, *Britton and Wilson* 15199.

HAITI: Croix-des-Bouquets, *Ekman* H 2157.

DOMINICAN REPUBLIC: Barahona, *Ekman* H 6957.

60256—36——4

15. UNIOLA L., Sp. Pl. 71. 1753

Spikelets, 3- to many-flowered, the lower 1 to 4 lemmas empty, the rachilla disarticulating above the glumes and between the florets; glumes compressed-keeled, rigid, usually narrow, nerved, acute or acuminate or rarely mucronate, lemmas compressed, sometimes conspicuously flattened, chartaceous, many-nerved, the nerves sometimes obscure, acute or acuminate, the empty ones at the base usually successively smaller, the uppermost usually reduced; palea rigid, sometimes bowed out in the winged keels. Rather tall, erect perennials, with flat or convolute blades and narrow or open panicles of compressed spikelets.

FIGURE 25.—*Uniola paniculata*. Plant, × 1/10; spikelets, × 1 (Kearney 2134).

Spikelets 8 to 10 mm broad, in a drooping panicle............ 1. U. PANICULATA.
Spikelets 2 to 4 mm wide, in a narrow erect panicle.......... 2. U. VIRGATA.

1. Uniola paniculata L., Sp. Pl. 71. 1753. Carolina. SEA-OATS.

A robust tufted smooth perennial, often 2 m tall, with long, tough, involute blades and long panicles of pale heavy spikelets, commonly 2.5 cm long; spikelets oval, 1.5 to 2.5 cm long; lemmas about 1 cm long (fig. 25).

Sandy seacoasts, Virginia to South America. In Cuba called "arana."

BAHAMAS: New Providence, *Geogr. Soc. Baltimore* 109; *Dewey* 570; *Eggers* 4119.

CUBA: Playa de Bacuranao, *Léon* 889. Bahía Honda, *Ekman* 10564. Playa de Marianao, *Léon* 964; *Van Hermann* 895. Cabañas, *Palmer and Riley* 751. Varedero Beach, *Killip* 13945. Cayo Sabinal, *Shafer* 701. Without locality, *Wright* 2823.

2. Uniola virgata (Poir.) Griseb., Fl. Brit. W. Ind. 531. 1864.

Poa virgata Poir., in Lam., Encycl. 5: 78. 1804. Santo Domingo.

Uniola racemiflora Trin., Mém. Acad. St. Pétersb. VI. Sci. Nat. 2^1: 55. 1836. Santo Domingo.

Uniola sparta Trin., Linnaea 10: 307. 1836. Cuba.

Plants in large clumps with many sterile shoots, the culms less robust than in *U. paniculata*, 1 to 2 m tall, the closely involute blades hard and very flexuous, the panicle stiffly erect, 40 to 60 cm long, the slender stiff branches narrowly ascending, 2 to 4 cm long; spikelets about 5 mm long. Panicle sometimes spikelike. Blades usually very scabrous on the margins.

Rocky seacoast, West Indies.

BAHAMAS: Eleuthera, *Geogr. Soc. Baltimore* 349. New Providence, *Geogr. Soc. Baltimore* 7, 301; *Curtiss* 131; *Eggers* 4333.

CUBA: Boca de Canasí, *Léon* 13174. Postelillo, *Ekman* 15411. Cajobabo, *Léon* 12317. Guantanamo, *Ekman* in 1922; *Hioram* 2168. Punta Brava, *Rugel* 870. Uvero Alto, *Léon* 14674. Bahía de Manatí, *Léon* 15751.

JAMAICA: Cane River Valley near coast, *Harris* 11312. Healthshire Hills, *Harris* 11622; *Hitchcock* 9761 (*Amer. Gr. Nat. Herb.* 698).

HAITI: Cabaret, *Leonard* 11801, 11857, 11861, 12043. Monte Cabrete, *Cook, Scofield, and Doyle* 72. Source-Matelas, *Ekman* H 2149. Jean Rabel, *Leonard* 12849, 13009. St. Marc, *Leonard* 3418. Randelle, *Ekman* H 677. Ennery, *Leonard* 8850a, 8880. Tortuga Island, *Leonard* 11527, 15394. Gonaïve Island, *Leonard* 3414.

DOMINICAN REPUBLIC: Higüey, *Ekman* H 12224. Monción, *Valeur* 215, 799. Santo Domingo, *Eggers* 2361. Puerto Plata, *Eggers* 2517. Azua, *Rose* 3825. Barahona, *Fuertes* 808; *Ekman* H 6724. Guayubín, *Abbott* 873, 896. Puerto Francés, *Abbott* 1215. Sosúa, *Ekman* H 14477.

PUERTO RICO: Guanica, *Chase* 6526; *Britton, Cowell, and Brown* 4890. Cabo Rojo, *Sintenis* 839, 840; *Britton, Cowell, and Brown* 4708. Guayanilla, *Shafer* 1992. Cayo Muertos, *Britton, Cowell, and Brown* 5002. Cayo Puerto Real, *Shafer* 2768. Puerto Diablo, *Shafer* 2938.

VIRGIN ISLANDS: St. Thomas, *Eggers* in 1882. Little St. James Island, *Britton and Rose* 1414.

16. DACTYLIS L., Sp. Pl. 71. 1753

Spikelets few-flowered, compressed, finally disarticulating between the florets, nearly sessile in dense 1-sided fascicles, these borne at the ends of the few branches of a panicle; glumes unequal, carinate, acute, hispid-ciliate on the keel; lemmas compressed-keeled, mucronate, 5-nerved, ciliate on the keel. Perennials, with flat blades and fascicled spikelets.

1. Dactylis glomerata L., Sp. Pl. 71. 1753. Europe. ORCHARD GRASS.

Rather coarse roughish perennial commonly about 1 m tall; blades flat; panicles of few to several branches naked at base, bearing toward the ends clusters of densely crowded, sparsely pilose spikelets 0.8 to 1 cm long.

Commonly cultivated in the United States as a meadow grass and frequent as an escape. In England called cocksfoot. Not grown in the West Indies.

JAMAICA: Cinchona, *Harris* 11779. Without locality, *Hart* 744.

17. GYNERIUM Willd.; Beauv., Ess. Agrost. 138. pl. 24. f. 6. 1812

Plants dioecious; spikelets several-flowered; pistillate spikelets with long-attenuate glumes and smaller long-silky lemmas; staminate spikelets with shorter glumes and glabrous lemmas. Large perennial reed.

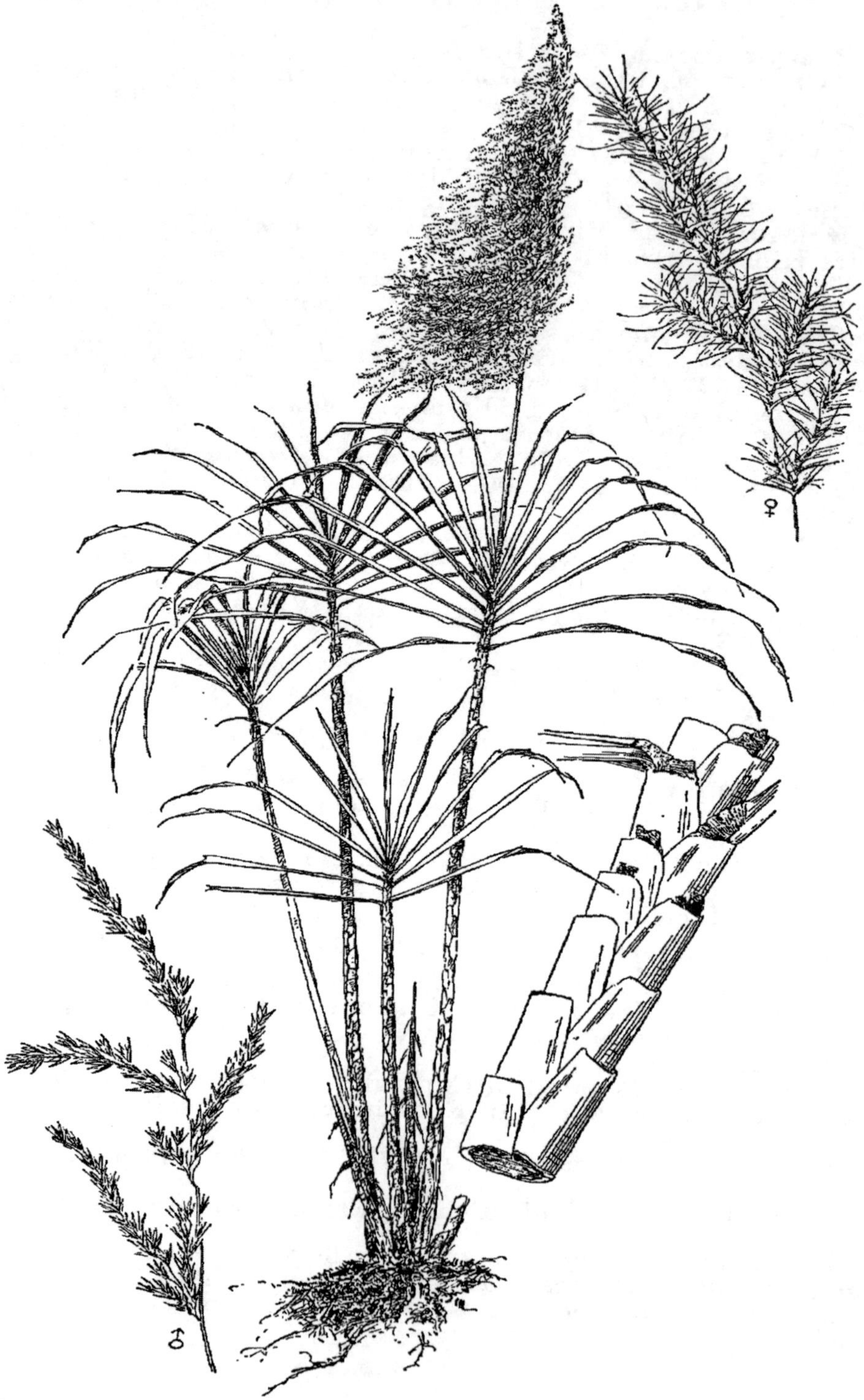

FIGURE 26.—*Gynerium sagittatum.* Plant, much reduced. Portion of culm showing imbricate sheaths, × ½; and staminate branch, × 1 (Leonard 5309); pistillate branch, × 1 (Chase 6442).

1. Gynerium sagittatum (Aubl.) Beauv., Ess. Agrost. 138. pl. 24. f. 6. 1812. WILD CANE.

Saccharum sagittatum Aubl., Pl. Guian. 1: 50. 1775. French Guiana.

Gynerium saccharoides Humb. and Bonpl., Pl. Aequin. 2: 105. pl. 115. 1813. Venezuela.

Arundo saccharoides Poir., in Lam., Encycl. Sup. 4: 703. 1816.

Aira gigantea Steud., Syn. Pl. Glum. 1: 224. 1854. Antilles.

Stout reeds often 10 m tall, the culms clothed below with old sheaths, the blades having fallen; blades sharply serrulate, commonly 2 m long and 4 to 6 cm wide (forming a great fan-shaped summit to the sterile culms); panicles pale, plumy, densely flowered, 1 m or more long, the main axis erect, the branches drooping; pistillate panicles silky from the villous florets; staminate panicles glabrous (fig. 26).

River banks and low ground, forming dense colonies, West Indies and southern Mexico to South America. Found throughout the West Indies except the Bahamas. Called in Cuba "caña de Castilla." The stems are used for lattices and light construction work.

18. ARUNDO L., Sp. Pl. 81. 1753

Spikelets several-flowered, the florets successively smaller, the summits of all about equal, the rachilla glabrous, disarticulating above the glumes and between the florets; glumes somewhat unequal, membranaceous, 3-nerved, narrow, tapering into a slender point, about as long as the spikelet; lemmas thin, 3-nerved, densely long-pilose, gradually narrowed at the summit, the nerves ending in slender teeth, the middle one longer, extending into a straight awn. Tall perennial reeds, with broad linear blades and large plumelike terminal panicles.

1. Arundo donax L., Sp. Pl. 81. 1753. Europe. GIANT REED, CARRIZO.

Culms stout, in large clumps, 2 to 6 m tall, sparingly branching, from thick knotty rhizomes; blades numerous, elongate, 5 to 7 cm wide on the main culm, conspicuously distichous, spaced evenly along the culm, the margins scabrous; panicle dense, erect, 30 to 60 cm long; spikelets 12 mm long (fig. 27).

River banks and moist ground, warmer parts of the Old World. Cultivated in America for ornament and occurring from Texas to California and southward to South America as an escape. Found on nearly all of the West Indian islands, including Bermuda and the Bahamas. In Cuba called "güín." The woody stems are used for lattices and light construction work.

19. PHRAGMITES Trin., Fund. Agrost. 134. 1820.

Spikelets several-flowered, the rachilla clothed with long silky hairs, disarticulating above the glumes and at the base of each joint between the florets, the lowest floret staminate or neuter; glumes 3-nerved, or the upper 5-nerved, lanceolate, acute, unequal, the first about half as long as the second, the latter shorter than the florets; lemmas

FIGURE 27.—*Arundo donax*. Plant, × ½: spikelet and floret, × 3 (Biltmore Herb. 7514).

FIGURE 28.—*Ph-agmites communis.* Plant, × ⅓; spikelet and floret, × 3 (Hitchcock 5078).

narrow, long-acuminate, glabrous, 3-nerved, the florets successively smaller, the summits of all about equal; palea much shorter than the lemma. Perennial reeds, with broad, flat linear blades and large terminal panicles.

1. Phragmites communis Trin., Fund. Agrost. 134. 1820.

COMMON REED.

Arundo phragmites L., Sp. Pl. 81. 1753. Europe.

Arundo occidentalis Sieber; Schult., Mant. 2: 289. 1824. Martinique, *Sieber* 31.

Phragmites martinicensis Trin.; Steud., Nom. Bot. ed. 2, 2: 324. 1841. Martinique, *Sieber* 31.

Phragmites phragmites Karst., Deutsch. Fl. 379. 1880.

Culms erect, 2 to 4 m tall, with stout creeping rhizomes and often also with stolons; blades flat, 1 to 5 cm wide; panicle tawny, 15 to 40 cm long, the branches ascending, rather densely flowered; spikelets 12 to 15 mm long, the florets exceeded by the hairs of the rachilla (fig. 28).

Swamps throughout the temperate regions of the world, extending into the Tropics. Called sometimes "wild cane."

BAHAMAS: New Providence, *Brace* 3901. Watlings Island, *Geogr. Soc. Baltimore* 521.

JAMAICA: Ferry River, *Maxon* 2187; *Harris* 11576. Black River, *Hitchcock* 9648. Cockpit River, *Ridley* 95.

HAITI: Port-au-Prince, *Ekman* H 5935. Roche à Bateau, *Ekman* H 298.

DOMINICAN REPUBLIC: Santo Domingo, *Rose* 3798; *Ekman* H 11167. Cabral, *Abbott* 1998. Arroyo Leonor, *Valeur* 513. Without locality, *Faris* 98; *Wright, Parry, and Brummel* 619.

PUERTO RICO: Herrera, *Eggers* 1195. Humacao, *Eggers* 712. Guanica, *Heller* 6289.

LEEWARD ISLANDS: Guadeloupe, *Duss* 4035.

WINDWARD ISLANDS: Martinique, *Duss* 1283. St. Lucia, *Box* 189.

TOBAGO: *Hitchcock* 10231.

20. TRIODIA R. Br., Prodr. Fl. Nov. Holl. 1: 182. 1810

Spikelets several-flowered; glumes nearly equal in length; lemmas broad, rounded on the back, the apex from minutely emarginate or toothed to deeply and obtusely lobed, 3-nerved, the lateral nerves near the margins, the midnerve excurrent between the lobes as a minute point or as a short awn, the lateral nerves often excurrent as minute points, usually all the nerves pubescent below. Erect tufted perennials, rarely rhizomatous or stoloniferous, the blades usually flat, the inflorescence an open or contracted panicle.

1. Triodia eragrostoides Vasey and Scribn., Contrib. U. S. Natl. Herb. 1: 58. 1890. Texas.

Culms slender, 50 to 100 cm tall; panicle open, 10 to 30 cm long; spikelets on slender pedicels, 1 to 10 mm long, oblong, mostly 6- to 10-flowered, scarcely 5 mm long; lemmas about 2 mm long, obtuse, obscurely pubescent along the midnerve on the lower half, the margins pubescent, the midnerve minutely excurrent (fig. 29).

Dry ground, rocks, and cliffs, Florida Keys, Cuba, Texas, and northern Mexico.

CUBA: Viñales, Sierra de la Guazasa, *Ekman* 16606.

FIGURE 29.—*Triodia eragrostoides*. Panicle, × 1; two views of floret, × 5 (Swallen 1471).

21. STREPTOGYNE Beauv., Ess. Agrost. 80. pl. 16. f. 8. 1812

Spikelets several-flowered, subsessile in a long 1-sided raceme; glumes unequal, much shorter than the elongate terete callus-tipped florets; lemmas firm, tapering into a slender awn; palea about as long as the lemma; stigmas 3, elongate, persistent, coiled, the mature fruits hanging by these entangled stigmas. Perennial with flat blades and slender erect raceme.

1. Streptogyne crinita Beauv., Ess. Agrost. 80. pl. 16. f. 8. 1812.

Erect perennial, 1 to 1.5 m tall, with elongate leaves mostly aggregate at the base and reaching beyond the base of the inflorescence; blades 1 to 1.5 cm wide; raceme slender, 30 to 50 cm long, the axis rather firm, the short-pediceled slender spikelets appressed, about 3 cm long, excluding the slender awns and curled stigmas (fig. 30).

Rich woods, Veracruz and Trinidad to Brazil. "Carolina", the locality given with the original description, is an error. Beauvois also mentions Guiana.

TRINIDAD: Caparo Forest, *Broadway* 4982. Tabaquite, *Hitchcock* 10122. Without locality, *Bot. Gard. Herb.* 3367; *Crueger.*

22. ORTHOCLADA Beauv., Ess. Agrost. 69. pl. 14. f. 9. 1812

Spikelets articulated below the glumes, 1-flowered with a prolongation of the rachilla, or 2-flowered, the florets distant; glumes and lemmas acuminate. A broad-leaved perennial with diffuse panicle.

1. Orthoclada laxa (L. Rich.) Beauv., Ess. Agrost. 70, 149, 168. 1812.

Aira laxa L. Rich., Act. Soc. Hist. Nat. Paris 1: 106. 1792. Cayenne.

Panicum rariflorum Lam., Encycl. 4: 746. 1798. Cayenne.

Orthoclada rariflora Beauv., Ess. Agrost. 70. pl. 14. f. 9. 1812.

Stoloniferous perennial; flowering culms ascending, leafy, simple, commonly 1 m long; blades slender-petioled, lanceolate, mostly 12 to 15 cm long, about 2.5 cm wide; panicle large, as broad as long, the long, slender, naked branches and capillary branchlets at first erect, finally stiffly divergent, bearing 1 to few spikelets at the extremities; glumes narrow, acute, 4 and 5 mm long; lemmas 6 to 7 mm long, acuminate or short-awned (fig. 31).

Rich woods, southern Mexico to Brazil; also in Guadeloupe and Trinidad.

FIGURE 30.—*Streptogyne crinita*, × ½ (Pittier 10602).

FIGURE 31.—*Orthoclada laxa*, × ½ (Donnell Smith 8791, Tuerckheim II. 1036).

LEEWARD ISLANDS: Guadeloupe, *Duss* 3522.

TRINIDAD: Valencia, *Eggers* 1399; *Broadway* in 1926. Guiaco, *Broadway* 4954. Caparo Forest, *Broadway* 4927. Mount Tocuche, *Britton, Hazen, and Mendelson* 1365. Port-of-Spain, *Hitchcock* 9969 (*Amer. Gr. Nat. Herb.* 696). Tabaquite, *Hitchcock* 10128 (*Amer. Gr. Nat. Herb.* 697).

23. ZEUGITES P. Br., Civ. Nat. Hist. Jam. ed. 2, 341 and Index II. 1789

(*Senites* Adans., Fam. Pl. 2: 39, 604. 1763. No generic description.)

Spikelets few to several-flowered, the lowest floret perfect, the others staminate, the rachilla joint between the perfect and staminate florets elongate; glumes and fertile lemma herbaceous, broad, with transverse veins between the nerves, obtuse or truncate, the glumes about half as long as the lemma; sterile lemmas membranaceous, narrower, acute. Broad-leaved perennials, with terminal panicles.

Culms clambering; blades 2 to 4 cm long____________________1. Z. AMERICANA.
Culms very slender, trailing, rooting at the nodes; blades 1 to 2 cm long.
2. Z. HAITIENSIS.

1. Zeugites americana Willd., Sp. Pl. 4: 204. 1805. Based on *Apluda zeugites* L.

Apluda zeugites L., Syst. Nat. ed. 10. 2: 1306. 1759. Jamaica.

Zeugites jamaicensis Raeuschel, Nom. Bot. ed. 3, 270. 1797. Name only. Jamaica.

Senites zeugites Nash; Hitchc., Contrib. U. S. Natl. Herb. 12: 127. 1908.

Loosely tufted branching glabrous clambering perennial 0.5 to 1 m tall; culms glossy brown or black, resembling fern stipes; blades on slender, often spreading petioles, ovate, 2.5 to 4 cm long; panicles mostly 5 to 7 cm long, loosely flowered, the branches and pedicels capillary; glumes and fertile lemma truncate (fig. 32).

Rich woods, above 1,000 m altitude. Blue Mountains, Jamaica, eastern Cuba and Hispaniola.

CUBA: Sierra Maestra, *Léon* 11334; *Bucher* 61; *Ekman* 7071.

JAMAICA: Cinchona, *Perkins* 1082; *Harris* 11418, 11431; *Harris and Lawrence* 15270; *Maxon* 1198; *Hitchcock* 9709. Gordon Town, *Hart* 789. Abbey Green, *Hitchcock* 9360 (*Amer. Gr. Nat. Herb.* 695); *Harris* 11584. Blue Mountain Peak, *Nichols* 115; *Orcutt* 2902. Catherines Peak, *Hitchcock* 9733; *Eggers* 3579. Sir Johns Peak, *Harris* 11596. Morces Gap Road, *Harris* 11327. Maccasucker Bump, *Maxon* 9593. Mossmans Peak, *Maxon* 9674. Sugar Loaf, *Maxon* 9972. New Haven Gap, *Maxon* 2673.

HAITI: Mission, *Leonard* 3863. Massif de la Selle, *Ekman* H 1282, H 1452.

DOMINICAN REPUBLIC: San José de Ocoa, *Ekman* H 12014.

2. Zeugites haitiensis (Pilger) Urban, Symb. Antill. 8: 51. 1920.

Zeugites americana subsp. *haitiensis* Pilger, in Urban, Symb. Antill. 6: 3. 1909. Haiti, *Picarda* 1523.

Senites haitiensis Hitchc. and Chase, Contrib. U. S. Natl. Herb. 18: 392. 1917.

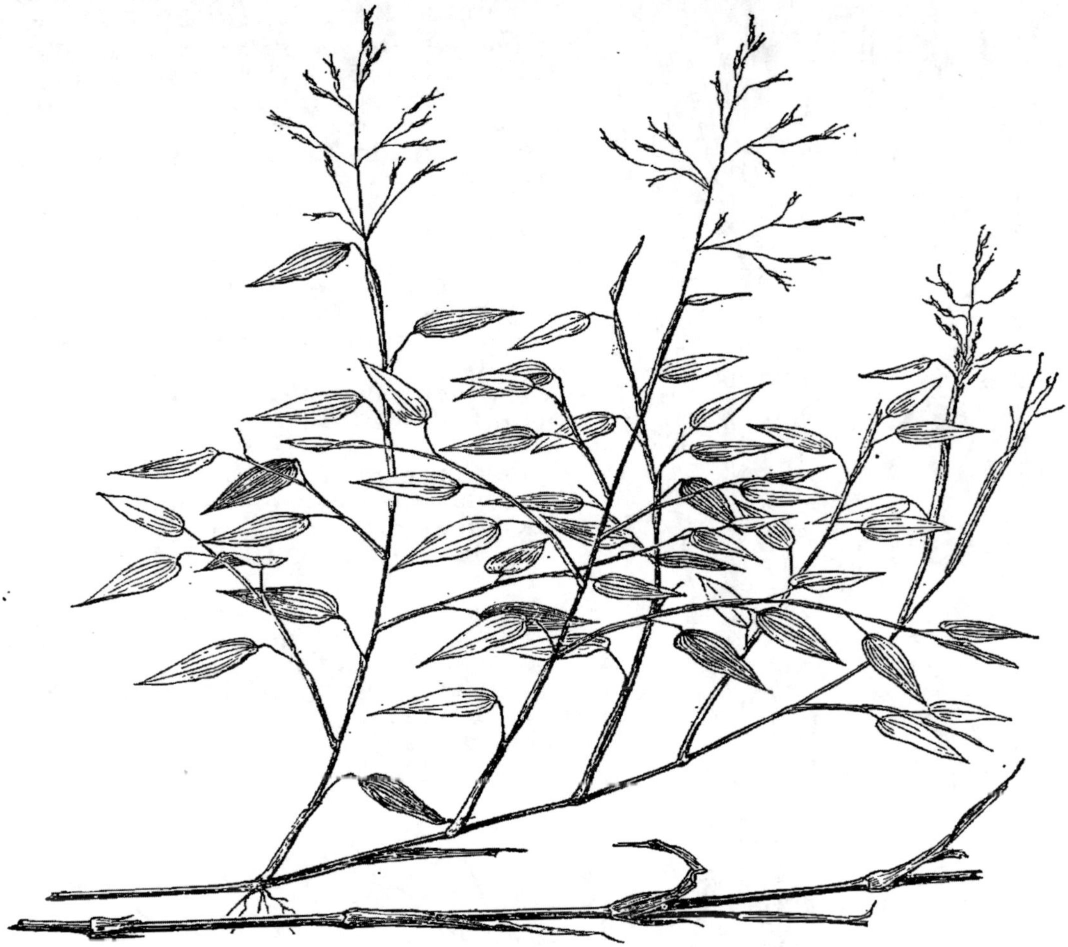

FIGURE 32.—*Zeugites americana*, × ½ (Hitchcock 9709).

Culms very slender, trailing, rooting at the nodes; blades ovate, 1 to 2 cm long.

Rocky shaded places, Hispaniola.

HAITI: Furcy, *Picarda* 1523. Ma Blanche, *Ekman* H 577. Morne la Visite, *Ekman* H 1650. Torbeek, *Ekman* H 5308. Petite Riviere de l'Artibonite Pérodin, *Ekman* H 3457.

DOMINICAN REPUBLIC: Santiago, *Ekman* H 16325.

24. PAPPOPHORUM Schreb.; Vahl, Symb. Bot. 3: 10. 1794

Spikelets, 1- to 3-flowered, the upper sterile; glumes thin, subequal; lemma subindurate, dissolving at the summit into about 13 slender awns, the second and third florets reduced, closely appressed to the palea, the awns of all the florets together forming a pappuslike crown, falling attached to the fruit. Tufted perennials with narrow panicles.

1. Pappophorum pappiferum (Lam.) Kuntze, Rev. Gen. Pl. 3²: 365. 1898.

Saccharum pappiferum Lam., Tabl. Encycl. 1: 155. 1791. South America. The type, with the name in Lamarck's script, was examined in the Lamarck Herbarium in Paris in 1935, by A. S. Hitchcock.

Pappophorum alopecuroideum Vahl, Symb. Bot. 3: 10. 1794. Vahl's statement "Ad fodinas Insulae Spanish Town Americae legit Du. v. Rohr" may refer to Spanish Town, Jamaica, but we have no specimens from that island.

Pappophorum laguroideum Schrad.; Schult., Mant. 2: 342. 1824. West Indies.

Perennial; culms erect, 1 m or more tall; blades elongate, involute; panicles silky, pale or whitish, dense, narrow or spikelike, 15 to 50 cm long, softly bristly with the numerous delicate awns (fig. 33).

Rocky soil, southern Mexico to South America and the West Indies.

CUBA: Vicinity of Habana, *Ekman* 952, 13149; *Léon* 2010, 4151, 9028; *Hitchcock* 254.

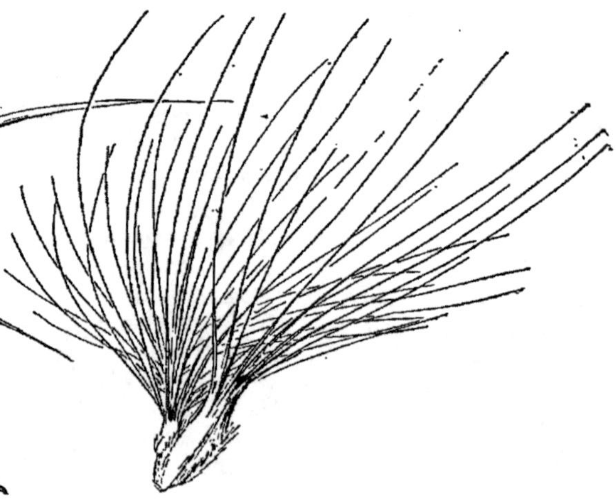

FIGURE 33.—*Pappophorum pappiferum*. Plant, × ½; spikelet, × 10 (Ekman 1 11...

PUERTO RICO: Mona Island, *Hess* 444; *Britton, Cowell, and Hess* 1777. Desecheo, *Hess* 427, 1607. Punta Aguila, *Britton, Cowell, and Brown* 4689.

VIRGIN ISLANDS: St. Thomas, *Eggers* in 1881, 1882.

LEEWARD ISLANDS: Antigua, *Box* 69, 87, 106. Guadeloupe, *Duss* 3164.

WINDWARD ISLANDS: Martinique, *Duss* 1329.

TRINIDAD: *Bot. Gard. Herb.* 3310.

TRIBE 3. HORDEAE

25. HORDEUM L., Sp. Pl. 84. 1753. BARLEY

Spikelets 1-flowered, in clusters of 3 at each joint of an articulate rachis, the middle spikelet sessile, perfect, the lateral spikelets stipitate, reduced to the awnlike glumes; glumes and lemmas awned.

1. **Hordeum pusillum** Nutt., Gen. Pl. 1: 87. 1818. Missouri Valley. LITTLE BARLEY.

Low, usually branched, annual with cylindric spikes 3 to 8 cm long, a part of the glumes dilated above the base.

Open dry ground, western United States, but introduced eastward and in Bermuda.

BERMUDA: *Brown* 694.

WHEAT (*Triticum aestivum* L.) and RYE (*Secale cereale* L.) are occasionally grown in the mountain regions and sometimes may be spontaneous but do not persist. *Triticum spinulosum* Lag. (Gen. et Sp. Nov. 7. 1816) described from Havana, collected by Balthazar Boldo, may belong to *T. aestivum.*

PARIANA SYLVESTRIS Nees (Agrost. Bras. 295. 1829), a Brazilian species, is mentioned by Grisebach [16] as having been found in St. Vincent by Guilding, "perhaps introduced."

26. LOLIUM L., Sp. Pl. 83. 1753. RYEGRASS

Spikelets several-flowered, solitary and sessile, placed edgewise to the continuous rachis, one edge fitting to the alternate concavities, the rachilla disarticulating above the glumes and between the florets; first glume wanting (except on the terminal spikelet), the second outward, strongly 3- to 5-nerved, equaling or exceeding the second floret; lemmas rounded on the back, 5- to 7-nerved, obtuse, acute, or awned. Annuals or perennials, with flat blades and simple terminal flat spikes.

Glume longer than the spikelet; annual------------------1. L. TEMULENTUM.
Glume shorter than the spikelet; perennial--------------2. L. MULTIFLORUM.

1. **Lolium temulentum** L., Sp. Pl. 83. 1753. Europe. DARNEL.

Lolium maximum Willd., Sp. Pl. 1: 462. 1797. Jamaica.

Lolium temulentum var. *leptochaeton* A. Br., Flora 1: 252. 1834. Europe.

---

[16] Fl. Brit. W. Ind. 528. 1864.

Culms 60 to 90 cm tall; blades 3 to 6 mm wide; spike strict, 15 to 20 cm long; glume about 2.5 cm long. Our specimens are awnless, var. *leptochaeton*.

Introduced from Europe.

CUBA: Habana, *Léon* 1583, 5052.

2. **Lolium multiflorum** Lam., Fl. Franç. 3: 621. 1778. Europe.
ITALIAN RYEGRASS.

Lolium italicum A. Br., Flora 17: 241. 1834. Europe.

Culms 30 to 60 cm tall; blades 2 to 4 mm wide; spike often subfalcate, 15 to 25 cm long; spikelets 10- to 20-flowered; lemmas 7 to 8 mm long, at least the upper awned (fig. 34).

Introduced from Europe. Used for pasture in the United States, but not grown in the West Indies.

BERMUDA: *Brown, Britton, and Bisset* 2137.

JAMAICA: Gordon Town, *Hart* 739.

TRIBE 4. AVENEAE

27. KOELERIA Pers., Syn. Pl. 1: 97. 1805

Spikelets 2- to 4-flowered, compressed, the rachilla disarticulating above the glumes and between the florets, prolonged beyond the perfect florets as a slender bristle or bearing a reduced or sterile floret at the tip; glumes usually about equal in length but unequal in shape, the lower narrow and sometimes shorter, 1-nerved, the upper somewhat broader above the middle, wider than the lower, 3- to 5-nerved; lemmas somewhat scarious and shining, the lowermost a little longer than the glume, obscurely 5-nerved, acute or short-awned, the awn, if present, borne just below the apex. Slender annuals or perennials with narrow blades and narrow dense panicles.

1. **Koeleria phleoides** (Vill.) Pers., Syn. Pl. 1: 97. 1805.

Festuca phleoides Vill., Fl. Delph. 7. 1785. Europe.

Annual; culms erect, 10 to 25 cm tall; sheaths and blades pilose, the blades flat, lax, 1 to 3 mm wide; panicles dense, spikelike, 1 to 4 cm long, 5 to 10 mm wide; glumes villous; lemmas glabrous, the lower about 3 mm long, the delicate awn 2 to 3 mm long.

Waste places, Bermuda. A native of Europe, introduced here and there in North America.

BERMUDA: *Brown* 473, 600, 605, 617; *Brown, Britton, and Bissett* 1956.

28. SPHENOPHOLIS Scribn., Rhodora 8: 142. 1906.
WEDGEGRASS

Spikelets 2- or 3-flowered, the pedicel disarticulating below the glumes, the rachilla produced beyond the upper floret as a slender bristle; glumes unlike in shape, the first narrow, acute, 1-nerved, the second broadly obovate, 3- to 5-nerved, somewhat coriaceous; lemmas firm, scarcely nerved, awnless, the first a little shorter or a little longer than the second glume. Slender perennials with flat blades and narrow panicles.

FIGURE 34.—*Lolium multiflorum*. Plant, × ½; spikelet, × 3; floret, × 5 (Suksdorf 5142).

1. Sphenopholis obtusata (Michx.) Scribn., Rhodora 8: 144. 1906.
PRAIRIE WEDGEGRASS.

Aira obtusata Michx., Fl. Bor. Amer. 1: 62. 1803. Florida.
Eatonia obtusata A. Gray, Man. ed. 2: 558. 1856.

Culms tufted, erect, 30 to 50 cm tall; blades flat, 1 to 5 mm wide; panicle narrow, contracted or spikelike, more or less lobed or interrupted, 3 to 8 cm long, pale or purplish; spikelets 2 to 3 mm long; glumes 2.3 to 2.5 mm long; lemmas scaberulous, about 2.5 mm long, the third, when present, reduced (fig. 35).

Pinelands and grassy plains, Hispaniola, at upper altitudes (1,200 to 2,300 m); United States and Mexico.

DOMINICAN REPUBLIC: Constanza, *Tuerckheim* 3319; *Ekman* H 13934. Valle Nuevo, *Ekman* H 13868. San José de Ocoa, *Ekman* H 12033.

29. TRISETUM Pers., Syn. Pl. 1: 97. 1805

Spikelets usually 2-flowered, sometimes 3- to 5-flowered, the rachilla prolonged behind the upper floret, usually villous; glumes somewhat unequal, acute, the second usually longer than the first floret; lemmas usually short-bearded at the base, 2-toothed at the apex, the teeth often awned, bearing from the back below the cleft apex a straight and included, or usually bent and exserted, awn. Tufted perennials with narrow blades and mostly dense panicles.

1. Trisetum spicatum (L.) Richt., Pl. Eur. 1: 59. 1890.
SPIKE TRISETUM.

Aira spicata L., Sp. Pl. 64. 1753. Lapland.

Culms tufted, erect, 30 to 70 cm tall; sheaths pubescent; blades flat, pubescent, mostly basal, 1 to 3 mm wide; panicle contracted, dense and spikelike or somewhat lobed or interrupted, 5 to 8 cm long; spikelets 5 to 7 mm long (fig. 36).

Open ground and pineland, at high altitudes, Hispaniola; Arctic regions of the Northern Hemisphere, extending south in the mountains to the Southern Hemisphere.

HAITI: Grand-Gosier, *Ekman* H 6867.

DOMINICAN REPUBLIC: Sierra de los Comisarios, *Ekman* H 6803. Valle Nuevo, *Eggers* 2227, 2228; *Tuerckheim* 3133. San José de Ocoa, *Ekman* H 11714.

30. DESCHAMPSIA Beauv., Ess. Agrost. 91. pl. 18. f. 3. 1812.
HAIRGRASS

Spikelets, 2-flowered, disarticulating above the glumes, the hairy rachilla prolonged behind the upper floret as a stipe, this sometimes bearing a reduced floret; glumes about equal, acute or acutish, membranaceous; lemmas thin, truncate and 2- to 4-toothed at the summit, bearing a slender awn from or below the middle, the awn straight, bent, or twisted. Slender annuals or perennials with shining spikelets in narrow or open panicles.

FIGURE 35.—*Sphenopholis obtusata*. Plant, × ½; glumes and floret, × 10 (Hitchcock 1453).

FIGURE 36.—*Trisetum spicatum*. Plant, × ½; spikelet and floret, × 5 (Rydberg and Bessey 3593).

1. Deschampsia domingensis Hitchc. and Ekman, sp. nov.[17]

Culms tufted, erect, 60 to 90 cm tall, from slender creeping rhizomes; sheaths glabrous, pale, somewhat papery; ligule membranaceous, acuminate, 8 mm long; shorter on the innovations; blades folded or involute, glabrous, elongate, laxly upright, flexuous, mostly less than 1 mm wide when folded; panicle open, 10 to 20 cm long, the branches capillary, flexuous, scabrous, spreading, usually naked for half their length or more, the lower as much as 10 cm or more long; spikelets on capillary pedicels, somewhat aggregate toward the ends of the branchlets; callus hairs 0.5 to 2 mm long, rather scant, the rachilla pilose; glumes 5 to 6 mm long; lemmas 2.5 to 4 mm long, thin, 4-toothed at summit, the teeth acuminate, the 2 outer 0.5 mm long; awn from near the base of the lemma, geniculate, the straight segment above the bend about 5 mm long; palea as long as the lemma (fig. 37).

FIGURE 37.—*Deschampsia domingensis.* Portion of panicle, × 1; spikelet, × 5 (type).

Type in the United States National Herbarium, no. 1502064, collected in moist pinelands, in Los Vallecitos del Yaque, prov. Azua, Cordillera Central, Dominican Republic, altitude about 2,500 m, October 2, 1929, by E. L. Ekman (no. H 13633b).

This species in habit resembles *D. caespitosa* (L.) Beauv., but differs in the slender rhizomes, the flexuous panicle branches, the insertion of the bent exserted awn at the base of the lemma, and in other details.

DOMINICAN REPUBLIC: Los Vallecitos del Yaque, *Ekman* H 13633a, H 13633b. Valle Nuevo, altitude 2,400 m, on rocks at a brook, *Ekman* H 13747. Sabana Alta, altitude 2,935 m, moist pine forest, *Ekman* H 13802. San Juan, Lomas de la Medianía, altitude 2,500 m, at the headwaters of a brook, "common above 2,500 m", *Ekman* H 13554.

[17] Culmi caespitosi erecti 60–90 cm alti, e rhizomatibus gracilibus: ligula 8 mm longa: laminae involutae graciles elongatae flexuosae circa 0.5 mm crassae; panicula patens 10–20 cm longa, ramis capillaribus flexuosis scabris patentibus infra nudis; glumae 5–6 mm longae; lemmata 2.5–4 mm longa, paulum supra basin aristam geniculatum emittens, aristae parte recta circa 5 mm longa.

31. AVENA L., Sp. Pl. 79. 1753

Spikelets 2 to several-flowered, the rachilla bearded, disarticulating above the glumes and between the florets; glumes about equal, membranaceous or papery, several-nerved, longer than the lower floret, usually exceeding the upper floret; lemmas indurate, except toward the summit, 5- to 9-nerved, bidentate at the apex, bearing a dorsal bent and twisted awn (this straight and reduced in *Avena sativa*). Annuals with open panicles of large spikelets.

Lemmas glabrous or nearly so ______ 1. A. SATIVA.
Lemmas pubescent with long brown hairs ______ 2. A. FATUA.

1. Avena sativa L., Sp. Pl. 79. 1753. OAT.

Culms rather stout, erect, 50 to 100 cm tall; blades flat, 5 to 10 mm wide; panicle 5 to 20 cm long or, in cultivated specimens, larger; spikelets mostly 2-flowered; glumes 2 to 3 cm long, striate-nerved; lemmas glabrous or nearly so, the awn often poorly developed.

Widely cultivated in temperate regions, often escaped but not persistent. Seldom grown in the West Indies.

BERMUDA: *Collins* 335.

CUBA: Habana, *Léon* 809.

JAMAICA: Summit of Blue Mountain Peak, *Hitchcock* 9369. Gordon Town, *Hart.*

2. Avena fatua L., Sp. Pl. 80. 1753. WILD OAT.

Differing from *A. sativa* chiefly in the long stiff brownish hairs on the florets and rachilla; awn stout, geniculate, twisted below, 3 to 4 cm long (fig. 38).

A weed in temperate regions, rare in the Tropics.

JAMAICA: Gordon Town, *Hart* 1493.

32. HOLCUS L., Sp. Pl. 1047. 1753 [18]

(*Notholcus* Nash; Hitchc., in Jepson, Fl. Calif. 1: 126. 1912)

Spikelets 2-flowered, the pedicel disarticulating below the glumes, the rachilla curved and somewhat elongate below the first floret, not prolonged above the second floret; glumes about equal, longer than the two florets; first floret perfect, its lemma awnless; second floret staminate, its lemma awned on the back. Perennials with flat blades and contracted panicles.

1. Holcus lanatus L., Sp. Pl. 1048. 1753. Europe. VELVET GRASS.

Notholcus lanatus Nash; Hitchc., in Jepson, Fl. Calif. 1: 126. 1912.

Perennial, 0.5 to 1 m tall, grayish-velvety throughout, the pale, rather densely flowered narrow panicle usually 8 to 10 cm long; glumes about 4 mm long; first floret 2 mm long, the second smaller, with a hooklike awn.

Pastures and waste places at upper altitudes. A native of Europe; introduced in America and occasionally cultivated as a meadow grass. Not grown in the West Indies.

JAMAICA: Without locality, *Hart* 748.

HAITI: Furcy, *Cook, Scofield, and Doyle* 35.

[18] See p. 407, footnote 9, for discussion of the name *Holcus*.

FIGURE 38.—*Avena fatua*. Plant, × ½; spikelet and floret, × 2 (Umbach).

33. DANTHONIA Lam. and DC., Fl. Franç. 3: 32. 1805. OATGRASS

Spikelets several-flowered, the rachilla readily disarticulating above the glumes and between the florets; glumes about equal, broad and papery, acute, mostly exceeding the uppermost floret; lemmas rounded on the back, obscurely several-nerved, the base with a strong callus, the apex bifid, the lobes acute, usually extending into slender awns, a stout awn arising from between the lobes; awn flat, tightly twisted below, geniculate, exserted, including three nerves of the lemma. Tufted perennials with few-flowered panicles of rather large spikelets.

Glumes 6 to 12, rarely to 15, mm long; lower lemmas 5 to 6 mm long. 1. D. DOMINGENSIS.
Glumes 20 to 22 mm long; lower lemmas 8 to 9 mm long--- 2. D. OBTORTA.

1. Danthonia domingensis Hack. and Pilger, in Urban, Symb. Antill. 6: 1. July 15, 1909. Santo Domingo, *Eggers* 2227b.

Danthonia shrevei Britton; Nash, Torreya 9: 210. October 26, 1909. Jamaica, *Shreve* in 1906.

Culms erect, 30 to 60 cm tall, finally forming large dense tussocks raised above the general level of the soil; leaves aggregate at the base, the blades usually elongate and overtopping the panicles, from rather coarse to subfiliform, involute, scabrous toward the ends; panicle 10 to 15 cm long, rather open; spikelets 12 to 15 mm long, 3 to 6-flowered; glumes 6 to 12 mm long, rarely longer; lemmas villous, 5 to 6 mm long, the awned lobes nearly as long, the main awn spreading, the terminal segment about 1 cm long; rachilla joints villous, noticeable between the florets (fig. 39, *A*).

On cleared slopes near the summit of Sir Johns Peak, altitude about 2,000 m, the only known locality in Jamaica, and Hispaniola in the mountains, 1,800 to 2,700 m.

JAMAICA: Sir Johns Peak, Harris 10914, 11429 (*Amer. Gr. Nat. Herb.* 647), 11594, 11629 (*Amer. Gr. Nat. Herb.* 648); *Hitchcock* 9720; *Shreve* in 1906.

HAITI: High ridge of La Selle, 2,400 to 2,500 m, "common", *Ekman* H 3153. Roberjot, *Ekman* H 1424. Pétionville, *Ekman* H 5997. Marigot, *Ekman* H 10048.

DOMINICAN REPUBLIC: Sierra de los Comisarios, *Ekman* H 6809. Constanza, *Tuerckheim* 3414. Loma Rosilla, *Fuertes* 1776. Valle Nuevo, *Eggers* 2227b. Monción, *Ekman* H 12830. Los Vallecitos del Yaque, *Ekman* H 13659.

2. Danthonia obtorta Chase, sp. nov.[19]

Habit similar to that of the preceding, the lower sheaths somewhat firmer; blades elongate, equaling or overtopping the panicle, involute, slender, narrower at base than the firm summit of the sheath, the lower part curved forward, bringing the upper surface downward; this surface pilose with fragile hairs, the blades otherwise glabrous and smooth; panicle 13 to 16 cm long, loose; spikelets 2 to 2.5 cm long, 7- to 9-flowered, the slender villous rachilla joints strongly zigzag; glumes 2 to 2.2 cm long; lemmas villous on the lower half, 8 to 9 mm long (to the base of central awn) the awned lobes nearly

[19] Perennis caespitosa; culmi erecti, 40–55 cm alti; laminae elongatae involutae, basi tortae pilosae; panicula 13–16 cm longa, sublaxa; spiculae magnae; glumae 2–2.2 cm longae; lemmata 8–9 mm longa, basi pilosa; arista 17–20 mm longa.

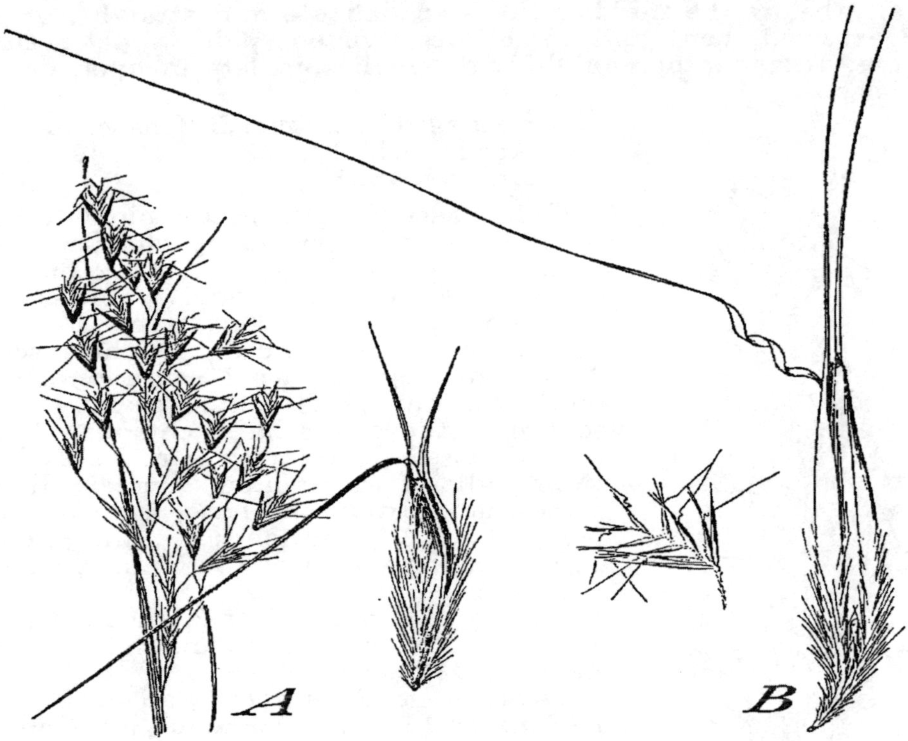

FIGURE 39.—*A, Danthonia domingensis.* Panicle, × ½; floret, × 5 (Ekman 12830). *B, D. obtorta.* Spikelet, × 1; floret, × 5 (type).

as long, the main awn spreading, the terminal segment 15 to 17 mm long (fig. 39, *B*).

Closely related to *Danthonia domingensis*, but the spikelets much larger, the blades not widened at base, bent forward with a twist, a character found in some grasses of windswept areas, like high paramos. The specific name refers to this twisted base.

Type in the United States National Herbarium, no. 1385638, collected near the highest peak of Morne de la Selle, 2,700 m, Gauthier, Massif de la Selle, Haiti, February 1, 1925, by Erik L. Ekman (no. H 3164).

An immature specimen was collected at Valle Nuevo, prov. La Vega, Dominican Republic, *Ekman* H 13748.

TRIBE 5. AGROSTIDEAE

34. CALAMAGROSTIS Adans.; Roth, Tent. Fl. Germ. 1: 33. 1788.

REEDGRASS

Spikelets 1-flowered, the rachilla disarticulating above the glumes, usually prolonged behind the palea as a short, commonly hairy bristle; glumes about equal, acute or acuminate; lemma shorter and usually more delicate than the glumes, the callus bearing a tuft of hairs which are often copious and as long as the lemma, awned from the back, usually below the middle, the awn delicate and straight, or stouter and exserted, bent and sometimes twisted; palea shorter than the lemma. Slender perennials with small spikelets in open or narrow panicles.

FIGURE 40.—*Calamagrostis leonardii*. Panicle, × 1; spikelet, × 5 (type).

1. **Calamagrostis leonardii** Chase, Jour. Wash. Acad. Sci. 17: 72. f. 1. 1927. Haiti, *Leonard* 4325.

Culms ascending from a geniculate base, 60 to 100 cm tall, producing slender rhizomes; ligule 3 to 4 mm long; blades lax, flat, 6 to 20 cm long, 2 to 5 mm wide, scabrous; panicle pale, nodding, narrow but rather loose, 12 to 20 cm long, the slender branches ascending, 2 to 5 cm long; glumes 4.5 mm long, scabrous on the back and keel; lemma about 4 mm long, scabrous, the callus hairs copious, about half as long as the lemma; awn from a little above the middle of the lemma, slender, divergent; somewhat flexuous at base, 4 to 5 mm long; palea about 3.5 mm long; rachilla joint about one-third the length of the lemma, long-pilose (fig. 40).

Grassy places, 1,300 to 2,100 m, Hispaniola.

HAITI: Pétionville, *Ekman* H 1113. Furcy, *Leonard* 4325, 4370.

DOMINICAN REPUBLIC: San José de Ocoa, *Ekman* H 11949. Sierra de los Comisarios, *Ekman* H 6812. Valle Nuevo, *Ekman* H 13809.

35. AGROSTIS L., Sp. Pl. 61. 1753. BENTGRASS

Spikelets, 1-flowered, disarticulating above the glumes, the rachilla usually not prolonged; glumes equal or nearly so, acute, acuminate, or sometimes awn-pointed, carinate, usually scabrous on the keel, and sometimes on the back; lemma obtuse, usually shorter and thinner in texture than the glumes, awnless or dorsally awned, often hairy on the callus; palea usually shorter than the lemma, 2-nerved in only a few species, usually small and nerveless or obsolete. Mostly perennials, the small spikelets in open or narrow panicles.

Palea present.
- Panicle contracted, somewhat lobed, the branches floriferous nearly to base; glumes scabrous on back and keels. 1. A. VERTICILLATA.
- Panicle open, the branches naked at base; glumes scabrous only on keels. 2. A. ALBA.

Palea wanting.
Culms 60 cm tall, leafy, spikelets about 2 mm long............3. A. CANINA.
Culms 15 to 40 cm tall; the leaves mostly near the base; spikelets 2.5 to 3 mm long..4. A. HIEMALIS.

1. Agrostis verticillata Vill., Prosp. Pl. Dauph. 16. 1779. Europe.

Culms decumbent or spreading, 20 to 40 cm or even as much as 1 m long; blades flat; panicles dense, more or less interrupted or lobed, 5 to 10 cm, or sometimes 15 cm, long; spikelets about 2 mm long, the glumes scabrous; lemma and palea about 1 mm long.

Ditches and moist places, Jamaica; a native of the Mediterranean region; widely introduced in warm temperate regions from southern United States to Argentina.

JAMAICA: Road to Strawberry Hill, Blue Mountains (altitude 1,300 m), *Harris* 12895.

2. Agrostis alba L., Sp. Pl. 63. 1753. Europe. REDTOP.

Culms erect or ascending from a decumbent or more or less creeping base, 30 to 60 cm tall, or even taller; blades flat, 1 to 5 mm wide; panicles open but rather narrow, mostly 10 to 15 cm long, many-flowered, the lower branches spreading, verticillate; spikelets 2 to 2.5 mm long; glumes glabrous except the keels; palea about half as long as the lemma (fig. 41).

The West Indian specimens are mostly fine-leaved, with decumbent or creeping culms.

Open ground and moist places at upper altitudes in Jamaica and Hispaniola; a native of Europe; widely cultivated in temperate regions and introduced at high altitudes in the Tropics. Not grown in the West Indies.

JAMAICA: Blue Mountain Peak, *Harris* 12664, 12666; *Hitchcock* 9368. Yallahes River course, *Harris* 12492. Morces Gap, *Harris* 12894. North slope of Catherines Peak, *Hitchcock* 9735 (sterile). Gordon Town, *Hart* 927.

HAITI: Furcy (altitude 1,300 m), *Leonard* 4516.

3. Agrostis canina L., Sp. Pl. 62. 1753. Europe. VELVET BENT.

Culms decumbent, about 60 cm tall; blades flat; panicle somewhat open, 5 to 15 cm long; spikelets 2 mm long; lemma awned, the awn geniculate, about 3 mm long.

Grassy summit of Blue Mountain Peak; native of Europe; occasional in pastures and lawns in the United States, and sometimes used there on golf greens. Not grown in the West Indies.

JAMAICA: Blue Mountain Peak, *Harris* 12667.

The single specimen cited above is not representative. The tall culms are leafy and the panicle contracted and somewhat distorted as if diseased.

4. Agrostis hiemalis (Walt.) B. S. P., Prel. Cat. N. Y. 68. 1888. TICKLE GRASS.

Cornucopiae hyemalis Walt., Fl. Carol. 73. 1788. South Carolina.
Agrostis scabra Willd., Sp. Pl. 1: 370. 1797. North America.

Culms tufted, erect or somewhat spreading at base, 15 to 40 cm tall; sheaths scaberulous; ligule membranaceous, thin, oblong, erose, 3 mm long; blades flat or, especially on the innovations, involute, scabrous, 3 to 10 cm long, 0.5 to 2 mm wide; panicles pale or purple, open, 5 to 15 cm long, pyramidal to oblong-pyramidal, the branches very scabrous, ascending or spreading, capillary, naked below for more

FIGURE 41.—*Agrostis alba*. Plant, × ½; 2 spikelets and floret, × 5 (Chase 5191).

than half their length, the branchlets also naked below, the lower branches in verticils; spikelets somewhat approximate on the branchlets, slender-pediceled; glumes acute, glabrous except the scabrous keels, the first about 2.5 to 3 mm long, the second a little shorter; lemma obtuse, about 2 mm long, minutely pilose at base, awned or awnless, the awn when present attached above the middle, curved or bent but not twisted or distinctly geniculate, exserted about 1 mm; palea wanting; anthers 0.4 to 0.5 mm.

Pine woods and open ground, Hispaniola in the mountains, 1,000 to 2,500 m altitude.

HAITI: Pétionville, *Ekman* H 1115, H 10088. Croix-des-Bouquets, *Ekman* H 7693. Mérion, *Ekman* H 3181. Furcy, *Leonard* 4318, 4593.

DOMINICAN REPUBLIC: Constanza, *Tuerckheim* 3227, 3413, 3558; *Ekman* H 14095. Loma Rosilla, *Fuertes* 1783. Valle Nuevo, *Ekman* H 13857. Top of Pelona (3,150 m), *Ekman* H 13648. Los Vallecitos del Yaque, *Ekman* H 13638. San José de Ocoa, *Ekman* H 11686.

This form of *A. hiemalis* approaches the mountain form found in the White Mountains of New Hampshire and in other mountains of the eastern part of the United States. It differs in being usually more lax and spreading. The mountain form [20] referred to has been called *Trichodium montanum* Torr., *Agrostis oreophila* Trin., *A. laxiflora* var. *montana* Tuckerm., and *A. torreyi* Tuckerm. The spikelets are awned or awnless.

The West Indian specimens are rather diverse among themselves but no more so than specimens in the United States. Ekman's no. 11686 is 60 cm tall, leafy, rather lax, the blades 3 mm wide, while *Ekman* H 13857 is 10 cm tall, the blades about 0.5 mm wide. Dr. Ekman wrote "there is but one species in Santo Domingo of this group", that is, the diverse specimens all belong to one species. The following specimens cited above are awned, the others awnless; *Ekman* H 1115, H 3181, H 7693, H 10088; *Leonard* 4318, 4593; *Tuerckheim* 3227, 3557.

36. POLYPOGON Desf., Fl. Atlant. 1: 66. 1798

Spikelets, 1-flowered, the pedicel disarticulating a short distance below the glumes, leaving a short-pointed callus attached; glumes equal, entire or 2-lobed, awned from the tip or from between the lobes, the awn slender, straight; lemma much shorter than the glumes, hyaline, usually bearing a slender straight awn shorter than the awns of the glumes. Annuals or perennials with flat blades and dense bristly panicles.

Plants annual; panicle dense and silky------------------1. P. MONSPELIENSIS.
Plants perennial; panicle lobed or interrupted, not silky-------2. P. LUTOSUS.

1. Polypogon monspeliensis (L.) Desf., Fl. Atlant. 1: 67. 1798.
RABBITFOOT GRASS.

Alopecurus monspeliensis L., Sp. Pl. 61. 1753. Europe.

Annual; culms 10 to 30 cm tall; blades flat, 2 to 4 mm wide, the sheaths inflated; panicles dense, 2 to 6 cm long, about 1 cm thick, silky with numerous awns; spikelets about 1.5 mm long, the awns about 5 mm long (fig. 42).

[20] For a further discussion of this form see North American Species of Agrostis, U. S. Dept. Agr., Bur. Plant Indus. Bull. 68: 43. 1905.

FIGURE 42.—*Polypogon monspeliensis.* Plant, × ½; glumes and floret, × 10 (Chase 5584).

Roadsides and waste places, Bermuda; native of the Old World, widely introduced in America.

BERMUDA: *Harshberger* in 1905; *Brown* 714.

2. **Polypogon lutosus** (Poir.) Hitchc., U. S. Dept. Agr. Bull. 772: 138. 1920. DITCH POLYPOGON.

Agrostis littoralis With., Bot. Arr. Veg. Brit. ed. 3. 2: 129. pl. 23. 1796. Not *A. littoralis* Lam., 1791. England.

Polypogon littoralis J. E. Smith, Comp. Fl. Brit. 13. 1800.

Agrostis lutosa Poir., in Lam., Encycl. Sup. 1: 249. 1810. Europe.

Perennial; culms geniculate at base, 30 to 80 cm tall; blades flat; panicle oblong, 5 to 15 cm long, more or less interrupted or lobed; spikelets about 2 mm long, the awns 2 to 3 mm long (fig. 43).

Ditches and waste places, Bermuda; native of Europe, widely introduced in the warmer parts of America.

BERMUDA: *Brown* 698; *Collins* 138.

FIGURE 43.—*Polypogon lutosus.* Panicle, × 1; glumes and floret, × 10 (Hitchcock 2686).

37. PHLEUM L., Sp. Pl. 59. 1753

Spikelets 1-flowered, laterally compressed, disarticulating above the glumes; glumes equal, membranaceous, keeled, abruptly mucronate or awned; lemma shorter than the glumes, hyaline, broadly truncate, 3- to 5-nerved; palea narrow, nearly as long as the lemma. Annuals or perennials, with erect culms, flat blades, and dense, cylindric panicles.

1. **Phleum pratense** L., Sp. Pl. 59. 1753. Europe. TIMOTHY.

Culms tufted, erect, 50 to 100 cm tall; blades flat, 3 to 5 mm wide; panicle cylindric, dense, spikelike, mostly 5 to 10 cm long; spikelets 2 to 3 mm long (fig. 44).

Commonly cultivated as a meadow grass in temperate regions, but not grown in the West Indies. Established on the summit of Blue Mountain Peak around the rest house.

JAMAICA: Blue Mountain Peak, *Harris* 12665; *Hitchcock* 9374.

38. MUHLENBERGIA Schreb.; Gmel., Syst. Nat. 2: 171. 1791

Spikelets 1-flowered, the rachilla disarticulating above the glumes; glumes usually shorter than the lemma, obtuse to acuminate or awned, the first sometimes small, rarely obsolete; lemma firm-membranaceous, 3- to 5- nerved, with a very short, usually minutely pilose callus, the apex acute, extending into a straight or flexuous awn, or sometimes only mucronate. Species of the West Indies perennial.

Panicle diffuse; blades involute, elongate .... 1. M. CAPILLARIS.
Panicle narrow, the branches appressed or ascending; blades flat, mostly less than 10 cm long .... 2. M. PARVIGLUMIS.

FIGURE 44.—*Phleum pratense*. Plant, × ½ glumes and floret, × 10 (Mearns 2209).

1. Muhlenbergia capillaris (Lam.) Trin., Gram. Unifl. 191. 1824.

Stipa capillaris Lam., Tabl. Encycl. 1: 158. 1791. Carolina.

Culms tufted, slender, erect, 40 to 70 cm tall; blades involute, elongate, slender or almost capillary, numerous, commonly overtopping the panicle; panicle large, diffuse, purplish; the numerous branches capillary; spikelets narrow, 3 mm long; glumes acute, about 1 mm long, equal or nearly so; awn of lemma capillary, somewhat flexuous, 5 to 8 mm long (fig. 45).

Savannas and rocky soil, eastern United States and Mexico, and the northern West Indies.

BAHAMAS: Andros Island, *Small and Carter* 8794. New Providence, *Britton and Brace* 403.

CUBA: Remates, *Ekman* 11186. Laguna Jovero, *Shafer* 11043. La Coloma, *Roig and Chrysler* 3293. Guanimar, *Wright* 3836. Habana, *Léon* 2011. Batabanó, *Léon* 5756. Cayo Cruz, *Shafer* 2795. Isla de Pinos, *Ekman* 11631.

PUERTO RICO: Arecibo, *Chase* 6557.

2. Muhlenbergia parviglumis Vasey, Contrib. U.S. Natl. Herb. 3: 71. 1892. Texas, *Nealley*.

Culms rather loosely tufted, erect or spreading and leaning, about 30 cm tall; blades flat, spread-

FIGURE 45.—*Muhlenbergia capillaris*. Plant, × ½; glumes and floret, × 10 (Scribner).

ing, minutely scabrous, long-acuminate, 5 to 10 cm long, 1 to 2 mm wide; panicles narrow, 5 to 10 cm long, the branches appressed or ascending; glumes less than 0.5 mm long, somewhat unequal, obtuse or acutish; lemma narrow, scaberulous toward the narrowed minutely bifid tip, about 2 mm long; awn capillary, somewhat flexuous, about 1.5 cm long (fig. 46).

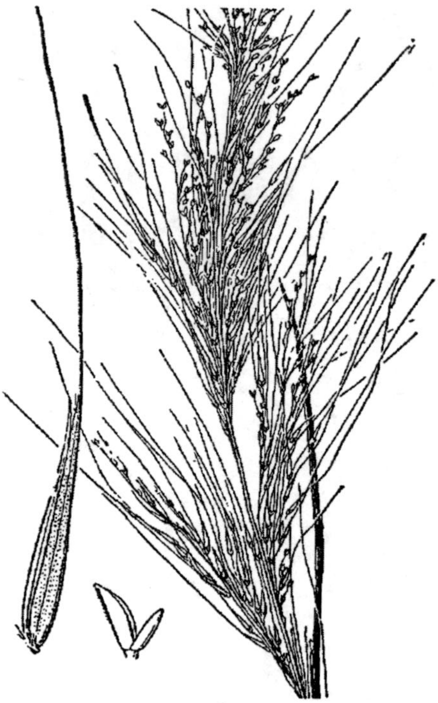

FIGURE 46.—*Muhlenbergia parviglumis.* Panicle, × 1; glumes and floret, × 10 (Vasey).

Limestone hills, Cuba; Texas and northern Mexico.

CUBA: Viñales, Loma de la Bandera, north of Pinar del Río, *Ekman* 16547.

39. SPOROBOLUS R. Br., Prodr. Fl. Nov. Holl. 169. 1810. DROPSEED

Spikelets, 1-flowered, the rachilla disarticulating above the glumes; glumes usually unequal, the second often as long as the spikelet; lemma membranaceous, 1-nerved, awnless; palea usually prominent and as long as the lemma or longer; seed often free from pericarp. Species of West Indies all perennial, except *S. bahamensis* and *S. tenuissimus*.

Plants annual. Panicle open; spikelets about 1 mm long.
  Glumes nearly equal, 0.3 to 0.4 mm long. 1. S. BAHAMENSIS.
  Glumes unequal, the first one-fourth, the second half as long as the spikelet. 2. S. TENUISSIMUS.
Plants perennial.
  Creeping rhizomes present. Panicles pale, spikelike; leaves conspicuously distichous---------10. S. VIRGINICUS.
  Creeping rhizomes wanting.
    Panicle large and diffuse, at least half the entire height of the plant. 3. S. BRASILIENSIS.
    Panicle narrow, contracted or if somewhat open not diffuse, less than one-third the entire height of the plant.
      Glumes both shorter than the spikelet.
        Glumes nearly equal, about 0.5 mm long; branches of panicle slender, somewhat loosely arranged and spreading; basal sheaths scarcely compressed------------------------------------4. S. INDICUS.
        Glumes unequal, the first about one-third as long as the spikelet, the second a little longer; branches of the panicle short, contiguous, the panicle thus rather compact and spikelike; basal sheaths compressed------------------------------------5. S. POIRETII.
      Glumes unequal, the second as long as the spikelet.
        Spikelets 1.5 mm long; panicle pyramidal-------6. S. PYRAMIDATUS.
        Spikelets 2 to 4 mm long; panicle elongate-oblong.
          Panicle green or whitish; spikelets about 2 mm long. 7. S. DOMINGENSIS.
          Panicle purple; spikelets 3 to 4 mm long.
            Basal sheaths copiously felty-ciliate; spikelets about 4 mm long. 8. S. CUBENSIS.
            Basal sheaths not felty; spikelets 3 mm long--9. S. PURPURASCENS.

1. Sporobolus bahamensis Hack., Oesterr. Bot. Ztschr. 52: 56. 1902.
Acklins Island, Bahamas, *Eggers* 3905.

Annual; culms slender, erect, 15 to 30 cm tall; blades loosely involute, mostly 4 to 6 cm long, about 1 mm thick, glabrous; panicle oblong, open, about half the length of the entire culm, 3 to 4 cm wide, the branches capillary, ascending or spreading, mostly solitary, glabrous, naked on the lower part; spikelets a little more than 1 mm long, somewhat clustered, short-pediceled, the lateral pedicels shorter than the spikelet, glabrous; glumes shorter than the spikelet, nearly equal, 0.3 to 0.4 mm long, the first acutish, the second broader, obtuse; lemma and palea equal, obtuse; fruit a little shorter than the lemma.

Known only from the Bahamas.

BAHAMAS: Acklins Island, *Eggers* 3905; *Brace* 4251.

In the Grasses of the West Indies [21] this species was referred to *S. atrovirens* (H. B. K.) Kunth, of Mexico, which differs in being perennial and in having slightly smaller spikelets short-pediceled along one side of the branches, the first glume only 0.2 mm long.

2. Sporobolus tenuissimus (Schrank) Kuntze, Rev. Gen. Pl. 3 [2]: 369. 1898.

Panicum tenuissimum Schrank, Denkschr. Bot. Ges. Regensb. 2: 26. 1822. Brazil.

Agrosticula muralis Raddi, Agrost. Bras. 33. pl. 1. f. 2. 1823. Brazil.

Sporobolus muralis Hitchc. and Chase, Contrib. U. S. Natl. Herb. 18: 368. 1917.

Annual; culms slender, erect, compressed, glabrous, 25 to 75 cm tall, blades flat, 5 to 15 cm long, 1 to 3 mm wide; panicles about half the length of the entire culm, narrow, open, 3 to 6 cm wide, the branches and branchlets glabrous, capillary, spreading; spikelets glabrous, about 1 mm long on slender glabrous pedicels; first glume about one-quarter, the second about half the length of the spikelet.

Waste ground, Lesser Antilles to Brazil.

VIRGIN ISLANDS: St. John, *Raunkaier* 1333. Tortola, *Britton and Shafer* 698. St. Croix, *Ricksecker* 290.

WINDWARD ISLANDS: Martinique, *Duss* 4508; *Hitchcock* 16460. St. Lucia, *Box* 183; *Hitchcock* 16470; *Kemp* 13, 33; *Glasgow* 6.

LEEWARD ISLANDS: Guadeloupe, *Stehlé* 275.

TRINIDAD: Port-of-Spain, *Broadway* 7415. Botanic Garden, *Broadway* 7941.

3. Sporobolus brasiliensis (Raddi) Hack., Bull. Herb. Boiss. (2) 4 [3]: 278. 1904.

Aira brasiliensis Raddi, Agrost. Bras. 36. 1823. Brazil.

Eragrostis airoides Nees, Agrost. Bras. 509. 1829. Brazil.

Culms erect, about 1 m tall; blades elongate, flat or loosely involute, scabrous on the upper surface, 2 to 3 mm wide; panicles rather more than half the entire length of the plant, 6 to 15 cm wide, open, the slender branches, branchlets, and pedicels spreading; spikelets 1.3 mm

[21] Contrib. U. S. Natl. Herb. 18: 369. 1917.

long, often 2-flowered; glumes somewhat unequal, a little shorter than the spikelet, acute.

Savannas, Cuba; Brazil.

CUBA: Bahía Honda, *Ekman* 17438. Cuchillas de San Sebastián, *Léon and Shafer* 3467; *Shafer and Léon* 13722. Chirigota, *Wright* 3827.

4. **Sporobolus indicus** (L.) R. Br., Prodr. Fl. Nov. Holl. 1: 170. 1810.

Agrostis indica L., Sp. Pl. 63. 1753. Jamaica.

Agrostis elongata Lam., Tabl. Encycl. 1: 162. 1791. Tropical America.

Sporobolus lamarckii Hamilt., Prodr. Pl. Ind. Occ. 4. 1825. Based on *Agrostis elongata* Lam.

Sporobolus jacquemontii Kunth, Rév. Gram. 2: 427. pl. 127. 1831. Santo Domingo.

Vilfa jacquemontii Trin., Mém. Acad. St. Pétersb. VI. Sci. Nat. 4^1: 92. 1840.

Vilfa indica Trin.; Steud., Nom. Bot. ed. 2. 2: 767. 1841.

Culms tufted, erect, 60 to 100 cm tall, with numerous leafy shoots at base; sheaths not noticeably compressed; blades elongate, slender, flexuous, mostly 1 to 2 mm wide; panicles 15 to 30 cm long; spikelets short-pediceled, mostly along the under side of the branches, 1.5 to 1.8 mm long; glumes nearly equal, about 0.5 mm long (fig. 47, *B*).

Grassy hills and dry savannas, Bahamas and Mexico to Colombia and Brazil. Throughout the Bahamas and the West Indies; probably to be found on all the islands. In Cuba called "espartillo" and "espartillo fino."

5. **Sporobolus poiretii** (Roem. and Schult.) Hitchc., Bartonia 14: 32. 1932. SMUTGRASS.

Agrostis compressa Poir., in Lam., Encycl. Sup. 1: 258. (no. 78) 1810. Not *A. compressa* Willd., 1790. Carolina.

Axonopus poiretii Roem. and Schult. Syst. Veg. 2: 318. 1817. Based on *Agrostis compressa* Poir., no. 78.

Agrostis tenuissima Spreng., Syst. Veg. 1: 258. 1825. Not *Sporobolus tenuissimus* Kuntze, 1898. West Indies and South America.

Vilfa berteroana Trin., Mém. Acad. St. Pétersb. VI. Sci. Nat. 4^1: 100. 1840. Santo Domingo.

Sporobolus berteroanus Hitchc. and Chase, Contrib. U. S. Natl. Herb. 18: 370. 1917.

Culms erect, tufted, 50 to 100 cm tall, the basal sheaths compressed; blades elongate, flat, folded or loosely involute, tapering into a long slender involute flexuous tip, 1 to 4 mm wide; panicle sometimes almost spikelike, usually 15 to 30 cm long, often red-brown from the exposed fruits at maturity or blackish from the effects of a fungus; spikelets 1.7 to 2 mm long; glumes obtuse, somewhat erose, the first about one-third as long as the spikelet, the second a little longer; fruit red-brown, mucilaginous on wetting (fig. 47, *A*).

Open ground, grassland, and waste places, southern United States to Argentina. Throughout the West Indies, probably to be found on all the islands. Because the inflorescence is frequently attacked by a black fungus the grass is often called smutgrass. This species was

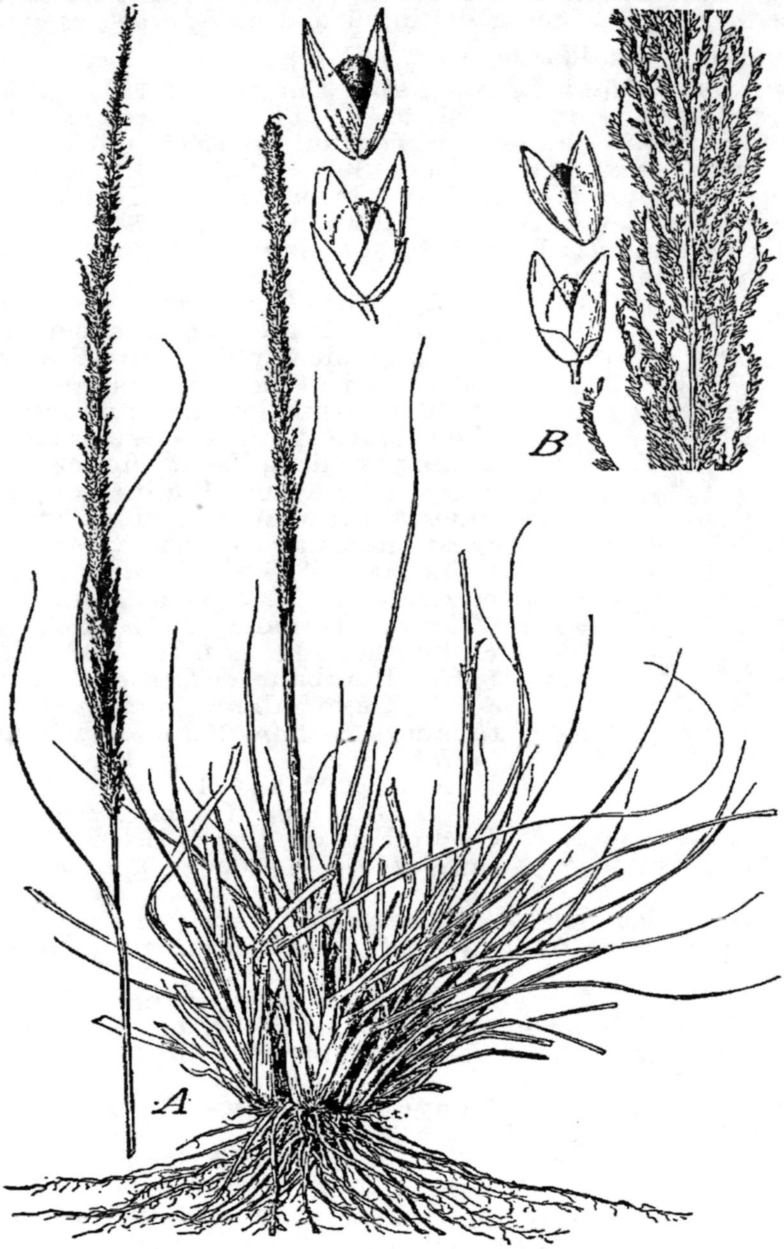

FIGURE 47.—*A*, *Sporobolus poiretii*. Plant, × ½; spikelet and floret, × 10 (Chase 7043). *B*, *S. indicus*. Panicle, × 1; spikelet and floret, × 10 (Léon 867).

included with the preceding under *Sporobolus indicus* by earlier botanists [22] and has been described as *Sporobolus indicus* by others, the preceding species being distinguished as *Sporobolus jacquemontii*.

6. Sporobolus pyramidatus (Lam.) Hitchc.

Agrostis pyramidata Lam., Tabl. Encycl. 1: 161. 1791. South America, the specimen from Richard. The type was examined by A. S. Hitchcock in the Lamarck Herbarium in 1935.

Vilfa arguta Nees, Agrost. Bras. 395. 1829. Brazil.

Sporobolus argutus Kunth, Rév. Gram. 1: Sup. XVII. 1830.

Vilfa richardi Steud., Syn. Pl. Glum. 1: 153. 1854. Antilles.

Agrostis pyramidalis Rich.; Steud., Syn. Pl. Glum. 1: 153. 1854. As synonym of the preceding.

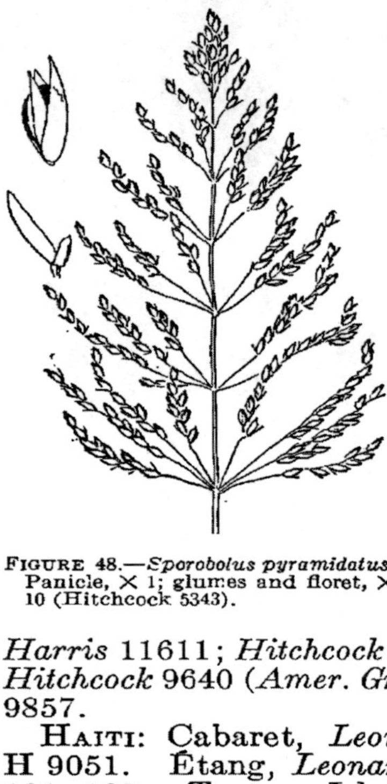

FIGURE 48.—*Sporobolus pyramidatus*. Panicle, × 1; glumes and floret, × 10 (Hitchcock 5343).

Low tufted glabrous perennial; culms spreading; blades short, rather thick, subinvolute; panicles pale, many-flowered, at first contracted, at maturity narrowly pyramidal or oblong; spikelets 1.5 mm long; first glume about half as long as the spikelet, the second as long as the spikelet (fig. 48).

Open sandy or alkaline soil, at low altitudes, southwestern United States and the West Indies to Argentina.

BAHAMAS: Grand Turk Island, *Millspaugh* 9384. Long Cay, *Brace* 4133.[23]

CUBA: Habana, *Léon* 285, 868, 6185; *Ekman* 94, 142; *Hitchcock* 235; *Baker* 1799, 1818. Batabanó, *Hitchcock* 236. Gaza, *Léon* 5467. Cayo Sabinal, *Ekman* 15513. Guantánamo, *Britton* 2035. Without locality, *Wright* 3828. Isla de Pinos, *Britton and Wilson* 15092, 15404.

JAMAICA: Old Harbor, *Ridley* 131, 133. Cockpit River, *Harris* 12463, 12467. Kingston, *Harris* 11503; *Hitchcock* 9318. Salt Ponds, *Harris* 11321. Healthshire Hills, *Harris* 11611; *Hitchcock* 9760. Rockfort, *Harris* 11306. Black River, *Hitchcock* 9640 (*Amer. Gr. Nat. Herb.* 634). Savanna-la-Mar, *Hitchcock* 9857.

HAITI: Cabaret, *Leonard* 11834. Port-au-Prince, *Ekman* H 319, H 9051. Étang, *Leonard* 3574. Gonaïves, *Cook, Scofield, and Doyle* 191, 193. Tortuga Island, *Leonard* 11415. Gonaïve Island, *Leonard* 3257, 3272, 3274.

DOMINICAN REPUBLIC: Guayubín, *Abbott* 867, 1004. Barahona, *Fuertes* 1291. Santiago, *Ekman* H 15979.

PUERTO RICO: Guanica, *Sintenis* 3416b; *Britton and Shafer* 1862, 1873. Punta Aguila, *Britton, Cowell, and Brown* 4684. Cuamo, *Sintenis* 3307. Cabo Rojo, *Sintenis* 549. Boqueron, *Chase* 6500. Ponce, *Chase* 6496. Mona Island, *Britton, Cowell, and Hess* 1780, 1875; *Hess* 453.

VIRGIN ISLANDS: Anegada, *Fishlock* 53. St. Croix, *Ricksecker* 279.

[22] Fl. Brit. W. Ind. 533. 1864.
[23] Fl. Baham. 33. 1920.

LEEWARD ISLANDS: Antigua, *Wullschlaegel; Box* 78.
WINDWARD ISLANDS: Barbados, *Freeman* 5024; *Hitchcock* 16508.
TRINIDAD: Cedros, *Broadway* 4919; *Hitchcock* 10163.

7. **Sporobolus domingensis** (Trin.) Kunth, Rév. Gram. 1: Sup. XVII. 1830.

Vilfa domingensis Trin., in Spreng., Neu. Entd. 2: 59. 1821. Santo Domingo.

Agrostis domingensis Schult., Mant. 3 (Add. 1): 570. 1827.

Sporobolus inordinatus Mez, Repert. Sp. Nov. Fedde 17: 294. 1921. Cuba, *Ramon de la Sagra*.

Resembling *S. pyramidatus;* culms stouter, 30 to 80 cm tall; panicles contracted, densely flowered, the branches appressed, the lower sometimes ascending; spikelets 2 mm long or sometimes somewhat less (fig. 49).

Sandy or alkaline soil, Bahamas and Greater Antilles; southern Florida.

BAHAMAS: New Providence, *Britton and Brace* 336. Anguilla Isles, *Wilson* 8001. Soldiers Road, *Geogr. Soc. Baltimore* 260. Fortune Island, *Hitchcock* in 1890.

CUBA: Habana, *Ekman* in 1921. Caibarién, *Fernando* 1, 307. Cienfuegos Bay, *Britton and Wilson* 5758. Cayo Sabinal, *Ekman* 15470. Santa Lucea, *Shafer* 972. Cayo Guajaba, *Shafer* 691. Guantánamo Bay, *Hioram* 2, 5; *Britton* 2125. Manzanillo, *Shafer* 12344.

JAMAICA: Montego Bay, *Ridley* 110.

HAITI: Cabaret, *Leonard* 11997, 11997a. Sources Puantes, *Ekman* H 2158. Gonaïve Island, *Leonard* 5203. Tortuga Island, *Leonard* 11422, 15318, 15319.

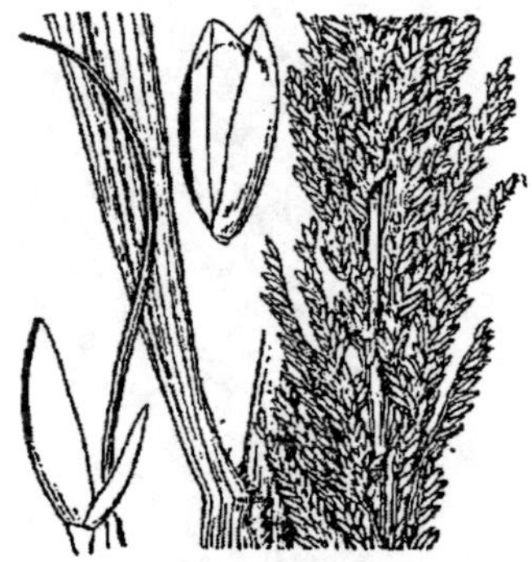

FIGURE 49.—*Sporobolus domingensis.* Plant, × 1; glumes and floret, × 10 (Hitchcock 530).

8. **Sporobolus cubensis** Hitchc., Contrib. U. S. Natl. Herb. 12: 237. 1909. Isla de Pinos, *Curtiss* 392.

Culms densely tufted, erect, 30 to 50 cm tall, the innovations numerous, lower sheaths felty-ciliate; blades flat or involute, firm and rather stiff, 10 to 15 cm long, 1 to 2 mm wide, ciliate near base; panicles narrowly pyramidal, erect, 10 to 15 cm long, usually bronze-green, the branches in indistinct verticils, spreading or the lower finally reflexed, 2 to 3 cm long; spikelets about 4 mm long, acute, somewhat secund along the lower side of the branches, the lateral pedicels about 0.5 mm long; first glume gradually acute, a little more than half as long as the spikelet, the second as long as the lemma. The basal part of the tuft usually shows the effect of fire burning off the upper part.

Sandy barrens, Cuba to Puerto Rico; British Guiana and Costa Rica to Bolivia.

CUBA: Hanábana, *Wright* 3427. Herradura, *Ekman* in 1922; *Hitchcock* 237. Isla de Pinos, *Ekman* 12541; *Britton and Wilson* 14141, 14422, 14975; *Curtiss* 392.

HAITI: Maissade, *Ekman* H 3252.

DOMINICAN REPUBLIC: Cuenca, *Ekman* H 13338.

PUERTO RICO: Mayaguez, *Heller* 4590.

9. Sporobolus purpurascens (Swartz) Hamilt., Prodr. Pl. Ind. Occ. 5. 1825.

Agrostis purpurascens Swartz, Prodr. Veg. Ind. Occ. 25. 1788. Jamaica.

Culms erect, 30 to 50 cm tall; blades mostly basal, 4 to 8 mm wide, ciliate near base; panicles condensed, brownish drab, 8 to 15 cm long,

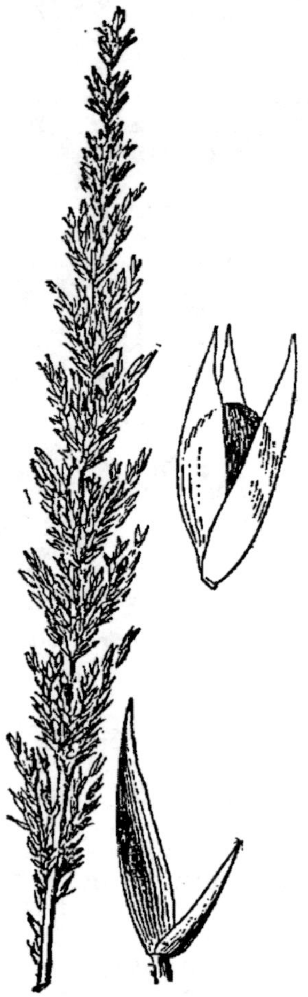

FIGURE 50.—*Sporobolus purpurascens*. Panicle, × 1; glumes and floret, × 10 (Hitchcock).

FIGURE 51.—*Sporobolus virginicus*. Plant, × 1; glumes and floret, × 10 (Nash 2467).

the short branches in whorls; spikelets 3 mm long; first glume less than half as long as the spikelet; second glume as long as the spikelet (fig. 50).

Grassy slopes, pine barrens, and savannas, southern United States, West Indies, and eastern Mexico to Bolivia and Brazil.

CUBA: San Julián, *Ekman* 11115; *Léon* 6923, 6984. Herradura, *Léon* 15953. Pinar del Río, *Wright* 3427a; *Britton* 10022. Laguna Jovero, *Shafer* 10757. Isla de Pinos, *Britton and Wilson* 14292.

JAMAICA: Westphalia, *Harris* 11434, 11568. Road to Salt Hill, *Harris* 11365. Below Sir Johns Peak, *Harris* 11598. Newcastle, *Hitchcock* 9340. Bull Head Mountain, *Hitchcock* 9525. Cinchona, *Hitchcock* 9716. Barican, *Hitchcock* 9573. North slope Catherines Peak, *Hitchcock* 9736. Gordon Town, *Hart* 735.

WINDWARD ISLANDS: Martinique, *Duss*.

10. Sporobolus virginicus (L.) Kunth, Rév. Gram. 1: 67. 1829.

Agrostis virginica L., Sp. Pl. 63. 1753. Virginia.

Agrostis littoralis Lam., Tabl. Encycl. 1: 161. 1791. Tropical America.

Vilfa virginica Beauv., Ess. Agrost. 16, 149, 182. 1812.

Sporobolus littoralis Kunth, Rév. Gram. 1: 68. 1829.

Culms 15 to 70 cm tall or even as much as 1 m, erect from extensively creeping hard scaly rhizomes; leaves numerous, conspicuously distichous, the sheaths overlapping; blades firm, involute-pointed, 3 to 15 cm long, 2 to 5 mm wide; panicles spikelike, somewhat narrowed above and below, 2 to 10, rarely to 15, cm long; spikelets 2 mm long or slightly longer; first glume a little more than half as long as the spikelet, the second as long as the spikelet (fig. 51).

In the Grasses of the West Indies [24] *Sporobolus littoralis* was recognized as distinct. Further collections show complete intergradation between large specimens referred to it and characteristic *S. virginicus*. Lamarck's type of *Agrostis littoralis*, examined in the Paris Herbarium in 1935, proves to be an intermediate specimen, the panicle 6 cm long.

Saline or sandy soil along the coast, Virginia to Brazil, and all warm countries of the Eastern Hemisphere. Common throughout the West Indies. Extensive colonies of sterile plants often found along sandy beaches.

40. ARISTIDA L., Sp. Pl. 82. 1753. THREE-AWN

Spikelets 1-flowered, the rachilla disarticulating obliquely above the glumes; glumes narrow, acute, acuminate, or awn-tipped; lemma indurate, narrow, terete, convolute, with a hard, sharp-pointed, usually minutely bearded callus at base, terminating above in a usually trifid awn. Species of the West Indies all perennial except *A. adscensionis*.

Lateral awns minute or obsolete .... 1. A. TERNIPES.
Lateral awns well developed (short in *A. laevigata*).
  Plants annual .... 2. A. ADSCENSIONIS.
  Plants perennial.
    Column of awn 10 mm long, twisted .... 3. A. SPICIFORMIS.
    Column of awn, if present, much shorter than 10 mm.
      Panicle open, the branches stiffly ascending or spreading.
        Lateral awns one-fourth as long as the central or less. 4. A. LAEVIGATA.
        Lateral awns half as long as the central or a little more. 5. A. PRADANA.
      Panicle narrow, the branches appressed or somewhat ascending; lateral awns usually about as long as the central, sometimes shorter but at least half as long.
        First glume one-half to two-thirds as long as the second.
          Awns contorted at base, about 1 cm long .... 6. A. FRAGILIS.
          Awns not contorted at base, 2 to 2.5 cm long .... 7. A. EGGERSII.

[24] Contrib. U. S. Natl. Herb. 18: 369. 1917.

First glume about as long as the second or a little shorter.
Beak of lemma 3 to 4 mm long, distinctly twisted--8. A. NEGLECTA.
Beak of lemma, if present, not twisted.
Awns at maturity about equally divergent, not spirally contorted at base.
Blades flat at least toward the base.
Culms mostly more than 1 m tall; blades 3 to 5 mm wide. 9. A. ERECTA.
Culms mostly less than 70 cm tall; blades mostly not more than 1 mm wide--------------------------10. A. VILFIFOLIA.
Blades involute.
Blades short and stiff, mostly less than 3 cm long, usually approximate in pairs; culms very stiff and wiry. 11. A. CURTIFOLIA.
Blades mostly more than 5 cm long, not approximate in pairs.
Panicle loose; awns 2 to 3 cm long--12. A. PORTORICENSIS.
Panicle rather dense; awns 1 to 2.5 cm long.
Callus of lemma nearly 2 mm long; first glume 1 cm long; lemma a little longer than the glumes; awns 2 cm long. 13. A. CHASEAE.
Callus of lemma about 0.5 mm long.
Culms erect; blades as much as 30 cm long; first glume about 7 mm long; lemma about 8 mm long; awns 1.5 to 2.5 cm long-----------14. A. SWARTZIANA.
Culms spreading and branching at base; blades 5 to 15 cm long; first glume 4 to 5 mm long; lemma 6 to 7 mm long; awns 1 to 1.5 cm long. 15. A. COGNATA.
Awns at maturity unequally divergent or spirally contorted at base.
Central awn horizontally spreading or somewhat reflexed, the lateral awns erect; awns not contorted at base; blades flat toward base-------------------------------16. A. AFFINIS.
Central awn not more divergent than the others; awns all contorted at base; blades involute.
Awns 1.5 to 3 cm long.
Lemma 7 mm long, glabrous, the awns strongly contorted at base; plants rather stout, the blades as much as 20 cm long, the panicles as much as 30 cm long. 17. A. BRITTONORUM.
Lemma 10 mm long, scabrous on the upper half, the awns weakly contorted at base; plants slender, the blades 5 to 10 cm long, the panicles 7 to 15 cm long. 18. A. CALCICOLA.
Awns about 1 cm long.
First glume glabrous on the keel-----------19. A. ROSEI.
First glume scabrous on the keel------20. A. REFRACTA.

1. Aristida ternipes Cav., Icon. Pl. 5: 46. 1799. Panama.

SPIDER GRASS.

Streptachne scabra H. B. K., Nov. Gen. et Sp. 1: 124. pl. 40. 1815. Mexico.

Aristida scabra Kunth, Rév. Gram. 1: 62. 1829.

Streptachne cubensis A. Rich., in Sagra, Hist. Cuba 11: 311. 1850. Cuba.

Erect perennial; culms 50 to 100 cm tall; blades flat, involute above, tapering into a fine point, 2 to 3 mm wide; panicle open, one-third to half the entire length of the culm, the branches few, distant, spreading, scabrous, mostly naked at base; spikelets appressed at the ends of the branches; glumes about equal, 8 to 10 mm long; lemma gradually narrowed into a laterally compressed scabrous falcate beak, this extending into a single arcuate awn 10 to 15 mm long; lateral awns minute or obsolete. In arid situations the blades may be narrow and nearly all involute (fig. 52).

Rocky hills and dry plateaus, Arizona to Colombia; Bahamas, Cuba, and Hispaniola.

BAHAMAS: Nassau, *Curtiss* 75; *Hitchcock* in 1890. Inagua, *Nash and Taylor* 926.

CUBA: Pinar del Río, *Wright* 3835. Vicinity of Habana, *Léon* 280, 958, 959, 8518; *Wilson* 9488; *Hitchcock* 496, 497. Guanabacoa, *Léon and Shafer* 3443; *Hitchcock* 23238. Santiago de Cuba, *Ekman* 8474; *Britton and Cowell* 12857.

HAITI: Port-de-Pai, *Ekman* H 3626.

DOMINICAN REPUBLIC: Peninsula de Barahona, *Ekman* H 7029.

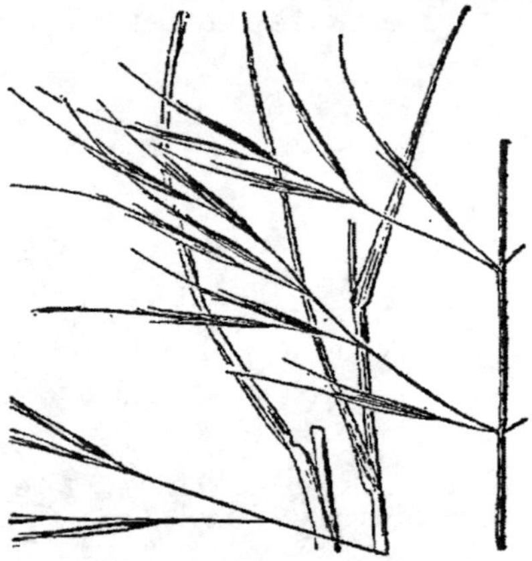

FIGURE 52.—*Aristida ternipes*, × 1 (Griffiths 7271).

2. Aristida adscensionis L., Sp. Pl. 82. 1753. Ascension Island.

Aristida maritima Steud., Syn. Pl. Glum. 1: 137. 1854. Guadeloupe.

Aristida debilis Mez, Repert. Sp. Nov. Fedde 17: 151. 1921. Based in part on a specimen collected in Jamaica by MacNab.

Annual, much branched at base; culms 10 to 80 cm tall; panicles narrow, erect, 5 to 10 cm long in the smaller plants; first glume 5 to 7 mm long, the second 8 to 10 mm long; lemma 8 to 9 mm long, compressed toward the scarcely beaked summit; awns about equal, 10 to 15 mm long, equally divergent, flat and straight at base. Extremely variable in appearance, ranging from dwarf plants with narrow compact panicles to larger plants, as much as 70 cm tall, with flexuous panicles (fig. 53).

FIGURE 53.—*Aristida adscensionis*, × 1 (Earle 559).

Open dry ground and waste places, throughout the warmer parts of America and the Old World. Grisebach[25] refers this species to *A. stricta* Michx.

BAHAMAS: Crooked Island, *Brace* 4633. Long Island, *Britton and Millspaugh* 6309. Long Cay, *Brace* 4077. Fortune Island, *Hitchcock* in 1890.

JAMAICA: Kingston, *Britton and Hollick* 1746; *Harris* 11500, 12452. Gordon Town, *Harris* 11513. Flamstead, *Harris* 11474. Musgrave Road, *Harris* 11480.

HAITI: Port-au-Prince, *Leonard* 3451, 15878, 15881; *Buch* 2041. Jean Rabel, *Leonard* 12968. Môle-St.-Nicolas, *Leonard* 13343. Cabaret, *Leonard* 11852, 11863, 11960. St. Michel de l'Atalaye, *Leonard* 7095. Morne-à-Cabrits, *Ekman* H 960.

[25] Fl. Brit. W. Ind. 534. 1864.

DOMINICAN REPUBLIC: Guayubín, *Abbott* 955. Valverde, *Ekman* H 13096.

PUERTO RICO: Boqueron, *Chase* 6506, 6510. Guanica, *Sintenis* 3438, 3766. Cabo Rojo, *Sintenis* 553. Mona Island, *Hess* 437.

VIRGIN ISLANDS: St. Croix, *Thompson* 22; *Ricksecker* 64; *Rose* 3211.

LEEWARD ISLANDS: Antigua, *Wullschlaegel; Box* 127. Guadeloupe, *Duss* 3159.

WINDWARD ISLANDS: Montserrat, *Shafer* 18.

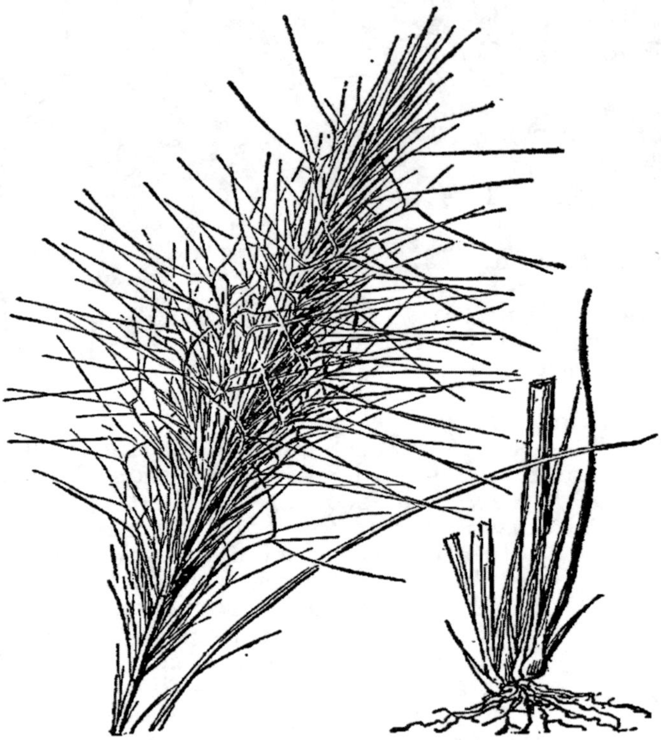

FIGURE 54.—*Aristida spiciformis*, × 1 (Combs and Baker 1115).

3. Aristida spiciformis Ell., Bot. S. C. and Ga. 1: 141. 1816. South Carolina.

Culms tufted, stiffly erect, 50 to 100 cm tall; panicle erect, dense and spikelike, mostly 10 to 15 cm long, the branches short and appressed, the whole panicle more or less spirally twisted; lemma, excluding the slender callus 1 mm long, about 4 mm long, extending into a twisted column 10 mm long; awns about equal, 1.5 to 2 cm long, spreading (fig. 54).

Some of the material from the United States has larger spikelets than that from the West Indies.

Sandy barrens in thickets or pine woods, southern United States, Cuba, and Puerto Rico.

CUBA: Pinar del Río, *Ekman* 17811. Isla de Pinos, *Britton and Wilson* 14198.

PUERTO RICO: Campo Alegre, *Chase* 6614 (*Amer. Gr. Nat. Herb.* 765).

4. Aristida laevigata Hitchc. and Ekman, N. Amer. Fl. 17: 390. 1935. Cuba, *Ekman* in 1922.

Culms cespitose, erect, glabrous, several-noded, 60 to 100 cm tall; sheaths glabrous; ligule a ciliate membrane less than 0.5 mm long; blades closely involute, firm, somewhat curved or flexuous, 0.5 to 1 mm thick when rolled, smooth on the outer surface, 10 to 20 cm long, villous on the upper surface near the base and around the summit of the sheath; panicles long-exserted, 20 to 30 cm long, the branches mostly solitary, distant, stiffly ascending, the lowermost as much as 15 cm long, the branchlets appressed along the branches, the axis of the panicle and the branches glabrous; glumes nearly equal, 1-nerved, obscurely scaberulous toward apex, otherwise glabrous even as to the keels, about 12 mm long, the first acuminate, the second mucronate from a rather broad bifid apex; lemma 12 to 14 mm long, including the 1 mm long short-pilose callus, glabrous, narrowed above but scarcely beaked, awns very unequal, the central widely spreading or somewhat reflexed, 12 to 20 mm long, obscurely scabrous at the base, the lateral divergent, 2 to 5 mm long, more slender than the central.

Known only from the type locality, pinelands at the headwaters of Río Piloto, Sierra de Nipe, prov. Oriente, Cuba, 750 m altitude. Besides the type collection, Ekman collected in the same locality nos. 2511, 9880, and 15058. The species is allied to *A. ternipes* and *A. divaricata* Humb. and Bonpl.

5. **Aristida pradana** Léon, Bull. Torrey Bot. Club 53: 458. 1926. Cuba, *Léon* 12299.

Culms tufted, erect, wiry, 60 to 80 cm tall, "simple and naked, the upper leaves of the culm, if any, reduced to the elongate, strongly adherent and mostly bladeless sheath"; blades firm, closely involute from the base, flexuous, as much as 60 cm long or more; panicle 25 to 35 cm long, narrow, the branches appressed, "finally divergent or spreading", the lower ones distant, as much as 8 cm long; "glumes unequal, 10 to 12 mm long the first caducous"; lemma 15 to 17 mm long, including the 1 mm long short-pilose callus, narrowed above into an obscure beak; awns unequal, the central one spreading, 2 to 3 cm long, the lateral ascending, half as long as the central or a little more.

Arid rocky siliceous hillside, Peladeros de Jauco, southwest of Baricoa, Cuba, *Léon* 12299.

Known only from the type collection. The duplicate type specimen in the United States National Herbarium is incomplete and the first glume has disappeared. The quoted parts of the above description are taken from the original description. The species is allied to *A. pansa* Woot. and Standl. of southwestern United States.

6. **Aristida fragilis** Hitchc. and Ekman, N. Amer. Fl. 17: 393. 1935. Cuba, *Ekman* 16784.

Culms cespitose, erect, glabrous, wiry, 30 to 50 cm tall, two to several nodes approximate near the base; sheaths glabrous, the culm-sheath 2 to 5 cm long, mostly bladeless, those of the innovations pilose at the summit, bearing involute blades 1 to 10 cm long; ligule a ciliate membrane 0.5 mm long; panicles narrow, rather soft, 10 to 20 cm long, the branches appressed, 1 to 3 cm long, the upper overlapping, the lower somewhat distant; glumes 1-nerved, acute, the first minutely scabrous on the keel and on the sides toward the summit, about 4 mm long; the second glabrous, somewhat narrowed toward the summit, about 7 mm long; lemma about 7 mm long including the minutely and softly pubescent rather slender callus a little more than 1 mm long; awns equal, finally horizontally spreading, contorted at base, about 1 cm long.

Pinelands on white sand, Cuba.

Cuba: San Juan y Martínez (Pinar del Río), *Ekman* 16784. La Grifa, *Ekman* 11247. Pábalo, *Ekman* 11417.

7. Aristida eggersii Hitchc., Contrib. U. S. Natl. Herb. 22: 560. 1924. Cuba, *Eggers* 5389.

Culms tufted, slender, spreading or decumbent at base, 20 to 40 cm tall; blades involute, falcate or flexuous, mostly less than 10 cm long, often much shorter; panicle narrow, 3 to 10 cm long, the branches distant, short and appressed, few-flowered; glumes unequal, the first 5 to 6 mm long, about half as long as the second; lemma about 1 cm long, including the 1 mm long callus, gradually narrowed and scaberulous above; awns about equal, 2 to 2.5 cm long, all spreading nearly horizontally, flat at base and scarcely contorted. Ekman's no. H 13158 agrees with this description except that the glumes are longer (about 8 and 13 mm).

Pastures and exposed hillsides, Cuba and Hispaniola.

Cuba: Guantánamo, *Ekman* 10227, 15755; *Britton* 2177. La Caimanera, *Eggers* 5389; *Ekman* 15742.

Dominican Republic: Monte Cristi, *Ekman* H 13158.

8. Aristida neglecta Léon; Hitchc., Contrib. U. S. Natl. Herb. 22: 567. 1924. Loma de las Jatas, Guanabacoa, Cuba, *Ekman* in 1921.

Culms loosely tufted, erect, wiry, several-noded, 40 to 60 cm tall; sheaths shorter than the internodes, distributed along the culm; blades stiff and firm, soon involute, sharp-pointed, usually not over 5 cm long, often shorter, less than 1 mm wide, or some of the earlier ones wider; panicles narrow, 5 to 10 cm long, the branches distant, rather stiffly ascending, 1 to 2 cm long, bearing 1 or 2 branchlets at base, few-flowered; glumes equal or nearly so, 7 to 9 mm long, acuminate or awn-pointed; lemma about 1 cm long, the callus less than 1 mm long, the body glabrous, gradually tapering into a scabrous twisted beak as long as or a little longer than the body; awns about equal, divergent, 10 to 15 mm long, slightly or distinctly contorted at base. With age the lower sheaths become open or flattened, and often lose their blades, giving the culms a naked knotty appearance.

Sandy savannas, pine barrens, and dry hills, Cuba and Hispaniola.

Cuba: Guane, *Shafer* 10364, 10630; *Léon* 7030, 7031. Pinar del Río, *Hitchcock* 23254, 23261, 23304, 23312. Viñales, *Killip* 13572. Herradura, *Ekman* 17731. Remates, *Ekman* 11165, 11300, 11339. San Diego de los Baños, *Léon* 4844; *Ekman* 17763. La Grifa, *Ekman* 11244. San Juan, *Ekman* 16785. Mantua, *Ekman* 11083. Consolación del Sur, *Ekman* 10868. San Juan y Martínez, *Ekman* 13793. Guanabacoa, *Léon* 871, 872, 874, 2875, 5015; *Hitchcock* 500, 23236; *Wilson and Léon* 11645; *Ekman* 45, 10897. Madruga, *Léon* 3455, 6374. Minas, *Léon* 5213. Soledad, *Hitchcock* 23328. Baragua, *Hitchcock* 23365. Placetas del Sur, *Léon* 6425. Manacos, *Léon* 5834. Sancti Spíritus, *Léon* 8993. Motembo, *Léon* 8639. Camagüey, *Ekman* 15323. Holguín, *Shafer* 1183. Guara, *Hitchcock* 23408. Victoria de las Tunas, *Ekman* 15584. Caimanera, *Hioram and Ramsden* 7. Eastern Cuba, *Wright* 737. Western Cuba, *Wright* 3433. Isla de Pinos, *Britton and Wilson* 14414.

Haiti: Marmelade, *Leonard* 8248. St. Michel de l'Atalaye, *Leonard* 7291, 7422, 7795. Mirebalais, *Ekman* H 2294. Camache, *Buch* 1075.

Dominican Republic: Moncion, *Ekman* H 12635. Santiago, *Ekman* H 16221.

9. Aristida erecta Hitchc., Contrib. U. S. Natl. Herb. 12: 236. 1909. Cuba, *Wright* 3432.

Culms erect, rather stout, as much as 1.5 m tall; blades flat, becoming involute especially toward the much-attenuate tip, as much as 1 m long, 3 to 5 mm wide; panicles narrow, as much as 50 cm long, the numerous very scabrous branches ascending or appressed, the lower as much as 10 cm long or even longer, all spikelet-bearing from the base, the spikelets crowded on erect rather stout pedicels 2 to 3 mm long; glumes acuminate or awn-tipped, the first 3-nerved, 12 to 15 mm long, the second 1-nerved, 2 to 3 mm shorter than the first; lemma 12 to 13 mm; awns divergent, the central 2 to 3 cm long, the lateral somewhat shorter.

Savannas of western Cuba.

CUBA: Santa Cruz de los Pinos, *Ekman* 17681 (*Amer. Gr. Nat. Herb.* 787). Herradura, *Hitchcock* 23441; *Tracy* 9076. San Diego (Pinar del Río), *Léon* 4852. Gaune, *Léon* 6918. Without locality, *Wright* 3432. Isla de Pinos, *Britton and Wilson* 14959.

10. Aristida vilfifolia Henr., Med. Rijks Herb. Leiden 54B: 671. 1928. Cuba, *Amer. Gr. Nat. Herb.* 791.

Culms rather loosely tufted, erect, slender and wiry, 30 to 60 cm tall; blades flat or often involute, becoming curved or flexuous, thickened on the margins, mostly 3 to 5 cm long, sometimes as much as 8 cm, on the innovations sometimes shorter, mostly not more than 1 mm wide; panicles erect, narrow, 5 to 15 cm long, the branches short and appressed, approximate or often distant, especially below; glumes about equal, acute, 6 to 8 mm long; lemma 6 to 7 mm long, including the 0.5 mm long callus; central awn spreading, 10 to 15 mm long, the lateral awns erect or somewhat spreading, usually about two-thirds as long as the central, all nearly straight at base, sometimes contorted (*Wright* 3831, 3832).

Sandy woods and savannas, Bahamas, Cuba, and Hispaniola.

In the Grasses of the West Indies [26] this species was referred to *A. gyrans* Chapm. of Florida. In the North American Species of *Aristida* [27] it was referred to *A. purpurascens* Poir., of the southern United States.

BAHAMAS: New Providence, *Eggers* 4447.

CUBA: Pinar del Río, *Hitchcock* 23258, 23266, 23282, 23309. Los Palacios, *Léon* 7395. Herradura, *Hitchcock* 232; *Tracy* 9095. Chirigota, *Wright* 3831, 3832. Camagüey, *Ekman* (*Amer. Gr. Nat. Herb.* 791). Baraguá, *Hitchcock* 23375. Sierra de Nipe, *Ekman* 3086. Isla de Pinos, *Taylor* 20; *Palmer and Riley* 995.

HAITI: Acul-Samedi, *Ekman* H 9909.

DOMINICAN REPUBLIC: Jarabaco, *Ekman* H 14160.

11. Aristida curtifolia Hitchc., Contrib. U. S. Natl. Herb. 12: 235. 1909. Cuba, *Wright* 736.

Culms densely tufted, stiffly erect, wiry, 20 to 60 cm tall, the alternate nodes often shortened, thus bringing the leaves together in approximate pairs; blades short, thickish, stiffly spreading, flat or mostly soon involute, 5 to 20 mm long, 0.5 to 1 mm wide, or the upper reduced to mere awns 2 to 3 mm long; panicles narrow, nearly

[26] Contrib. U. S. Natl. Herb. 18: 366. 1917.
[27] Contrib. U. S. Natl. Herb. 22: 571. 1924.

simple, 5 to 10 cm long, the spikelets nearly sessile; glumes nearly equal, 8 to 9 mm long, acute; lemma 5 to 6 mm long, the callus 0.5 mm long; awns about equal, 10 to 12 mm long, spreading but not curved or contorted at base (fig. 55).

Dry hills and barrens, Cuba.

CUBA: Las Posas "in cuabales", *Ekman* 12739. Guanabacoa, *Ekman* 10898, 10899; *Hitchcock* 498, 23231; *Léon* 873, 4645; *Baker and Hasselbring* 7211. San Miguel de los Baños, *Killip* 13831, 13858, 13889, 13902. Pastelillo, *Ekman* 15410. Santiago de Cuba, *Ekman* 8953, 15628. Río Seboruco to Falls of Río Mayarí, *Shafer* 3694. Holguín, *Ekman* 15738. Mayarí, *Ekman* 15863. Without locality, *Wright* 736.

12. **Aristida portoricensis** Pilger, in Urban, Symb. Antill. 4: 100. 1903. Puerto Rico, *Sintenis* 77.

Culms tufted, often in large bunches, slender, erect or spreading at base, 30 to 50 cm tall; blades involute, somewhat curved or flexuous, mostly 5 to 10 cm long, scarcely 1 mm thick when rolled; panicles narrow, loose, few-flowered, mostly 3 to 8 cm long, the few distant branches rather stiffly ascending, mostly floriferous from the base; glumes awn-pointed, the first about 7 mm long, the second about 10 mm long; lemma 10 to 12 mm long including the 1 mm long callus and the 2 to 3 mm long slightly twisted scabrous neck; awns about equal, divergent or horizontally spreading, 2 to 3 cm long, slightly contorted at base.

Stony or barren slopes, Puerto Rico.

PUERTO RICO: Mayaguez, *Sintenis* 77; *Chase* 6269, 6298, 6812; *Britton, Cowell, and Brown* 4361; *Holm* 40.

13. **Aristida chaseae** Hitchc., Contrib. U. S. Natl. Herb. 22: 575. 1924. Boqueron, Puerto Rico, *Chase* 6507.

Culms few in a tuft, widely spreading, 50 to 60 cm long; blades involute, 10 to 15 cm long; panicles narrow, 10 to 15 cm long; glumes equal or somewhat unequal, 10 to 13 mm long, acuminate or awn-pointed; lemma about 12 mm long, narrowed at the summit but scarcely beaked, scaberulous on the upper half; callus 1 mm long, densely pilose, the upper hairs about 1 mm long; awns equal, somewhat divergent, flat at base, not contorted, about 2 cm long.

Open stony hills, Puerto Rico, known only from the type collection.

14. **Aristida swartziana** Steud., Syn. Pl. Glum. 1: 137. 1854. Jamaica.

Culms tufted, with numerous erect innovations, 40 to 70 cm tall; blades involute; mostly erect, as much as 30 cm long, about 1 mm wide; panicles narrow, loose and interrupted, as much as 15 cm long, the branches ascending, 1 to 3 cm long, usually rather lax, several-flowered; first glume about 7 mm long, the second about 1 mm longer; lemma about as long as the second glume or a little longer; callus 0.5 mm long, the pubescence short and soft; awns about equal, ascending or somewhat spreading, 15 to 25 mm long.

Rocky savannas and open ground, Jamaica, Hispaniola, and Leeward Islands. Described by Swartz as *A. adscensionis* L.

JAMAICA: New Forest, southern Manchester, *Hitchcock* 9845 (*Amer. Gr. Nat. Herb.* 790). Lititz Savanna, *Harris* 12440. Healthshire Hills, *Harris* 9542. Gordon Town, *Hart* 864.

FIGURE 55.—*Aristida curtifolia*. Plant, × 1; glumes and floret, × 2 (type).

60256—36——7

HAITI: Port-au-Prince, *Ekman* H 2019.
LEEWARD ISLANDS: Antigua, *Box* 38, 62.

15. Aristida cognata Trin. and Rupr., Mem. Acad. St. Pétersb. VI. Sci. Nat. 5[1]: 127. 1842. St. Thomas.

Culms ascending, 20 to 40 cm tall; blades involute, 5 to 15 cm long, about 1 mm wide; panicles narrow, loose, 5 to 15 cm long, the branches rather distant, ascending, mostly closely flowered, 1 to 2 cm long; glumes acuminate, the first 4 to 5 mm long, the second 1 to 2 mm longer; lemma 6 to 7 mm long, gradually narrowed into a scaberulous beak about 1 mm long; callus about 0.7 mm long, the hairs short and soft, awns about equal, ascending, 10 to 15 mm long.

Dry hillsides, Virgin Islands and Montserrat.

VIRGIN ISLANDS: St. Thomas, *Britton and Shafer* 119; *Rose* 3189; *Eggers* in 1882. St. Croix, *Benzon*. St. John, *Eggers* 3003.

WINDWARD ISLANDS: Montserrat, *Shafer* 48, 430.

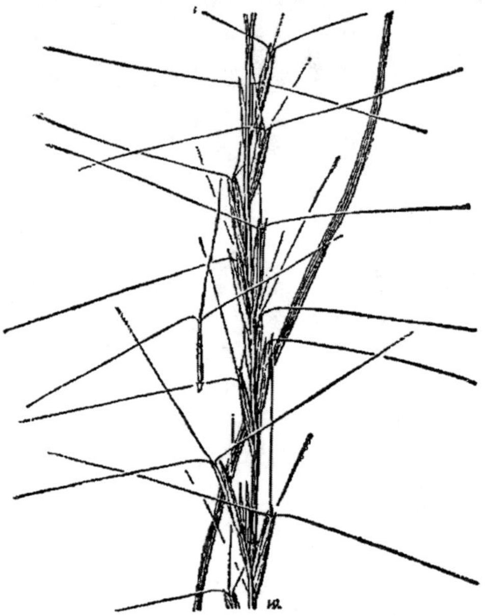

FIGURE 56.—*Aristida affinis*, × 1 (Combs 688).

16. Aristida affinis (Schult.) Kunth, Rév. Gram. 1: 61. 1829.

Chaetaria affinis Schult., Mant. 2: 210. 1824. Pennsylvania.

Aristida virgata var.? *palustris* Chapm., Fl. South. U. S. 555. 1860. Florida.

Aristida palustris Vasey, Descr. Cat. Grasses U. S. 35. 1885.

Culms tufted from a hard thickened base, stiffly erect, rather stout, 1 to 1.5 m tall; panicle narrow and virgate, as much as 50 cm long; glumes about equal, mucronate, about 12 mm long; lemma about 8 mm long, glabrous, the callus 1 mm long, short-pubescent; central awn horizontally spreading, 1.5 to 3 cm long, the lateral erect, two-thirds to three-fourths as long (fig. 56).

Low pine barrens, southern United States and Cuba.

CUBA: Pinar del Río, *Ekman* 17870. Remates, *Ekman* 11230.

17. Aristida brittonorum Hitchc., Contrib. U. S. Natl. Herb. 22: 584. 1924. Isla de Pinos, *Britton, Britton, and Wilson* 14169.

Culms rather stout, erect, 60 to 100 cm tall; blades firm, involute, stiffly erect, the basal as much as 30 cm long and 0.8 mm thick when rolled; panicles narrow, interrupted, 20 to 30 cm long, the branches appressed, the lower as much as 5 cm long; glumes acuminate, the first 7 to 10 mm long, the second 10 to 12 mm long; lemma about 7 mm long, the sharp callus 1 mm long, the pubescence fine and short, the beak about 1 mm long; awns about equal, 1.5 to 2 cm long, widely spreading, all contorted at base.

White sand in pineland, Isla de Pinos, Cuba.

CUBA: Isla de Pinos, *Britton, Britton, and Wilson* 14169; *Ekman* 11983, 12024, 12495.

18. Aristida calcicola Hitchc. and Ekman, N. Amer. Fl. 17: 405. 1935. Cuba, *Ekman* 15774.

Perennial; culms densely cespitose, erect, slender, wiry, glabrous, about 2-noded, sometimes branching, 30 to 50 cm tall; sheaths glabrous, pilose at the throat; ligule a ciliate membrane about 0.5 mm long; blades flat or mostly involute, glabrous beneath, scabrous-pubescent on the upper surface, usually 5 to 10 cm long, those of the culms often shorter, mostly less than 1 mm wide when flat; panicles narrow, 7 to 15 cm long, the few branches appressed, bearing 1 to few spikelets; glumes somewhat unequal, acuminate, about 1 cm long, the first 1 to 2 mm shorter than the second, glabrous except the keel of the first; lemma 8 to 10 mm long, slender, scabrous on the upper part, the callus rather slender, densely short-pilose, about 1 mm long; awns about equal, about equally divergent, 1.5 to 3 cm long, somewhat contorted at base.

Limestone hillsides, Cuba and Hispaniola.

Cuba: Guantánamo, *Ekman* 15774.

Dominican Republic: Monte Cristi, *Ekman* H13158.

19. Aristida rosei Hitchc., Contrib. U. S. Natl. Herb. 22: 584. 1924. Dominican Republic, *Rose, Fitch, and Russell* 4027.

Culms tufted, slender, wiry, often firm and stiff, erect, 30 to 80 cm tall; blades involute, ascending or spreading, from less than 5 cm to more than 15 cm long; panicles narrow, rather lax, 5 to 20 cm long, the branches and pedicels delicate, appressed or ascending, few-flowered, the lower distant; the first glumes acuminate, mucronate, 5 to 8 mm long, the second 1 to 2 mm longer; lemma 6 to 7 mm long, the callus 0.5 mm long, rather finely pubescent, the beak indistinct, about 1 mm long; awns about equal, divergent, only minutely scabrous, 1 to 1.5 cm long, contorted at base.

Dry or rocky slopes, Cuba and Hispaniola.

Cuba: Pinar del Río City, *Ekman* 17800.

Haiti: Ennery, *Leonard* 8824, 8850; *Ekman* H 2454. Cabaret, *Leonard* 12108. Môle-St.-Nicolas, *Leonard* 13215, 13313. Croix-des-Bouquets, *Ekman* H 2161, H 2316, H 2316b. Gros-Morne, *Ekman* H 4938. Habitation Prince, *Picarda* 1554. Port-au-Prince, *Ekman* H 2019, H 9281.

Dominican Republic: Azua, *Rose, Fitch, and Russell* 4027. Santiago, *Ekman* H 15965.

20. Aristida refracta Griseb., Cat. Pl. Cub. 228. 1866. Cuba, *Wright* 3431.

Culms usually densely tufted with numerous innovations, erect, slender, 20 to 60 cm tall; blades filiform-involute, mostly less than 10 cm long; sometimes as much as 20 cm long; panicles narrow, rather lax, 5 to 15 cm long, the branches ascending, at maturity rather stiff, few-flowered, sometimes as much as 3 cm long; glumes unequal or nearly equal, the second mucronate from a bifid apex; lemma about 4.5 mm long, the callus 0.5 mm long, short-pilose, the summit scarcely beaked; awns about equal, or the lateral a little shorter, about 1 cm long, contorted at base.

Dry slopes and pine woods, Greater Antilles.

Cuba: Pinar del Río, *Wright* 3833, 3834; *Hitchcock* 23255, 23262. Guane, *Léon* 6942, 6971, 7307, 7308, 8971; *Shafer* 10414. Mántua, *Shafer* 11254. Laguna Jovero, *Shafer* 10718, 10864. Cajálbana, *Léon*

4846. San Diego de los Baños, *Léon* 4845. Herradura, *Hitchcock* 233, 499; *Ekman* 17749. San Julián, *Ekman* 11107. Las Pozas, *Ekman* 12737. La Grifa, *Ekman* 11246. Chirigota, *Léon* 7444, 7454; *Wright* 3431. Guanabacoa, *Baker and Hasselbring* 7208; *Hitchcock* 231, 23226; *Léon* 875, 2641, 4646, 4718, 5605, 5606. Baraguá, *Hitchcock* 23373. Manacas, *Léon* 5830, 5863, 5874. Motembo, *Léon* 11338, 11340, 11342; *Ekman* 16816a. Placetas del Sur, *Léon* 8179. Manajanabo, *Léon* 5276. Camagüey, *Ekman* in 1922 (*Amer. Gr. Nat. Herb.* 792). Woodfred, *Shafer* 2990, 3080. Cajobabo, *Léon* 12316. Guara, *Hitchcock* 23425, 23426. Holguín, *Ekman* 15719. Loma Menqura, *Shafer* 3858. Without locality, *Wright* 3430. Isla de Pinos, *Britton and Wilson* 15369.

JAMAICA: Ashley Hall, *Harris* 12734. Lititz Savanna, *Harris* 12433. New Forest, *Hitchcock* 9853 (*Amer. Gr. Nat. Herb.* 793).

HAITI: Acul-Samedi, *Ekman* H 9908. St. Michel de l'Atalaye, *Ekman* H 9402.

DOMINICAN REPUBLIC: Monción, *Ekman* H 12634.

PUERTO RICO: Mayaguez, *Britton, Cowell, and Brown* 4358. Boqueron, *Chase* 6508.

TRIBE 6. ZOYSIEAE

41. LEPTOTHRIUM Kunth, Rév. Gram. 1: 156. 1829

Spikelets solitary; glumes much exceeding the single minute floret, the tips diverging, the first subulate, not at all clasping, the second laterally compressed above; pedicel falling with the spikelet, forming a pointed callus. Densely tufted perennial with slender rigid short-jointed culms branching toward the summit, short stiff divergent blades, and partially included spikes of narrow spikelets along a slender axis.

1. **Leptothrium rigidum** Kunth, Rév., Gram. 1: 156. 1829. "America calidior."

Culms 30 to 40 cm tall; blades 1 to 3 cm long; spikes 5 to 10 cm long, flexuous; spikelets about 8 mm long, at first erect, becoming divergent or reflexed (fig. 57).

In sand along the seacoast, Jamaica, Venezuela, and Santa Marta, Colombia.

JAMAICA: Palisadoes, Port Royal, *Hitchcock* 9753; *Harris* (*Amer. Gr. Nat. Herb.* 287) 11357; *Britton and Hollick* 1729.

42. ANTHEPHORA Schreb., Beschr. Gräs. 2: 105. pl. 44. 1810

Spikelets in clusters of 4, the indurate first glumes united at base, forming a pitcher-shaped pseudo-involucre, the clusters subsessile and erect on a slender flexuous continuous axis; glumes rigid, acute, or produced into short awns. Ours annual with flat blades and narrow spikes.

1. **Anthephora hermaphrodita** (L.) Kuntze, Rev. Gen. Pl. 2: 759. 1891.

Tripsacum hermaphroditum L., Syst. Nat. ed. 10. 2: 1261. 1759. Jamaica.

Anthephora elegans Schreb., Beschr. Gräs. 2: 105. 1810. Jamaica.

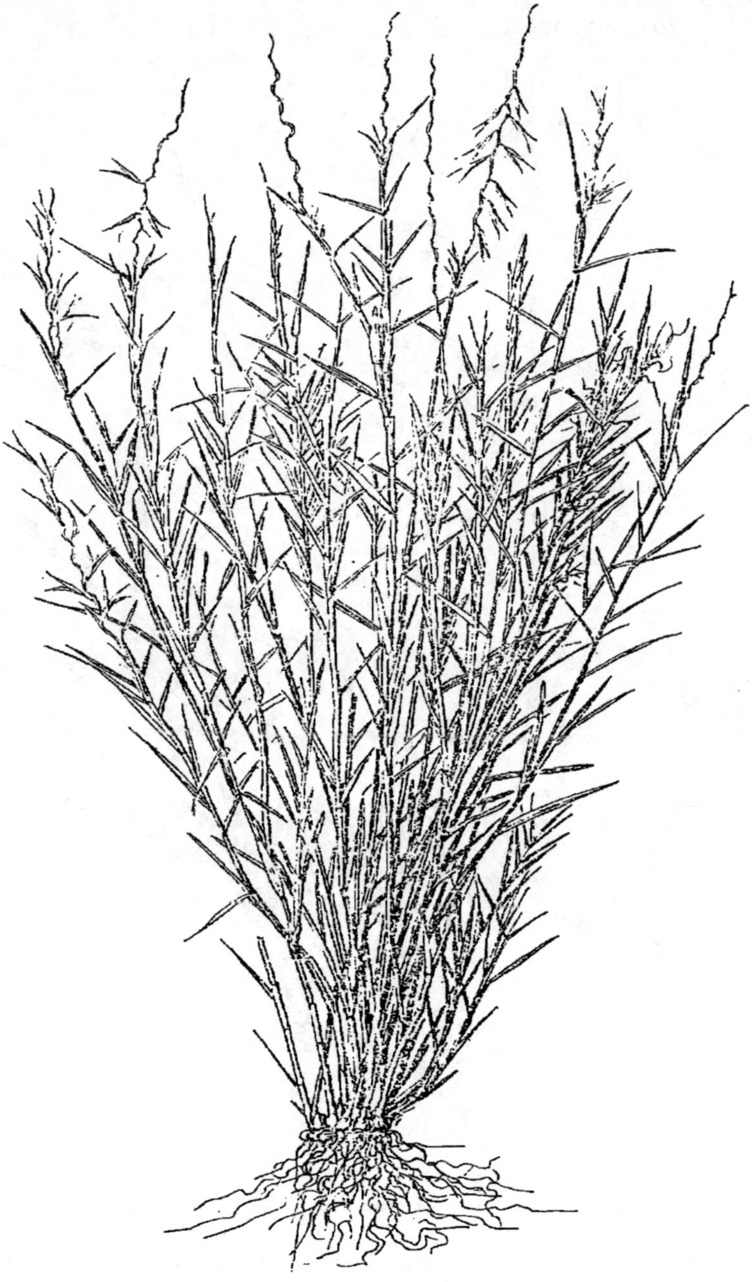

FIGURE 57.—*Leptothrium rigidum*. Plant, × ½ (Harris, Amer. Gr. Nat. Herb. 287).

Anthephora villosa Spreng., Neu. Entd. 3: 14. 1822. West Indies, the pubescent form.

Cenchrus villosus Spreng., Syst. Veg. 1: 301. 1825.

FIGURE 58.—*Anthephora hermaphrodita*, × ½ (Harris 12679).

Leafy ascending or decumbent branching annual; culms mostly 20 to 50 cm tall; blades flat, thin, 5 to 10 mm wide; spikes erect, 5 to 10 cm long; glumes 5 to 7 mm long (fig. 58).

A common weed throughout the West Indies and other parts of tropical America.

43. TRAGUS Hall., Stirp. Helv. 2: 203. 1768.

(*Nazia* Adans., Fam. Pl. 2: 581. 1763. No generic description)

Spikelets 1-flowered, in small spikes of 2 to 5, the spikes subsessile, falling entire, the spikelets sessile on a very short zigzag rachis, the first glumes small, thin, or wanting, appressed to the rachis, the second glumes of the two lower spikelets strongly convex with 3

FIGURE 59.—*Tragus berteronianus.* Plant, × ½; bur and spikelet, × 5 (Hitchcock 3745).

thick nerves bearing a row of squarrose, stout hooked prickles along each side, the 2 second glumes forming the halves of a little bur, the upper 1 to 3 spikelets reduced and sterile; lemmas and palea thin, the lemma flat, the palea strongly convex. Low annuals with flat blades and narrow spikes.

1. Tragus berteronianus Schult., Mant. 2: 205. 1824. Santo Domingo.

Culms branched at base, spreading, 10 to 40 cm long; blades firm, mostly less than 5 cm long, 2 to 4 mm wide, the cartilaginous margin bearing stiff white hairs or short slender teeth; racemes dense, 4 to 10 cm long, 4 to 5 mm thick; burs 2 to 3 mm long, nearly sessile, the apex scarcely exceeding the spines (fig. 59).

This species has been erroneously referred to *Tragus alienus* (Spreng.) Schult. (*Lappago aliena* Spreng.; *Nazia aliena* Scribn.).

Open arid ground, southwestern United States and the West Indies to Brazil. Occurs on probably all the islands.

TRIBE 7. CHLORIDEAE

44. LEPTOCHLOA Beauv., Ess. Agrost. 71, 166. pl. 15. f. 1. 1812

SPRANGLETOP

Spikelets 2- to several-flowered, sessile or short-pediceled, approximate or somewhat distant along one side of a slender rachis, the rachilla disarticulating above the glumes and between the florets; glumes unequal or nearly equal, awnless or mucronate, 1-nerved, usually shorter than the first lemma; lemmas obtuse or acute, sometimes 2-toothed and mucronate or short-awned from between the teeth, 3-nerved, the nerves sometimes pubescent. Annuals or perennials with flat blades and numerous racemes scattered along a common axis forming a long or sometimes short panicle.

Plants annual.
  Sheaths, at least the upper, papillose-hispid ---------- 1. L. FILIFORMIS.
  Sheaths glabrous or scabrous.
    Lemmas awned, the awn sometimes short ---------- 2. L. FASCICULARIS.
    Lemmas awnless.
      Florets acuminate; sheaths scabrous ---------- 4. L. SCABRA.
      Florets obtuse; sheaths glabrous or slightly scabrous.
        Spikelets 5 to 7 mm long, 6- to 9-flowered, lead-color. 3. L. UNINERVIA.
        Spikelets 2 to 3 mm long, 3- or 4-flowered, pale. 5. L. NEALLEYI.
Plants perennial.
  Spikes slender, 15 to 20 cm long ---------- 8. L. LONGA.
  Spikes mostly less than 10 cm long.
    Blades involute ---------- 9. L. MONTICOLA.
    Blades flat or loosely involute in drying.
      Sheaths and blades glabrous, usually somewhat glaucous; awnless or the awns shorter than body of lemma ---------- 6. L. VIRGATA.
      Sheaths sparsely papillose-hispid; blades sparsely villous on the upper surface near the base; awns or some of them about as long as their lemmas ---------- 7. L. DOMINGENSIS.

1. Leptochloa filiformis (Lam.) Beauv., Ess. Agrost. 71, 166. 1812.
RED SPRANGLETOP.

Festuca filiformis Lam., Tabl. Encycl. 1: 191. 1791. Tropical America.

Eleusine mucronata Michx., Fl. Bor. Amer. 1: 65. 1803. Illinois.

Rabdochloa? mucronata Beauv., Ess. Agrost. 84, 176. 1812.

Leptochloa mucronata Kunth, Rév. Gram. 1: 91. 1829.

Leptochloa brachiata Steud., Syn. Pl. Glum. 1: 209. 1854. Guadeloupe.

Plants often purplish or reddish; culms erect or often branching and geniculate below, 40 to 70 cm tall, or often dwarf: blades flat, thin, as much as 1 cm wide; panicle somewhat viscid, of numerous approximate slender racemes 5 to 15 cm long on an axis mostly half the entire length of the culm; spikelets, 3- to 4-flowered, 1 to 2 mm long; glumes acuminate, longer than the first floret, often as long as the spikelet; lemmas awnless, pubescent on the nerves, 1.5 mm long (fig. 60).

FIGURE 60.—*Leptochloa filiformis*. Plant, × ½; spikelet and floret, × 10 (Ruth 51).

Fields and open ground, Virginia to California, south to South America. A common weed in fields throughout the West Indies, except the Bahamas. *Leptochloa mucronata* var. *multiflora* Eggers [28] is listed, without description, from St. Croix.

2. Leptochloa fascicularis (Lam.) A. Gray, Man. 588. 1848.

Festuca fascicularis Lam., Tabl. Encycl. 1: 189. 1791. South America.

Festuca polystachya Michx., Fl. Bor. Amer. 1: 66. 1803. Illinois.

Festuca thouini Steud., Syn. Pl. Glum. 1: 311. 1854. Santo Domingo.

Somewhat succulent; culms erect to spreading or prostrate, freely branching, 30 to 100 cm tall; blades flat to loosely involute; panicles more or less included, mostly 10 to 20 cm long, often smaller, the racemes several to numerous, as much as 10 cm long, usually ascending or appressed, or at maturity spreading; spikelets usually overlapping, 7 to 12 mm long, 6- to 12-flowered; lemmas 4 to 5 mm long, the lateral nerves pubescent below, acuminate, the awn from short to as long as the body (fig. 61).

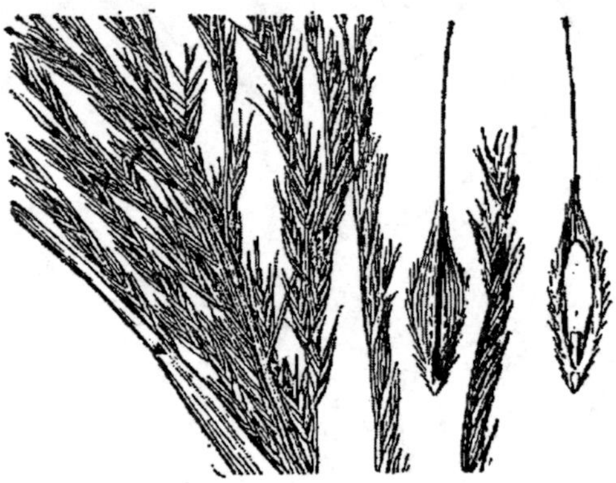

FIGURE 61.—*Leptochloa fascicularis*. Panicle, × 1; two views of floret, × 10 (Hitchcock 7876).

Ditches and moist ground, United States, Mexico, and the West Indies.

BAHAMAS: Great Exuma, *Britton and Millspaugh* 3108. New Providence, *Britton and Brace* 504.

CUBA: Habana, *Léon* 753, 864, 1509, 2020. Batabanó, *Hitchcock* 251; *Ekman* 889. Romelie, *Eggers* 4834. Corrientes Bay, *Britton and Cowell* 9984. Central Orosco, *Ekman* 10570. Baraguá, *Hitchcock* 23337. Guantánamo, *Léon* 3911. Without locality, *Wright* 3812, 3822.

JAMAICA: Black River, *Hitchcock* 9643. Port Henderson, *Ridley* 132. Savanna-la-Mar, *Hitchcock* 9863. St. Anns Bay, *Britton* 2519. Ferry Pen, *Harris* 12498.

HAITI: Étang, *Leonard* 3520. Cape Haitien, *Ekman* H 2750. Port-au-Prince, *Ekman* H 2105; *Buch* 1801, 1869. Miragoane, *Ekman* H 7257. Gourjon, *Ekman* H 6453.

VIRGIN ISLANDS: St. Croix, *Thompson* 407; *Ricksecker* 306.

LEEWARD ISLANDS: Antigua, *Box* 8, 33, 34, 47.

3. Leptochloa uninervia (Presl) Hitchc. and Chase, Contrib. U. S. Natl. Herb. 18: 383. 1917.

Megastachya uninervia Presl, Rel. Haenk. 1: 283. 1830. Mexico.

Leptochloa imbricata Thurb., in S. Wats., Bot. Calif. 2: 293. 1880. California.

Perennial, resembling *L. fascicularis*, rather sparingly branching, usually strictly erect, the panicle more oblong in outline, with shorter,

[28] Vidensk. Medd. Naturhist. Forening. Copenhagen (III) 8: 151. 1876.

denser-flowered racemes; spikelets, 5 to 7 mm long, 6- to 9-flowered, lead-color; glumes broader, more obtuse; lemmas scarcely narrowed toward tip, apiculate but not awned, the lateral nerves more or less excurrent (fig. 62).

Ditches and wet open ground, southwestern United States, Cuba, and Jamaica, and south to Argentina and Chile.

CUBA: Guantánamo, *Hioram* 1359.

JAMAICA: Salt Ponds, *Harris* 12309, 12311.

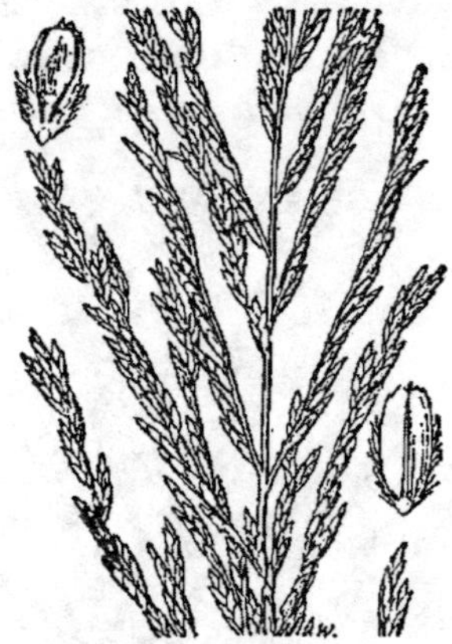

FIGURE 62.—*Leptochloa uninervia*. Panicle, × 1; two views of floret, × 10 (Tharp 3123).

4. Leptochloa scabra Nees, Agrost. Bras. 435. 1829. Brazil.

Annual; culms erect, about 1 m tall, somewhat robust and succulent; sheaths and blades scabrous, the blades elongate, 8 to 12 mm wide; panicle 20 to 40 cm long, not more than 7 cm wide, the slender racemes crowded, 4 to 8 cm long, ascending or somewhat drooping, usually curved or flexuous; spikelets crowded, mostly 3-flowered, about 3 mm long; lemmas acute, awnless, the nerves pubescent (fig. 63).

Ditches and shallow swamps, Louisiana, the West Indies, and Central America to Brazil.

DOMINICAN REPUBLIC: Villa Vásquez, *Ekman* H 13127a.

PUERTO RICO: Aguirre, *Britton and Earle* 6495. Rio Piedras, *Stevenson* 2987. Cabo Rojo, *Sintenis* 844. Tabucoa, *Sintenis* 5103. Coamo, *Sintenis* 3282. Guayanilla, *Shafer* 1981. Bayamon, *Hioram* 5, 325; *Chase* 6392. Anasco, *Heller* 4535. Ponce, *Britton and Brown* 5512; *Chase* 6493. Rio Grande, *Chase* 6715. Mayaguez, *Chase* 6289.

FIGURE 63.—*Leptochloa scabra*. Panicle, × 1; two views of floret, × 10 (Tracy 8388).

TRINIDAD: Cedros, *Broadway* 4937; *Hitchcock* 10137. Arima, *Hitchcock* 10293. California, *Hitchcock* 10106. Port-of-Spain, *Hitchcock* 10012. Pointe Gourde, *Britton and Broadway* 2652. Moruga, *Britton and Broadway* 2431. Palo Seco, *Broadway* 9238.

TOBAGO: *Broadway* 4739; *Hitchcock* 10259.

5. Leptochloa nealleyi Vasey, Bull. Torrey Bot. Club 12: 7. 1885. Texas.

Annual, usually erect and rather robust; culms mostly 1 to 1.5 m tall, simple or sparingly branched at the base; sheaths glabrous or slightly scabrous, mostly keeled; blades elongate, flat to loosely involute; panicle commonly 25 to 50 cm long, not more than 4 cm wide, the racemes subverticillate, overlapping, 2 to 4 cm long, appressed or ascending; spikelets crowded, 3- or 4-flowered, 2 to 3 mm long;

lemmas about 1.5 mm long, the apex obtuse, the nerves sparingly pubescent, the lateral close to the margin (fig. 64).

Wet woods, Texas, Mexico, and Cuba.

CUBA: Tiffin, *Shafer* 2904.

6. Leptochloa virgata (L.) Beauv., Ess. Agrost. 166. 1812.

Cynosurus virgatus L., Syst. Nat. ed. 10. 2: 876. 1759. Jamaica.

FIGURE 64.—*Leptochloa nealleyi.* Panicle. × 1; two views of floret, × 10 (Fisher 25).

Eleusine virgata Pers., Syn. Pl. 1: 87. 1805.

Leptostachys virgata Meyer, Prim. Fl. Esseq. 74. 1818.

Oxydenia virgata Nutt.; Jacks., Ind. Kew. 3: 392. 1894.

Leptochloa perennis Hack., Inf. Est. Centr. Agron. Cuba 1: 411. 1906. Cuba, *Baker* 4617.

Perennial; culms wiry, erect, 50 to 100 cm tall; blades flat; racemes several to many, slender, laxly ascending, 5 to 10 cm long, the lower distant, the others often aggregate; spikelets nearly sessile, mostly 3- to 5-flowered; lemmas 1.5 to 2 mm long, awnless or the lower with a short awn (fig. 65).

Open ground and grassy slopes, Mexico and the West Indies to South America. To be found on probably all of the West Indian islands.

7. Leptochloa domingensis (Jacq.) Trin., Fund. Agrost. 133. 1820.

Cynosurus domingensis Jacq., Misc. Austr. 2: 363. 1781. Probably Santo Domingo.

Rabdochloa domingensis Beauv. Ess. Agrost. 84, 176. 1812.

Chloris gracilis H. B. K., Nov. Gen. et Sp. Pl. 1: 168. 1816. Peru.

Leptochloa virgata var. *gracilis* Nees; Griseb., Fl. Brit. W. Ind. 538. 1864.

Leptochloa virgata var. *domingensis* Link; Griseb., Fl. Brit. W. Ind. 538. 1864.

Resembling *L. virgata;* sheaths and blades sparsely pilose; panicles more elongate, the racemes shorter and more numerous; lemmas

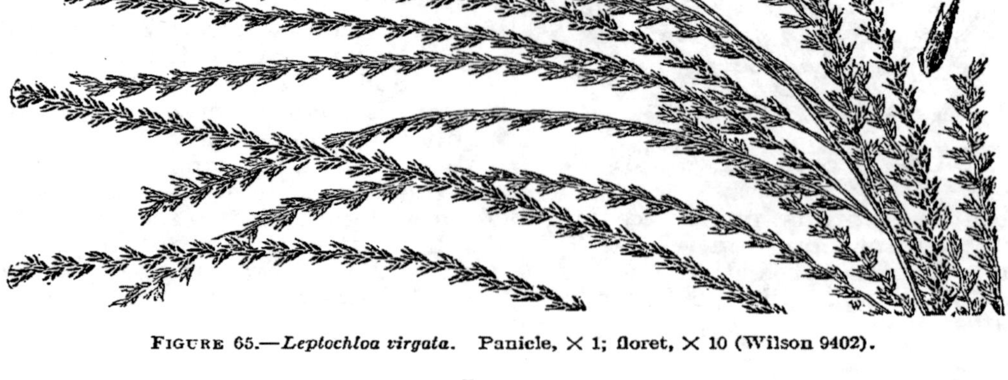

FIGURE 65.—*Leptochloa virgata.* Panicle, × 1; floret, × 10 (Wilson 9402).

appressed-pubescent on the internerves, awned, the awn of the lower florets of the spikelet 1 to 3 mm long (fig. 66).

Open ground and grassy banks, Florida, Mexico, and the West Indies.

BAHAMAS: New Providence, *Hitchcock* in 1890. Eleuthera, *Hitchcock* in 1890.

CUBA: Habana, *Ekman* 419a, 13122. Sancti Spíritus, *Léon* 863b. San Antonio, *Eggers* 5349. Santiago de Cuba, *Léon* 862, 865, 9767. Without locality, *Wright* 3436.

JAMAICA: Hope Gardens, *Ridley* 120, 122. Kingston, *Hitchcock* 9253. Halls Delight, *Harris* 11261. Spanish Town, *Ridley* 128. Guava Ridge, *Harris* 11291, 11367, 11601. Barican, *Hitchcock* 9563. Ewarton, *Hitchcock* 9455. Alligator Pond, *Hitchcock* 9836; *Harris* 12447. East of Hope, *Harris* 12346. Lititz, *Harris* 11713, 11718.

HAITI: Gonaïve Island, *Leonard* 3106, 3300, 5123, 5145. Port-au-Prince, *Ekman* H 1986. St. Marc, *Leonard* 2946. Tortuga Island, *Leonard* 15466. Bourdarie, *Buch* 1209.

DOMINICAN REPUBLIC: Las Salinas, *Fuertes* 1428. Rincón, *Fuertes* 1283. Santiago, *Ekman* H 16042.

FIGURE 66.—*Leptochloa domingensis*. Panicle, × 1; floret, × 10 (Hitchcock 10055).

LEEWARD ISLANDS: St. Kitts, *Box* 166. Antigua, *Wullschlaegel*.

TRINIDAD: Chacachacare, *Hitchcock* 10055 (*Amer. Gr. Nat. Herb.* 671). Mona Island, *Broadway* 5900. Port-of-Spain, *Hitchcock* 9994, 10196; *Britton and Hazen* 1689.

8. Leptochloa longa Griseb., Fl. Brit. W. Ind. 538. 1864. Trinidad.

Perennial; culms about 1.5 m tall, decumbent at base; blades 1.5 to 2.5 cm wide, the collar pilose; racemes several, very slender, spreading, loosely flowered, somewhat fascicled, 15 to 20 cm long; spikelets about 3-flowered; lemmas about 3 mm long, the awn about as long as the lemma or a little longer.

Rich shady banks, Trinidad.

TRINIDAD: Manzanilla, *Hitchcock* 10377. San Fernando, *Hitchcock* 10082 (*Amer. Gr. Nat. Herb.* 672). Without locality, *Bot. Gard. Herb.* 3359; *Crueger*.

9. Leptochloa monticola Chase, Jour. Wash. Acad. Sci. 17: 73. f. 2. 1927. Haiti, *Leonard* 4751.

Perennial; culms densely tufted, erect, rigid, about 1 m tall; blades involute, 20 to 30 cm long, 2 to 6 mm wide (when flattened); panicle about 30 cm long, 8 cm wide, the numerous racemes approximate, stiffly ascending, the middle ones about 10 cm long; spikelets rather distant, 8 to 10 mm long, 6- to 7-flowered; lemmas about 5 mm long, densely pilose on the lower part of the nerves (fig. 67).

Higher mountains of Hispaniola.

HAITI: Pétionville, *Ekman* H 1352, H 1576. Badeau, *Ekman* H 7777. Furcy, *Leonard* 4751. Massif de la Selle, *Ekman* H 1576, H 3075.

DOMINICAN REPUBLIC: San José de Ocoa, *Ekman* H 11874.

45. GOUINIA Fourn., Mex. Pl. 2: 103. 1886

Spikelets, few-flowered, short-pedicellate, appressed, in slender elongate racemes, these racemosely arranged; glumes and lemmas keeled, the lemmas densely villous on the nerves, awned, the uppermost much reduced but awned. Erect or ascending perennials with linear blades and terminal panicles of slender racemes.

Blades 1 to 2 mm wide .... 1. G. GRACILIS.
Blades 5 to 12 mm wide .... 2. G. VIRGATA.

FIGURE 67.—*Leptochloa monticola.* Spikelet and floret, × 5 (type).

FIGURE 68.—*Gouinia gracilis.* Glumes and floret, × 5 (type).

1. Gouinia gracilis Ekman; Swallen, Amer. Jour. Bot. 22: 33. f. 1. 1935. Cuba, *Ekman* in 1922.

Culms slender, branching, sprawling or leaning, 70 cm long or more; blades flat or usually involute, as much as 14 cm long, not more than 2 mm wide; panicles 5 to 15 cm long, the branches stiffly spreading or reflexed, the lower as much as 4.5 cm long; spikelets 2- or 3-flowered, short-pedicellate, stiffly and abruptly spreading or reflexed; lemmas 4 to 6 mm long, the awn 5 to 9 mm long (fig. 68).

Thickets, Cuba.

CUBA: Holguín, *Ekman* in 1922, 3255. Mendoza, *Ekman* 11486.

2. Gouinia virgata (Presl) Scribn., U. S. Dept. Agr., Div. Agrost. Bull. 4: 10. 1897.

Bromus virgatus Presl, Rel. Haenk. 1: 263. 1830. Mexico.

Festuca laxiflora A. Rich., in Sagra, Hist. Cuba 11: 318. 1850. Habana, Cuba.

FIGURE 69.—*Gouinia virgata*, × ½ (Palmer 77 in 1895).

Diplachne virgata Hack., Oesterr. Bot. Ztschr. 52: 276. 1902.

Culms erect from a knotty base, usually about 1 m tall; blades flat, 5 to 15 mm wide; panicle 15 to 35 cm long, the branches stiffly spreading, the lower usually about 12 cm long, spikelet-bearing from the base; spikelets mostly 2- or 3-flowered; lemma 8 to 10 mm long, the awn 1 to 1.5 cm long (fig. 69).

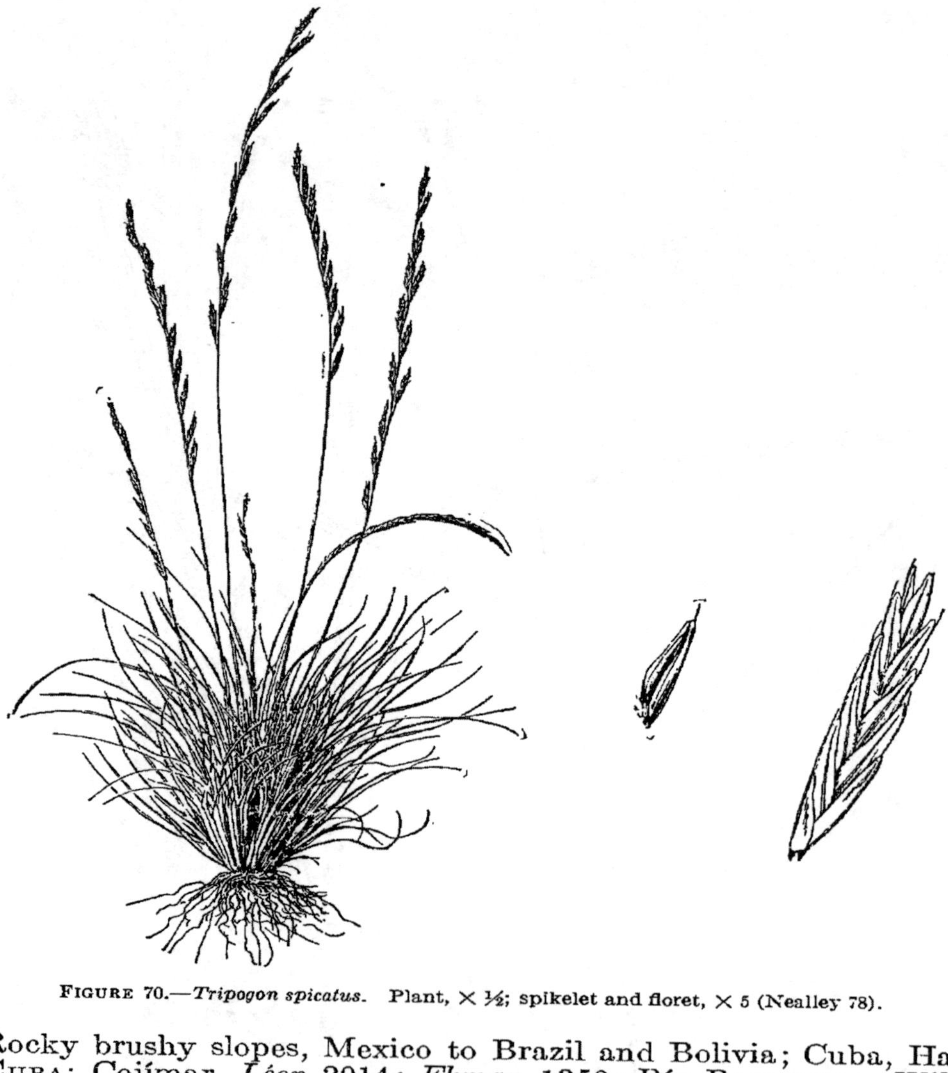

FIGURE 70.—*Tripogon spicatus*. Plant, × ½; spikelet and floret, × 5 (Nealley 78).

Rocky brushy slopes, Mexico to Brazil and Bolivia; Cuba, Haiti.

CUBA: Cojímar, *Léon* 2014; *Ekman* 1359; Río Bacuranao, *Wilson and Léon* 11594.

HAITI: Hinche, *Ekman* H 6137.

46. TRIPOGON Roth; Roem. and Schult., Syst. Veg. 2: 600. 1817

Spikelets, several- to many-flowered, sessile, erect in a single spike; glumes shorter than the lowermost floret; lemmas awned from between the lobes of the minutely two-lobed summit. Low tufted perennials with narrow blades and slender solitary spikes, the spikelets somewhat distant.

1. Tripogon spicatus (Nees) Ekman, Arkiv. Bot. 11⁴: 36. 1912.

Bromus spicatus Nees, Agrost. Bras. 471. 1829. Brazil.

Tricuspis simplex Griseb., Mem. Amer. Acad. (n. s.) 8: 532. 1862. Cuba, *Wright* 1551.

Leptochloa spicata Scribn., Acad. Nat. Sci. Phila. Proc. 1891: 304. 1892.

Culms slender, mostly less than 10 cm tall; blades subfiliform, aggregated at the base of the plant; spike about half the entire height of the plant; spikelets appressed, about 5 mm long (fig. 70).

Sterile hills, Texas to Argentina; central Cuba, Haiti.

CUBA: Santayana, *Ekman* 15356. Motembo, *Léon* 9416.

HAITI: St. Michel, *Ekman* H 8371.

47. LEPTURIDIUM Hitchc. and Ekman, gen. nov.[29]

Spikelets 2-flowered in two rows on one sde of a continuous triangular rachis, the pedicels very short; glumes about equal, awnless, the midnerve broad, greenish, firm, the margins thin, apparently no lateral nerves; lower floret slightly exceeding the first glume, the second floret more or less reduced, the internode of the rachilla slender, somewhat flexuous, the callus minutely pilose; lemma of first floret thin, minutely and rather sparsely villous, 3-nerved, the midnerve evident, the lateral nerves near the margins, obscure, the midnerve extending into a minute mucro between two very short teeth; palea narrow, a little shorter than the lemma, deeply sulcate on the back, thin like the lemma; second lemma similar to the first, smaller or sometimes much reduced, the rachilla enlarged and pilose below the floret; paleap resent in the larger second florets, but empty; stamens 3, brown.

Perennial with short firm distichous blades and terminal spikes.

The genus is not closely allied to any other genus. The structure of the spikelet would place it near *Gymnopogon* which differs in having several spikes in an inflorescence and in having usually remote awned spikelets.

Type species, *Lepturidium insulare* Hitchc. and Ekman.

1. Lepturidium insulare Hitchc. and Ekman, sp. nov.[30]

Perennial; culms cespitose rather wiry, spreading, decumbent at base, or prostrate, 10 to 30 cm long; sheaths overlapping, several to many on the lower half of the flowering culms, pilose or villous around the summit and the base of the blade; blades stiffly ascending, rather conspicuously distichous, flat, becoming involute, glabrous, 1 to 2 mm wide, mostly 1 to 2 cm long, the tip hard, obtuse, somewhat boat-shaped; spike solitary, erect, stiff, mostly 5 to 8 cm long, the base enclosed in the uppermost sheath or slightly exserted; glumes about 3 mm long, oblong-linear, the midnerve hard; lemma of first floret about 2.5 mm long; second floret nearly as long as the first or reduced to a minute rudiment, the rachilla joint slender, 1 to 1.5 mm long; stamens 3, about 0.5 mm long (fig. 71).

[29] Spiculae 2-florae multae in spica solitaria terminale; glumae aequales 1-nerviae; floscula inferior glumam primam subequans tenuis 3-nervia mucronata; floscula superior parva vel minuta, rachilla gracili.

[30] Planta perennis; culmi subrigidi 10–30 cm alti, nodis multis; laminae rigidae distichae 1–2 cm longae, 1–2 mm latae; glumae 3 mm longae; lemma inferius sparse villosum.

60256—36——8

Type in the United States National Herbarium, no. 1296125, collected in white sand, saline flats, Santa Bárbara, Isla de Pinos, Cuba, November 3, 1920, by E. L. Ekman (no. 12060).

Other specimens, both from Isla de Pinos, are: Santa Bárbara, *Ekman* 12023; Los Indios, *Ekman* 12155.

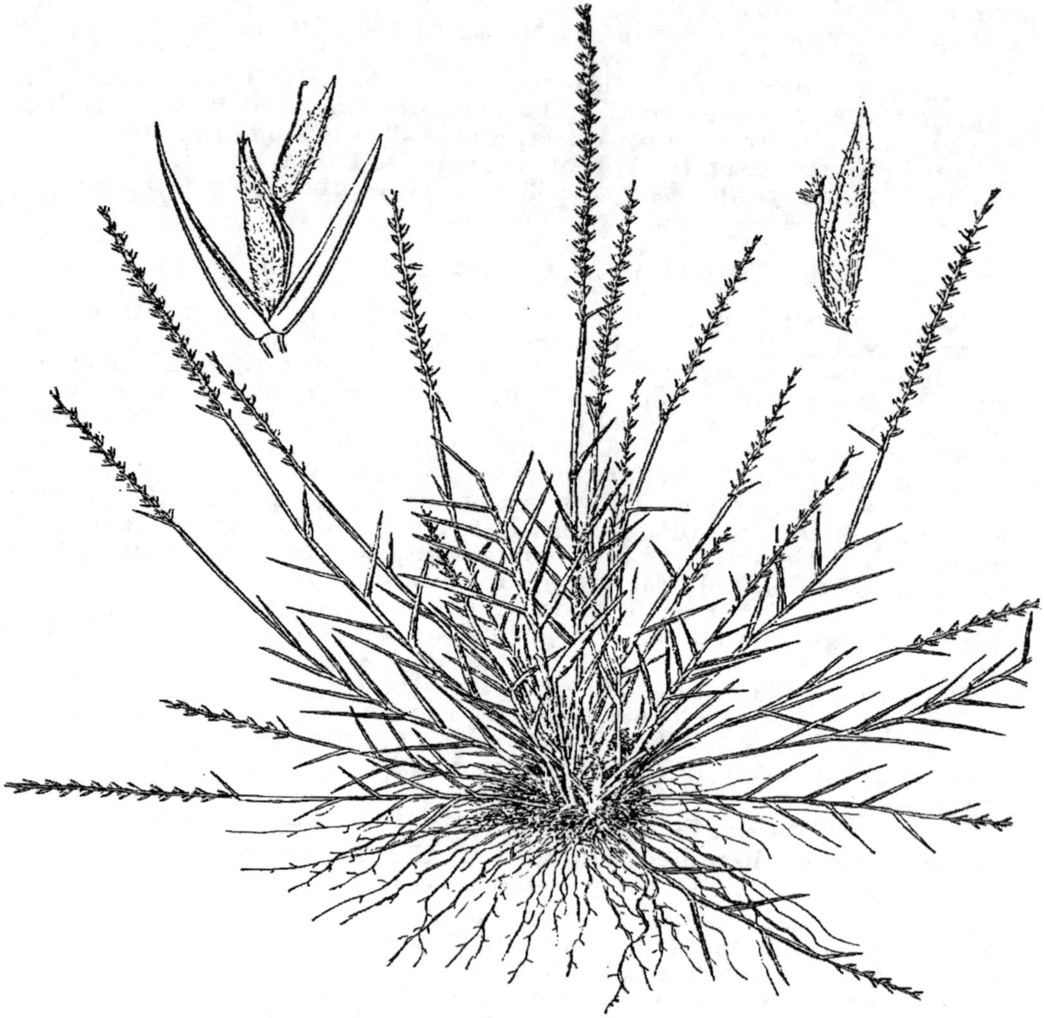

FIGURE 71.—*Lepturidium insulare.* Plant, × ½; spikelet and floret, × 10 (type).

No pistils have been found in the specimens examined. The species may be dioecious. On one specimen (no. 12155), there is an auriculate extension of the margin of the rachis below many of the spikelets, forming a glumelike point by the side of the spikelet. This appears to be an abnormality. In aspect the sterile plants somewhat resemble those of *Cenchrus distichophyllus*.

48. ELEUSINE Gaertn., Fruct. et Sem. 1: 7. pl. 1. f. 11. 1788

Spikelets, few- to several-flowered, compressed, sessile and closely imbricate, in two rows along one side of a rather broad rachis, the latter not prolonged beyond the spikelets; rachilla disarticulating above the glumes and between the florets, glumes unequal, rather broad, acute, 1-nerved, shorter than the first lemma; lemmas acute, with 3 strong green nerves close together forming a keel, the uppermost somewhat reduced; seed dark brown, roughened by fine ridges, loosely enclosed in the thin pericarp. Annuals, with two to several rather stout spikes, digitate at the summit of the culms, sometimes with one or two a short distance below, or rarely with a single terminal spike.

Spikes in a terminal whorl, sometimes with a spike below...... 1. E. INDICA.
Spikes in more than one whorl........................ 2. E. VERTICILLATA.

1. Eleusine indica (L.) Gaertn., Fruct. et Sem. 1: 8. 1788.
GOOSEGRASS.

Cynosurus indicus L., Sp. Pl. 72. 1753. India.

Branching at base, ascending or prostrate, very smooth; culms compressed, usually less than 50 cm long; blades flat or folded, 3 to 8 mm wide; spikes mostly 2 to 6, flat, 4 to 15 cm long (fig. 72).

Open ground and waste places. A common weed of warm and warm-temperate regions. Introduced in America. To be found on all the West Indian islands. In Cuba called "pata de gallina" and "grama de caballo."

2. Eleusine verticillata Roxb., Fl. Ind. 1: 346. 1820. India.

Annual; culms rather slender, 30 to 60 cm tall; spikes in a terminal whorl of 3 to 5 and several below in 2 or 3 whorls or opposite or alternate; spikelets 8- to 12-flowered; glumes aristulate; lemmas mucronate.

Pastures and open ground. Tropical regions of the Old World; introduced in Haiti.

HAITI: Cul-de-Sac, *Ekman* H 941. L'Arcahaie, *Ekman* H 6671.

49. DACTYLOCTENIUM Willd., Enum. Pl. 1029. 1809

Spikelets, 3- to 5-flowered, compressed, sessile and closely imbricate, in two rows along one side of the rather narrow flat rachis, the end projecting in a point beyond the spikelets; rachilla disarticulating above the first glume and between the florets; glumes somewhat unequal, broad, 1-nerved, the first persistent upon the rachis, the second mucronate or short-awned below the tip, deciduous; lemmas firm, broad, keeled, acuminate or short-awned, 3-nerved, the lateral nerves indistinct, the upper floret reduced; the palea about as long as the lemma; seed subglobose, ridged or wrinkled, enclosed in a thin, early-disappearing pericarp. Annuals or perennials, with flat blades and two to several short thick spikes, digitate and widely spreading at the summit of the culms.

1. Dactyloctenium aegyptium (L.) Richt., Pl. Eur. 1: 68. 1890.
CROWFOOT GRASS.

Cynosurus aegyptius L., Sp. Pl. 72. 1753. Africa, Asia, America.
Eleusine aegyptiaca Desf., Fl. Atlant. 1: 85. 1798.

FIGURE 72.—*Eleusine indica.* Plant, × ½; spikelet, floret, and seed (without pericarp), × 5 (Fredholm 5331).

FIGURE 73.—*Dactyloctenium aegyptium.* Plant, × ½; spikelet, floret, and seed (without pericarp), × 5 (Small and Heller 378).

Culms compressed, spreading with ascending ends, rooting at the nodes, branching, commonly forming mats, usually 20 to 40 cm long; blades flat, ciliate; spikes 1 to 5 cm long (fig. 73).

Open ground and waste places. A common weed in warm countries. Introduced in America. To be found on all the West Indian islands. In Cuba called "pata de gallina."

50. CYNODON L. Rich.; Pers., Syn. Pl. 1: 85. 1805

(*Capriola* Adans., Fam. Pl. 2: 31, 532. 1763. Ineffectively published)

Spikelets, 1-flowered, awnless, sessile in two rows along one side of a slender continuous rachis, the rachilla disarticulating above the glumes and prolonged behind the palea as a slender naked bristle, this sometimes bearing a rudimentary lemma; glumes narrow, acuminate, 1-nerved, about equal, shorter than the floret; lemma strongly compressed, pubescent on the keel, firm, 3-nerved, the lateral nerves close to the margins. Perennials with creeping stolons or rhizomes, short blades, and several slender digitate spikes.

1. Cynodon dactylon (L.) Pers., Syn. Pl. 1: 85. 1805.

BERMUDA GRASS.

Panicum dactylon L., Sp. Pl. 58. 1753. Europe.
Capriola dactylon Kuntze, Rev. Gen. Pl. 2: 764. 1891.

Culms low, extensively creeping, wiry, compressed, the flowering shoots 10 to 30 cm tall, or in moist shady places 50 cm tall or even more; blades on the stolons short and spreading, flat, the sheath pilose at the throat; spikes usually 3 to 5, digitate, slender, arcuate-spreading, 2.5 to 5 cm long; spikelets about 2 mm long, the lemma longer than the glumes (fig. 74).

Common in open, rather dry ground in the warmer parts of both hemispheres; apparently introduced in America. To be found on probably all the islands of the West Indies. A common and well-known pasture grass, called Bermuda grass in the United States and Bahama grass in the English West Indies. In the Spanish islands it is called "grama", "hierba fina", and "hierba del prado", and because of its digitate spikes, "pata de gallina." In Antigua it is called "devil's grass"; in Haiti called chiendent. Bermuda grass is commonly used for lawns and pasture throughout the West Indies.

51. SPARTINA Schreb.; Gmel., Syst. Nat. ed. 13. 2: 123. 1791

CORDGRASS

Spikelets, 1-flowered, much flattened laterally, sessile and usually closely imbricate, on one side of a continuous rachis, disarticulating below the glumes, the rachilla not produced beyond the floret; glumes keeled, 1-nerved, acute or short-awned, the first shorter, the second often exceeding the lemma; lemma firm, keeled, the lateral nerves obscure, narrowed to a rather obtuse point; palea 2-nerved, keeled and flattened, the keel between or at one side of the nerves. Stout perennials with tough leaves and 2 to many spikes racemose on a main axis.

Spikes ascending or somewhat spreading; spikelets closely imbricate; second glume very scabrous on the keel .... 1. S. PATENS.
Spikes appressed in a narrow close inflorescence; spikelets imbricate only at the tip; second glume nearly glabrous .... 2. S. BRASILIENSIS.

1. Spartina patens (Ait.) Muhl., Descr. Gram. 55. 1817.
SALTMEADOW SORDGRASS.

Dactylis patens Ait., Hort. Kew. 1: 104. 1789.
Trachynotia juncea Michx., Fl. Bor. Amer. 1: 64. 1803. South Carolina.
Spartina juncea Willd., Enum. Pl. 81. 1809.

FIGURE 74.—*Cynodon dactylon.* Plant, × ½; spikelet and two views of floret, × 5 (Kearney).

Spartina patens var. *juncea* Hitchc., Rhodora 8: 210. 1906.
Culms erect, usually 1 m or more tall, tough and wiry, with stout scaly creeping rhizomes; blades involute, extending into a long fine point; spikes mostly 2 to 8, ascending or spreading, 4 to 6 cm long; spikelets closely imbricate, 6 to 8 mm long, the second glume scabrous on the keel (fig. 75).

Sandy sea beaches and salt marshes, southeastern United States and the West Indies.

BERMUDA: *Brown and Britton* 313; *Collins* 162.
BAHAMAS: Eleuthera, *Geogr. Soc. Baltimore* 415.
CUBA: Morillo, *Ekman* 17428.
JAMAICA: Black River, *Hitchcock* 9638.
HAITI: Aux Cayes, *Ekman* H 746.
DOMINICAN REPUBLIC: Peninsula de Barahona, *Ekman* H 7060. Perrero, *Ekman* H 13169.

PUERTO RICO: Arecibo, *Chase* 6562. Santurce, *Chase* 6349. Aguada, *Chase* 6603. Guanajibo, *Britton, Cowell, and Brown* 4357. Vieques Island, *Chase* 6699.

VIRGIN ISLANDS: St. Croix, *Borgesen* in 1906. Buck Island. *Borgesen* in 1906.

LEEWARD ISLANDS: Antigua, *Box* 102. Guadeloupe, *Duss* 3162

FIGURE 75.—*Spartina patens*. Panicle, × 1; spikelet, × 5 (Killip 6359).

2. Spartina brasiliensis Raddi, Agrost. Bras. 21. 1823. Brazil.

Culms erect from extensively creeping rhizomes, 50 to 100 cm tall; blades erect, 3 to 5 mm wide; spikes few, appressed, 4 to 8 cm long; spikelets about 1 cm long, slightly overlapping, the second glume glabrous or nearly so on the keel.

Tidal flats, Trinidad to Brazil.

TRINIDAD: Erin Beach, growing in salt water, *Broadway* 9287.

SPARTINA CYNOSUROIDES (L.) Roth, Catal. Bot. 3: 10. 1806. In the United States National Herbarium there is a specimen said to come from the Bahama Islands. The species occurs from Massachusetts to Florida and Louisiana but is not otherwise known from the Bahamas.

52. GYMNOPOGON Beauv., Ess. Agrost. 41. pl. 9. f. 3. 1812

Spikelets, 1- or rarely 2- or 3-flowered, nearly sessile, appressed and usually remote in two rows along one side of a slender continuous rachis, the rachilla disarticulating above the glumes and prolonged behind the 1 or more fertile florets as a slender stipe, bearing a rudiment of a floret, this sometimes with 1 or 2 slender awns; glumes narrow, acuminate, 1-nerved, usually longer than the floret; lemmas narrow, 3-nerved, the lateral nerves near the margin, the apex minutely bifid, bearing between the teeth a slender awn, or rarely awnless. Perennials or rarely annuals, with short, flat, stiff blades, numerous stiff, slender, divergent spikes loosely scattered along the upper part of the culm, or sometimes aggregate toward the summit, the spikes often deflexed at maturity.

Spikes 2 to 4 cm long, aggregate at the summit of the naked culms; annual. 1. G. FOLIOSUS.
Spikes 10 to 25 cm long, scattered along the upper part of the culms; perennial.
  Blades ovate-lanceolate, 2 to 5 cm long; culms mostly not more than 30 cm tall .... 2. G. AMBIGUUS.
  Blades linear-lanceolate, 3 to 7 cm long; culms 50 to 100 cm tall .. 3. G. SPICATUS.

1. **Gymnopogon foliosus** (Willd.) Nees, Agrost. Bras. 426. 1829.

Chloris foliosa Willd., Sp. Pl. 4: 924. 1806. St. Thomas.

Biatherium foliosum Desv., Opusc. 72. 1831.

Annual; culms wiry, erect or decumbent at base, short-jointed, 15 to 50 cm tall; blades numerous, short, squarrose, mostly 1 to 2 cm long, sharp-pointed; spikes 3 to 7, erect or ascending, 2 to 3 cm long; glumes 3 to 4 mm long; lemma 2.5 mm long, the awn 1.5 cm long.

White barren sands, Puerto Rico, Hispaniola, and St. Thomas to Brazil.

PUERTO RICO: Laguna Tortuguero, *Britton* 7955. Campo Alegre, *Chase* 6611, 6789 (*Amer. Gr. Nat. Herb.* 661).

DOMINICAN REPUBLIC: "Santo Domingo" in Trinius Herbarium.

2. **Gymnopogon ambiguus** (Michx.) B. S. P., Prel. Cat. N. Y. 69. 1888.

Andropogon ambiguus Michx., Fl. Bor. Amer. 1: 58. 1803. Carolina.

Culms 30 to 60 cm tall, in small clumps with short scaly rhizomes, suberect to spreading, rigid, sparingly branching; leaves numerous, approximate with overlapping sheaths, or the lower rather distant; blades spreading, 5 to 15 mm, mostly about 10 mm wide, the base rounded-truncate; spikes 10 to 20 cm long, floriferous from base, the lower spikelets often remote; glumes 4 to 6 mm long; lemma with an awn 4 to 6 mm long, the rudiment bearing a delicate shorter awn (fig. 76).

Dry pine lands, southern United States; Hispaniola.

DOMINICAN REPUBLIC: Constanza, *Ekman* H 14023. El Tetero, *Ekman* H 13721. San Juan, *Ekman* H 13538. San José de Ocoa, *Ekman* H 11932.

3. **Gymnopogon spicatus** (Spreng.) Kuntze, Rev. Gen. Pl. 3^2: 354. 1898.

Polypogon spicatus Spreng., Syst. Veg. 1: 243. 1825. Brazil.

Gymnopogon filiformis Griseb., Fl. Brit. W. Ind. 538. 1864. Trinidad.

Perennial; culms slender, wiry, 50 to 100 cm tall; blades thickish, linear-lanceolate, 3 to 7 cm long; inflorescence commonly nearly half the entire length of the plant; spikes slender, divaricate, 15 to 25 cm long, naked or nearly so for the lower one-third to half their length.

Sterile hills, Trinidad to Argentina.

TRINIDAD: Without locality, *Bot. Gard. Herb.* 3361.

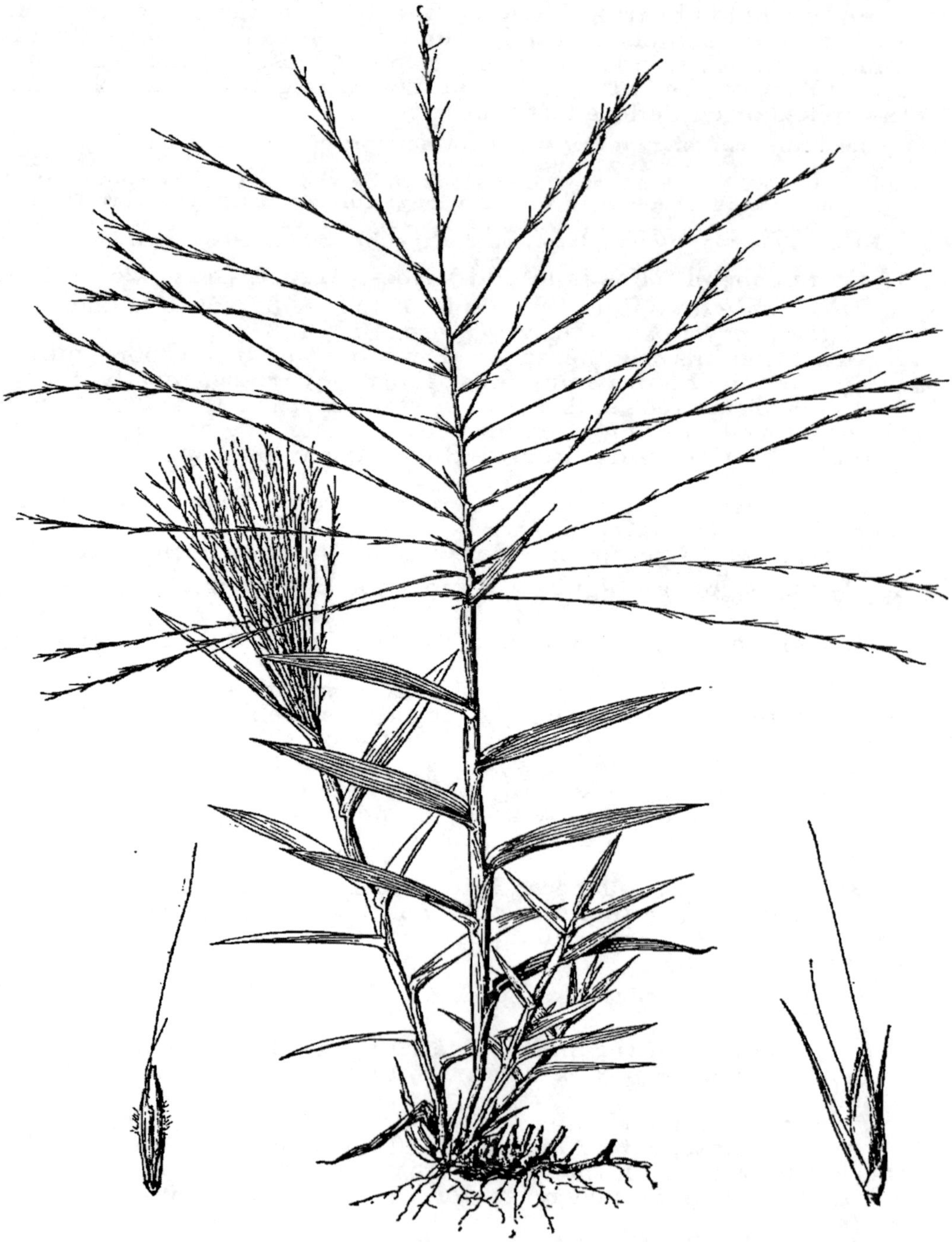

FIGURE 76.—*Gymnopogon ambiguus.* Plant, × ½; spikelet and floret, × 5 (Tracy 8292).

53. SAUGETIA Hitchc. and Chase, Contrib. U. S. Natl. Herb. 18: 378. 1917

Spikelets, 2-flowered, the first perfect, the second neuter and much reduced; glumes thin, unequal, 1-nerved, acuminate, shorter than the floret; first floret stipitate, the lemma firm, minutely 2-toothed at the apex, 3-nerved, the midnerve produced into a delicate awn; palea slightly shorter than the lemma. acute, sulcate between the nerves; second floret reduced to a minute lemma on an elongate slender rachilla joint. Cespitose perennials with slender wiry branching culms, narrow blades, and 1 to 3 slender spikes, the spikelets subsessile, contiguous but scarcely imbricate along one side of a slender continuous rachis, closely appressed to it.

Plants 20 to 40 cm tall, the culms and blades slender and delicate; spikes solitary -- 1. S. FASCICULATA.
Plants 50 to 80 cm tall, the culms and blades much coarser; spikes usually 2, sometimes 1 or 3 -- 2. S. PLEIOSTACHYA.

1. Saugetia fasciculata Hitchc. and Chase, Contrib. U. S. Natl. Herb. 18: 378. 1917. Cuba, *Léon* 6901.

Plants in dense hard tufts, glabrous throughout; culms 40 to 50 cm tall, erect or the summit leaning, the internodes elongate, branching at most of the nodes, the branches mostly fascicled, commonly one of them elongate, the others reduced to leafy shoots of overlapping sheaths and short spreading blades, these branchlets forming conspicuous tufts along the main culms and branches; sheaths 5 to 8 mm long, with broad papery margins, a tuft of delicate white hairs 1 mm long at the summit, these wanting on old sheaths, the sheaths of the branchlets reduced; ligule obsolete; blades filiform, crescent-shaped in cross section, scarcely 0.5 mm wide when flattened out, flexuous, the primary blades as much as 10 cm long, those of the branchlets 1 to 3 cm long; spikes long-exserted, erect, 3 to 5 cm long, the rachis subfiliform, slightly concavo-convex, the spikelets fitting into the concavities; spikelets distant by about their own length to half their length, 3.6 to 3.8 mm long excluding the awn; glumes lanceolate-subulate, the first 0.7 to 0.8 mm long, the second 2 to 2.5 mm long; floret stipitate, the stipe 0.5 mm long, bearded with erect hairs 0.4 to 0.5 mm long; lemma 3.2 mm long (excluding the awn), about 0.4 mm wide, glabrous, the lateral nerves near the margin, the midnerve becoming strong toward the summit and produced into a delicate flexuous erect, minutely scabrous awn 12 to 16 mm long; palea minutely scabrous on the nerves; second floret reduced to a narrow pointed 1-nerved lemma about 1.2 mm long, the slender glabrous erect rachilla joint 1.8 mm long (fig. 77).

Limestone ground in thickets and on limestone cliffs, Cuba and Hispaniola.

CUBA: Mendoza, *Ekman* 18172. San Julián, south of Guane, *Léon* 6901, 7312, 7474; *Wright* 3894. Jauco Abajo, southern Baracoa region, *Léon* 12312.

DOMINICAN REPUBLIC: Río Mao, *Valeur* 177. Moncíón, *Ekman* H 12606, H 13059, H 13081.

In one specimen (*Léon* 12312) some of the inflorescences consist of two spikes. In all the others the spikes are solitary.

FIGURE 77.—*Saugetia fasciculata*. Plant, × ½; glumes and floret, × 5 (Léon 7312).

A fragmentary specimen of this peculiar grass was collected by Wright "in small skirts of woods bordering the Savana San Julián" in 1865 (no. 3894) and was listed in Sauvalle's Flora Cubana[31] without description as "*Muhlenbergia spicata* Munn" and by Hitchcock[32] as an unidentified specimen. The few weatherworn spikelets on the Wright specimen were too much broken to permit of diagnosis. Brother León at our request kindly visited the locality and sent us a specimen of this apparently very rare species. His letter in regard to this collection is of interest:

> I visited the Savana San Julián in company with Father Modesto Roca of Guanabacoa. The first two days I did not see any kind of Bouteloua [from the broken Wright specimen we had guessed it to be a species of that genus], not knowing on what border of the savanna were the skirts of woods, and the savanna has a circuit of 40 to 50 kilometers. At last * * * we went to a small wood (Cayo Gabino) on the northeastern border of the hacienda [of Señor D. J. M. Lamas] and there I saw a tufted grass which I supposed might be the long lost species of Wright, though at first sight it called to my mind the idea of a small *Arthrostylidium*, having some resemblance to my no. 4853 [*Arthrostylidium capillifolium*]. I noted with pleasure that it agreed exactly with your description. Unluckily there remained very few flowers. I entered the wood at different places all around but could not find more of it.

It is noteworthy that in his field notes Wright called his number 3894 "*Arthrostylidium*."

2. Saugetia pleiostachya Hitchc. and Ekman, sp. nov.[33]

Culms glabrous, many-noded, straggling, 50 to 80 cm tall, the branches appressed, often fascicled, the lower internodes elongate; sheaths glabrous, firm, shorter than the internodes, densely villous at the truncate summit; ligule a very short densely ciliate membrane; blades glabrous, slender, wiry, flat and about 1.5 mm wide or mostly filiform, involute, the margins scabrous with fine sharp points; inflorescence of 1 to 3 falcate spikes, 8 to 12 cm long, the second and third spike attached 10 to 15 mm below the terminal one and closely appressed to it, the rachis slender, triangular; spikelets appressed, imbricate, about 1 mm apart on the rachis; first glume a slender minute bristle; second glume very narrow or setiform, 2 to 4 mm long; lemma slightly raised on a minutely pilose stipe, narrow, somewhat terete, acute, about 4 mm long, awned from just below the apex, the awn very slender, 1 to 2 cm long, the tip very fine, flexuous; palea narrow, about as long as the lemma, ending in 2 very fine teeth; rudiment minute, the rachilla joint about 2 mm long, lying in the sulcus of the incurved margins of the lemma, awnless or with a minute fine awn.

Type in the United States National Herbarium, no. 1296127, collected on jurassic limestone, top of Cerro de Mendoza, Mendoza, Province of Pinar del Río, Cuba, June 26, 1920, by E. L. Ekman (no. 11483).

Another collection from the same locality was made in 1923 by Dr. Ekman (no. 16746).

In its technical character this species agrees closely with *S. fasciculata*. It differs in its larger size, coarser foliage, the usually 2 spikes

[31] P. 191.

[32] Contrib. U. S. Nat. Herb. 12: 246. 1909.

[33] Perennis; culmi glabri multinodii tenues 50–80 cm alti ramosi, ramis appressis; laminae glabrae tenues planae vel plerumque filiformes, marginibus scabris; spicae 1–3 tenues falcatae 8–20 cm longae appressae; gluma prima minuta setiformis; gluma secunda setiformis 2–4 mm longa; lemma angustum, acutum circa 4 mm longum aristatum, arista tenuissima 1–2 cm longa; palea bisetosa; rudimentum minutum.

nearly twice as long, and in the larger spikelets. *S. fasciculata* is now known from several localities. It is uniformly smaller and more delicate than *S. pleiostachya.*

54. CHLORIS Swartz, Prodr. Veg. Ind. Occ. 25. 1788. FINGERGRASS

Spikelets with 1 perfect floret, sessile, in two rows along one side of a continuous rachis, the rachilla disarticulating above the glumes, produced beyond the perfect floret and bearing 1 to several reduced florets consisting of empty lemmas, these often truncate, and, if more than one, the smaller ones enclosed in the lower, forming a usually club-shaped rudiment; glumes somewhat unequal, the first shorter, narrow, acute; lemma keeled, usually broad, 1- to 5-nerved, often villous on the callus and villous or long-ciliate on the keel or marginal nerves, awned from between the short teeth of a bifid apex, the awn slender or sometimes reduced to a mucro, the sterile lemmas awned or awnless. Perennials or annuals with flat or folded blades and 2 to many often showy digitate spikes.

Lemmas awnless; spikes dark brown (Eustachys) -------------- 1. C. PETRAEA.
Lemmas awned; spikes pale or purplish.
  Sterile floret narrow, the apex acute or obtuse but not truncate.
    Plants 1 to 1.5 m tall, with stout creeping stolons ---------- 2. C. GAYANA.
    Plants lower; stolons wanting or poorly developed.
      Spikes numerous, at least 10, ascending even when mature. 3. C. RADIATA.
      Spikes fewer than 10, usually not more than 6.
        Culms leafy throughout; spikes erect or ascending --- 4. C. RUPESTRIS.
        Culms naked or with a few remote short blades. Spikes often reflexed at maturity.
          Spikelets divergent, somewhat distant. Plant delicate. 5. C. CRUCIATA.
          Spikelets appressed, imbricate.
            Culms slender, wiry; blades filiform or narrow ---- 6. C. EKMANII.
            Culms stouter; blades flat or folded, 1 to 3 mm wide.
              Leaves pubescent; awns 1.5 to 2.5 cm long ---- 9. C. ARENARIA.
              Leaves glabrous; awns 1 to 2 cm long.
                Lemma pilose-ciliate on upper part of margins; callus pilose; rudiment rather broad and prominent --- 8. C. CUBENSIS.
                Lemmas minutely pilose or nearly glabrous on the margins; callus nearly glabrous; rudiment not prominent, mostly enclosed in the margins of the lemma -- 7. C. SAGRAEANA.
  Sterile floret broad, truncate, broadest at the summit. Spikelets pectinately arranged.
    Plants perennial, commonly more than 1 m tall; spikes flexuous, 8 to 10 cm long ------------------------------------ 10. C. POLYDACTYLA.
    Plants annual, usually less than 75 cm tall; spikes less than 8 cm long.
      Awn of fertile lemma not longer than the body; lemma long-ciliate on keel and margins ------------------------------ 11. C. CILIATA.
      Awn of fertile lemma at least twice as long as the body.
        Sterile florets 2; sterile lemmas (rudiment) nearly as broad as long; fertile lemma without tuft of hairs ------------- 12. C. INFLATA.
        Sterile floret 1; sterile lemma narrow, more than twice as long as broad, hairy on the keel and margins ---------- 13. C. VIRGATA.

1. **Chloris petraea** Swartz, Prodr. Veg. Ind. Occ. 25. 1788. Jamaica.

Eustachys petraea Desv., Nouv. Bull. Soc. Philom. Paris 2: 189. 1810.

Schultesia petraea Spreng., Pl. Pugill. 2: 17. 1815.

Chloris swartzii C. Muell., Bot. Ztg. 19: 341. 1861. Based on *C. petraea* Swartz.

Chloris swartziana Doell, in Mart., Fl. Bras. 2[3]: 68. 1878. Based on *C. petraea* Swartz.

Glabrous glaucous sparingly stoloniferous perennial; culms flat, ascending; sheaths keeled, often in pairs, especially in robust plants; blades flat, thickish, oblong or linear, obtuse; spikes few to several, the rachis and glumes pale green, the florets chestnut; spikelets 2 mm long; second glume bilobed, the midnerve excurrent as a short awn; lemma awnless, a little exceeding the second glume (fig. 78).

Open ground, mostly near the seashore, southern United States and eastern Mexico, to Trinidad and Panama.

BERMUDA: *Collins* 144; *Brown* 523; *Brown and Britton* 60.

BAHAMAS: New Providence, *Eggers* 4092; *Geogr. Soc. Baltimore* 99, 261. Andros, *Small and Carter* 8918. Anguilla Isles, *Wilson* 7947.

CUBA: Habana, *Ekman* 369; *Hitchcock* 238; *Léon* 961; *Liebmann* 235. Cayo Sabinal, *Shafer* 716. Cayo Paredon Grande, *Shafer* 2739. Without locality, *Wright* 3817. Isla de Pinos, *Britton and Wilson* 14947; *Palmer and Riley* 969.

JAMAICA: Port Antonio, *Fredholm* 3305. Buff Bay, *Hitchcock* 9767. Mouth of Cockpit River, *Harris* 12464. Montego Bay, *Maxon* 1562; *Hitchcock* 9672. Claremont, *Hitchcock* 9485. Moneague, *Hitchcock* 9453. Savanna-la-Mar, *Hitchcock* 9883. Spanish Town, *Hitchcock* 9297. Ipswich, *Hitchcock* 9591. Black River, *Harris* 12543. Gordon Town, *Hart* 2079. Grand Cayman, *Millspaugh* 1255.

HAITI: Miragoane, *Eyerdam* 402. Aux Cayes, *Ekman* H 44. Tortuga Island, *Leonard* 13889, 13893; *Ekman* H 4157.

DOMINICAN REPUBLIC: Santo Domingo City, *Ekman* H 11416.

FIGURE 78.—*Chloris petraea*. Plant, × 1; florets, × 5 (Curtiss).

PUERTO RICO: Santurce, *Heller* 6422; *Chase* 6347. Condado, *Britton and Brown* 6629. Boqueron, *Chase* 6512. Cabo Rojo, *Sintenis* 555. Bayamon, *Sintenis* 1031. Mayaguez, *Chase* 6183. Vega Baja, *Heller* 1317. Vieques Island, *Chase* 6702. Mona Island, *Hess* 446. Without locality, *Eggers* 708.

WINDWARD ISLANDS: Barbados, *Hitchcock* 16509; *Miller* 48.

TRINIDAD: *Bot. Gard. Herb.* 3377.

2. Chloris gayana Kunth, Rév. Gram. 1: 89. 1829; 2: 293. pl. 58. 1830. Africa. RHODES GRASS.

Perennial; culms stout, erect or ascending, usually 1 to 1.5 m tall, with stout creeping stolons; blades flat, numerous, elongate, 2 to 5 mm wide; spikes several to numerous, digitate, 5 to 10 cm long, spikelets closely imbricate, about 4 mm long; lower floret glabrous on the keel, appressed hispid along the margin, the hairs longer toward the summit, about 3 mm long, the awn about 5 mm long; second floret smaller than the first but not much reduced, glabrous, the awn about 3 mm long; third floret about 2 mm long, truncate, mucronate, sometimes a rudimentary fourth floret present (fig. 79).

Cultivated in the warmer parts of America for forage and soon escaping into fields and waste places. The West Indian specimens appear to be all cultivated, but the species is likely to be found naturalized. Rhodes grass gives promise of value in the drier parts of the West Indies.

CUBA: Soledad, *Jack* 6596, 8321.
JAMAICA: Richmond Park, *Harris* 12707.
HAITI: Fond-Blanc, *Ekman* H 9890.

3. Chloris radiata (L.) Swartz, Prodr. Veg. Ind. Occ. 26. 1788.

Agrostis radiata L., Syst. Nat. ed. 10. 2: 873. 1759. Jamaica.
Cynosurus scoparius Lam., Encycl. 2: 188. 1786. "St. Domingue."
Chloris gracilis Durand, Chlor. Sp. 10. 1808. Jamaica. This work has not been seen. A specimen so named, apparently by Durand, in the herbarium of the Institut Botanique, Montpellier, is *C. radiata*.

Chloris durandiana Schult., Mant. 2: 341. 1824. Based on *Chloris gracilis* Durand.

Chloris glaucescens Steud., Syn. Pl. Glum. 1: 206. 1854. Guadeloupe.

Weedy branching decumbent-ascending annual; sheaths broad, compressed; blades thin, flat or folded, scaberulous or sparsely pilose; spikes slender, somewhat flexuous; second glume narrow, awn-pointed, 2 mm long; lemma narrow, 2.5 mm long, the awn 5 to 10 mm long; rudiment narrow, scarcely 1 mm long, diverging a little from the fertile lemma and not as long as this, the awn as much as 5 mm long (fig. 80).

Grassy banks, pastures, and waste places, Mexico and the West Indies to Paraguay. A common weed, to be found on probably all the West Indian islands.

4. Chloris rupestris (Ridley) Hitchc.

Gymnopogon rupestris Ridley, Jour. Linn. Soc. 27: 73. 1890. Brazil.

Chloris angustiflora Areschoug, Svensk. Freg. Eugenies Resa 1910: 118. 1910; Repert. Sp. Nov. Fedde 10: 300. 1912. Ecuador.
Chloris leptantha Hitchc., in Urban, Symb. Antill. 7: 166. 1912. Bonaire.

Chloris luetzelburgii Hitchc., Biol. Soc. Wash. Proc. 36: 197. 1923. Brazil.

Annual; culms 30 to 100 cm tall; blades flat, acuminate, scabrous, 5 to 15 cm long, 1 to 6 mm wide; spikes 5 to 8, slender, ascending or appressed, 6 to 12 cm long, aggregate on an axis as much as 5 cm long; spikelets narrow, loosely imbricate, with 1 perfect floret and a narrow rudiment; lemma about 5 mm long, about 0.4 mm thick, the margins short-ciliate toward the summit, the awn about 5 mm long; rudiment 1 to 2 mm long, the awn a little shorter than that of the first floret. Slender spikes of cleistogamous spikelets borne in the lower sheaths.

Open dry ground, fields, and waste places, the West Indies to Brazil and Ecuador.

FIGURE 79.—*Chloris gayana*. Plant, × ½; florets, × 5 (Hitchcock 13667).

FIGURE 80.—*Chloris radiata*, × ½ (Sintenis 28).

CUBA: Caimanera Naval Station, *Hioram and Ramsden* 1.

JAMAICA: Port Henderson, *Ridley* 130. Hope Gardens, *Ridley* 75, 90. Rockfort, *Ridley* 91; *Harris* 12675. Kingston, *Ridley* 115; *Harris* 11502, 12212. Gordon Town, *Harris* 11515. Grants Pen, *Harris* 12211. Spanish Town Road, *Harris* 12476.

HAITI: Anse-à-Pitre, *Ekman* H 6999. Jean Rabel, *Leonard* 12581, 13797.

DOMINICAN REPUBLIC: Las Salinas, *Fuertes* 1421.

5. Chloris cruciata (L.) Swartz, Prodr. Veg. Ind. Occ. 25. 1788.

Agrostis cruciata L., Syst. Nat. ed. 10. 2: 893. 1759. Jamaica.

Chloris humboldtiana Steud., Syn. Pl. Glum. 1: 205. 1854. Cuba.

Chloris brevigluma Wright, An. Acad. Cien. Habana 8: 200. 1871. Cuba, *Wright* 1848 [error for 1548] in part.

Perennial but sometimes appearing to be annual; culms delicate, filiform, densely tufted, erect or geniculate at base, sometimes straggling, branching from the lower nodes, 10 to 30 cm tall; blades flat or usually folded or involute, slender, soft, mostly less than 5 cm long, the uppermost sometimes less than 1 cm long; spikes usually 2 to 4, delicate, 1 to 3 cm long, finally widely spreading or somewhat reflexed; spikelets on distinct pedicels 0.2 to 0.5 mm long, finally horizontally spreading, pale, about 3 mm long; awns delicate, 5 to 10 mm long.

Stony slopes, Cuba, Jamaica, and Hispaniola.

CUBA: Guanabacóa, *Curtiss* 584; *Ekman* 279, 13547; *Hitchcock* 239, 240, 23233; *Léon* 896; *Wilson and Léon* 11637. Habana, *Léon* 4786, 11495, 11573. Hanábana, *Wright* 1548. Western Cuba, *Wright* 1549.

JAMAICA: Troy, *Harris* 12588, 12647. Yallahs Valley, *Perkins* 1481. Guava Ridge, *Hart* 680; *Eggers* 3724. Gordon Town, *Hitchcock* 9376; *Hart* 841. Ewarton, *Hitchcock* 9428. Red Hills, *Hitchcock* 9469. Stony Hill, *Harris* 11341. Clifton, *Harris* 11375. Mount Hybla, *Harris* 11393. Cold Spring Gap, *Harris* 11392. Alligator Pond, *Hitchcock* 9820. Kingston, *Hitchcock* 9276 (*Amer. Gr. Nat. Herb.* 651). Ipswich, *Hitchcock* 9597. Arntully, *Orcutt* 2592. Farm Hill, *Orcutt* 3380, 3739. Halberstadt, *Maxon* 8766.

HAITI: Between Cerca-Carivajal and Bois-Charles, on rocks in River Samaná, *Ekman* H 6067.

6. Chloris ekmanii Hitchc., sp. nov.[34]

Perennial; culms densely tufted, slender or capillary, geniculate at base, 10 to 30 cm tall, rarely taller; blades slender, mostly folded or involute, usually less than 10 cm long and less than 1 mm wide when flat; spikes 2 to 5, mostly 3 or 4, slender, rather flexuous, usually 1.5 to 3 cm long, finally horizontally spreading or reflexed; spikelets loosely overlapping, appressed; glumes narrow, acuminate, the second about as long as the lemma, the first about half as long; lemma narrow, about 3 mm long, shining, pale, minutely pilose along the margin near the summit, otherwise glabrous, the awn 7 to 8 mm long; rudiment narrow, about 1 mm long, mostly hidden by the fertile lemma, the awn shorter than that of the fertile floret.

Type in the United States National Herbarium, no. 1387451, collected in pastures at Babujal, Jagüey Grande, prov. Matanzas, Cuba, August 2, 1923, by E. L. Ekman (no. 16954).

Dry grassy or rocky slopes or in pine woods, Cuba, Jamaica, and Hispaniola. The species differs from *C. sagraeana* in the more delicate habit, the narrower blades, the shorter and more slender spikes, and the less imbricate spikelets.

CUBA: Cajalbana, *Léon* 4855. La Grifa, *Ekman* 11252. Habana, *Léon* 287, 4788. Guanabacoa, *Hitchcock* 23229, 23240; *Léon* 856.

[34] A *C. sagraeana* differt plantis gracilioribus, laminis angustioribus, spicis tenuioribus brevibusque.

Babujal, *Ekman* 16954. Soledad, *Hitchcock* 23329. Baragua, *Hitchcock* 23357, 23377, 23384. Pitajones, *Shafer* 12225. Trinidad, *Ekman* 13975. Sancti Spíritus, *Sergius* 2569. Iron mine, south of Guara, *Hitchcock* 23412, 23427.

JAMAICA: Ewarton, *Hitchcock* 9458 (*Amer. Gr. Nat. Herb.* 652). Troy, *Hitchcock* 9810. New Forest, *Hitchcock* 9847. Montego Bay, *Hitchcock* 9695. Inverness, *Harris* 12727. Lititz, *Harris* 12434, 12697. Alligator Pond, *Hitchcock* 9823.

HAITI: Roche, *Ekman* H 723.

DOMINICAN REPUBLIC: Guayubín, *Abbott* 916. El Maniclito, *Ekman* H 11310.

7. **Chloris sagraeana** A. Rich., in Sagra, Hist. Cuba 11:315. 1850. Cuba, *Ramon de la Sagra*.

Chloris eleusinoides Griseb., Fl. Brit. W. Ind. 539. 1864. Jamaica and Antigua.

Chloris morales-coelloi Léon, Bull. Torrey Bot. Club 53: 458. 1926. Cuba, *Léon* 12320.

Perennial; culms mostly slender, cespitose, erect or ascending from a geniculate base, 20 to 60 cm tall; blades flat or folded, 1 to 2 mm wide, glabrous, the sheaths compressed; spikes mostly 3 to 6, sometimes more, mostly 3 to 5 cm long; spikelets imbricate; glumes narrow, acuminate, 2 and 3 mm long; lemma about 3 mm long, narrow, minutely pilose on the margins above and on the callus, the awn about 1 cm long, purplish, flexuous; rudiment small, narrow, usually enclosed in the margins of the lemma, the awn somewhat shorter than that of the lemma.

Dry or rocky soil, West Indies.

Chloris ekmanii, *C. sagraeana*, and *C. cubensis* form a polymorphous group. Most of the specimens fall into one of the three species, but there are a few intermediate specimens.

BAHAMAS: Nassau, *Curtiss* 81. Without locality, *Geogr. Soc. Baltimore* 97 in part.

CUBA: Guanabacoa, *Léon* 857; *Hitchcock* 23245. Vicinity of Habana, *Léon* 1965, 2560, 4783, 4787, 4807, 12453, 12454, 12455; *Ekman* 389; *Baker* in 1907; *Ausovin* 779; *Hitchcock* 242. Guantánamo, *Hioram* 1379. Monte Verde, *Wright* 1549. Eastern Cuba, *Wright* 1548, 3818.

JAMAICA: Ashley Hall, *Harris* 12738. Savanna-la-Mar, *Hitchcock* 9890 (*Amer. Gr. Nat. Herb.* 653).

HAITI: Grande Cayemite, *Eyerdam* 336. Gros-Morne, *Leonard* 9839. Dutreuil, *Ekman* H 10748. Cabaret, *Leonard* 12067. Jean Rabel, *Leonard* 12552, 13804. Môle-St.-Nicolas, *Leonard* 13255. Tortuga Island, *Ekman* H 4058, H 4171. Pétionville, *Leonard* 4984. Pignon, *Cook, Scofield, and Doyle* 138.

DOMINICAN REPUBLIC: Mao, *Abbott* 1042.

LEEWARD ISLANDS: Barbuda, *Danforth* 3. Antigua, *Box* 122; *Wullschlaegel*. Guadeloupe, *Duss* 4110.

WINDWARD ISLANDS: Barbados, *Hitchcock* 16499.

A robust form has been called *C. morales-coelloi* Léon, the type of which is *Léon* 12320, from Cajobabo, southern Baracoa region, Cuba. It resembles *C. cubensis* but is not pilose at base and lacks the cilia on the upper part of the margins of the lemma. Also the rudiment is smaller, as in *C. sagraeana*. The following specimens appear to belong to this form, though there is no definite line between these and the usual form of *C. sagraeana*.

CUBA: Triscornia, *Hitchcock* 241. Mariel, *Ekman* 12837. Cajobabo, *Léon* 12320.

HAITI: Port-de-Pai, *Leonard* 11051. Ennery, *Leonard* 8835. Port-au-Prince, *Ekman* H 2107. Miragoane, *Ekman* H 9042.

DOMINICAN REPUBLIC: Vásquez, *Ekman* H 13128. Without locality, *Wright, Parry, and Brummel* 610.

8. Chloris cubensis Hitchc. and Ekman, sp. nov.[35]

Perennial; culms erect or spreading at base, sometimes decumbent and rooting, occasionally forming stolons, glabrous, more or less compressed, 50 to 75 cm tall; sheaths glabrous, somewhat villous at the throat, the basal usually rather strongly compressed and keeled, mostly shorter than the internodes; ligule a ciliate membrane about 0.3 mm long; blades flat or folded, scaberulous and sometimes sparsely villous on the upper surface especially at the base, glabrous beneath, mostly 5 to 10 cm long, the basal sometimes elongate, the upper reduced, 1 to 2 or rarely 3 mm wide; racemes usually 5 to 7, distant, 5 to 7 cm long, ascending; spikelets rather closely imbricate, appressed or ascending, pale or purplish; glumes narrow, the first about 2 mm long, the second about 3 mm long; fertile lemma about 3 mm long, pilose at base, ciliate on the upper half of the margins, the hairs as much as 1 mm long, sometimes sparsely pilose along the middle of the keel, the awn from about 0.5 mm below the apex, 1 to 2 cm long, capillary, slightly flexuous; rudiment about 1.5 mm long, oblong, the awn shorter than that of the fertile floret.

Type in the United States National Herbarium, no. 1387446, collected at Gamboa, prov. Oriente, Cuba, August 26, 1922, by E. L. Ekman (no. 14960).

In the Grasses of the West Indies[36] this species was referred to *C. orthonoton* Doell of Brazil which is strongly stoloniferous, with wider lemmas and shorter awns. The smaller specimens have been referred to *C. sagraeana*, which has more slender culms, and shorter, finally reflexed spikes.

Dry open ground, Cuba, Jamaica, Haiti, and Leeward Islands.

CUBA: Herradura, *Hitchcock* 243. Vicinity of Habana, *Léon* 859, 860, 12456; *Ekman* 13469. Gamboa, *Ekman* 14960. Holguín, *Ekman* in 1922.

JAMAICA: Cockpit (Vere), *Harris* 12462.

HAITI: Tortuga Island, *Leonard* 12538; *Ekman* H 4058.

LEEWARD ISLANDS: Antigua, *Box* 35.

9. Chloris arenaria Hitchc. and Ekman, sp. nov.[37]

Chloris eleusinoides var. *vestita* Greenm., in Combs, Acad. Sci. St. Louis Trans. 7: 477. 1897. Cuba, *Combs* 631.

Perennial; culms cespitose, erect or somewhat geniculate at base, glabrous, 30 to 50 cm tall; sheaths compressed-keeled, puberulent; ligule a ciliate membrane about 0.5 mm long; blades firm, flat or folded, puberulent, the basal 5 to 10 cm long, the culm blades shorter,

---

[35] A *C. sagraeana* differt planta robustiore spicis longioribus crassioribus ascendentibus, lemmate ad basin et supra ad margines pilosociliato, rudimento majore.

[36] Contrib. U. S. Natl. Herb. 18: 376. 1917.

[37] Perennis; culmi erecti glabri 30–50 cm alti; vaginae laminaeque puberulae, vaginis compressis, laminis planis vel conduplicatis 5–10 cm longis 1–2 mm latis; racemi 5–6 digitati ascendentes vel denique reflexi 3–6 cm longi; spiculae imbricatae; glumae acuminatae, prima 3 mm longa, secunda 5 mm longa; lemma fertile 3.5 mm longum, callo puberulo, marginibus superne pilosociliatis; arista 1.5–2.4 cm longa; rudimentum anguste oblongum 2 mm longum, arista 1–2 cm longa.

the uppermost 5 to 10 mm long, the basal blades as much as 3 mm wide, but mostly much narrower; racemes mostly 5 or 6, digitate, pubescent at base, ascending or finally reflexed, 3 to 6 cm long, stramineous; spikelets imbricate, appressed; glumes narrow, acuminate, the first 3 mm long, the second 5 mm long; fertile lemma 3.5 mm long, including the narrow, puberulent callus, pilose-ciliate along the upper part of the margins, the awn about 1.5 to 2.5 cm long; rudiment narrowly oblong, 2 mm long, the awn somewhat shorter than that of the fertile lemma.

Type in the United States National Herbarium, no. 1387449, collected in pinelands on white sand, La Grifa, prov. Pinar del Río, June 14, 1920, by E. L. Ekman (no. 11253).

The species is allied to *C. sagraeana* from which it differs in the puberulent foliage, the longer glumes and awns, and in the firm erect innovations.

Pinelands, Cuba.

CUBA: La Grifa, *Ekman* 11252, 11253; *Wright* 3819. Cienfuegos, *Combs* 631.

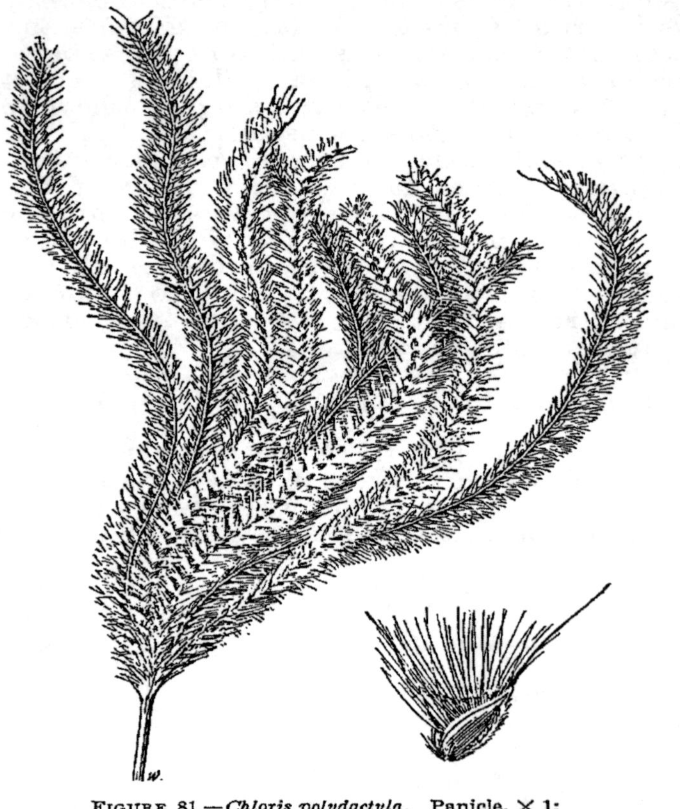

FIGURE 81.—*Chloris polydactyla.* Panicle, × 1; florets, × 5 (Simpson).

10. Chloris polydactyla (L.) Swartz, Prodr. Veg. Ind. Occ. 26. 1788.

Andropogon barbatus L., Syst. Nat. ed. 10. 2: 1305. 1759. Jamaica.

Andropogon polydactylon L., Sp. Pl. ed. 2. 1483. 1763. Jamaica.

Chloris barbata Nash, Bull. Torrey Bot. Club 25: 443. 1898. Not *C. barbata* Swartz, 1797 (this based on *Andropogon barbatus* L., 1771, from the East Indies).

Culms rather stout, commonly more than 1 m tall; blades about 1 cm wide; spikes 5 to 10, pale, usually 8 to 10 cm long, strongly flexuous; spikelets closely imbricate, silky; first lemma about 2.5 mm long; broad, pubescent on the keel, long-ciliate on the margins, the hairs 2 mm long, the awn about as long as the lemma; second lemma shorter and narrower than the first, the awn about 2 mm long (fig. 81).

Savannas and grassy slopes, Florida and the West Indies to Brazil.

BAHAMAS: New Providence, *Curtiss* 80; *Geogr. Soc. Baltimore* 262.

JAMAICA: Ipswich, *Maxon and Killip* 1492; *Hitchcock* 9622. Inverness, *Harris* 12743. Lucea, *Hitchcock* in 1891. Ewarton, *Hitchcock*

9459. Gordon Town, *Hitchcock* 9322 (*Amer. Gr. Nat. Herb.* 656); *Hart* 929. Bog Walk, *Hitchcock* 9302. Montego Bay, *Hitchcock* 9676. Savanna-la-Mar, *Hitchcock* 9865. New Forest, *Hitchcock* 9842. Lititz, *Hitchcock* 11654. Yardley Chase, *Harris* 9665. Without locality, *Wullschlaegel* 1116. Grand Cayman, *Millspaugh* 1271.

HAITI: Grande Cayemite, *Eyerdam* 329; *Ekman* H 8941. Aux Cayes, *Ekman* H 846.

LEEWARD ISLANDS: Antigua, *Hitchcock* 16394; *Box* 26. Common on this island.

11. Chloris ciliata Swartz, Prodr. Veg. Ind. Occ. 25. 1788. Jamaica.

Chloris propinqua Steud., Syn. Pl. Glum. 1: 204. 1854. Guadeloupe.

Erect or spreading annual; culms 30 to 60 cm tall or sometimes taller; blades flat, as much as 5 mm wide; spikes pale, 4 to 6, strongly flexuous, 3 to 6 cm long, the florets conspicuously silky-ciliate; fertile lemma about 2.5 mm long, strongly ciliate on the keel and marginal nerves, the awn 1 to 1.5 mm long; rudiment of 2 or 3 sterile lemmas, triangular-truncate, not longer than the fertile lemma, awnless (fig. 82).

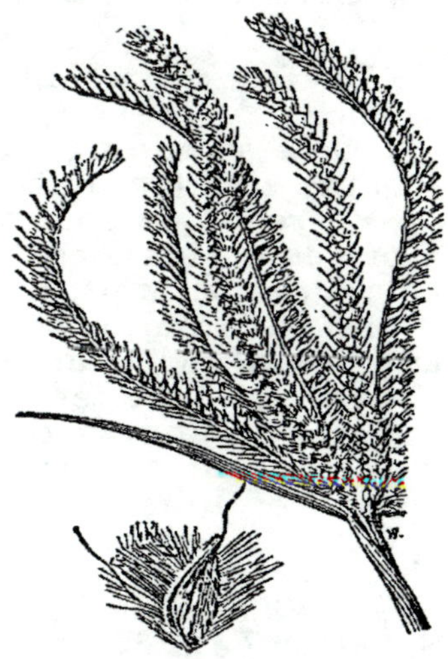

FIGURE 82.—*Chloris ciliata*. Panicle, × 1; florets, × 5 (Tracy 8886).

Open ground and waste places, Texas and the West Indies to Argentina.

BAHAMAS: New Providence, *Curtiss* 72.

CUBA: Guane, *Shafer* 10393. Herradura, *Hitchcock* 245. Habana, *Tracy* 9085, 9106; *Curtiss* 600; *Ekman* 1192; *Léon* 574. Santiago de las Vegas, *Tracy* 9115; *Hitchcock* 244. Trinidad, *Wright* 743. Santiago de Cuba, *Léon* 856½.

JAMAICA: Southern Manchester, *Harris* 12689. Inverness, *Harris* 12755. Ipswich, *Hitchcock* 9592. Ewarton, *Hitchcock* 9430 (*Amer. Gr. Nat. Herb.* 655). Montego Bay, *Hitchcock* 9671. Savanna-la-Mar, *Hitchcock* 9856. Halfmoon Bay, *Hitchcock* 9757. Hope Gardens, *Hitchcock* 9309. New Forest, *Hitchcock* 9829. Flamstead, *Harris* 11473.

HAITI: Ennery, *Leonard* 8814. Port-de-Pai, *Ekman* H 4324. Jean Rabel, *Leonard* 12934. Port-au-Prince, *Ekman* H 8145; *Hitchcock* 19872, 22955. St. Marc, *Leonard* 2973. Gonaïve Island, *Leonard* 3371. Tortuga Island, *Leonard* 12444, 15584.

DOMINICAN REPUBLIC: Barahona, *Fuertes* 908. Jaina, *Ekman* H 12486.

PUERTO RICO: Ponce, *Chase* 6495.

VIRGIN ISLANDS: St. Croix, *Ricksecker* 42; *Thompson* 13; *Hitchcock* 16338. St. Thomas, *Eggers* in 1882.

LEEWARD ISLANDS: Barbuda, *Danforth* 6. Antigua, *Hitchcock* 16392; *Box* 31. Guadeloupe, *Duss* 3158b.

WINDWARD ISLANDS: Martinique, *Duss* 1273; *Hahn*. Barbados, *Hitchcock* 16514.

12. Chloris inflata Link, Enum. Pl. 1: 105. 1821.

Andropogon barbatum L., Mant. Pl. 2: 302. 1771. Not *A. barbatum* L., 1759. East Indies.

Chloris barbata Swartz, Fl. Ind. Occ. 1: 200. 1797. Based on *Andropogon barbatum* L. Mant. 2: 302. 1771.

Chloris paraguaiensis Steud., Syn. Pl. Glum. 1: 204. 1854. Paraguay.

Tufted annual, 30 to 75 cm tall; culms and sheaths strongly compressed; blades long, lax; spikes about 10, usually flexuous, commonly purplish-tinged, 4 to 6 cm long; first lemma 2 mm long, the awn about 6 mm long; rudiment of 2 triangular-obtuse lemmas about 1 mm long, the awn of the first about as long as that of the fertile lemma, the awn of the second short (fig. 83).

Waste places, a common weed at low altitudes, Mexico and the West Indies to Argentina. Type grown in the Berlin Botanic Garden from seed said to come from "California," probably from Mexico. Probably to be found on all the West Indian islands.

13. Chloris virgata Swartz, Fl. Ind. Occ. 1: 203. 1797. Antigua.
FEATHER FINGERGRASS.

Chloris elegans H. B. K., Nov. Gen. et Sp. 1: 166. pl. 49. 1816. Mexico.

Culms ascending, 20 to 40 cm tall, scarcely compressed, the upper sheaths slightly inflated, glabrous in the throat; spikes mostly 5 or 6, suberect, somewhat flexuous in age, 3 to 5 cm long; fertile lemma 3 mm long, broadest above the middle, villous on the keel to a little below the summit, and long pilose on the margins near the tip, the awn 5 to 8 mm long; rudiment a little more than 2 mm long gradually broadened to an oblique truncate apex, the awn somewhat shorter than that of the fertile lemma (fig. 84).

Open ground, fields, and waste places, the West Indies and southwestern United States to Argentina; a common weed in warm countries of both hemispheres.

CUBA: Candelaria, *Ekman* 17595. Herradura, *Hitchcock* 249. Campo Florido, *Léon* 3461. Vento, *Shafer* 483; *Baker* 1183. Mazarra, *Baker* 4023. Soledad, *Hitchcock* 23336. Fomento, *Léon* 6434. Sancti Spíritus, *Léon* 858. Corojo, *Léon* 3964. Bayamo, *Shafer* 12394.

HAITI: Port-au-Prince, *Ekman* H 9098; *Hitchcock* 19879. Artibonite Valley, *Cook, Scofield, and Doyle* 213. L'Arcahaie, *Ekman* H 9054.

DOMINICAN REPUBLIC: Santiago, *Ekman* H 16020.

LEEWARD ISLANDS: Barbuda, *Danforth* 5. Guadeloupe, *Stehlé* 108.

55. TRICHLORIS Fourn., Mex. Pl. 2: 142. 1886

Spikelets, 1- to few-flowered, nearly sessile, in two rows along one side of a continuous slender rachis, the rachilla disarticulating above the glumes and prolonged behind the uppermost perfect floret, bearing a reduced, usually awned floret; glumes unequal, acuminate or short-awned, the body shorter than the lower lemma; lemmas narrow, 3-nerved, the marginal nerves sometimes pubescent, these and the midnerve extending into awns, the central long and slender, the lateral often much shorter. Erect, slender, tufted perennials, with flat blades and numerous erect or ascending spikes, aggregate but scarcely digitate at the summit of the culms.

FIGURE 83.—*Chloris inflata*, × ½ (Rose, Fitch, and Russell 3534).

FIGURE 84.—*Chloris virgata*. Plant, × ½; glumes and florets, × 5 (Tracy 8173).

1. Trichloris pluriflora Fourn., Mex. Pl. 2: 142. 1886.

Culms 50 to 100 cm tall; blades 5 to 10 mm wide; inflorescence somewhat loose and feathery; spikes 7 to 15 cm long; fertile lemma about 4 mm long, the others successively shorter, the middle awns of all 5 to 15 mm long, somewhat spreading, the lateral awns short or obsolete (fig. 85).

Plains and dry woods, southern Texas and Mexico; Cuba; South America.

CUBA: Casa Blanca, Habana, *Ekman* 16879.

56. BOUTELOUA Lag., Var. Cien. 2[4]: 134. 1805. GRAMA

Spikelets, 1-flowered, with the rudiments of 1 or more florets above, sessile, in two rows along one side of the rachis; glumes unequal, 1-nerved, acuminate or awn-tipped, the first shorter and narrower; lemma as long as the second glume or a little longer, 3-nerved, the nerves extending into short or often rather long awns, the internerves usually extending into teeth; palea 2-nerved, sometimes 2-awned; rudiment various, usually 3-awned, a second rudimentary floret sometimes present. Perennials or sometimes annuals, with few to many spikes racemose on a common axis, sometimes solitary, the spikelets few to many in each spike, rarely solitary, pectinate or more loosely arranged and appressed, the rachis of the spike usually produced beyond the insertion of the spikelets.

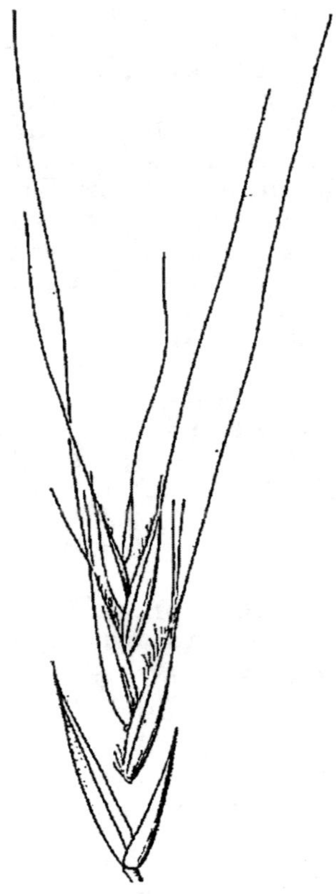

FIGURE 85.—*Trichloris pluriflora*. Glumes and florets, × 5 (Griffiths 6484).

Plants annual. Culms widely spreading..5. B. DISTICHA.
Plants perennial.
Spikes numerous, usually more than 10.
Awns very short; culms about 30 cm tall. 1. B. VANEEDENII.
Awns conspicuous, about as long as the spikelet; culms mostly less than 20 cm tall. 2. B. JUNCEA.
Spikes mostly less than 10.
Spikes divergent, rather distant, slender. 3. B. AMERICANA.
Spikes less distant, broader and shorter. 4. B. HETEROSTEGA.

FIGURE 86.—*Bouteloua vaneedenii*. Panicle, × 1; spikelet, × 5 (Ekman 15546).

1. Bouteloua vaneedenii Pilger, in Urban, Symb. Antill. 6: 2. 1909. Anguilla, *Boldingh* 3512.

Perennial; culms cespitose, erect, slender, about 30 cm tall; blades involute, filiform, glabrous; spikes 10 to 20, on an axis 8 to 15 cm long, 2 to 5 mm apart, finally reflexed, 5 to 8 mm long; spikelets mostly 2 to each spike; awns very short (fig. 86).

Dry littoral limestone rocks, Cuba, Anguilla, and Venezuela (*Pittier* 11338).

CUBA: Pastelillo, *Ekman* 15546.

LEEWARD ISLANDS: Anguilla, *Boldingh* 3512.

2. **Bouteloua juncea** (Desv.) Hitchc., Contrib. U. S. Natl. Herb. 17: 343. 1913.

Triathera juncea Desv.; Beauv., Ess. Agrost. 40. pl. 9. f. 4. 1812. Hispaniola.

Eutriana juncea Trin., Gram. Unifl. 238. 1824.

Eutriana ledebouri Trin., Gram. Unifl. 238. 1824. Haiti.

Atheropogon domingensis Spreng., Syst. Veg. 1: 293. 1825. Hispaniola.

Triaena juncea Griffiths, Contrib. U. S. Natl. Herb. 14: 354. 1912.

A low delicate perennial, prostrate below, geniculate at the lower nodes, the branches commonly in pairs or fascicles; nodes and summit of the sheaths pilose; blades flat or folded, 8 to 12 mm long, about 1.5 mm wide; racemes of few to several minute spikes, the spikelet solitary, pilose at base, 3 to 4 mm long; glumes lanceolate, acuminate, the first one-third, the second slightly over half the length of the spikelet; fertile lemma narrow, with 3 erect scabrous teeth at the summit, the palea 2-toothed, shorter; sterile floret about equaling the fertile lemma, consisting of 3 slender scabrous awns.

Arid open ground, eastern Cuba, Puerto Rico, and Hispaniola.

CUBA: Guantánamo, *Britton* 1964.

HAITI: Jean Rabel, *Leonard* 12622. Bombardopolis, *Leonard* 13593. Cabaret, *Leonard* 11788, 11853. Bassin Bleu, *Leonard* 14902. Artibonite, *Cook, Scofield, and Doyle* 212. St. Michel de l'Atalaye, *Leonard* 7096. Gros-Morne, *Leonard* 9868. Croix-des-Bouquets, *Ekman* H 2147. Cape Haitien, *Ekman* H 2717. Anse-à-Pitre, *Ekman* H 6683. Anse-à-Veau, *Ekman* H 5416. Gonaïves, *Buch* 1010.

DOMINICAN REPUBLIC: Guayubín, *Abbott* 864. Monción, *Ekman* H 13058. San Juan, *Ekman* H 13393. Without locality, *Poiteau*.

PUERTO RICO: Guanica, *Britton, Cowell, and Brown* 4918.

3. **Bouteloua americana** (L.) Scribn., Acad. Nat. Sci. Phila. Proc. 1891: 306. 1891.

Aristida americana L., Syst. Nat. ed. 10. 2: 879. 1759. Jamaica.

Aristida antillarum Poir., in Lam., Encycl. Sup. 1: 451. 1810. Antilles.

Bouteloua litigiosa Lag., Gen. et Sp. Nov. 5. 1816. Jamaica.

Chaetaria antillarum Beauv.; Roem. and Schult., Syst. Veg. 2: 395. 1817.

Aristida subbiflora Steud., Syn. Pl. Glum. 1: 138. 1854. Guadeloupe.

Eutriana antillarum Steud., Syn. Pl. Glum. 1: 217. 1854.

Bouteloua elatior Griseb., Fl. Brit. W. Ind. 537. 1864. Antigua.

Aristida adscensionis var. *americana* Kuntze, Rev. Gen. Pl. 3: 340. 1898.

Perennial, mostly prostrate-spreading; culms branching, 30 to 60 cm long; blades flat or loosely involute, 2 to 3 mm wide; spikes 3 to 7, about 2 cm long; glumes 3 and 4 mm long; lemma 3-awned, the central awn 3 mm long, the lateral 1 mm; rudiment with 3 awns about 1 cm long (fig. 87).

Open dry ground, West Indies and Central America to Brazil.

CUBA: Habana, *Léon* 780, 890, 4725, 4789; *Curtiss* 546 (in part). La Gloria, *Shafer* 244. Soledad, *Hitchcock* 23324. Guara, *Hitchcock* 23395. Isla de Pinos, *Ekman* 11789. Without locality, *Wright* 3816.

JAMAICA: Vicinity of Kingston, *Harris* 11369, 11372, 11500, 12674; *Hitchcock* 9743, 9744; *Ridley* 76, 112. Alligator Pond, *Hitchcock* 9824. Savanna-la-Mar, *Hitchcock* 9860. Black River, *Hitchcock* 4633 (*Amer. Gr. Nat. Herb.* 380). Mount Charles, *Harris* 11559. Mount Hybla, *Harris* 11443. Musgrave Road, *Harris* 11481. Mount Faraway, *Harris* 11451. Robertsfield, *Harris* 11394. Montego Bay, *Hitchcock* 9662. Gordon Town, *Hart* 559.

HAITI: St. Michel de l'Atalaye, *Leonard* 7205. Ennery, *Leonard* 9476. Gros-Morne, *Leonard* 9865. Étroite, *Leonard* 3403. Port-au-Prince, *Ekman* H 2188. St. Marc, *Ekman* H 6645.

DOMINICAN REPUBLIC: Rincón, *Fuertes* 1376. Maniel de Ocoa, *Tuerckheim* 3616.

PUERTO RICO: Coamo Springs, *Chase* 6539. Guayama, *Chase* 6754. Fajardo, *Chase* 6662. Vieques Island, *Chase* 6666; *Shafer* 2501.

VIRGIN ISLANDS: St. Jan, *Britton and Shafer* 280, 633. St. Thomas, *Eggers* in 1876. St. Croix, *Thompson* 616; *Ricksecker* 78. Virgin Gorda, *Fishlock* 274.

LEEWARD ISLANDS: Antigua, *Box* 117; *Wullschlaegel* 619. Guadeloupe, *Duss* 3160. Dominica, *Jones* 64.

WINDWARD ISLANDS: Montserrat, *Shafer* 215. Martinique, *Duss* 1326. Grenada, *Broadway* 217, 1670; *Elliott* 138; *Hitchcock* 17666.

TOBAGO: *Broadway* 4385; *Hitchcock* 10215; *Eggers* 5650.

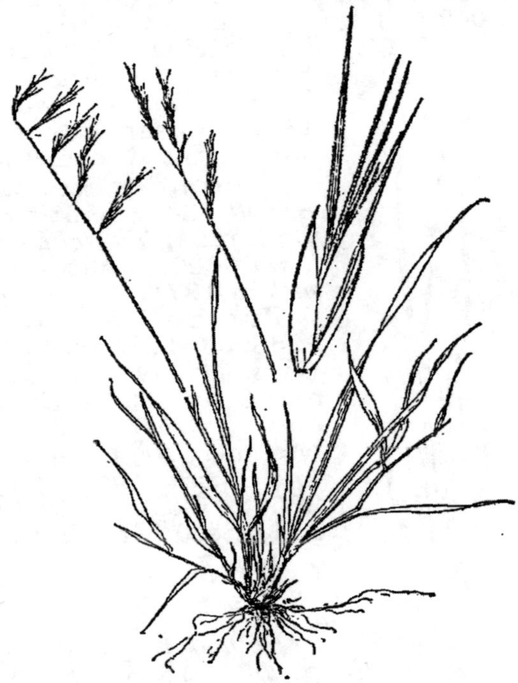

FIGURE 87.—*Bouteloua americana*. Plant, × ½; spikelet, × 5 (Harris 11451).

4. **Bouteloua heterostega** (Trin.) Griffiths, Contrib. U. S. Natl. Herb. 14: 414. 1912.

Heterosteca juncifolia Desv., Nouv. Bull. Soc. Philom. Paris 2: 188. 1810. Antilles. Not *Bouteloua juncifolia* Lag., 1816.

Eutriana heterostega Trin., Gram. Unifl. 242. 1824. Antilles.

Bouteloua humboldtiana Griseb., Mem. Amer. Acad. n. ser. 8: 532. 1862. Cuba, *Wright* 734, 739.

Bouteloua porphyrantha Wright, Anal. Acad. Cienc. Habana 8: 201. 1871. Cuba, *Wright* 734, 739, 3816.

Heterosteca rhadina Nash, Bull. Torrey Bot. Club 30: 386. 1903. Puerto Rico, *Heller* 6057.

Perennial; culms usually widely spreading or leaning, 30 to 50 cm long or sometimes longer: blades flat or involute, filiform or as much as 2 mm wide; inflorescence 3 to 10 cm long; spikes mostly 3 to 7, ascending or spreading, 1 to 2 cm long, oblong; spikelets mostly 4 to 8, rather closely imbricate; awns 3 to 8 mm long (fig. 88).

CUBA: Vicinity of Habana, *Léon* 293, 861, 3479, 4147, 4792, 8980; *Hitchcock* 460; *Curtiss* 546 (in part); *Ekman* 35, in 1921. Triscornia, *Hitchcock* 452; *Tracy* 9088; *Van Hermann* 1873. Guanabacoa, *Hitchcock* 23244; *Léon* 9124. Sancti Spíritus, *Shafer* 12060. Guantánamo, *Britton* 2148. Santiago de Cuba, *Ekman* 7913. Bayamo, *Shafer* 12386. Eastern Cuba, *Wright* 739. Isla de Pinos, *Britton and Wilson* 15155. Without locality, *Wright* 3815.

HAITI: Port-au-Prince, *Ekman* H 9108; *Hitchcock* 19881; *Buch* 2042. Étang, *Leonard* 3508. Hinche, *Cook, Scofield, and Doyle* 143, 145. St. Michel de l'Atalaye, *Leonard* 7111, 7336, 7789. Ennery, *Leonard* 8809. Gros-Morne, *Leonard* 9987. Miragoane, *Eyerdam* 575. Môle-St.-Nicolas, *Leonard* 13219. Jean Rabel, *Leonard* 12562. St. Marc, *Leonard* 2880. St. Roc, *Buch* 1831.

FIGURE 88.—*Bouteloua heterostega.* Spikelet, × 5 (Léon 861).

DOMINICAN REPUBLIC: Nigua, *Faris* 555. Guayubín, *Abbott* 934. Santiago, *Raunkiaer* 939; *Ekman* H 16495. Contanza, *Tuerckheim* 3275. Maniel de Ocoa, *Tuerckheim* 3600. Without locality, *Wright, Parry, and Brummel* in 1871.

PUERTO RICO: Bayamon, *Stahl* 2. Mayaguez, *Chase* 6268, 6301; *Holm* 117; *Britton and Cowell* 4074. Maricao, *Chase* 6227. Ponce, *Chase* 6327, 6484, 6485½; *Britton and Cowell* 1321; *Britton, Cowell, and Brown* 5382; *Britton and Marble* 1778. Boqueron, *Chase* 6504. Punta Melones, *Britton and Brown* 4648. San German, *Britton and Cowell* 4017. Cayey, *Sintenis* 2203. Arroyo, *Sintenis* 2267. Coamo, *Britton and Brown* 5947; *Sintenis* 1959. Palo Seco, *Hioram* 837.

5. **Bouteloua disticha** (H. B. K.) Benth., Jour. Linn. Soc. Bot. 19: 105. 1881.

Polyodon distichum H. B. K. Nov. Gen. et Sp. 1: 175. pl. 55. 1816. Ecuador.

Annual; culms widely spreading or straggling, 20 to 100 cm long; blades flat, more or less pilose on the margins and upper surface, 2 to 5 mm wide; spikes several to many, sometimes 30 or more, approximate on an axis 10 to 20 cm long, 5 to 10 mm long (excluding awns); spikelets mostly 2 to 5 in each spike; awns 5 to 10 mm long.

Open ground and dry hills, Ecuador and northern Peru; Cuba, probably introduced.

CUBA: Vicinity of Habana, *Ekman* 13478; *Léon* 299, 749, 12467; *Van Hermann* 320; *Wilson and Léon* 11590; *Curtiss* 537; *Wilson* 9160; *Johnston* 1108; *Hitchcock* 23222.

57. OPIZIA Presl, Rel. Haenk. 1: 293. pl. 41. f. 1. 1830

Plants monoecious (sometimes dioecious); pistillate spikelets in a single loose 1-sided spike; first glume minute or obsolete; second glume nearly as long as the floret; fertile lemma subindurate, broad, 3-awned, enclosing a broad palea with keels crested above, the rachilla joint below the 3-awned rudimentary floret adnate to the lower part of the keel; staminate spikelets awnless, imbricate in short spikes, these racemose. Low stoloniferous perennial with flat blades and small spikes.

FIGURE 89.—*Opizia stolonifera*, × ½ (Pringle 4566).

1. **Opizia stolonifera** Presl, Rel. Haenk. 1: 293. pl. 41. f. 1. 1830. Mexico.

Forming dense mats, the shoots on the stolons mostly fascicled, the slender flowering culms 5 to 10 cm tall; blades flat, 1 to 2 mm wide; pistillate spikes short-exserted, bristly with awns about 5 mm long; staminate spikes 1 to 3, long-exserted, 1 to 1.5 cm long (fig. 89).

Open ground and pastures, southern Mexico; Cuba, probably introduced; Trinidad, introduced.

CUBA: Vicinity of Habana, *Ekman* 36, 13251; *Hitchcock* 268, 23243; *Curtiss* 571; *Léon* 274, 288.

TRINIDAD: Port-of-Spain, introduced in lawns and parks, *Bain* 13082.

TRIBE 8. PHALARIDEAE

58. ANTHOXANTHUM L., Sp. Pl. 28. 1753

Spikelets with 1 terminal perfect floret and 2 sterile lemmas, the rachilla disarticulating above the glumes, the sterile lemmas falling attached to the fertile floret; glumes unequal, acute or mucronate; sterile lemmas shorter than the glumes, empty, awned from the back; fertile lemma shorter than the sterile ones, awnless; palea 1-nerved, rounded on the back, enclosed in the lemma. Sweet-smelling annuals or perennials with flat blades and narrow panicles.

1. **Anthoxanthum odoratum** L., Sp. Pl. 28. 1753. Europe.

SWEET VERNALGRASS.

Perennial, culms erect, 30 to 60 cm tall; blades flat, 1 to 6 mm wide; panicles spikelike, oblong or lanceolate, greenish yellow or bronze, 2 to 7 cm long; spikelets about 6 to 8 mm long (fig. 90).

Cultivated and escaped in pastures in temperate regions of the world; introduced in America.

JAMAICA: Cinchona, *Harris* 9499, 11302, 11453, 11525, 11599, 11849, 12353, 12455, 12481; *Hitchcock* 9698. St. Helens Gap, *Maxon and Killip* 607. Morces Gap, *Orcutt* 5555. Gordon Town, *Hart* 742.

HAITI: Pays-Pourri, *Ekman* H 7749.

59. PHALARIS L., Sp. Pl. 54. 1753

Spikelets laterally compressed, with 1 terminal perfect floret and 2 sterile lemmas below, disarticulating above the glumes, arranged in usually dense spikelike panicles; glumes equal, boat-shaped, often winged on the keel; sterile lemmas reduced to 2 small scales (rarely only 1); fertile lemma coriaceous, shorter than the glumes, enclosing the faintly 2-nerved palea. Annual or perennial erect grasses, with flat blades.

1. **Phalaris canariensis** L., Sp. Pl. 54. 1753. Europe and the Canary Islands.

CANARY GRASS.

Annual; culms erect, 30 to 60 cm tall; blades flat, 3 to 8 mm wide; panicles dense, ovoid, 2 to 3 cm long; spikelets whitish, 5 to 6 mm long, the glumes with a green stripe down the side, the keel with a broad wing (fig. 91).

Waste places; a native of Europe and Africa but now widely distributed in temperate regions.

BERMUDA: *Brown, Britton, and Bisset* 1963.

CUBA: Habana, *Léon and Ekman* 4265.

FIGURE 90.—*Anthoxanthum odoratum*. Plant, × ½; spikelet, sterile lemmas, and fertile floret, × 5 (Biltmore Herb. 74b).

60256—36——10

FIGURE 91.—*Phalaris canariensis*. Plant, × ½; spikelet and floret, × 5 (Mearns 3376).

TRIBE 9. ORYZEAE

60. ORYZA L., Sp. Pl. 333. 1753

Spikelets, 1-flowered, laterally compressed, disarticulating below the glumes; glumes 2, much shorter than the lemma, narrow; lemma rigid, keeled, 3-nerved (with 2 thin additional marginal nerves seen only in section), sometimes awned; palea similar to the lemma, narrower, keeled, 2-nerved near the margin, apparently no midnerve (a thin midnerve seen only in section). Annual or perennial swamp grasses with flat blades and spikelets in open or rather dense panicles.

Plants annual; cultivated and sparingly escaped. Spikelets 8 to 10 mm long.
1. O. SATIVA.

Plants perennial; native species.
Spikelets about 9 mm long 2. O. PERENNIS.
Spikelets about 5 mm long 3. O. LATIFOLIA.

1. Oryza sativa L., Sp. Pl. 333. 1753. Africa and India. RICE.

Erect annual up to 1 m or more in height; blades flat, as much as 1.5 cm wide; panicles rather compact, many-flowered, drooping when large or heavy with fruit; spikelets oblong, 7 to 10 mm long; glumes 2 to 3 mm long; lemma hard, ridged by the lateral nerves, more or less hispidulous, the awn variable, several centimeters long or wanting (fig. 92).

Cultivated throughout tropical and warm temperate regions at low altitudes; more or less persistent in fields and ditches.

The native species from which cultivated rice originated is not known with certainty. There are wild forms found in India and China which appear to be the prototype of rice or a degenerate form arising from rice which has gone wild. Such forms differ chiefly in habit, the culm often decumbent, widespreading, and rooting at the nodes.

2. Oryza perennis Moench, Meth. Pl. 197. 1794.

Perennial; culms erect, 1 to 2 m tall; blades elongate, 7 to 14 mm wide; panicle narrow, 15 to 20 cm long, the branches ascending or appressed; spikelets about 9 mm long, the tip of lemma and palea purple, the awn purplish, 7 to 10 cm long.

Swamps and wet places, Cuba, Hispaniola, and Brazil. The original specimens described by Moench were cultivated in the botanical garden at Marburg.

CUBA: Pinar del Río, *Ekman* in 1923; *Hitchcock* 23275. Without locality (probably Pinar del Río), *Wright* 3838. Isla de Pinos, *Ekman* 12014.

DOMINICAN REPUBLIC: Guerra, *Ekman* H 13349.

The author collected this wild rice in Cuba in situations where it seemed to be native. Dr. Ekman, who also collected it in Cuba, states:

> It is not a weed and has never been found among cultivated rice. It grows in pineland swamps far from human dwellings as, for instance, in Ciénaga de Lanier, Isla de Pinos, where rice has never been cultivated. It is, I repeat it, absolutely out of the question that it could be an escaped form of the cultivated rice. It is, moreover, perennial, not annual, as *O. sativa*.

3. Oryza latifolia Desv., Jour. Bot. Desv. (II) 1: 77. 1813. Puerto Rico.

Oryza sativa var. *latifolia* Doell, in Mart., Fl. Bras. 2[2]: 7. 1871.

Rather robust perennial; culms 2 m or more tall; blades thin, flat, scabrous, commonly 50 to 60 cm long and 4 to 5 cm wide; panicles large many-flowered; spikelets about 5 mm long, the erect awn 10 to 15 mm long, short-pediceled along the upper half to two-thirds of the long slender ascending branches.

Swamps, ditches, and wet places, Guatemala and the West Indies to Brazil. The type locality, "Habitat in Carolina, insulaque Portorici", is clearly erroneous as to Carolina. The type specimen in the

FIGURE 92.—*Oryza sativa*. Plant, × ½; spikelet, × 5 (cult.).

Paris Herbarium is without locality. The awn is described by Desvaux as being "brevissima." Later, Hamilton[38] described the species from a specimen in Desvaux's herbarium without mentioning the awn. In Desvaux's specimen the awns are about 10 to 14 mm long. The habitat is here given as "in parte Hispanica Hispaniolae."

CUBA: Sabanaso, *Ekman* 6540. Gamboa, *Ekman* in 1922.

HAITI: Port Margot, *Ekman* H 4806.

DOMINICAN REPUBLIC: Sánchez, *Abbott* 2944.

PUERTO RICO: Mayaguez, *Hess* 107.

TRINIDAD: St. Joseph, *Hitchcock* 10023. Cedros, *Hitchcock* 10144. Without locality, *Bot. Gard. Herb.* 1674; *Crueger.*

61. LEERSIA Swartz, Prodr. Veg. Ind. Occ. 21. 1788 (Conserved)

(*Homalocenchrus* Mieg., Act. Helv. Phys. Math. 4: 307. 1760.)

Spikelets, 1-flowered, strongly compressed laterally, disarticulating from the pedicel; glumes wanting; lemma chartaceous, broad, oblong, boat-shaped, usually 5-nerved, the lateral pair of nerves close to the margins, the intermediate nerves sometimes faint; palea as long as the lemma, much narrower, usually 3-nerved, the lateral nerves close to the margins, the margins firmly held by the margins of the lemma; stamens six or fewer. Perennials usually with creeping rhizomes, flat scabrous blades, and open panicles.

Panicle contracted, the branches ascending, spikelet-bearing from near the base; spikelets hispid ---------- 1. L. HEXANDRA.
Panicle open, the branches slender, spreading, naked below; spikelets smooth or sometimes sparsely hispid.
 Spikelets 2 mm long; blades about 5 mm wide ---------- 2. L. MONANDRA.
 Spikelets 2.5 mm long; blades 1 to 2 cm wide ---------- 3. L. GRANDIFLORA.

1. Leersia hexandra Swartz, Prodr. Veg. Ind. Occ. 21. 1788. Jamaica.

Oryza hexandra Doell, in Mart., Fl. Bras. 2^2: 10. 1871.

Homalocenchrus hexandrus Kuntze, Rev. Gen. Pl. 2: 777. 1891.

Scabrous aquatic perennial; culms slender, 50 to 100 or even 200 cm tall, erect from a creeping base, often producing extensively creeping stolons with short, flat blades, mostly 15 to 20 cm long and about 8 mm wide; panicles contracted, many-flowered, pale or purplish, the branches ascending, spikelet-bearing from near the base; spikelets hispid, 3 to 3.5 mm long (fig. 93).

Swamps and ditches, southern United States and the West Indies to Argentina.

CUBA: Herradura, *Ekman* in 1923 (*Amer. Gr. Nat. Herb.* 986); *Hitchcock* 494. Mordozo, *Léon* 5944. Habana, *Léon* 1510, 4191, 5749. Baraguá, *Hitchcock* 23370, 23371. Ciénaga de Zapata, *Léon* 9514. Alto Cedro, *Ekman* 10059. Without locality, *Wright* 3434, 3837.

JAMAICA: Castleton, *Harris* 12450. Temple Hill, *Harris* 12715. Ipswich, *Hitchcock* 9584.

HAITI: Petite Rivière de l'Artibonite, *Ekman* H 3371.

[38] Prodr. Pl. Ind. Occ. 7 1825.

Dominican Republic: Jarabaco, *Ekman* H 14142, H 14177. Sánchez, *Abbott* 62, 1118, 1440. Guayubín, *Abbott* 979.

Puerto Rico: Catano, *Goll* 846. Campo Alegre, *Chase* 6797, 6799. San Juan, *Chase* 6397, 6781. Mayaguez, *Chase* 6291.

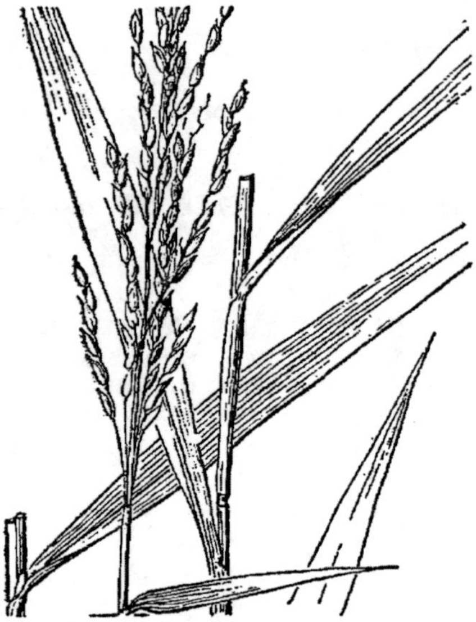

Figure 93.—*Leersia hexandra*, × 1 (Wurzlow).

Windward Islands: Martinique, *Duss* 4021.

Trinidad: St. Joseph, *Hitchcock* 10031. Manzanilla, *Hitchcock* 10367. Arima, *Hitchcock* 10315.

2. Leersia monandra Swartz, Prodr. Veg. Ind. Occ. 21. 1788. Jamaica.

Paspalum cubense Spreng., Neu. Entd. 3: 12. 1822. Cuba.

Oryza monandra Doell, in Mart., Fl. Bras. 2^2: 9. 1871.

Homalocenchrus monandrus Kuntze, Rev. Gen. Pl. 2: 777. 1891.

Densely tufted perennial; culms erect, 50 to 100 cm tall; blades elongate linear, often grayish, 3 to 6 mm wide; panicles open, mostly 10 to 15 cm long, the few very slender remote branches spreading, naked on the lower part; spikelets imbricate, pale, suborbicular, glabrous, 1.5 mm long (fig. 94).

Rocky woods and limestone hills, Florida to Brazil. In Cuba called "hierba de venado" and "guinea cimarrona."

Cuba: Sumidero, *Shafer and Léon* 13670; *Léon and Shafer* 3468. Mariel, *Ekman* in 1921. Pinar del Río, *Hitchcock* 23321. Sierra Guane, *Shafer* 10549. Tiffin, *Shafer* 1089. Río Jipero, *Eggers* 5404a. Guantánamo, *Léon* 3779. Guara, *Hitchcock* 23400. Bayate, *Ekman* 4825. Without locality, *Wright* 731.

Jamaica: Ferry River, *Harris* 11326, 11788; *Hitchcock* 9749. Gordon Town, *Harris* 11459. Guara Ridge, *Harris* 11331. Kingston, *Hitchcock* 9466. Alligator Pond, *Hitchcock* 9822. Inverness, *Harris* 12744. Bog Walk, *Hitchcock* 9307. Without locality, *Hart* 1525.

Haiti: St. Michel de l'Atalaye, *Leonard* 7473, 7625, 8485. St. Raphael, *Leonard* 7663. Port-de-Pai, *Ekman* H 3928. Jean Rabel, *Leonard* 12919. Gonïave Island, *Leonard* 3080, 3082, 5126. Tortuga Island, *Leonard* 11691.

Figure 94.—*Leersia monandra*, × 1 (Nealley).

Dominican Republic: Monción, *Ekman* H 13057. Mao, *Abbott* 1037.

Puerto Rico: Ponce, *Chase* 6490. Guanica Bay, *Chase* 6524. Coamo, *Sintenis* 3228; *Britton and Brown* 6057.

3. Leersia grandiflora (Doell) Prodoehl, Bot. Arch. Mez 1: 219. 1922.

Oryza monandra var. *grandiflora* Doell in Mart. Fl. Bras. 2^2: 9. 1871. Brazil.

Homalocenchrus grandiflorus Hitchc., Contrib. U. S. Natl. Herb. 17: 273. 1913.

Culms erect, without rhizomes, 1 to 2 m tall; blades 1 to 2 cm wide; panicles large and open, the slender branches about 15 cm long; spikelets 2 to 2.5 mm long.

Shady banks and borders of streams, Mexico to Brazil; Guadeloupe and Martinique.

LEEWARD ISLANDS: Guadeloupe, *Duss* 3146.

WINDWARD ISLANDS: Martinique, *Duss* 775.

TRIBE 10. ZIZANIEAE

62. LUZIOLA Juss.; Gmel., Syst. Nat. ed. 13. 2: 637. 1791

Spikelets, unisexual, 1-flowered, disarticulating from the pedicel, the staminate and pistillate flowers in separate panicles on the same plant; both glumes wanting; lemma and palea about equal, thin, several to many nerved, lanceolate or oblong, acuminate; stamens several ("6 to 18"); stigmas long, plumose; grain free, globose, smooth. Perennials with flat blades and terminal and axillary panicles.

Blades 7 to 10 mm wide; inflorescence many-flowered ....3. L. SPRUCEANA.
Blades 1 to 3 mm wide; inflorescence few-flowered.
  Fruit 2 mm long ....2. L. BAHIENSIS.
  Fruit 1.5 mm long ....1. L. PERUVIANA.

1. Luziola peruviana Gmel., Syst. Nat. ed. 13. 2: 637. 1791. Peru.

More or less decumbent, spreading, apparently annual; culms 10 to 30 cm long, blades flat, 1 to 2 mm wide; panicles spreading, 2 to 3 cm long; pistillate spikelets 2 to 3 mm long, with striate lemma and palea; fruit globose, smooth, a little more than 1 mm long; staminate spikelets 5 mm long (fig. 95).

Swamps, shallow water, and wet ground, southern United States and Cuba to Uruguay and Peru. Grisebach[39] records this species from Trinidad.

CUBA: Mordazo, *Léon* 5941.

2. Luziola bahiensis (Steud.) Hitchc., Contrib. U. S. Natl. Herb. 12: 234. 1909.

Caryochloa bahiensis Steud., Syn. Pl. Glum. 1: 5. 1854. Bahia, Brazil.

Luziola alabamensis Chapm., Fl. South. U. S. 584. 1860. Alabama.

Luziola longivalvula Doell, in Mart., Fl. Bras. 2^2: 17. 1871. Brazil.

Plants stoloniferous; culms slender, tufted, about 10 cm tall; blades flat, narrow, linear, elongate, 2 to 4 mm wide, gradually narrowed toward the base; staminate panicles narrow terminating the main culm; spikelets about 4 mm long, striate-nerved; pistillate panicles open, the few branches spreading; spikelets 3 to 4 mm long, lanceolate; fruit obscurely striate, 2 mm long (fig. 96).

In streams or in mud, Alabama and Greater Antilles to Brazil. Extremely variable in appearance according to the depth of water in which the specimen grew. Plants growing in places from which water has receded are low and widely creeping.

[39] Fl. Brit. W. Ind. 535. 1864.

FIGURE 95.—*Luziola peruviana*. Plant, × ½; pistillate and staminate spikelets, × 5 (Curtiss 6871).

CUBA: Pinar del Río, *Wright* 3813. Isla de Pinos, *Britton and Wilson* 15190; *Ekman* 12267.

DOMINICAN REPUBLIC: Jarabaco, *Ekman* H 14132. Villa Altagracia, *Ekman* H 11207. Sánchez, *Ekman* H 15939.

3. Luziola spruceana Benth.; Doell, in Mart., Fl. Bras. 2^2: 18. 1871. Brazil.

Culms thick, soft and spongy, freely branching; sheaths broad, as much as 30 cm long; ligule delicate, as much as 3 cm long; blades firm, flat, as much as 50 cm long and 2 cm wide, narrowed and folded toward the base; staminate panicles open, 10 to 15 cm long; spikelets 5 mm long; stamens 6; pistillate panicles on shorter branches, the branches numerous, approximate on a short axis, finally reflexed; spikelets 5 mm long, acuminate: fruit about 2 mm long.

Ponds, lagoons, and quaking bogs, Cuba and Hispaniola; Trinidad to Brazil.

CUBA: Laguna de Ariguanabo (prov. Habana), *Ekman* 13436 (*Amer. Gr. Nat. Herb.* 987); *Léon* 4193 (growing in water 1 m deep).

HAITI: Bayeux, *Ekman* H 4802. Miragoane, *Ekman* H 6471.

DOMINICAN REPUBLIC: Jaina, *Ekman* H 13354; *Faris* 266, 394. Santo Domingo City, *Ekman* H 11589. Higüey, *Ekman* H 12173.

TRINIDAD: Without locality, *Broadway* 1626.

TOBAGO: *Broadway* 3100.

63. PHARUS L., Syst. Nat. ed. 10. 2: 1269. 1759

FIGURE 96.—*Luziola bahiensis*, × 1 (Mohr).

Spikelets 1-flowered, unisexual, in pairs appressed along the main branches of the inflorescence, one pistillate and sessile, the other staminate and long-pediceled; pistillate spikelet terete; glumes about equal, membranaceous, several-nerved; lemma rather thin in anthesis but becoming indurate in fruit, longer than the glumes, with a minute bent beak, the back clothed to a varying degree with thickly set uncinate hairs, these becoming adhesive organs in fruit, the edges sharply folded inward and the whole lemma becoming involute in fruit; palea very narrow, as long as the lemma, 2-nerved, membranaceous, folded around the long style; stigmas 3; staminate spikelet laterally compressed on a stiff pedicel as long as the pistillate spikelet; glumes thin, the first shorter, 1-nerved, the second 3-nerved; lemma as long as the second glume; stamens 6. Erect perennials (the base sometimes decumbent) with broad flat blades and open panicles, the blades with fine transverse veins between the longitudinal nerves, petioled (the petiole with a single twist reversing the upper and under surfaces of the blade), the nerves running obliquely from midrib to margin.

Culms creeping at base .... 3. P. PARVIFOLIUS.
Culms erect or nearly so.
 Fruit pubescent only at tip, slightly exceeding the glumes ... 2. P. LATIFOLIUS.
 Fruit pubescent all over. 2 to 3 times as long as the glumes .... 1. P. GLABER.

1. **Pharus glaber** H. B. K. Nov. Gen. et Sp. 1: 196. 1816. Venezuela.

Pharus lappulaceus Lam., in Tuss., Fl. Antill. 2. pl. 8. 1818. Not *P. lappulaceus* Aubl., 1775. Jamaica.

Pharus brasiliensis Raddi, Agrost. Bras. 21. 1823. Brazil.

Pharus lancifolius Desv.; Hamilt., Prodr. Pl. Ind. Occ. 8. 1825. Antilles.

Erect glabrous perennial 50 to 75 cm tall; blades oblanceolate, acuminate, commonly 15 to 25 cm long and 3 to 5 cm wide; panicles large, open, fragile, the few branches stiffly ascending or spreading, the appressed oblong brown spikelets about 1 cm long; fruit densely clothed with hooked hairs, the panicles readily breaking up, the pieces attaching themselves by the hooked hairs to passing objects.

Rich woods, Mexico and the West Indies to Brazil. Found in the Greater Antilles and in the Lesser Antilles as far south as Martinique.

2. **Pharus latifolius** L., Syst. Nat. ed. 10. 2: 1269. 1759. Jamaica.

Pharus ovalifolius Desv.; Hamilt., Prodr. Pl. Ind. Occ. 8. 1825. Antilles.

Similar to *P. glaber,* the blades on the average broader, the fruits longer, tapering at the summit, pubescent only near the tip (fig. 97).

Rich woods, West Indies and Central America to Brazil. Sometimes called wild oats.

Cuba: Sumidero, *Shafer and Léon* 13544. Sierra de Anafe, *Léon* 1999. Guape, *Linden* 1811. Bayate, *Ekmàn* 9853.

Jamaica: Mill Bank, *Maxon* 9335. Bath, *Nichols* in 1903. Ipswich, *Harris* 12365. Peckham Woods, *Harris* 12786. Mount Diablo, *Ridley* 71. Windsor, *Miller* 1441.

Haiti: St. Louis du Nord, *Ekman* H 3771. Tortuga Island, *Leonard* 12390.

Dominican Republic: Barahona, *Fuertes* 614. Sánchez, *Abbott* 190. Without locality, *Wright, Parry, and Brummel* 605 (in part *P. glaber*).

Puerto Rico: Dorado, *Chase* 6627. Utuado, *Britton and Cowell* 1034.

Leeward Islands: Guadeloupe, *Duss* 2700.

Windward Islands: Martinique, *Duss* 781. Grenada, *Broadway* in 1897, in 1905.

Trinidad: Caparo, *Broadway* 4930. Port-of-Spain, *Hitchcock* 10042, 10046. San Fernando, *Hitchcock* 10103 (*Amer. Gr. Nat. Herb.* 312).

3. **Pharus parvifolius** Nash, Bull. Torrey Bot. Club 35: 301. 1908. Haiti, *Nash and Taylor* 1482.

Differing from *P. glaber* in having a creeping and rooting base; blades narrowly elliptic-lanceolate to narrowly elliptic-oblanceolate, rarely as much as 3 cm wide; inflorescence averaging smaller; spikelets about as in *P. glaber* (fig. 98).

Rich woods, West Indies to Brazil.

Cuba: Sierra Maestra, *Ekman* 10351; *Léon* 10317. Jagüey, *Maxon* 4155; *Eggers* 4939. Viñales, *Léon* 14372.

Jamaica: Claremont, *Hitchcock* 9474 (*Amer. Gr. Nat. Herb.* 313).

Haiti: Port-de-Pai, *Ekman* H 3825.

FIGURE 97.—*Pharus latifolius*, × ½ (Hitchcock 10103, Amer. Gr. Nat. Herb. 312).

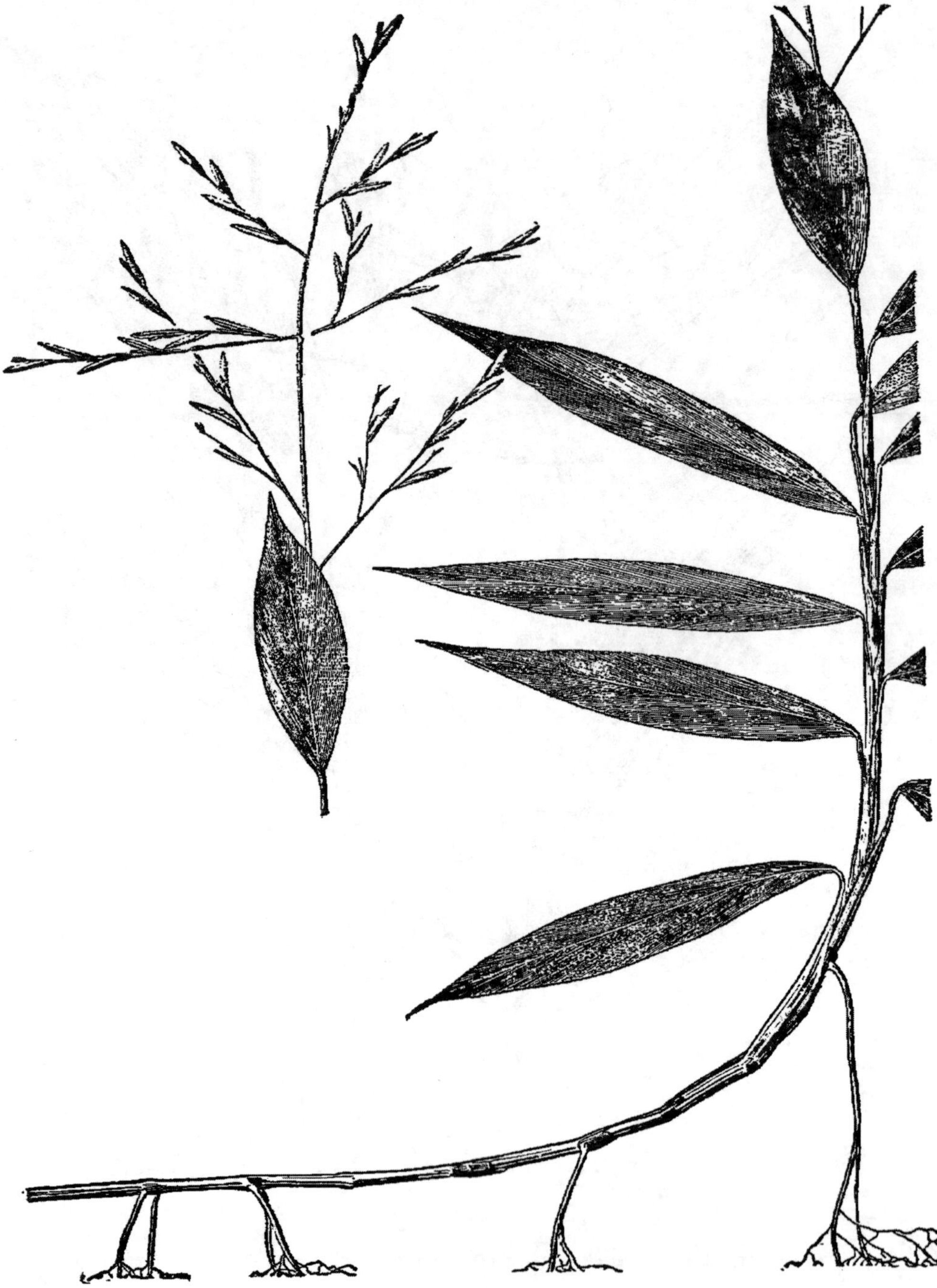

FIGURE 98.—*Pharus parvifolius*, × ½ (Miller 1231).

DOMINICAN REPUBLIC: Villa Altagracia, *Ekman* H 11186. Sánchez, *Abbott* 197. Río San Juan, *Miller* 1231.

TRINIDAD: Tabaquite, *Britton, Freeman, and Nowell* 2609; *Hitchcock* 10124. Southern Watershed Reserve, *Britton, Hazen, and Mendelson* 1097. Tamana, *Broadway* 4955. Siparia, *Broadway* 4988. Maracas Falls, *Broadway* 6703. Without locality, *Bot. Gard. Herb.* 3364.

TRIBE 11. MELINIDEAE

64. ARUNDINELLA Raddi, Agrost. Bras. 36. pl. 1. f. 3. 1823

Spikelets, short-pedicellate in large panicles; glumes acuminate, the tips widely spreading, the second longer than the first and the sterile lemma; fertile lemma minute, bearded on the callus, bearing a long slender awn from the apex. Perennial or sometimes annual, often robust grasses with narrow blades and open or contracted panicles.

Awn tightly twisted below, the column shorter than the second glume.
1. A. CONFINIS.

Awn not tightly twisted below, the part below the bend exceeding the glume.
- Blades broad and flat, 1 to 2 cm wide; plants robust, 1.5 to 2 m tall; sheaths appressed-villous.
2. A. DEPPEANA.
- Blades narrow and more or less folded or convolute; plants slender, mostly less than 1 m tall; sheaths usually smooth ---- 3. A. BERTERONIANA.

1. Arundinella confinis (Schult.) Hitchc. and Chase, Contrib. U. S. Natl. Herb. 18: 290. 1917.

Piptatherum confine Schult., Mant. 2: 184. 1824. Martinique, *Sieber* 265.

Arundinella martinicensis Trin., Gram. Pan. 62. 1826. Martinique. *Sieber* 262.

Tufted erect perennial with strong slender simple culms up to 2.5 m tall, flat blades, scabrous at least on the upper surface, and rather densely flowered oblong panicles 20 to 40 cm long (fig. 99).

FIGURE 99.—*Arundinella confinis*. Panicle, × ½; spikelet and floret, × 10 (Chase 6815).

Grassy slopes, West Indies and southern Mexico to Paraguay. The Cuban name is "cañuela de sabana."

CUBA: Pinar del Río, *Roig* 3154. Sancti Spíritus, *Léon* 6526. Baraguá, *Hitchcock* 23382. Caibarién, *Ekman* 16309. San Serapio, *Léon* 16202. Bayate, *Ekman* 6734. San Juan de Buenavista, *Wright* 3478. Loma Menqura, *Shafer* 3981.

JAMAICA: Nevis Bank, *Harris* 11519. Troy, *Harris* 12652; *Hitchcock* 9814. Newcastle, *Ridley* 74.. Gordon Town, *Hitchcock* 9326. Upper Clarendon, *Harris* 12247. Abbey Green, *Hitchcock* 9383. Flamstead, *Harris* 11462; *Eggers* 3514. Berwick, *Harris* 11452, 11533.

HAITI: Plaisance, *Leonard* 9415. Ennery, *Leonard* 8968. Marmelade, *Leonard* 8220. Caille la Croix, *Leonard* 7860. Furcy, *Leonard* 4467. Pétionville, *Ekman* H 1833. Mirebalais, *Ekman* H 5509.

DOMINICAN REPUBLIC: Cuenca, *Ekman* H 11062. Sánchez, *Ekman* H 14733. Pimentel, *Abbott* 668. Without locality, *Wright, Parry, and Brummel* 626.

PUERTO RICO: Maricao, *Britton and Cowell* 4089; *Sintenis* 361. Utuado, *Barrett* 101; *Britton and Cowell* 895. Lares, *Chase* 6594. Ponce, *Heller* 6256. Aguada, *Sintenis* 5797. Mayaguez, *Chase* 6815; *Heller* 4355; *Holm* 75. Caguas, *Heller* 934.

LEEWARD ISLANDS: Guadeloupe, *Duss* 4153. Dominica, *Jones* 2.

WINDWARD ISLANDS: Martinique, *Duss* 559.

TRINIDAD: St. Joseph, *Hitchcock* 10182; *Broadway* 9347. San Fernando, *Hitchcock* 10109. Without locality, *Bot. Gard. Herb.* 3227, 3375.

TOBAGO: *Broadway* 4620; *Hitchcock* 10277, 10280 (*Amer. Gr. Nat. Herb.* 289).

2. Arundinella deppeana Nees, in Steud., Syn. Pl. Glum 1: 115. 1854. Mexico.

Arundinella phragmitoides Griseb., Cat. Pl. Cuba 234. 1866. Cuba, *Wright* 3479.

Culms erect, as much as 2.5 m tall; sheaths appressed-pilose, especially toward summit; blades flat, as much as 2.5 cm wide; panicle as much as 70 cm long, the branches ascending, very numerous, closely overlapping, mostly 10 to 15 cm long; spikelets approximate on the branches, overlapping, 4 to 5 mm long; awn about 1 cm long.

Moist places, Cuba; Mexico to Brazil.

CUBA: Pinar del Río, *Britton* 10048; *Palmer and Riley* 70. San Blas, *Jack* 6457. San Diego, *Léon* 4847. Madruga, *Curtiss* 662. Santa Clara, *Léon* 3973. Manacas, *Léon* 5916. El Porvenir, *Britton and Wilson* 5282. Without locality, *Otto* 268; *Wright* 3479. San Miguel de los Baños, *Killip* 13844. Cayajabos, *Léon* 13224.

3. Arundinella berteroniana (Schult.) Hitchc. and Chase, Contrib. U. S. Natl. Herb. 18: 290. 1917.

Trichochloa berteroniana Schult., Mant. 2: 209. 1824. Santo Domingo.

Muhlenbergia berteroniana Kunth, Rév. Gram. 1: 64. 1829.

Arundinella cubensis Griseb., Mem. Amer. Acad. (n. s.) 8: 533. 1862. Cuba, *Wright* 1552.

Smaller and more slender than *A. deppeana*; blades often folded or involute, usually less than 5 mm wide; panicle less dense and fewer flowered.

Moist places and rocky river banks, Cuba and Hispaniola; Mexico to Brazil.

CUBA: Sancti Spíritus, *Léon* 2570. Banao Mountains, *Léon* 4009; *Ekman* 16211, 16212 (*Amer. Gr. Nat. Herb.* 988). Without locality, *Wright* 1552.

HAITI: Pétionville, *Ekman* H 1370. Las Caobas, *Ekman* H 3249.

DOMINICAN REPUBLIC: Santiago, *Raunkiaer* 934. Monción, *Ekman* H 12666.

65. ACHLAENA Griseb., Cat. Pl. Cub. 228. 1866

Spikelets jointed with the pedicel, disarticulating at maturity, the base narrowed to a pointed stipe or callus minutely barbed at the base or point; first glume subulate, extending into a slender awn; second glume narrow, somewhat indurate, narrowed into a slender awn; sterile lemma empty, rather hard, shorter than the second glume, awnless; fertile lemma rather thin, hyaline, awnless, acuminate, about as long as the sterile lemma, the palea like the glume but shorter. Tufted perennial with narrow blades and open panicle.

From Grisebach's description of the genus it is evident that he failed to note the palea, mistaking the sterile lemma for the fertile lemma (flos fertilis) and the fertile lemma for the palea, stating as he does that the palea is 1-nerved. Bentham and Hooker [40] and Hackel [41] follow Grisebach in this disposition of the genus, probably lacking material for verification of Grisebach's description. Hackel places the genus in Oryzeae, and elsewhere describes a specimen of *Achlaena piptostachya* as *Arthropogon stipitatus*. Grisebach states that there is but 1 stamen; we find 3, as did Hackel in the plant he described under *Arthropogon*. *Achlaena* is closely allied to the South American *Arthropogon* or is possibly congeneric.

1. **Achlaena piptostachya** Griseb., Cat. Pl. Cub. 229. 1866. Cuba, *Wright* 3487.

Arthropogon stipitatus Hack., Sitzungsber. Akad. Wiss. Math. Naturw. (Wien) 89 [1] : 125. 1884. Cuba, *Ramon de la Sagra*.

Culms stiffly erect, 50 to 100 cm tall; blades linear, firm, flat or involute, abruptly sharp-pointed, mostly clustered toward the base; panicle long-exserted, erect, 7 to 15 cm long, the branches stiffly spreading or reflexed, fascicled below, somewhat glutinous; spikelets appressed along the outer half of the main branches of the panicle; first glume, including awn, 1 to 2 cm long; second glume scaberulous, about 4 mm long, the awn about 3 cm long (fig. 100).

Open woods, dry slopes, and savannas, Cuba and Jamaica.

CUBA: San Isidro, *Britton, Wilson, and Léon* 13945. Bahía Honda, *Wilson* 9215. San Diego de los Baños, *Léon* 4383. Pinar del Río, *Hitchcock* 23291; *Baker and Abarca* 3447; *Britton and Cowell* 9732. Viñales, *Killip* 13556. Soledad, *Hitchcock* 23333. San Miguel de los Baños, *Killip* 13837. Canasí, *Léon* 12940. Baraguá, *Hitchcock* 23347. Guara, *Hitchcock* 23410. Sierra de Nipe, *Ekman* 9688, in 1922 (*Amer. Gr. Nat. Herb.* 800). Isla de Pinos, *Curtiss* 236; *Britton and Wilson* 14316; *Palmer and Riley* 913. Without locality, *Wright* 3487.

JAMAICA: Askenish (Dolphin Head), *Britton and Hollick* 2194.

---

[40] Gen. Pl. 3: 1117. 1883.

[41] In Engl. and Prantl, Pflanzenfam. 2^2: 41. 1887.

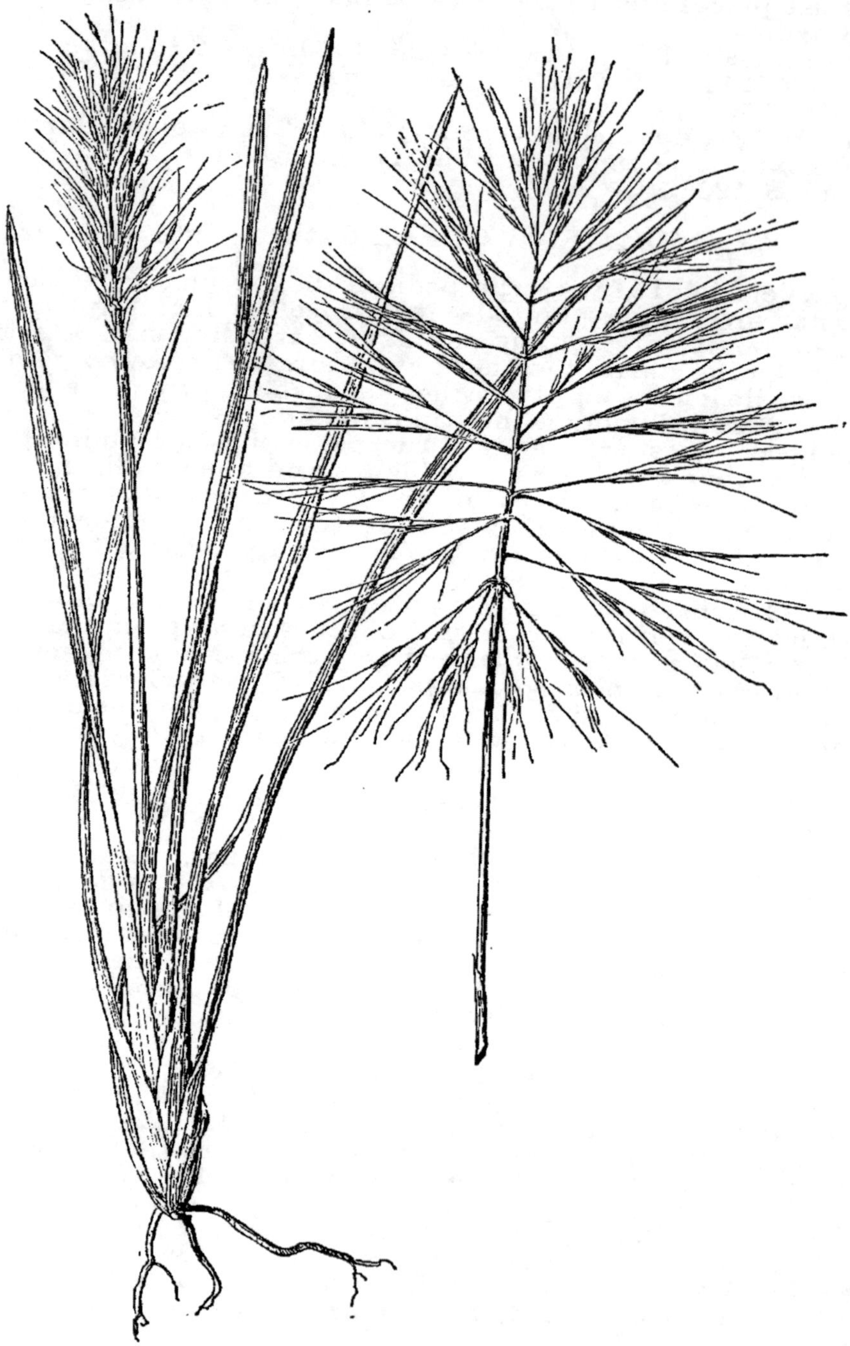

FIGURE 100.—*Achlaena piptostachya*, × ½ (Léon 4383).

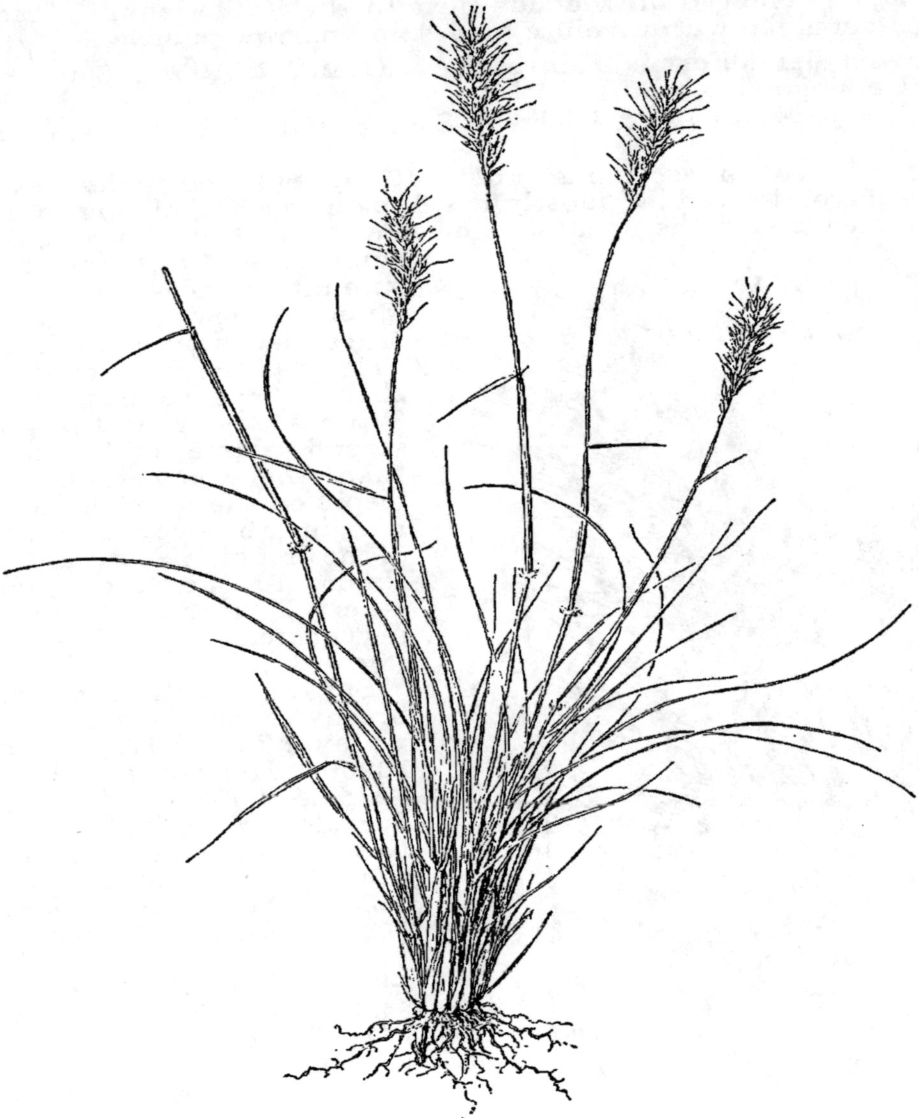

FIGURE 101.—*Reynaudia filiformis*, × ½ (Hitchcock 495).

66. REYNAUDIA Kunth, Rév. Gram. 1: 195. pl. 9. 1830

Spikelets perfect, articulated with the pedicel; glumes keeled, strongly nerved, awned from between the lobes of the bifid apex; sterile lemma awn-tipped from the bilobed summit; fertile lemma thin, nerveless, shorter than the sterile lemma, strongly compressed, keeled, the tip of the keel sometimes extended as a minute mucro, with 2 pairs of obscure lateral nerves; palea wanting; caryopsis flat, oblong, the embryo on the side next to the fertile lemma. Slender tufted perennial with involute blades and narrow panicle.

1. **Reynaudia filiformis** Kunth, Rév. Gram. 2: 195. 1830. Santo Domingo.

Polypogon cubensis A. Rich., in Sagra, Hist. Cuba 11: 313. 1850. Cuba.

Culms erect or ascending, 15 to 40 cm tall, the nodes bearded; blades involute, slender, mostly basal; panicle erect, oblong to linear, contracted and rather densely flowered, 3 to 6 cm long; spikelets compressed, 3 to 4 mm long, the summit purple-tinged; first glume 3-nerved or obscurely 5-nerved, a little more than half as long as the spikelet, the awn slightly flexuous, purplish, 2 or 3 times as long as the glume; second glume a little shorter than the spikelet, 5-nerved, hispid on the lower half of the margins, the awn similar to that of the first glume; sterile lemma similar to the second glume, 3-nerved, glabrous, the midnerve extended as a short mucro (fig. 101).

FIGURE 102.—*Melinis minutiflora*. Plant, × 1; spikelet, × 10 (Moldenke 453).

Savannas, palm barrens, and brushy slopes, Greater Antilles.

CUBA: Pinar del Río, *Hitchcock* 23260. Herradura, *Hitchcock* 495; *Léon* 15950; *Tracy* 9070. Sumidero, *Léon* 3480. Guanabacoa, *Wilson and Léon* 11632; *Léon* 848. Baraguá, *Hitchcock* 23358. Motembo, *Ekman* 16815. Sagua la Grande, *Léon* 14221. Eastern Cuba, *Wright* 3428.[42] Western Cuba, *Wright* 3428. Isla de Pinos, *Curtiss* 371; *Taylor* 44; *Britton and Wilson* 15188.

JAMAICA: Manchester, *Wullschlaegel* 1370.

HAITI: Mount Organisé, *Ekman* H 6230.

DOMINICAN REPUBLIC: Higüey, *Ekman* H 12208. Santo Domingo, *Wright, Parry, and Brummel* 623. Guarabo, *Abbott* 2804. Cotuy, *Abbott* 787a, 797. Pimentel, *Abbott* 663.

67. MELINIS Beauv., Ess. Agrost. 54. pl. 11. f. 4. 1812

Spikelets, 1-flowered with a sterile lemma below as in *Panicum*, disarticulating from the short slender pedicels; first glume very small, the second about equaling the sterile lemma, two-lobed at apex,

[42] Part of *Wright* 3428 came from western Cuba and part from eastern Cuba (Contrib. U. S. Natl. Herb. 12: 235. 1909).

mucronate between the lobes, nerved; sterile lemma similar to the second glume, the awn straight, long, and slender; fertile lemma and palea whitish, somewhat cartilaginous, shorter than the sterile lemma, awnless; palea a little shorter than its lemma. Spreading branching perennial with small spikelets in panicles.

1. **Melinis minutiflora** Beauv., Ess. Agrost. 54. pl. 11. f. 4. 1812. Brazil. MOLASSES GRASS.

Glandular throughout; culms 1 m or more long, rooting at the lower nodes, pubescent especially about the nodes; sheaths pilose; blades pubescent, 10 to 15 cm long, 5 to 10 mm wide; panicle 15 to 20 cm long, dark purple, rather closely flowered, the branches ascending; spikelets about 2 mm long, the straight delicate awn about 1 cm long. When fresh the plant emits a sweetish pungent odor (fig. 102).

Cultivated for forage. Called also zacate gordura. Described from Brazil where, however, it appears to be introduced. Native of Africa. As it escapes readily from cultivation it will undoubtedly soon become established here and there. Molasses grass is a good forage plant and its use will probably increase throughout the West Indies. The following are cultivated specimens.

DOMINICAN REPUBLIC: Monción, *Ekman* H 12654.
PUERTO RICO: Mayaguez, *Chase* 6826.
LEEWARD ISLANDS: Dominica, *Jones* 1.

TRIBE 12. PANICEAE

68. TRISCENIA Griseb., Mem. Amer. Acad. n. ser. 8: 534. 1862

Spikelets much as in *Panicum*, narrowly lanceolate, acuminate, deciduous from the pedicels; first glume acute, about half as long as the spikelet, 3-nerved, the base overlapping; second glume as long as the spikelet, acuminate, 5-nerved; sterile lemma similar to the second glume, 3-nerved, containing no palea or stamens; fertile lemma shorter than the second glume and sterile lemma, narrow, somewhat acuminate, thin but somewhat chartaceous, not green like the glumes and sterile lemma; palea like its lemma in texture, nearly enclosed in the flat edges of the lemma. Low tufted perennial with narrow few-flowered panicles.

This genus has been included in the tribe Melinideae by Hitchcock and Chase [43] and in Tristegineae by Hackel [44], but the structure of the spikelet is entirely that of Paniceae. The fertile floret is rather thin but papery and distinctly different from the glumes and sterile lemma; the structure is similar to that of *Hymenachne*, but the palea is nearly enclosed in the edges of the lemma. *Triscenia* also approaches *Ichnanthus*, but there are no wings at the base of the fertile lemma and no prominent scars as found in those species that lack wings.

1. **Triscenia ovina** Griseb., Mem. Amer. Acad. (n. s.) 8: 534. 1863. Cuba, *Wright* 756.

Panicum nudiculme Mez, Bot. Jahrb. Engler 56 (Beibl. 125): 6. 1921. Based on *Triscenia ovina* Griseb.

Culms slender, 20 to 50 cm tall; blades filiform, glabrous, mostly basal, about half as long as the culm, the innovations numerous;

[43] Contrib. U.S. Natl. Herb. 18: 263. 1917.
[44] Engl. and Prantl, Pflanzenfam. 2^2: 32. 1887; True Grasses 68. 1890.

panicles slender, few-flowered, the ascending branches distant; spikelets appressed, on short slender pedicels, glabrous, 3 mm long (fig. 103).

Stream borders in mountains or hills; Cuba, common in Oriente.

CUBA: Sierra Maestra, valley of Río Yara, *Ekman* in 1922 (*Amer. Gr. Nat. Herb.* 989). Nagua, *Léon* 10889. Sierra de Nipe, *Ekman*

FIGURE 103.—*Triscenia ovina.* Plant, × ½; spikelet and floret, × 10 (Wright 756).

10148. Baracoa, *Ekman* 4324. Piedra Gorda, *Shafer* 3668. Pinal Creek, *Wright* 756.

Dr. Ekman states on one of his labels that the species is known also from Camagüey and from Pinar del Río, but the author has seen no specimens from there.

69. LEPTOCORYPHIUM Nees, Agrost. Bras. 83. 1829

Spikelets lanceolate, 1-flowered with a sterile lemma below; first glume obsolete; second glume and sterile lemma 3- and 5-nerved, the latter a little longer than the former and about as long as the fruit; fertile lemma slightly cartilaginous-indurate, chestnut with a white delicate hyaline summit; palea not enclosed above, the 2 nerves obscurely visible. Tufted perennial with narrow blades and silky panicle.

1. Leptocoryphium lanatum (H. B. K.) Nees, Agrost. Bras. 84. 1829.

Paspalum lanatum H. B. K., Nov. Gen. et Sp. 1: 94. pl. 29. 1815. Mexico.

Milium lanatum Roem. and Schult, Syst. Veg. 2: 322. 1817.

Anthaenantia lanata Benth., Jour. Linn. Soc. Bot. 19: 39. 1881.

Slender erect perennial up to 1 m tall; blades long, narrow, often involute; panicles oblong, loose, many-flowered, pale, the branchlets capillary; spikelets silky-pilose, the hairs at first appressed, at maturity spreading (fig. 104).

Dry hills and pine barrens, southern Mexico and the West Indies to northern South America.

CUBA: Herradura, *Tracy* 9048, 9071, 9132; *Earle* 682; *Hitchcock* 482; *Ekman* in 1922 (*Amer. Gr. Nat. Herb.* 707). San Diego de los Baños, *Léon* 4564. Sumidero, *Léon* 3465; *Shafer and Léon* 13609. Pinar del Río, *Wright* 3429; *Hitchcock* 23268; *Palmer and Riley* 440. Sabana de Motembo, *Léon* 9347. Manacas, *Léon* 5827. San Miguel de los Baños, *Killip* 13854. Sancti Spíritus, *Léon* 853. "La Magdalena" Cayamas, *Baker* 4555. Baraguá, *Hitchcock* 23367. Paso Estancia, *Shafer* 1683. Bayate, *Ekman* 4956. Isla de Pinos, *Palmer and Riley* 972; *Curtiss* 393; *Britton and Wilson* 14173.

HAITI: St. Michel de l'Atalaye, *Ekman* H 3253; *Sweet* in 1925. Lamielle, *Ekman* H 6203. Bonao, *Ekman* H 5827.

DOMINICAN REPUBLIC: Guerra, *Ekman* H 13348.

PUERTO RICO: Mayaguez, *Britton and Hess* 2699; *Chase* 6272, 6810; *Holm* 192, 193.

TRINIDAD: San Fernando, *Hart* 3368. O'Meara Savanna, *Britton and Hazen* 1562.

70. TRICHACHNE Nees, Agrost. Bras. 85. 1829

(*Valota* Adans., Fam. Pl. 2: 495. 1763. No generic description)

Spikelets lanceolate, in pairs, short-pedicellate, in two rows along one side of a narrow rachis; first glume minute, glabrous; second glume and sterile lemma about as long as the fruit, 3- to 5-nerved, copiously silky; fertile lemma cartilaginous, lanceolate, acuminate, usually brown, the flat white hyaline margins broad. Perennials, the slender racemes erect or nearly so, aggregate along the upper part of the main axis, forming a white or brownish silky panicle.

Racemes few, usually about 3; blades short, mostly not over 3 cm long; plants 20 to 40 cm tall .... 1. T. EGGERSII.
Racemes numerous; blades elongate; plants usually more than 50 cm tall.
  Lower panicle branches in a fascicle on one side of the axis; spikelets densely clothed with tawny or brown silky hairs much exceeding the spikelet. .... 2. T. INSULARIS.
  Lower panicle branches in a whorl; spikelets sparsely villous, the hairs shorter than the spikelet .... 3. T. LAXA.

FIGURE 104.—*Leptocoryphium lanatum.* Plant, × ½; floret, × 10 (Chase 6272).

1. **Trichachne eggersii** (Hack.) Henr., Med. Rijks Herb. Leiden 61: 10. 1930.

Panicum eggersii Hack., Oesterr. Bot. Ztschr. 51: 292. 1901. St. Thomas, *Eggers* 295.

Valota eggersii Hitchc. and Chase, Contrib. U. S. Natl. Herb. 18: 292. 1917.

Digitaria eggersii Henr., Blumea 1: 97. 1934.

Culms slender, branching, 20 to 40 cm tall, decumbent at base; blades flat, puberulent, 1 to 5 cm long, 2 to 4 mm wide; panicles of 2 or 3 erect racemes 2 to 5 cm long; spikelets 3 to 4 mm long.

Stony slopes, Virgin Islands.

VIRGIN ISLANDS: St. Thomas, *Eggers* 3, 295. Virgin Gorda, *Fishlock* 209.

2. **Trichachne insularis** (L.) Nees, Agrost. Bras. 86. 1829. SOURGRASS.

Andropogon insularis L., Syst. Nat. ed. 10. 2: 1304. 1759. Jamaica.

Panicum lanatum Rottb., Act. Lit. Univ. Hafn. 1: 269. 1778. Jamaica.

Milium villosum Swartz, Prodr. Veg. Ind. Occ. 24. 1788. Jamaica.

Panicum leucophaeum H. B. K., Nov. Gen. et Sp. 1: 97. 1815. Venezuela and Colombia.

Panicum insulare Meyer, Prim. Fl. Esseq. 60. 1818.

Saccharum polystachyum Sieb.; Kunth, Enum. Pl. 1: 124. 1833. Martinique.

Panicum saccharoides A. Rich., in Sagra, Hist. Cuba 11: 306. 1850. Cuba.

Panicum falsum Steud., Syn. Pl. Glum. 1: 67. 1854. Cuba.

Panicum duchaissingii Steud., Syn. Pl. Glum. 1: 93. 1854. Guadeloupe.

Tricholaena insularis Griseb., Abh. Ges. Wiss. Göttingen 7: 265. 1857.

Tricholaena saccharoides Griseb., Syst. Unt. Veg. Karaib. 117. 1857.

Digitaria leucophaea Stapf, in Thiselt. Dyer, Fl. Cap. 7: 382. 1898.

Syntherisma insularis Millsp. and Chase, Field Mus. Bot. 1: 473. 1902.

Valota insularis Chase, Biol. Soc. Wash. Proc. 19: 188. 1906.

Digitaria insularis Mez; Ekman, Arkiv. Bot. 13: 22. 1913.

Rather coarse tufted weedy grass; culms 50 to 150 cm tall; sheaths sparsely hirsute; blades flat, usually scabrous, as much as 25 cm long and 1 cm wide; panicles silky, tawny at maturity, 10 to 30 cm long, the numerous racemes 10 to 15 cm long; spikelets about 4 mm long, very silky (fig. 105).

Open ground and waste places in the Tropics and Subtropics of America at low altitudes.

This species is often called "sourgrass", a name which is occasionally applied to other large unpalatable grasses such as species of *Paspalum* and *Andropogon*. In Cuba it is one of the grasses called "barba de indio", and "rabo de zorra." In St. Kitts it is called "long grass." To be found in probably all of the West Indian islands.

3. **Trichachne laxa** (Reichenb.) Hitchc.

Reimaria laxa Reichenb.; Spreng., Tent. Sup. Syst. Veg. 2. 1828. Surinam.

Valota laxa Hitchc. and Chase, Contrib. U. S. Natl. Herb. 18: 292. 1917.

FIGURE 105.—*Trichachne insularis.* Plant, × ½; spikelet and floret, × 10 (Baker and Wilson 602).

Digitaria laxa Parodi, Physis 9: 13, 18. 1928.

Culms in large tufts, decumbent at base, 1 to 2 m tall; sheaths tuberculate-hispid; blades flat, glabrous or nearly so, 5 to 20 cm long, 5 to 15 mm wide; panicle 15 to 25 cm long, the numerous rather slender racemes usually 15 to 20 cm long, widely spreading; spikelets narrowly lanceolate, acuminate, rather sparsely silky pilose, 4 to 5 mm long. The stiff hairs of the sheaths break off in handling and penetrate the skin.

Open moist ground, southern West Indies to Paraguay.

WINDWARD ISLANDS: Grenada, *Broadway* 1782.

TRINIDAD: Pitch Lake, *Hitchcock* 10084 (*Amer. Gr. Nat. Herb.* 553). Cedros, *Hitchcock* 10143. San Fernando, *Bot. Gard. Herb.* 3374. Port-of-Spain, *Hitchcock* 9954.

TOBAGO: *Hitchcock* 10246; *Broadway* 4851.

71. DIGITARIA Heist.; Scop., Fl. Carn. ed. 2. 1: 52. 1772
CRABGRASS

(*Syntherisma* Walt., Fl. Carol. 76. 1788)

Spikelets solitary or in twos or threes, subsessile or short-pediceled, alternate in two rows on one side of a 3-angled winged or wingless rachis; spikelets lanceolate or elliptic, plano-convex; first glume minute or wanting; second glume equaling the sterile lemma or shorter; fertile lemma cartilaginous, the hyaline margins pale. Erect or prostrate annuals or perennials, the slender racemes digitate or somewhat scattered, but aggregate along the upper part of the culms.

Rachis wing-margined, the green wings as wide as the whitish midrib or wider.
- First glume small but evident ---- 1. D. SANGUINALIS.
- First glume obsolete or wanting.
  - Rachis sparsely beset with spreading long hairs ---- 2. D. HORIZONTALIS.
  - Rachis with no long hairs.
    - Pedicels with a ring of short stiff hairs at summit; spikelets with stripes of dense capitellate hairs ---- 3. D. ARGYROSTACHYA.
    - Pedicels not hairy at summit.
      - Second glume about half as long as the spikelet. Plant creeping and rooting at the nodes ---- 4. D. SEROTINA.
      - Second glume as long as the spikelet.
        - Spikelets 2 mm long ---- 6. D. ISCHAEMUM.
        - Spikelets 1.5 mm long.
          - Culms erect or decumbent at base ---- 5. D. VIOLASCENS.
          - Culms forming long stolons ---- 7. D. LONGIFLORA.

Rachis not winged or the margin much narrower than the midrib.
- Spikelets glabrous or nearly so.
  - Spikelets 1.5 mm long; second glume shorter than the spikelet; obtuse. 10. D. CURVINERVIS.
  - Spikelets 2.5 mm long; second glume as long as the spikelet, acute. 13. D. EKMANII.
- Spikelets pubescent.
  - Spikelets 1.5 mm long (disregarding the hairs extending beyond the end).
    - Hairs on the spikelet extending beyond the apex as a stiff brownish brushlike tip ---- 11. D. ARGILLACEA.
    - Hairs on spikelet not extending beyond the spikelet as a brushlike tip. 9. D. PANICEA.
  - Spikelets 2 mm long.
    - Hairs extending beyond the spikelet as a short brushlike tip. 12. D. PINETORUM.
    - Hairs not extending beyond the spikelet as a brushlike tip - 8. D. VILLOSA.

FIGURE 106.—*Digitaria sanguinatis.* Plant, ×½; two views of spikelet, and floret, × 10 (Norton 566).

1. Digitaria sanguinalis (L.) Scop., Fl. Carn. ed. 2. 1: 52. 1772. CRABGRASS.

Panicum sanguinale L., Sp. Pl. 57. 1753. America, Europe.
Digitaria marginata Link, Enum. Pl. 1: 102. 1821. Brazil.
Digitaria fimbriata Link, Hort. Berol. 1: 226. 1827. Brazil.
Syntherisma sanguinalis Dulac, Fl. Haut. Pyr. 77. 1867.
Syntherisma fimbriata Nash, Bull. Torrey Bot. Club 25: 302. 1898.

Spreading branching annual often rooting at the nodes; sheaths pilose; blades more or less pilose; racemes few to several, ascending or spreading, 5 to 10 cm long, in 1 or 2 whorls; spikelets about 3 mm long, the first glume small but distinct (fig. 106).

A common weed in cultivated soil and waste places throughout the temperate and tropical regions of both hemispheres. To be found on all the West Indian islands. An excellent fodder grass. In Cuba this is one of the grasses called "pata de gallina."

FIGURE 107.—*Digitaria horizontalis*. Plant, × 1; spikelet and floret, × 10 (Nash 996).

2. Digitaria horizontalis Willd., Enum. Hort. Berol. 92. 1809. Santo Domingo.

Milium digitatum Swartz, Prodr. Veg. Ind. Occ. 24. 1788. Jamaica. Not *Digitaria digitata* Buse, 1854.
Axonopus digitatus Beauv., Ess. Agrost. 12, 154. 1812.
Digitaria setigera Roth; Roem. and Schult., Syst. Veg. 2: 474. 1817. India.
Panicum horizontale Meyer, Prim. Fl. Esseq. 54. 1818.
Digitaria setosa Desv.; Hamilt., Prodr. Pl. Ind. Occ. 6. 1825. Antilles.
Digitaria jamaicensis Spreng., Syst. Veg. 1: 272. 1825. Jamaica.
Paspalum digitatum Kunth, Rév. Gram. 1: 24. 1829.
Panicum hamiltonii Kunth, Rév. Gram. 1: Sup. IX. 1830. Antilles.
Syntherisma setosa Nash, Bull. Torrey Bot. Club 25: 300. 1898.
Syntherisma digitata Hitchc., Contrib. U. S. Natl. Herb. 12: 142. 1908.
Digitaria digitata Urban, Symb. Antill. 8: 24. 1920. Not *Digitaria digitata* Buse, 1854. Based on *Milium digitatum* Swartz.

Decumbent branching stoloniferous weedy annual with pilose sheaths and pubescent, often velvety, flat blades, and 5 to 15 very slender lax racemes up to 8 cm long, subdigitate or in fascicles along a slender axis; spikelets narrow, about 2.5 mm long; first glume obsolete or wanting (fig. 107).

A common weed in fields, open ground, and waste places, tropical regions of both hemispheres. To be found in probably all of the West Indian islands. In Cuba sometimes called "pata de gallina fina" (fine henfoot).

3. Digitaria argyrostachya (Steud.) Fernald, Rhodora 22: 103. 1920.

Panicum argyrostachyum Steud., Syn. Pl. Glum. 1: 40. 1854. Java.

Syntherisma argyrostachya Hitchc. and Chase, Contrib. U. S. Natl. Herb. 18: 294. 1917.

Annual; culms erect or spreading, 10 to 60 cm tall; sheaths glabrous; blades flat, 3 to 5 mm wide, sparsely pilose on the upper surface; racemes slender, erect or ascending, mostly 2 to 4, 4 to 10 cm long; spikelets 2 mm long.

A weed in cultivated soil, introduced in Jamaica.

JAMAICA: Cinchona, *Harris* 11271, 11413; *Hitchcock* 9705.

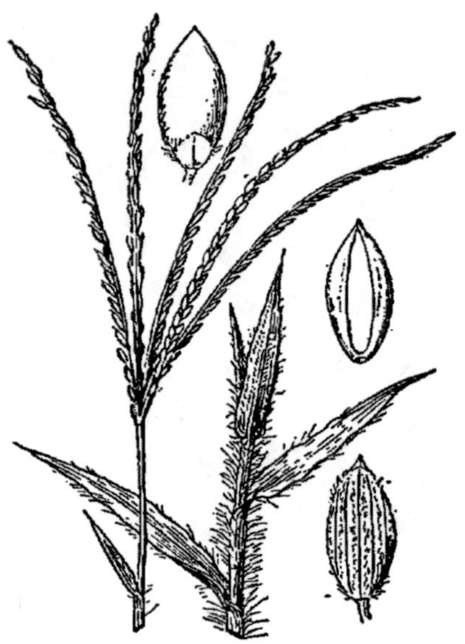

FIGURE 108.—*Digitaria serotina*. Plant, × 1; two views of spikelet, and floret, × 10 (Tracy 4653).

4. Digitaria serotina (Walt.) Michx., Fl. Bor. Amer. 1: 46. 1803.

Syntherisma serotina Walt., Fl. Carol. 76. 1788. South Carolina.

Culms creeping and rooting, forming mats, the flowering ones ascending, 20 to 30 cm tall; sheaths and blades pilose; racemes 3 to 5 on an axis about 1 cm long, 3 to 5 cm long, the rachis flat, a little less than 1 mm wide, the margins wider than the midrib; spikelets oblong-elliptic, minutely pubescent, about 1.5 mm long (fig. 108).

Sandy soil, Coastal Plain of the United States from Delaware to Mississippi; also in western Cuba.

CUBA: Laguna Jovero, *Shafer* 10769. Habana, *Ekman* 1057, 11515; *Léon* 4332.

5. Digitaria violascens Link, Hort. Berol. 1: 229. 1827. Brazil.

Panicum violascens Kunth, Rév. Gram. 1: 33. 1829.

Paspalum chinensis Nees, in Hook. and Arn., Bot. Beechey Voy. 231. 1836. China.

Paspalum minutiflorum Steud., Syn. Pl. Glum. 1: 17. 1854. Not *P. minutiflorum* Desv., 1831. China.

Syntherisma helleri Nash, Minn. Bot. Stud. 1: 798. pl. 44. 1897. Hawaii.

Syntherisma violascens Nash, in Brown, Acad. Nat. Sci. Phila. Proc. 61: 488. 1909.

Digitaria chinensis A. Camus, Not. Syst. Lecomte 4: 48. 1923. Not *D. chinensis* Hornem., 1819.

Syntherisma chinensis Hitchc., Contrib. U. S. Natl. Herb. 22: 468. 1922.

Annual; culms decumbent and rooting at the base or sometimes erect, 30 to 60 cm tall; sheaths glabrous; blades glabrous, mostly 3 to 6 mm wide; racemes mostly 2 to 5, sometimes 6 or 7, slender, ascending, often curved, 5 to 10 cm long; rachis flat, wing-margined, 1 mm wide or somewhat less, glabrous; spikelets elliptic, 1.5 mm long, cinereous-pubescent; first glume wanting; second glume and sterile lemma equal, about as long as the dark brown fertile lemma (fig. 109).

Open ground, fields, waste places, and moist grassland, China to India and Australia; introduced in the American Tropics.

BERMUDA: *Collins* 146; *Brown and Britton* 57.

JAMAICA: St. Andrew, *Harris* 12714. Cinchona, *Harris* 11269, 11271½, 12484; *Hitchcock* 9703. Castleton, *Harris* 11283; *Hitchcock* 9396. Abbey Green, *Hitchcock* 9354 (*Amer. Gr. Nat. Herb.* 556). Gordon Town, *Hart* 688, 756; *Hitchcock* 9328.

PUERTO RICO: Mayaguez, *Chase* 6255.

TRINIDAD: Port-of-Spain, *Hitchcock* 10008, 10328. Las Lilas, *Britton* 2515. Piarco Savanna, *Britton and Hazen* 716. Princes Town, *Broadway* 1922. Mora Forest, *Broadway* 7752. Tamana Main Road, *Broadway* 4961. Without locality, *Bot. Gard. Herb.* 3433.

6. Digitaria ischaemum (Schreb.) Schreb.; Muhl., Descr. Gram. 131. 1817. SMOOTH CRABGRASS.

Panicum ischaemum Schreb.; Schweigger and Koerte, Spec. Fl. Erlang. 16. 1804. Europe.

Digitaria humifusa Pers., Syn. Pl. 1: 85. 1805.

Syntherisma glabrum Schrad., Fl. Germ. 1: 163. 1806.

Digitaria glabra Beauv., Ess. Agrost. 51. 1812.

Syntherisma ischaemum Nash, N. Amer. Fl. 17: 151. 1912.

Spreading annual weed resembling *D. sanguinalis*, but with glabrous foliage; spikelets 2 mm long; first glume wanting.

Common in eastern United States; Virgin Islands; introduced from Europe.

VIRGIN ISLANDS: St. Croix, *Benzon*.

7. Digitaria longiflora (Retz.) Pers., Syn. Pl. 1: 85. 1805.

Paspalum longiflorum Retz., Obs. Bot. 4: 15. 1786. India.

Panicum longiflorum Gmel., Syst. Nat. 2: 158. 1791.

Syntherisma longiflora Skeels, U. S. Dept. Agr., Bur. Plant Indus. Bull. 261: 30. 1912.

Perennial; culms widely creeping; sheaths glabrous; blades flat, glabrous, those of the stolons 1 to 3 cm long; fertile culms ascending 20 to 40 cm long; racemes often 2, sometimes 3 or 4, 3 to 6 cm long, usually curved, the rachis flat, 0.5 to 0.8 mm wide, the margin wider than the midrib; spikelets elliptic, minutely pubescent, 1.5 mm long (fig. 110).

Ditches and sandy savannas, tropical regions of the Old World; introduced in the American Tropics.

CUBA: Pinar del Río, *Hitchcock* 23269, 23279, 23286; *Ekman* 17288; *Roig* 3954, 4200; *Léon* 12861, 16151, 16425.

LEEWARD ISLANDS: Antigua, *Box* 63, 182.

WINDWARD ISLANDS: St. Lucia, *Box* 199.

TRINIDAD: Long Stretch, *Broadway* 6551.

8. Digitaria villosa (Walt.) Pers., Syn. Pl. 1: 85. 1805.

Syntherisma villosa Walt., Fl. Carol. 77. 1788. South Carolina.

?*Panicum domingense* Zuccagni, in Roemer, Coll. Bot. 123. 1809. Santo Domingo.

FIGURE 109.—*Digitaria violascens*. Plant, × ½ (Hitchcock 1032S).

Panicum leucocomum Scribn., U. S. Dept. Agr., Div. Agrost. Bull. 7 (ed. 2): 58. 1898. Florida.

Syntherisma leucocoma Nash, Bull. Torrey Bot. Club 25: 295. 1898. Florida.

Digitaria leucocoma Urban, Symb. Antill. 8: 24. 1920.

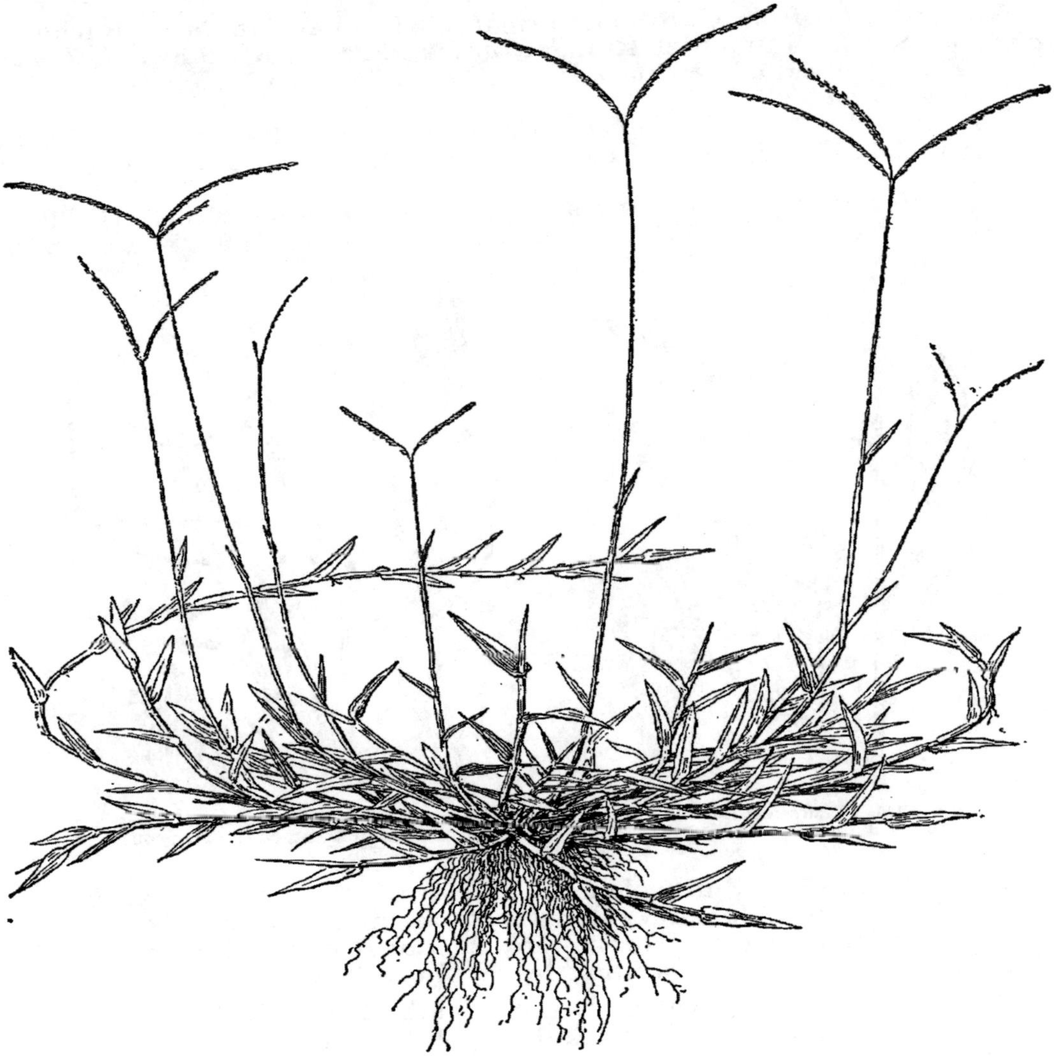

FIGURE 110.—*Digitaria longiflora*, × ½ (Hitchcock 14186).

Erect cespitose perennial (or annual according to Ekman), 50 to 120 cm tall; sheaths pubescent or glabrate; blades narrow, sometimes loosely involute; panicles of several erect or ascending racemes 8 to 15 cm long, the rachis narrowly winged; spikelets about 2 mm long; first glume wanting; second glume a little shorter than the fruit, cinereous-pubescent, some of the hairs capitellate; sterile lemma like the second glume, about as long as the chestnut-apiculate fruit (fig. 111).

Sandy woods and open ground, southeastern United States, West Indies, and Central America.

BAHAMAS: Andros, *Brace* 4882. New Providence, *Britton and Brace* 701.

CUBA: La Grifa la Catolina, *Wright* 3884. Laguna Santa Bárbara, *Ekman* 18116. Pinar del Río, *Hitchcock* 23264. Matanzas, *Ekman* in 1923. Baraguá, *Hitchcock* 23385. Mordazo, *Ekman* 17026. Manacas, *Léon* 9289.

HAITI: Hinche, *Cook, Scofield, and Doyle* 146. Pétionville, *Ekman* H 1388, H 1747. Port-au-Prince, *Ekman* 1991. Gros-Morne, *Ekman* H 4920.

DOMINICAN REPUBLIC: Constanza, *Tuerckheim* 3459; *Ekman* H 13904. Santiago, *Ekman* H 16377. Sánchez, *Ekman* H 15942. Monción,

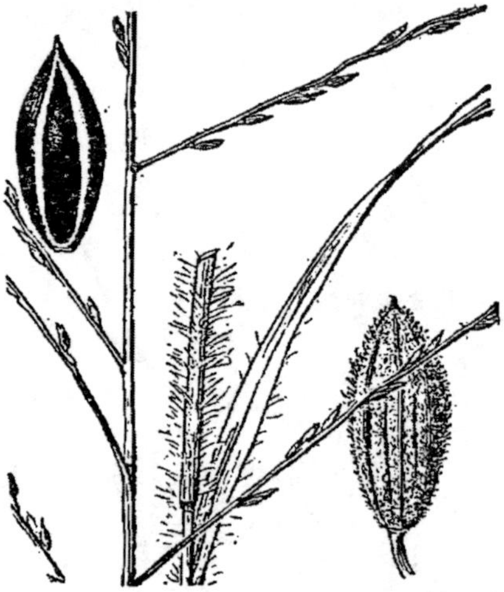

FIGURE 111.—*Digitaria villosa.* Plant, × 1; spikelet and floret, × 10 (Curtiss 5300).

FIGURE 112.—*Digitaria panicea.* Plant, × 1; spikelet and floret, × 10 (Tracy 9058).

Ekman H 12637. Punta Icacos, *Ekman* H 15785. Azua, *Ekman* H 13509. Without locality, *Wright, Parry, and Brummel* 622.

PUERTO RICO: Laguna Tortuguero, *Britton, Cowell, and Brown* 3858. San Juan, *Chase* 6784. Campo Alegre, *Chase* 6806.

9. Digitaria panicea (Swartz) Urban, Symb. Antill. 8: 23. February, 1920; Fernald, Rhodora 22: 103. June, 1920.

Milium paniceum Swartz, Prodr. Veg. Ind. Occ. 24. 1788. Jamaica.

Agrostis jamaicensis Poir., in Lam., Encycl. Suppl. 1: 258. 1810. Jamaica.

Axonopus paniceus Beauv., Ess. Agrost. 12, 154. 1812.

Syntherisma paniceum Nash, N. Amer. Fl. 17: 152. 1912.

More slender than *D. villosa*, probably annual; blades folded or involute, flexuous, about 1 mm wide; racemes mostly 1 to 3, erect, 5 to 20 cm long, usually 10 to 15 cm, very slender, loosely flowered; spikelets about 1.5 mm long, the capitellate hairs rather stiff and appressed (fig. 112).

There is a slight uncertainty in the application of the name *Milium paniceum*. The original description applies to the species described above. The amplified description[45] also applies with the exception of "Raches 3-quetrae, margine membranaceae." The rachis is only minutely margined. There is no specimen of *Milium paniceum* in the Swartz Herbarium, but there are three specimens sent by Swartz to other herbaria, one at Munich, one at Madrid, and one in the DeCandolle Herbarium. All these specimens are *Digitaria panicea* as here understood. The habitat given by Swartz is "in aridis sabulosis Jamaicae australis." This species resembles *D. filiformis* of the United States under which name Grisebach[46] and Nash[47] include it, but differs in having longer, more numerous racemes, longer folded or subinvolute blades, and slightly larger spikelets with longer pubescence.

Open grassy places, subtropical Florida, West Indies, and Central America.

BAHAMAS: New Providence, *Britton and Brace* 486.

CUBA: Baraguá, *Hitchcock* 23361, 23379. Sancti Spíritus, *Léon* 952. Tunas, *Léon* 6745. Sierra de Nipe, *Ekman* in 1922. Eastern Cuba, *Wright* 1544 (in part). Isla de Pinos, *Britton, Wilson, and Léon* 6060, 15247.

JAMAICA: Barican, *Hitchcock* 9574.

HAITI: Jean Rabel, *Leonard* 13032. Pétionville, *Ekman* H 1732.

DOMINICAN REPUBLIC: Sierra de los Comisarios, *Ekman* H 6804.

PUERTO RICO: Campo Alegre, *Chase* 6435.

10. Digitaria curvinervis (Hack.) Fernald, Rhodora 22: 103. 1920.

Panicum curvinerve Hack., Oesterr. Bot. Ztschr. 51: 335. 1901. Cuba, *Wright* 1544 in part.

Syntherisma curvinervis Hitchc. and Chase, Contrib. U. S. Natl. Herb. 18: 295. 1917.

Annual; culms slender, 20 to 60 cm tall; sheaths and blades sparsely or rather densely pilose or nearly glabrous, the blades flat, 2 to 5 mm wide; racemes mostly 2 to 4, sometimes 1 or several, 2 to 10 cm long; spikelets elliptic, glabrous, strongly nerved, 1.5 mm long, rarely nearly 2 mm long, 0.5 mm wide; first glume wanting; second glume about three-fourths as long as the spikelet, the internerves hyaline, 3-nerved, the outer nerves incurved and joined with the midnerve near the apex; sterile lemma 5-nerved, the outer pair incurved to the midnerve at apex; fruit dark brown with a whitish tip.

Sandy soil, Cuba and Hispaniola. The type collection mixed with two other species.

CUBA: Pan de Guajaibon, *Ekman* 17482. Santa Cruz de los Pinos, *Ekman* 17688. Las Pozas, *Ekman* 12738. Pinar del Río, *Wright* 1544. San Diego de los Baños, *Léon* 4439. Motembo, *Léon* 8689.

DOMINICAN REPUBLIC: San Juan, *Ekman* H 13399.

11. Digitaria argillacea (Hitchc. and Chase) Fernald, Rhodora 22: 104. 1920.

Syntherisma argillacea Hitchc. and Chase, Contrib. U. S. Natl. Herb. 18: 296. 1917. Puerto Rico, *Chase* 6221.

---

[45] Fl. Ind. Occ. 1: 179. 1797.
[46] Fl. Brit. W. Ind. 543. 1864.
[47] Fl. N. Amer. 17: 150. 1912.

Annual (according to Ekman); culms slender, erect or decumbent at base, 15 to 60 cm tall; blades flat, 3 to 4 mm wide, more or less pilose; panicles long-exserted; racemes usually 3 or 4, 1 to 8 cm long, the rachis very narrowly margined; spikelets 2 mm long; first glume obsolete or wanting; second glume about three-fourths the length of the spikelet; sterile lemma as long as the spikelet, this and the glume densely pubescent, the hairs, some as much as 1 mm long, exceeding the spikelet as a brushlike tip, fruit dark brown.

Savannas and open rocky slopes, West Indies and Central America.

CUBA: Santa Cruz de los Pinos, *Ekman* 17687. Pinar de Cajálbana, *Ekman* 17309. Herradura, *Tracy* 9104. Habana, *Léon* 4785. Guanabacoa, *Léon* 4715; *Hitchcock* 23232. San Miguel de los Baños, *Léon* 8874, 8875. Manacas, *Léon* 5843. Motembo mines, *Léon* 8629. Zaza de Tunas, *Léon* 898. Sancti Spíritus, *Léon* 2790. Santiago de Cuba, *Ekman* 7700.

HAITI: Pétionville, *Ekman* H 1351. Hinche, *Ekman* H 6176.

DOMINICAN REPUBLIC: Constanza, *Ekman* H 13903.

PUERTO RICO: Mayaguez, *Chase* 6271, 6277. Maricao, *Chase* 6221.

12. Digitaria pinetorum Hitchc., sp. nov.[48]

Perennial; culms slender, cespitose, sometimes loosely so, erect, 30 to 80 cm tall; sheaths glabrous or the lower pubescent; ligule a membrane 0.5 mm long; blades slender, flat or involute, mostly less than 2 mm wide, minutely pubescent or glabrate; racemes long-exserted, usually 1 or 2, sometimes 3, 4 to 10 cm long, sometimes as much as 20 cm, the rachis about 0.3 mm wide, with a very narrow margin, the spikelets in pairs or threes, the longer pedicels 2 mm long; spikelets lanceolate-elliptic, 2 to 2.2 mm long, densely appressed-pubescent between the nerves, the brownish hairs extending a little beyond the spikelet as a brushlike tip; first glume wanting; second glume slightly shorter than the spikelet, 3-nerved; sterile lemma as long as the spikelet, 5-nerved; fruit dark brown at maturity.

Type in the United States National Herbarium, no. 1387398, collected in pinelands, Los Indios, towards La Siguanéa, Isla de Pinos, November 10, 1920, by E. L. Ekman (no. 12175).

Pinelands, Cuba.

CUBA: Herradura, *Hitchcock* 483, 484; *Tracy* 9077. Isla de Pinos, *Ekman* 12175; *Britton and Wilson* 15361, 15368.

13. Digitaria ekmanii Hitchc., sp. nov.[49]

Perennial; culms decumbent and rooting at base, glabrous, rather stout, 50 to 100 cm tall; sheaths compressed-keeled, glabrous or the lower papillose-hispid toward the base; ligule membranaceous, rather prominent, about 3 mm long; blades flat, finely pubescent, 5 to 15 cm long, 2 to 4 mm wide; racemes 7 to 10, on an axis 2 to 3 cm long, erect or ascending, 7 to 12 cm long, the rachis triangular, scabrous, somewhat flexuous, 0.3 mm wide, the margins much narrower than the midrib; spikelets narrowly lanceolate, acute, glabrous

[48] Perennis; culmi graciles erecti 30–80 cm alti; laminae graciles, planae vel involutae 0.5–2 mm latae; racemi 1–2 (–3), 4–10 (–20) cm longi, rachi 0.3 mm lata margine angustissimo; spiculae lanceolato-ellipticae 2–2.2 mm longae dense pubescentes; fructus brunneus.

[49] Perennis; culmi decumbentes 50–100 cm longi; vaginae glabrae vel inferiores nonnihil papilloso-hispidae; laminae planae tenuiter pubescentes 5–15 cm longae 2–4 mm latae; racemi 7–10 erecti vel ascendentes 7–12 cm longi, rachi 0.3 mm lata margine angustissimo; spiculae anguste lanceolatae acutae, glabrae 2.5 mm longae; gluma prima nulla; gluma secunda spiculam equans; fructus pallidus.

or nearly so, about 2.5 mm long, in pairs, the longer pedicel 2 to 3 mm long; first glume obsolete or wanting; second glume as long as the spikelet, obtusish, 3-nerved; sterile lemma as long as the spikelet, acute, 5-nerved; fertile lemma as long as the spikelet, pale, acute.

Type in the United States National Herbarium, no. 1161280, collected in wet places in pinelands, Herradura, prov. Pinar del Río, Cuba, June 26, 1922, by E. L. Ekman.

This species has been referred to [50] *Syntherisma simpsoni* (Vasey) Nash, of Florida, which differs in having spikelets 3 mm long, the second glume and sterile lemma 7-nerved.

The type specimen has glabrous spikelets. In the other two specimens cited the spikelets are minutely pubescent along the nerves.

CUBA: Herradura, *Ekman* in 1922. Damují (Pinar del Río), *Ekman* 10938. Isla de Pinos, *Curtiss* 521.

72. STENOTAPHRUM Trin., Fund. Agrost. 175. 1820

Spikelets embedded in one side of an enlarged and flattened corky rachis disarticulating at maturity, the spikelets remaining attached; first glume small; second glume and sterile lemma about equal, the latter with a palea or staminate flower; fertile lemma chartaceous. Stoloniferous perennials with short flowering culms, rather broad short obtuse blades, and flat terminal and axillary racemes.

1. **Stenotaphrum secundatum** (Walt.) Kuntze, Rev. Gen. Pl. 2: 794. 1891. ST. AUGUSTINE GRASS.

Ischaemum secundatum Walt., Fl. Carol. 249. 1788. South Carolina.

Rottboellia stolonifera Poir., in Lam., Encycl. 6: 310. 1804. Puerto Rico.

Stenotaphrum americanum Schrank, Pl. Rar. Hort. Monac. pl. 98. 1820. Described from a cultivated plant.

Stenotaphrum glabrum var. *americanum* Doell, in Mart., Fl. Bras. 2^2: 300. 1877.

Stenotaphrum dimidiatum var. *americanum* Hack., in Stuck., An. Mus. Nac. Buenos Aires 21: 57. 1911.

Extensively creeping, the flat stolons with long internodes and short leafy branches, the sheaths equitant; flowering culms 10 to 30 cm tall, the blades commonly 10 to 15 cm long; racemes 5 to 10 cm long; spikelets 4 to 6 mm long (fig. 113).

Open grassland, at low altitudes, especially near the coast, southern United States to Argentina. An excellent pasture grass. Used for lawns in loamy or mucky soils. In Cuba called "camalote", "cambute", "gramon de costa", and "cañamazo amargo." Bermuda Islands and Bahamas to Trinidad and Tobago; to be found on probably all the West Indian islands.

73. THRASYA H.B.K., Nov. Gen. et Sp. 1: 120. pl. 39. 1815

Inflorescence a single terminal spikelike raceme, the rachis usually with membranaceous wings, partially embracing the row of spikelets; spikelets apparently subsessile and solitary in a single row, but actually in pairs, the spikelets of each pair back to back, the pedicel

[50] Contrib. U. S. Natl. Herb. 12: 210. 1909; 18: 294. 1917.

of the primary spikelet adnate to the midnerve of the rachis; first glume minute, often hyaline; second glume shorter than the spikelet; sterile lemma subindurate, thinner down the middle, at maturity splitting to the base (the margins of the split rolling inward), or deeply sulcate only, the sterile palea nearly as long as its lemma, the margins firm, enclosing a staminate flower or empty; fruit cartilaginous-indurate, commonly with stiff hairs at the summit. Slender branching perennials, with narrow blades.

Rachis ciliate with stiff hairs; blades pilose, at least on the margin.
1. T. PASPALOIDES.
Rachis not ciliate; blades glabrous or nearly so----------2. T. ROBUSTA.

1. Thrasya paspaloides H. B. K., Nov. Gen. et Sp. 1: 121. pl. 39. 1815. Venezuela.

Panicum thrasya Trin., Mém. Acad. St. Pétersb. VI. Sci. Nat. 1: 228. 1834. Based on *Thrasya paspaloides* H. B. K.

Thrasya trinitensis Mez, Repert. Sp. Nov. Fedde 15: 125. 1918. Trinidad, *Broadway* 5294.

Perennial; culms erect, slender, densely tufted, 25 to 50 cm tall,

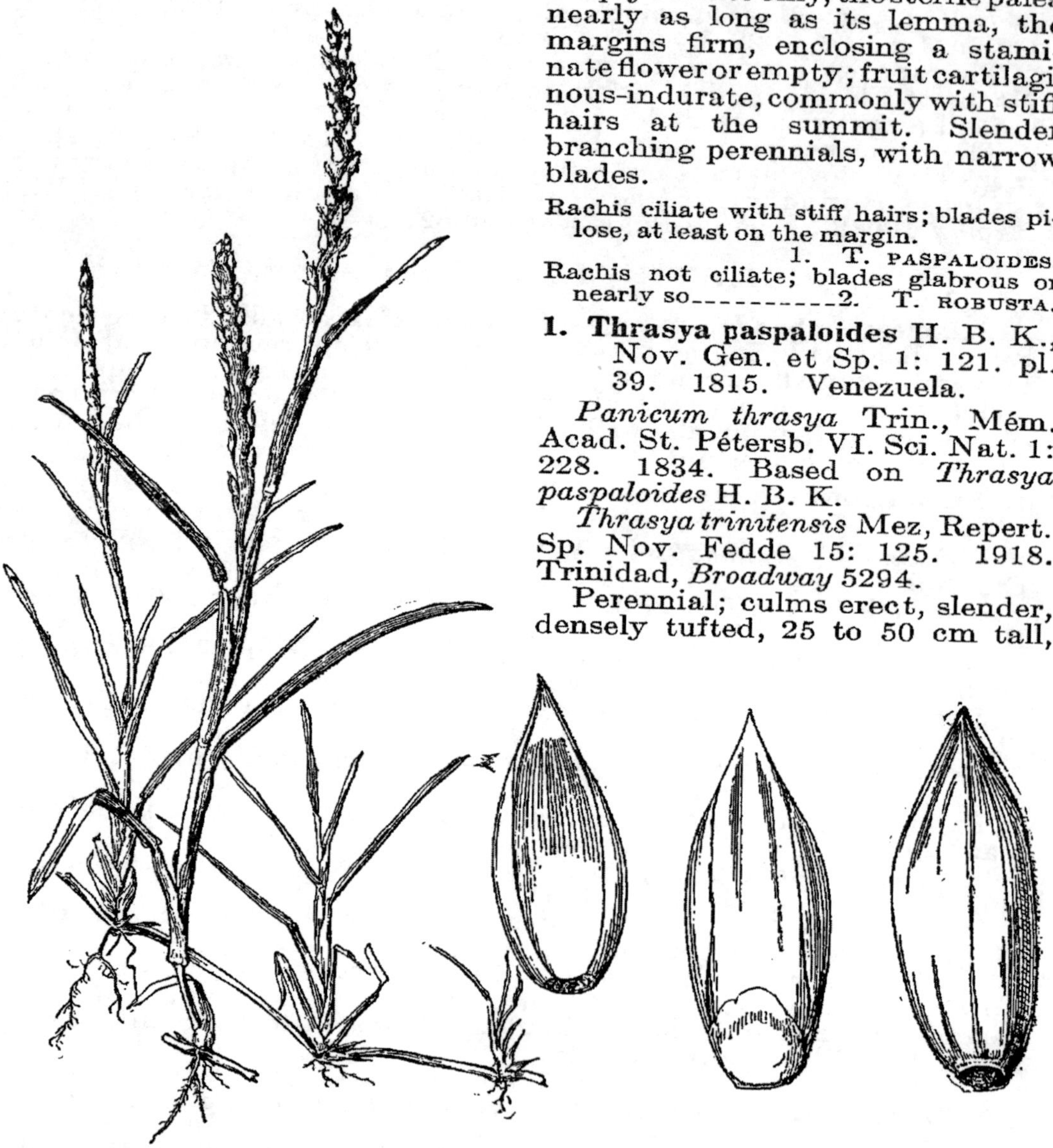

FIGURE 113.—*Stenotaphrum secundatum*. Plant, × ½; two views of spikelet, and fertile floret, × 10 (Tracy 1408).

at length branching from the upper nodes; blades flat, narrow, pilose at least on the margin; racemes arcuate, long-exserted, 3 to 5 cm long, the rachis ciliate with stiff hairs; spikelets stiffly ciliate, about 3 mm long (fig. 114).

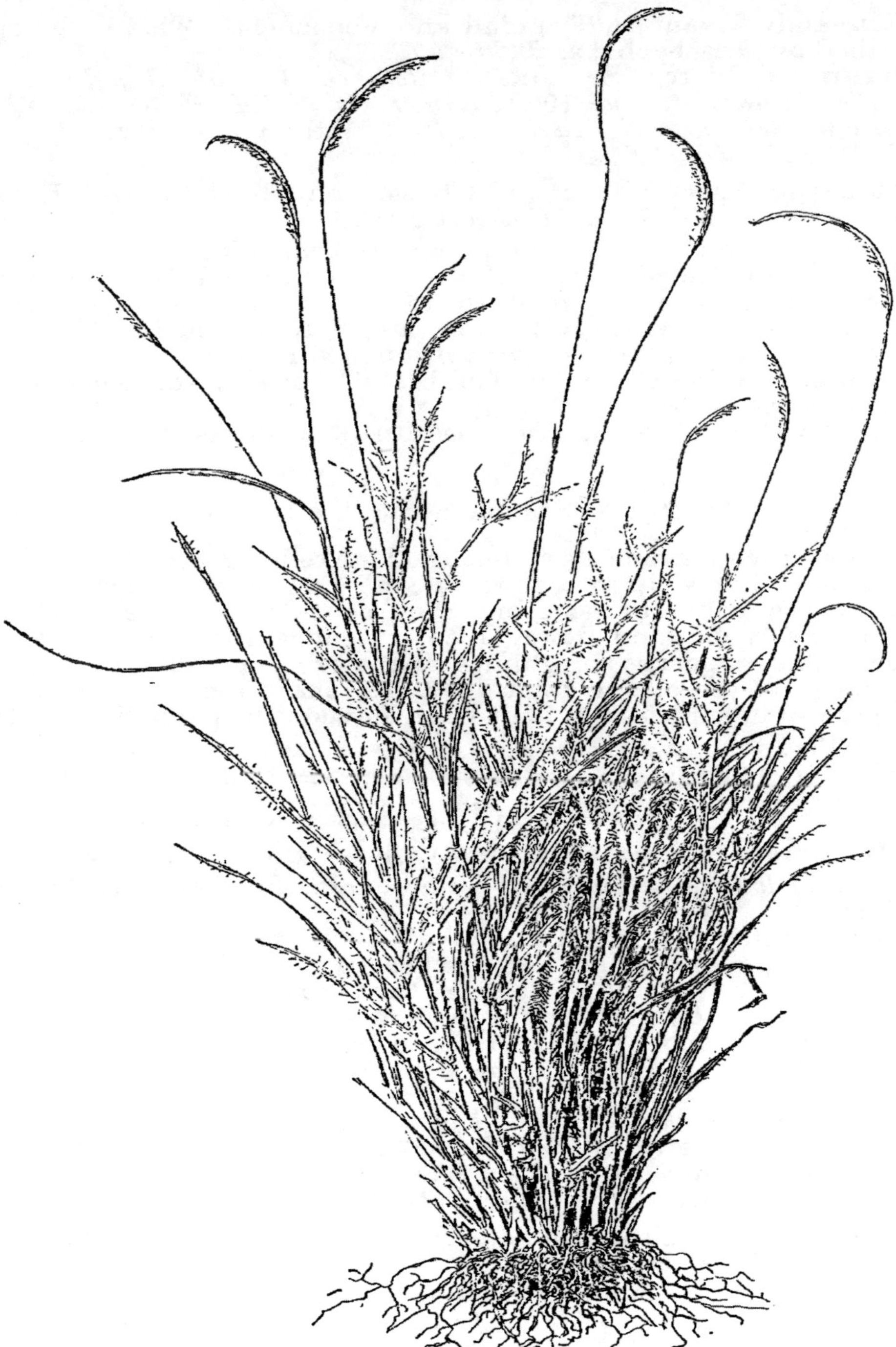

FIGURE 114.—*Thrasya paspaloides*, × ½ (Hitchcock 10335, Amer. Gr. Nat. Herb. 557).

Wet sandy savannas, Trinidad and Venezuela. This is the species described by Grisebach [51] as *T. hirsuta.*

TRINIDAD: Piarco Savanna, *Hitchcock* 10335; *Broadway* 5294. Aripo Savanna, *Hitchcock* 10081 (*Amer. Gr. Nat. Herb.* 557). O'Meara Savanna, *Britton and Hazen* 1576. Without locality, *Bot. Gard. Herb.* 3373; *Crueger* 43.

2. Thrasya robusta Hitchc. and Chase, Contrib. U. S. Natl. Herb. 18: 297. 1917. Trinidad, *Hitchcock* 10187.

Perennial; culms erect, rather stout, branching, 1 to 1.5 m tall; blades flat or folded, firm, ciliate, crisp puberulent on the upper surface, 15 to 30 cm long, 4 to 15 mm wide, the upper reduced; racemes 1 (or occasionally 2), arcuate, 8 to 14 cm long, the rachis 2 to 3 mm wide; spikelets 3.2 mm long, villous.

Savannas, Trinidad and Colombia ("Pipiral", southeast of Quetame, *Pennell* 1719).

TRINIDAD: St. Joseph, *Hitchcock* 10187. Piarco Savanna, *Hitchcock* 10352.

74. MESOSETUM Steud., Syn. Pl. Glum. 1: 118. 1854

Inflorescence a single erect terminal spikelike raceme, the spikelets subsessile, solitary, in two rows on one side of a slender rachis, the back of the fruit turned from the rachis, ventricose on the side toward the rachis and fitting into its concavities, the back of the spikelet flat or nearly so; glumes and sterile lemma usually bearing stiff hairs on the strong lateral nerves, the midnerve of the sterile lemma faint or suppressed; fruit ventricose on the palea side. Slender perennials.

Racemes 6 to 12 cm long; second glume (outer one) three-fourths as long as the spikelet .... 1. M. LOLIIFORME.
Racemes 3 to 4 cm long; second glume exceeding the spikelet .. 2. M. WRIGHTII.

1. Mesosetum loliiforme (Hochst.) Chase, Bot. Gaz. 51: 302. 1911.

Panicum loliiforme Hochst.; Steud., Syn. Pl. Glum. 1: 56. 1854. Surinam.

Culms tufted, erect, 15 to 60 cm tall, with long leafy stolons; blades flat, papillose-pilose, the lower 10 to 15 cm long, 1 to 4 mm wide, those of the stolons lanceolate, 2 to 3 cm long; spikes pale, long-exserted, 3 to 15 cm long: spikelets whitish, 4 mm long (fig. 115).

Sandy pine woods, Cuba, Trinidad, and south to Brazil.

CUBA: Pinar del Río, *Hitchcock* 23256, 23267, 23280, 23307; *Léon* 3469. Mangas, *Ekman* in 1921. Herradura, *Ekman* 10690, 10724; *Tracy* 9058: *Hitchcock* 485. Matatosa, *Wright* 3449. Manacas, *Léon* 5867. Baraguá, *Hitchcock* 23374. Isla de Pinos, *Britton and Wilson* 15353; *Palmer and Riley* 889, 986; *Curtiss* 396; *Taylor* 31.

TRINIDAD: Piarco Savanna, *Hitchcock* 10336.

2. Mesosetum wrightii Hitchc., Contrib. U. S. Natl. Herb. 12: 211. 1909. Cuba, *Wright* 3859.

Culms usually decumbent at base, tufted or ascending from the long leafy stolons, 10 to 20 cm tall; blades flat, sparsely hispidulous, 2 to 5 cm long, 1 to 2 mm wide, those of the stolons a little wider;

[51] Fl. Brit. W. Ind. 540. 1864.

FIGURE 115.—*Mesosetum loliiforme*, × ½ (Hitchcock 485).

spikes mostly 2 to 3 cm long; spikelets 4 mm long, greenish, less hirsute than the preceding.

Sandy pine woods, Cuba.

CUBA: Salado, *Ekman* 11552. La Caloma, *Ekman* in 1923 (*Amer. Gr. Nat. Herb.* 990). Dayaniguas, *Wright* 3859. Hatüey, *Léon* 9211. Placetas del Sur, *Léon* 6430. Camagüey, *Ekman* 15551.

75. ERIOCHLOA H. B. K., Nov. Gen. et Sp. 1: 94. 1815
CUPGRASS

Spikelets dorsally compressed, more or less pubescent, solitary or sometimes in pairs, short-pedicellate or subsessile, in two rows on one side of a narrow, usually hairy rachis, the pedicels often clothed with long, stiff hairs, the back of the fertile lemma turned from the rachis; lower rachilla joint thickened, forming a more or less ringlike, usually dark-colored callus below the second glume, the first glume reduced to a minute sheath about this and adnate to it; second glume and sterile lemma about equal, acute or acuminate; fertile lemma indurate, minutely papillose-rugose, mucronate or awned, the awn often readily deciduous, the margins slightly inrolled. Annuals or perennials with terminal panicles consisting of several or many spreading or appressed racemes, usually rather closely arranged along the main axis.

Blades filiform .... 1. E. SETOSA.
Blades flat, 2 to 15 mm wide.
  First glume present; plant long-decumbent or stoloniferous. .... 5. E. POLYSTACHYA.
  First glume obsolete; plants erect or decumbent at base.
    Plants annual .... 3. E. BOXIANA.
    Plants perennial.
      Fertile lemma mucronate or with an awn as much as 0.2 mm long; racemes 2 to 6; culms 15 to 60 cm tall .... 2. E. EKMANII.
      Fertile lemma with an awn about 1 mm long; racemes several to many; culms usually 1 m or more tall .... 4. E. PUNCTATA.

1. Eriochloa setosa (A. Rich.) Hitchc.

Piptatherum setosum A. Rich., in Sagra, Hist. Cuba 11: 311. 1850. Cuba. The type, bearing the name in Richard's script, was examined in the Paris Herbarium in 1935 and proves to be the same as *Eriochloa filifolia*. Richard's description is misleading in some respects, and the species was referred by Grisebach,[52] on the description, to his *Andropogon setosus*, which is the basis of *Sorghastrum setosum* (Griseb.) Hitchc. Grisebach, however, gives a description of his own and, though using the same specific epithet, does not base his species on that of Richard.

Eriochloa filifolia Hitchc., Contrib. U. S. Natl. Herb. 12: 207. 1909. Guanabacoa, Cuba, *Hitchcock* in 1906.

Perennial; culms tufted, slender, 15 to 40 cm tall; blades filiform, 5 to 15 cm long, the uppermost reduced; inflorescence long-exserted; racemes usually 2 to 4, 1 to 2 cm long, the rachis slender; spikelets mostly 5 to 8, rather loosely arranged on pedicels as much as 1 mm long, lanceolate, about 3.5 mm long, appressed-villous, the second glume and sterile lemma acuminate or somewhat awn-tipped; fertile lemma about 2 mm long, tipped with a slender awn about 1 mm long.

Sterile hills, Cuba.

CUBA: Guanabacoa, *Hitchcock* in 1906, 23223; *Léon* 851, 2687, 5607, 9127 (*Amer. Gr. Nat. Herb.* 991); *Wilson and Léon* 11642;

[52] Cat. Pl. Cub. 235. 1866.

Ekman 573, 1279. 10904. Batabanó, *Léon* 13709. San Miguel de los Baños, *Léon* 8856. Sabana de Motembo, *Léon* 9380, 11346.

2. Eriochloa ekmanii Hitchc., sp. nov.[53]

Perennial; culms slender, tufted, decumbent at base, branching, 15 to 60 cm tall, the nodes puberulent; sheaths puberulent, especially at the margins and around the throat and collar; ligule a row of stiff hairs 0.5 to 1 mm long; blades flat or somewhat involute, more or less puberulent, 3 to 15 cm long, 1 to 3 mm wide; panicle contracted, 3 to 8 cm long, the axis slender, scabrous and somewhat puberulent; racemes mostly 2 to 6, appressed or ascending, 1 to 3 cm long, rather distant on the axis, the rachis slender, scaberulous; spikelets mostly solitary, sometimes in pairs, rather loosely arranged, 2.5 to 3 mm long, 0.8 to 1 mm wide, the pedicels 0.3 to 0.5 mm long, often bearing 1 or 2 stiff hairs; second glume and sterile lemma equal, rather sparsely appressed-pilose, acuminate or awn-tipped; fertile lemma 1.8 to 2 mm long, apiculate or with an awn as much as 0.2 mm long.

Type in the U. S. National Herbarium, no. 1385555, collected in savannas near Mir, prov. Oriente, Cuba, August 22, 1916, by Dr. E. L. Ekman (no. 7509).

The species differs from *E. setosa* in the flat blades and the apiculate or short-awned fertile lemma. In the Grasses of the West Indies[54] it was referred to *Eriochloa ramosa* (Retz.) Kuntze, which differs in the stouter and taller culms, broader blades, larger panicles, paired spikelets, and in the usually naked base of the racemes.

CUBA: Tiffin (prov. Camagüey), *Ekman* 15391. Adelaida, *Léon* 15804. Zaza de Tunas (prov. Santa Clara), *Léon* 852. Mir, *Ekman* 7509. Without locality, *Wright* 3886.

3. Eriochloa boxiana Hitchc., in Swallen, Carneg. Inst. Wash. Publ. 436: 339. 1934. Antigua, *Box* 43.

Annual; culms branching, decumbent and spreading at base, rooting at the lower nodes, 30 to 40 cm tall, glabrous, minutely puberulent at the nodes; blades flat, ascending, glabrous beneath, puberulent on the upper surface, 5 to 12 cm long, 2 to 3 mm wide, the apex long-acuminate; panicle contracted, 7 to 11 cm long, the racemes numerous; racemes appressed or ascending, overlapping, 1.5 to 2 cm long; spikelets in pairs, imbricate; lanceolate-acuminate, 4.5 to 5 mm long, including the awn-tip, appressed pilose on the lower two-thirds, the tip minutely scaberulous, the pedicels about 0.5 mm long, bearing a few slender hairs; basal ring not prominent, pale, the first glume wanting; second glume extending into an awn nearly 1 mm long; sterile lemma smaller and a little shorter than the glume, acuminate-tipped rather than awned; fertile lemma elliptic-oblong, tipped with an awn 0.5 mm long (fig. 116).

Damp or swampy open land, Antigua, Yucatan, and Colombia. The species is named for Harold E. Box, entomologist at the Antigua

[53] Perennis; culmi tenues caespitosi erecti, basi decumbentes glabri 20–60 cm alti; nodis puberulis; vaginae puberulae, collo pubescente; laminae planae 5–15 cm longae 1–3 mm latae puberulae acuminatae; panicula contracta 3–8 cm longa, axi scabro tenue; racemi 2–6 appressi 1–3 cm longi, a basi floriferi, rachi scabra; spiculae plerumque solitariae 2.5–3 mm longae 0.8–1 mm latae, pedicellis 0.3–0.5 mm longis; gluma secunda mucronata, arista usque ad 0.2 mm longa; lemma fertile 1.8–2 mm longum, arista usque ad 0.2 mm longa.

[54] Contrib. U. S. Natl. Herb. 18: 298. 1917.

Sugar Factory, who has submitted a fine collection of the grasses of Antigua. Mr. Box states that the species is frequent in one locality.

LEEWARD ISLANDS: Antigua, Parrys bridge, *Box* 43.

4. Eriochloa punctata (L.) Desv.; Hamilt., Prodr. Pl. Ind. Occ. 5. 1825.

Milium punctatum L., Syst. Nat. ed. 10. 2: 872. 1759. Jamaica.

Agrostis punctata Lam., Encycl. 1: 58. 1783.

Oedipachne punctata Link, Hort. Berol. 1: 51. 1827.

Helopus punctatus Nees, Agrost. Bras. 16. 1829.

Monachne punctata Nash, Bull. Torrey Bot. Club 30: 374. 1903.

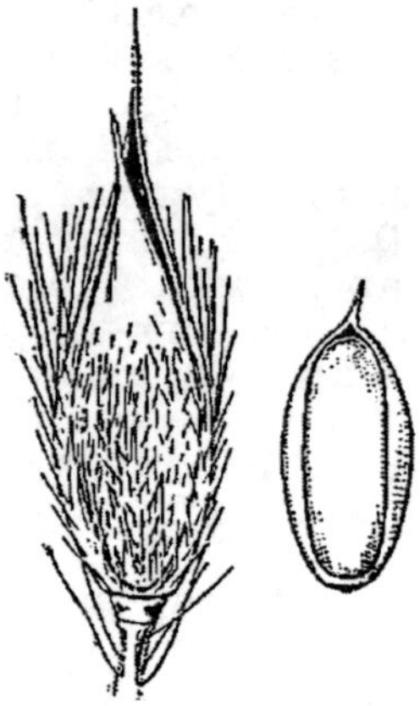

FIGURE 116.—*Eriochloa boxiana*. Spikelet and floret, × 10 (type).

FIGURE 117.—*Eriochloa punctata*. Panicle, × 1; floret, × 10 (Hitchcock 9661).

Glabrous branching perennial; culms ascending from a decumbent base, commonly 1 m or more tall; blades flat, 10 to 15 mm wide; racemes, several to many, narrowly ascending, the axis pubescent and villous; spikelets lanceolate, acute, about 4 mm long, appressed-pubescent on the lower half; fruit about 2 mm long, the awn hispidulous, about 1 mm long (fig. 117).

Swamps, ditches, and wet places, southern United States to Argentina.

CUBA: Habana, *Léon* 850, 2686, 3448, 4315. Coliseo, *Léon* 8828. Yumurí Mountains, *Rugel* 889. Eastern Cuba, *Wright* 1542. Isla de Pinos, *Ekman* 12037.

JAMAICA: Montego Bay, *Hitchcock* 9679. Appleton, *Hitchcock* 9661 (*Amer. Gr. Nat. Herb.* 300). Windsor, *Maxon and Killip* 269.

HAITI: Fond-des-Negres, *Ekman* H 7161. Aux Cayes, *Ekman* H 759. Gourjon, *Ekman* H 6454. Miragoane, *Ekman* H 7232.

DOMINICAN REPUBLIC: Santiago, *Ekman* H 16528. Sánchez, *Ekman* H 14791. Matanzos, *Ekman* H 15900.

PUERTO RICO: Vega Baja, *Britton and Cowell* 1451. San Juan, *Chase* 6380; *Hioram* 361. Sierra de Luquillo, *Chase* 6712. Ponce, *Heller* 6298. Mayaguez, *Chase* 6251; *Hess* 122. Cayey, *Sintenis* 2386. Rio Piedras, *Britton and Matz* 7055. Adjuntas, *Chase* 6467, 6477; *Sintenis* 4253. Fajardo, *Sintenis* 1227b.

VIRGIN ISLANDS: St. Croix, *Ricksecker* 467. St. Thomas, *Eggers* in 1881. Tortola, *Fishlock* 107; *Britton and Shafer* 761.

LEEWARD ISLANDS: Antigua, *Hitchcock* 16387; *Box* 73; *Wullschlaegel* 607. Guadeloupe, *Duss* 2709. Dominica, *Jones* 36.

WINDWARD ISLANDS: Montserrat, *Shafer* 536. Martinique, *Duss* 540. Barbados, *Dash* 602. Grenada, *Broadway* 1530, 4617.

TRINIDAD: St. Joseph, *Hitchcock* 10031½, 10167. Cedros, *Hitchcock* 10141 (*Amer. Gr. Nat. Herb.* 301).

TOBAGO: *Hitchcock* 10250; *Broadway* 4603.

5. **Eriochloa polystachya** H. B. K., Nov. Gen. et Sp. 1: 95. pl. 31. 1815. Ecuador. MALOJILLA.

Monachne subglabra Nash, Bull. Torrey Bot. Club 30: 374. 1903. Puerto Rico, *Heller* 380.

Eriochloa punctata var. *subglabra* Urban, Symb. Antill. 4: 85. 1903.

Eriochloa subglabra Hitchc., Contrib. U. S. Natl. Herb. 12: 208. 1909.

A stoloniferous perennial with erect flowering culms 1 to 2 m tall, bearded nodes, flat spreading blades, and terminal panicles of several to many loosely ascending or spreading branches, the spikelets usually in pairs, first glume developed as a minute broad loose membrane.

Swamps, ditches, and moist ground, West Indies to Brazil and Ecuador. A good forage grass. In Puerto Rico this species is confused with Pará grass, which it resembles in habit, and the name "malojilla" is applied to both. The two species are not infrequently found growing together.

CUBA: Habana, *Ekman* 18298.

JAMAICA: Savanna-la-Mar, *Hitchcock* 9859.

PUERTO RICO: Dorado, *Britton and Brown* 6683. Condado, *Britton and Brown* 5769. Rio Piedras, *Stevenson* 2304; *Chase* 6360 (*Amer. Gr. Nat. Herb.* 302); *Johnston* 10. Mayaguez, *Holm* 56; *Chase* 6254, 6554; *Britton* 2366. Catano, *Britton* 8829. Lecheria, *Goll* 23. Pueblo Viejo, *Hioram* 134. Bayamon, *Hioram* 327; *Sintenis* 1228. Rio Canas, *Britton* 9336. Ponce, *Britton and Brown* 5513. Santurce, *Chase* 6350. Arecibo, *Chase* 6445. Vega Baja, *Chase* 6795. Sierra Luquillo, *Chase* 6714. Fajardo, *Chase* 6656; *Britton and Shafer* 1523. Utuado, *Chase* 6458.

LEEWARD ISLANDS: Guadeloupe, *Hitchcock* 16400.

TRINIDAD: Port-of-Spain, *Hitchcock* 9951, 9970, 10332. Aripo Savanna, *Hitchcock* 10071. St. Anns, *Broadway* 7784.

76. BRACHIARIA Griseb., in Ledeb., Fl. Ross. 4: 469. 1853.

Spikelets dorsally compressed, solitary, rarely in pairs, subsessile in two rows on one side of a 3-angled, sometimes narrowly winged rachis, the first glume turned toward the axis; second glume and sterile lemma about equal, 5- to 7-nerved, the lemma enclosing a hyaline palea and sometimes a staminate flower; fertile lemma indurate, usually papillose-rugose, the margins inrolled, the apex rarely mucronate or bearing a short awn. Annuals or perennials with linear blades and several spreading or appressed racemes along a common axis.

Spikelets 2 mm long, pubescent .... 2. B. ERUCAEFORMIS.
Spikelets 4 mm long, glabrous .... 1. B. EXTENSA.

1. **Brachiaria extensa** Chase, Contrib. U. S. Natl. Herb. 28: 240. 1929. Based on *Paspalum platyphyllum* Griseb.

Paspalum platyphyllum Griseb., Cat. Pl. Cub. 230. 1866. Not *P. platyphyllum* Schult. 1827. Cuba, *Wright* 3441.

Panicum platyphyllum Munro; Wright, An. Acad. Cien. Habana 8: 206. 1871.

Brachiaria platyphylla Nash., in Small, Fl. Southeast. U. S. 81. 1903.

Glabrous; culms ascending from a creeping base, rather freely branching; blades flat, 5 to 10 cm long, about 1 cm wide; inflorescence included at base of 1 to 4 rather distant finally spreading racemes with a flat rachis and sessile ovoid spikelets appearing to be in a single row (fig. 118).

Moist sandy soil, Louisiana, Texas, Cuba; also Argentina.

CUBA: Sumidero, *Shafer* 13850; *Shafer and Léon* 13637, 13724. Herradura, *Ekman* in 1922 (*Amer. Gr. Nat. Herb.* 710). San Diego de los Baños, *Léon* 4522, 4848. Sabinilla, *Wright* 3867. Jagüey Chico (prov. Santa Clara), *Ekman* 16999. Without locality, *Wright* 3441, 3853.

2. Brachiaria erucaeformis (J. E. Smith) Griseb., in Ledeb., Fl. Ross. 4: 469. 1833.

Panicum erucaeforme J. E. Smith, in Sibth., Fl. Graec. Prodr. 1: 40. 1806. Greece.

Panicum isachne Roth; Roem. and Schult., Syst. Veg. 2: 458. 1817. India.

Brachiaria isachne Stapf, in Prain, Fl. Trop. Afr. 9: 552. 1919.

Annual; culms decumbent-spreading, rooting at

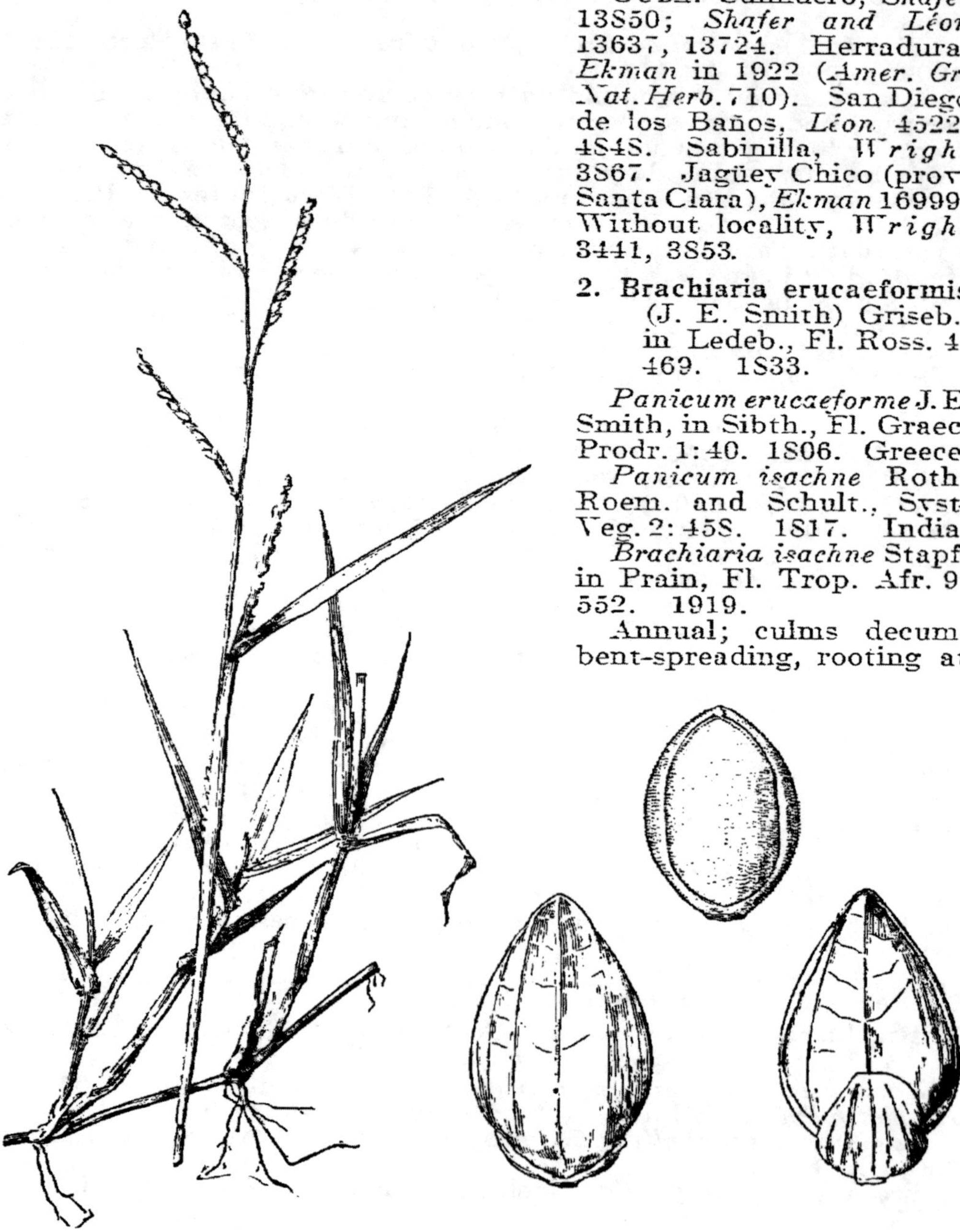

FIGURE 118.—*Brachiaria extensa*. Plant, × ½; two views of spikelet and floret, × 10 (Nealley).

the lower nodes, branching, the flowering branches 20 to 30 cm tall; blades flat, sparsely pilose, 4 to 6 cm long, 3 to 5 mm wide; panicle 5 to 8 cm long; racemes several, appressed or ascending, 5 to 20 mm long; spikelets pubescent, 2 mm long (fig. 119).

A weed in cultivated fields, Barbados; warmer parts of the Old World.

LEEWARD ISLANDS: Antigua, *Box* 9, 67.

WINDWARD ISLANDS: Barbados, *Bot. Sta. Herb.* 448; *Hitchcock* 16525 (*Amer. Gr. Nat. Herb.* 708).

77. AXONOPUS Beauv., Ess. Agrost. 12, 154. 1812

Spikelets depressed biconvex, not turgid, oblong, usually obtuse, solitary, sessile, and alternate, in two rows on one side of a 3-angled rachis, the back of the fertile lemma turned from the axis; first glume wanting; second glume and sterile lemma equal, the lemma without a palea; fertile lemma and palea indurate, the lemma oblong-elliptic, usually obtuse, the margins slightly inrolled. Stoloniferous or tufted perennials, rarely annuals, with usually flat or folded, abruptly rounded or somewhat pointed blades, and few or numerous, slender, spikelike racemes, digitate or racemose along the main axis.

FIGURE 119.—*Brachiaria erucaeformis*. Panicle, × 1; two views of spikelet, and floret, × 10 (cult.).

Rachis bearing conspicuous stiff spreading golden yellow hairs. (Sec. CABRERA.)
  Plants annual; rachis over 1 mm wide, extending beyond the spikelets ---- 1. A. APPENDICULATUS.
  Plants perennial; rachis slender, about 0.5 mm wide, not extending beyond the spikelets. 2. A. AUREUS.
Rachis not bearing stiff hairs. (AXONOPUS proper.)
  Plants annual, the delicate racemes 2 or 3. 3. A. CAPILLARIS.
  Plants perennial.
    Plants stoloniferous, the racemes 2 to 5.
      Spikelets about 2.5 mm long ---------------------- 4. A. COMPRESSUS.
      Spikelets 4 to 5 mm long ------------------------- 5. A. FURCATUS.
    Plants not stoloniferous.
      Racemes 100 or more, the axis elongate ----------------- 8. A. ANCEPS.
      Racemes 4 to several.
        Blades glabrous; racemes several; spikelets acute. 7. A. LEPTOSTACHYS.
        Blades, at least when young, ciliate and more or less villous; racemes few; spikelets obtuse ---------------------- 6. A. EQUITANS.

1. Axonopus appendiculatus (Presl) Hitchc. and Chase, Contrib. U. S. Natl. Herb. 18: 300. 1917.

Paspalum appendiculatum Presl, Rel. Haenk. 1: 211. 1830. Panama.

Slender sparingly branching annual with long smooth orange-colored internodes; blades flat, thin, yellowish green, sparsely hispid or glabrous; racemes 2 to 8, subdigitate, 3 to 6 cm long, the flat green rachis bearing a row of stiff golden hairs on each margin and down the center between the 2 rows of small glabrous spikelets sunken in the rachis.

Open grassy hillsides, Trinidad to Brazil. A strikingly beautiful species.

TRINIDAD: St. Joseph, *Hitchcock* 10173 (*Amer. Gr. Nat. Herb.* 559).

2. **Axonopus aureus** Beauv., Ess. Agrost. 12. 1812. Type locality not indicated.

Paspalum aureum H. B. K., Nov. Gen. et Sp. 1: 93. 1815.

Tall slender branching perennial; culms wiry, compressed; blades flat, rather firm, spreading; racemes 4 to 15, subdigitate, slender, golden brown, the stiff orange-yellow hairs in tufts below the spikelets as well as along the margins; spikelets about 1.3 mm long, glabrous or sparingly appressed-hispid.

Wet sandy savannas, Puerto Rico and northern South America. This species is described by Grisebach[55] under the name *Paspalum pulchrum*.

PUERTO RICO: San Juan, *Chase* 6764 (*Amer. Gr. Nat. Herb.* 560). Rio Piedras, *Stevenson* 3282.

TRINIDAD: Piarco Savanna, *Hitchcock* 10339. Without locality, *Crueger*.

3. **Axonopus capillaris** (Lam.) Chase, Biol. Soc. Wash. Proc. 24: 133. 1911.

Paspalum capillare Lam., Tabl. Encycl. 1: 176. 1791. Tropical America.

Anastrophus capillaris Nash, N. Amer. Fl. 17: 161. 1912.

Annual; culms slender, glabrous, ascending, branching, 10 to 30 cm tall; blades thin, 2.5 to 5 cm long, about 4 mm wide; racemes 2 or 3, delicate, about 2.5 cm long, on long subcapillary peduncles; spikelets glabrous, 1.3 mm long.

Forming patches on moist open ground, Central America to Trinidad and Brazil.

TRINIDAD: Pitch Lake, *Hitchcock* 10101 (*Amer. Gr. Nat. Herb.* 561).

4. **Axonopus compressus** (Swartz) Beauv., Ess. Agrost. 12. 1812. CARPET GRASS.

Milium compressum Swartz, Prodr. Veg. Ind. Occ. 24. 1788. Jamaica.

Paspalum platicaulon Poir., in Lam., Encycl. Sup. 5: 34. 1804. Puerto Rico.

Agrostis compressa Poir., in Lam., Encycl. Sup. 1: 259 [not 258]. 1810. Not *A. compressa* Willd., 1790.

Paspalum compressum Raspail, Ann. Sci. Nat. Bot. 5: 301. 1825.

Paspalum laticulmum Spreng., Syst. Veg. 1: 245. 1825. West Indies.

Digitaria platicaulis Desv., Opusc. 62. 1831.

Digitaria domingensis Desv.; Kunth, Enum. Pl. 1: 49. 1833, as synonym of *Paspalum platycaule* Poir.

Paspalum filostachyum A. Rich.; Steud., Syn. Pl. Glum. 1: 20. 1854. Antilles.

Anastrophus compressus Schlecht.; Doell, in Mart., Fl. Bras. 2^2: 102. 1877, as synonym of *Paspalum platicaulon*.

Anastrophus platycaulis Schlecht; Jacks., Ind. Kew. 1: 118. 1893.

Paspalum raunkiaerii Mez, Repert. Sp. Nov. Fedde 15: 60. 1917. St. Jan.

Nearly glabrous perennial, under favorable conditions producing long leafy stolons with short broad obtuse blades; flowering culms

[55] Fl. Brit. W. Ind. 543. 1864.

erect or ascending, compressed; blades rather thin, 8 to 10 mm wide; racemes 2 to 5, slender, along a short axis, 2 or 3 axillary peduncles often produced from the upper node; spikelets glabrous or nearly so, 2 to 3 mm long (fig. 120).

This species is exceedingly variable in habit; in dry ground it sometimes has blades not more than 2 or 3 mm wide.

Moist grassland, fields, partial shade, common at low altitudes, throughout the West Indies. Southern United States to Argentina; also in the warmer parts of the Old World.

An important pasture grass throughout the West Indies. Readily propagating by stolons, it tends to drive out other species, thus becoming dominant in lowland pastures. In Cuba this grass is called "cañamazo dulce", "cañamazo de sabana", and "cañamazo macho."

5. Axonopus furcatus (Flügge) Hitchc., Rhodora 8: 205. 1906.

Paspalum furcatum Flügge, Monogr. Pasp. 114. 1810. Carolina.

Anastrophus furcatus Nash, N. Amer. Fl. 17: 162. 1912.

Plants stoloniferous; culms in tufts, erect or decumbent at base, as much as 1 m tall; blades mostly 5 to 10 mm wide; glabrous, ciliate or even hirsute; racemes 2 at the summit of the culm, spreading, 5 to 10 cm long; spikelets 4 to 5 mm long, glabrous, acute, the midnerve of the glume evident (fig. 121).

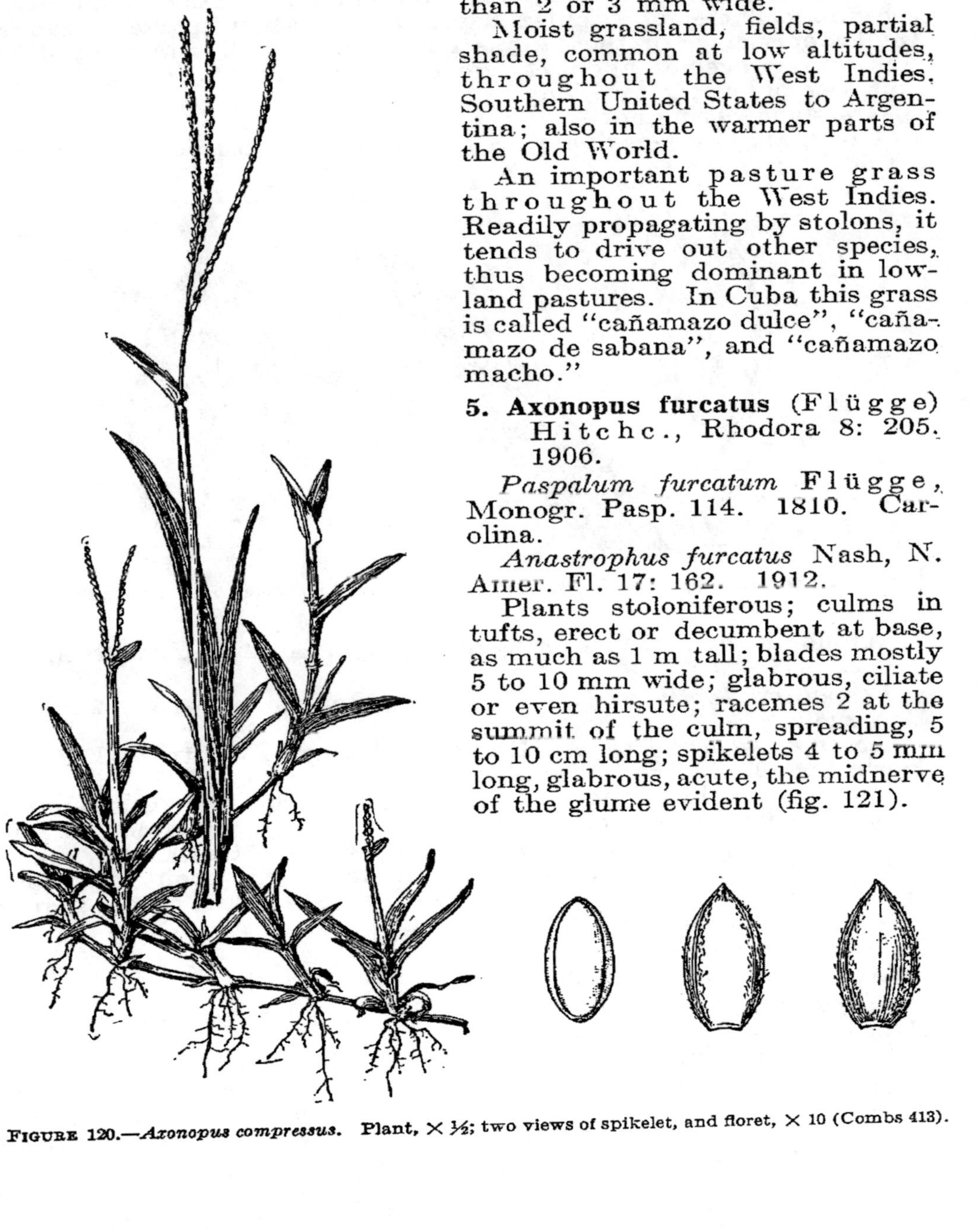

FIGURE 120.—*Axonopus compressus*. Plant, × ½; two views of spikelet, and floret, × 10 (Combs 413).

Marshes, river banks, and moist pine barrens, southern United States and Cuba.

CUBA: Habana, *Ekman* 16928.

6. **Axonopus equitans** Hitchc. and Chase, Contrib. U. S. Natl. Herb. 18: 301. 1917. Trinidad, *Hitchcock* 9988.

Perennial; culms erect, 40 to 60 cm tall; blades rather stiffly ascending, flat from a folded base, ciliate, rather sparsely villous on the lower surface or the cauline glabrate, 15 to 20 cm long, 4 to 10 mm wide; racemes about 4, erect or ascending, 7 to 15 cm long; spikelets oblong, 2 mm long.

Grassland, Trinidad.

TRINIDAD: Port-of-Spain, *Hitchcock* 9988. St. Joseph, *Hitchcock* 10193.

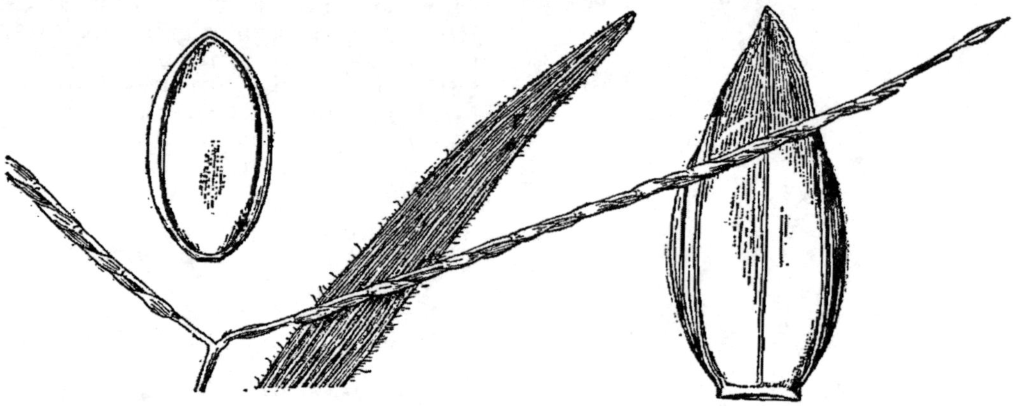

FIGURE 121.—*Axonopus furcatus*. Plant, × 1; spikelet and floret, × 10 (Combs 1205).

7. **Axonopus leptostachys** (Flügge) Hitchc., Contrib. U. S. Natl. Herb. 22: 471. 1922.

Paspalum leptostachyum Flügge, Monogr. Pasp. 123. 1810. Venezuela.

Axonopus macrostachyus Hitchc. and Chase, Contrib. U. S. Natl. Herb. 18: 301. 1917. Trinidad, *Hitchcock* 10093.

Perennial; culms erect, 1 to 1.5 m tall; sheaths keeled but not strongly compressed; blades flat, stiffly erect, glabrous, as much as 50 cm long, 4 to 7 mm wide; racemes about 12, slender, erect or stiffly ascending, 15 to 25 cm long, the main axis about 12 cm long; spikelets acute, 3 mm long, minutely silky at base and on the margins.

Low, open ground, Trinidad to Brazil.

TRINIDAD: Pitch Lake, *Hitchcock* 10093.

8. **Axonopus anceps** (Mez) Hitchc.

Paspalum anceps Mez, Repert. Sp. Nov. Fedde 15: 61. 1917. Brazil.

Perennial; culms flat, 1.5 m tall; sheaths broad, keeled, overlapping, hirsute, densely hairy on the collar; blades elongate, rather stiff, sparsely pilose; panicle 30 cm long; racemes numerous, laxly spreading, 6 to 12 cm long, densely woolly in the axils; spikelets plump, oval, 2 mm long, silky pubescent in lines.

In Grasses of the West Indies [56] this species was referred to *Axonopus pellitus* (Nees) Hitchc. and Chase. Nees' type of *Paspalum pellitum* and also Mez's of *P. anceps* have since been examined in the Berlin Herbarium.

Open grassland, Trinidad to Brazil.

TRINIDAD: Pitch Lake, *Hitchcock* 10094.

78. REIMAROCHLOA Hitchc., Contrib. U. S. Natl. Herb. 12: 198. 1909

Spikelets strongly dorsally compressed, lanceolate, acuminate, rather distant, subsessile, and alternate in two rows along one side of a narrow, flattened rachis, the back of the fertile lemma turned toward it; both glumes wanting, or the second sometimes present in the terminal spikelet; sterile lemma about equaling the fruit, the sterile palea obsolete; fertile lemma scarcely indurate, faintly nerved, acuminate, the margins inrolled at the base only, the palea free nearly half its length. Spreading or stoloniferous perennials, with flat blades and slender racemes, these subdigitate or racemose along the upper part of the culm, stiffly spreading or reflexed at maturity.

Spikelets 2 to 3 mm long, silky along the margin; racemes several. 1. R. BRASILIENSIS.

Spikelets about 5 mm long, glabrous; racemes 2 or 3 ---- 2. R. OLIGOSTACHYA.

1. Reimarochloa brasiliensis (Spreng.) Hitchc., Contrib. U. S. Natl. Herb. 12: 198. 1909.

Agrostis brasiliensis Spreng., Nov. Prov. Hal. 45. 1819. Brazil.

Reimaria brasiliensis Schlecht., Bot. Ztg. 10: 17. 1852.

Panicum oxyanthum Steud., Syn. Pl. Glum. 1: 41. 1854. Santo Domingo.

Culms tufted, branching, stoloniferous, the ascending flowering branches scarcely more than 10 cm tall; sheaths loose; blades flat, rather lax, mostly less than 10 cm long, pubescent or pilose; racemes delicate, digitate, about 10, finally spreading or reflexed, 2 to 3 cm long; spikelets about 3 mm long, acuminate, silky along the margin.

Wet ground around ponds, Cuba to Brazil.

CUBA: Hanábana, *Wright* 3437. Las Mangas, *Ekman* 13085. Habana, *Ekman* 757. Santiago de las Vegas, *Ekman* in 1923 (*Amer. Gr. Nat. Herb.* 992). San Francisco, *Ekman* 10976. Isla de Pinos, *Curtiss* 497.

DOMINICAN REPUBLIC: Higüey, *Ekman* H 12176. Santo Domingo, *Ekman* H 10994. Without locality, *Poiteau*.

2. Reimarochloa oligostachya (Munro) Hitchc., Contrib. U. S. Natl. Herb. 12: 199. 1909.

Reimaria oligostachya Munro; Benth., Jour. Linn. Soc. Bot. 19: 34. 1882. Florida.

Stouter than the preceding, the flat culms often elongate, decumbent with ascending ends; racemes 1 to 3, terminal and axillary, stiff, at maturity widely divergent or deflexed; spikelets glabrous, about 5 mm long (fig. 122).

Wet soil around ponds, Florida and Cuba.

CUBA: Hanábana, *Wright* 3854.

[56] Contrib. U. S. Natl. Herb. 18: 301. 1917.

60256—36——13

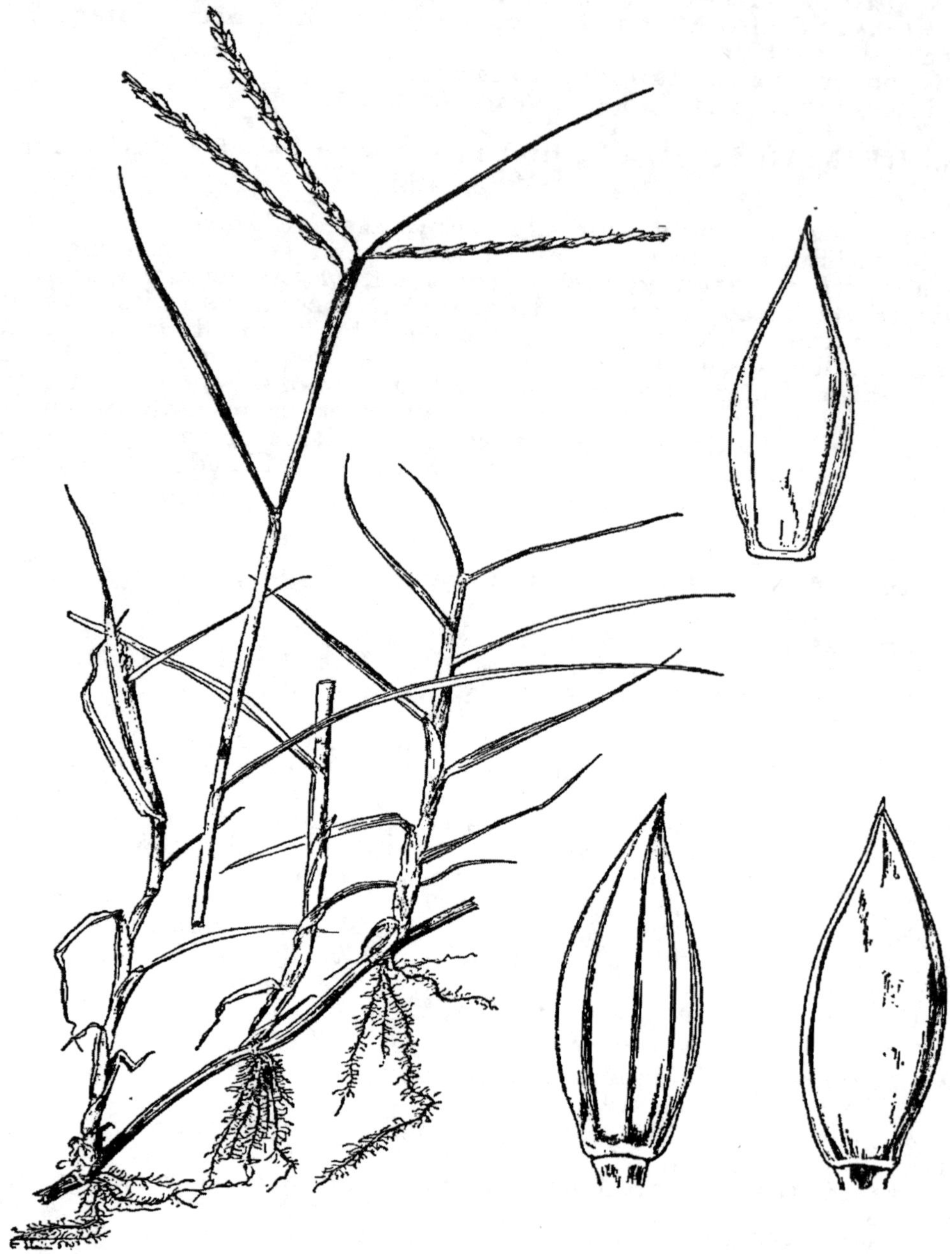

FIGURE 122.—*Reimarochloa oligostachya*. Plant, × 1; two views of spikelet, and floret, × 10 (Curtiss 3596A).

79. PASPALUM L., Syst. Nat. ed. 10. 2: 855. 1759

Spikelets plano-convex, usually obtuse, subsessile, solitary or in pairs, in two rows on one side of a narrow or dilated rachis, the back of the fertile lemma toward it; first glume usually wanting; second glume and sterile lemma commonly about equal, the former rarely wanting; fertile lemma usually obtuse, chartaceous-indurate, the margins inrolled. Annuals or perennials, with one to many spike-like racemes, these single or paired at the summit of the culms or racemosely arranged along the main axis.

Full synonymy and more complete descriptions are to be found in the North American Species of Paspalum.[57]

Rachis membranaceous or foliaceous, mostly broad and winged.
  Spikelets clothed with long silky hairs; rachis brightly colored. (Subgenus CERESIA.)
    Culms simple; racemes solitary or paired ---------- 1. P. STELLATUM.
    Culms branching; racemes not paired, 2 to 7 on the main culm, solitary on the branches ---------- 2. P. HETEROTRICHON.
  Spikelets glabrous (or minutely pubescent in *P. repens*); rachis green or dull.
    Plants perennial.
      Racemes persistent on the axis; rachis with a spikelet at the apex. Second glume developed.
        Spikelets 2 mm long, obovate-oval ---------- 3. P. DISSECTUM.
        Spikelets more than 3 mm long, pointed ---------- 4. P. SERRATUM.
      Racemes falling from the axis; rachis extending beyond the uppermost spikelet ---------- 5. P. REPENS.
    Plants annual ---------- 6. P. RACEMOSUM.
Rachis not membranaceous, foliaceous, nor winged. (Slightly winged in a few species but spikelets not silky.)
  Inflorescence a large flabellate panicle of numerous racemes. Spikelets solitary.
    Spikelets glabrous or minutely ciliate ---------- 59. P. FASCICULATUM.
    Spikelets obscured by their long silky hairs ---------- 75. P. SACCHAROIDES.
  Inflorescence not flabellate.
    Racemes 2, conjugate or nearly so at the summit of the culm, rarely a third below.
      Spikelets elliptic to narrowly ovate.
        Plants with creeping rhizomes or stolons.
          Second glume pubescent; spikelets relatively turgid - 9. P. DISTICHUM.
          Second glume and sterile lemma glabrous; spikelets flattened.
            Blades erect or ascending, involute-setaceous -- 8. P. DISTACHYON.
            Blades spreading, tapering from base to apex, the margins involute ---------- 7. P. VAGINATUM.
        Plants tufted, not rhizomatous or stoloniferous.
          Spikelets not transversely wrinkled ---------- 16. P. LINEARE.
          Spikelets transversely wrinkled ---------- 44. P. INSULARE.
      Spikelets suborbicular, broadly ovate, or obovate.
        Spikelets concavo-convex, sparsely long-silky around the margins; plant stoloniferous ---------- 56. P. CONJUGATUM.
        Spikelets plano-convex (rarely biconvex, not silky margined; plants not stoloniferous).
          Plants annual, small, slender; spikelets not more than 1.5 mm long.
            Spikelets orbicular, some of them beaded with globular hairs. 48. P. MULTICAULE.
            Spikelets obovate, glabrous or minutely pubescent. 49. P. CLAVULIFERUM.
          Plants perennial; spikelets 1.8 to 3 mm long, solitary.
            Spikelets golden brown, transversely marked with dark lines. 15. P. SERPENTINUM.
            Spikelets green, not marked.
              Rhizome stout, horizontal, forming tough sod.
                Spikelets 2.5 to 3 mm long ---------- 12. P. NOTATUM.
                Spikelets less than 2.5 mm long ---------- 13. P. MINUS.
              Rhizome none or short and vertical ---------- 14. P. PUMILUM.

[57] Contrib. U. S. Natl. Herb. 28: 1–310. 1929.

Racemes 1 to many, racemose or fascicled on the axis, not conjugate.
Second glume wanting ---------- 73. P. PULCHELLUM.
Second glume developed.
First glume developed on at least one of the pair of spikelets.
Plants with stout scaly rhizomes; spikelets glabrous. First glume often obsolete ---------- 24. P. UNISPICATUM.
Plants without rhizomes; culms more or less tufted.
Spikelets not more than 2 mm long.
Plants decumbent, creeping.
First glume small, about equally developed on all spikelets 20. P. DECUMBENS.
First glume obsolete or only occasionally developed. 21. P. NUTANS.
Plants erect or ascending, not creeping. First glume of secondary spikelet elongate ---------- 22. P. DISPAR.
Spikelets more than 2 mm long. Plants not decumbent.
Spikelets glabrous ---------- 23. P. PILOSUM.
Spikelets sparsely pubescent ---------- 25. P. LANGEI.
First glume normally wanting.
Racemes terminal and axillary, the axillary sometimes hidden in the sheaths; terminal inflorescence of 1 to 3, rarely 6, racemes.
Plants rooting at the lower nodes ---------- 21. P. NUTANS.
Plants erect to widely spreading but not rooting at the nodes.
Blades densely grayish-villous, not ciliate ----- 17. P. DEBILE.
Blades ciliate, not villous.
Spikelets about 2 mm long, not pointed - 18. P. CILIATIFOLIUM.
Spikelets about 1.8 mm long, slightly pointed. 19. P. PROPINQUUM.
Racemes terminal on the primary culm or leafy branches, no truly axillary racemes.
Plants annual.
Spikelets with a broad firm notched margin - 74. P. FIMBRIATUM.
Spikelets not margined.
Spikelets not more than 1.5 mm long, elliptic; fruit pale. Plants annual.
Spikelets solitary.
Spikelets orbicular, usually beaded with globular hairs. 48. P. MULTICAULE.
Spikelets elliptic, not beaded ----- 50. P. PARVIFLORUM.
Spikelets in pairs ---------- 49. P. CLAVULIFERUM.
Spikelets 2 to 3 mm long; fruit dark brown.
Spikelets 2.4 to 3 mm long, commonly appressed-pubescent. 70. P. CONVEXUM.
Spikelets not more than 2.2 mm long, glabrous.
Rachis scarcely 1 mm wide ---- 71. P. MELANOSPERMUM.
Rachis 2 to 2.5 mm wide ---------- 72. P. BOSCIANUM.
Plants perennial.
Racemes solitary, subcylindric; spikelets solitary (sometimes paired in *P. saugetii*).
Plants stoloniferous. Culms rarely more than 10 cm tall.
Glume and sterile lemma not beaked nor wrinkled. 51. P. BREVE.
Glume and sterile lemma beaked beyond the fruit, deeply wrinkled ---------- 52. P. EDMONDI.
Plants not stoloniferous.
Sterile lemma wrinkled or crumpled.
Foliage conspicuously pubescent; blades flat or subinvolute.
Raceme cylindric; rachis straight ------ 43. P. NANUM.
Raceme rather flat, scarcely cylindric; rachis flexuous. 44. P. INSULARE.
Foliage glabrous or nearly so; blades concavo-convex in cross section.
Glume and sterile lemma scarcely crumpled. 40. P. FILIFORME

Glume and sterile lemma inflated and crumpled.
Spikelets 2 mm long; glume and sterile lemma not pointed beyond the fruit--41. P. DISTORTUM.
Spikelets 2.7 to 3 mm long; glume and sterile lemma pointed beyond the fruit-42. P. LINDENIANUM.
Sterile lemma not wrinkled nor crumpled.
Spikelets 3 to 3.3 mm long.
Spikelets glabrous, in pairs--------37. P. ROCANUM.
Spikelets pubescent, solitary.
Blades elongate, glabrous--38. P. ALTERNIFLORUM.
Blades less than 20 cm long, conspicuously pilose. 39. P. ROTTBOELLIOIDES.
Spikelets not more than 1.8 mm long.
Blades not more than 1 mm wide, concavo-convex or subterete in cross section.
Plants delicate; blades capillary, subterete. 47. P. CAPILLIFOLIUM.
Plants wiry; blades concavo-convex. 40. P. FILIFORME.
Blades or some of them 2 mm or more wide; flat or involute.
Spikelets elliptic, glabrous--------45. P. RUPESTRE.
Spikelets oval, pubescent----------46. P. SAUGETII.
Racemes 2 to many.
Glume and sterile lemma conspicuously crumpled. 42. P. LINDENIANUM.
Glume and sterile lemma not crumpled or but slightly so.
Plants creeping, rooting at the nodes.
Spikelets suborbicular------------53. P. ORBICULATUM.
Spikelets more or less elliptic.
Spikelets pubescent, blunt--------54. P. REPTATUM.
Spikelets glabrous, or obscurely pubescent at base only, subacute------------55. P. AMPHICARPUM.
Plants not creeping, sometimes rooting at 1 or 2 nodes of a decumbent base, if so, spikelets in pairs.
Spikelets conspicuously silky-ciliate around the margin, the hairs as long as the spikelet or longer.
Racemes commonly 3 to 5; culms geniculate at base. 57. P. DILATATUM.
Racemes commonly 12 to 18; culms erect. 58. P. URVILLEI.
Spikelets not conspicuously ciliate.
Fruit dark brown and shining; spikelets glabrous or minutely appressed-pubescent.
Spikelets obovate, turgid; sterile lemma wrinkled just within the margin-----66. P. PLICATULUM.
Spikelets elliptic, depressed, not turgid.
Plants subaquatic; rachis 1.5 to 2 mm wide. 67. P. WRIGHTII.
Plants terrestrial; rachis 1 mm wide.
Racemes not more than 5 cm long; foliage glabrous----------68. P. MOTEMBENSE.
Racemes 8 to 15 cm long; sheaths and blades hirsute at their junction. 69. P. URBANIANUM.
Fruit pale to stramineous (brown but not shining in *P. virgatum*).
Plants robust; culms commonly more than 1 m, often 2 m tall; spikelets normally in pairs.
Culms freely branching. Racemes 10 to 45; spikelets elliptic, glandular-pubescent. 65. P. CORYPHAEUM.

Culms simple or with a few simple branches.
  Blades firm, with sharp-cutting edges.
    Spikelets pubescent, at least toward the summit; blades flat, more or less arcuate-spreading............60. P. VIRGATUM.
    Spikelets glabrous; blades V-shaped in cross section, ascending.
      Spikelets suborbicular, crowded; rachis ciliate.
        Panicle not pyramidal, the racemes rarely more than 50; glume and sterile lemma rather firm in texture. 63. P. MILLEGRANA.
        Panicle elongate-pyramidal, the racemes commonly more than 70, short and crowded at the summit; glume and sterile lemma fragile. 64. P. DENSUM.
      Spikelets obovate-elliptic; rachis not ciliate.
        Racemes slender; spikelets not crowded; rachis 0.7 mm wide..61. P. SECANS.
        Racemes thick; spikelets somewhat crowded; rachis 1 mm wide. 62. P. ARUNDINACEUM.

Plants not robust; if more than 1 m tall, culms relatively slender.
  Spikelets 2 mm or more long.
    Spikelets about 3 mm long, pubescent.
      Blades 6 to 14 mm wide; spikelets oval. 10. P. PUBIFLORUM.
      Blades very narrow, involute; spikelets lanceolate....38. P. ALTERNIFLORUM.
    Spikelets 2 to 2.5 mm long, glabrous.
      Spikelets broadest in the middle.
        Racemes 2 to 4, the rachis greenish, 1.2 to 1.5 mm wide......37. P. ROCANUM.
        Racemes mostly 4 to 7, the rachis dark purple, 1.5 to 2 mm wide. 11. P. LIVIDUM.
      Spikelets broadest above the middle.
        Pedicels pubescent; spikelets 2.2 to 2.5 mm long....36. P. PLEOSTACHYUM.
        Pedicels glabrous or scaberulous; spikelets about 2 mm long.
          Spikelets subangular-obovate, 1.4 mm wide.....27. P. OLIGOSTACHYUM.
          Spikelets obovate-elliptic, 1.1 mm wide. 34. P. BAKERI.
  Spikelets less than 2 mm long.
    Spikelets glabrous, 1.6 to 1.9 mm long, oval. 26. P. NESIOTES.
    Spikelets more or less pubescent.
      Spikelets subhemispheric, 1.3 to 1.4 mm long, pubescent..28. P. PANICULATUM.
      Spikelets elliptic or oval.
        Racemes usually solitary, sometimes 2. 46. P. SAUGETII.
        Racemes usually more than 2.
          Spikelets 1.3 mm long, oval, pubescent. 30. P. BLODGETTII.
          Spiketets 1.5 to 1.8 mm long, or as much as 2 mm in *P. laxum*.
            Primary pedicel nearly as long as the spikelet, the spikelets not crowded........32. P. MOLLE.

Primary pedicel much shorter than its spikelet, the spikelets crowded.
Nodes glabrous; spikelets pale, stramineous or brownish, 1.7 to 2 mm long__35. P. LAXUM.
Nodes or some of them appressed-pubescent; spikelets green or purplish.
Rhizomes long, scaly.
29. P. MARITIMUM.
Rhizomes wanting.
Ligule obsolete or minute.
31. P. CAESPITOSUM.
Ligule 1.5 to 2 mm long.
33. P. ACUTIFOLIUM.

1. **Paspalum stellatum** Humb. and Bonpl., in Flügge, Monogr. Pasp. 62. 1810. Colombia.

Culms simple, erect, or decumbent at base, 40 to 80 cm tall, slender, wiry; sheaths papillose-hirsute, or the upper glabrate; blades involute-setaceous, papillose-pilose; racemes solitary or paired, 2.5 to 10 cm long; rachis 5 to 7 mm wide, the margins membranaceous; spikelets about 3 mm long, almost hidden under the dense glistening white hairs (fig. 123).

Savannas and open rocky slopes, southern Mexico to Argentina; Hispaniola.

HAITI: St. Michel, *Leonard* 7289, 7526, 7537a. Between Morne Sala and Morne Basil, *Ekman* H 2484. Hinche, *Ekman* H 6428. Mirebalais, *Ekman* H 2302. Miragoane, *Ekman* H 7246.

DOMINICAN REPUBLIC: Leonor, *Valeur* 498. Monción, *Ekman* H 13015.

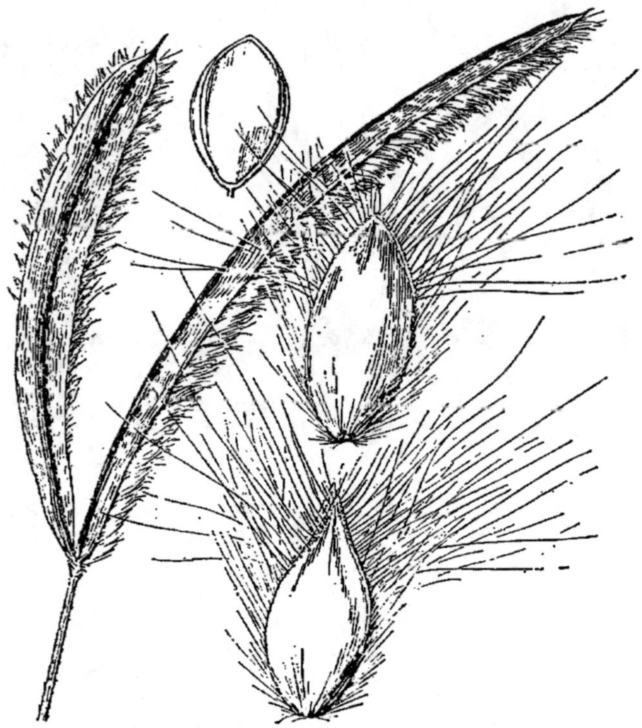

FIGURE 123.—*Paspalum stellatum*. Panicle, × 1; two views of spikelet, and floret, × 10 (Sello 5686).

2. **Paspalum heterotrichon** Trin., Gram. Icon. 3: pl. 285. 1831. Brazil.

Paspalum heterotrichum var. *paucispicatum* Hack., Notizbl. Bot. Gart. Berlin 1: 328. 1897. Haiti, *Picarda* 1525.

Culms very slender, 50 to 90 cm tall, finally branching and leaning or clambering among other vegetation; blades firm, more or less involute; racemes 2 to 7, 1 to 2 cm distant, 1 to 6 cm long; rachis 3 to 4 mm wide, the margins membranaceous; spikelets about 2.5 mm long, partially hidden by the copious white hairs; one hair of the marginal fringe bristlelike, much exceeding the others (fig. 124).

Open grassy hillsides and savannas, Panama to Peru and southern Brazil; Hispaniola.

HAITI: St. Michel, *Buch* 1091; *Leonard* 7537, 7793, 7795a. Mirebalais, *Ekman* H 2274. Ennery, *Leonard* 8957. Morne Faure, *Christ* 1800. Miragoane, *Ekman* H 7247. Trouin, *Ekman* H 2401. Furcy, *Leonard* 4298.

DOMINICAN REPUBLIC: Constanza, *Ekman* H 14018. San Juan, *Ekman* H 13404.

FIGURE 124.—*Paspalum heterotrichon*. Panicle, × 1; two views of spikelet, and floret, × 10 (type and Malme 1562B).

3. Paspalum dissectum (L.) L., Sp. Pl. ed. 2. 81. 1762.

Panicum dissectum L., Sp. Pl. 57. 1753. (Probably Delaware.)

Subaquatic perennial; culms creeping, rooting at the nodes, the flowering branches ascending; blades flat, thin, 3 to 6 cm long, 4 to 5 mm wide; inflorescence terminal and axillary; racemes 2 to 4, 2 to 3 cm long, usually erect, falling entire, the rachis membranaceous, 2 to 3 mm wide; spikelets 2 mm long (fig. 125).

On muddy or sandy banks of ponds and ditches or in shallow water, southeastern United States; Cuba.

CUBA: Laguna Santa María, *Ekman* 17269. Hanábana, *Wright* 169 in 1865. Eastern Cuba, *Wright* 3440.

4. Paspalum serratum Hitchc. and Chase, Contrib. U. S. Natl. Herb. 18: 306. 1917. Jamaica, *Hitchcock* 9795.

Aquatic glabrous perennial; culms as much as 1.7 m long; blades flat, soft, thin, 4 to 9 cm long, 3 to 7 mm wide; racemes 2, rarely 1, 12 to 15 mm distant, 3 to 5 cm long; rachis about 3 mm wide; spikelets about 3.3 mm long (fig. 126).

In ponds and sluggish streams, Cuba and Jamaica.

CUBA: Jagüey Chico, *Ekman* 16990.

JAMAICA: Troy, *Hitchcock* 9795; *Harris* 12582, 12598. Inverness, *Harris* 12719. Without locality, *Alexander*.

5. Paspalum repens Bergius, Act. Helv. Phys. Math. 7: 129. pl. 7. 1762. Dutch Guiana.

Aquatic perennial, the submerged culms as much as 2 m long, with inflated sheaths; blades flat, 10 to 20 cm long, 12 to 15 mm wide; panicles 10 to 15 cm long; racemes numerous, solitary or 2 or 3 together, tardily falling entire, 3 to 5 cm long, the rachis 1.5 mm wide; spikelets 1.5 to 2 mm long, whitish, glabrous or pubescent (fig. 127).

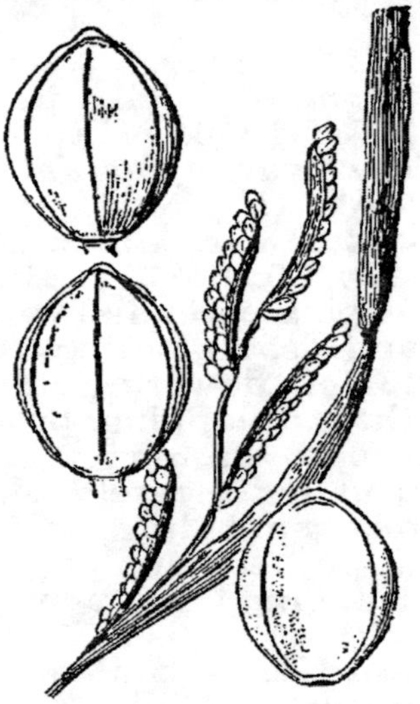

FIGURE 125.—*Paspalum dissectum.* Panicle × 1; two views of spikelet, and floret, × 10 (Commons 85).

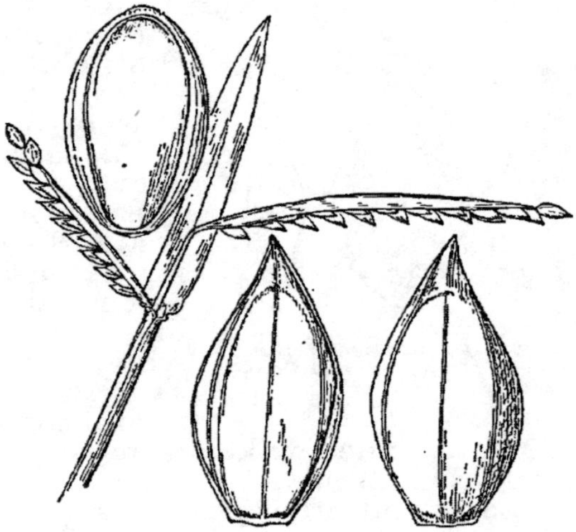

FIGURE 126.—*Paspalum serratum.* Panicle, × 1; two views of spikelet, and floret, × 10 (type).

Floating in sluggish streams or standing water or creeping in wet places, southeastern United States, West Indies, and Central America to Paraguay.

JAMAICA: Cornwall, *Harris* 12557. Shettlewood, *Harris* 11641. Westmoreland, *Harris* 11812. Middle Quarters, *Hitchcock* 9582.

TRINIDAD: Caroni Savanna, *Hart* 4194.

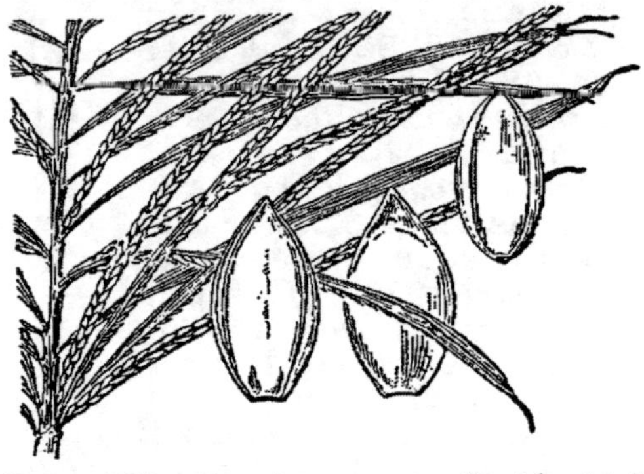

FIGURE 127.—*Paspalum repens.* Panicle, × 1; two views of spikelet, and floret, × 10 (Hitchcock 9179).

6. Paspalum racemosum Lam., Tabl. Encycl. 1: 176. 1791. Peru.

Annual; culms widely spreading or clambering, as much as 1 m long; blades flat, thin, 4 to 12 cm long, 1 to 2 cm wide, acuminate, glabrous; panicle ferruginous or dark purple, 10 to 20 cm long; racemes numerous, falling entire, 1 to 2 cm long; rachis about 1 mm wide; spikelets about 2.7 mm long, the glume rugulose on the lower part, the sterile lemma fluted or deeply wrinkled crosswise (fig. 128).

In recently disturbed soil, fields, waste places, and roadsides, Ecuador and Peru; introduced as an ornamental in the West Indies and escaped.

CUBA: Habana, *Léon* 759.

DOMINICAN REPUBLIC: Without locality, *Poiteau.*

7. Paspalum vaginatum Swartz, Prodr. Veg. Ind. Occ. 21. 1788. Jamaica.

Digitaria foliosa Lag., Gen. et Sp. Nov. 4. 1816. Habana.

Paspalum brachiatum Trin.; Nees, Agrost. Bras. 62. 1829, as synonym. Martinique.

Paspalum foliosum Kunth, Rév. Gram. 1: 25. 1829.

Paspalum inflatum A. Rich., in Sagra, Hist. Cuba 11: 298. 1850. Habana.

Paspalum distichum var. *vaginatum* Swartz; Griseb., Fl. Brit. W. Ind. 541. 1864.

Paspalum vaginatum var. *nanum* Doell, in Mart., Fl. Bras. 2 [2]: 75. 1877. Brazil.

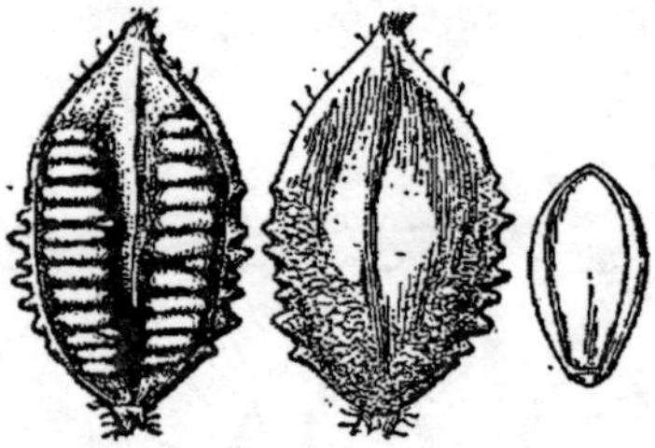

FIGURE 128.—*Paspalum racemosum*. Two views of spikelet, and floret, × 10 (Peru).

Extensively creeping perennial with horizontal rhizomes and also stoloniferous, forming extensive colonies; flowering culms 8 to 60 cm tall; sheaths overlapping, broad and loose; blades 2.5 to 15 cm long, 3 to 8 mm wide; racemes usually 2, rarely as many as 5, at first erect, spreading or reflexed at maturity, 1.5 to 7.5 cm long; rachis 1 to 2 mm wide; spikelets mostly 3.5 to 4 mm long, acute, pale, glabrous (fig. 129).

Seacoasts and brackish sands, southeastern United States, Mexico, and West Indies to Argentina, Baja California to Chile, Tropics of Eastern Hemisphere.

BERMUDA: *Brown and Britton* 100.

BAHAMAS: Nassau, *Geogr. Soc. Baltimore* 546; Hog Island, *Britton and Brace* 340.

CUBA: Arroyo Mántua, *Ekman* 11003. Habana, *Curtiss* 751; *Ekman* 13392; *Léon* 811, 14168. Playa del Rosario, *Léon and Roca* 7287. Playa de Marianao, *Palmer and Riley* 848. Tunas, *Léon* 6734. Santiago de Cuba, *Léon and Voisard* 930. Castillo de Jagua, *Léon* 15590. Western Cuba, *Wright* 947, 3854.

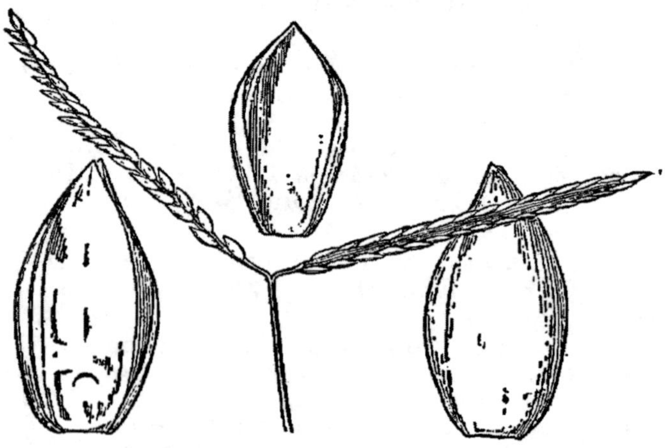

FIGURE 129.—*Paspalum vaginatum*. Panicle, × 1; two views of spikelet, and floret, × 10 (Hitchcock 9866).

JAMAICA: Montego Bay, *Hitchcock* 9667. Savanna-la-Mar, *Hitchcock* 9866. Black River, *Hitchcock* 9641. Buff Bay, *Hitchcock* 9775. Gordon Town, *Hart* 860. Kingston, *Hitchcock* 9317 (*Amer. Gr. Nat. Herb.* 563); *Harris* 12661.

HAITI: Cape Haitien, *Ekman* H 2756. Tortuga Island, *Leonard* 14096.

DOMINICAN REPUBLIC: Higüey, *Ekman* H 12222.

PUERTO RICO: Mona Island, *Hess* 439. Mayaguez, *Chase* 6307; *Sintenis* 6857. Santurce, *Chase* 6343. Humacao, *Eggers* 691. Vieques Island, *Chase* 6694.

VIRGIN ISLANDS: St. Croix, *Benzon*; *Paulsen* 313.

LEEWARD ISLANDS: Antigua, *Hitchcock* 16383. Guadeloupe, *Hitchcock* 16409.

WINDWARD ISLANDS: Martinique, *Duss* 545 in part; *Sieber* 20, 367. Barbados, *Bot. Station Herb.* 277.

TRINIDAD: Port-of-Spain, *Hitchcock* 10050. San Fernando, *Hitchcock* 10108. Cedros, *Hitchcock* 10139.

TOBAGO: Scarborough, *Broadway* 4655; *Hitchcock* 10287. Studley Park, *Broadway* 3045.

8. Paspalum distachyon Poit.; Trin., Mém. Acad. St. Pétersb. VI. Sci. Nat. 1: 142. 1834. Santo Domingo.

Culms erect, 15 to 40 cm tall, slender, wiry, with hard yellow rhizomes; blades 6 to 15 cm long, 1 to 2 mm wide, drying involute; racemes 2, 1.2 to 5 cm long, erect; spikelets about 3 mm long (fig. 130).

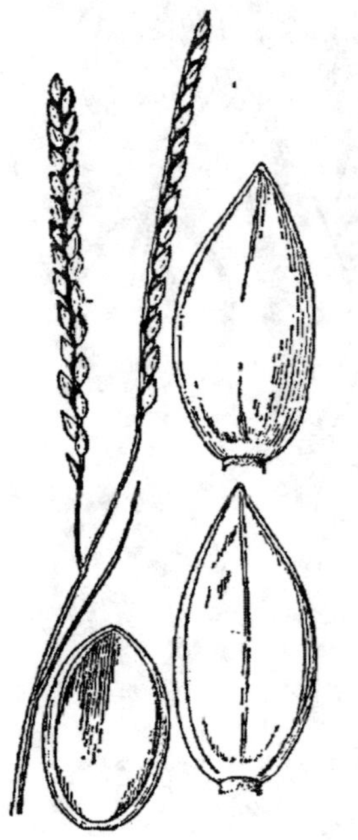

FIGURE 130.—*Paspalum distachyon.* Panicle, × 1; two views of spikelet, and floret, × 10 (Hitchcock 9678).

Moist or dry brackish or alkaline soil, mostly near the coast, West Indies.

CUBA: Habana, *Léon* 2614, 2783. Ciénaga de Zapata, *Léon* 9534. Baraguá, *Hitchcock* 23340, 23341. Tiffin, *Shafer* 2874, 2905. Guantánamo, *Hioram* 12. Jamaica, *Hioram and Baptiste* 1289. Júcaro, *Léon* 15639, 15641. Isla de Pinos, *Ekman* 12423.

JAMAICA: Montego Bay, *Hitchcock* 9678. Savanna-la-Mar, *Hitchcock* 9864. Black River, *Harris* 12548; *Hitchcock* 9642. Inverness, *Harris* 11695, 12716.

HAITI: Cape Haitien, *Ekman* H 2749, H 2756. Port-au-Prince, *Buch* 1760.

DOMINICAN REPUBLIC: Santiago, *Ekman* H 16536.

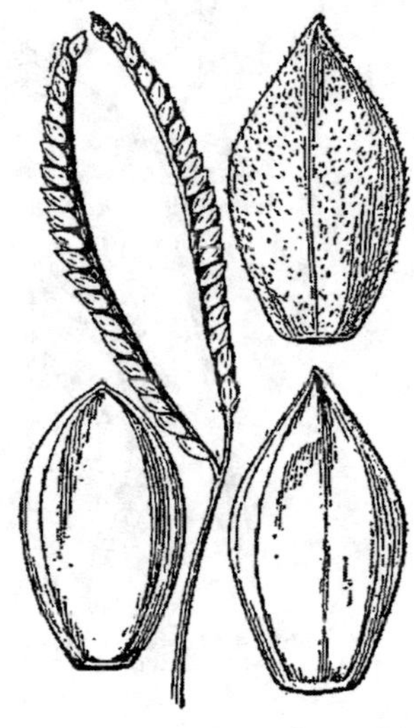

FIGURE 131.—*Paspalum distichum.* Panicle, × 1; two views of spikelet, and floret, × 10 (Hitchcock 9394).

LEEWARD ISLANDS: Dominica (probably *Poiteau*).

9. Paspalum distichum L., Syst. Nat. ed. 10. 2: 855. 1759. Jamaica.
KNOTGRASS.

Widely creeping perennial with slender rhizomes, extensively stoloniferous; flowering culms 6 to 50 cm tall; blades flat, 3 to 12 cm long, 2 to 6 mm wide; racemes usually 2, rarely as many as 4, erect to reflexed, commonly incurved, 1.5 to 7 cm long; spikelets 2.5 to 3.5 mm long, acute, the glume minutely appressed-pubescent; first glume frequently developed (fig. 131).

Ditches and wet, rarely brackish places, southern United States to Chile; warm regions of Eastern Hemisphere. Common throughout the West Indies and to be found on probably all the islands.

10. Paspalum pubiflorum Rupr.; Fourn., Mex. Pl. 2: 11. 1886. Mexico.

Culms rather robust, decumbent and rooting at base, 40 to 100 cm tall; blades flat, usually 10 to 15 cm long, 6 to 14 mm wide; racemes usually 3 to 5, 2 to 10 cm long, rather thick; spikelets about 3 mm long, pubescent (fig. 132).

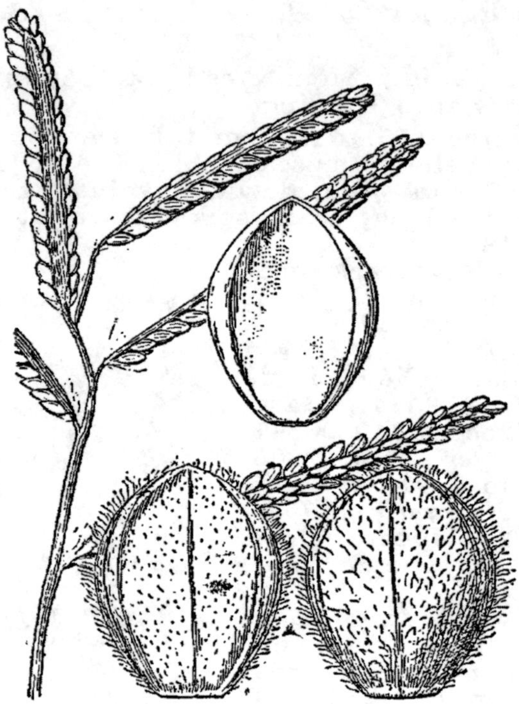

FIGURE 132.—*Paspalum pubiflorum.* Panicle, × 1; two views of spikelet, and floret, × 10 (Hitchcock 5555).

FIGURE 133.—*Paspalum lividum.* Panicle, × 1; two views of spikelet, and floret, × 10 (Arsène 3176).

Moist open ground, Louisiana to Mexico; Cuba.

CUBA: Habana, *Ekman* 10 (*Amer. Gr. Nat. Herb.* 908), 16800; *Léon* 1986. Cerro, *Ekman* 938.

11. Paspalum lividum Trin., in Schlecht., Linnaea 26: 383. 1854. Mexico. LONGTOM.

Culms 50 to 100 cm tall, from a decumbent or creeping base; blades usually 15 to 25 cm long, 3 to 6 mm wide; racemes usually 4 to 7, thick, somewhat flexuous, erect or ascending, 1.5 to 5 cm long; rachis 1.5 to 2 mm wide, dark livid purple; spikelets 2 to 2.5 mm long (fig. 133).

Low ground, wet savannas, and swamps, and along streams and ditches, southern United States and Mexico to Argentina; Cuba.

This species was referred to *P. denticulatum* Trin. in the Grasses of the West Indies.

CUBA: Habana, *Baker, Tracy, and Hasselbring* 3096; *Ekman* 1253, 1257; *Léon* 571, 937, 4635; *Tracy* 9119. Arroyo Apolo, *Léon* 272. Marianao, *Léon* 588. Macagua, *Ekman* 16805.

12. Paspalum notatum Flügge, Monogr. Pasp. 106. 1810. St. Thomas. BAHIA GRASS.

Paspalum taphrophyllum Steud., Syn. Pl. Glum. 1: 19. 1854. Martinique.

Culms 15 to 50 cm tall from short stout woody horizontal rhizomes; leaves mostly basal; racemes 2, very rarely 3, subconjugate, thick, usually 4 to 7 cm long; spikelets ovate to obovate, 2.5 to 3.8 mm long (fig. 134).

Open ground, savannas, and pastures, up to 2,000 m, Mexico to Argentina and nearly throughout the West Indies. An important forage constituent of lowland pastures.

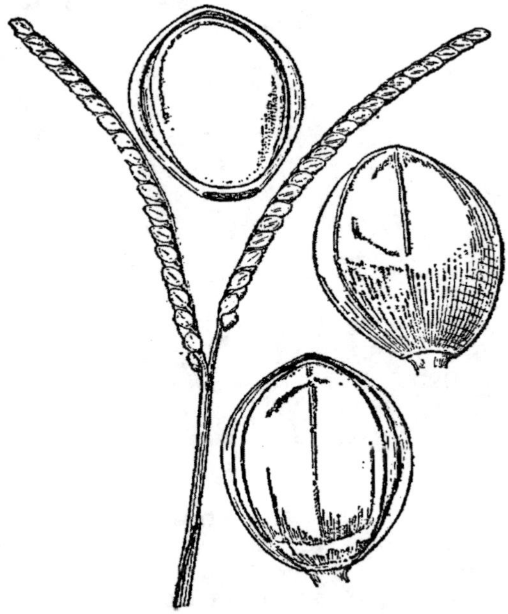

FIGURE 134.—*Paspalum notatum*. Panicle, × 1; two views of spikelet, and floret, × 10 (Chase 6639).

CUBA: Guane, *Léon* 6989. Sierra la Guira, *Léon* 5167. San Diego de los Baños, *Léon* 4526. Herradura, *Baker* 2968; *Hitchcock* 454. San Ramón, *Ekman* 13052. Mariel, *Ekman* in 1921 (*Amer. Gr. Nat. Herb.* 914). Habana, *Baker, Tracy, and Hasselbring* 3097; *Ekman* 1251; *Léon* 117b, 928; *Tracy* 9118. Guanabacoa, *Hitchcock* 23224; *Léon* in 1907. La Magdalena, *Baker* 2. Placetas del Sur, *Léon* 6423. Mordazo, *Ekman* 17096. Baraguá, *Hitchcock* 23360. Soledad, *Jack* 6125, 7576. Isla de Pinos, *Palmer and Riley* 1119. Without locality, *Wright* 3438 in part.

JAMAICA: Troy, *Hitchcock* 9784. Claremont, *Hitchcock* 9495. Holly Mount, *Hitchcock* 9450 (*Amer. Gr. Nat. Herb.* 564). New Forest, *Hitchcock* 9821. Lititz Savanna, *Harris* 12443. Bull Head Mountain, *Hitchcock* 9540. Kingston, *Hitchcock* 9471. Westphalia, *Harris* 11570. Blue Mountains, *Perkins* 1488. Cinchona, *Harris* 9497; *Hitchcock* 9696, 9711. Castleton Gardens, *Hitchcock* 9395, Hardware Gap, *Harris* 11544.

HAITI: Port-Margot, *Ekman* H 2927. Boche á Bateau, *Ekman* H 734. Aux Cayes, *Ekman* H 863.

DOMINICAN REPUBLIC: Samaná Peninsula, *Abbott* 152; *Ekman* H 15607. Guerra, *Ekman* H 11016.

PUERTO RICO: Mayaguez, *Chase* 6287, 6314; *Holm* 173. Maricao, *Britton, Cowell, and Brown* 4476; *Chase* 6236. Lares, *Chase* 6585. Bayamon, *Hioram* 347. Vega Beja, *Chase* 6424. San Juan, *Chase* 6344, 6401. Catano, *Chase* 6639. Rio Piedras, *Chase* 6779; *Hioram*

807. El Yunque, *Chase* 6729. Colonia San Miguel, *Britton and Shafer* 1624.

LEEWARD ISLANDS: Antigua, *Wullschlaegel* 593; *Box* 99, 142. Dominica, *Hitchcock* 16421.

WINDWARD ISLANDS: Martinique, *Duss* 558. Grenada, *Broadway* 1793½.

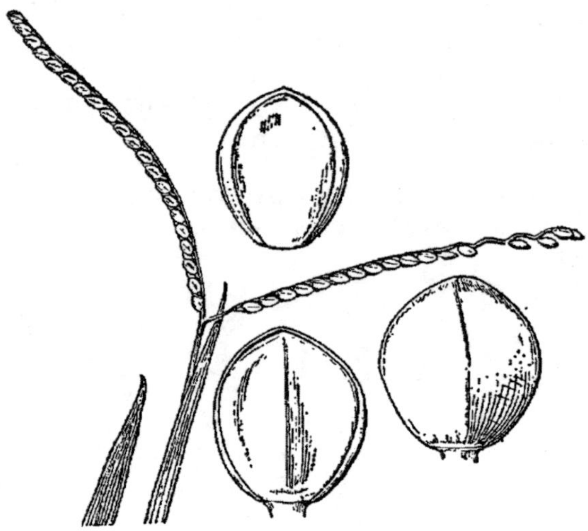

FIGURE 135.—*Paspalum minus*. Panicle, × 1; two views of spikelet, and floret, × 10 (type collection).

13. Paspalum minus Fourn., Mex. Pl. 2: 6. 1886. Mexico.

Similar to *P. notatum*, commonly in denser mats, on the average smaller, the culms rarely more than 30 cm tall; racemes more slender, less rarely 3; spikelets 2 to 2.5 mm long (fig. 135).

Open slopes and savannas up to 1,500 m, Texas, Mexico, and the West Indies to Paraguay and Bolivia.

CUBA: Arroyo del Sumidero, *Léon and Shafer* 13670; *Shafer and Léon* 13677. Herradura, *Hitchcock* 455, 23439; *Tracy* 9093. Cajálbana, *Léon and Charles* 4856. San Diego de los Baños, *Léon* 4468. Pinar del Río, *Hitchcock* 23284, 23305. Mordazo, *Ekman* 17093. Isla de Pinos, *Britton and Wilson* 14695; *Palmer and Riley* 978. Without locality, *Wright* 3438 in part.

JAMAICA: Bull Head Mountain, *Hitchcock* 9540½.

HAITI: Las Cahobas, *Cook, Scofield, and Doyle* 103.

DOMINICAN REPUBLIC: Cotuy, *Abbott* 830, 850.

PUERTO RICO: Trujillo Alto, *Chase* 6368.

14. Paspalum pumilum Nees, Agrost. Bras. 52. 1829. Brazil.

Culms usually 15 to 35 cm tall, the rhizomes, if present, short and nearly vertical; blades 1.5 to 12 cm long, 2 to 7 mm wide, glabrous or pubescent; racemes 2, recurved-ascending, 2 to 7 cm long, slender; spikelets 1.6 to 2 mm long, glabrous (fig. 136).

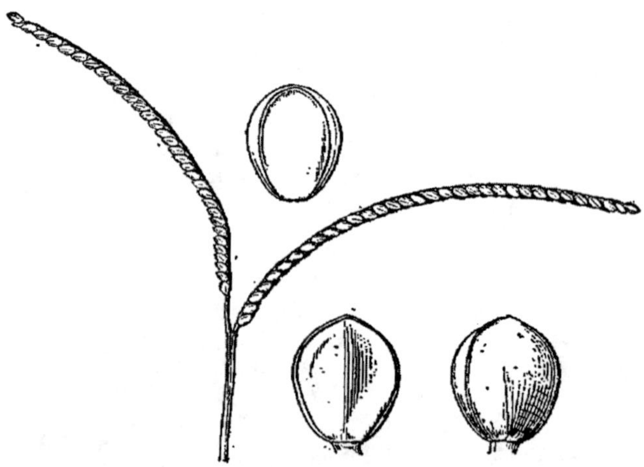

FIGURE 136.—*Paspalum pumilum*. Panicle, × 1; two views of spikelet, and floret; × 10 (type and Hitchcock 10350).

Sandy savannas and moist open ground, mostly at low altitudes, West Indies to Uruguay and Chile.

LEEWARD ISLANDS: Dominica, *Jones* 39.
TRINIDAD: Piarco Savanna, *Hitchcock* 10350; *Warming* 808. Valencia, *Broadway* 6946.

15. Paspalum serpentinum Hochst.; Steud., Syn. Pl. Glum. 1: 22. 1854. Dutch Guiana.

Culms simple, erect, 50 to 60 cm tall, naked above; lower sheaths crowded, grayish villous, the upper glabrous; blades firm, flat or involute, 3 to 5 mm wide; racemes 2, subconjugate, 6 to 8 cm long; rachis slender, flexuous; spikelets suborbicular, flattish, 2.6 mm long, glabrous, yellowish brown with irregular transverse markings of dark brown (fig. 137).

Wet sandy savannas, Trinidad, the Guianas, and Brazil.

TRINIDAD: Piarco Savanna, *Hitchcock* 10337.

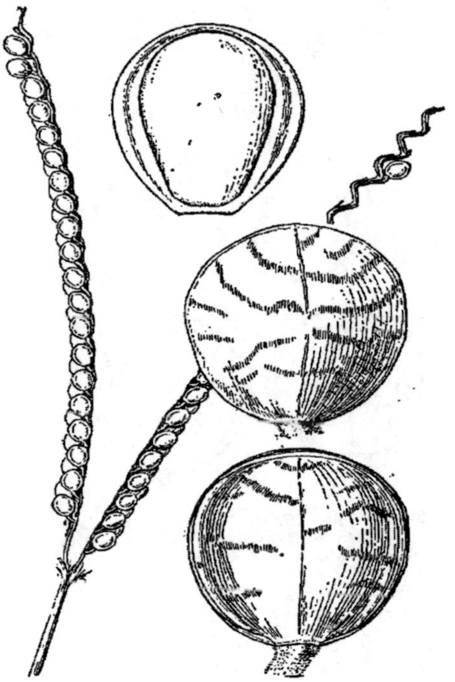

FIGURE 137.—*Paspalum serpentinum*. Panicle, × 1; two views of spikelet, and floret, × 10 (type and Hitchcock 10337).

16. Paspalum lineare Trin., Gram. Pan. 99. 826. Brazil.

Paspalum neesii Kunth, Rév. Gram. 1: 25. 1829. Brazil.

Culms slender, 40 to 80 cm tall, the nodes appressed-pubescent; blades narrow, conduplicate, the upper surfaces grown together; racemes 2, approximate, erect, 3 to 5 cm long; spikelets not imbricate, elliptic, 4 to 4.5 mm long, glabrous except at the very base (fig. 138).

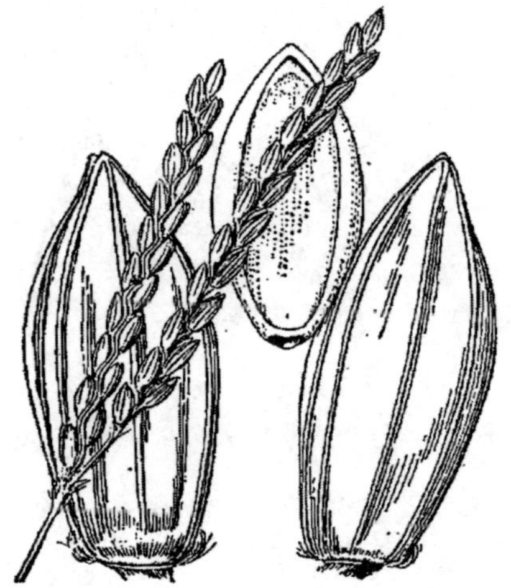

FIGURE 138.—*Paspalum lineare*. Panicle × 1; two views of spikelet, and floret, × 10 (type and Glaziou 22493).

Savannas, Costa Rica to Argentina; Cuba and Hispaniola.

CUBA: Herradura, *Baker* 3459; *Ekman* 10737. Between Zarzal and Nagua, *Léon* 11336; *Ekman* 14146. Isla de Pinos, *Britton and Wilson* 15114; *Curtiss* 379.

DOMINICAN REPUBLIC: Cuenca, *Ekman* H 11061, H 13338.

17. Paspalum debile Michx., Fl. Bor. Amer. 1: 44. 1803. Carolina.

Culms slender, ascending, with a cluster of short leafy shoots at base; blades flat, rather thin, pilose on both surfaces, conspicuously ciliate; racemes 4 to 6 cm long, usually 2 on the terminal culm, solitary on the axillary peduncles; spikelets broadly ovate, 1.6 to 1.8 mm long, minutely pubescent (fig. 139).

Sandy, mostly dry soil, barrens, and pine woods, eastern United States, Mexico, and Cuba.

CUBA: Herradura, *Hitchcock* 471. Cojimar, *Ekman* 1094. Santa Fé, *Léon* 8783.

18. Paspalum ciliatifolium Michx., Fl. Bor. Amer. 1: 44. 1803. Carolina.

Culms slender, erect to spreading, 35 to 90 cm tall; sheaths glabrous or pubescent along the margin, or the lower pubescent; blades flat, 7 to 20 mm wide, usually ciliate along the margin; racemes 1 to 3,

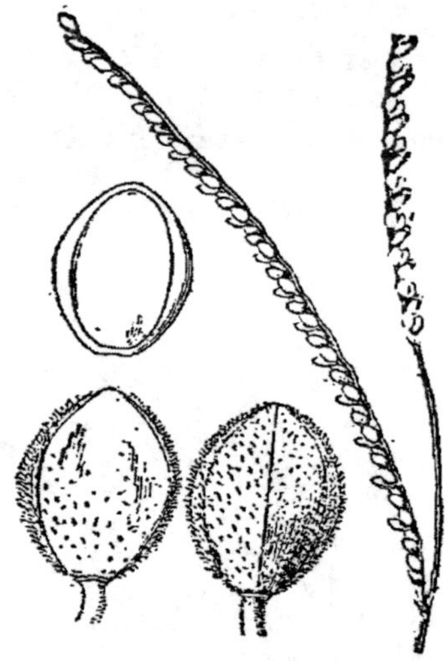

FIGURE 139.—*Paspalum debile.* Panicle, × 1; two views of spikelet, and floret, × 10 (Nash 946).

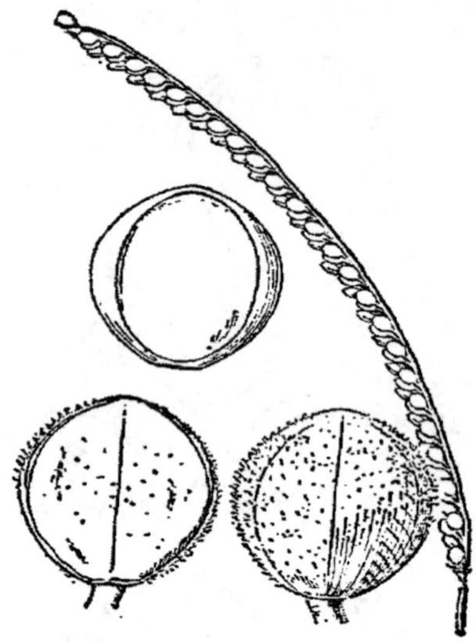

FIGURE 140.—*Paspalum ciliatifolium* Raceme, × 1; two views of spikelet, and floret, × 10 (Nash 1426).

slender, arching, commonly 7 to 10 cm long; spikelets about 2 mm long, elliptic-obovate, glabrous or minutely pubescent (fig. 140).

Open ground or open woods, mostly sandy soil, southeastern United States, Honduras, and the West Indies.

CUBA: Western Cuba, *Wright* 3442. Marianao, *Léon* 779. Baraguá, *Hitchcock* 23342.

HAITI: Aux Cayes, *Ekman* H 66.

19. Paspalum propinquum Nash, Bull. N. Y. Bot. Gard. 1: 291. 1899. Florida.

Differing from *P. ciliatifolium* in having a more strongly developed rhizome; blades narrower and firmer; spikelets smaller (about 1.8 mm long), slightly pointed (fig. 141).

Sandy savannas and sand barrens overlying limestone, peninsular Florida and the West Indies; Veracruz to Panama.

This species was referred by Grisebach [58] to *P. setaceum.*

[58] Fl. Brit. W. Ind. 542. 1864.

BERMUDA: Hillcrest, *Collins* 155 in part. Hamilton, *Brown and Britton* 56.

BAHAMAS: Inagua, *Hitchcock* in 1890.

CUBA: Arroyo Mántua, *Ekman* 10960, 11021. Candeleria, *Léon* 12702. Bacunagua, *Léon* 15068. Savanna de Chirigota, *Léon* 7455. Habana, *Léon* 2738, 3478, 7521, 13604, 15824. Cojimar, *Léon* 5604. Isla de Pinos, *Ekman* 11652; *Britton and Wilson* 15665. Without locality, *Wright* 3845.

JAMAICA: Claremont, *Hitchcock* 9520. Appleton, *Hitchcock* 9654. Ipswich, *Hitchcock* 9598.

HAITI: Vallière, *Ekman* H 4501. Bayeux, *Ekman* H 2601.

DOMINICAN REPUBLIC: Jaina, *Faris* 11; *Ekman* H 12484. Santo Domingo City, *Ekman* H 11385. Peninsula de Samana, *Ekman* H 15365.

PUERTO RICO: Mayaguez, *Chase* 6282. Quebradillas, *Chase* 6572. Barcelonita, *Chase* 6439. Campo Alegre, *Chase* 6433, 6613. Vega Baja, *Britton, Britton, and Brown* 6950. San Juan, *Chase* 6634½. Playa de Fajardo, *Chase* 6661.

LEEWARD ISLANDS: Antigua, *Wullschlaegel* 697; *Box* 103, 108.

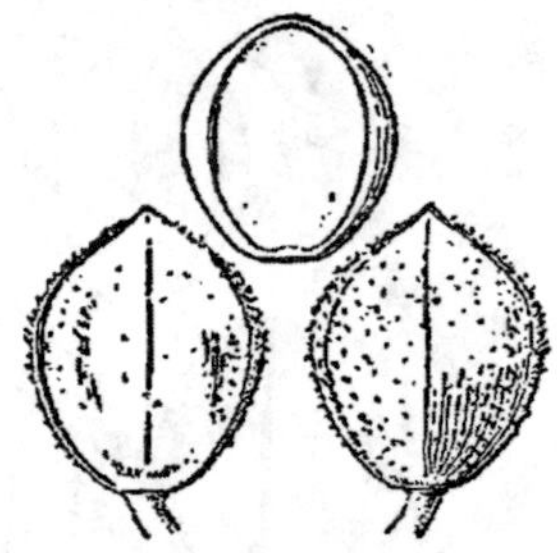

FIGURE 141.—*Paspalum propinquum.* Two views of spikelet, and floret, × 10 (type).

WINDWARD ISLANDS: Barbados, *Hitchcock* 16500. St. Lucia, *Box* 321.

20. Paspalum decumbens Swartz, Prodr. Veg. Ind. Occ. 22. 1788. Jamaica.

Panicum decumbens Roem. and Schult., Syst. Veg. 2: 429. 1817.

Culms spreading or creeping, freely branching, 10 to 70 cm long; blades flat, commonly 5 to 10 cm long, 6 to 12 mm wide, more or less pubescent; peduncles 2 to 8 from the uppermost sheath; racemes solitary (very rarely 2), 1 to 3.5 cm long, arcuate; spikelets crowded, 1.7 mm long, obovate; first glume present; second glume about half as long as the spikelet (fig. 142).

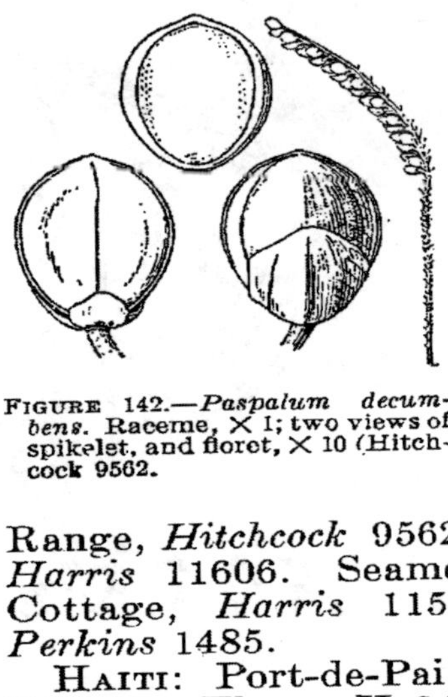

FIGURE 142.—*Paspalum decumbens.* Raceme, × 1; two views of spikelet, and floret, × 10 (Hitchcock 9562.

Open or partly shaded slopes, up to 1,600 m, often a weed in waste ground, Guatemala and the West Indies to Brazil and Bolivia.

CUBA: Pinar del Río, *Wright* 3851. San Diego de los Baños, *Léon* 4569. Sierra de los Órganos, *Ekman* 12966. Isla de Pinos, *Curtiss* 327.

JAMAICA: Bull Head Mountain, *Hitchcock* 9553 (*Amer. Gr. Nat. Herb.* 573). Upper Clarendon, *Harris* 12255. Ram's Horn Range, *Hitchcock* 9562. Hardware Gap, *Harris* 11545. Castleton, *Harris* 11606. Seamens Valley, *Maxon and Killip* 58. Claverty Cottage, *Harris* 11522. Mattis River, *Maxon and Killip* 190; *Perkins* 1485.

HAITI: Port-de-Pai. *Ekman* H 3693. Plaisance, *Leonard* 9336. Pérodin, *Ekman* H 3483. Caille la Croix, *Leonard* 7840, 7855.

DOMINICAN REPUBLIC: Villa Altagracia, *Ekman* H 11182.

PUERTO RICO: Mayaguez, *Chase* 6170, 6176, 6186; *Holm* 88. Rosario, *Chase* 6264. Monte Alegrillo, *Chase* 6235. Monte Montoso, *Britton and Cowell* 4118. Yauco, *Britton* 7225. Adjuntas, *Britton and Shafer* 2135; *Chase* 6473; *Heller* 6354. San Juan, *Chase* 6399, 6648. Trujillo Alto, *Chase* 6361. Las Cruces, *Britton and Britton* 9068. Cayey, *Chase* 6340. Rio Grande, *Chase* 6718. Mameyes, *Cowgill* 627. Fajardo, *Britton and Shafer* 1680.

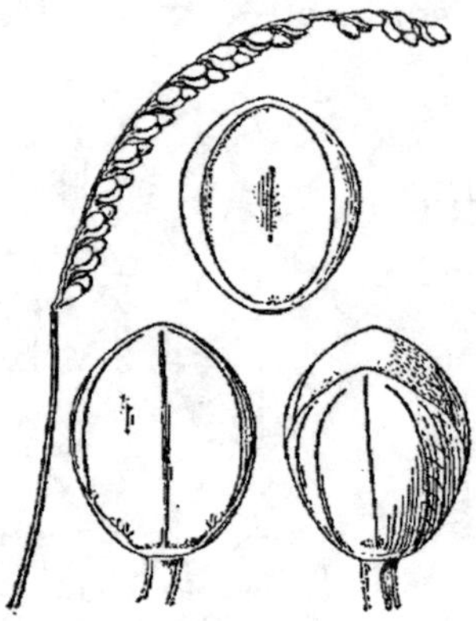

FIGURE 143.—*Paspalum nutans*, Raceme, × 1; two views of spikelet, and floret, × 10 (Raddi).

TRINIDAD: St. Ann, *Britton and Hazen* 1688. Port-of-Spain, *Hitchcock* 9957½. St. Joseph, *Hitchcock* 10175. Arima, *Hitchcock* 10308. Piarco Savanna, *Hitchcock* 10353. O'Meara Savanna, *Britton and Hazen* 1582. Masacas, *Broadway* in 1925. Cedros, *Hitchcock* 10135. Aripo Road, *Broadway* 8030. Without locality, *Finlay* 39; *Bot. Gard. Herb.* 2271.

21. Paspalum nutans Lam., Tabl. Encycl. 1: 175. 1791. South America.

Paspalum lloydii Nash, N. Amer. Fl. 17: 178. 1912. Dominica, *Lloyd* 590.

Resembling *P. decumbens* in habit; primary peduncle often with 2 to 4 racemes, the others with only one; racemes 2 to 6 cm long; spikelets 1.8 to 2 mm long; first glume obsolete or occasionally developed especially on the secondary spikelet; second glume three-fourths as long as the spikelet (fig. 143).

Partly shaded slopes and banks and mossy cliffs, to 1,000 m altitude, Honduras and the Leeward Islands to Brazil.

LEEWARD ISLANDS: St. Kitts, *Hitchcock* 16351; *Box* 147, 153. Nevis, *Box* 167. Guadeloupe, *Duss* 4059. Dominica, *Bryant* 5.

WINDWARD ISLANDS: "Martinique et Guadeloupe", *Husnot* 77. Grenada, *Broadway* 1729. St. Lucia, *Box* 188.

TRINIDAD: St. Ann, *Broadway* 4914, 5331. Port-of-Spain, *Chase* 9930; *Hitchcock* 9957, 9982, 10040, 10200. St. Joseph, *Hitchcock* 10015. Mount Tucuche, *Britton, Hazen, and Mendelson* 1249. Arima, *Hitchcock* 10299, 10301. Belmont, *Broadway* 2811. Blanchisseuse Road, *Broadway* 7665.

22. Paspalum dispar Chase, Contrib. U. S. Natl. Herb. 28: 96. f. 50. 1929. Dominican Republic, *Ekman* H 6248.

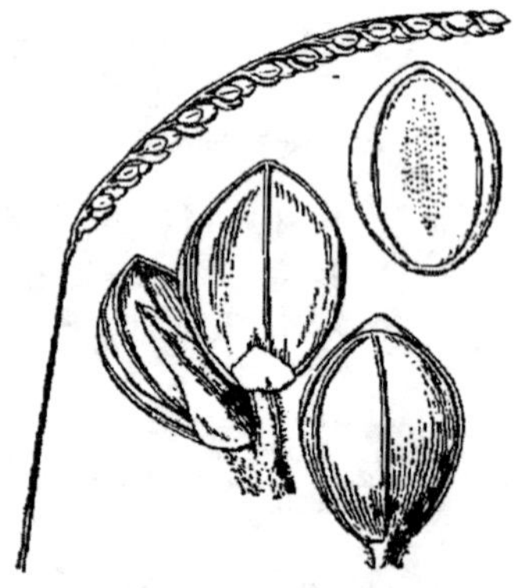

FIGURE 144.—*Paspalum dispar*. Raceme, × 1; two views of spikelet, and floret, × 10 (type).

Culms erect or ascending, 12 to 35 cm tall, the nodes pilose; blades flat, 4 to 15 cm long, 3 to 6 mm wide, finely pubescent; peduncles 2 or 3 from the upper sheath, the secondary ones at first concealed; racemes solitary, 1.5 to 4.5 cm long, arcuate; spikelets elliptic-obovate, 1.9 mm long; first glume small and nerveless on the primary spikelet, 1-nerved, pointed, and two-thirds as long as the spikelet on the secondary (fig. 144).

Brushy slopes, and pinelands, Hispaniola.

DOMINICAN REPUBLIC: Restauración, *Ekman* H 6248. Constanza, *Ekman* H 13928. San José de Ocoa, *Ekman* H 11595. Villa

Altagracia, *Ekman* H 11255. Bayaguana, *Ekman* H 11095. Moncíon, *Ekman* H 12629. San Juan, *Ekman* H 13426.

23. Paspalum pilosum Lam., Tabl. Encycl. 1: 175. 1791. Tropical America.

Dimorphostachys pilosa Fourn., Mex. Pl. 2: 14. 1886.

Culms ascending or spreading, 40 to 115 cm tall; blades flat or the margins revolute, 10 to 40 cm long, 3 to 8 mm wide, harshly pubescent; peduncles slender, elongate, 1 to 4 from the upper and middle sheaths; racemes solitary, arcuate, 6 to 17 cm long; spikelets 2.6 to 3 mm long, elliptic; first glume minute on the primary spikelet, small to half the length of the spikelet, pointed and eccentric on the secondary (fig. 145).

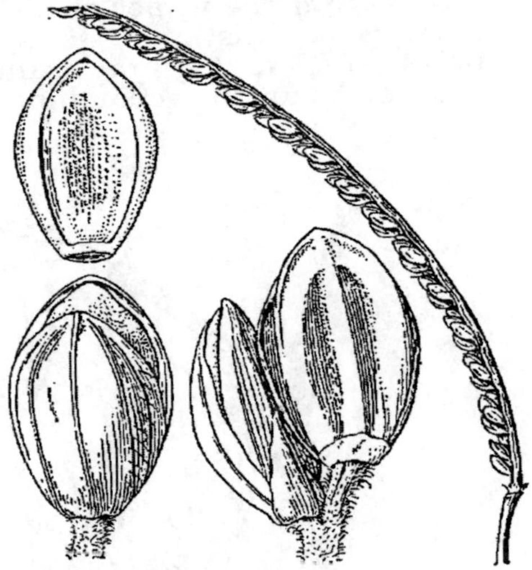

FIGURE 145.—*Paspalum pilosum*. Raceme, × 1; two views of spikelet, and floret, × 10 (Hitchcock 8130).

Open sparsely wooded slopes and brushy savannas, mostly in rather moist soil, lowlands, and up to 1,500 m, Costa Rica to Bolivia and southern Brazil; Trinidad.

TRINIDAD: Port-of-Spain, *Hitchcock* 9987. St. Joseph, *Hitchcock* 10189. Aripo Savanna, *Hitchcock* 10075. Pitch Lake, *Broadway* 2603; *Hitchcock* 10088. La Brea, *Broadway* 4969.

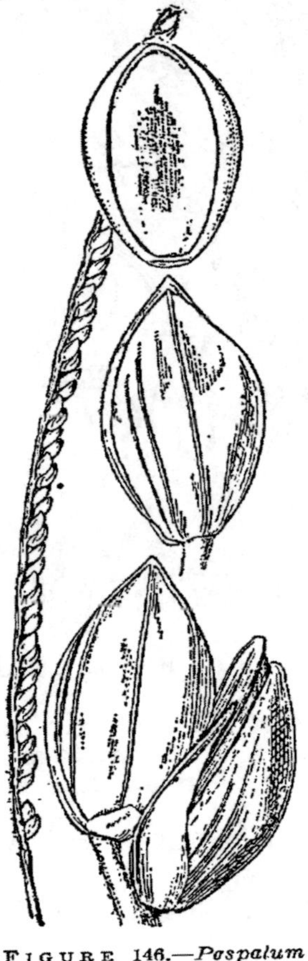

FIGURE 146.—*Paspalum unispicatum*. Raceme, × 1; two views of spikelet, and floret, × 10 (type).

24. Paspalum unispicatum (Scribn. and Merr.) Nash, N. Amer. Fl. 17: 193. 1912.

Panicum unispicatum Scribn. and Merr., U. S. Dept. Agr., Div. Agrost. Bull. 24: 14. 1901. Mexico.

Culms erect, 50 to 80 cm tall; blades flat, 10 to 30 cm long, 8 to 15 mm wide, stiffly papillose-ciliate on the margin, and more or less so on the surface; peduncles commonly 2 from the upper sheath; racemes 1 or sometimes 2, 6 to 20 cm long; spikelets 3 to 3.5 mm long; first glume minute on the primary spikelet, larger and acuminate on the secondary (fig. 146).

Meadows, savannas, open slopes, and banks, up to 1,500 m, southern Texas to Venezuela and Argentina; Cuba.

CUBA: Guane, *Ekman* 11093. Habana, *Léon* 2401. Zaza de Tunas, *Léon* 947. Sancti Spíritus, *Clements* 2427; *Léon* 4099, 5582; *Sergius* 2411, 2682. Soledad, *Jack* 6149, 8273.

25. Paspalum langei (Fourn.) Nash, N. Amer. Fl. 17: 179. 1912.

Dimorphostachys langei Fourn., Mex. Pl. 2: 14. 1886. Mexico.

Dimorphostachys ciliifera Nash, in Small, Fl. Southeast. U. S. 78, 1327. 1903. Florida.

Paspalum ciliiferum Hitchc., Contrib. U. S. Natl. Herb. 12: 201. 1909.

Culms ascending, 30 to 100 cm tall; blades flat, 10 to 40 cm long, 6 to 15 mm wide, usually glabrous or nearly so; peduncles slender, 1 to 3 from the upper sheath; racemes 2 to 5, arcuate, 3.5 to 11 cm long, rather distant; spikelets 2.2 to 2.6 mm long, finally brown, pubescent; first glume minute on the primary spikelet, larger and acuminate on the secondary (fig. 147).

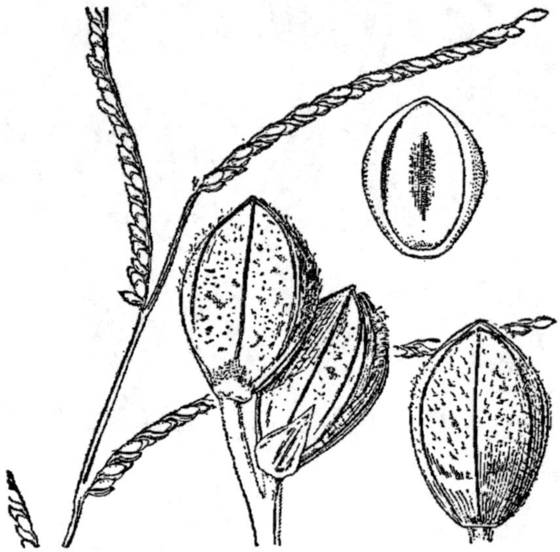

FIGURE 147.—*Paspalum langei*. Panicle, × 1; two views of spikelet, and floret, × 10 (Pringle 3991).

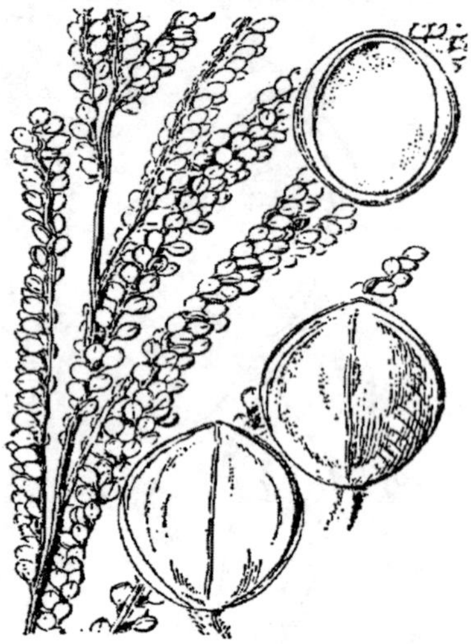

FIGURE 148.—*Paspalum nesiotes*. Panicle, × 1; two views of spikelet, and floret, × 10 (type).

Moist woods and shaded slopes and banks mostly at low altitudes, Florida and Texas to Venezuela.

CUBA: Mariel, *Ekman* 11497 (*Amer. Gr. Nat. Herb.* 934). Habana, *Léon* 934. Guatao, *Léon* 6321. Tapaste, *Léon* 4183. Arroyo Naranjo, *Léon* 587. Marianao, *Léon* 1511. Rio Bacuranao, *Wilson and Léon* 11602. Matanzas, *Britton and Wilson* 148.

HAITI: Morne Cap-Rouge, *Ekman* H 5948. Trouin, *Ekman* H 2376.

26. Paspalum nesiotes Chase, Contrib. U. S. Natl. Herb. 28: 117. f. 67. 1929. St. Lucia, *Hitchcock* 16471.

Culms 45 to 120 cm tall; blades flat or folded, 25 to 50 cm long, 6 to 11 mm wide, glabrous or scabrous; panicles long-exserted; racemes 5 to 11, arching, 4 to 10 cm long; spikelets about 2 mm long, glabrous (fig. 148).

Known only from St. Lucia and Martinique.

WINDWARD ISLANDS: Martinique, *Duss* in 1879. St. Lucia, *Hitchcock* 16471.

27. Paspalum oligostachyum Salzm.; Steud., Syn. Pl. Glum. 1: 23. 1854. Bahia.

Culms ascending to spreading, 25 to 75 cm tall; sheaths softly pubescent with spreading hairs; blades flat, densely velvety pubescent, 8 to 25 cm long, 7 to 13 mm wide; racemes usually 3 to 5, spreading, 3 to 10 cm long; spikelets 2 mm long, obovate, bronze-green, mottled with purplish brown, obscurely appressed-pubescent (fig. 149).

Wooded slopes and clay banks, Trinidad to eastern Brazil.

TRINIDAD: Monos, *Broadway* 7437.

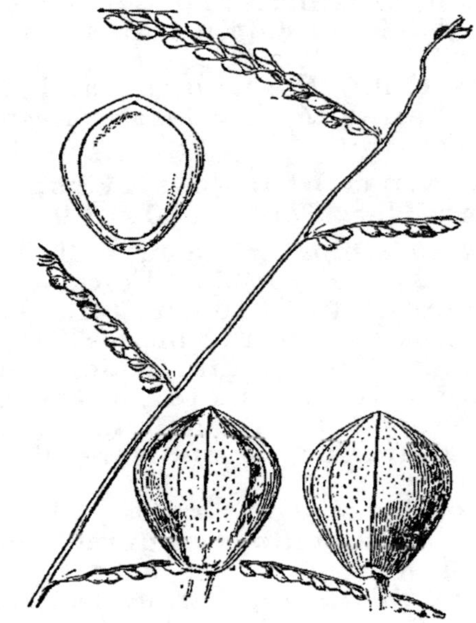

FIGURE 149.—*Paspalum oligostachyum.* Panicle, × 1; two views of spikelet, and floret, × 10 (type collection).

FIGURE 150.—*Paspalum paniculatum.* Panicle, × 1; two views of spikelet, and floret, × 10 (Ledru, and Duss 549).

28. Paspalum paniculatum L., Syst. Nat. ed. 10. 2: 855. 1759. Jamaica.

Paspalum hemisphericum Poir., in Lam. Encycl. 5: 31. 1804. Puerto Rico.

Paspalum strictum Pers., Syn. Pl. 1: 86. 1805. Santo Domingo.

Paspalum affine Bello, An. Soc. Espan. Hist. Nat. 12: 125. 1883. Puerto Rico.

Panicum paniculatum Kuntze, Rev. Gen. Pl. 3^2: 363. 1898.

Paspalum paniculatum minor Scribn., Field Mus. Bot. 2: 24. 1900. Jamaica.

Culms erect or decumbent at base, mostly 50 to 100 cm tall; sheaths papillose-hispid; blades flat, mostly 10 to 25 cm long, 10 to 20 mm wide, more or less hispid; panicle usually 8 to 20 cm long, of several to many arched-spreading, somewhat fascicled racemes, the lower 4 to 12 cm long; spikelets about 1.3 mm long, subhemispheric, pubescent (fig. 150).

Moist open ground and brushy slopes, along ditches, and a weed in cultivated and waste places, up to 2,000 m, Mexico and the West Indies to Argentina.

29. Paspalum maritimum Trin., Mém. Acad. St. Pétersb. VI. Sci. Nat. 1: 148. 1834. Bahia, Brazil.

Culms ascending to spreading, 30 to 50 cm tall, sometimes branching, with hard scaly horizontal rhizomes, often stoloniferous; sheaths ciliate on the margin and pilose on the keel toward the summit; blades flat, rather firm, 6 to 50 cm long, 8 to 20 cm wide, bearded back of the ligule; racemes mostly 3 to 7 (1 or 2 on the branches), ascending-arcuate, 4 to 9 cm long, somewhat approximate; spikelets 1.7 to 2 mm long, brown-speckled and softly pilose. Often forms extensive sterile colonies.

Sandy or rocky soil near the coast, Cuba, the Guianas, and Brazil.

CUBA: San José, Matanzas, *Léon and Acuña* 4471.

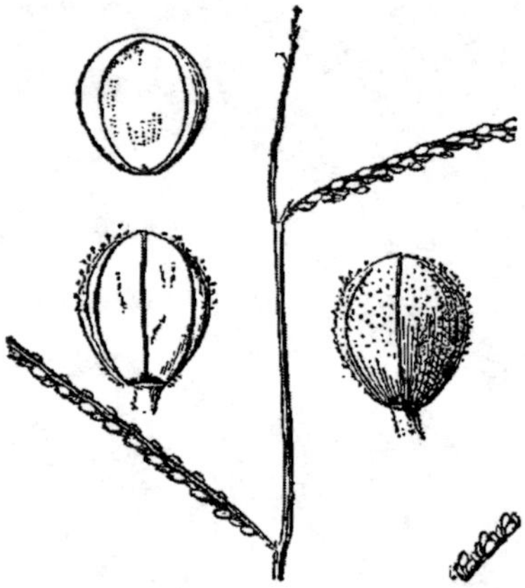

FIGURE 151.—*Paspalum blodgettii*. Panicle, × 1; two views of spikelet, and floret, × 10 (Simpson).

30. Paspalum blodgettii Chapm., Fl. South. U. S. 571. 1860. Florida.

Paspalum simpsoni Nash, Bull. Torrey Bot. Club 24: 39. 1897. Florida.

Culms erect, 40 to 100 cm tall; sheaths more or less pubescent; blades flat, 5 to 25 cm long, 5 to 10 mm wide; racemes commonly 3 to 8, remote, or the upper approximate, 2 to 8 cm long; spikelets about 1.3 mm long, glandular-pubescent (fig. 151).

Open or brushy calcareous soil; southern Florida, Yucatan, Honduras, and the West Indies.

BAHAMAS: Nassau, *Curtiss* 165; *Hitchcock* in 1890.

CUBA: Madruga, *Léon* 6354. Batabanó, *Ekman* 12604; *Hitchcock* 470. Motembo, *Léon* 8628. Sabana de San Marcos, *Léon* 9182. Baraguá, *Hitchcock* 23346. Santiago de Cuba, *Léon* 954. Jauco, *Léon* 11690, 11719. Isla de Pinos, *Britton, Britton, and Wilson* 15359; *Britton, Wilson, and Léon* 15790; *Millspaugh* 1408. Eastern Cuba, *Wright* 3443 in part.

JAMAICA: Montego Bay, *Hitchcock* 9668. Savanna-la-Mar, *Hitchcock* 9874. Troy, *Harris* 12620; *Hitchcock* 9816. Ipswich, *Hitchcock* 9599½, 9624; *Maxon and Killip* 1519. Black River, *Harris* 12546. New Forest, *Hitchcock* 9833. Between Ewarton and Linstead, *Hitchcock* 9417, 9464. Bog Walk, *Harris* 12560. Between Bog Walk and Spanish Town, *Hitchcock* 9295 (*Amer. Gr. Nat. Herb.* 571). Claremont, *Hitchcock* 9476, 9480. Buff Bay, *Hitchcock* 9766. Stony Hill, *Harris* 12703. Mount Diablo, *Maxon and Killip* 459; *Ridley* 3. Kingston, *Hitchcock* 9470.

HAITI: St. Louis du Nord, *Leonard* 14381. Môle-St.-Nicolas, *Leonard* 13216. Aux Cayes, *Ekman* H 42. Rousselin, *Ekman* H 10478. Tortuga Island, *Leonard* 11472, 13890, 13903, 13933, 15504, 15550.

DOMINICAN REPUBLIC: Santo Domingo City, *Ekman* H 11415. Higüey, *Ekman* H 12230. Peninsula de Samaná, *Ekman* H 15000.

PUERTO RICO: Joyuda, *Britton, Stevens, and Hess* 2398. Aguadilla, *Chase* 6579, 6580, 6605.

31. Paspalum caespitosum Flügge, Monogr. Pasp. 161. 1810. Santo Domingo.

Paspalum gracile Poir., in Lam., Encycl. Supp. 4: 313. 1816. Not *P. gracile* Rudge, 1805. Santo Domingo.

Paspalum heterophyllum Desv.; Poir., in Lam., Encycl. Sup. 4: 315. 1816. Santo Domingo.

Paspalum poiretii Roem. and Schult., Syst. Veg. 2: 878. 1817. Based on *P. gracile* Poir.

Culms densely cespitose, erect, slender, 30 to 60 cm tall, the base hard and slightly enlarged; blades flat in sheltered situations but commonly folded or involute, 5 to 20 cm long, 4 to 10 mm wide, narrowed to the base; racemes commonly 3 to 5, remote, rather thick, ascending or somewhat spreading, usually 1.5 to 4 cm long; spikelets crowded, about 1.5 mm long, sparsely appressed-pubescent or nearly glabrous (fig. 152).

FIGURE 152.—*Paspalum caespitosum*. Panicle, × 1; two views of spikelet, and floret, × 10 (Poiteau).

Mostly in partly shaded humus in limestone soil, or rock, southern Florida, Central America, and the West Indies.

BAHAMAS: Andros Island, *Brace* 5258; *Small and Carter* 8658, 8823. Great Exuma, *Britton and Millspaugh* 3089.

CUBA: Habana, *Ekman* 176; *Léon* 768, 2381, 3701, 7501, 8981. Río Almendares, *Ekman* 331. Columbia, *Léon* 268, 935, 936. Cojimar, *Hitchcock* 464, 465. Tapaste, *Léon* 3676. Triscornia, *Hitchcock* 467; *Tracy* 9087. Batabanó, *Hitchcock* 466. Sagua de Grande, *Léon* 9469. Caya Paloma, *Shafer* 2578. Guara, *Hitchcock* 23419. Santiago de Cuba, *Léon* 953. Guantánamo, *Britton* 2175; *Ekman* 2890. Jauco, *Léon* 11713, 12314. Isla de Pinos, *Britton and Wilson* 14890. Without locality, *Wright* 769, 3443 in part.

JAMAICA: Montego Bay, *Maxon and Killip* 1609. Lititz, *Harris* 12699. Walderston, *Harris* 12758. New Forest, *Hitchcock* 9832 (*Amer. Gr. Nat. Herb.* 568). Inverness, *Harris* 12726, 12748. Cane River Valley, *Harris* 11408, 12317. Mount Diablo, *Maxon and Killip* 504.

HAITI: St. Michel de l'Atalaye, *Leonard* 7186, 7418. Môle-St.-Nicolas, *Leonard* 13283, 13284, 13305a, St. Marc, *Leonard* 2911, 2915. Morne-à-Cabrits, *Ekman* H 1017. Gonaïve Island, *Leonard* 5126. Port-de-Pai, *Leonard* 12359. Port-au-Prince, *Hitchcock* 19885; *Leonard* 2827. Ètang Saumatre, *Leonard* 4216. Jean Rabel, *Leonard* 12708, 13005. Tortuga Island, *Leonard* 11315, 11333, 15552, 15586.

DOMINICAN REPUBLIC: Jaina, *Faris* 4, 109. Without locality, *Poiteau*. Santo Domingo City, *Ekman* H 11144.

PUERTO RICO: Mona Island, *Britton, Cowell, and Hess* 1656, 1839; *Hess* 435, 436. Quebradillas, *Chase* 6574 (*Amer. Gr. Nat. Herb.* 569). Penuelas, *Chase* 6489. Vega Baja, *Chase* 6427.

32. Paspalum molle Poir., in Lam., Encycl. 5: 34. 1804. St. Thomas.

Paspalum portoricense Nash, Bull. Torrey Bot. Club 30: 377. 1903. Puerto Rico, *Heller* 524.

Culms slender, spreading, 10 to 50 cm tall; blades flat or, in exposed situations, involute, 6 to 12 cm long, 2 to 7 mm wide; racemes commonly 2 or 3, slender, distant, ascending or arcuate-spreading, 1.5 to 7 cm long; spikelets about 1.7 mm long, elliptic, sparsely appressed-pubescent (fig. 153).

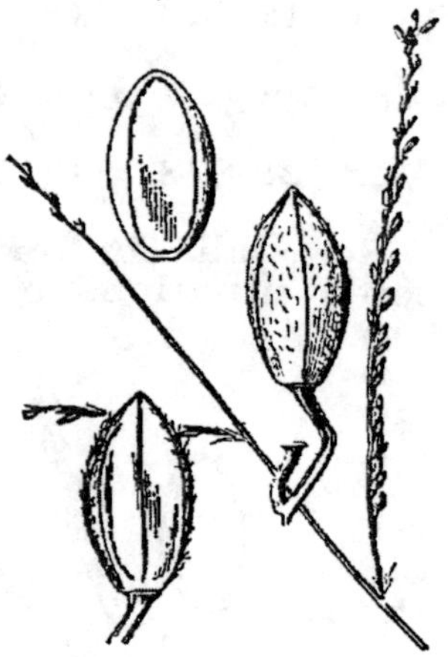

FIGURE 153.—*Paspalum molle*. Panicle, × 1; two views of spikelet, and floret, × 10 (Chase 6232, Amer. Gr. Nat. Herb. 570).

Open but humid slopes, mostly in red clay, West Indies to Brazil.

BAHAMAS: Crooked Island, *Brace* 4805.

PUERTO RICO: Mayaguez, *Chase* 6262, 6322, 6820. Monte Alegrillo, *Chase* 6232 (*Amer. Gr. Nat. Herb.* 570). Aguadilla, *Chase* 6607, 6608. Vega Baja, *Chase* 6428. Cayey, *Chase* 6338, 6741; *Heller* 524; *Sintenis* 2451.

VIRGIN ISLANDS: St. Thomas, *Ledru* (Lamarck Herb., Paris).

LEEWARD ISLANDS: Antigua, *Box* 93, 100.

33. Paspalum acutifolium Léon, in Britton, Mem. Torrey Bot. Club 16: 58. 1920. Cuba, *Léon and Roca* 8164.

Culms erect or geniculate below, 20 to 40 cm tall, the nodes appressed-pilose; blades firm, flat from a folded base, 6 to 17 cm long, 4 to 8 mm wide; racemes 2 to 4, ascending to arcuate spreading, 2 to 8 cm long, the common axis 1 to 3.5 cm long; spikelets about 1.8 mm long, oblong-elliptic, obscurely pubescent near the margin or glabrous (fig. 154).

Sandy or gravelly siliceous soil, palm barrens and savannas, Cuba. Originally described from Motembo, prov. Santa Clara.

CUBA: Canasí, *Léon* 13079, 13119. La Cumbre, *Ekman* 18980. Sabana de Motembo (Placetas del Sur), *Léon and Roca* 8164.

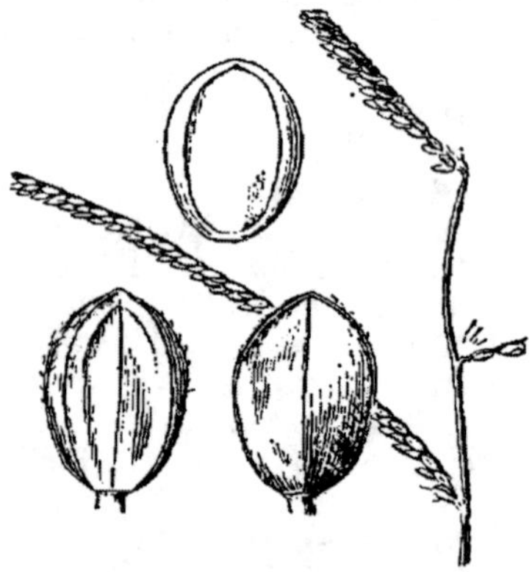

FIGURE 154.—*Paspalum acutifolium*. Panicle, × 1; two views of spikelet, and floret, × 10 (type).

34. Paspalum bakeri Hack., Inf. Est. Centr. Agron. Cuba 1: 410. 1906. Cuba, *Baker* 1824.

Culms widely spreading, 20 to 55 cm long; blades folded at base, commonly flat above, 2 to 10 cm long, 2 to 4 mm wide; racemes 2 to 4, stiffly ascending, 2.5 to 7 cm long, the common axis 1 to 5 cm long; spikelets about 2 mm long, glabrous (fig. 155).

Sandy seashores and coral reefs, Bahamas, western Cuba, and Leeward Islands.

BAHAMAS: Inagua, *Nash and Taylor* 1353.

CUBA: Mariel, *Ekman* 12838 (*Amer. Gr. Nat. Herb.* 942). Habana, *Léon* 956, 2625. Between Morro and Cojimar, *Ekman* 798. Triscornia, *Hitchcock* 475. Yumuri Mountains, *Rugel* 869. Matanzas, *Ekman* 17207; *Léon* 14675. Palma Sola, *Wright* 298. Isla de Pinos, *Britton and Wilson* 14939; *Britton, Wilson, and Léon* 15294, 15337.

LEEWARD ISLANDS: Barbuda, *Danforth* 1.

35. **Paspalum laxum** Lam., Tabl. Encycl. 1: 176. 1791. (Probably St. Croix.)

Paspalum glabrum Poir., in Lam., Encycl. 5: 30. 1804. Puerto Rico.

Paspalum milioideum Desv.; Poir., in Lam., Encycl. Sup. 4: 315. 1816. Puerto Rico.

Paspalum miliare Spreng., Syst. Veg. 1: 247. 1825. Based on *P. milioideum* Desv.

?*Paspalum sinuosum* Desv., Opusc. 57. 1831. Antilles.

Paspalum floribundum Desv., Opusc. 58. 1831. Antilles?

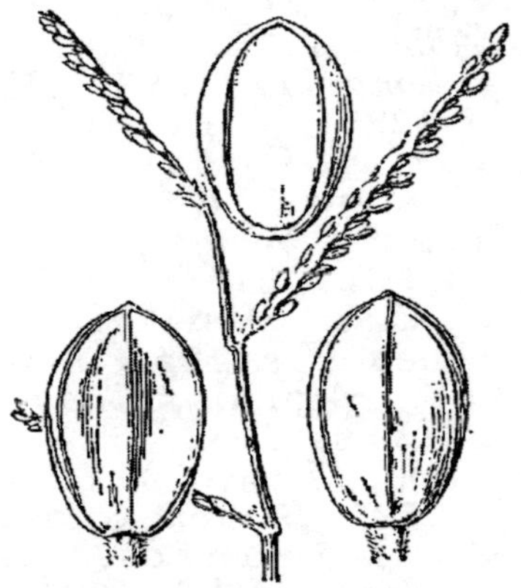

FIGURE 155.—*Paspalum bakeri.* Panicle, × 1; two views of spikelet, and floret, × 10 (type).

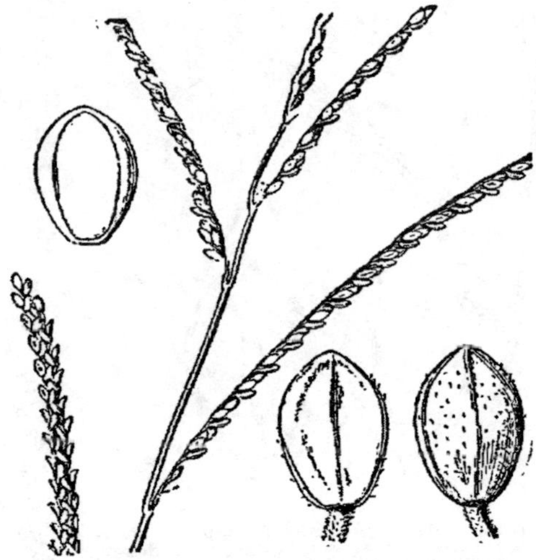

FIGURE 156.—*Paspalum laxum.* Panicle, × 1; two views of spikelet, and floret, × 10 (Richard's specimen in Paris Herbarium).

Paspalum richardii Steud., Syn. Pl. Glum. 1: 17. 1854. Antilles, probably St. Croix.

Paspalum rhizomatosum Steud., Syn. Pl. Glum. 1: 17. 1854. Guadeloupe.

Paspalum koleopodum Steud., Syn. Pl. Glum. 1: 18. 1854. Guadeloupe.

Paspalum helleri Nash, Bull. Torrey Bot. Club 30: 376. 1903. Puerto Rico.

Paspalum tenacissimum Mez, Bot. Jahrb. Engler 56 (Beibl. 125): 11. 1921. Puerto Rico.

Culms mostly erect, 50 to 75 cm tall; blades commonly more or less involute, mostly 20 to 30 cm, sometimes to 50 cm, long, 3 to 8 mm wide, narrowed to the base; racemes usually 3 to 5, sometimes more, arcuate-spreading, 3 to 10 cm long; spikelets 1.7 to 2 mm long, elliptic-obovate, the glume appressed-pubescent (fig. 156).

Sandy and limestone soils, Key West and the West Indies.

BAHAMAS: New Providence, *Britton and Brace* 404; *Curtiss* 156; *Geogr. Soc. Baltimore* 267. Andros Island, *Geogr. Soc. Baltimore* 197. Fortune Island, *Hitchcock* in 1890.

CUBA: Between Carabela Grande and Carabela Chica, *Roig* 3204. Habana, *Léon* 3446, 15825. Cayo Paloma, *Shafer* 2569. Guara, *Hitchcock* 23418. Preston, *Ekman* 3475. Santiago de Cuba, *Léon* 951. Guantánamo, *Britton* 1902. Jauco, *Léon* 12305, 12313.

JAMAICA: Montego Bay, *Hitchcock* 9674.

HAITI: St. Louis du Nord, *Leonard* 14281, 14396, 14410. Môle-St.-Nicolas, *Leonard* 13155, 13179. Port-de-Pai, *Ekman* H 3593, H 3624; *Leonard* 11034, 11110, 12335, 12356, 15244, 15656. Port-à-l-Ecu, *Leonard* 13882. Bayeux, *Ekman* H 2555. Cabaret, *Leonard* 11998. Jean Rabel, *Leonard* 12884, 13789. Aux Cayes, *Ekman* H 43. Morne-à-Bateau, *Ekman* H 8043. Gonaïve Island, *Ekman* H 8837; *Leonard* 3339. Navassa Island, *Ekman* H 10812. Tortuga Island, *Ekman* H 4156; *Leonard* 11314, 11318.

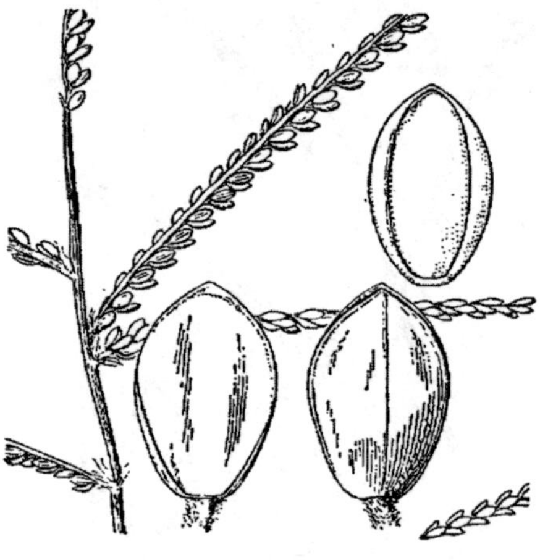

FIGURE 157.—*Paspalum pleostachyum*. Panicle, ×1; two views of spikelet, and floret, ×10 (Ekman 15756).

DOMINICAN REPUBLIC: Jaina, *Faris* 105. Jovero, *Abbott* 2880a. Cape Samaná, *Abbott* 1172. Santo Domingo City, *Ekman* H 11365. Higüey, *Ekman* H 12231. Peninsula de Samaná, *Ekman* H 15336, H 15359, H 15808. Matanzas, *Ekman* H 15910. Without locality, *Wright, Parry, and Brummel* 607, 617, 618.

PUERTO RICO: Mona Island, *Hess* 434. Desecheo, *Hess* 425. Aguadilla, *Chase* 6605½. Aguada, *Chase* 6601. Mayaguez, *Chase* 6182, 6279, 6300, 6313. Joyuda, *Chase* 6306 (*Amer. Gr. Nat. Herb.* 572); *Britton, Stevens, and Hess* 2395. Boqueron, *Britton, Cowell, and Brown* 4636, 4639; *Chase* 6499. Punta Aguila, *Britton, Cowell, and Brown* 4686, 4690. Morillos de Cabo Rojo, *Britton, Cowell, and Brown* 4717. Quebradillas, *Chase* 6573, 6575. Lares, *Chase* 6584, 6591. Arecibo, *Chase* 6446. Campo Alegre, *Chase* 6437, 6618, 6625. Manati, *Chase* 6609. Guanica, *Britton, Cowell, and Brown* 4909. Condado, *Britton and Brown* 6630. Vega Baja, *Chase* 6423. Catano, *Chase* 6635. Santurce, *Chase* 6346; *Heller* 10, 164; *Hioram* 804. Cangrejos, *Stevenson* 2292. Bayamon, *Chase* 6408. Pueblo Viejo, *Chase* 6402; *Hioram* 111, 2717. Rio Piedras, *Chase* 6759. Trujillo Alto, *Chase* 6367, 6369. Cayo Muertos, *Britton, Cowell, and Brown* 5041. Salinas, *Chase* 6756. Between Rio Grande and Fajardo, *Britton and Brown* 7038. Fajardo, *Chase* 6658. Humacao, *Eggers* in 1881. Culebra Island, *Britton and Wheeler* 190. Vieques Island, *Chase* 6678, 6697.

VIRGIN ISLANDS: St. Thomas, *Eggers* in 1876, 1880, 1881, 1882; *Friedrichsthal* 183; *Hitchcock* 16313. St. Croix, *Hitchcock* 16336; *Ricksecker* 410; *Thompson* 449, 463. Anagada, *Britton and Fishlock* 986, 1041. Virgin Gorda, *Fishlock* 108. Tortola, *Britton and Shafer* 694, 880. St. John, *Britton and Shafer* 257, 292, 506.

LEEWARD ISLANDS: Antigua, *Hitchcock* 16378; *Box* 23, 24, 32, 40, 42, 46, 97, 107. St. Kitts, *Box* 134, 163, 164. Barbuda, *Danforth* 9. Dominica, *Jones* 47.

WINDWARD ISLANDS: Martinque, *Duss* 551. Barbados, *Dash* 584; *Freeman* 5026. Grenada, *Broadway* in 1905.

36. Paspalum pleostachyum Doell, in Mart., Fl. Bras. 2^2: 58. 1877. Brazil.

Culms ascending to spreading, 40 to 100 cm tall; sheaths ciliate on the margin, usually villous on the collar; blades firm, flat from a folded base, often drying subinvolute, 15 to 25 cm long, 4 to 8 mm wide; racemes 3 to 15, commonly 4 to 8, at length stiffly spreading, 7 to 14 cm long, on an axis 4 to 11 cm long; spikelets 2.2 to 2.5 mm long, elliptic-obovate, glabrous (fig. 157).

On rocks or in sand or clay, seacoast, Cuba to Brazil.

CUBA: Guantánamo, *Ekman* 15756.

HAITI: Cabaret, *Leonard* 11982. Tortuga Island, *Ekman* H 4132; *Leonard* 11529, 13902, 13940.

WINDWARD ISLANDS: Grenada, *Broadway* in 1905.

37. Paspalum rocanum Léon, in Britton, Mem. Torrey Bot. Club 16: 57. 1920. Cuba, *Léon and Roca* 8233.

Culms simple, 40 to 75 cm tall; sheaths keeled; blades conduplicate, 10 to 30 cm long, 3 to 7 mm wide (flattened out); racemes 2 to 4, ascending to spreading, 2.5 to 9 cm long, 1 to 2 cm distant on the slender axis; spikelets 2.1 to 2.5 mm long, elliptic, minutely pointed (fig. 158).

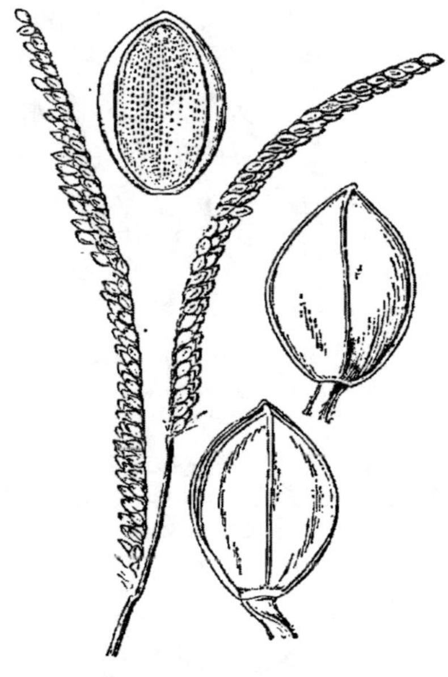

FIGURE 158.—*Paspalum rocanum.* Panicle, × 1; two views of spikelet, and floret, × 10 (duplicate type).

Palm barrens, sometimes in moist places and brushy savannas, Cuba.

CUBA: Sabana de Motembo, *Léon and Roca* 8233; *Léon and Loustalot* 9382, 11337; *Ekman* 16819 (*Amer. Gr. Nat. Herb.* 943). Baños de Santa Rosalia, *Léon and Loustalot* 9392. San Miguel de los Baños (prov. Matanzas), *Léon and Roca* 8871.

38. Paspalum alterniflorum A. Rich., in Sagra, Hist. Cuba 11: 299. 1850. Cuba.

Paspalum dolichophyllum Hack., Inf. Est. Centr. Agron. Cuba 1: 409. 1906. Habana, *Baker and Zarragoitia* 4545.

Culms 30 to 100 cm tall; blades erect at base, elongate, nearly equaling the culm, mostly 1.5 to 3 mm wide, drying involute; racemes 1 to 5, commonly 2 or 3, suberect or ascending, 7 to 12 cm long, 1 to 3 cm distant on the axis; spikelets 3 mm long, ovate-oblong, subacute or blunt; glume and sterile lemma silky pubescent on the lower part, pointed beyond the fruit (fig. 159).

Open ground, pastures, and savannas, Cuba, common in the western part, rare eastward, and in Haiti.

CUBA: Mariel, *Ekman* in 1921 (*Amer. Gr. Nat. Herb.* 944). Habana, *Baker, Tracy, and Hasselbring* in 1907; *Léon* 2556, 3473; *Tracy* 9105. Marianao, *Léon* 581. Arroyo Apolo, *Léon* 564, 585. Vibora, *Baker* 2587; *Léon* 943, 945. Guanabacoa, *Ekman* 594; *Léon* 2561. Calabazar,

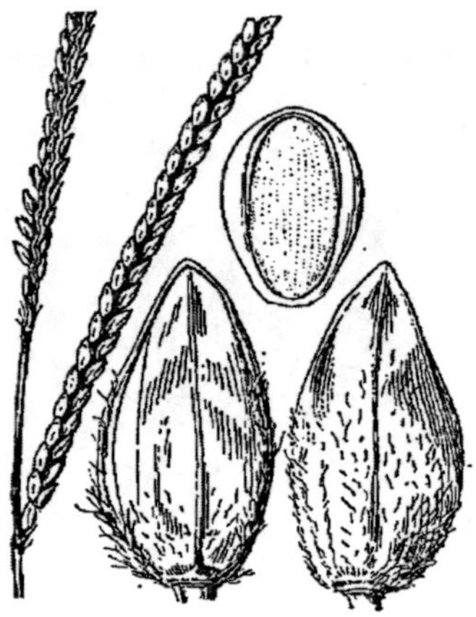

FIGURE 159.—*Paspalum alterniflorum.* Panicle, × 1; two views of spikelet, and floret, ×10 (Baker, Tracy, and Hasselbring).

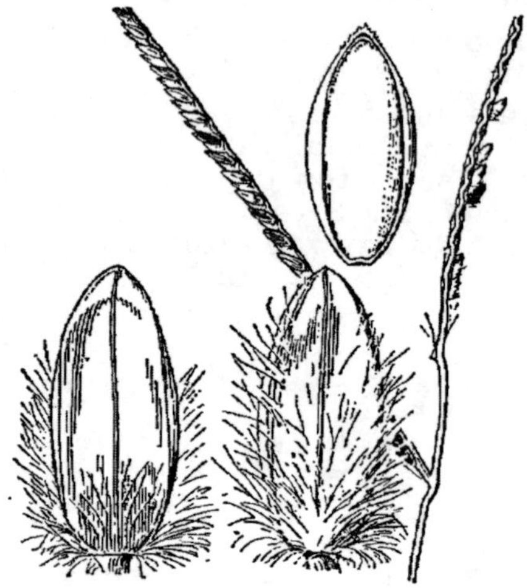

FIGURE 160.—*Paspalum rottboellioides.* Panicle, × 1; two views of spikelet, and floret, × 10 (duplicate type).

Baker and Zarragoitia 4545. Hanábana, *Wright* 167 in 1865. Caibarien, *Fernando* 36. Manatí, *Léon* 5680. Cupey, *Ekman* 6294. Without locality, *Liebmann* 194, 201; *Rugel* 753a; *Wright* 3841.

HAITI: St. Michel, *Ekman* H 8351; *Nash and Taylor* 1445. Between Anse-à-Veau and Petit Trou des Nippes, *Ekman* H 5401.

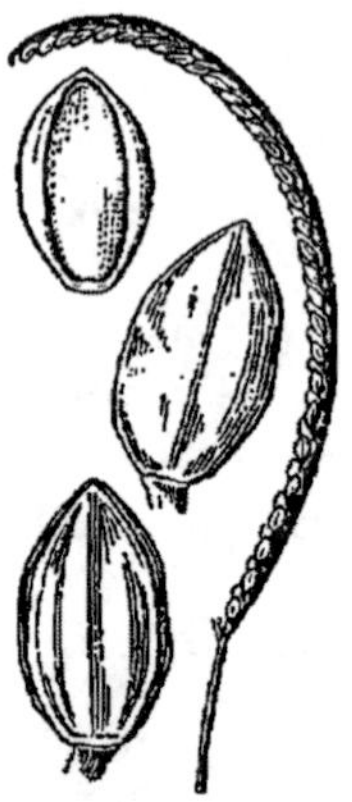

FIGURE 161.—*Paspalum filiforme.* Raceme, × 1; two views of spikelet, and floret, × 10 (type).

39. Paspalum rottboellioides Wright, An. Acad. Cien. Habana 8: 204. 1871. Cuba, *Wright* 3864.

Culms slender, 20 to 75 cm tall; blades spreading, 5 to 18 cm long, 1 to 1.5 mm wide, mostly involute, papillose-pilose; racemes 1 or 2, ascending or spreading, straight or nearly so, 4 to 12 cm long, the axis 1 to 2 cm long; spikelets 3 to 3.3 mm long, oblong-elliptic, the glume long-villous, the sterile lemma villous at base (fig. 160).

Sandy pinelands and savannas, western Cuba and Isla de Pinos.

CUBA: Herradura, *Ekman* in 1922 (*Amer. Gr. Nat. Herb.* 945). Vuelto-abajo, *Wright* 3864. Isla de Pinos, *Britton and Wilson* 14697; *Curtiss* 375; *Ekman* 12219; *Taylor* 41.

40. Paspalum filiforme Swartz, Prodr. Veg. Ind. Occ. 22. 1788.

Paspalum swartzianus Flügge, Monogr. Pasp. 96. 1810. Based on *P. filiforme* Swartz.

Paspalum leptocaulon Nash, N. Amer. Fl. 17: 181. 1912. Jamaica, *Britton* 1475.

Culms densely cespitose in large tussocks, reclining, slender, 20 to 70 cm long, with short flowering culms intermixed; blades mostly 20 to 50 cm long, about 1 mm wide, plano-convex; raceme solitary, arcuate, 3 to 8 cm long; spikelets 1.6 to 1.8 mm long, ovate-elliptic, glabrous (fig. 161).

Savannas, open or wooded slopes, Cuba, Jamaica, and Hispaniola.

CUBA: Guane, *Ekman* 11095. Remates, *Ekman* 11197. El Rangel, *Léon* 14047. Sabana de Chirigota, *Léon* 7452. Mariel, *Ekman* in 1921 (*Amer. Gr. Nat. Herb.* 946). San Miguel de Casanova, *Léon* 12472, 12558. Sabana de Motembo, *Léon* 9346. Manatí, *Léon* 6009. Without locality, *Wright* 3848.

JAMAICA: Savanna-la-Mar, *Hitchcock* 9885. Troy, *Hitchcock* 9809 (*Amer. Gr. Nat. Herb.* 566). Lacovia, *Britton* 1475.

HAITI: "Hispaniola", *Swartz*.

DOMINICAN REPUBLIC: Santo Domingo City, *Ekman* H 10908. Higüey, *Ekman* H 12234. Peninsula de Samaná, *Ekman* H 15829.

41. Paspalum distortum Chase, Contrib. U. S. Natl. Herb. 28: 142. f. 85. 1929. Jamaica, *Harris* 12569.

Culms slender, 15 to 50 cm tall; blades 15 to 40 cm long, 1 to 1.5 mm wide, involute, commonly somewhat tortuous; raceme solitary, arcuate, 2.5 to 6 cm long; spikelets 2 mm long, ovate to somewhat rhomboid, the glume and sterile lemma irregularly crumpled, glabrous (fig. 162).

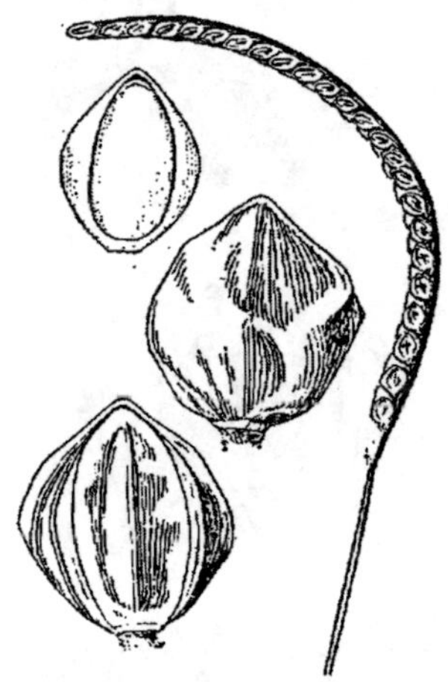

FIGURE 162.—*Paspalum distortum.* Raceme, × 1; two views of spikelet, and floret, × 10 (type).

Open hillsides, especially on serpentine rocks, Cuba, Haiti, and Jamaica.

CUBA: Cajálbana, *Léon* 4857. Habana, *Léon* 946. Guanabacoa, *Léon* 7057. San Miguel de Casanova, *Léon* 12473. Sabana del Tibisial, *Léon* 6661. Manajanabo, *Léon* 5273. Banao Mountains, *Léon* 8042. Baraguá, *Walker* in 1925. Sierra Maestra, *Ekman* 14691. El Yunque, *Shafer* 7732. Baracoa, *Ekman* 3597. Isla de Pinos, *Curtiss* 374.

JAMAICA: Troy, *Harris* 12564, 12569; *Hitchcock* 9789. Cockpit Country, *Britton* 465. Bull Head Mountain, *Hitchcock* 9544. Claremont, *Hitchcock* 9518. Between Ewarton and Linstead, *Hitchcock* 9438½.

HAITI: Aux Cayes, *Ekman* H 7. Cotrail, *Ekman* H 10740.

DOMINICAN REPUBLIC: Puerta Plata, *Ekman* H 14584.

42. Paspalum lindenianum A. Rich., in Sagra, Hist. Cuba 11: 299. 1850. Cuba, *Linden* 1813.

Paspalum longifolium Steud., Syn. Pl. Glum. 1: 21. 1854. Not *P. longifolium* Roxb., 1820. Cuba, *Linden* 1813.

Paspalum megaphyllum Steud., Syn. Pl. Glum. 1: 464. 1854. Based on *P. longifolium* Steud.

Culms commonly 40 to 70 cm tall, cespitose in dense tussocks, the leaves of the numerous sterile shoots usually about equaling the culm; blades 20 to 50 cm long, 1 mm wide, plano-convex; racemes 1 or 2, rarely 3 or 4, arcuate or nearly straight, mostly 6 to 10 cm long;

spikelets 2.5 to 2.8 mm long, irregularly ovate-rhomboid, the glume and sterile lemma deeply crumpled (fig. 163).

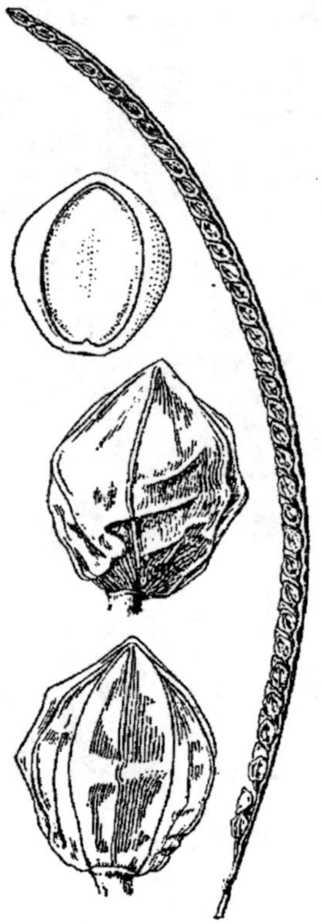

FIGURE 163.—*Paspalum lindenianum*. Raceme, × 1; two views of spikelet, and floret, × 10 (Hitchcock 9873).

Open or brushy places, mostly on limestone hills, Cuba, Jamaica, and Haiti.

CUBA: Mariel, *Ekman* 12908 (*Amer. Gr. Nat. Herb.* 947). Playa de Marianao, *Léon* 5272. Habana, *Léon* in 1909. Guanabacoa, *Ekman* 264; *Hitchcock* 463, 23242; *Léon* 944, 7346. Madruga, *Léon* 3457. Calvario, *Léon* 945b. La Sierra, *Jack* 7848. San Miguel de Casanova, *Léon* 12471. Hanábana, *Wright* 769. Saltadura, *Linden* 1813. Baraguá, *Hitchcock* 23348, 23363. Soledad, *Hitchcock* 23326. Isla de Pinos, *Curtiss* 523; *Palmer and Riley* 949.

JAMAICA: Montego Bay, *Hitchcock* 9663. Savanna-la-Mar, *Hitchcock* 9873. Cornwall, *Harris* 12551. Between Ewarton and Linstead, *Hitchcock* 9438. Between Bog Walk and Spanish Town, *Hitchcock* 9294. Lucea, *Harris* 12559.

HAITI: Marmelade, *Leonard* 8434. Mirebalais, *Cook, Scofield, and Doyle* 87. Pétionville, *Leonard* 4830. Between Décayette and Dupréné, *Ekman* H 2045.

DOMINICAN REPUBLIC: Moca, *Ekman* H 12557.

43. Paspalum nanum Wright; Griseb., Cat. Pl. Cuba 230. 1866. Cuba, *Wright* 176.

Paspalum caudicatum Wright, An. Cienc. Habana 8: 205. 1871. Cuba, *Wright* 3866.

Culms erect, mostly 15 to 25 cm tall; sheaths densely pubescent; blades 3 to 13 cm long, 3 to 4.5 mm wide, flat or drying involute, the lower surface velvety, the upper pilose; raceme solitary, 1.5 to 4 cm long, arcuate or nearly straight; spikelets 2.4 to 2.8 mm long, oval-elliptic, the glume and sterile lemma somewhat crumpled (fig. 164).

Low sandy pinelands and brushy savannas, central and western Cuba and Isla de Pinos. Apparently rare.

CUBA: La Coloma, *Ekman* 17831. Santiago de los Baños, *Léon* 4570. Herradura, *Ekman* 10784, 14093 (*Amer. Gr. Nat. Herb.* 948), 14104; *Hitchcock* 462. Vuelto-abajo, *Wright* 3866. Hanábana, *Wright* 176. Isla de Pinos, *Ekman* 12190. Without locality, *Wright* 3842.

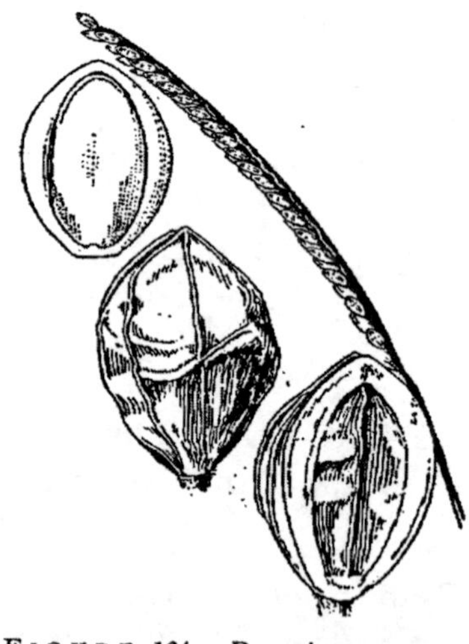

FIGURE 164.—*Paspalum nanum*. Raceme, × 1; two views of spikelet, and floret, × 10 (Wright 3842).

44. Paspalum insulare Ekman; Chase, Contrib. U. S. Natl. Herb. 28: 145. f. 88. 1929. Isla de Pinos, *Ekman* 11957.

Culms erect or ascending, 40 to 55 cm tall, the nodes densely appressed-pubescent; sheaths densely papillose-pilose; blades flat,

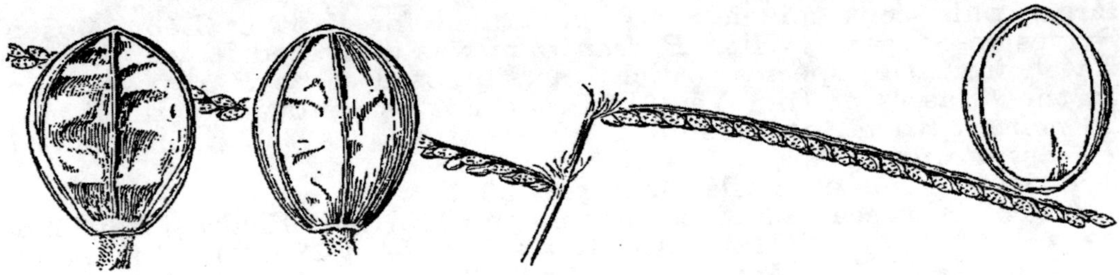

FIGURE 165.—*Paspalum insulare.* Racemes, × 1; two views of spikelet, and floret, × 10 (type).

6 to 16 cm long, 3 to 5 mm wide, papillose-pilose; racemes 1 or 2, approximate, arcuate to horizontally spreading, 3 to 6.5 cm long; spikelets about 2.5 mm long, obovate-elliptic, cross-wrinkled (fig. 165).

Sandy savannas, pinelands, and moist places, Isla de Pinos.

CUBA: Isla de Pinos, Santa Bárbara, *Ekman* 11957, 12220; *Taylor* 40.

45. Paspalum rupestre Trin., Linnaea 10: 293. 1836. Cuba.

Paspalum leoninum Chase, in Hitchc., Bot. Gaz. 51: 301. 1911. Cuba, *Léon* 950.

Culms from suberect to radiate-reclining; blades folded at base, flat above, or subinvolute, 3 to 12 cm long, 1.5 to 4 mm wide, glabrous; raceme solitary, straight or falcate, 1.2 to 4.5 cm long; spikelets mostly about 1.3 mm long, elliptic (fig. 166).

Open rocky slopes, mostly serpentine, Cuba, Haiti, and Puerto Rico.

CUBA: San Claudio, *Ekman* 12998. Guanabacoa, *Hitchcock* 23234 *Léon* 949, 2691, 11010. San Miguel de Casanova, *Léon* 12470. Campo Florido, *Léon* 3482. Amaro, *Léon* 9142. Ciénaga de Zapata, *Roig and Cremata* 2116. Sancti Spíritus, *Léon* 950. Guara, *Hitchcock* 23417, 23419½, 23424. Baraguá, *Hitchcock* 23355. Sierra de Nipe, *Ekman* in 1922 (*Amer. Gr. Nat. Herb.* 949). El Yunque, *Shafer* 7729. Jauco, *Léon* 12302. Baracoa, *Wright* 3445 in part.

HAITI: Gros-Morne, *Ekman* H 4919.

DOMINICAN REPUBLIC: Monción, *Ekman* H 12630.

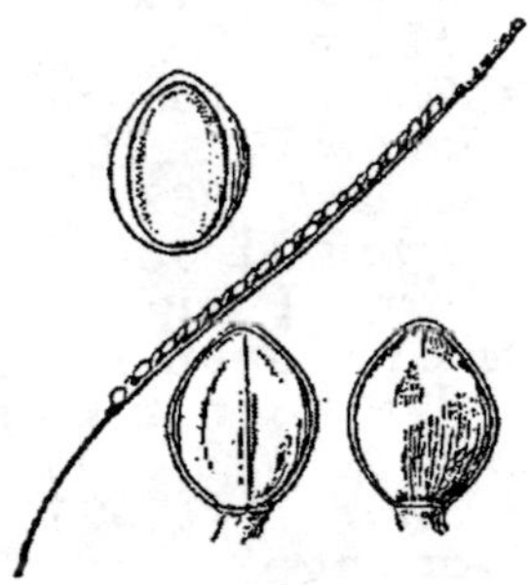

FIGURE 166.—*Paspalum rupestre.* Raceme, × 1; two views of spikelet, and floret, × 10 (Léon 950).

PUERTO RICO: Mayaguez, *Chase* 6178 (*Amer. Gr. Nat. Herb.* 567), 6259, 6274, 6275, 6299, 6312, 6315, 6323, 6811, 6813; *Holm* 152. Maricao, *Chase* 6220, 6246.

46. Paspalum saugetii Chase, Contrib. U. S. Natl. Herb. 28: 147. f. 90. 1919. Cuba, *Léon* 8982.

Culms slender, wiry, leaning or spreading, 15 to 40 cm tall, more or less twisted and tortuous; blades rather thick, usually flat when fresh, folded or involute in drying, more or less tortuous, 3 to 15 cm long, 3 to 7 mm wide; racemes commonly solitary, sometimes a second 1 to 1.5 cm distant, 2 to 4 cm long; spikelets 1.3 to 1.6 mm long, oval, appressed-pubescent (fig. 167).

Rocky, mostly limestone soil in the Greater Antilles.

This species has been confused with *Paspalum rupestre* Trin., from which it differs in its less delicate habit and longer foliage, and in the larger pubescent spikelets. It is named for Brother Léon, Joseph Sylvestre Sauget. When *P. leoninum* was described it was differentiated from this species, which was supposed to be *P. rupestre* Trin. In the Grasses of the West Indies this was tentatively referred to *P. poiretii* Roem. and Schult., but that proves to be the same as *P. caespitosum.*

BAHAMAS: Fortune Island, *Eggers* 3995.

CUBA: Between Cape San Antonio and Morro de Piedras, *Roig* 3255. Habana, *Ekman* 697; *Léon* 286, 948, 1527, 3694, 4664, 7499, 8982. Cojimar, *Baker and O'Donovan* 4417; *Ekman* 16904 (*Amer. Gr. Nat. Herb.* 950); *Hitchcock* 459, 461; *Léon* 5602; 13671. Triscornia, *Hitchcock* 458. Puentes Grandes, *Léon* 935b. Banao Mountains, *Léon* 3980. Cupey, *Ekman* 6337. Guantánamo, *Hioram* 2633. Jauco, *Léon* 12450. Baracoa, *Shafer* 3951; *Wright* 3444 in part, 3445 in part.

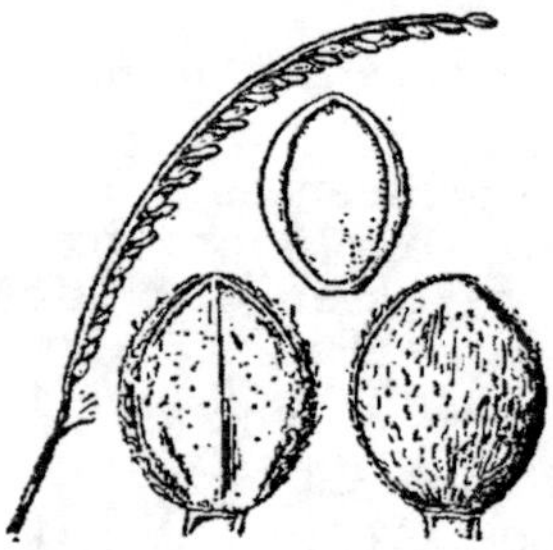

FIGURE 167.—*Paspalum saugetii.* Raceme, × 1; two views of spikelet, and floret, × 10 (type).

JAMAICA: Troy, *Harris* 12620a. Ipswich, *Hitchcock* 9599. New Forest, *Hitchcock* 9832. Bull Head Mountain, *Hitchcock* 9533. Between Ewarton and Moneague, *Hitchcock* 9442. Between Ewarton and Linstead, *Hitchcock* 9465. Claremont, *Hitchcock* 9482, 9516. Yardley Chase, *Harris* 9674. Constant Spring, *Hitchcock* 9275. Buff Bay, *Hitchcock* 9765.

HAITI: Tortuga Island, *Ekman* H 4228. Ennery, *Leonard* 8810, 10030. Môle-St.-Nicolas, *Leonard* 13208, 13283a. Port-au-Prince, *Ekman* H 2210; *Leonard* 15750. *Hitchcock* 19886, 19890. Mission, *Leonard* 3627. Fond Parisien, *Leonard* 4075. Étang Pénéte, *Ekman* H 334. Morne à Cabrits, *Ekman* H 1018. Morne Rouge, *Ekman* H 690. Aux Cayes, *Ekman* H 61. Jean Rabel, *Leonard* 13762.

DOMINICAN REPUBLIC: Jaina, *Faris* 89, 107. Azua, *Rose, Fitch, and Russell* 4079. San José de Ocoa, *Ekman* H 11921. Guerra, *Ekman* H 11018. Santo Domingo City, *Ekman* H 11121, H 12512. Constanza, *Ekman* H 13927.

PUERTO RICO: Aguada, *Chase* 6598. Lares, *Chase* 6588. Between Aguadilla and San Sebastian, *Chase* 6597.

47. Paspalum capillifolium Nash, N. Amer. Fl. 17: 181. 1912. Cuba, *Britton and Wilson* 6116.

Culms few, delicate, reclining, 10 to 35 cm long, sometimes loosely twisted and sinuous with a mass of filiform curled foliage at base; blades folded and curled, 3 to 15 cm long, about 0.3 mm wide as folded; racemes solitary, straight, 2 to 4 cm long, very slender, mostly cylindric; spikelets 1.7 mm long, elliptic (fig. 168).

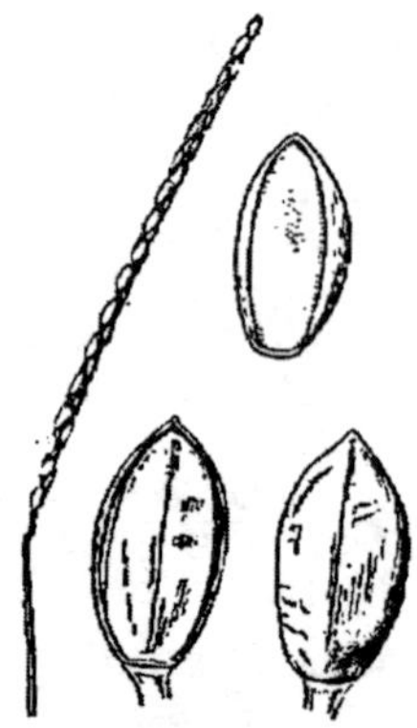

FIGURE 168.—*Paspalum capillifolium.* Raceme, × 1; two views of spikelet, and floret, × 10 (Léon 9376).

Palm barrens and savannas, Cuba.

CUBA: Santa Clara, *Britton and Wilson* 6116. Sabana de Motembo *Léon* 8223. Baños de Santa Rosalia, *Léon* 9376. Santayana, *Ekman* 19046. Holguín, *Ekman* 7565.

48. Paspalum multicaule Poir., in Lam., Encycl. Sup. 4: 309. 1816. Brazil.

Annual; culms in dense tufts, often forming mats, spreading or ascending, 20 to 45 cm tall; blades flat, drying revolute and often tortuous, 2 to 15 cm long, 1.5 to 2.5 mm wide, papillose-pilose; racemes 2, paired, divergent, commonly 2 to 4 cm long, yellowish; spikelets 1.2 to 1.4 mm long, subhemispheric, beaded with subglobular hairs (fig. 169).

Moist eroded places in savannas and open usually disturbed or washed ground, southern Mexico to Brazil and Bolivia.

CUBA: Laguna Santa Bárbara, *Ekman* 18115. Mendoza, *Shafer* 10862. Herradura, *Baker and Abarca* 4185; *Hitchcock* 472. Chiragota, *Wright* 3844 in part. Isla de Pinos, *Britton and Wilson* 14805.

DOMINICAN REPUBLIC: Cotuy, *Abbott* 850b. Cuenca, *Ekman* H 11005.

TRINIDAD: Piarco Savanna, *Broadway* 2126; *Hitchcock* 10340; *Warming* 839. O'Meara Savanna, *Britton and Hazen* 1572. Pitch Lake, *Hitchcock* 10102 (*Amer. Gr. Nat. Herb.* 574).

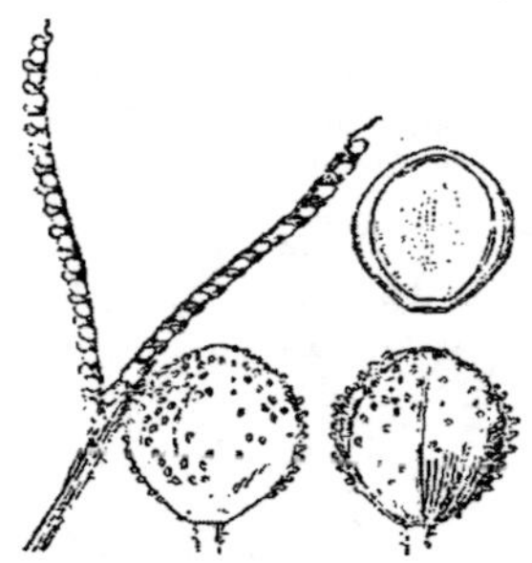

FIGURE 169.—*Paspalum multicaule.* Racemes, × 1; two views of spikelet, and floret, × 10 (Otto).

49. Paspalum clavuliferum Wright, An. Acad. Cien. Habana 8: 203. 1871; Fl. Cub. 195. 1873. Cuba, *Wright* 3444 in part.

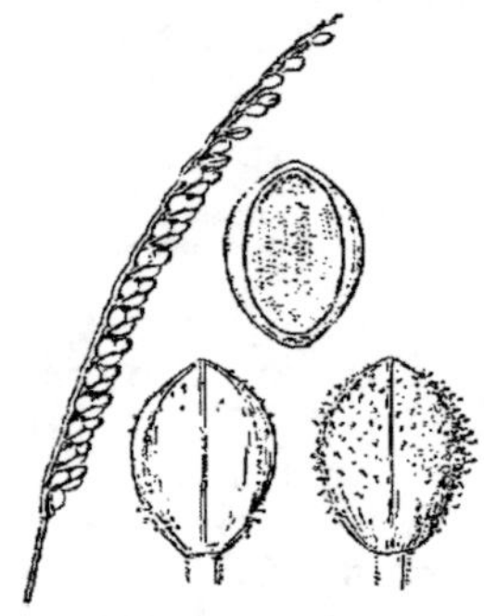

FIGURE 170.—*Paspalum clavuliferum.* Raceme, × 1; two views of spikelet, and floret, × 10 (duplicate type).

Annual; culms erect to spreading, branching, 5 to 45 cm tall; blades flat, 3 to 16 cm long, 1.5 to 3 mm wide, papillose-pilose; racemes solitary or paired, rarely with a third below, arcuate, 1 to 5.5 cm long; spikelets 1.2 to 1.4 mm long, elliptic-obovate, the glume pubescent with capitellate hairs (fig. 170).

Moist spots in sandy savannas and barrens, eroded places in open and brushy slopes, waste and cultivated ground, southern Mexico to Brazil; Cuba to Puerto Rico.

CUBA: La Coloma, *Ekman* in 1923 (*Amer. Gr. Nat. Herb.* 954). Cajálbana, *Léon* 4858. Jagüey Chico, *Ekman* 16982. Gavilanes, *Léon* 6655. Placetas del Sur, *Léon* 6417, 6418. Zaza de Tunas, *Léon* 942. Baraguá, *Hitchcock* 23379½. Guara, *Hitchcock* 23430. Eastern Cuba, *Wright* 3444 in part.

HAITI: Acul-Samedi, *Ekman* H 9911.

DOMINICAN REPUBLIC: San Juan, *Ekman* H 13402. Higüey, *Ekman* H 12209. Monción, *Ekman* H 12631. Guerra, *Ekman* H 11019.

PUERTO RICO: Campo Alegre, *Stevenson* 2454.

50. Paspalum parviflorum Rohdé; Flügge, Monogr. Pasp. 98. 1810. Puerto Rico.

Annual, densely tufted, conspicuously pilose; culms branching, ascending or spreading, 4 to 17 cm tall; blades 1.5 to 6.5 cm long, 1 to 2 mm wide; racemes 2 to 4, 2 to 10 mm distant, spreading or reflexed, 6 to 25 mm long, the rachis strongly zigzag; spikelets not imbricate, 0.8 mm long, oblong-elliptic, the glume and sterile lemma tearing apart in the middle and reduced to a rim around the spikelet (fig. 171).

Sandy savannas and sand barrens, Panama to Brazil; Puerto Rico.

PUERTO RICO: Without locality, *Rohdé* in 1809 (British Museum).

51. Paspalum breve Chase, in Urban, Symb. Antill. 7: 166. 1912. Cuba, *Léon* 1996.

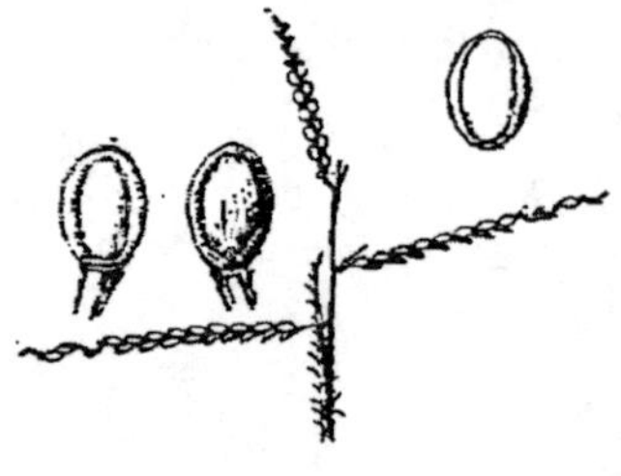

FIGURE 171.—*Paspalum parviflorum.* Panicle, × 1; two views of spikelet, and floret, × 10 (Chase 8001).

Stoloniferous perennial often forming dense leafy mats; culms subfiliform, 5 to 10 cm tall; blades mostly 3 to 6 cm long, 2 to 4 mm wide, flat or folded or subinvolute in drying; racemes usually solitary about 10 mm long; spikelets 1.4 mm long, broadly oval, fruit brownish (fig. 172).

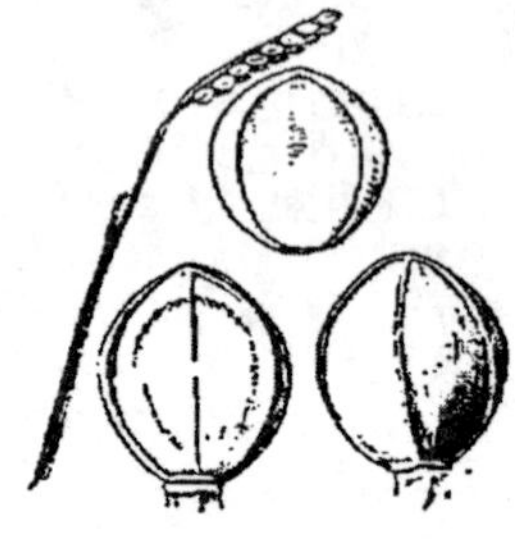

FIGURE 172.—*Paspalum breve.* Raceme, × 1; two views of spikelet, and floret, × 10 (type).

Stony, mostly calcareous, slopes, Cuba and Hispaniola.

CUBA: Gorge of Taco Taco River, *Léon* 15060. Marianao, *Léon* 1996, 3477. Serro de Esperón, *Killip* 13512. Cojimar, *Léon* 1997. Bacuranao, *Wilson and Léon* 2872, 11599. Sierra de Anafe, *Ekman* 16906. Sancti Spíritus, *Léon* 4100. Manatí, *Léon* 5681½. Bayate, *Ekman* 9843. Loma del Gato, *Léon* 9811.

HAITI: La Source, *Ekman* H 3379. Grande Riviere, *Ekman* H 449. Pestel, *Eyerdam* 357. Dame-Marie, *Ekman* H 10480.

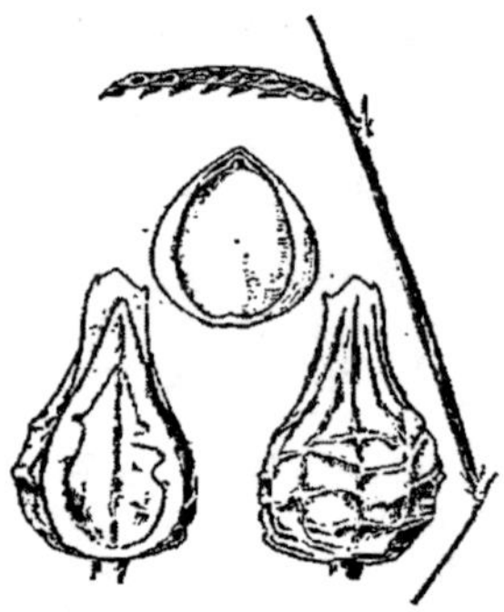

FIGURE 173.—*Paspalum edmondi.* Raceme, × 1; two views of spikelet, and floret, × 10 (duplicate type).

DOMINICAN REPUBLIC: Santo Domingo City, *Ekman* H 10957.

52. Paspalum edmondi Léon, in Britton, Mem. Torrey Bot. Club 16: 58. 1920. Cuba, *Léon and Edmond* 8607.

Low stoloniferous perennial with short slender rhizomes; culms filiform, 2 to 6 cm tall, the stolons as much as 15 cm long; foliage conspicuously spreading-pilose; blades flat, 1 to 6 cm long, 1 to 2 mm wide; raceme solitary, 10 to 15 mm long; spikelets 1.5 to 2 mm long, broadly ovate, the apex prolonged into a prominent beak; glume irregularly transversely wrinkled, less so at maturity; fruit brown (fig. 173).

Palms barrens on serpentine, Cuba.

CUBA: Motembo, *Ekman* 16822; *Léon and Edmond* 8607, 8682.

53. Paspalum orbiculatum Poir., in Lam., Encycl. 5: 32. 1804. Puerto Rico.

Paspalum pusillum Vent.; Flügge, Monogr. Pasp. 100. 1810. St. Thomas and Puerto Rico.

Paspalum lenormandi Husnot, Bull. Soc. Linn. Normand. (II) 5: 259. 1871. Martinique.

Low creeping perennial, with long leafy stolons, often forming dense mats; culms 10 to 60 cm long, decumbent and rooting at the nodes, the flowering branches 5 to 20 cm tall; blades flat, 1 to 6 cm long, 1.5 to 7 mm wide; racemes commonly 3 or 4, ascending or spreading, 0.6 to 2.3 cm long, 1 to 10 mm distant; spikelets 1 to 1.2 mm long, subhemispheric, greenish golden, turning brown between the pale margins; fruit reddish (fig. 174).

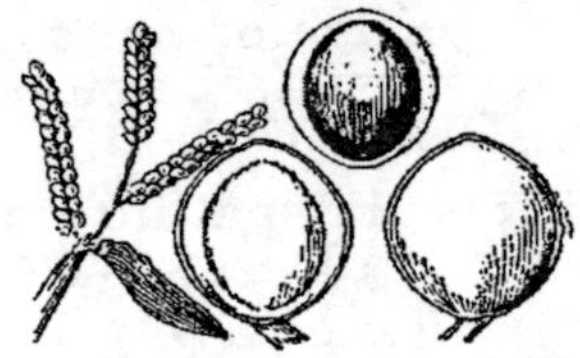

FIGURE 174.—*Paspalum orbiculatum.* Panicle, × 1; two views of spikelet, and floret, × 10 (duplicate type).

Moist open ground along streams and ditches, in savannas and old fields, southern Mexico and the West Indies to Paraguay.

CUBA: Guantánamo, *Ekman* 15806. Cajóbabo, *Léon* 12315.

DOMINICAN REPUBLIC: Cuenca, *Ekman* H 10959. Jarabaco, *Ekman* H 14191.

PUERTO RICO: Mayaguez, *Britton and Hess* 2835. Guaynabo, *Whetzel, Kern, and Toro* in 1924. Pueblo Viejo, *Sintenis* 1229. San Juan, *Heller* 664. Cayey, *Chase* 6739. Sierra de Naguabo, *Britton and Cowell* 2186.

WINDWARD ISLANDS: Antigua, *Box* 187. Martinique, *Duss* 4507. St. Lucia, *Box* 187.

TRINIDAD: St. Joseph, *Hitchcock* 10016 (*Amer. Gr. Nat. Herb.* 575). Oropuche Lagoon, *Britton, Hazen, and Freeman* 1139.

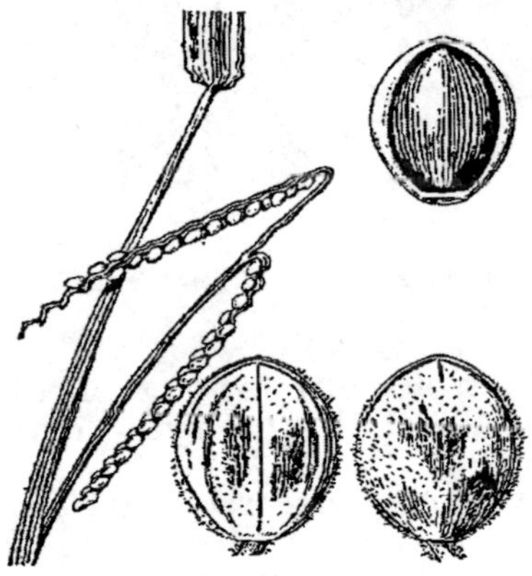

FIGURE 175.—*Paspalum reptatum.* Racemes, × 1; two views of spikelet, and floret, × 10 (type).

54. **Paspalum reptatum** Hitchc. and Chase, Contrib. U. S. Natl. Herb. 18: 318. 1917. Cuba, *Léon and Cazanas* 5850.

Creeping subaquatic perennial; culms 30 to 100 cm or more long, decumbent and rooting at the nodes; blades flat, 3 to 10 cm long, 2 to 5 mm wide, velvety pubescent to glabrous; racemes 2 or 3, commonly overtopped by the upper leaf, divergent or reflexed, 1 to 4 cm long, 5 to 10 mm distant; spikelets 1.5 to 1.7 mm long, elliptic-obovate, finely pubescent, yellowish green blotched with brown; fruit reddish brown. Cleistogamous spikelets are borne in minute sheaths at the very base (fig. 175).

In mud or shallow water, margins of ponds and depressions in savannas, Cuba and Jamaica.

CUBA: Pinar del Rio, *Ekman* 18249 (*Amer. Gr. Nat. Herb.* 957). Manacas, *Léon* 5850. Jagüey Chico, *Ekman* 16983.

JAMAICA: Inverness, *Harris* 12717.

55. **Paspalum amphicarpum** Ekman, in Chase, Contrib. U. S. Natl. Herb. 28: 161. f. 103. 1929. Cuba, *Ekman* 17565.

Glabrous widely creeping aquatic or subaquatic perennial with solitary cleistogamous spikelets borne on short subterranean branches from the base or from rooting nodes; culms 50 to 75 cm or more long, decumbent and rooting at the nodes, the flowering branches 30 to 40 cm long; blades folded at base, flat above, 5 to 15 cm long, 3 to 6 mm wide; racemes 2 or 3, divergent, 2 to 4.5 cm long, 4 to 15 mm distant; spikelets 2.5 to 2.7 mm long, elliptic, subacute, pointed beyond the fruit; fruit brownish; subterranean spikelets 4 to 5 mm long (fig. 176).

Edge of ponds, known only from Pinar del Río, Cuba.

CUBA: Laguna de Piedras, Mangas, *Ekman* 17565 (*Amer. Gr. Nat. Herb.* 958).

56. Paspalum conjugatum Bergius, Act. Helv. Phys. Math. 7: 129. pl. 8. 1762. Dutch Guiana. SOUR PASPALUM.

Extensively creeping perennial, with long leafy stolons; culms as much as 2 m long, rooting at the nodes, compressed, wiry, the flowering branches 20 to 50 cm tall; blades flat, commonly 8 to 12 cm long, 5 to 15 mm wide; racemes 2, paired or nearly so, rarely a third below,

FIGURE 176.—*Paspalum amphicarpum.* Racemes, × 1; two views of aerial spikelet, and floret and cleistogamous spikelet and floret, × 10 (type).

widely divaricate, often arcuate, usually 8 to 12 cm long; spikelets 1.4 to 1.8 mm long, flattened, ovate, pale yellow, the margin fringed with long silky hairs (fig. 177).

A common weed in cultivated and waste ground, southern United States to Argentina; throughout the West Indies. The species is said by some to be an excellent forage grass, but Maza and Roig [59] state that it is eaten by cattle only when they are driven to it by hunger. The common name "sour grass" given to this species by Grisebach would indicate that it was unpalatable. In Cuba it is called "cañamazo" and "cañamazo hembro."

56a. Paspalum conjugatum var. **pubescens** Doell, in Mart. Fl. Bras. 2^2:55. 1877. Brazil.

On the average coarser, the blades somewhat firmer, pubescent; spikelets 1.7 to 2.2 mm long, the silky hairs more copious.

Along ditches and banks, Mexico and the Lesser Antilles to Brazil.

VIRGIN ISLANDS: St. Thomas, *Eggers* in 1881.

WINDWARD ISLANDS: Grenada, *Broadway* 1744. St. Kitts, *Box* 150.

[59] Est. Expt. Agron. Bol. 22: 57. 1914.

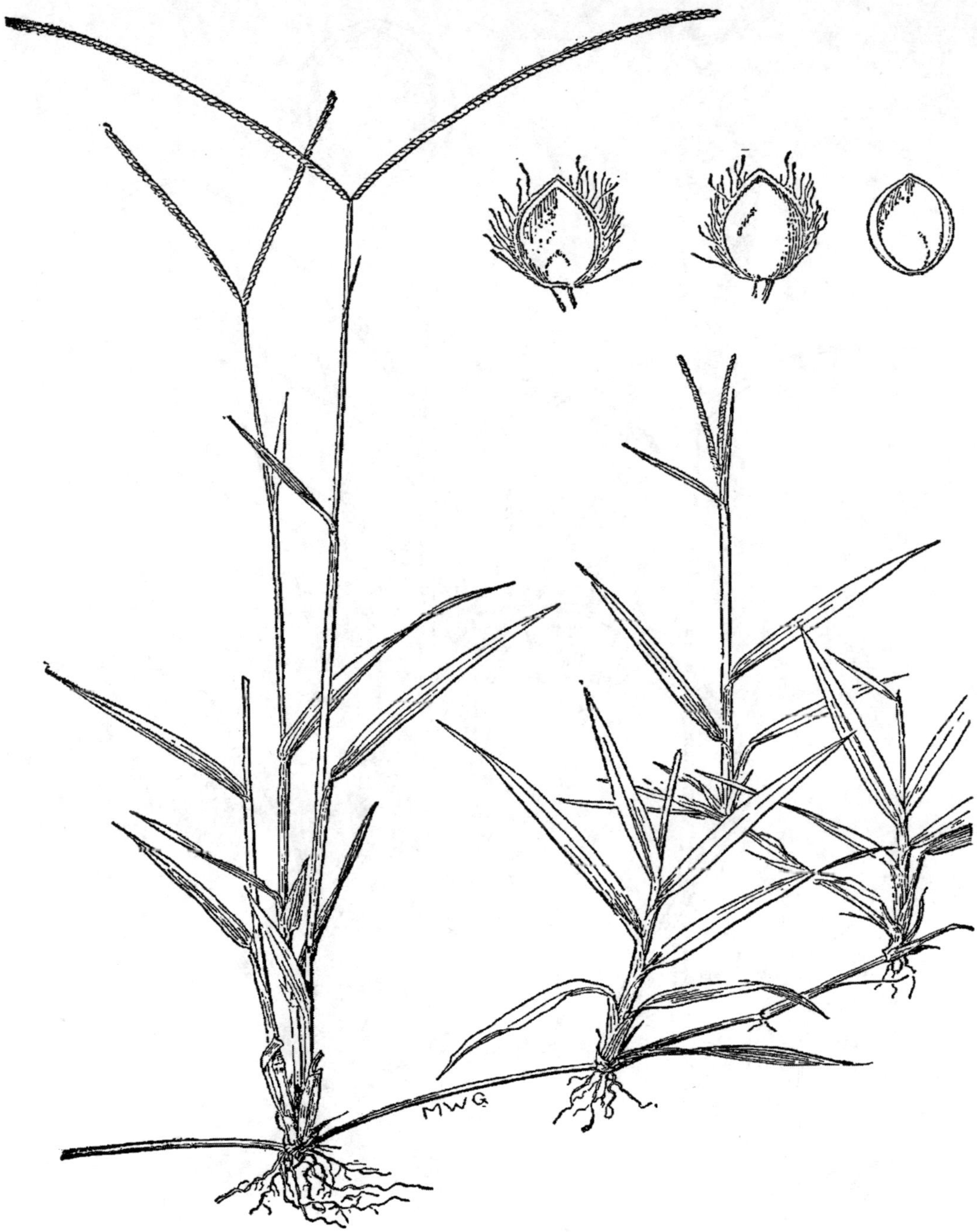

FIGURE 177.—*Paspalum conjugatum*. Plant, × ½; two views of spikelet, and floret, × 10 (Baker 90).

FIGURE 178.—*Paspalum dilatatum*. Plant, × ½; two views of spikelet, and floret, × 10 (Hitchcock 297).

57. Paspalum dilatatum Poir., in Lam., Encycl. 5: 35. 1804. Argentina. PASPALUM.

Culms ascending or erect, 40 to 175 cm tall; blades flat, commonly 10 to 25 cm long, 3 to 12 mm wide; racemes commonly 3 to 5, ascending or drooping, about 6 to 8 cm long; spikelets 2.8 to 3.8 mm long, ovate, pointed, depressed plano-convex, fringed with long white silky hairs (fig. 178).

Pastures and waste ground, sparingly introduced in the West Indies; southeastern United States; native of South America from Brazil to Argentina. Cultivated in the southern United States, where it is considered a valuable pasture grass. Called paspalum or paspalum grass and recently Dallis grass.

BERMUDA: Agricultural Station, *Brown, Britton, and Bisset* 2005. Shelley Bay, *Collins* 156.

CUBA: Mariel, *Ekman* 12855 (*Amer. Gr. Nat. Herb.* 962).

JAMAICA: Richmond Park, *Harris* 12708.

HAITI: St. Louis du Nord, *Leonard* 14387.

DOMINICAN REPUBLIC: Jaina, *Faris* 329.

58. Paspalum urvillei Steud., Syn. Pl. Glum. 1: 24. 1854. Brazil. VASEY GRASS.

Paspalum larrañagai Arech., An. Mus. Nac. Montevideo 1: 60. pl. 2. 1894. Uruguay.

Paspalum vaseyanum Scribn., U. S. Dept. Agr., Div. Agrost. Bull. 17: 32. f. 328. 1899. Southern United States.

Culms erect, 1 to 2.5 m tall; lower sheaths hirsute; blades flat, commonly 20 to 30 cm long, 3 to 15 mm wide; panicle erect, 10 to 40 cm long; racemes mostly 12 to 18, ascending, approximate, the lower 7 to 14 cm long, the upper gradually shorter; spikelets about 2.5 mm long (2 to 3 mm), ovate, abruptly pointed, flattened, fringed with long, silky hairs (fig. 179).

Along ditches and roadsides, and in waste ground, southern United States; native from Brazil to Argentina; introduced sparingly in Cuba. Known as Vasey grass in the United States, where it is sometimes cut for hay.

CUBA: Baraguá, *Hitchcock* 23353.

59. Paspalum fasciculatum Willd.; Flügge, Monogr. Pasp. 69. 1810. Brazil.

Large extensively creeping leafy stoloniferous perennial, the stolons as much as 5 m long; culms as much as 2 m tall and 1 cm thick at base; blades flat, ascending to spreading, 20 to 60 cm long, 1.2 to 3 cm wide; panicle flabellate, of usually 12 to 20 ascending racemes, 7 to 17 cm long, aggregate on a short axis; spikelets 4 to 4.5 mm long, elliptic, silky-ciliate on the margin (fig. 180).

Borders of streams, low ground, and swamps, southern Mexico to Ecuador and Argentina.

WINDWARD ISLANDS: St. Lucia, *Box* 191 (sterile).

TRINIDAD: St. Joseph, *Hitchcock* 10029.

TOBAGO: Plymouth, *Hitchcock* 10281.

60. Paspalum virgatum L., Syst. Nat. ed. 10. 2: 855. 1759. Jamaica. CORTADERO.

Paspalum virgatum var. *jacquinianus* Flügge, Monogr. Pasp. 190. 1810. Caribbean Islands.

FIGURE 179.—*Paspalum urvillei.* Plant, × ½; two views of spikelet, and floret, × 10 (Chase 4388).

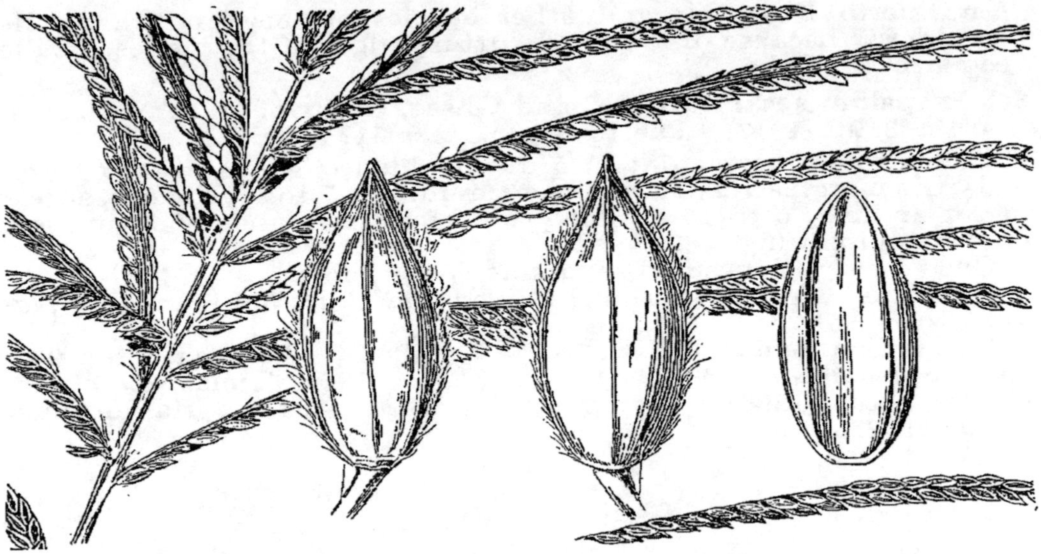

FIGURE 180.—*Paspalum fasciculatum*. Panicle, × 1; two views of spikelet, and floret, × 10 (Hitchcock 7899)

Paspalum virgatum var. *stramineum* Griseb., Fl. Brit. W. Ind. 543 1864. Jamaica and Antigua.

Paspalum leucocheilum Wright, An. Acad. Cien. Habana 8: 203. 1871. Isla de Pinos, *Blain*.

Culms robust, 1 to 2 m tall; blades flat, elongate, 1 to 2.5 cm wide; panicle 15 to 25 cm long; racemes mostly 10 to 16, ascending to drooping, the lower 5 to 15 cm long; spikelets about 2.5 mm long, obovate, pubescent along the margin (fig. 181).

Open moist or swampy ground, Mexico and throughout the West Indies to Brazil.

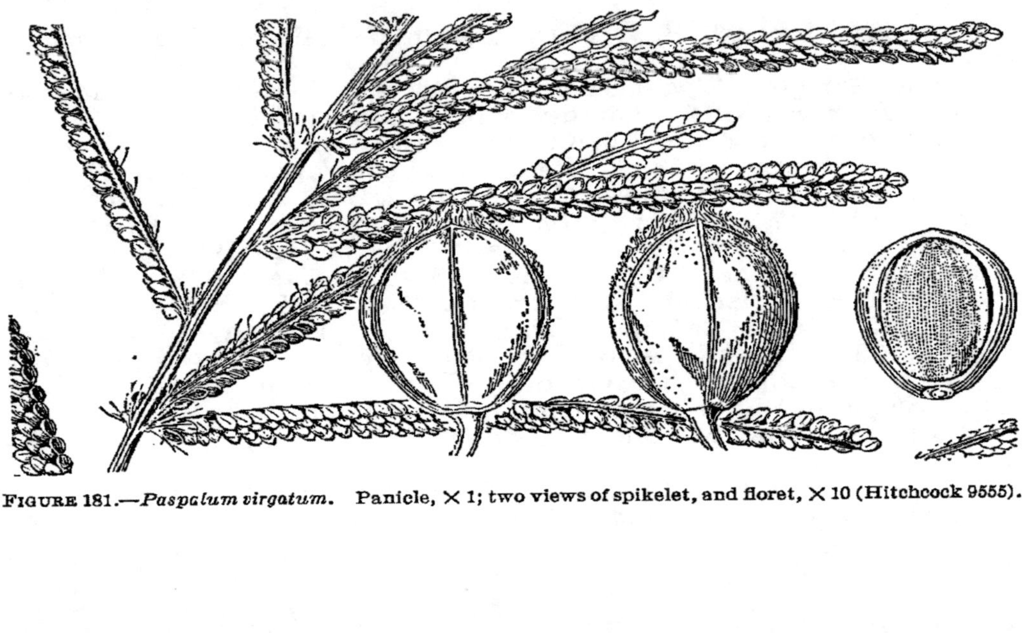

FIGURE 181.—*Paspalum virgatum*. Panicle, × 1; two views of spikelet, and floret, × 10 (Hitchcock 9555).

In Puerto Rico this and other species of this group are called "cortadero" because of the cruel cutting edges of the blades. Called "caguazo" in Cuba.

61. Paspalum secans Hitchc. and Chase, Contrib. U. S. Natl. Herb. 18: 319. 1917. Puerto Rico, *Chase* 6174.

Culms robust, erect, 1 to 1.5 m tall; blades elongate, 5 to 10 mm wide, the margins very sharp; racemes mostly 7 to 12, slender, spreading or arching, 6 to 15 cm long; spikelets pale, about 2.5 mm long, obovate-elliptic (fig. 182).

Open brushy slopes and savannas, West Indies.

Bahamas: New Providence, *Britton and Brace* 598. Inagua, *Nash and Taylor* 956.

Cuba: Santiago de los Baños, *Léon* 4366½. Habana, *Léon* 931b, 932. Soledad, *Jack* 6201. Cano, *Ekman* 184. Tunas, *Léon* 6743. Canasí, *Léon* 12961. Baraguá, *Hitchcock* 23343. Isla de Pinos, *Ekman* 12223.

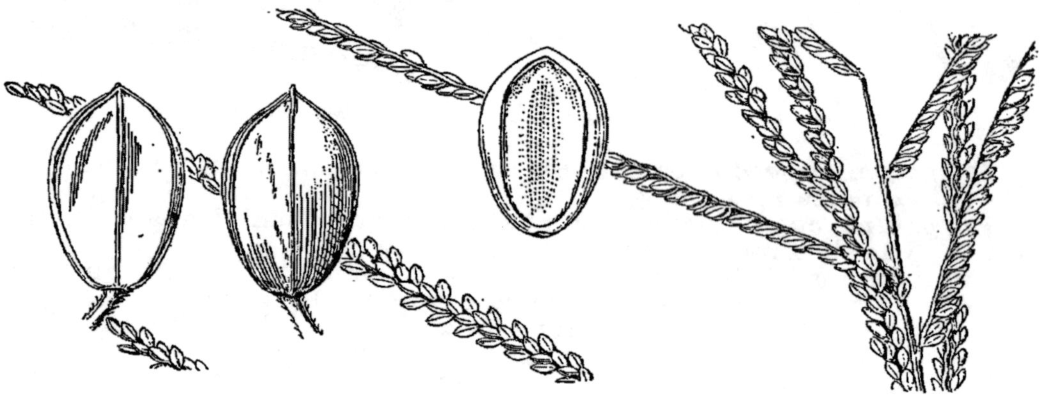

Figure 182.—*Paspalum secans*. Panicle, × 1; two views of spikelet, and floret, × 10 (type).

Jamaica: Montego Bay, *Hitchcock* 9670. Black River, *Hitchcock* 9649.

Haiti: Gourjon, *Ekman* H 6451. Between Les Anglais and Chardonnier, *Ekman* H 384. Tortuga Island, *Leonard* 11702.

Dominican Republic: Monción, *Ekman* H 12611; *Valeur* 417. Matanzas, *Ekman* H 15899. Peninsula de Samaná, *Ekman* H 15362.

Puerto Rico: Mayaguez, *Chase* 6261 (*Amer. Gr. Nat. Herb.* 577), *Chase* 6150, 6174, 6309; *Holm* 84. Maricao, *Chase* 6193, 6238. Arecibo, *Chase* 6444, 6559. Lares, *Chase* 6581. Between Utuado and Adjuntas, *Chase* 6465. Campo Alegre, *Chase* 6787. Between Ponce and Santa Isabel, *Britton and Brown* 5518. Bayamon, *Chase* 6382, 6387, 6409. Catano, *Chase* 6641. Rio Piedras, *Chase* 6372; *Wetmore* 167. Trujillo Alto, *Sein* 321. Caguas, *Britton and Cowell* 1405; *Sintenis* 2539. Rio Grande, *Chase* 6707, 6716, 6723. Loma Icaco, *Shafer* 3415. Vieques Island, *Chase* 6698.

Virgin Islands: St. Thomas, *Foster*. St. Croix, *Hitchcock* 16323; *Ricksecker* 434.

Leeward Islands: Antigua, *Wullschlaegel* 603; *Box* 41, 56, 96, 113. Guadeloupe, *Hitchcock* 16408.

62. Paspalum arundinaceum Poir., in Lam., Encycl. Sup. 4: 310. 1816. Cayenne.

Culms robust, erect, 1 to 2 m tall; blades elongate, 5 to 10 mm wide; racemes usually 12 to 18, rather thick, ascending, 8 to 20 cm long, approximate or fascicled, the axis 10 to 20 cm long; spikelets about 2.5 mm long, obovate-elliptic (fig. 183).

In marshes and low open ground, West Indies, Guatemala, and French Guiana.

CUBA: Pinar del Río, *Hitchcock* 23293. Herradura, *Hitchcock* 478. Guanajay, *Palmer and Riley* 813. Habana, *Tracy* 9125, 9126. Cano, *Ekman* 184. Batabanó, *Baker and Wilson* 2303; *Hitchcock* 477. Hanábana, *Wright* 3446 in part. Cayamas, *Baker* 3626.

JAMAICA: Black River, *Harris* 12544; *Hitchcock* 9644. Bull Head Mountain, *Hitchcock* 9536. Between Ewarton and Linstead, *Hitchcock* 9457. Annotta Bay, *Harris* 12469a.

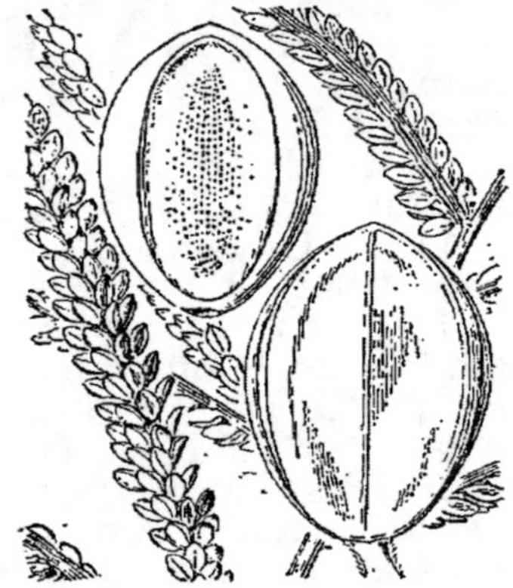

FIGURE 183.—*Paspalum arundinaceum.* Panicle, × 1; spikelet and floret, × 10 (Hitchcock 9457).

HAITI: Plaisance, *Cook, Scofield, and Doyle* 174. Trouin, *Ekman* H 2435. Gourjon, *Ekman* H 6452. Fond Parisien, *Leonard* 4174, 4187. Ennery, *Leonard* 9079. Bassïn Bleu, *Leonard* 15033.

DOMINICAN REPUBLIC: Pimentel, *Ekman* H 13240. Santo Domingo City, *Ekman* H 11576. Santiago, *Ekman* H 16091.

LEEWARD ISLANDS: Antigua, *Hitchcock* 16375.

63. Paspalum millegrana Schrad., in Schult., Mant. 2: 175. 1824. Brazil.

Paspalum underwoodii Nash, Bull. Torrey Bot. Club 30: 375. 1903. Puerto Rico, *Underwood and Griggs* 149.

Culms erect, robust, 1 to 2 m tall; blades elongate, 7 to 15 mm wide; racemes commonly 12 to 25, rather thick, ascending to spread-

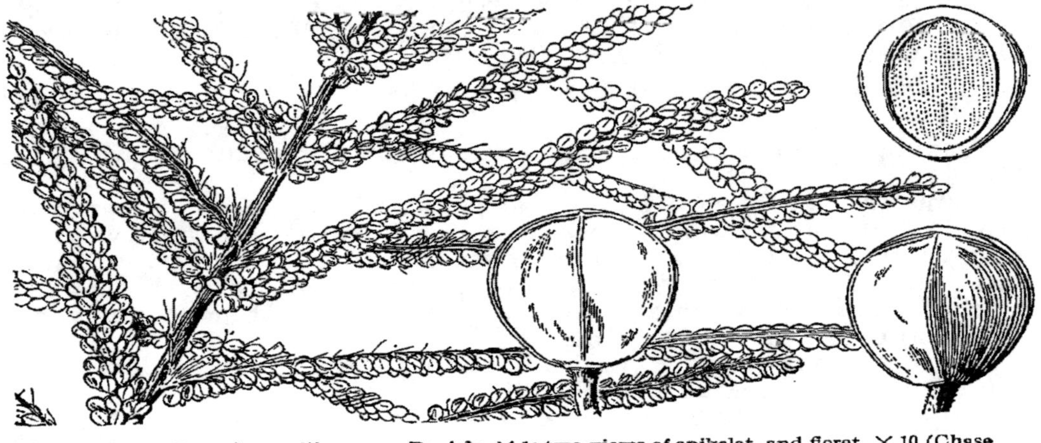

FIGURE 184.—*Paspalum millegrana.* Panicle, × 1; two views of spikelet, and floret, × 10 (Chase 7840).

ing, approximate, 6 to 16 cm long; spikelets 2 to 2.4 mm long, obovate-suborbicular, flattened, pale to leaden-purplish (fig. 184).

Moist savannas, along ditches, and in low open ground. Central America and the West Indies to Brazil.

BAHAMAS: New Providence, *Krebs* (Copenhagen Herb).

CUBA: Santiago de Los Baños, *Léon* 4364. Pinar del Río, *Hitchcock* 23259. Habana, *Léon* 931, 4157, 4160; *Tracy* 9121. Guanabacoa, *Léon* 2870. Bajucal, *Van Hermann* 347. Cano, *Léon* 1987. Santiago de las Vegas, *Van Hermann* 142. Tunas, *Léon* 6735. San Marcos Savanna, *Léon* 9183. San Miguel de los Baños, *Killip* 13920. Lagoon Mojabraga, *Léon* 9413. Between Camagüey and Santayana, *Britton* 2361. Baraguá, *Hitchcock* 23366. Sierra de Nipe, *Ekman* 10118. Bayate, *Ekman* 6176. Without locality, *Wright* 3446 in part, 3840.

JAMAICA: Savanna-la-Mar, *Hitchcock* 9869. Troy, *Harris* 12657. Bull Head Mountain, *Hitchcock* 9557. Savoy, *Harris* 11620. Ashley Hall, *Harris* 12730. Annotta Bay, *Harris* 12469, 12534, 12658, 12660. Buff Bay, *Hitchcock* 9776.

HAITI: Aux Cayes, *Ekman* H 256, H 861.

DOMINICAN REPUBLIC: Jaina, *Faris* 267. Pimentel, *Ekman* H 13242. Sabana Guabatico, *Ekman* H 13322.

PUERTO RICO: Mayaguez, *Chase* 6316 (*Amer. Gr. Nat. Herb.* 578); *Chase* 6153, 6164, 6187, 6257½, 6303; *Goll* 923; *Heller* 4368; *Sintenis* 1223 in part; *Underwood and Griggs* 149. Maricao, *Chase* 6237. Arecibo, *Chase* 6441, 6565. Campo Alegre, *Chase* 6626. Vega Baja, *Britton and Cowell* 1449; *Chase* 6793, 6794. Bayamon, *Chase* 6373, 6646. Catano, *Chase* 6637. San Juan, *Chase* 6356, 6359, 6785. Rio Piedras, *Cowgill* 691; *Wetmore* 176. Trujillo Alto, *Chase* 6761 6775½. Mameyes, *Chase* 6650. Rio Grande, *Chase* 6725. Fajardo, *Chase* 6655, 6704. Humacao, *Eggers* 676. Vieques Island, *Chase* 6687.

LEEWARD ISLANDS: Antigua, *Box* 186. Guadeloupe, *Balbis* in 1822; *Hitchcock* 16411.

WINDWARD ISLANDS: St. Lucia, *Box* 186.

TRINIDAD: Cedros, *Broadway* 4921; *Hitchcock* 10145. Icacos, *Hitchcock* 10156. Dabadie, *Broadway*. Manzanilla, *Hitchcock* 10366.

TOBAGO: Scarborough, *Hitchcock* 10285. Milford Road, *Broadway* 3066. Old Grange Road, *Broadway* 4696.

64. **Paspalum densum** Poir., in Lam., Encycl. 5: 32. 1804. Puerto Rico.

Paspalum paniceum J. E. Smith, in Rees's Cycl. 26: no. 14. 1813. Jamaica.

Culms erect; robust, 1 to 2 m tall; blades elongate, 1 to 2 cm wide; panicle 12 to 30 cm long, dense, tapering upward; racemes 50 to 100, rather thick, the lower 5 to 9 cm long, the others successively shorter and more crowded, the rachis conspicuously ciliate with stiff hairs 2 to 5 mm long; spikelets about 2 mm long, suborbicular, tan to brownish or purplish (fig. 185).

Marshes, wet savannas, and low open ground, or in shallow water, West Indies to Panama and Brazil.

CUBA: Mántua, *Ekman* 11085. Hanábana, *Wright* 3447. Rodrigo, *Léon* 9135. Placetas del Sur, *Léon* 6420. Baraguá, *Hitchcock* 23381.

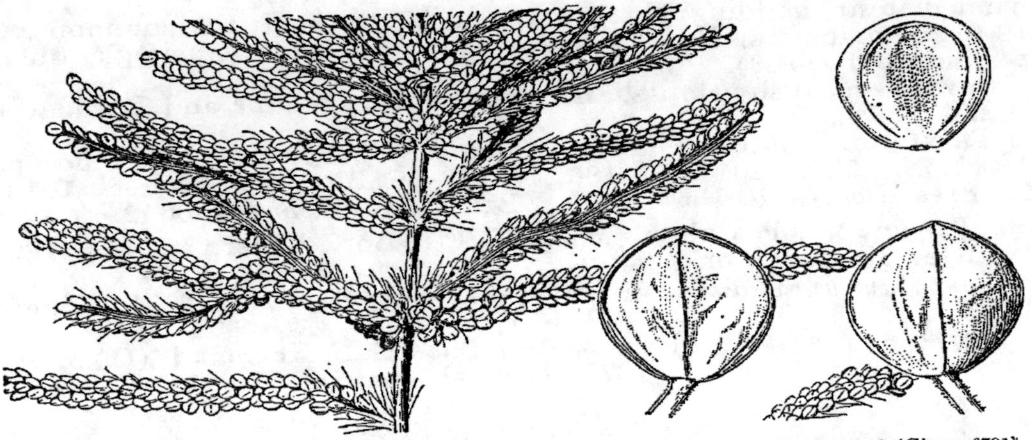

FIGURE 185.—*Paspalum densum.* Panicle × 1; two views of spikelet, and floret, × 10 (Chase 6791).

JAMAICA: Bull Head Mountain, *Hitchcock* 9556 (*Amer. Gr. Nat. Herb.* 579), Killits, *Harris* 11149. Appleton, *Hitchcock* 9657. Bog Walk, *Harris* 12214.

HAITI: Marmelade, *Leonard* 8357. Caille la Croix, *Leonard* 7989. St. Michel de l'Atalaye, *Ekman* H 9416. Petite-Riviere de l'Artibonite, *Ekman* H 3430.

DOMINICAN REPUBLIC: Pimentel, *Abbott* 671; *Ekman* H 13241. Leonor, *Valeur* 505. Sabana de la Mar, *Ekman* H 15663.

PUERTO RICO: Vega Baja, *Chase* 6791. Between Bayamon and Cantano, *Stahl* 42.

VIRGIN ISLANDS: St. Thomas, *Riedley.*

LEEWARD ISLANDS: Guadeloupe, *Duss* 4224.

TRINIDAD: St. Joseph, *Hitchcock* 10025. St. Augustine, *Hart* 2155. Longdenville, *Broadway* 2618. Claxton Bay, *Hitchcock* 10115.

65. Paspalum coryphaeum Trin., Gram. Pan. 114. 1826. Brazil.

Paspalum violascens Mez, Repert. Sp. Nov. Fedde 15: 73. 1917. Trinidad, *Bot. Gard. Herb.* 2175.

Culms 1 to 4 m tall, with short hard rhizomes; blades flat, elongate, 1 to 2 cm wide, puberulent to nearly glabrous; racemes 10 to 45, some-

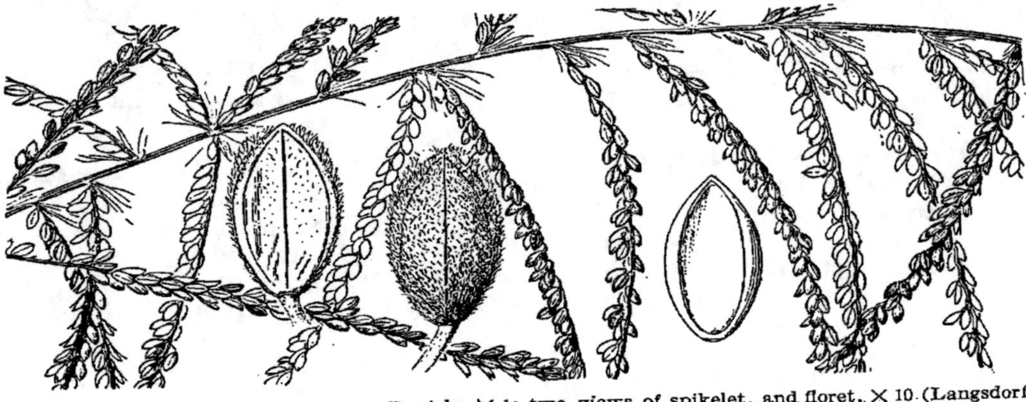

FIGURE 186.—*Paspalum coryphaeum.* Panicle, × 1; two views of spikelet, and floret, × 10 (Langsdorff, and Chase 9058).

what distant, nodding, the lower 6 to 12 cm long, the common axis 10 to 25 cm long; spikelets 2 to 2.5 mm long, elliptic, finely glandular-pubescent (fig. 186).

Savannas, brushy slopes, and river banks, Panama and Trinidad to Brazil.

TRINIDAD: Botanic Garden, *Broadway* 2175, 5947. St. Joseph, *Hitchcock* 10183, 10184, 10186, 10192. California, *Hitchcock* 10107. La Brea, *Bot. Gard. Herb.* 2262. Brighton, *Hitchcock* 10092.

66. Paspalum plicatulum Michx., Fl. Bor. Amer. 1: 45. 1803. Georgia and Florida.

Paspalum undulatum Poir., in Lam., Encycl. 5: 29. 1804. Puerto Rico.

Paspalum antillense Husnot, Bull. Soc. Linn. Normand. (II) 5: 260. 1871. Guadeloupe.

Panicum plicatulum Kuntze, Rev. Gen. Pl. 3^2: 363. 1898.

Culms erect or ascending, 50 to 100 cm tall, rather slender; blades mostly folded at base, elongate, 3 to 10 mm wide; racemes 2 to several, usually 3 to 10, 2 to 10 cm long; spikelets usually 2.5 to 2.8 mm long, obovate-oval, the sterile lemma wrinkled transversely just inside the margin; fruit dark brown (fig. 187).

Open ground or wood borders, southeastern United States to Argentina; throughout the West Indies.

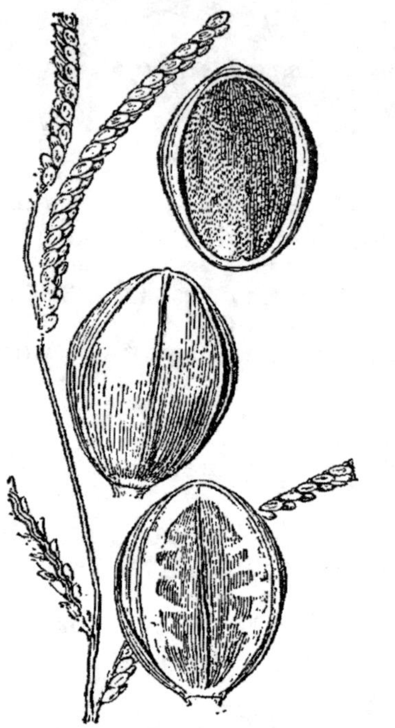

FIGURE 187.—*Paspalum plicatulum.* Panicle, × 1; two views of spikelet, and floret, × 10 (Chase 7061).

FIGURE 188.—*Paspalum wrightii.* Panicle, × 1; two views of spikelet, and floret, × 10 (type).

67. Paspalum wrightii Hitchc. and Chase, Contrib. U. S. Natl. Herb. 18: 310. 1917. Cuba, *Wright* 3843.

Subaquatic; culms about 1.5 m tall, erect from a decumbent or floating base; blades flat, elongate, about 5 mm wide, long-pilose just back of the ligule; racemes 5 to 9, ascending, 4 to 8 cm long, the axis 8 to 10 cm long; spikelets about 2.5 mm long, elliptic; fruit brown (fig. 188).

Margin of pools and streams, Gulf Coast, Texas, and western Cuba, sometimes forming dense colonies.

CUBA: Pinar del Río, *Wright* 3843. Arroyo Mateo Sánchez, *Ekman* 17910 (*Amer. Gr. Nat. Herb.* 978).

68. Paspalum motembense Léon, in Britton, Bull. Torrey Bot. Club 53: 457. 1926. Cuba, *Léon and Loustalot* 9354.

Culms about 60 cm tall, erect, with a short rhizome; blades mostly folded, elongate, 5 to 8 mm wide; racemes several, ascending, the lower about 5 cm long, the upper gradually shorter, the axis about 15 cm long; spikelets 2.5 mm long, elliptic; fruit brown (fig. 189).

Grassy places, Cuba. Known only from the type collection, from Motembo, Province of Santa Clara.

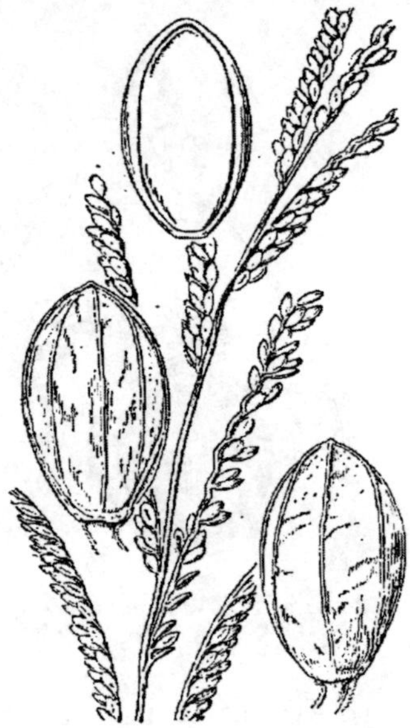

FIGURE 189.—*Paspalum motembense.* Panicle, × 1; two views of spikelet, and floret, × 10 (type).

69. Paspalum urbanianum Ekman, sp. nov.[60]

Perennial with a short scaly rhizome; culms 80 to 100 cm tall erect, appressed branches from the lower nodes, the lower part slightly spongy, clothed with overlapping old sheaths; leaves numerous, crowded toward the base, the sheaths papillose-hirsute toward the summit, usually conspicuously so on the collar; ligule membranaceous, scarcely 1 mm long; blades terete, the margins grown together above the hispid base, stiff but rather brittle, 30 to 60 cm long (the uppermost reduced) 1.5 to 2 mm thick, erect or ascending, sharp-pointed; racemes 3 to 5, slender, narrowly ascending, purplish-brown, 8 to 15 cm long, 3 to 5 cm distant on a slender common axis; rachis 0.7 to 0.8 mm wide, flexuous, sometimes naked at base; spikelets in pairs or solitary on short scabrous pedicels, not crowded, sometimes distant, often unsymmetrical, 3.5 to 3.8 mm long, about 1.5 mm wide, elliptic, acute; glume and sterile lemma equal, pointed beyond the fruit, glabrous or very obscurely pubescent, 5-nerved, the outer pair of nerves obscure, thin, the lemma sometimes faintly wrinkled; fruit 3 mm long, minutely papillose-striate, chestnut-brown, the apex and margin of the lemma paler (fig. 190).

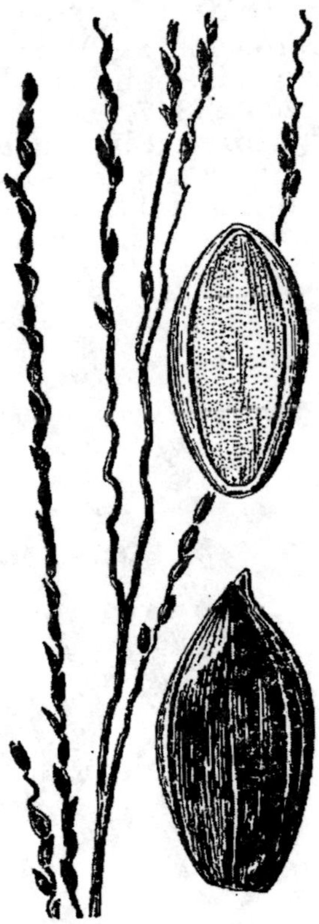

FIGURE 190.—*Paspalum urbanianum.* Panicle, × 1; spikelet and floret, × 10 (type).

Type in the United States National Herbarium, no. 1502227, collected in a moist place, about 2,000 m altitude, Loma Tina, prov. Azua, in the Cordillera Central, Dominican Republic, October 9, 1929, by E. L. Ekman (no. H 13712).

[60] Perenne; culmi 80-100 cm alti erecti; folia numerosa; vaginae summo hispidae; laminae elongata; suberectae cylindricae subrigidae pungentes; racemi 3–5 purpurei 8–15 cm longi; rachis 0.7–0.8 mm lata spiculae geminae 3.5–3.8 mm longae 1.5 mm latae acutae glabrae vel obscure pubescentes; fructus 3 mm longus castaneus.

The base of the type specimen and of *Ekman* H 13603 suggest that the plants were growing in deep humus, such as is often found in open ground above timberline. A note by Dr. Ekman on H 13603 reads: "Silt flats, about 1,950 m, very abundant. One of the very few plants characteristic of the high mountain group west of Constanza. As a rule all plants found in this region grow also in the Los Valles region." No. H 13542 is said to form vast colonies. Known only from Cordillera Central, prov. Azua, Dominican Republic.

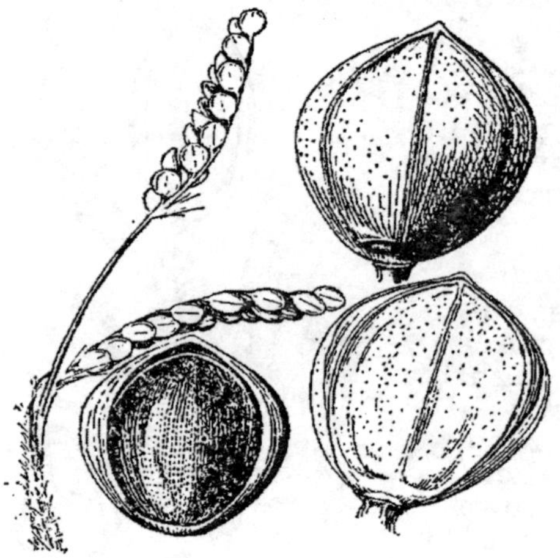

FIGURE 191.—*Paspalum convexum*. Panicle, × 1; two views of spikelet, and floret, × 10 (Palmer 592 in 1866).

DOMINICAN REPUBLIC: Loma Tina, *Ekman* H 13712. San Juan, Arroyo del Oro, *Ekman* H 13542; Lomas de la Medianía, *Ekman* H 13603.

70. Paspalum convexum Humb. and Bonpl., in Flügge, Monogr. Pasp. 175. 1810. Mexico.

Paspalum hemicryptum Wright, An. Acad. Cien. Habana 8: 204. 1871. Cuba, *Wright* 3847.

Tufted leafy branching usually spreading annual; culms usually 20 to 40 cm tall; blades flat, ratherlax, 5 to 20 cm long, 3 to 11 mm wide; racemes usually 2 or 3, thick, 2 to 4 cm long; spikelets 2.2 to 3 mm long, obovate-suborbicular, appressed-pubescent to glabrous; fruit dark brown (fig. 191).

Open ground, cultivated and waste places, Mexico to Brazil; Cuba and Trinidad, probably introduced.

CUBA: El Salado, *Wright* 3847. Gamboa, *Ekman* 15008.

TRINIDAD: La Brea, *Broadway* 4983. Pitch Lake, *Broadway* 9012½.

71. Paspalum melanospermum Desv., in Poir., in Lam., Encycl. Sup. 4: 315. 1816. Cayenne.

Paspalum olivaceum Hitchc. and Chase, Contrib. U. S. Natl. Herb. 18: 310. 1917. Guadeloupe, *Duss* 3915.

Leafy nearly glabrous annual; culms 40 to 70 cm long, ascending from a decumbent base; blades lax, flat, 10 to 15 cm long, 5 to 10 mm wide; racemes 2 to 7, arcuate-spreading, 1 to 6 cm long, the slender subflexuous axis 4 to 8 cm long; spikelets 2 mm long, obovate, brown; fruit dark brown (fig. 192).

FIGURE 192.—*Paspalum melanospermum*. Panicle, × 1; two views of spikelet, and floret, × 10 (Duss 3915).

Open moist ground, northern South America; Guadeloupe and Martinique, probably introduced.

LEEWARD ISLANDS: Guadeloupe, *Duss* 3915; *Husnot* 76 in part.

WINDWARD ISLANDS: Martinique, *Duss* 4012; *Hitchcock* 16445.

72. Paspalum boscianum Flügge, Monogr. Pasp. 170. 1810. Carolina. BULL PASPALUM.

Rather succulent branching annual; culms mostly 20 to 60 cm long, ascending to widely spreading; blades flat, mostly 15 to 30 cm long, 8 to 10 mm wide; racemes usually 4 to 11, 2.5 to 9 cm long,

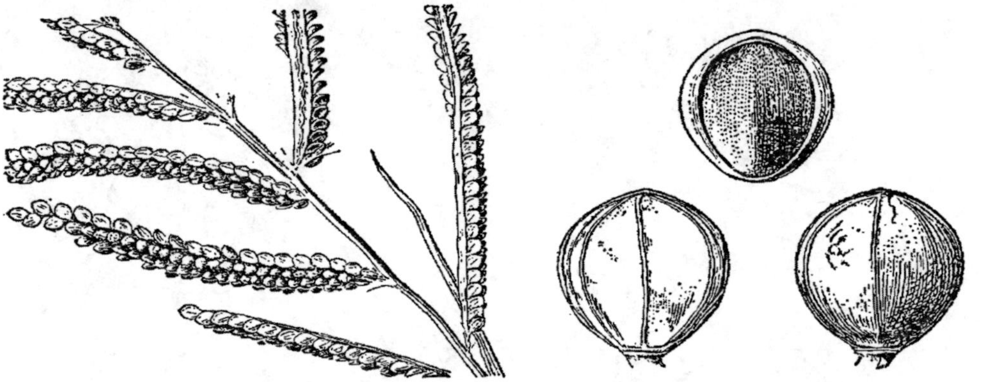

FIGURE 193.—*Paspalum boscianum*. Panicle, × 1; two views of spikelet, and floret, × 10 (Kearney 152).

the rachis 2 to 2.5 mm wide; spikelets 2 to 2.2 mm long, obovate-suborbicular; fruit brown (fig. 193).

In the Grasses of the West Indies this species was described under *P. melanospermum* Desv.

Moist or wet open ground, along ditches and ponds, sometimes a weed in cultivated soil, southeastern United States; West Indies to Brazil.

DOMINICAN REPUBLIC: Azua, *Ekman* H 13673. Cuenca, *Ekman* H 11002. Higüey, *Ekman* H 12177. Constanza, *Ekman* H 14070. Sabana de la Mar, *Ekman* H 15551.

PUERTO RICO: Mayaguez, *Chase* 6172. Maricao, *Chase* 6234. Sierra Luquillo, *Chase* 6724; *Hioram* 367.

VIRGIN ISLANDS: St. Thomas, *Herb. Ventenat* (Delessert Herb.).

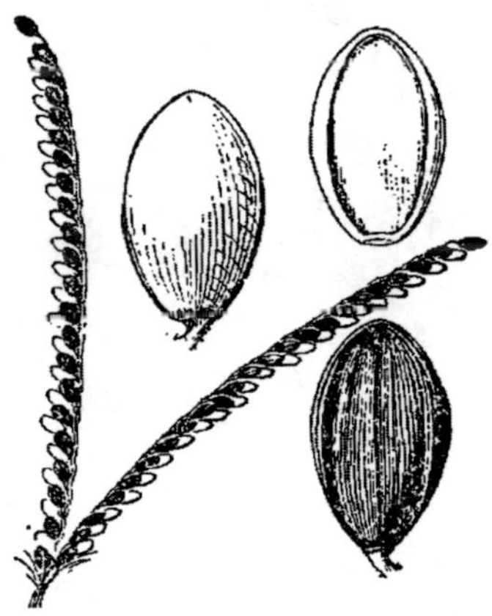

FIGURE 194.—*Paspalum pulchellum*. Racemes, × 1; two views of spikelet, and floret, × 10 (Hitchcock 10066).

73. Paspalum pulchellum Kunth, Mèm. Mus. Hist. Nat. 2: 68. 1815. Based on *Reimaria elegans* Humb. and Bonpl.

Reimaria elegans Humb. and Bonpl.; Flügge, Monogr. Pasp. 216. 1810. Not *Paspalum elegans* Flügge, op. cit. 183. Venezuela.

Culms erect, slender, 25 to 75 cm tall; blades flat, becoming involute, 5 to 25 cm long, 1.5 to 4 mm wide, papillose-pilose; racemes usually 2, approximate, or somewhat distant, 2 to 9 cm long; spikelets 1.7 to 2 mm long, elliptic, the glume wanting, the sterile lemma often dark purple (fig. 194).

Sandy mostly moist savannas and pinelands, Guatemala to Brazil; Cuba, Hispaniola, and Trinidad.

FIGURE 195.—*Paspalum fimbriatum.* Plant, × ½ (Chase 6296); two views of spikelet, and floret, × 10 (Hitchcock 9773).

CUBA: Guane, *Léon* 6936. Herradura, *Baker and Dimmock* 4813; *Ekman* in 1922 (*Amer. Gr. Nat. Herb.* 984); *Hitchcock* 469. Hanábana, *Wright* 171. San Marcos, *Léon* 9185. Placetas del Sur, *Léon* 8156. Nagua, *Léon* 11344. Isla de Pinos, *Britton and Wilson* 14282; *Ekman* 11715. Without locality, *Wright* 3439.

DOMINICAN REPUBLIC: Matas, *Eggers* 2439. Cuenca, *Ekman* H 13304. Monción, *Ekman* H 13014. Sabana de la Mar, *Ekman* H 15609.

TRINIDAD: Comuto Station, *Hitchcock* 10066. Arouca, *Hitchcock* 10338.

74. Paspalum fimbriatum H. B. K., Nov. Gen. et Sp. 1: 93. pl. 28. 1815. Colombia.

Annual; culms erect, 25 to 100 cm tall; blades flat, mostly 10 to 20 cm long, 5 to 12 mm wide; racemes 3 to 8, ascending or spreading, 2.5 to 8 cm long, the axis 8 to 10 cm long; spikelets about 2.3 mm long, with a broad firm notched wing, the wing and spikelet together about 3 mm long and wide (fig. 195).

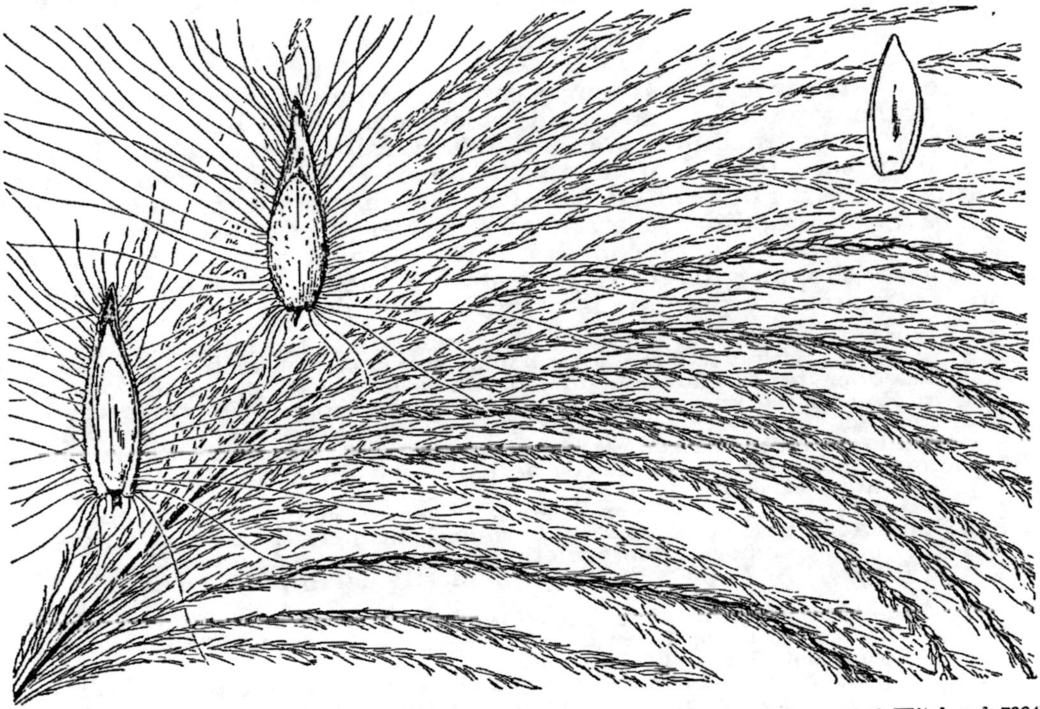

FIGURE 196.—*Paspalum saccharoides*. Panicle, × ½; two views of spikelet, and floret, × 10 (Hitchcock 7904)

Savannas, open and waste ground, Panama, the West Indies, and northern South America. To be found on probably all the islands of the West Indies.

75. Paspalum saccharoides Nees, in Trin., Gram. Icon. 1: pl. 107. 1827. Based on *Saccharum polystachyum* Swartz.

Saccharum polystachyum Swartz, Prodr. Veg. Ind. Occ. 21. 1788. Not *Paspalum polystachyum* R. Br., 1810. St. Christopher.

Panicum saccharoides Kunth, Rév. Gram. 2: 237. pl. 30. 1830.

Tricholaena saccharoides Griseb., Syst. Unt. Veg. Karaib. 117. 1857.

Paspalum polystachyum Kuntze, Rev. Gen. Pl. 2: 786. 1891. Not *P. polystachyum* R. Br., 1810.

Robust branching perennial growing in tough clumps; culms 1 to 2 m long, often decumbent or creeping at base; blades flat, 15 to 30 cm long, 8 to 15 mm wide; panicle subflabellate, feathery; racemes numerous, slender, silky, drooping, 15 to 30 cm long, the axis short; spikelets 2.5 to 3 mm long, lanceolate, acuminate, bearing a fringe of pale silky hairs as much as 5 to 8 mm long (fig. 196).

Open brushy or jungly slopes, mostly in moist spots, Costa Rica and the Lesser Antilles to Bolivia.

LEEWARD ISLANDS: St. Kitts, *Box* 151. Dominica, *Imray* 311.

WINDWARD ISLANDS: Martinique, *Duss* 1317. Grenada, *Broadway* 62, 2919, and in 1905; *Smith* 192, 843.

TRINIDAD: Cedros, *Hitchcock* 10134. Without locality, *Broadway* in 1919.

TOBAGO: Adelphi, *Broadway* 3979. Center of island, *Hitchcock* 10278.

80. PANICUM L., Sp. Pl. 55. 1753

Spikelets more or less compressed dorsiventrally, arranged in open or compact panicles, rarely in racemes; glumes herbaceous, nerved, usually very unequal, the first often minute, the second typically equaling the sterile lemma, the latter of the same texture and simulating a third glume, bearing in its axil a membranaceous or hyaline palea and sometimes a staminate flower, the palea rarely wanting; fertile lemma chartaceous-indurate, typically obtuse, the nerves obsolete, the margins inrolled over an enclosed palea of the same texture. Annuals or perennials of various habit.

1a. Axis of branchlets produced beyond the base of the uppermost spikelet as a point or bristle 1 to 6 mm long, sometimes nearly obsolete. Culms cespitose, a slender rhizome developed in some species, usually found in *P. leonis*, often in *P. utowanaeum*, but rarely in the others (Subgenus PAUROCHAETIUM).
  Second glume about as long as fruit, this and the sterile lemma faintly reticulate; first glume rounded or truncate ---------------- 89. P. CHAPMANI.
  Second glume about two-thirds as long as fruit, neither this nor the sterile lemma reticulate; first glume usually acute.
    Panicles strict, 15 to 35 cm long; spikelets spreading ---- 92. P. PRADANUM.
    Panicles not strict, mostly subflexuous, not more than 10 cm long; spikelets not spreading (a few sometimes slightly spreading).
      Blades 4 to 7 mm wide, thickish, mostly flat, 5 to 15 cm long. 94. P. LEONIS.
      Blades 1 to 3 mm wide, flat to involute.
        Spikelets 1.4 to 1.5 mm long ---------------- 91. P. DISTANTIFLORUM.
        Spikelets 1.8 to 2.5 mm long.
          Blades flat or folded toward the apex, mostly 3 to 8 cm (rarely to 12 cm) long, the basal crowded in a tuft, those of the culm spreading ------------------------------------ 90. P. OPHITICOLA.
          Blades of the innovations involute, 8 to 20 cm long, ascending, the basal not in a dense tuft ---------------- 93. P. UTOWANAEUM.

1b. Axis of branchlets not produced into a bristle. (In *P. geminatum* the somewhat flattened axis pointed but not bristle-form.)
  2a. Basal leaves usually distinctly different from those of the culm, forming a winter rosette; culms at first simple, the spikelets of the primary panicle not perfecting seed, later usually becoming much branched, the small secondary panicles with cleistogamous fruitful spikelets (Subgenus DICHANTHELIUM).
    Foliage soft and lax, the flat blades prominently ciliate; plants branching from the base, finally forming rosettes or cushions (*Laxiflora*).
      Spikelets papillose-pilose; sheaths retrorsely pilose --- 59. P. XALAPENSE.
      Spikelets glabrous; sheaths not retrorsely pilose.
        Blades glabrous on the surface ------------------ 60. P. POLYCAULON.
        Blades pilose on the surface ---------------------- 61. P. STRIGOSUM.

Foliage not soft and lax; plants branching from the culm nodes.
- 3a. Blades long, stiff, conspicuously striate, tapering from base to apex; autumnal phase bushy-branched above; spikelets turgid, attenuate at base, mostly pustulose-pubescent (*Angustifolia*).
  - Nodes bearded ---------- 62. P. CHRYSOPSIDIFOLIUM.
  - Nodes not bearded.
    - Autumnal blades flat; lower panicle branches spreading or deflexed. 64. P. ANGUSTIFOLIUM.
    - Autumnal blades involute; lower panicle branches more or less ascending.
      - Spikelets 3 to 3.5 mm long, pointed ---------- 63. P. FUSIFORME.
      - Spikelets less than 3 mm long, not pointed or obscurely so.
        - Plants glabrous or nearly so; autumnal culm erect. 66. P. NEURANTHUM.
        - Plants pubescent, at least on the lower half.
          - Spikelets about 2.4 mm long; vernal blades 7 to 12 cm long; autumnal blades not falcate ------ 65. P. ARENICOLOIDES.
          - Spikelets about 2 mm long; vernal blades 4 to 6 cm long; autumnal blades much crowded, falcate. 67. P. ACICULARE.
- 3b. Blades not long and stiff; culms not bushy-branched.
  - Spikelets subglobose or pyriform.
    - Blades spreading, rarely over 5 cm long and 5 mm wide; spikelets pyriform; autumnal phase bushy-branching (*Lancearia*).
      - Spikelets about 1.5 mm long ---------- 83. P. PORTORICENSE.
      - Spikelets about 2 mm long.
        - Blades firm, glabrous above; culms stiffly ascending. 85. P. LANCEARIUM.
        - Blades lax, softly puberulent on both surfaces; culms decumbent. 84. P. PATULUM.
    - Blades erect, 7 to 13 cm long, 7 to 14 mm wide, spikelets sphaeroidal (*Sphaerocarpa*).
      - Culms spreading; panicle nearly as broad as long; spikelets about 1.7 mm long ---------- 78. P. SPHAEROCARPON.
      - Culms erect or ascending; panicle never more than two-thirds as broad as long; spikelets about 1.1 mm long. 79. P. ERECTIFOLIUM.
  - Spikelets not subglobose nor pyriform-elliptic.
    - 4a. Ligule of conspicuous hairs usually 3 to 5 mm long.
      - Sheaths glabrous or only the lowermost somewhat pubescent; spikelets not more than 1.3 mm long (*Spreta*).
        - Culms and sheaths glabrous ---------- 73. P. LONGILIGULATUM.
        - Culms and sheaths appressed-pubescent.
          - Spikelets 1.2 to 1.3 mm long ---------- 71. P. LEUCOTHRIX.
          - Spikelets 1 mm long ---------- 72. P. WRIGHTIANUM.
      - Sheaths strongly pubescent (*Lanuginosa*).
        - Spikelets about 2 mm long. (See also *P. viscidellum*.) 74. P. ACUMINATUM.
        - Spikelets about 1.5 mm long.
          - Blades velvety-puberulent with long hairs intermixed. 75. P. ALBEMARLENSE.
          - Blades villous ---------- 76. P. AUBURNE.
    - 4b. Ligule obsolete or nearly so (manifest in *P. viscidellum*).
      - Spikelets about 3 mm long, elliptic, pubescent; blades somewhat cordate (*Commutata*) ---------- 88. P. JOORII.
      - Spikelets less than 3 mm long.
        - Blades of midculm elongate; plant villous or velvety (*Scoparia*).
          - Spikelets 2.5 mm long ---------- 86. P. SCOPARIUM.
          - Spikelets less than 2 mm long ---------- 87. P. VISCIDELLUM.
        - Blades of midculm not elongate.
          - Nodes bearded (*Dichotoma*) ---------- 68. P. NITIDUM.
          - Nodes not bearded.
            - Sheaths crisp- or appressed-pubescent (*Columbiana*). 77. P. WILMINGTONENSE.
            - Sheaths glabrous.
              - Culms slender, rarely less than 40 cm tall (*Dichotoma*).
                - Spikelets about 1.5 mm long --- 70. P. CAERULESCENS.
                - Spikelets about 2 mm long ------ 69. P. ROANOKENSE.

Culms delicate, usually less than 40 cm tall, spikelets not more than 1.5 mm long (*Ensifolia*).
Spikelets about 1 mm long; blades not white-margined. 82. P. CHAMAELONCHE.
Spikelets about 1.5 mm long; blades white-margined.
Uppermost culm blades much reduced. 80. P. ALBOMARGINATUM.
Uppermost culm blades about as long as the others. 81. P. TRIFOLIUM.

2b. Basal leaves similar to the culm leaves, not forming a winter rosette; spikelets all fertile.
5a. Plants annual.
Spikelets laterally compressed; second glume carinate. Panicles small, few-flowered ---------------------------------- 53. P. TRIGONUM.
Spikelets not laterally compressed; second glume not carinate.
Spikelets plano-gibbous, the second glume swollen, bristly and burlike at maturity; first glume nearly as long as the minute spikelet. 58. P. HIRTUM.
Spikelets not plano-gibbous nor burlike.
Panicles consisting of more or less secund spikelike racemes; fruit transversely rugose; glumes and sterile lemma usually reticulate-veined (*Fasciculata*).
Spikelets strongly reticulate-veined, 2 to 3 mm long, glabrous. 4. P. FASCICULATUM.
Spikelets scarcely reticulate-veined or only near the apex.
Spikelets not more than 2 mm long, glabrous -- 3. P. REPTANS.
Spikelets more than 3 mm long, pubescent.
Rachis pilose with bristly hairs; plants more or less velvety. 5. P. MOLLE.
Rachis scabrous but not bristly.
Spikelets glabrous ---------------------- 7. P. ADSPERSUM.
Spikelets tuberculate-hispid --------- 6. P. ECHINULATUM.
Panicles more or less diffuse.
Blades ovate-lanceolate -------------------- 43. P. TRICHOIDES.
Blades linear.
First glume not more than one-fourth the length of the spikelet, truncate or triangular-tipped ---- 8. P. DICHOTOMIFLORUM.
First glume usually as much as half the length of the spikelet, acute or acuminate.
Inflorescence elongate, composed of several approximate implicate panicles --------------------- 15. P. CAYENNENSE.
Inflorescence not as above.
Panicles more than half the length of the entire plant. 13. P. CAPILLARE.
Panicles not more than one-third the entire height of the plant ------------------------- 14. P. HIRTICAULE.
5b. Plants perennial.
6a. Spikelets short-pediceled along one side of the panicle branches, forming more or less spikelike racemes.
Spikelets more or less pubescent or hispid.
Spikelets 4 mm long; blades 2 to 4 cm wide -- 55. P. ASPERIFOLIUM.
Spikelets less than 3 mm long; blades mostly less than 1 cm wide.
Sterile lemma glandless; second glume inflated-gibbous. 48. P. VENEZUELAE.
Sterile lemma bearing a pair of crateriform glands. 41. P. PULCHELLUM.
Spikelets glabrous.
Blades lanceolate or ovate-lanceolate; glumes strongly carinate.
Blades not more than 5 cm, usually 2 or 3 cm, long; second glume rather blunt and shorter than the sterile lemma. 39. P. STOLONIFERUM.
Blades 5 to 11 cm long; second glume acute, nearly equaling the sterile lemma ------------------------- 40. P. FRONDESCENS.

Blades linear, often elongate; glumes not carinate or but slightly so.
Fruit transversely rugose.
Nodes bearded............ 2. P. PURPURASCENS.
Nodes not bearded............ 1. P. GEMINATUM.
Fruit not rugose.
Spikelets not expanded at maturity by an enlarged sterile palea, pointed............32. P. POLYGONATUM.
Spikelets expanded at maturity by the enlarged sterile palea.
Blades narrowed toward the base............36. P. LAXUM.
Blades cordate or truncate at base.
Spikelets 2 mm long; panicle branches erect or nearly so............37. P. STEVENSIANUM.
Spikelets not more than 1.6 mm long; panicle branches spreading or ascending.
Panicles one-third to half as wide as long; spikelets not conspicuously secund, somewhat irregularly disposed; blades cordate-clasping..35. P. BOLIVIENSE.
Panicles rarely one-fourth as wide as long; spikelets conspicuously secund and regularly disposed.
Culms as much as 2 m long; panicles 25 to 30 cm long............33. P. MILLEFLORUM.
Culms not more than 1 m tall; panicles 5 to 15 cm long............34. P. PILOSUM.

6b. Spikelets in open or sometimes in contracted or congested panicles, but not in 1-sided spikelike racemes.
Fruit transversely rugose............19. P. MAXIMUM.
Fruit not transversely rugose.
Culms more or less succulent. Plants glabrous or nearly so throughout, aquatic or subaquatic.
First glume not more than one-fifth the length of the spikelet.
Spikelets 4 to 5 mm long; fruit long-acuminate............ 12. P. ELEPHANTIPES.
Spikelets 2 to 3 mm long; fruit not acuminate.
Spikelets 2 mm long............10. P. LACUSTRE.
Spikelets about 3 mm long............11. P. AQUATICUM.
First glume one-third to one-half the length of the spikelet.
Culms erect, panicle contracted............31. P. CONDENSUM.
Culms long-decumbent at base; panicle open...54. P. GRANDE.
Culms not succulent.
First glume not more than one-fifth the length of the spikelet or wanting (occasionally a long glume developed in *P. discrepans.*)
Fruit felty villous at base and apex; first glume often minute or wanting; fruit keeled, pubescent at apex.57. P. DISCREPANS.
Fruit not felty villous; first glume evident; fruit not keeled, sparsely pubescent all over............42. P. SCHIFFNERI.
First glume more than one-fifth the length of the spikelet.
Sterile palea enlarged and indurate at maturity, expanding the spikelet............38. P. EXIGUIFLORUM.
Sterile palea, if present, not enlarged and indurate.
First glume less than one-third the length of the spikelet, blunt............9. P. BARTOWENSE.
First glume usually more than one-third the length of the spikelet.
7a. Plants forming conspicuous hard creeping rhizomes.
First glume less than half the length of the spikelet; spikelets not more than 2.5 mm long.
Panicle loosely flowered; first glume truncate, about one-fifth the length of the spikelet....20. P. REPENS.
Panicles rather densely flowered; first glume triangular, about one-third the length of the spikelet............ 21. P. GOUINI.
First glume more than half the length of the spikelet; spikelets 3 to 4 mm long.
Culms decumbent or creeping at base, mostly 2 to 4 m tall............23. P. ALTUM.

Culms erect.
Panicles strongly contracted, elongate; seacoast plants growing in large bunches.
24. P. AMARULUM.
Panicles open, rather narrow; plants of low ground but not littoral, the culms solitary or few in a clump--------22. P. VIRGATUM var. CUBENSE.
7b. Plants not forming creeping scaly rhizomes.
Fruit crested at apex; spikelets 5.5 to 6 mm long.
56. P. ZIZANIOIDES.
Fruit not crested.
Panicles narrow and few-flowered; culms erect and wiry; blades drying involute.
Second glume and sterile lemma exceeding the fruit; spikelets somewhat pointed.
Pedicels bearing a few long hairs-26. P. TENERUM.
Pedicels puberulent, without long hairs.
30. P. BEYERI.
Second glume and sterile lemma not exceeding the fruit; spikelets rather blunt.
Pedicels bearing a few long stiff erect hairs at the summit-----------------27. P. CARICOIDES.
Pedicels not hairy.
Spikelets attenuate at base, about 2 mm long; leaves more or less pilose.
28. P. STENODOIDES.
Spikelets not attenuate at base, about 1.5 mm long; leaves glabrous----29. P. STENODES.
Panicles open or contracted.
Panicles 40 to 60 cm long, the numerous elongate branches in verticils---------52. P. MERTENSII.
Panicles mostly much less than 40 cm long; branches not verticillate.
First glume not pointed, two-thirds the length of the spikelet or more; spikelets blunt.
Panicles not more than 6 cm long; plants somewhat glaucous, relatively small; blades mostly less than 8 cm long.
Culms very slender, decumbent or creeping; blades 1 to 3 cm long-45. P. PARVIFOLIUM.
Culms firm, erect or decumbent at base only; blades 3 to 8 cm long-46. P. CYANESCENS.
Panicles 10 to 20 cm long, diffuse; plants tall or stout.
Blades gradually narrowed from a clasping base, stiff, striate, erect or ascending.
47. P. NERVOSUM.
Blades not clasping at base.
Spikelets viscid, 3 mm long.
50. P. GLUTINOSUM.
Spikelets not viscid, 2 to 2.3 mm long.
49. P. SELLOWII.
First glume pointed, usually less than two-thirds as long as the spikelets.
Spikelets sparsely hirsute------51. P. RUDGEI.
Spikelets glabrous.
Culms straggling; spikelets minute.
44. P. TRICHANTHUM.
Culms erect or stiffly ascending.
Culms tall and stout, usually more than 1 m tall.
Sheaths hirsute-------18. P. HIRSUTUM.
Sheaths glabrous-----25. P. PETERSONII.
Culms slender, less than 1 m tall.
Blades 1 to 3 mm wide; plants spreading or ascending------16. P. DIFFUSUM.
Blades mostly more than 5 mm wide; plants erect--17. P. GHIESBREGHTII.

1. Panicum geminatum Forsk., Fl. Aegypt. Arab. 18. 1775. Egypt.

Paspalidium geminatum Stapf, in Prain, Fl. Trop. Afr. 9: 583. 1920.

Perennial, glabrous throughout; culms cespitose, 25 to 80 cm tall, spreading from a decumbent base; blades 10 to 20 cm long, 3 to 6 mm wide, flat; panicle 12 to 30 cm long, the racemes 12 to 18, erect, or nearly so, rather distant; spikelets glabrous, a little more than 2 mm long (fig. 197).

Moist ground, ditches, and swamps, mostly near the coast, tropical regions of both hemispheres, in America extending north into southern Florida and Texas; throughout the West Indies.

This species has sometimes been referred to *P. paspalodes* Pers.

2. Panicum purpurascens Raddi, Agrost. Bras. 47. 1823. Brazil. PARA GRASS.

Panicum barbinode Trin., Mém. Acad. St. Pétersb. VI. Sci. Nat. 1: 256. 1834. Bahia.

Panicum guadaloupense Steud., Syn. Pl. Glum. 1: 61. 1854. Guadeloupe.

Perennial, sending out widely creeping stolons; culms decumbent at base, rooting at the lower nodes, 2 to 6 m long or even more, sometimes ascending into bushes and trees; nodes densely villous; sheaths villous; blades 10 to 15 mm wide, glabrous; panicle 12 to 20 cm long, with several rather distant racemes; spikelets 3 mm long, glabrous (fig. 198).

Cultivated and waste ground, especially in moist places, tropical America. To be found on all the West Indian islands.

A valuable forage grass in the Tropics at low altitudes, used for pasture and for cut green feed. In common with *Eriochloa polystachya* called "malojilla" in Puerto Rico; in Cuba called "hierba del Paral", "hierba bruja", and "paraná"; in the English islands called "Dutch grass" and "Scotch grass."

Panicum purpurascens Raddi had previously been discarded because of the earlier *P. purpurascens* Opiz (1822) which, however, is a nomen nudum.

Some botanists have referred this species to *Panicum muticum* Forsk. described from Egypt, or to *P. numidianum* Lam., also described from Egypt ("Nubia"). In the author's opinion *P. purpurascens* is different from *P. numidianum* to which *P. muticum* should probably be referred. The Egyptian plant differs in having pubescent but not villous nodes, more acute spikelets, no long hairs on the rachis and pedicels, and a larger first glume. *Panicum purpurascens* occurs in tropical Africa whence it may have been introduced into Brazil.

3. Panicum reptans L., Syst. Nat. ed. 10. 2: 870. 1759. Jamaica.

Panicum grossarium L., Syst. Nat. ed. 10. 2: 871. 1759. Jamaica.

Panicum prostratum Lam., Tabl. Encycl. 1: 171. 1791. Santo Domingo.

Panicum caespitosum Swartz, Fl. Ind. Occ. 1: 146. 1797. Jamaica.

Panicum insularum Steud., Syn. Pl. Glum. 1: 61. 1854. Lesser Antilles.

Brachiaria prostrata Griseb., Abh. Ges. Wiss. Göttingen 7: 263. 1857.

FIGURE 197.—*Panicum geminatum*. Plant, × ½; two views of spikelet, and floret, × 10 (Tracy 9395).

FIGURE 198.—*Panicum purpurascens.* Plant, × ½; two views of spikelet, and floret, × 10 (Hitchcock 9693).

Panicum prostratum var. *pilosum* Eggers, Fl. St. Croix and Virgin Isl. 104. 1879. St. Croix.

Urochloa reptans Stapf, in Prain, Fl. Trop. Afr. 9: 601. 1920.

Plants annual, spreading, usually prostrate; culms slender, freely branching, 10 to 30 cm tall; blades lanceolate or ovate-lanceolate, 1.5 to 6 cm long, 4 to 12 mm wide, cordate, glabrous or puberulent, ciliate at base; inflorescence long-exserted, 2 to 6 cm long; racemes spikelike, 3 to 12, 2 to 3 cm long; spikelets about 2 mm long, glabrous; first glume rounded or truncate, less than 0.5 mm long (fig. 199).

Moist open ground and a frequent weed in waste places and cultivated soil, Florida to Texas, southward to northern South America; also in tropical regions of the Eastern Hemisphere. Probably to be found on all the West Indian islands. In Cuba called "San Juan de Castillo."

4. **Panicum fasciculatum** Swartz, Prodr. Veg. Ind. Occ. 22. 1788. Jamaica. BROWNTOP MILLET.

Panicum fuscum Swartz, Prodr. Veg. Ind. Occ. 23. 1788. Jamaica.

Panicum flavescens Swartz, Prodr. Veg. Ind. Occ. 23. 1788. Jamaica.

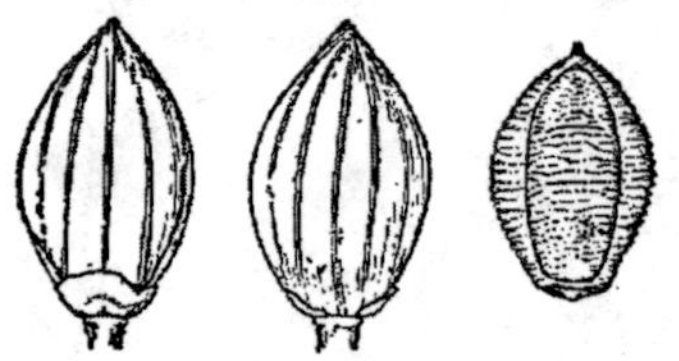

FIGURE 199.—*Panicum reptans*. Two views of spikelet, and floret, × 10 (type of *P. prostratum* Lam.).

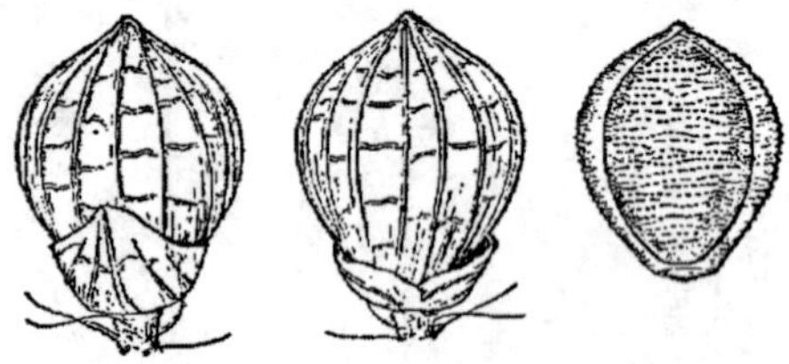

FIGURE 200.—*Panicum fasciculatum*. Two views of spikelet, and floret, × 10 (type).

Panicum chartaginense Swartz, Prodr. Veg. Ind. Occ. 22. 1788. Cartagena.

Panicum fusco-rubens Lam., Tabl. Encycl. 1: 171. 1791. Caribbean Islands.

Panicum fastigiatum Poir., in Lam., Encycl. Sup. 4: 277. 1816. Based on *P. fasciculatum* Swartz.

Panicum illinoniense Desv., Opusc. 91. 1831.

Panicum reticulatum Griseb., Abh. Ges. Wiss. Göttingen 7: 264. 1857. Caribbean Islands or Panama.

Panicum fuscum var. *fasciculatum* Griseb., Fl. Brit. W. Ind. 547. 1864.

Panicum fasciculatum var. *flavescens* Doell, in Mart., Fl. Bras. 2^2: 205. 1877.

Panicum fasciculatum var. *fuscum* Doell, in Mart., Fl. Bras. 2^2: 205. 1877.

Annual, erect or spreading from a decumbent base, 30 to 100 cm tall; sheaths glabrous or papillose-hispid; blades flat, 6 to 20 mm wide, glabrous or sparsely hispid; panicle 10 to 20 cm long, of several racemes 5 to 10 cm long, solitary or fascicled along the main axis; spikelets 2 to 2.5 mm long, bronze to yellow or brown, glabrous, pointed, reticulate-veined; first glume one-third as long as the spikelet (fig. 200).

Moist open ground, often a weed in fields and waste places, southern Florida and Texas, Mexico, and throughout the West Indies to central South America. In Cuba called "súrbana."

5. **Panicum molle** Swartz, Prodr. Veg. Ind. Occ. 22. 1788. (Probably Jamaica.)

Annual, resembling *P. fasciculatum* but more or less pubescent all over; spikelets about 3.5 mm long, pilose (fig. 201).

Open ground, often a weed in fields, Greater Antilles, Mexico, and Central America to Argentina. In Cuba called "súrbana." This species was referred by Grisebach[61] to *Panicum chartaginense.*

CUBA: Gamboa, *Ekman* 14953. Without locality, *Reed.*

JAMAICA: Hope Gardens, *Hitchcock* 9350 (*Amer. Gr. Nat. Herb.* 9). Kingston, *Alexander* in 1849; *Hitchcock* in 1890. Healthshire Hills. *Hitchcock* 9758. Gordon Town, *Hitchcock* 9323; *Harris* 11504. Musgrave Road, *Harris* 11483.

HAITI: Croix-des-Bouquets, *Ekman* H 971. Cape St. Marc, *Ekman* H 6650.

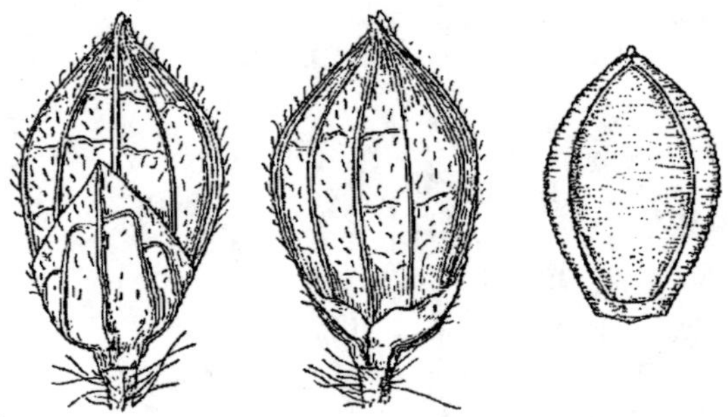

FIGURE 201.—*Panicum molle.* Two views of spikelet, and floret, × 10 (type).

6. **Panicum echinulatum** Mez, Notizbl. Bot. Gart. Berlin 7: 62. 1917. Paraguay.

Differing from *P. adspersum* chiefly in the tuberculate-hispid spikelets.

Fields and waste places, West Indies, probably introduced, Paraguay and Bolivia.

CUBA: Between Pastelillo and Tarafa, low forest, *Ekman* 15451. Trinidad, on the railroad track, *Ekman* 14023.

HAITI: Les Gonaïves, *Ekman* H 8515.

DOMINICAN REPUBLIC: Villa Vásquez, *Ekman* H 13126. Santiago, *Ekman* H 16387.

VIRGIN ISLANDS: St. Croix, *Eggers* in 1876.

LEEWARD ISLANDS: Nevis, *Box* 175.

7. **Panicum adspersum** Trin., Gram. Pan. 146. 1826. Santo Domingo.

Panicum thomasianum Steud.; Doell, in Mart., Fl. Bras. 2^2: 188. 1877. St. Thomas.

Panicum keyense Mez, Notizbl. Bot. Gart. Berlin 7: 61. 1917. Florida.

Culms ascending or spreading, commonly branching and rooting at the lower nodes, the flowering branches 30 to 100 cm tall; blades 5 to 15 cm long, 8 to 20 mm wide; panicles 6 to 15 cm long, the racemes spikelike, few to many, 3 to 10 cm long; spikelets fusiform, abruptly acuminate, 3.2 to 4 mm long, more or less hispidulous especially toward the summit (fig. 202).

Moist open ground, Florida and the West Indies.

BAHAMAS: Nassau, *Curtiss* 113. Anguilla Isles, *Wilson* 8066.

61 Fl. Brit. W. Ind. 546. 1864.

CUBA: Herradura, *Tracy* 9102. Sierra de Anafe, *Wilson* 11491. Cabanas, *Palmer and Riley* 746, 771. Habana, *Hitchcock* 159; *Ekman* 109; *Léon* 291, 570, 1978; *Curtiss* 748. Santiago de las Vegas, *Hitchcock* 147, 148; *Baker and Wilson* 512; *Tracy* 9109. Guines, *Léon* 924. Baraguá, *Hitchcock* 23350. Sancti Spíritus, *Léon* 925. Zaza del Sur, *Léon* 2776. Without locality, *Wright* 3869.

JAMAICA: Hope Gardens, *Harris* 11247; *Hitchcock* 9282 (*Amer. Gr. Nat. Herb.* 11), 9351 (*Amer. Gr. Nat. Herb.* 10). Gordon Town, *Harris* 11343, 11512. Yallahs Valley, *Harris* 11498. Black River, *Hitchcock* 9630. Ferry River, *Hitchcock* 9750; *Harris* 11785. Alligator Pond, *Hitchcock* 9830. Lititz, *Harris* 11714.

HAITI: Tortuga Island, *Leonard* 11447, 11956, 12096, 14067. Port-de-Pai, *Leonard* 11155. Port-au-Prince, *Hitchcock* 19882; *Ekman* H 323, H 8149. Gonaïves, *Cook, Scofield, and Doyle* 194. St. Marc, *Leonard* 2934, 2968. Fond Parisien, *Leonard* 4138. Pétionville, *Leonard* 4875. Cape Haitien, *Leonard* 5286. Tiburon, *Ekman* H 373.

DOMINICAN REPUBLIC: Barahona, *Fuertes* 43. Guayubín, *Abbott* 955a. Jaina, *Faris* 350. Santo Domingo, *Ekman* H 12528. Santiago, *Ekman* H 16385.

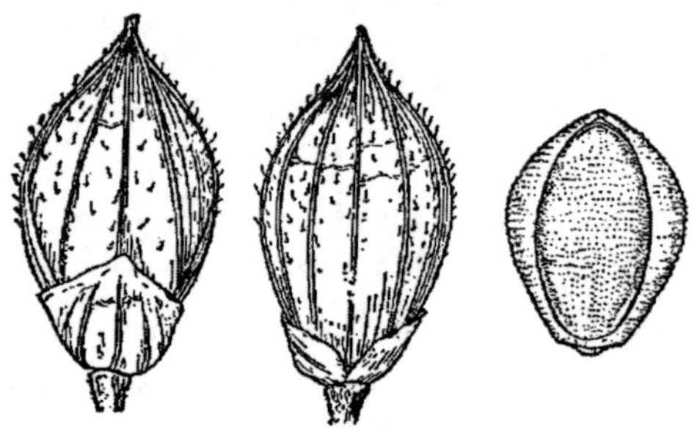

FIGURE 202.—*Panicum adspersum.* Two views of spikelet, and floret, × 10 (type).

PUERTO RICO: Mona Island, *Britton, Cowell, and Hess* 1761. Cayo Muertos, *Britton, Cowell, and Brown* 4991. Mayaguez, *Britton and Cowell* 4069; *Chase* 6286, 6302. Guanica Bay, *Chase* 6514. Aibonito, *Chase* 6333; *Sintenis* 1957. Bayamon, *Hioram* 315. Vieques Island, *Chase* 6686.

VIRGIN ISLANDS: St. John, *Britton and Shafer* 334. Tortola, *Britton and Shafer* 711. St. Croix, *Hitchcock* 16334; *Thompson* 14, 443; *Ricksecker* 66, 384. St. Thomas, *Hitchcock* 16315, 16316. Virgin Gorda, *Fishlock* 48, 53, 243.

LEEWARD ISLANDS: St. Kitts, *Box* 157. Antigua, *Hitchcock* 16379; *Box* 59, 118. Guadeloupe, *Duss* 3180.

8. **Panicum dichotomiflorum** Michx., Fl. Bor. Amer. 1: 48. 1803. Illinois.

Annual; culms freely branching, ascending or spreading from a geniculate base, 50 to 100 cm tall; sheaths glabrous; blades flat or more or less folded, glabrous, 10 to 50 cm long, 3 to 10 mm wide; panicles terminal and axillary, many-flowered, 10 to 20 cm long, the branches ascending to spreading; spikelets oblong-lanceolate, acute, glabrous, about 2.3 mm long; first glume truncate or broadly triangular, one-fifth to one-fourth the length of the spikelet; second glume and sterile lemma equal, 7-nerved (fig. 203).

Moist open ground, United States to Argentina.

BERMUDA: *Millspaugh* 126.

BAHAMAS: Hog Island, *Eggers* 4405, 4512. Watling Island, *Geogr. Soc. Baltimore* 489. Cat Cay, *Brace* 3742. Nassau, *Curtiss* 177.

CUBA: Herradura, *Tracy* 9055, 9342; *Britton and Earle* 6566. Remates, *Ekman* 11212. Laguna del Ariguanabo, *Léon* 2774, 2775, 4328, 7693. Santiago de las Vegas, *Hitchcock* 151. Batabanó, *Hitchcock* 150. Cayo de los Pavos, *Léon* 9507.

HAITI: Étang, *Leonard* 3493, 4233. Manneville, *Ekman* H 3060. Miragoane, *Ekman* H 7233.

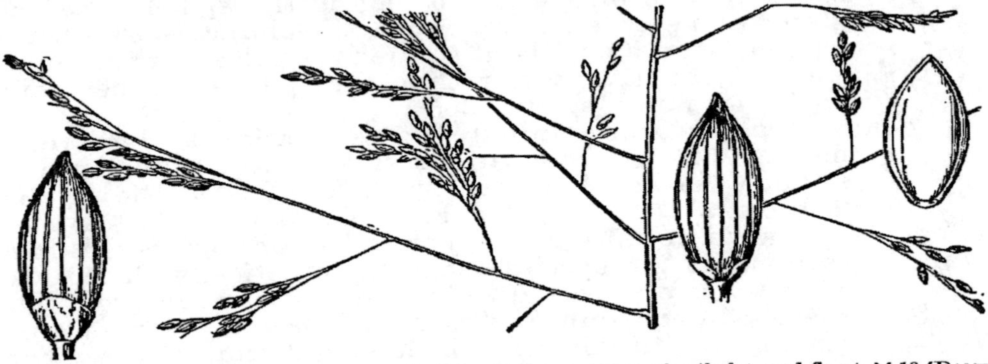

FIGURE 203.—*Panicum dichotomiflorum.* Panicle, × 1; two views of spikelet, and floret, × 10 (Deam).

9. Panicum bartowense Scribn. and Merr., U. S. Dept. Agr., Div. Agrost. Circ. 35: 3. 1901. Florida.

Simple or sparingly branched; culms erect or decumbent at base, sometimes only 20 to 30 cm tall but often 1 m or even 2 m tall; sheaths papillose-hispid; blades pilose on the upper surface; panicle and spikelets about as in *P. dichotomiflorum* (fig. 204).

Low moist ground, Florida to Cuba and Jamaica.

BAHAMAS: Great Bahama, *Britton and Millspaugh* 2706. North Bimini, *Brace* 3467 (both in Field Mus. Herb.).

CUBA: Carabela Grande, *Roig* 3205. Guanajay, *Ekman* 13013. Marianao, *Léon* 6142. Guines, *Léon* 7289. Batabanó, *Hitchcock* 149. Caibarién, *Fernando* 636. Without locality, *Wright* 3860. Isla de Pinos, *Ekman* 12400; *Britton, Wilson, and Léon* 15257.

JAMAICA: Black River, *Hitchcock* 9645 (*Amer. Gr. Nat. Herb.* 18).

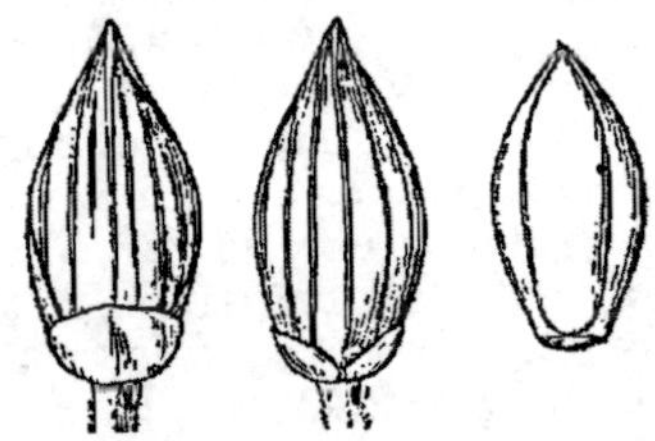

FIGURE 204.—*Panicum bartowense.* Two views of spikelet, and floret, × 10 (type).

10. Panicum lacustre Hitchc. and Ekman, sp. nov.[62]

Perennial; culms erect, glabrous, rather succulent below, 1 to 1.5 m tall, rooting at the lower nodes when growing in the water; sheaths glabrous (under water bladeless); ligule a laciniate membrane dissected into bristles, 1 to 2 mm long; blades flat, or folded at base, the middle and upper 15 to 30 cm long, about 2 mm wide, slightly scabrous, sparsely pilose on the upper surface, the lower shorter; panicle

[62] Culmi perennes erecti glabri succulenti 1–1.5 m alti; vaginae glabrae; laminae planae 15–30 cm longae 2 mm latae; panicula patens 20–30 cm longa, radiis ascendentibus, radiis secondariis appressis; spiculae oblongo-lanceolatae glabrae 2 mm longae; gluma prima 0.5–0.7 mm longa truncata; gluma secunda 5-nervis; lemma sterile glumam secundam aequans 7-nervis.

open, many-flowered, 20 to 30 cm long, the branches ascending, scabrous, the lower fascicled, the others solitary or in pairs, the branches of the second order appressed along the main branches, the basal part of the latter naked; spikelets oblong-lanceolate, glabrous, about 2 mm long, tinged with purple, the ultimate lateral pedicels 1 to 2 mm long; first glume truncate or broadly triangular, one-fourth to one-third as long as the spikelet; second glume and sterile lemma equal, the glume 5-nerved, the lemma 7-nerved, without stamens or palea; fertile lemma smooth, slightly shorter than the spikelet, rather thin; anthers 1 mm long (fig. 205).

FIGURE 205.—*Panicum lacustre*. Panicle branch, × 1; spikelet and floret, × 10 (type).

Type in the United States National Herbarium, no. 1387529, collected in water of 30 to 60 cm depth in Laguna de la Máquina, prov. Pinar del Río, Cuba, October 31, 1923, by Dr. E. L. Ekman (no. 17878).

Known only from the type collection, but Dr. Ekman states that the species occurs in practically all lagunas of the western part of Pinar del Río Province. The species differs from *P. dichotomiflorum* in being an erect perennial with smaller spikelets, and from *P. aquaticum* in the erect habit and smaller spikelets.

11. Panicum aquaticum Poir., in Lam., Encycl. Sup. 4: 281. 1816. Puerto Rico.

Panicum proliferum var. *strictum* Griseb., Cat. Pl. Cub. 232. 1866. Cuba, *Wright* 3456.

Perennial; culms usually decumbent at base and rooting at the nodes, the erect flowering branches 30 to 100 cm tall; sheaths glabrous; blades linear, 5 to 10 mm wide, flat or folded, usually pilose on the upper surface at least toward the base; panicles similar to those of *P. dichotomiflorum* but averaging smaller; spikelets 3 to 3.4 mm long, acuminate; fruit shorter than the spikelet, somewhat pointed (fig. 206).

Wet places or in shallow water, margins of streams and ponds at low altitudes, Mexico and the West Indies to Paraguay.

CUBA: Herradura, *Hitchcock* 23444; *Shafer* 10912. Jovero, *Léon* 15367. Pinar del Río, *Hitchcock* 23290; *Wright* 3861. El Sábalo, *Léon* 15097. Almacigos, *Wright* 3456 (in part). Habana, *Léon* 4155. Ariguanabo lagoon, *Léon* 1975, 1976. El Cano, *Léon* 1974. Guanabacoa, *Léon* 919. Puentes Grandes, *Ekman* 502, 18294. Motembo, *Léon* 9410. Manacas, *Léon* 5823, 5998. Marianao, *Léon* 5702. Isla de Pinos, *Britton and Wilson* 14803.

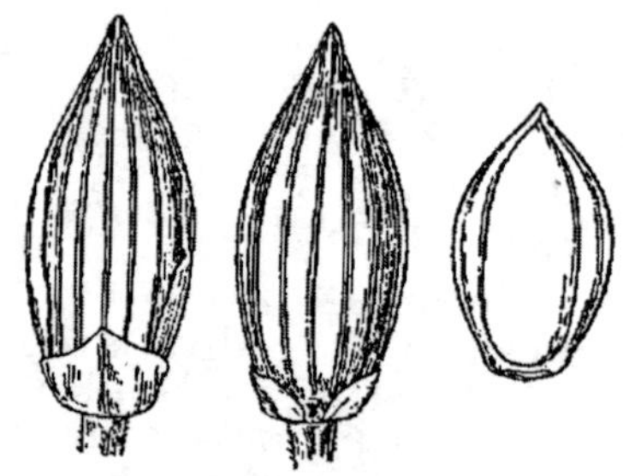

FIGURE 206.—*Panicum aquaticum*. Two views of spikelet, and floret, × 10 (type).

PUERTO RICO: Rio Piedras, *Stevenson* 3566; *Chase* 6778. Campo Alegre, *Chase* 6804. Adjuntas, *Chase* 6471. Utuado, *Britton and Cowell* 432.

LEEWARD ISLANDS: Guadeloupe, *Duss* 3178.

TRINIDAD: Pitch Lake, *Hitchcock* 10099 (*Amer. Gr. Nat. Herb.* 502).

12. Panicum elephantipes Nees, Agrost. Bras. 165. 1829. Brazil.

Perennial; culms ascending from a decumbent, often widely creeping base, rooting at the nodes, succulent, as much as 2 cm thick, 1 m or more tall; blades flat, as much as 20 mm wide; panicles large and open, as much as 40 cm long, the short branchlets appressed along the ascending branches; spikelets 4 to 5 mm long, lanceolate, acuminate, glabrous; first glume one-fifth to one-fourth the length of the spikelet, obtuse or acutish (fig. 207).

Ponds and shallow water at low altitudes, sometimes in large colonies, Central America and the West Indies to Argentina.

CUBA: Cabañas, *Ekman* 10504. Laguna de los Indios, *Roig* 3186. Habana, *Léon* 335, 9039. Laguna Origuanabo, *Léon* 13312. San Antonio, *Hitchcock* 152. Soledad, *Hitchcock* 23335.

JAMAICA: Savanna-la-Mar, *Hitchcock* 9878. Cabaritta River, *Harris* 11813. Montego Bay, *Ridley* 127. Middle Quarters, *Hitchcock* 9586 (*Amer. Gr. Nat. Herb.* 19).

HAITI: Miragoane, *Ekman* H 6539, H 7254. Dessolines, *Ekman* H 3024.

DOMINICAN REPUBLIC: Jaina, *Faris* 393; *Ekman* H 13352. Santo Domingo City, *Ekman* H 11149.

PUERTO RICO: Fajardo, *Sintenis* 938. San Juan, *Chase* 6407. Vega Baja, *Chase* 6415.

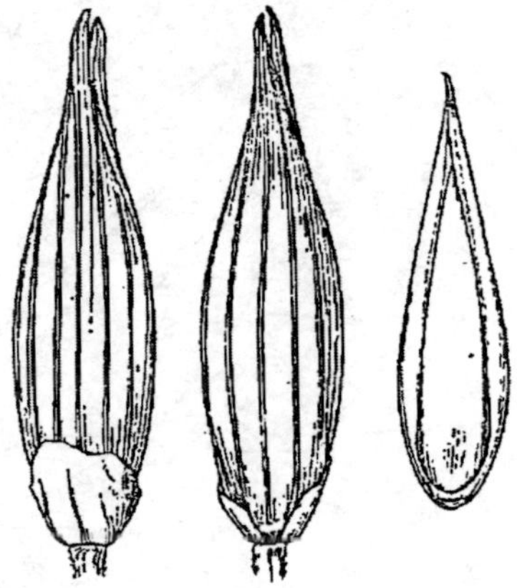

FIGURE 207.—*Panicum elephantipes.* Two views of spikelet, and floret, × 10 (type).

13. Panicum capillare L., Sp. Pl. 58. 1753. Virginia. WITCHGRASS.

Annual; culms erect, 20 to 80 cm tall; sheaths densely papillose hispid; blades 10 to 25 cm long, 5 to 15 mm wide, hispid on both surfaces; panicle diffuse, often half the length of the entire plant, breaking away at maturity; spikelets 2 mm long, glabrous, acute; first glume about half as long as the spikelet, acute (fig. 208).

Open ground and waste places, eastern United States; introduced in Bermuda and the Virgin Islands.

BERMUDA: *Collins* 151, 152; *Brown and Britton* 21.

VIRGIN ISLANDS: St. Croix, *Benzon* 42.

14. Panicum hirticaule Presl, Rel. Haenk. 1: 308. 1830. Mexico.

Annual; culms erect, 15 to 70 cm tall, glabrous or papillose-hispid, the nodes and sheaths hispid; blades flat, mostly glabrous or nearly so, 4 to 13 mm wide; panicles 5 to 15 cm long, open, usually reddish-brown; spikelets about 3 mm long, acuminate, glabrous; first glume half to three-fourths the length of the spikelet, acuminate (fig. 209).

Rocky or sandy soil, southwestern United States to Bolivia; Cuba and Haiti.

CUBA: Gamboa, *Ekman* 15009.

HAITI: Damien, *Ekman* H 9154, H 9991. Petite Rivière de l'Artibonite, *Picarda* 1654.

Dr. Ekman notes that this species is very common in fields around Port-au-Prince (no. H 9991).

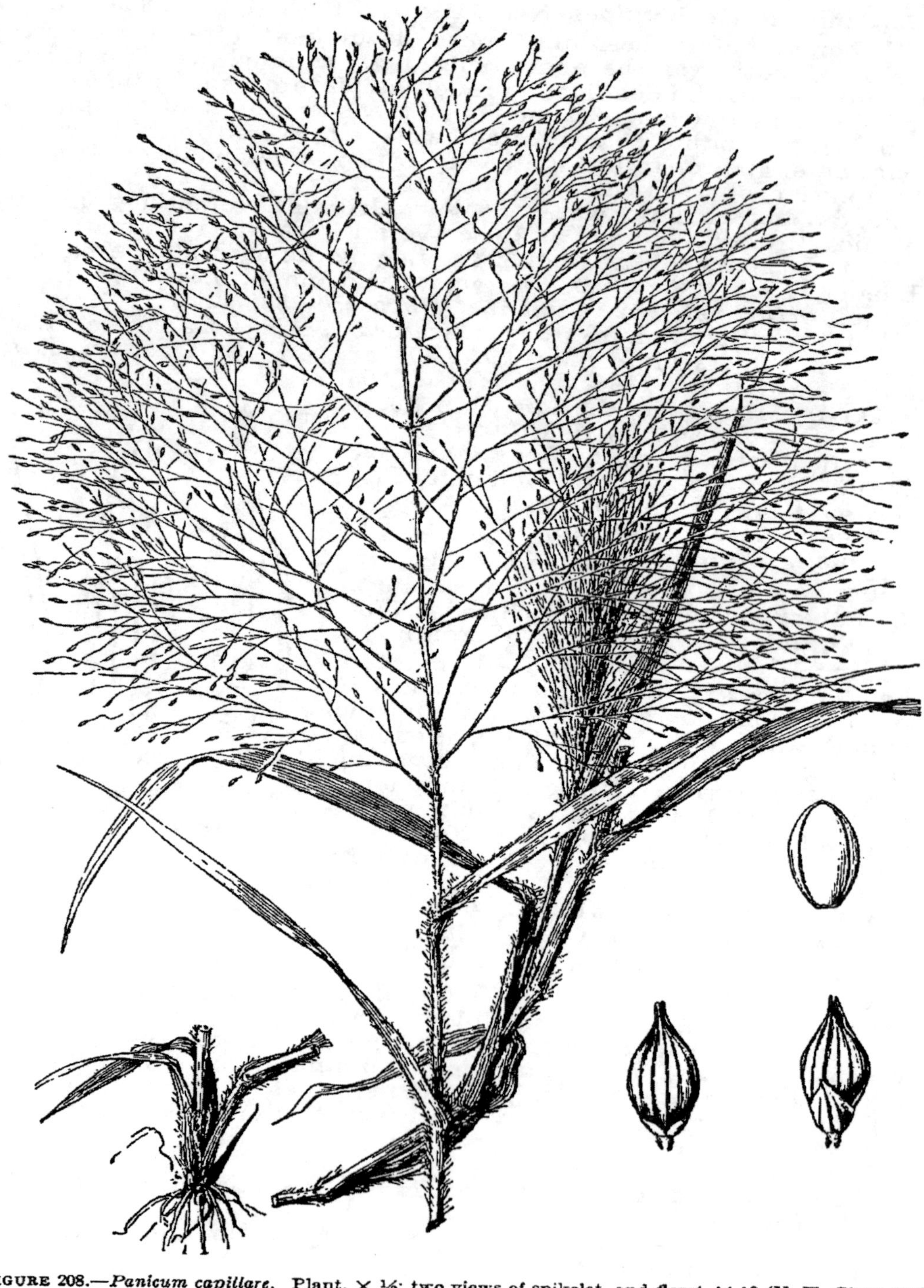

FIGURE 208.—*Panicum capillare*. Plant, × ½; two views of spikelet, and floret, × 10 (V. H. Chase 774).

Panicum miliaceum L., Sp. Pl. 58. 1753. Hog millet, broom-corn millet, introduced from the Old World and escaped from cultivation in the United States, has been found in Puerto Rico (*Stevenson* 3052) and St. Croix (*Benzon*).

15. Panicum cayennense Lam., Tabl. Encycl. 1: 173. 1791. Cayenne.

Annual; culms erect, often much branched at base, 20 to 50 cm tall; sheaths and blades pilose, the latter 4 to 10 mm wide; panicles terminal and axillary, open, 8 to 20 cm long; spikelets a little more than 2 mm long, obovoid, turgid, strongly nerved; first glume acute, half as long as the spikelet (fig. 210).

Open ground and pine woods, West Indies and Honduras to Brazil.

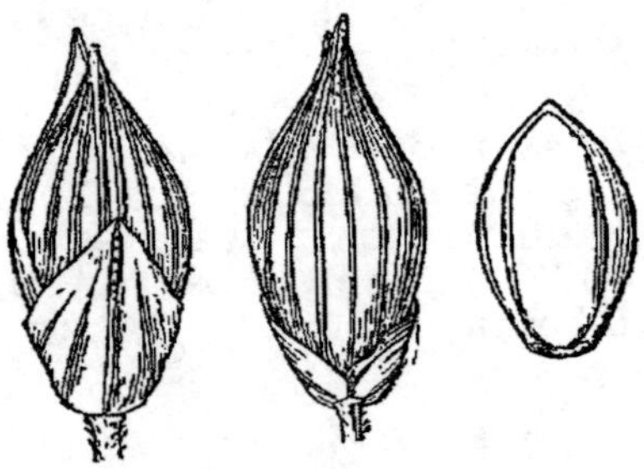

Figure 209.—*Panicum hirticaule*. Two views of spikelet, and floret, × 10 (type).

Cuba: Herradura, *Britton, Earle, and Gager* 6520; *Tracy* 9073. Pinar del Río, *Wright* 3865. Sierra de Cabra, *Britton and Gager* 7275. Laguna Jovero, *Shafer* 10910. Sumidero, *Léon and Shafer* 13717, 13719. Bayate, *Ekman* 10028. Isla de Pinos, *Curtiss* 267; *Taylor* 34; *Palmer and Riley* 1086; *Britton, Wilson, and Selby* 14455.

Jamaica: Hallis Savanna, *Harris* 12226.

Dominican Republic: Lagunas de Cenobí, *Valeur* 7. Bonao, *Ekman* H 11490. Cuenca, *Ekman* H 13306. El Valle, *Ekman* H 15694.

16. Panicum diffusum Swartz, Prodr. Veg. Ind. Occ. 23. 1788. Jamaica or Hispaniola.

Perennial; culms densely tufted, spreading or ascending from a decumbent base, 25 to 50 cm tall; sheaths glabrous or the lower some-

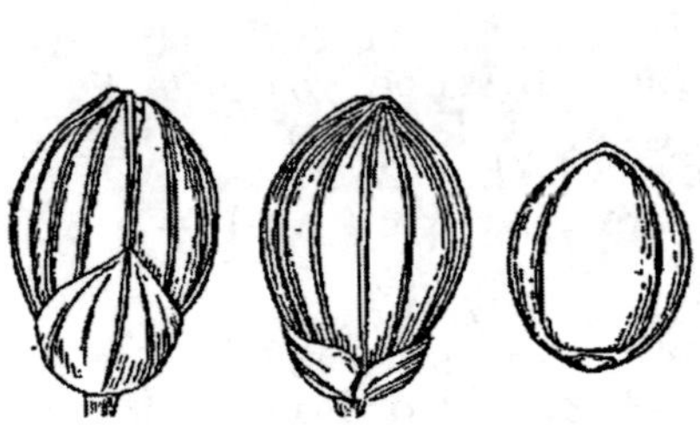

Figure 210.—*Panicum cayennense*. Two views of spikelet, and floret, × 10 (type).

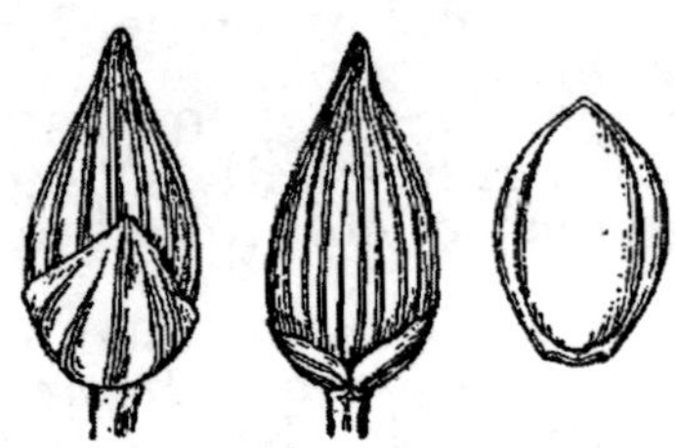

Figure 211.—*Panicum diffusum*. Two views of spikelet, and floret, × 10 (type).

times sparsely pubescent; blades 5 to 20 cm long, 1 to 3 mm wide, flat or drying subinvolute, sparsely pilose on the upper surface; panicles 5 to 10 cm long, the few branches stiffly spreading at maturity, bearing a few short-pediceled spikelets toward the ends; spikelets about 2.3 mm long, somewhat acuminate, glabrous; first glume acute, about half as long as the spikelet (fig. 211).

Banks, cliffs, and savannas, West Indies.

Bahamas: New Providence, *Britton and Brace* 424.

CUBA: Bahía, *Wilson* 9443. Guanajay, *Palmer and Riley* 802. Habana, *Léon* 190, 305 in part, 923, 2532. Santiago de las Vegas, *Wilson* 1405; *Van Hermann* 1444; *Tracy* 9111; *Baker and Wilson* 511. Triscornia, *Tracy* 9082. Cojimar, *Léon* 2559. Campo Florido, *Léon* 3449; *Ekman* 995. Jaimanito, *Ekman* 1200. Guanabacoa, *Hitchcock* 23227, 23239. Zaza de Tunas, *Léon* 923c. La Gloria, *Shafer* 385. Baraguá, *Hitchcock* 23368. Holguín, *Shafer* 1512. Manatí, *Léon* 5681. Mir, *Ekman* 7511. Retiro, *Wright* 3852, 3877. Eastern Cuba, *Wright* 1540. Isla de Pinos, *Curtiss* 384, 494.

JAMAICA: Ewarton, *Hitchcock* 9463.

HAITI: St. Michel de l'Atalaye, *Leonard* 7449. Aux Cayes, *Ekman* H 20. Source Matelas, *Ekman* H 2151. Mirebalais, *Cook, Scofield, and Doyle* 78. Jean Rabel, *Leonard* 12590, 13609, 13828. Port-de-Pai, *Leonard* 12237. Môle-St.-Nicolas, *Leonard* 13147. Bassin Bleu, *Leonard* 15090. Cabaret, *Leonard* 11875, 11900. Tortuga Island, *Leonard* 11576.

DOMINICAN REPUBLIC: Pimentel, *Abbott* 690. Guayubín, *Abbott* 1027. Azua, *Rose* 4410. San Juan, *Ekman* H 13390. Santiago, *Ekman* H 16237. Porto Plata, *Wright, Parry, and Brummel* 627.

PUERTO RICO: Mayaguez, *Chase* 6308; *Britton and Cowell* 4064. Quebradillas, *Chase* 6567, 6577 (*Amer. Gr. Nat. Herb.* 205).

VIRGIN ISLANDS: St. Thomas, *Britton and Shafer* 382; *Eggers* in 1882; St. Croix, *Eggers* in 1874; *Benzon*. St. John, *Eggers* 3068.

LEEWARD ISLANDS: Antigua, *Wullschlägel* 64.

WINDWARD ISLANDS: Martinique, *Hahn* 1232; *Duss* 536.

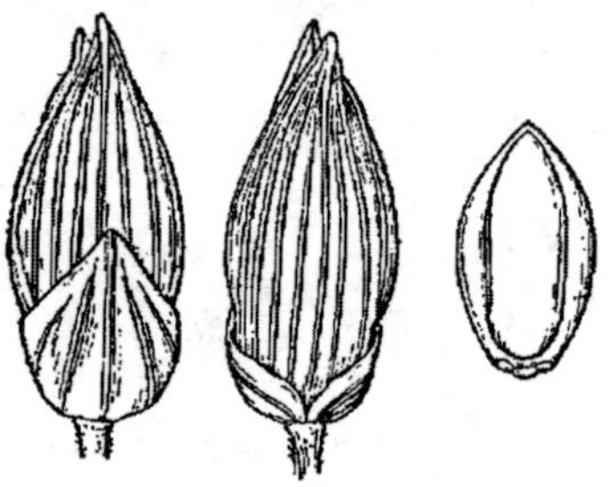

FIGURE 212.—*Panicum ghiesbreghtii*. Two views of spikelet, and floret, × 10 (type).

17. Panicum ghiesbreghtii Fourn., Mex. Pl. 2: 29. 1886. Mexico.

Panicum hirtivaginum Hitchc., Contrib. U. S. Natl. Herb. 12: 223. 1909. Cuba, *Wright* 758.

Perennial; culms erect, hispid, 60 to 80 cm tall, the nodes and sheaths hirsute; blades elongate, flat, hirsute, about 1 cm wide; panicle open, oblong, 20 to 30 cm long; spikelets 3 mm wide, glabrous, acute; first glume half as long as spikelet (fig. 212).

Low moist open ground and pastures, Mexico and West Indies to Brazil.

BAHAMAS: Crooked Island, *Brace* 4812.

CUBA: Herradura, *Hitchcock* 23443; *Tracy* 9068. Viñales, *Léon* 15339. Pinar del Río, *Hitchcock* 23292. San Diego de los Baños, *Léon* 4362, 4601. Bahía Honda, *Ekman* 12686. Habana, *Ekman* 776. El Calvario, *Léon* 922, 2674. Santiago de las Vegas, *Tracy* 9116. Soledad, *Hitchcock* 23322; *Eggers* 5406. Baraguá, *Hitchcock* 23351. Placetas del Sur, *Léon* 6429. Retiro, *Wright* 758. Baracoa, *Léon* 12304. Manatí, *Léon* 6005. La Perla, *Léon* 3783. Santiago de Cuba, *Léon* 3747. Guayabal, *Léon* 922b. Guara, *Hitchcock* 23397.

JAMAICA: Inverness, *Harris* 11691, 12161.

HAITI: Pilate, *Leonard* 9607. Plaisance, *Leonard* 9417. Port-au-Prince, *Ekman* H 1987; *Leonard* 15754. St. Michel de l'Atalaye, *Leonard* 7745. Marmelade, *Leonard* 8344. Port-à-Piment, *Ekman* H 420. St. Louis du Nord, *Leonard* 14338. Jean Rabel, *Leonard* 13744. Pétionville, *Leonard* 4901.

DOMINICAN REPUBLIC: Santiago, *Ekman* H 16129.

PUERTO RICO: Cayey, *Chase* 6744. Coamo Springs, *Chase* 6547. Tabucoa, *Sintenis* 4983.

LEEWARD ISLANDS: Antigua, *Hitchcock* 16382; *Box* 18, 39, 49, 89. Guadeloupe, *Duss* 3184.

18. Panicum hirsutum Swartz, Fl. Ind. Occ. 1: 173. 1797. Jamaica.

Perennial; culms robust, erect, as much as 1.5 m tall and 1 cm thick; sheaths hirsute with prickly fragile hairs; blades flat, mostly glabrous, 20 to 35 mm wide; panicles open, densely flowered, 20 to 35 cm long; spikelets about 2 mm long, acute, glabrous; first glume half as long as spikelet (fig. 213).

Open moist soil, Mexico and the West Indies to Brazil.

CUBA: Mangas, *Ekman* 17578. Caibarién, *Ekman* 16312. Matanzas, *Wright* in 1865. Guantánamo, *Léon* 3913. Preston, *Ekman* 3419. Guaro, *Hitchcock* 23396. Bayate, *Ekman* 6118, 6183, 10068.

HAITI: Anse-à-Taleur, *Ekman* H 4392. Aux Cayes, *Ekman* H 755.

DOMINICAN REPUBLIC: Pimentel, *Ekman* H 13275. Río Yaque del Sur, *Ekman* H 5791.

LEEWARD ISLANDS: Guadeloupe, *Duss* 3917. Antigua, *Box* 176.

WINDWARD ISLANDS: St. Lucia, *Box* 190.

TRINIDAD: Burkes pasture, *Bot. Gard. Herb.* 2295. La Brea, *Broadway* 4980. Mayaro, *Broadway* 2629. Manzanilla, *Myers* 4189.

TOBAGO: *Broadway* 4586, 4895.

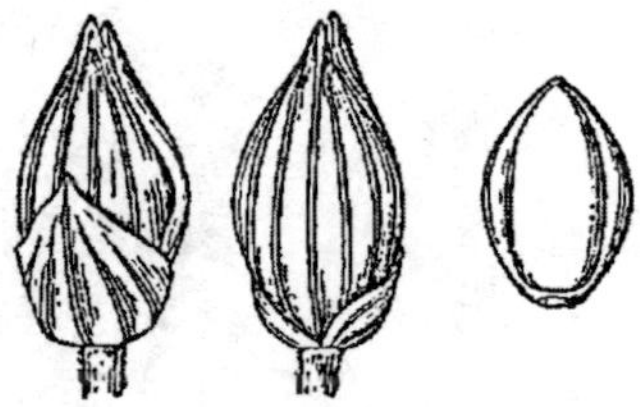

FIGURE 213.—*Panicum hirsutum.* Two views of spikelet, and floret, × 10 (type).

19. Panicum maximum Jacq., Coll. Bot. 1: 76. 1786. Guadeloupe. GUINEA GRASS.

Panicum polygamum Swartz, Prodr. Veg. Ind. Occ. 24. 1788. Jamaica.

Panicum laeve Lam., Tabl. Encycl. 1: 172. 1791. Santo Domingo and Mauritius.

Panicum jumentorum Pers., Syn. Pl. 1: 83. 1805. Based on *P. polygamum* Swartz.

Panicum trichocondylum Steud., Syn. Pl. Glum. 2: 74. 1854. Guadeloupe.

Perennial; culms cespitose, erect, 1 to 2.5 m tall, glabrous, the nodes densely hirsute; sheaths hirsute or glabrous; blades flat, elongate, 1 to 3.5 cm wide, glabrous except the margin, or hirsute on the upper surface near the base; panicle open, 20 to 50 cm long, the lower branches in whorls; spikelets oblong, glabrous, about 3 mm long; first glume one-third as long as spikelet; fruit transversely rugose (fig. 214).

Open ground, at low altitudes, escaped from cultivation, southern Florida, through Mexico and the West Indies to South America; a native of Africa and now widespread in the warmer parts of the Old World. An important forage grass throughout the Tropics of the world at low altitudes. Used for pasture, or cut and fed green. In Cuba called "hierba Guinea." To be found on all the islands.

20. Panicum repens L., Sp. Pl. ed. 2. 1: 87. 1762. Spain.

Perennial from extensively creeping rhizomes; culms erect, 30 to 80 cm tall; blades 2 to 5 mm wide; panicles open, 7 to 12 cm long, the branches stiffly ascending, naked at the base; spikelets about 2.5 mm long, glabrous; first glume one-fifth as long as spikelet, broad, truncate (fig. 215).

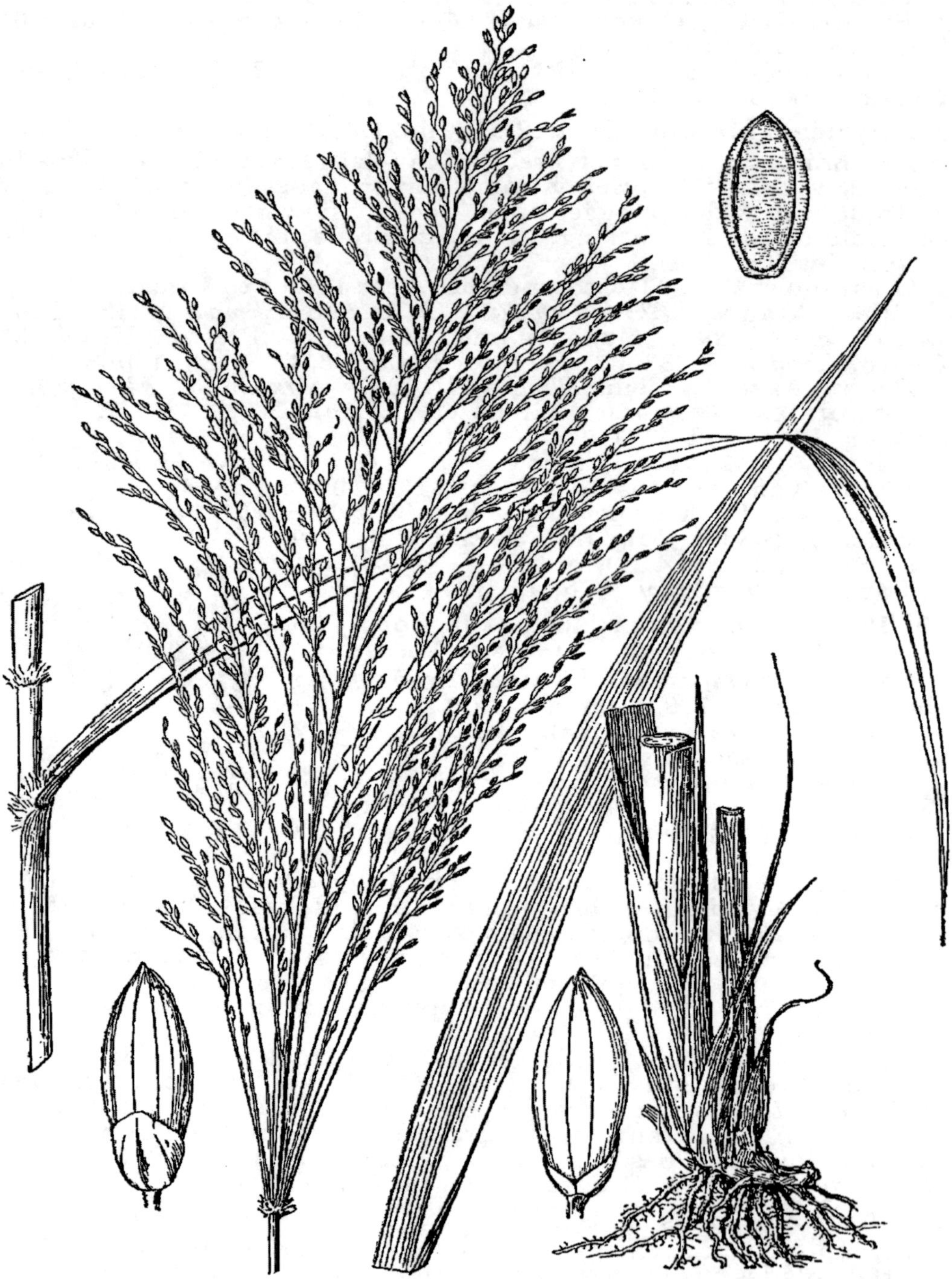

FIGURE 214.—*Panicum maximum*. Plant, × ½; two views of spikelet, and floret, × 10 (Combs and Baker 1170).

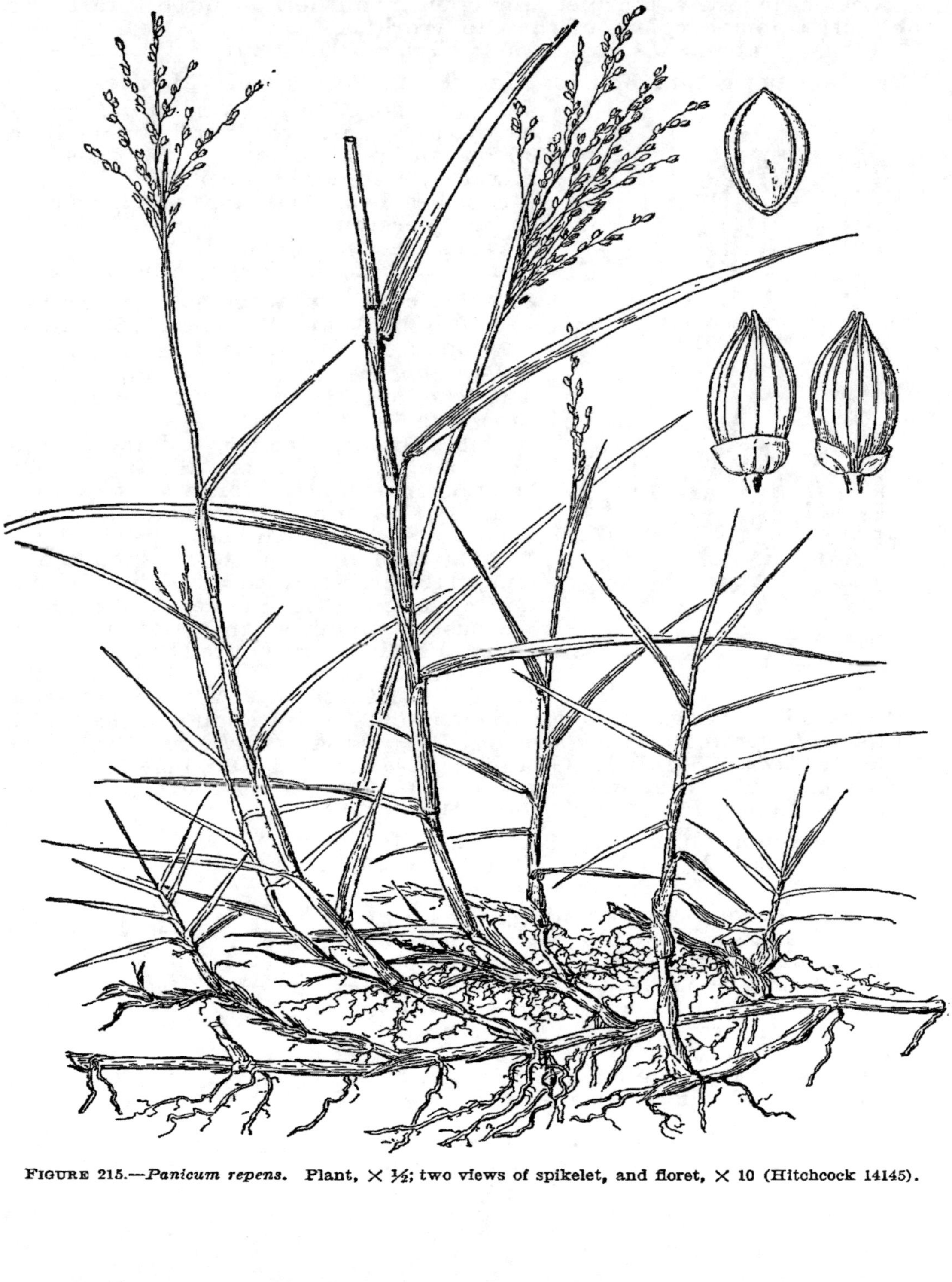

FIGURE 215.—*Panicum repens.* Plant, × ½; two views of spikelet, and floret, × 10 (Hitchcock 14145).

Sea beaches, extensively creeping, southern United States to Brazil; tropical regions of the Old World.

CUBA: Habana, *Léon* 296, 563; *Ekman* 702, 16301.

21. Panicum gouini Fourn., Mex. Pl. 2: 28. 1886. Mexico.

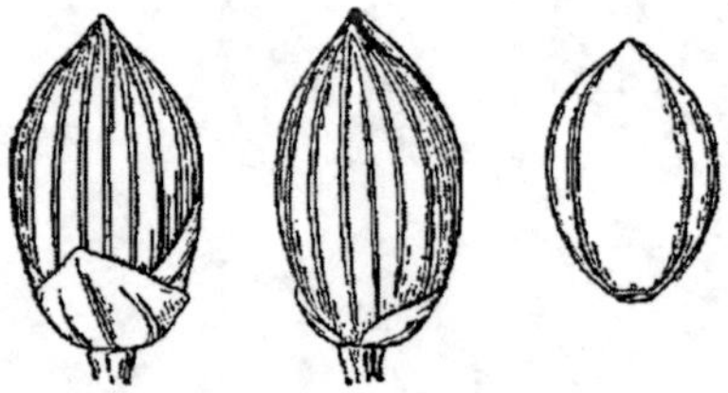

FIGURE 216.—*Panicum gouini.* Two views of spikelet, and floret, × 10 (type).

Plants like *P. repens* in habit; culms on the average lower, rarely more than 30 cm tall; panicle smaller, more densely flowered, commonly purple (fig. 216).

Sea beaches, Alabama to Louisiana; Cuba; Veracruz.

CUBA: Lomas de Camoa (prov. Habana), at a small laguna, *Ekman* 17554.

22. Panicum virgatum var. **cubense** Griseb., Cat. Pl. Cub. 233. 1866. Cuba, *Wright* in 1865.

Panicum virgatum var. *scorteum* Linder, Rhodora 24: 14. 1922. Bermuda, *Moore*, 2850.

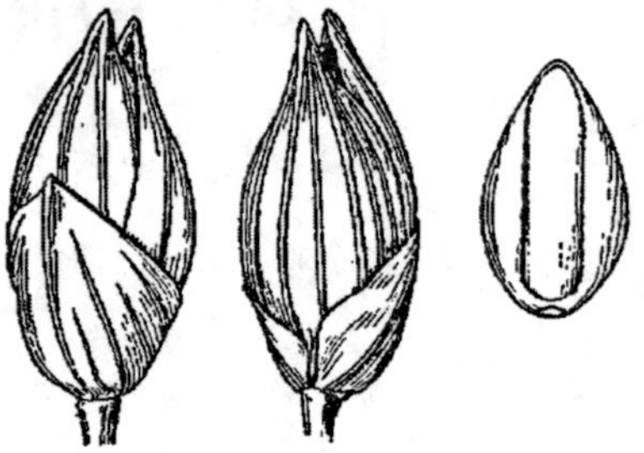

FIGURE 217.—*Panicum virgatum* var. *cubense.* Two views of spikelet, and floret, × 10 (type).

Culms erect, slender, solitary or few in a clump, 1 to 2 m tall, from scaly creeping rhizomes; blades 10 to 60 cm long, 3 to 12 mm wide, gradually long-acuminate, flat; panicles open oblong, 15 to 30 cm long; spikelets 2.8 to 3.2 mm long, glabrous, acute, the first glume about half as long as the spikelet (fig. 217).

Coastal marshes and wet places, Coastal Plain of the United States; Cuba.

CUBA: Remates, *Ekman* 11372, 11390, La Fé, *Ekman* 11322. Hanábana, *Wright* 3873. Laguna Jovero, *Shafer* 10927. Batabanó, *Ekman* 901, 12576; *Baker* in 1905; *Palmer and Riley* 1134; *Hitchcock* 153; *Killip* 13609; *Léon* 5754, 5755. Guanimar, *Léon* 7697, 14180, 14181. Guaní, *Fernando* 445. Baraguá, *Hitchcock* 23338. Ciénaga de Zapata, *Léon* 9575. Guines, *Léon* 7262; *Ekman* 16939.

23. Panicum altum Hitchc. and Chase, Contrib. U. S. Natl. Herb. 17: 488. f. 57. 1915. Panama.

Culms decumbent and straggling forming tangled masses, reedlike, as much as 6 mm in diameter, ascending to a height of 2 to 4 m, smooth and glaucous; blades flat, firm, 30 to 45 cm long, 8 to 15 mm wide; panicles ovoid, open, rather densely flowered, 20 to 30 cm long; spikelets 3.2 to 4 mm long, turgid, glabrous; first glume about two-thirds the length of the spikelet (fig. 218).

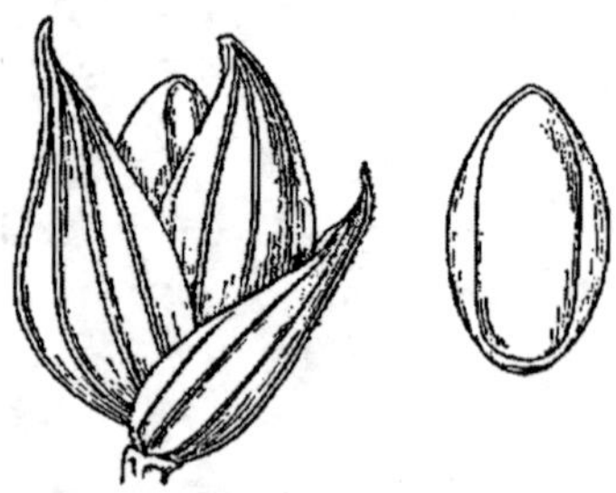

FIGURE 218.—*Panicum altum.* Spikelet and floret, × 10 (type).

Sandy marshes or flats near the coast, British Honduras to Trinidad.

TRINIDAD: Debadie, *Broadway* 5949. Port-of-Spain, *Hitchcock* 10053. Cedros, *Hitchcock* 10154, 10159.

TOBAGO: *Hitchcock* 10233; *Broadway* 3068.

24. Panicum amarulum Hitchc. and Chase, Contrib. U. S. Natl. Herb. 15: 96. f. 87. 1910. Virginia.

Plant glabrous throughout and somewhat glaucous, growing in large bunches; culms 1 to 2 m tall, robust; blades flat, more or less involute toward the slender tip, 20 to 50 cm long, 5 to 12 mm wide; panicle slightly nodding, many-flowered, compact, 15 to 30 cm long; spikelets ovate, acuminate, 4 to 5 mm long (fig. 219).

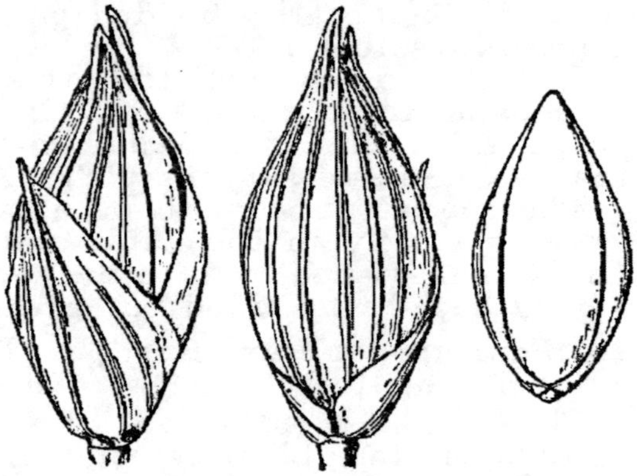

FIGURE 219.—*Panicum amarulum*. Two views of spikelet, and floret, × 10 (type).

Sandy seashores, southeastern United States, Mexico, Bahamas, and Cuba.

BERMUDA: *Collins* 139.

BAHAMAS: Great Bahama, *Britton and Millspaugh* 2739. New Providence, *Britton and Brace* 307, 493 (all in Field Mus. Herb.).

CUBA: Bahía Honda, *Ekman* 17290, 17291. Cayo Paredon Grande, *Shafer* 2735. Cayo Sabinal, *Ekman* 15500. Bahía de Manatí, *Léon* 16027.

25. Panicum petersonii Hitchc. and Ekman, sp. nov.[63]

Perennial; culms erect, tough, firm, glabrous, sparingly branched, about 2 m tall, the nodes not swollen; sheaths glabrous, passing insensibly into the blade, the lower coriaceous; ligule a very short densely ciliate membrane; blades erect, coriaceous, thick, crescent-shaped in cross section toward base, the edges sharp but smooth, gradually narrowed toward the tip and becoming flat with scabrous edges, the midrib appearing to occupy most of the tissue, 1 m long or more, the apex fine and scabrous, the middle part of the blade 2 to 3 mm wide; panicles terminal and axillary, the terminal ovoid, open but rather densely flowered, 15 to 25 cm long, the axis scabrous, the branches rather closely set, more or less fascicled, ascending, floriferous nearly to the base; spikelets short-pediceled and rather crowded on the branches of the second or third order, ovoid, glabrous, rather blunt, about 2.3 mm long; first glume

FIGURE 220.—*Panicum petersonii*. Portion of panicle, × 1; spikelet and floret, × 10 (type).

[63] Culmi erecti duri 2 m alti; vaginae glabrae; laminae durae rigidae erectae angustae 1 m longae 2–3 mm latae; panicula nonnihil patens 15–25 cm longa 10 cm lata; spiculae 2.3 mm longae glabrae obtusae; gluma prima circa 1 mm longa 3-nervis; gluma secunda 5-nervis; lemma sterile 5-nerve, quam gluma secunda paulo longius, palea et staminibus praeditum; lemma fertile lemma sterile aequans.

3- to 5-nerved, half as long as the spikelet or a little less; second glume 5-nerved, slightly shorter than the spikelet; sterile lemma 5-nerved, as long as the spikelet, staminate, the palea as long as the lemma, scabrous on the keels; fertile lemma as long as the sterile, pale, rather acute (fig. 220).

Type in the United States National Herbarium, no. 1296166, collected in temporarily flooded places, Mendoza, prov. Pinar del Río, Cuba, November 16, 1923, by E. L. Ekman (no. 18085).

Dr. Ekman also collected this species at Jagüey Chico, on the Hanábana River, prov. Santa Clara (no. 17010). Dr. Ekman states on the label that it is found on both sides of the Hanábana River (Santa Clara and Matanzas Provinces).

The species appears to be allied to *P. prionitis* Nees, of Brazil, agreeing closely in the habit and foliage but with larger spikelets. Dr. Ekman wished to have the species named for Mr. F. J. Peterson, a good friend who aided him greatly in Cuba.

26. Panicum tenerum Beyr., in Trin., Mém. Acad. St. Pétersb. VI. Sci. Nat. 1: 341. 1834. Georgia.

Plants in small tufts from a knotted crown; culms erect, stiff, wiry, 40 to 90 cm tall; blades erect, firm, 4 to 15 cm long, 2 to 4 mm wide; panicles 3 to 8 cm long, narrow, the branches appressed, the pedicels usually with a few long hairs at the summit; spikelets about 2.5 mm long, narrowly ovate, glabrous (fig. 221).

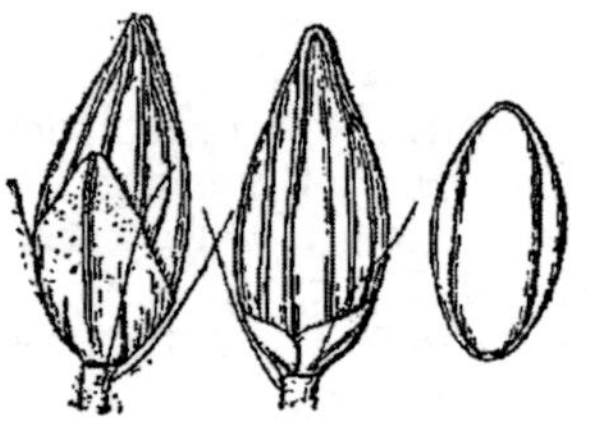

FIGURE 221.—*Panicum tenerum.* Two views of spikelet, and floret, × 10 (type).

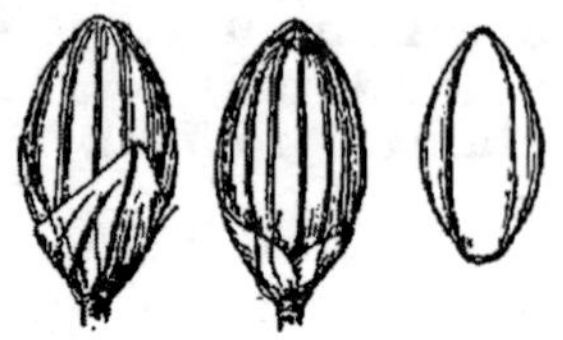

FIGURE 222.—*Panicum caricoides.* Two views of spikelet, and floret, × 10 (type).

Margins of swamps and wet places near the coast, southeastern United States, Bahamas, Cuba, and Puerto Rico.

BAHAMAS: Andros Island, *Brace* 7019, 7132 (both in Field Mus. Herb.).

CUBA: Pinar del Río, *Wright* 3870; *Hitchcock* 23272. Herradura, *Hitchcock* 154; *Tracy* 9080; *Ekman* 10759. Laguna Jovero, *Shafer* 10750. Laguna los Indios, *Shafer* 10807. Guane, *Léon* 6919. Jagüey Grande, *Ekman* 16965. Baraguá, *Hitchcock* 23378. Mordazo *Léon* 5977. Manacas, *Léon* 5856. Placetas del Sur, *Léon* 6416. Isla de Pinos, *Britton and Wilson* 14741, 15364, 15380, 15385.

DOMINICAN REPUBLIC: Cuenca, *Ekman* H 11009, 13331. El Valle, *Ekman* H 15653, H 15670, H 15701.

PUERTO RICO: Campo Alegre, *Chase* 6617.

27. Panicum caricoides Nees; Trin., Gram. Pan. 149. 1826; Agrost. Bras. 108. 1829. Brazil.

Culms tufted, erect, stiff and wiry, as much as 90 cm tall; blades appressed, narrower than the sheath, involute, 1 to 5 cm long; panicles narrow, nearly simple, 1 to 1.5 cm long, the pedicels bearing long erect white hairs at the summit; spikelets 1.5 to 1.8 mm long, glabrous (fig. 222).

Wet savannas, Trinidad to Brazil; Cuba.

CUBA: Manacas, *Léon* 9305. Mordazo, *Ekman* 17048. Isla de Pinos, *Britton and Wilson* 14282, 14701.

TRINIDAD: Aripo Savanna, *Hitchcock* 10069. O'Meara Savanna, *Britton and Hazen* 1564.

28. Panicum stenodoides Hubb., Amer. Acad. Proc. 49: 497. 1913. British Honduras.

Perennial; culms in dense tufts, erect, slender, wiry, 20 to 40 cm tall; blades erect, flat at base, involute toward the apex, 3 to 8 cm long, 1 to 2 mm wide, more or less papillose-pilose; panicles about 1 cm long, narrow, bearing 3 to 7 spikelets about 2 mm long; first glume half as long as the spikelet (fig. 223).

Open grassland and moist savannas, Central America, Trinidad.

TRINIDAD: Piarco Savanna, *Hitchcock* 10346.

29. Panicum stenodes Griseb., Fl. Brit. W. Ind. 547. 1864. Jamaica.

Perennial; culms in small tufts, slender and wiry, 25 to 50 cm tall, erect or reclining; blades 1 to 4 cm long, 1 to 2 mm wide, involute; panicles 1 to 2 cm long, 1 to 2 mm wide; spikelets about 1.5 mm long (fig. 224).

Borders of ponds and wet savannas at low altitudes, Central America and the West Indies to Brazil.

CUBA: El Salado, *Wright* 3871. Herradura, *Hitchcock* 155; *Léon* 15955. Guane, *Léon* 6998, 15354. Pinar del Río, *Hitchcock* 23263, 23281, 23297. Manacas, *Léon* 5868, 6045. Banao Mountains, *Léon* 5402. Isla de Pinos, *Britton and Wilson* 15346, 15623.

JAMAICA: Bull Head Mountain, *Hitchcock* 9534 (*Amer. Gr. Nat. Herb.* 46). Hollis Savanna, *Harris* 12227. Without locality, *Orcutt* 7829.

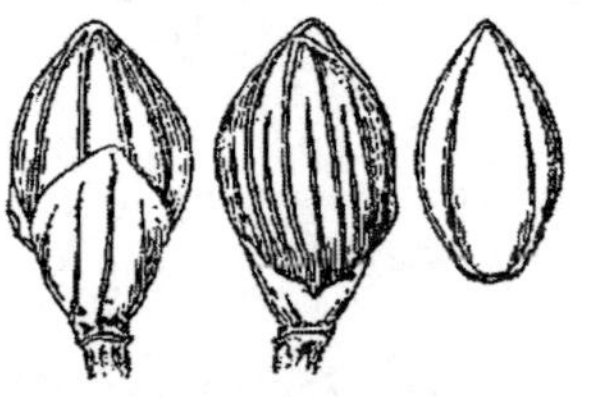

FIGURE 223.—*Panicum stenodoides.* Two views of spikelet, and floret, × 10 (type).

FIGURE 224.—*Panicum stenodes.* Two views of spikelet, and floret, × 10 (Wright 192).

HAITI: Acul-Samedi, *Ekman* H 9919.

DOMINICAN REPUBLIC: Santo Domingo, *Wright, Parry, and Brummel* 624. Sabana de la Mar, *Ekman* H 15610.

PUERTO RICO: San Juan, *Chase* 6769.

TRINIDAD: Piarco Savanna, *Hitchcock* 10347; *Broadway* 2151a. Aripo Savanna, *Hitchcock* 10069½.

30. Panicum beyeri Hitchc. and Ekman, sp. nov.[64]

Culms densely tufted, slender, weakly erect or reclining, glabrous, 50 to 130 cm tall; sheaths glabrous; ligule a line of hairs less than 0.5 mm long; blades numerous, glabrous, flat or mostly involute, very slender, elongate, 20 to 40 cm long or more, the broader ones as much as 1.5 mm wide, mostly less than 1 mm wide, lax or reclining; panicles very slender and elongate, as much as 35 cm long, the branches few, remote, appressed, few-flowered, 5 to 15 mm long, the axis and branches very minutely puberulent or scaberulous; spikelets somewhat oblique on the puberulent pedicels, narrowly elliptic, acute, often gaping, glabrous, about 3 mm long; first glume broadly acute, 3-nerved, 1 mm long; second glume and sterile lemma equal, narrowed to an obtuse point, 5-nerved, the lemma with a palea nearly as long as itself but with no stamens; fertile lemma rather soft, acute, a

[64] Culmi dense caespitosi gracillimi glabri 50–130 cm alti debiles vel reclinati; laminae gracillimae debiles planes vel involutae elongatae 20–40 cm longae, interdum 1.5 mm latae, plerumque 0.5–1 mm latae; panicula gracillima elongata 30–35 cm longa, ramis paucis remotis appressis paucifloris 5–15 mm longis; spiculae angustae glabrae acutae 3 mm longae.

little shorter than the spikelet, very minutely scaberulous at the tip, 5-nerved, the midnerve evident only at the tip, the intermediate pair indistinct, the lateral pair distinct near the margin on the ventral side of the floret, the margins of the lemma approximate but not in contact along the middle of the face; palea nearly as long as the lemma, scaberulous like the lemma at the acute tip, convex on the back, the 2 nerves wide apart, the apex enclosed at the tip (fig. 225).

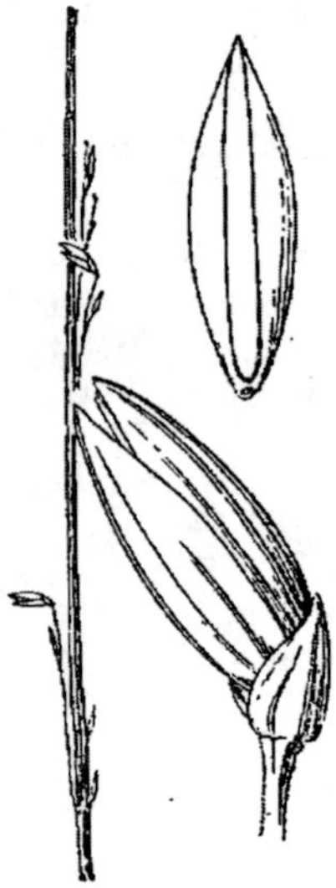

FIGURE 225.—*Panicum beyeri*. Portion of panicle, × 1; spikelet and floret, × 10 (type).

Type in the United StatesNational Herbarium, no. 1387466, collected along the edge of the Río Piloto, at 300 m altitude, Sierra de Nipe, prov. Oriente, Cuba, September 8, 1922, by E. L. Ekman (no. 15045).

The species was collected by Dr. Ekman (no. 10085) at the same locality, October 19, 1919, growing in moist sloping "manacales",[65] but the specimens are sterile. The species is said by Dr. Ekman to be very rare. It is named for M. K. Beyer, a Norwegian, who accompanied Dr. Ekman on many Sierra de Nipe excursions.

The species is not closely allied to any other, but for convenience is assigned to the group Tenera in which the culms are stiff and wiry. In habit it resembles *P. distantiflorum*, but the branches of the panicle do not end in a bristle, but frequently bear abortive spikelets, suggesting a trend toward elimination of the spikelet, as in *P. distantiflorum* and its allies.

31. Panicum condensum Nash, in Small, Fl. Southeast. U. S. 93. 1903. Florida.

Culms erect, 1 to 2 m tall; lower sheaths, especially on the innovations, compressed-keeled; blades flat from a usually folded base; panicles condensed, terminal and axillary, 10 to 25 cm long, rarely over 5 cm wide, the long solitary or fascicled branches erect, naked at base, with appressed branchlets bearing crowded spikelets on short pedicels; spikelets about 2.5 mm long, glabrous, acuminate (fig. 226).

FIGURE 226.—*Panicum condensum*. Two views of spikelet and floret, × 10 (type).

Borders of streams and ponds and in wet places, southeastern United States and the West Indies.

BAHAMAS: Nassau, *Curtiss* 174.

CUBA: Remates, *Ekman* 11178, 11389, 11393. San Diego de Tapias, *Ekman* 10616. Carabela Grande, *Roig* 3193. Hanábana, *Wright* 3862 in part. Guanimar, *Léon* 5062. Batabanó, *Léon* 13430, 13434, 13623, 13624, 14197, 14203; *Ekman* 12587. Campo Florido, *Léon* 4141; *Ekman* 13239. Sabana de San Marcos, *Léon* 9207. Sabana de Motembo, *Léon* 9344; *Ekman* 16820. Ciénaga de Zapata, *Léon* 9500, 9518; *Ekman* 16945. Santayana, *Ekman* 15362. Caibarién, *Léon* 468, 475, 478.

[65] "Wet forests up to 800 m in Cuba, characterized by a palm named 'manaca' (*Calyptrogyne occidentalis*)."—Letter from Brother Léon.

Holguín, *Shafer* 1438. Isla de Pinos, *Britton and Wilson* 14621; *Ekman* 11795, 12444.

JAMAICA: Black River, *Hitchcock* 9652 (*Amer. Gr. Nat. Herb.* 47). Savanna-la-Mar, *Hitchcock* 9884. Grosmond Marsh, *Harris* 11750.

HAITI: Port-au-Prince, *Ekman* H 2171; *Leonard* 10087; *Buch* 2047. Aux Cayes, *Ekman* H 25, H 264.

PUERTO RICO: San Juan, *Chase* 6351. Campo Alegre, *Chase* 6802.

LEEWARD ISLANDS: Guadeloupe, *Duss* 3919.

32. **Panicum polygonatum** Schrad., in Schult., Mant. 2: 256. 1824. Brazil.

Panicum potamium Trin., Gram. Pan. 239. 1826. Brazil.

Perennial; culms branching, widely spreading or creeping, as much as 100 cm long, the nodes densely pubescent; blades 3 to 13 cm long, 8 to 15 mm wide, cordate; panicles 7 to 20 cm long, the branchlets secund from the lower side of the branches, the rachises sparsely pilose with long weak hairs; spikelets 1.5 mm long, pointed, glabrous (fig. 227).

Swamps and moist soil along roadsides and in open woods, Mexico and Trinidad to Paraguay.

FIGURE 227.—*Panicum polygonatum*. Two views of spikelet, and floret, × 10 (type).

FIGURE 228.—*Panicum milleflorum*. Spikelet and floret, × 10 (type).

FIGURE 229.—*Panicum pilosum*. Spikelet and floret, × 10 (type).

TRINIDAD: Port-of-Spain, *Chase* 9935; *Hitchcock* 9953. Penal Rock Road, *Britton, Hazen, and Mendelson* 1091. Caparo, *Broadway* 2837. Aripo Savanna, *Hitchcock* 10077. Arima, *Hitchcock* 10297, 10306. Ortoire River, *Britton, Freeman, and Nowell* 2663. Tabaquite, *Hitchcock* 10132 (*Amer. Gr. Nat. Herb.* 57).

TOBAGO: *Broadway* 4476.

33. **Panicum milleflorum** Hitchc. and Chase, Contrib. U. S. Natl. Herb. 17: 494. f. 70. 1915. Canal Zone.

Panicum distichum var. *lancifolium* Griseb., Fl. Brit. W. Ind. 548. 1864. Trinidad, *Crueger* 84.

Differs from *P. pilosum* in its larger size, as much as 2 m tall, in its longer blades, as much as 40 cm long, in its longer panicles, as much as 35 cm long, and in its slightly smaller spikelets, 1.3 mm long (fig. 228).

Swamps near the coast, British Honduras to Brazil; Trinidad.

TRINIDAD: Without locality, *Crueger* 84 (*Bot. Gard. Herb.* 3195).

34. **Panicum pilosum** Swartz, Prodr. Veg. Ind. Occ. 22. 1788. Jamaica.

Panicum distichum Lam., Encycl. 4: 731. 1798. Jamaica.

Perennial; culms decumbent or creeping and rooting at the nodes, the branches and sometimes the main culms erect; nodes villous or sometimes glabrous; blades 4 to 20 cm long, 7 to 15 mm wide, broadest near the cordate or truncate base; panicles of 10 to 20 spikelike densely flowered racemes along an axis 5 to 15 cm long, the racemes 1 to 3 cm long, the rachis pilose; spikelets 1.5 mm long, glabrous (fig. 229).

Moist ground, ditches, and swamps, Mexico and the West Indies to Paraguay.

CUBA: Daraniguas, *Wright* 3451. Sumidero, *Shafer* 13505, *Shafer and Léon* 13533, 13535. Buenaventura, *Wilson* 9444. Herradura, *Van Hermann* 763; *Tracy* 9063. Marianao, *Léon* 1977. Sancti Spíritus, *Léon* 908. Banao Mountains, *Léon* 3982. Jauco, *Léon* 12306. Isla de Pinos, *Curtiss* 305; *Taylor* 36; *Britton and Wilson* 14638, 15807.

JAMAICA: Castleton, *Harris* 11280a; *Hitchcock* 9407. Troy, *Harris* 12566; *Hitchcock* 9782. Claverty Cottage, *Harris* 11524. Hollis Savanna, *Harris* 12254. Ipswich, *Hitchcock* 9626. Ramble, *Hitchcock* 9517. Bull Head Mountain, *Hitchcock* 9548. Ewarton, *Hitchcock* 9423. Port Morant, *Hitchcock* in 1890. Gordon Town, *Hart* 732. Navy Island, *Millspaugh* 1859. East of Seamens Valley, *Maxon and Killip* 106a. Mill Bank, *Maxon and Killip* 196. Mount Diablo, *Maxon and Killip* 489. Cedar Hurst, *Harris* 11547.

DOMINICAN REPUBLIC: Samaná Peninsula, *Abbott* 313; *Ekman* H 14835. Guarabo, *Abbott* 2802. La Nassa, *Faris* 268. Higüey, *Ekman* H 12133, H 12236; Villa Altagracia, *Ekman* H 11183.

FIGURE 230.—*Panicum boliviense*. Two views of spikelet, and floret, × 10 (type).

LEEWARD ISLANDS: St. Kitts, *Box* 137. Guadeloupe, *L'Herminier; Duss* 4154. Dominica, *Imray* 151, 312; *Hitchcock* 16441; *Jones* 20.

WINDWARD ISLANDS: Martinique, *Hitchcock* 16449. St. Lucia, *Hitchcock* 16478; *Kemp* 18. Grenada, *Broadway* 148.

TRINIDAD: Mount Tocuche, *Britton, Hazen, and Mendelson* 1252. Arima, *Hitchcock* 10309. Piarco Savanna, *Hitchcock* 10358. Tabaquite, *Hitchcock* 10121. Port-of-Spain, *Bot. Gard. Herb.* 3293; *Hitchcock* 9961, 10045. Cedros, *Hitchcock* 10147 (*Amer. Gr. Nat. Herb.* 59). Oropuche Lagoon, *Britton, Hazen, and Freeman* 1153. O'Meara Savanna, *Britton and Hazen* 1578. Ortoire River, *Britton, Freeman, and Nowell* 2533. La Brea, *Broadway* 4986.

TOBAGO: *Broadway* 4063; *Hitchcock* 10208, 10242, 10265; *Eggers* 5534.

35. Panicum boliviense Hack., Repert. Sp. Nov. Fedde 11: 19. 1912. Bolivia.

Perennial; culms decumbent, branching, as much as 1.5 m long; nodes glabrous; blades flat, gradually narrowed from a cordate-clasping base, 8 to 15 cm long, 1 to 2 cm wide; panicle 10 to 25 cm long, open; spikelets 1.5 mm long, glabrous (fig. 230).

Ditches, banks of streams, and moist open woodland, southern Mexico and Cuba to Paraguay.

CUBA: Mariel, *Ekman* 11499. Mendoza, *Léon* 6952. Baños San Vicente, *Britton and Gager* 7452. San Miguel de Casanova, *Léon* 12469. San Nicolás, *Léon* 7297. Marianao, *Léon* 1977. Batabanó, *Léon* 14234. Baraguá, *Hitchcock* 23369. Sancti Spíritus, *Léon* 909, 6515, 6574, 6606. Caibarién, *Fernando* 374. Omaro, *Léon* 9441. Manacas, *Léon* 5906. Banao, *Léon* 5460. Santa Rosa, *Léon* 10336. Guara, *Hitchcock* 23405. Isla de Pinos, *Curtiss* 464.

Haiti: Étang-Dérémond, *Ekman* H 10473. Aux Cayes, *Ekman* H 754.

Dominican Republic: Cuenca, *Ekman* H 10980, H 13305. Villa Altagracia, *Ekman* H 11204. Sosúa, *Ekman* H 14533.

Leeward Islands: Guadeloupe, *L'Herminier* 17. Dominica, *Hitchcock* 16419, 16435.

Windward Islands: Martinque, *Hitchcock* 16446. St. Lucia, *Box* 184, 322; *Hitchcock* 16483.

36. **Panicum laxum** Swartz, Prodr. Veg. Ind. Occ. 23. 1788. Jamaica.

Panicum diandrum Kunth, Rév. Gram 2: 393. pl. 110. 1831. Guadeloupe and Brazil.

More or less spreading, often rooting at the nodes of the decumbent base, culms 40 to 100 cm long; blades conduplicate or flat, 5 to 15 mm wide, narrowed to a rounded or subcordate base; panicles oblong, 5 to 30 cm long, composed of many slender, raceme-like branches, the lower distant, spreading, the upper ascending; branchlets mostly secund on the lower side of the branches, bearing 2 or 3 acutish spikelets 1 to 1.5 mm long (fig. 231).

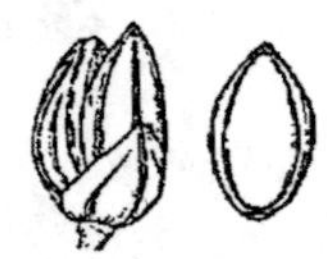

Figure 231.—*Panicum laxum*. Spikelet and floret, × 10 (type).

Ditches, banks, moist woods, and wet savannas, Mexico and the West Indies to Paraguay. Common in Cuba, Jamaica, Puerto Rico, and Trinidad. Other localities are listed below.

Haiti: Lamielle, *Ekman* H 6204.

Dominican Republic: Pimentel, *Abbott* 687, 688. Cuenca, *Ekman* H 10981. La Cumbre, *Ekman* H 12390.

Virgin Islands: Tortola, *Britton and Shafer* 791, 808.

Leeward Islands: Antigua, *Wullschlaegel* 623; *Box* 74, 82. Guadeloupe, *Duss* 3179. Dominica, *Jones* 21, 25.

Windward Islands: Barbados, *Dash* 450. St. Lucia, *Kemp* 11, 42.

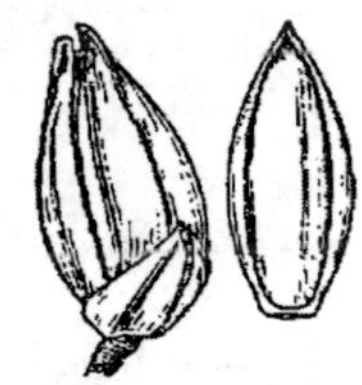

Figure 232.—*Panicum stevensianum*. Spikelet and floret, × 10 (type).

Grenada: *Broadway* 1870, 3712, 4668.

Tobago: *Hitchcock* 10245, 10272.

37. **Panicum stevensianum** Hitchc. and Chase, Contrib. U. S. Natl. Herb. 17: 498. f. 76. 1915. Puerto Rico, *Chase* 6616.

Perennial; culms compressed, prostrate-spreading, rooting at the nodes, 30 to 60 cm long, the flowering branches ascending; blades flat, 4 to 10 cm long, 5 to 10 mm wide, truncate-cordate at base; panicles 6 to 10 cm long, narrow, consisting of several appressed or ascending spikelike branches; spikelets about 2 mm long, glabrous, acute; first glume about one-fourth the length of the spikelet (fig. 232).

Borders of pools, ditches, and other wet places, Cuba and Puerto Rico.

Cuba: Batabanó, *Ekman* 12630, 13093; *Léon* 14200. Laguna Ariguanabo, *Ekman* 11516, 16929; *Léon* 9030. Laguna de Castellano, *Wilson* 9558; *Ekman* 16796.

Puerto Rico: Campo Alegre, *Chase* 6616.

38. **Panicum exiguiflorum** Griseb., Cat. Pl. Cub. 234. 1866. Based on *P. minutiflorum* Rich.

Panicum minutiflorum A. Rich., in Sagra, Hist. Cuba 11: 305. 1850. Not *P. minutiflorum* Rasp., 1825. Cuba.

Panicum laxum var. *variegatum* Griseb., Cat. Pl. Cub. 233. 1866. Cuba, *Wright* 3450.

Panicum tricolor Hack., Oesterr. Bot. Ztschr. 51: 370. 1901. Fortune Island, *Eggers* 3978.

Perennial; culms tufted, sometimes sending out prostrate stolons, decumbent at base, 15 to 50 cm tall; blades 2 to 6 cm long, 0.5 to 1.5 mm wide, glabrous; panicles 3 to 10 cm long, the branches few, spreading or reflexed at maturity; spikelets 1.5 mm long, glabrous, clustered on short branchlets; sterile palea enlarging at maturity, expanding the spikelet (fig. 233).

Low savannas and moist sandy woods, Cuba and Haiti.

BAHAMAS: Fortune Island, *Hitchcock* in 1890.

CUBA: Santa Cruz de los Pinos, *Ekman* in 1923 (*Amer. Gr. Nat. Herb.* 702). Herradura, *Hitchcock* 179; *Tracy* 9075. Pinar del Río, *Hitchcock* 23273, 23278. Guane, *Léon* 6948, 7004, 7008. Guanabacoa, *Ekman* 572; *Léon* 911, 913, 5608, 5624; *Hitchcock* 23241. Madruga, *Léon* 6377, 14690. San Juan de Buena Vista, *Wright* 755. Chirigota, *Wright* 3450, 3877 in part. Zaza de Tunas, *Léon*

FIGURE 233.—*Panicum exiguiflorum.* Spikelet and floret, × 10 (Wright 3450).

FIGURE 234.—*Panicum stoloniferum.* Spikelet and floret, × 10 (type).

FIGURE 235.—*Panicum frondescens* Spikelet and floret, × 10 (type).

902, 6730. Sancti Spíritus, *Léon* 2566. Gavilanes, *Léon* 6654. Manacas, *Léon* 9277. Soledad, *Hitchcock* 23330. Baraguá, *Hitchcock* 23356. Bayate, *Ekman* 2443. Isla de Pinos, *Britton and Wilson* 14699, 15381; *Taylor* 35.

HAITI: Morne Belanse, *Ekman* H 4916.

39. Panicum stoloniferum Poir., in Lam., Encycl. Sup. 4: 274. 1816. Cayenne.

Perennial; plants creeping, branching, 10 to 50 cm long; blades flat, 1 to 5 cm long, 3 to 15 mm wide; panicles 1 to 5 cm long, with few to several racemes 5 to 10 mm long; spikelets about 2.5 mm long, glabrous (fig. 234).

Moist shady places, Central America and the Lesser Antilles to Brazil.

WINDWARD ISLANDS: Martinique, *Duss* 1291 (Krug and Urban Herb.).

TRINIDAD: Maracas, *Broadway* 6078, 7239. Ortoire River, *Britton, Freeman, and Nowell* 2539. Caura River, *Britton and Hazen* 1204. Port-of-Spain, *Bot. Gard. Herb.* 2293. Arima, *Broadway* 2370. Oropuche, *Broadway* 5582. Blanchisseuse, *Broadway* 6907. Chaguanas, *Bot. Gard. Herb.* 3747. Without locality, *Crueger* 79.

40. Panicum frondescens Meyer, Prim. Fl. Esseq. 56. 1818. British Guiana.

Hymenachne frondescens Fourn., Mex. Pl. 2: 36. 1886.

Culms erect or ascending from a creeping base, 30 to 50 cm tall; blades 5 to 11 cm long, 12 to 20 mm long, acuminate, glabrous; panicles 5 to 11 cm long, with numerous approximate racemes 10 to 25 cm long; spikelets about 2.7 mm long, glabrous (fig. 235).

Swamps and wet places at low altitudes, Mexico and Lesser Antilles to Brazil.

LEEWARD ISLANDS: Guadeloupe, *L'Herminier* 137.

WINDWARD ISLANDS: *Smith and Smith* 187 (Krug and Urban Herb.).

TRINIDAD: Blanchisseuse, *Broadway* 2390. Arima, *Broadway* 2371. Oropuche, *Broadway* 6171. Mount Tamana, *Broadway* 7980. Without locality, *Crueger* 85.

41. Panicum pulchellum Raddi, Agrost. Bras. 42. 1823. Brazil.

Perennial; culms spreading or creeping, branching, the nodes pubescent; blades thin, flat, 1.5 to 4 cm long, 4 to 15 mm wide; panicles oblong, 2 to 12 cm long, the racemes 5 to 15 mm long; spikelets about 2 mm long, hispid, bearing on the sterile lemma 2 sessile glands (fig. 236).

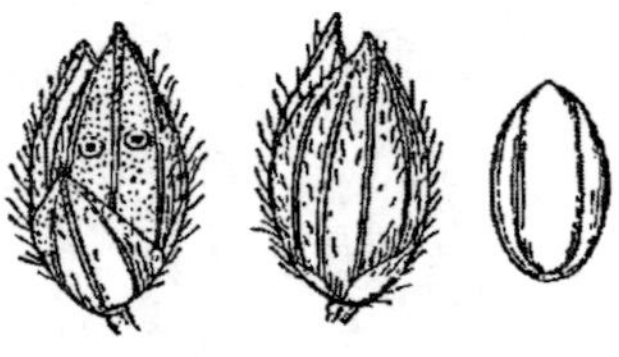

FIGURE 236.—*Panicum pulchellum*. Two views of spikelet, and floret, × 10 (Raddi).

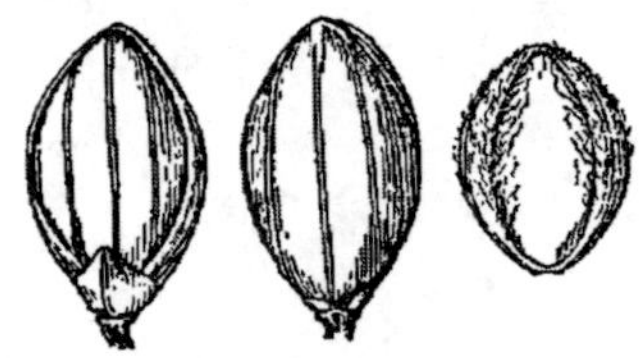

FIGURE 237.—*Panicum schiffneri*. Two views of spikelet, and floret, × 10 (type).

Moist shady places, southern Mexico and Windward Islands to Brazil.

WINDWARD ISLANDS: Martinique, *Duss* 767 (Krug and Urban Herb.).

42. Panicum schiffneri Hack., Ergeb. Bot. Exped. Akad. Wiss. Sudbras. 11. 1906. Brazil.

Perennial, branching and rooting at the nodes; culms ascending, 2 to 3 m long; sheaths papillose-hispid; blades 10 to 15 cm long, 12 to 25 mm wide, scabrous; panicles 10 to 15 cm long, the few slender scabrous branches remote, the spikelets approximate along the upper part; spikelets glabrous, elliptic, about 2 mm long; first glume less than one-fourth the length of the spikelet; fruit elliptic, 1.5 mm long, sparsely silky (fig. 237).

Wet shady banks and slopes, Mexico and the West Indies to Brazil.

HAITI: Pétionville, *Ekman* H 1927. Le Borgne, *Ekman* H 4791.

DOMINICAN REPUBLIC: Polo, *Abbott* 1808. Jarabaco, *Ekman* H 14178. Loma Diego de Ocampo, *Ekman* H 16301. Sierra de Ocoa, *Ekman* H 11646.

PUERTO RICO: Maricao, *Chase* 6198, 6247 (*Amer. Gr. Nat. Herb.* 512). Adjuntas, *Chase* 6474. Cayey, *Chase* 6745.

WINDWARD ISLANDS: Martinique, *Hahn* 616.

60256—36——18

43. Panicum trichoides Swartz, Prodr. Veg. Ind. Occ. 24. 1788. Jamaica.

Panicum capillaceum Lam., Tabl. Encycl. 1: 173. 1791. Puerto Rico.

Annual; culms erect or branched and spreading, the ascending ones 20 to 40 cm long; sheaths papillose-hirsute; blades ovate or ovate-lanceolate, thin, cordate, 2 to 6 cm long, 1 to 2 cm wide, glabrous or sparsely hirsute; panicles open and spreading, 5 to 20 cm long, the branches and pedicels capillary; spikelets about 1.3 mm long, elliptic, sparsely hirsute; first glume about half as long as the spikelet (fig. 238).

Damp shady places, often a weed in fields and groves, throughout tropical America. To be found on all the islands.

This species has been referred in some American floras to *P. brevifolium* L., of India.

44. Panicum trichanthum Nees, Agrost. Bras. 210. 1829. Brazil.

Perennial; culms branching and straggling, the ascending fertile ones 1 to 2 m long; blades oblong-lanceolate, 10 to 15 cm long, 10 to 15 mm wide, cordate, rather strongly nerved; panicles 10 to 30 cm

FIGURE 238.—*Panicum trichoides.* Two views of spikelet, and floret, × 10 (type).

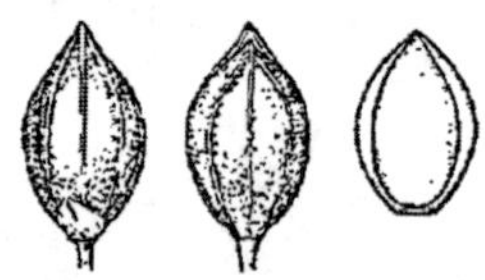

FIGURE 239.—*Panicum trichanthum.* Two views of spikelet, and floret, × 10 (Fendler 1643).

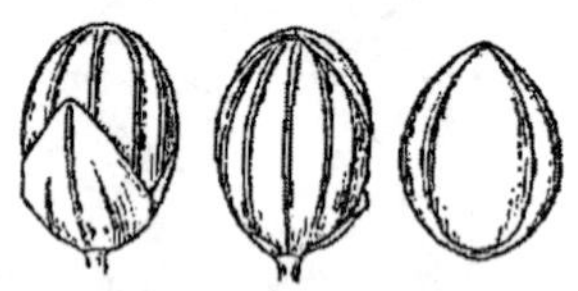

FIGURE 240.—*Panicum parvifolium.* Two views of spikelet, and floret, × 10 (type).

long, open and spreading; spikelets about 1.5 mm long, elliptic, acute; first glume less than one-fifth the length of the spikelets (fig. 239).

Moist thickets and river banks, Central America and the West Indies to Paraguay.

CUBA: Vento, *Curtiss* 598; *Léon* 557. Trinidad, *Wright* 753. Bayate, *Ekman* 4559, 6553. Romelia, *Eggers* 5350.

JAMAICA: Port Antonio, *Hitchcock* in 1890.

HAITI: Dondou, *Leonard* 8571. Port-de-Pai, *Leonard* 12269. Ennery, *Leonard* 9157. Cabaillon, *Ekman* H 845.

DOMINICAN REPUBLIC: Polo, *Abbott* 1773. Gros-Figuier, *Ekman* H 6763.

PUERTO RICO: Ponce, *Chase* 6487. Cayey, *Chase* 6748; *Sintenis* 2471. Rio Piedras, *Johnston* 143.

TRINIDAD: Arima, *Eggers* in 1883. Cedros, *Hitchcock* 10146. Port-of-Spain, *Hitchcock* 9943. Siparia, *Broadway* 4973.

45. Panicum parvifolium Lam., Tabl. Encycl. 1: 173. 1791. Tropical America.

Panicum oplismenoides Nash, Bull. Torrey Bot. Club 30: 381. 1903. Puerto Rico, *Heller* 1316.

Perennial, more or less glaucous; culms branching and creeping, rooting at the nodes, the ascending fertile ones 20 to 80 cm long;

blades 1 to 3 cm long, 2 to 6 mm wide, oblong-lanceolate, rounded or subcordate, spreading or reflexed, glabrous; panicles open, loosely few-flowered, 2 to 4 cm long; spikelets turgid, blunt, glabrous, 1.5 mm long; first glume a little more than half the length of the spikelet (fig. 240).

Wet savannas and margins of ponds and streams, Costa Rica and the West Indies to Paraguay.

CUBA: Pinar del Río, *Hitchcock* 23277; *Britton and Gager* 7075. Los Almacigos, *Wright* 3458. Herradura, *Hitchcock* 181, 23435; *Baker* 2078; *Britton, Earle, and Gager* 6494; *Tracy* 9060, 9079. Remates, *Ekman* 11359. Guane, *Shafer* 10659; *Léon* 6944, 15399. Laguna los Indios, *Shafer* 10803. Isla de Pinos, *Britton and Wilson* 14235, 15624; *Britton, Wilson, and Leon* 6053.

JAMAICA: Hollis Savanna, *Harris* 12221. James Hill Savanna, *Harris* 12839.

DOMINICAN REPUBLIC: Cuenca, *Ekman* H 10968. Rincón, *Ekman* H 13290. Jovero, *Abbott* 2539.

PUERTO RICO: Carolina, *Britton and Brown* 5720. Vega Baja, *Chase* 6796. Aguada, *Sintenis* 5719. San Juan, *Chase* 6358, 6630, 6763, 6786. Campo Alegre, *Chase* 6615, 6788. Catano, *Sintenis* 5719.

TRINIDAD: O'Meara Savanna, *Broadway* 2372. Aripo Savanna, *Hitchcock* 10065, 10080 (*Amer. Gr. Nat. Herb.* 72). Pitch Lake, *Hitchcock* 10100 (*Amer. Gr. Nat. Herb.* 210). Without locality, *Broadway* in 1918; *Crueger* 224.

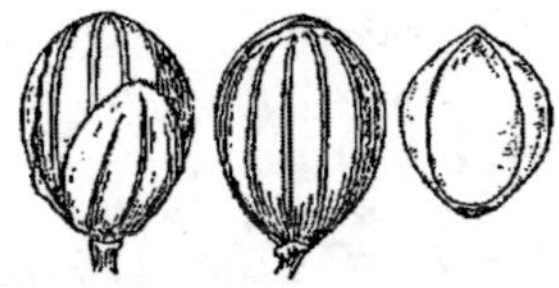

FIGURE 241.—*Panicum cyanescens*. Two views of spikelet, and floret, × 10 (type).

46. Panicum cyanescens Nees; Trin., Gram. Pan. 202. 1826; Agrost. Bras. 220. 1829. Brazil.

Perennial, bluish or glaucous; culms tufted, 30 to 50 cm tall; blades flat, rather firm, erect to spreading or reflexed, 3 to 8 cm long, 4 to 5 mm wide, oblong-lanceolate, glabrous; panicles open, 3 to 6 cm long; spikelets 1.5 mm long, turgid or subglobose, obtuse, glabrous; first glume obtuse, two-thirds as long as spikelet (fig. 241).

Swamps and wet savannas, Trinidad to Brazil; Cuba; British Honduras.

CUBA: Isla de Pinos, *Ekman* 12148; *Britton and Wilson* 14748a.

TRINIDAD: Aripo Savanna, *Hitchcock* 10067. Piarco Savanna, *Hitchcock* 10349, 10354, 10364. Without locality, *Finlay* 88; *Crueger* 20.

47. Panicum nervosum Lam., Encycl. 4: 747. 1798. Cayenne.

Stouter than *P. cyanescens*, the lower sheaths much overlapping; blades strongly nerved, cordate-clasping, widest near the base, gradually narrowing to a sharp point; panicle 10 to 15 cm long, open, the branches ascending.

Savannas, Trinidad to Brazil.

TRINIDAD: Aripo Savanna, *Broadway* 2377.

48. Panicum venezuelae Hack., Oesterr. Bot. Ztschr. 51: 368. 1901. Venezuela.

Panicum ineptum Hitchc. and Chase, Contrib. U. S. Natl. Herb. 17: 509. f. 98. 1915. Santo Domingo, *Bertero* 817.

Panicum berteronianum Mez, Bot. Jahrb. Engler 56 (Beibl. 125): 5. 1921. Not *P. berteronianum* Schult., 1854. Santo Domingo, *Bertero* 817.

Perennial; culms slender, widely spreading or creeping, the flowering branches ascending, 10 to 15 cm tall, the nodes pilose; sheaths pilose; blades flat, 3 to 7 cm long, 3 to 6 mm wide, pubescent on both surfaces; panicles 3 to 5 cm long, of few to several short spreading densely flowered branches, remote along the main pilose axis, the branches 4 to 6 mm long, bearing 1 to 8 subsessile spikelets about 2.5 mm long; first glume pubescent, half as long as the spikelet; second glume pubescent, gibbous, equaling the glabrous sterile lemma, both inflated (fig. 242).

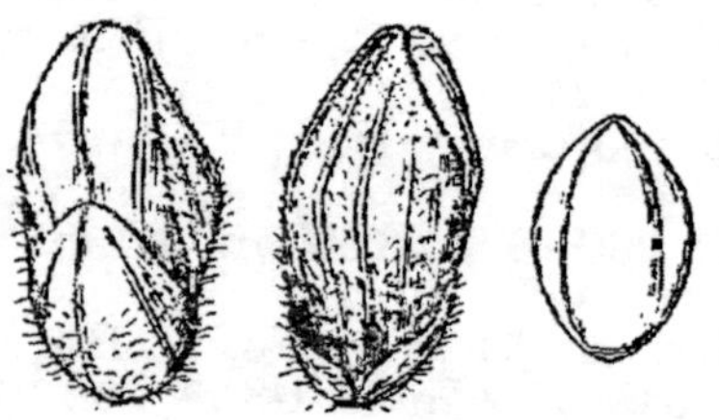

FIGURE 242.—*Panicum venezuelae.* Two views of spikelet, and floret, × 10 (type of *P. ineptum*).

Crevices of rocks and stony slopes, Cuba, Dominican Republic, Venezuela, and Brazil.

CUBA: Loma Barbí, Sierra Maestra, *Ekman* 15661. Loma del Gato, *Ekman* in 1922 (*Amer. Gr. Nat. Herb.* 703); *Léon* 10190.

DOMINICAN REPUBLIC: Monción, *Ekman* H 12608, H 13085. San José de las Matas, *Ekman* H 14602. Bajabonico, *Ekman* H 14499. Without locality, *Bertero* 817 (Krug and Urban Herb.).

49. Panicum sellowii Nees, Agrost. Bras. 153. 1829. Brazil.

Panicum valenzuelanum A. Rich, in Sagra, Hist. Cuba 11: 304. 1850. Cuba.

Panicum rugulosum var. *hirtiglume* Griseb., Cat. Pl. Cub. 233. 1866. Cuba, *Wright* 3455.

Perennial; culms branching and straggling, as much as 1 m long; blades thin, ovate-lanceolate, 4 to 15 cm long, 10 to 30 mm wide, more or less pubescent or velvety; panicles open, 10 to 20 cm long, the branches ascending or spreading; spikelets short-pediceled along the upper part, about 2 mm long, obovate, obtuse, papillose-hispidulous; first glume about two-thirds as long as the spikelet (fig. 243).

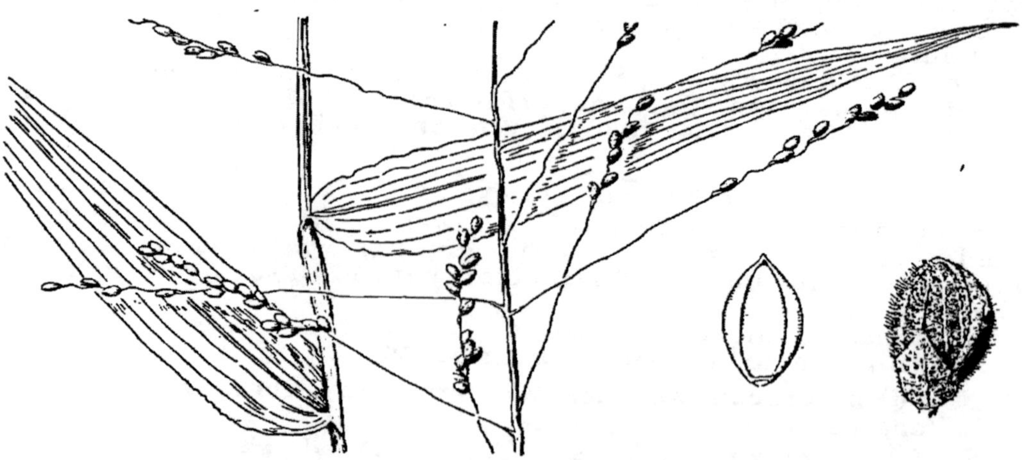

FIGURE 243.—*Panicum sellowii.* Plant, × 1; spikelet, and floret, × 10 (type and Hitchcock 23294).

In Grasses of the West Indies this species was referred to *Panicum millegrana* Poir. That species, differing chiefly in having long-pedicelled spikelets, is not known from North America, except for the type specimen of *P. patentissimum* Desv., said to be from "Saint-Domingue [and] la Nouvelle-Espagne." The type, in the Paris Herbarium, is labeled "Hispaniola." Like many localities cited by Desvaux it is probably erroneous.

Damp woods and shady banks, Mexico and Trinidad to Paraguay.

CUBA: Herradura, *Ekman* 10828; *Hitchcock* 180, 23440; *Tracy* 9098. Pinar del Río, *Hitchcock* 23296; *Wright* 3855. Viñales, *Killip* 13549. La Catalina, *Wright* 3455. Sumidero, *Shafer and Léon* 13562. Sierra de Cabra, *Britton and Gager* 7201. Cajálbana, *Léon* 4836. San Diego de los Baños, *Léon* 4595, 4602.

TRINIDAD: Port-of-Spain, *Hitchcock* 9979; *Broadway* 5909. Pitch Lake, *Hitchcock* 10087.

50. Panicum glutinosum Swartz, Prodr. Veg. Ind. Occ. 24. 1788. Jamaica.

Panicum obtusiflorum A. Rich., in Sagra, Hist. Cuba 11: 305. 1850. Cuba, *Linden* 2143.

Panicum lindeni Griseb., Cat. Pl. Cub. 233. 1866. Cuba, *Linden* 2143.

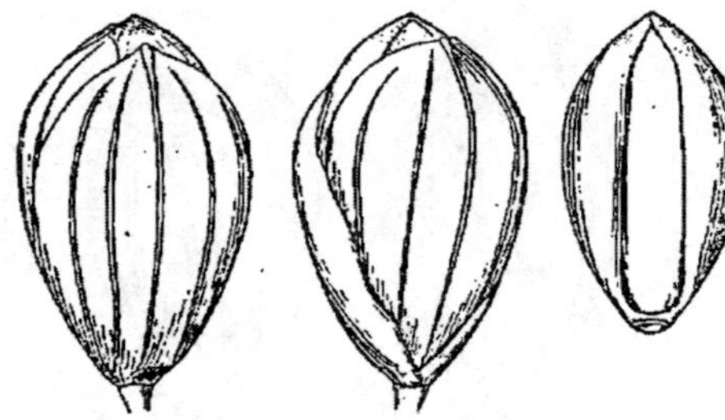

FIGURE 244.—*Panicum glutinosum*. Two views of spikelet, and floret, × 10 (type).

Perennial; culms erect from a geniculate or creeping and rooting base, 1 to 2 m tall; blades elongate-lanceolate, acuminate, 15 to 50 cm long, 15 to 25 mm wide; panicles open, 15 to 30 cm long, the lower branches verticillate, stiffly ascending; spikelets 3 mm long, turgid, obovoid, obtuse, glabrous but viscid; first glume nearly as long as the spikelet (fig. 244).

Mountain woods 500 to 2,000 m, Mexico and the West Indies to Paraguay.

CUBA: Sancti Spíritus Mountains, *Léon* 6620. Banao Mountains, *Léon* 3998. La Perla, *Léon* 3790; *Wright* 757. Gran Piedra, *Shafer* 9014. Alto de Iberia, *Ekman* 8298. Guara, *Hitchcock* 23416. Without locality, *Linden* 2143.

JAMAICA: Gordon Town, *Hart* 792; *Hitchcock* 9321; *Harris* 12431. Troy, *Maxon* 2816; *Hitchcock* 9785; *Harris* 12607. Ewarton, *Hitchcock* 9451. Abbey Green, *Hitchcock* 9370. Ipswich, *Hitchcock* 9627. Mount Diablo, *Ridley* 25, 38; *Maxon and Killip* 443. Cinchona, *Harris* 11264, 11440, 11508; *Hitchcock* 9708. Arntully, *Orcutt* 2643, 3110. Red Hills, *Harris* 11836. Salt Hill, *Harris* 11395. Newport, *Britton* 3193. Above Mattis River, *Maxon and Killip* 185. St. Helens Gap, *Maxon and Killip* 595. Without locality, *Wullschlägel* 1163.

HAITI: Kenskoff, *Buch* 956. Marmelade, *Leonard* 8212. Caille la Croix, *Leonard* 7854. Furcy, *Buch* 1540; *Leonard* 4337. Source Rouillé, *Ekman* H 6827. Ma Blanche, *Ekman* H 623.

DOMINICAN REPUBLIC: San Juan, *Ekman* H 13431. Lagunas de Cenobí, *Valeur* 54. Sabaneta, *Valeur* 520.

PUERTO RICO: Mayaguez, *Sintenis* 357. Cerro Gordo, *Sintenis* 2609. Maricao, *Chase* 6199, 6250 (*Amer. Gr. Nat. Herb.* 211). Adjuntas, *Chase* 6469.

51. Panicum rudgei Roem. and Schult., Syst. Veg. 2: 444. 1817. Based on *P. scoparium* Rudge.

Panicum scoparium Rudge, Pl. Guian. 1 : 21. pl. 29. 1805. Not *P. scoparium* Lam., 1798. British Guiana.

Perennial; culms robust, 30 to 100 cm tall, erect or somewhat geniculate; sheaths hirsute; blades thick, linear, 15 to 40 cm long, 5 to 10 mm wide, rather rigidly ascending, flat or folded, usually densely hirsute; panicles terminal and lateral, forming an oblong inflorescence, open, the branches stiff, the pedicels divaricate; spikelets 3.5 mm long, turgid, strongly nerved, sparsely hirsute; glumes and sterile lemma acuminate or abruptly pointed (fig. 245).

Savannas at low and medium altitudes, Central America and Jamaica to Brazil.

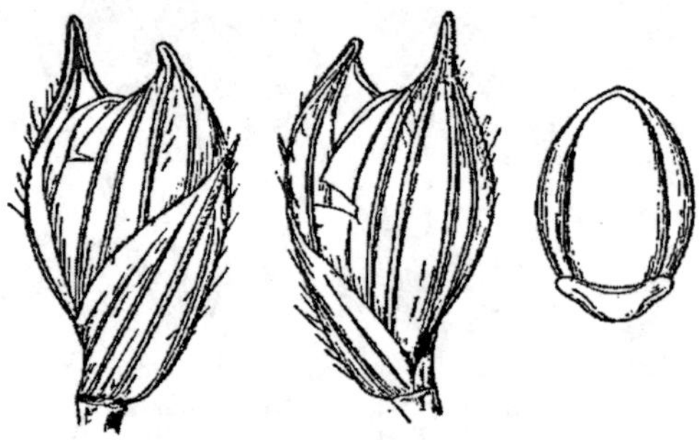

FIGURE 245.—*Panicum rudgei.* Two views of spikelet, and floret, × 10 (Salzmann).

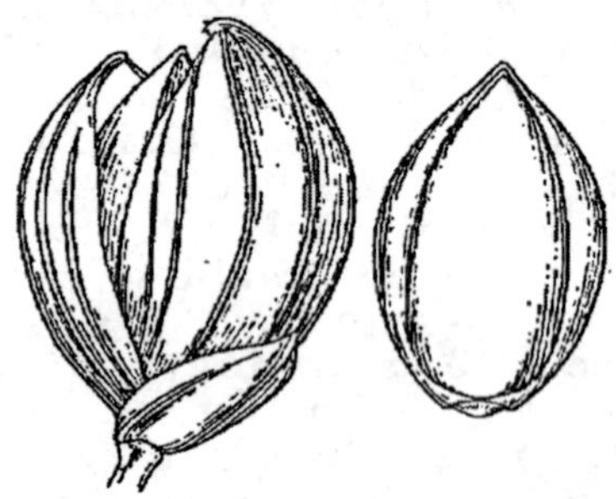

FIGURE 246.—*Panicum mertensii.* Spikelet and floret, × 10 (type of *P. altissimum* Meyer).

JAMAICA: Upper Clarendon, *Harris* 12235, 12845. Bunkers Hill Savanna, *Harris* 11170. Bull Head Mountain, *Hitchcock* 9528.

TRINIDAD: Piarco Savanna, *Britton and Hazen* 688. O'Meara Savanna, *Britton and Hazen* 1563. Pitch Lake, *Hitchcock* 10083 (*Amer. Gr. Nat. Herb.* 75). St. Joseph, *Hitchcock* 10181. Without locality, *Crueger.*

52. Panicum mertensii Roth, in Roem. and Schult., Syst. Veg. 2: 458. 1817. British Guiana.

Panicum altissimum Meyer, Prim. Fl. Esseq. 63. 1818. Not *P. altissimum* DC., 1813. British Guiana.

Panicum megiston Schult., Mant. 2: 248. 1824. Based on *P. altissimum* Meyer.

Perennial; culms robust, 1 to 2 m tall; sheaths papillose-hispid; blades elongate, 1.5 to 3 cm wide, glabrous; panicles 40 to 60 cm long, the stiff main axis striate-angled, the branches in distant verticils as many as 20 to 30 in a verticil; spikelets about 3.5 mm long, globular-obovoid, glabrous; first glume less than one-third the length of the spikelet (fig. 246).

Swamps and banks of ponds and rivers, Mexico and Trinidad to Paraguay; Cuba.

CUBA: Damnjí, *Ekman* 11004. Santa Cruz de los Baños, *Wright* 3872.

TRINIDAD: Cedros, *Broadway* 9286. Caroni Savanna, *Hart* 4197. Without locality, *Crueger*.

53. Panicum trigonum Retz., Obs. Bot. 3: 9. 1783. India.

Cyrtococcum trigonum A. Camus, Bull. Mus. Hist. Nat. [Paris] 27: 118. 1921.

Annual; culms branching, slender, 10 to 30 cm long; blades flat, lanceolate, sparsely pilose, 1 to 3 cm long, 3 to 5 mm wide; panicles few-flowered, 1 to 3 cm long, open or contracted; spikelets somewhat laterally compressed, pilose, about 1.7 mm long, the second glume keeled and bulged out at the middle.

Shady places, Trinidad; introduced.

TRINIDAD: Port-of-Spain, forming a thick carpet under trees in the Botanic Garden, *Hitchcock* 17661; *Broadway* 4891, 8017 (*Amer. Gr. Nat. Herb.* 706); *Bailey* in 1921.

54. Panicum grande Hitchc. and Chase, Contrib. U. S. Natl. Herb. 17: 529. f. 143. 1915. Canal Zone.

Panicum myrianthum Mez, Bot. Jahrb. Engler 56: Beibl. 125: 3. 1921. Guiana.

Perennial, gregarious, producing extensively creeping or floating leafy stolons about 5 mm thick; culms 1.5 to 2 m tall, the nodes densely hirsute; blades flat, as much as 1 m long and 6 cm wide, narrowed toward base and apex, glabrous, somewhat plicate; panicles as much as 60 cm long and 40 cm wide, open; spikelets 2.5 mm long, pointed, glabrous (fig. 247).

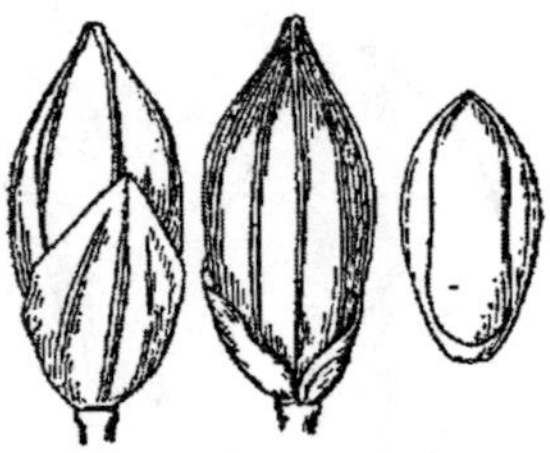

FIGURE 247.—*Panicum grande*. Two views of spikelet, and floret, × 10 (type).

Lakes, ponds, and swamps, near the coast, growing in the water, Central America to Brazil; Cuba, Trinidad.

CUBA: Baracoa, *Ekman* 3487.

TRINIDAD: St. Joseph, *Hitchcock* 10022. Manzanilla, *Hitchcock* 10376. Caroní, *Broadway* 5859. Cedros, *Hitchcock* 10148; *Broadway* 4957. Naset, *Broadway* 9110.

55. Panicum asperifolium (Desv.) Hitchc., Contrib. U. S. Natl. Herb. 22: 489. 1922.

Streptostachis asperifolia Desv., Nouv. Bull. Sci. Philom. Paris 2: 190. 1810. Tropical America.

Panicum streptostachys Spreng., Syst. Veg. 1: 316. 1825. Based on *Streptostachys aspera* Desv. (error for *asperifolia*).

Plants about 1 m tall from a decumbent base; sheaths glabrous or hirsute; blades thin, as much as 20 cm long and 3.5 cm wide, cordate-clasping; panicle of a few distant spreading branches, the spikelets and branchlets appressed; spikelets 4 mm long, oblong, obtuse, pubescent, the base hardened and ringlike; first glume as long as the spikelet.

Damp forests at low altitudes, Trinidad to Brazil.

TRINIDAD: Chaguasamas, near the sea, *Broadway* 6741.

56. Panicum zizanioides H. B. K., Nov. Gen. et Sp. 1: 100. 1815. Colombia.

Panicum oryzoides Swartz, Prodr., Veg. Ind. Occ. 23. 1788. Not *P. oryzoides* Ard., 1764. Jamaica.

Acroceras oryzoides Stapf, in Prain, Fl. Trop. Afr. 9: 622. 1920.

Perennial; culms decumbent and rooting at base, 50 to 100 cm tall, glabrous; sheaths glabrous except margins; blades flat, 4 to 15 cm long, 1 to 3 cm wide, cordate-clasping, glabrous or rarely pubescent; panicles 10 to 25 cm long, with a few ascending stiff branches 3 to 10 cm long, bearing appressed branchlets; spikelets 5.5 to 6 mm long, glabrous, abruptly short-pointed; first glume two-thirds as long as the spikelet (fig. 248).

Moist, usually shaded places at low altitudes, Mexico and the West Indies to Paraguay.

CUBA: Damují, *Ekman* 10936. Sumidero, *Shafer and Léon* 13635. Anafe, *Ekman* 226. Rincón, *Van Hermann* 545, 4477. Laguna Castellano, *Baker* 4334; *Wilson* 9567. San Nicolás, *Léon* 7297. Puentes Grandes, *Léon* 2743. Sancti Spíritus, *Léon* 903. Guara, *Hitchcock* 23394. Without locality, *Wright* 3466. Isla de Pinos, *Britton and Wilson* 14923.

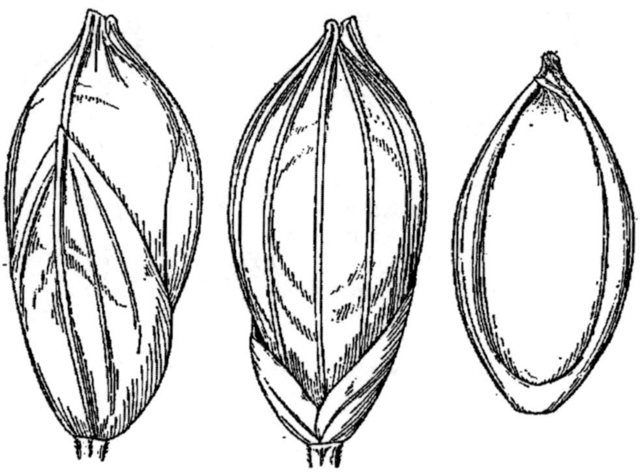

FIGURE 248.—*Panicum zizanioides*. Two views of spikelet, and floret, × 10 (Bonpland).

JAMAICA: Kingston, *Hitchcock* 9278. Castleton, *Hitchcock* 9398. St. Georges, *Harris* 11420. Port Antonio, *Maxon* 2109. Gordon Town, *Hart* 726. Temple Hill, *Harris* 11385. Chapelton, *Ridley* 28. Ipswich, *Hitchcock* 9609. Ewarton, *Hitchcock* 9419. Claremont, *Hitchcock* 9513. Troy, *Hitchcock* 9781; *Harris* 12654. Buff Bay, *Hitchcock* 9779. Montego Bay, *Hitchcock* 9684. Without locality, *Wullschlaegel* 1108; *Alexander Prior* in 1850.

HAITI: Mount Organisé, *Ekman* H 6219.

DOMINICAN REPUBLIC: Cuenca, *Ekman* H 11059. Pimental, *Abbott* 652. Los Haitises, *Ekman* H 15564.

TRINIDAD: Port-of-Spain, *Hitchcock* 9958. Toco, *Broadway* 2563. Mount Pleasant Estate, *Bot. Gard. Herb.* 2286. Blanchisseuse Road, *Broadway* 6740. Without locality, *Bot. Gard. Herb.* 3188.

TOBAGO: *Eggers* 5810; *Hitchcock* 10258; *Broadway* 4556.

57. Panicum discrepans Doell, in Mart., Fl. Bras. 2[2]: 252. 1877. Brazil.

Perennial; culms glabrous, ascending from a decumbent base, 20 to 40 cm tall; sheaths minutely pubescent or glabrous, the lowermost felty-pubescent; blades ascending or appressed, more or less pubescent, the lower often densely so, the upper sometimes glabrous, flat, those of the midculm 3 to 5 cm long, 3 to 5 mm wide; panicles ovoid, open but densely flowered, 4 to 7 cm long, pilose in the lowermost axil, the axis and branches smooth; spikelets elliptic, somewhat turgid, glabrous, about 1.3 mm long; first glume narrow, variable in length, sometimes half as long as spikelet, often wanting; second glume and sterile lemma equal, 3-nerved, the glume gibbous in the middle; fertile lemma felty-villous at base and apex, gibbous at the middle (fig. 249).

Edges of ponds and lagoons, Brazil; Cuba.

CUBA: Sábalo, edge of lagoon, *Ekman* in 1923 (*Amer. Gr. Nat. Herb.* 705). Herradura, moist places in pinelands, *Ekman* 14089.

58. Panicum hirtum Lam., Encycl. 4: 741. 1798. Cayenne.

Annual; culms slender, branching, decumbent, 20 to 40 cm tall; blades flat, thin, ovate to lanceolate, cordate-clasping at base, sparsely hispid, 2 to 6 cm long, 0.8 to 2 cm wide; panicles ovoid, 3 to 7 cm long, the branches delicate but stiffly ascending at a uniform angle, the spikelets recurved at right angles on capillary pedicels; spikelets strongly plano-convex, turgid, hispid, 1.2 mm long (fig. 250).

FIGURE 249.—*Panicum discrepans.* Panicle, × 1 (Ekman 14089); spikelet and floret, × 10 (type).

FIGURE 250.—*Panicum hirtum.* Spikelets and floret, × 10 (type).

Damp shady places, British Honduras; Trinidad to Brazil. In the Lamarck Herbarium at Paris is a specimen of this species "de Portorico le Dru", but the locality is probably an error, as it is not otherwise known from north of Trinidad.

TRINIDAD: Port-of-Spain, *Hitchcock* 10320. St. Joseph, *Hitchcock* 10177. Aripo Road, *Broadway* 6450. Dibe Valley, *Britton and Coker* 1754. Arima, *Hitchcock* 10310 (*Amer. Gr. Nat. Herb.* 546). Piarco Savanna, *Hitchcock* 10363. Blanchisseuse Road, *Broadway* 5929. Without locality, *Bot. Gard. Herb.* 3194.

59. Panicum xalapense H. B. K., Nov. Gen. et Sp. 1: 103. 1815. Mexico.

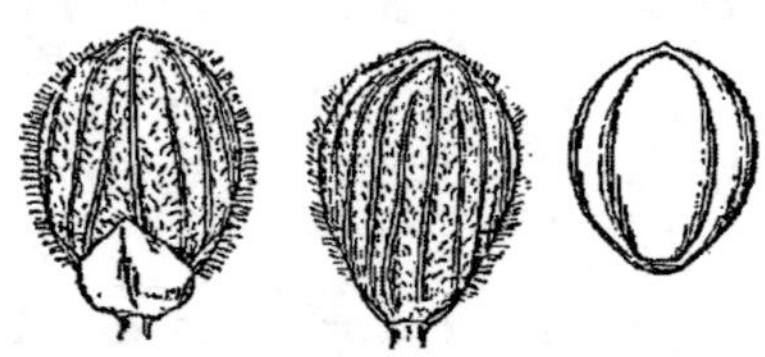

FIGURE 251.—*Panicum xalapense.* Two views of spikelet, and floret, × 10 (type).

Vernal phase with slender culms 20 to 60 cm tall, the nodes bearded with reflexed hairs; sheaths retrorsely pilose; blades 7 to 12 mm wide, pilose on both surfaces; panicles 5 to 10 cm long, open, few-flowered, the branches flexuous; spikelets 2 mm long, obovate, obtuse, pilose. Autumnal phase branching at the base, forming soft prostrate tufts or rosettes (fig. 251).

Moist banks and open woods at low and medium altitudes, eastern and southern United States and Mexico to Costa Rica; Cuba and Hispaniola.

CUBA: Consolación del Sur, *Ekman* 10860.

HAITI: Furcy, *Cook, Scofield, and Doyle* 36; *Leonard* 4346, 4501. Caille la Croix, *Leonard* 7920. St. Louis du Nord, *Leonard* 14503; *Ekman* H 4743. Mission, *Leonard* 3801, 3852. Pétionville, *Ekman* H 1095. Morne de la Selle, *Buch* 1364.

DOMINICAN REPUBLIC: Constanza, *Tuerckheim* 3059. Jarabaco, *Eggers* H 2129. Azua, *Ekman* H 11855. Jicomé, *Valeur* 293, 756.

60. Panicum polycaulon Nash, Bull. Torrey Bot. Club 24: 200. 1897. Florida.

Culms tufted, soon forming small mats or dense rosettes, the vernal culms 10 to 20 cm tall, the autumnal culms prostrate, scarcely exceeding the leaves; blades flat, mostly 3 to 6 cm long, 3 to 6 mm wide, usually strongly ciliate; panicles ovoid, few-flowered, 3 to 4 cm long, about as wide, the axis pilose; spikelets about 1.5 mm long, glabrous or rarely pubescent (fig. 252).

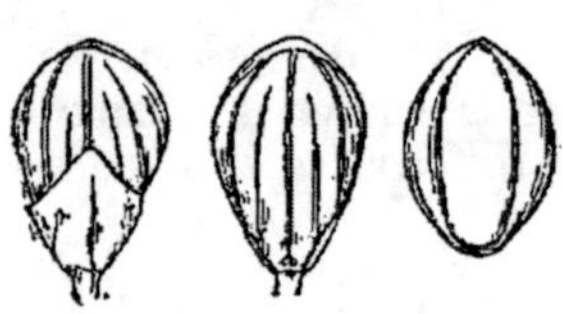

FIGURE 252.—*Panicum polycaulon.* Two views of spikelet, and floret, × 10 (type).

Sandy pine woods, Florida to Mississippi and the Greater Antilles.

CUBA: Pinar del Río, *Hitchcock* 23299. Herradura, *Hitchcock* 115; *Ekman* 10083. Sábalo, *Ekman* 11436a. Guara, *Hitchcock* 23411, 23429. Woodfred, *Shafer* 3083. Without locality, *Wright* 3875 in part. Isla de Pinos, *Ekman* 12123; *Palmer and Riley* 990.

JAMAICA: James Hill, *Harris* 12852. Hollis Savanna, *Harris* 12225. Barican, *Hitchcock* 9561. Bull Head Mountain, *Hitchcock* 9550.

DOMINICAN REPUBLIC: Cuenca, *Ekman* H 11068.

PUERTO RICO: Mayaguez, *Chase* 6276; *Holm* 59a. San Juan, *Chase* 6767. Campo Alegre, *Chase* 6621. Aguada, *Sintenis* 5724.

61. Panicum strigosum Muhl., in Ell., Bot. S. C. and Ga. 1: 126. 1816. Southern United States.

Vernal phase with culms 5 to 30 cm tall, the nodes pubescent; blades 3 to 6 cm long, 3 to 8 mm wide, ciliate and pilose; panicles 3 to 5 cm long, open, the branches pilose; spikelets about 1.5 mm long, glabrous. Autumnal phase a dense mat, as in *P. xalapense* (fig. 253).

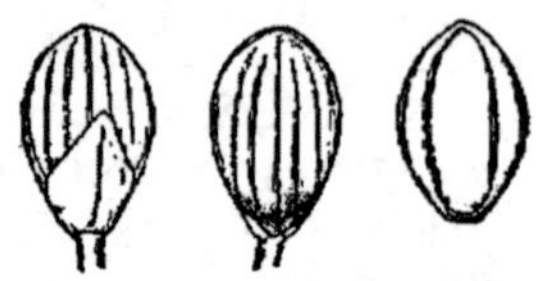

FIGURE 253.—*Panicum strigosum.* Two views of spikelet, and floret, × 10 (type).

Sandy woods and open moist ground, at low and medium altitudes, eastern and southern United States, and Mexico to Panama; Greater Antilles.

CUBA: Pinar del Río, *Ekman* 17874. El Guama, *Palmer and Riley* 213. Cajálbana, *Léon* 4829. Without locality, *Wright* 3875 in part. Isla de Pinos, *Britton and Wilson* 14411.

JAMAICA: Bull Head Mountain, *Hitchcock* 9551.

HAITI: Grand-Gosier, *Ekman* H 6857.

DOMINICAN REPUBLIC: El Tetero, *Ekman* H 13720.

62. Panicum chrysopsidifolium Nash, in Small, Fl. Southeast. U. S. 100. 1903. Florida.

Vernal culms ascending or spreading, grayish-villous, the nodes bearded; sheaths villous; blades 5 to 10 cm long, 3 to 5 mm wide, tapering from base to apex, conspicuously pointed, villous on both surfaces; panicles 4 to 6 cm long; spikelets 2 mm long, pubescent. Autumnal phase spreading and forming mats; blades flat, papery with age (fig. 254).

Sandy pine woods and palm barrens and wet savannas, southern United States and the Greater Antilles.

CUBA: Cajálbana, *Léon* 4835, 4840. Cayajabos, *Léon* 13227, 13566. Consolación del Sur, *Palmer and Riley* 481. Guane, *Shafer* 10639; *Léon* 7005. Herradura, *Hitchcock* 116. La Guira, *Léon* 5177. Banao Mountains, *Léon* 7944. Placetas del Sur, *Léon* 6422. Motembo, *Ekman* 16851. Without locality, *Wright* in 1865. Isla de Pinos, *Palmer and Riley* 982.

JAMAICA: Hollis Savanna, *Harris* 12228. Pedro Morass, *Harris* 11163. Bull Head Mountain, *Hitchcock* 9535 (*Amer. Gr. Nat. Herb.* 89).

HAITI: Gros-Morne, *Ekman* H 4907. Acul du Nord, *Ekman* H 2908. Grand-Gosier, *Ekman* H 6856.

DOMINICAN REPUBLIC: Constanza, *Ekman* H 14093. La Cumbre, *Ekman* H 11431. Monción, *Ekman* H 12680. Cotuy, *Abbott* 858. Monte Jicomé, *Valeur* 299.

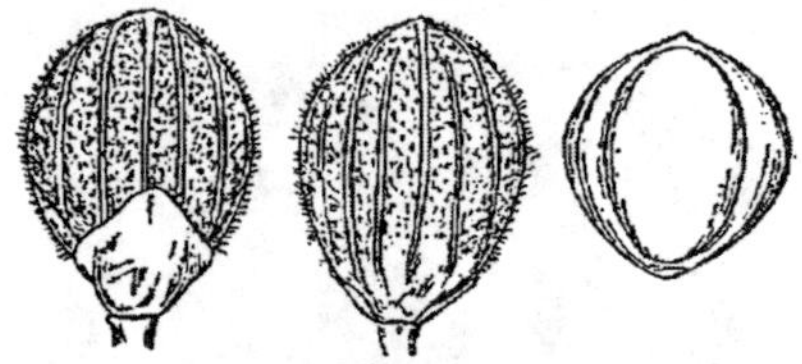

FIGURE 254.—*Panicum chrysopsidifolium*. Two views of spikelet, and floret, × 10 (type).

PUERTO RICO: San Juan, *Chase* 6766. Santurce, *Heller* 982. Tabonico, *Sintenis* 5985. Sierra de Naguabo, *Shafer* 3530 in part [with *P. leucothrix*].

63. Panicum fusiforme Hitchc., Contrib. U. S. Natl. Herb. 12: 222. 1909. Based on *P. neuranthum* var. *ramosum* Griseb.

Panicum neuranthum var. *ramosum* Griseb., Cat. Pl. Cub. 232. 1866. Not *P. ramosum* L., 1767. Cuba, *Wright* 3454.

Vernal culms erect, 30 to 70 cm tall; blades flat, gradually pointed, ascending, rather stiff, mostly 5 to 10 cm long, 4 to 8 mm wide, the lowermost softly pubescent beneath; panicles 4 to 10 cm long, the lower branches often reflexed; spikelets pubescent, fusiform, attenuate at base, about 3.5 mm long. Autumnal phase erect or reclining; blades soon involute, 3 to 5 cm long (fig. 255).

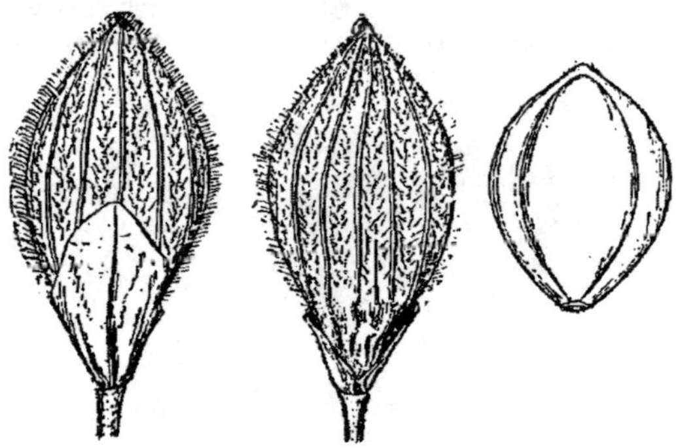

FIGURE 255.—*Panicum fusiforme*. Two views of spikelet, and floret, × 10 (type).

Sandy pine woods, Georgia to Mississippi, Greater Antilles; British Honduras.

CUBA: Herradura, *Hitchcock* 117, 23434; *Baker and Dimmock*, 4846; *Caldwell and Baker* 7139; *Tracy* 9074. Pinar del Río, *Hitchcock* 23257. Guane, *Shafer* 10484; *Léon* 7007. Laguna Jovero, *Shafer* 11049. Sabana de Chirigota, *Léon* 7451. Manacas, *Léon* 5840. La Cumbre, *Ekman* 13952. Guara, *Hitchcock* 23431. Western Cuba, *Wright* 3453 in part, 3454. Isla de Pinos, *Ekman* 11654.

JAMAICA: Bull Head Mountain, *Hitchcock* 9552. Hollis Savanna, *Harris* 12234.

64. Panicum angustifolium Ell., Bot. S. C. and Ga. 1: 129. 1816. Florida.

Vernal culms erect or nearly so, 30 to 50 cm tall, the lowermost internodes gray crisp-villous, the nodes glabrous; lower sheaths somewhat appressed-villous; blades stiffly ascending, long-acuminate, 8 to 12 cm long, 4 to 8 mm wide, the lowermost shorter and broader; panicles 4 to 10 cm long, loosely flowered, the branches at anthesis widely spreading, often reflexed; spikelets 2.5 to 3 mm long, autumnal phase stiffly ascending or somewhat topheavy-reclining, the blades flat, rather thin, and papery (fig. 256).

Sandy woods, southeastern United States; Cuba; Puerto Rico; Nicaragua.

CUBA: Isla de Pinos, *Curtiss* 406; *Britton and Wilson* 14305.

PUERTO RICO: El Yunque, *Britton* 7628.

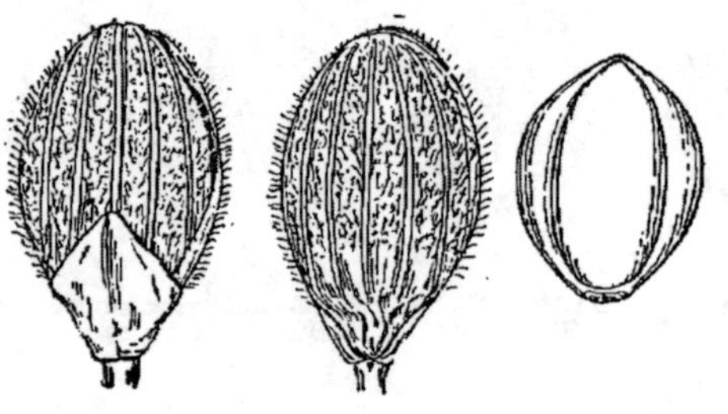

FIGURE 256.—*Panicum angustifolium.* Two views of spikelet, and floret, × 10 (type).

65. Panicum arenicoloides Ashe, Jour. Elisha Mitchell Sci. Soc. 16: 89. 1900. North Carolina.

Panicum orthophyllum Ashe, Jour. Elisha Mitchell Sci. Soc. 16: 90. 1900. North Carolina.

Vernal phase similar to that of *P. angustifolium;* spikelets about 2.5 mm long. Autumnal phase similar to that of *P. angustifolium,* but the blades soon involute (fig. 257).

Sandy pine woods, southeastern United States; Cuba; Guatemala; Honduras.

CUBA: Sierra de Nipe, *Ekman* 15189.

66. Panicum neuranthum Griseb., Cat. Pl. Cub. 232. 1866. Cuba, *Wright* 3453.

Vernal culms tufted, stiff, erect, glabrous, 30 to 60 cm tall; sheaths glabrous; blades erect or ascending, glabrous, 10 to 15 cm long, 3 to 5 mm wide; panicles narrow, 5 to 9 cm long, the branches narrowly ascending; spikelets 2 mm long, glabrous, not much attenuate at

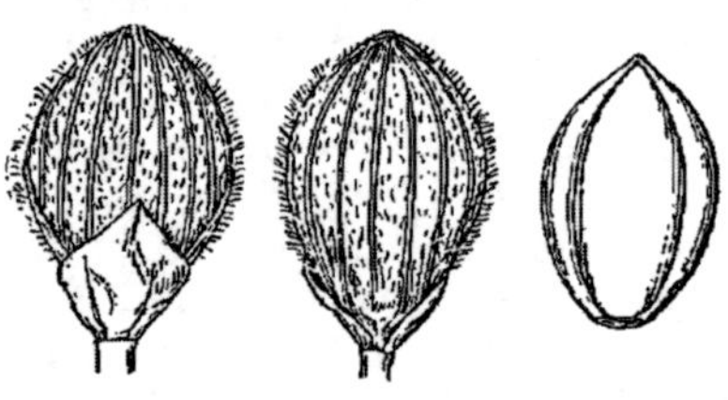

FIGURE 257.—*Panicum arenicoloides.* Two views of spikelet, and floret, × 10 (type).

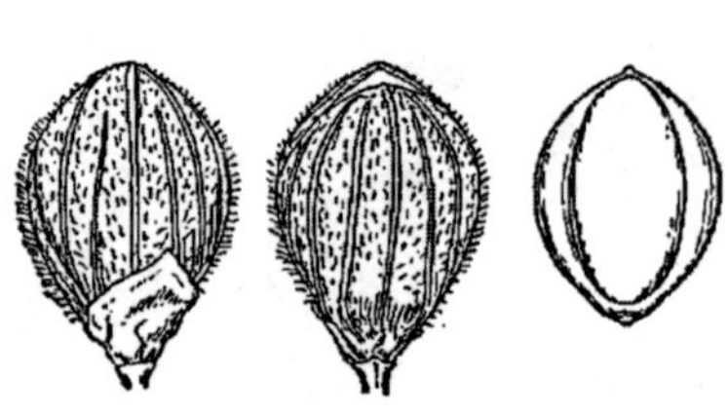

FIGURE 258.—*Panicum neuranthum.* Two views of spikelet, and floret, × 10 (type).

base. Autumnal phase similar to the vernal, but the blades shorter and involute (fig. 258).

Savannas and open ground, southern Florida to Mississippi; Bahamas; Cuba.

BAHAMAS: New Providence, *Britton and Brace* 599 (Field Mus. Herb.).

CUBA: Remates, *Ekman* 11182. Yaguaramas, *Ekman* 18395. Sabana del Guaní, *Fernando* 488. Mordazo, *Léon* 9245. Baracoa, *Wright* 3453 in part.

67. Panicum aciculare Desv.; Poir., in Lam. Encycl. Sup. 4: 274. 1816. Probably Puerto Rico.

Panicum setaceum Muhl., Descr. Gram. 99. 1817. Georgia.

Vernal phase similar to that of *P. angustifolium* but lower and more slender; spikelets about 2 mm long, very obtuse. Autumnal phase bushy-branched, the blades involute (fig. 259).

Pine woods, southeastern United States; the Greater Antilles; Honduras. The type is erroneously said to come from the East Indies, but it probably came from the West Indies.

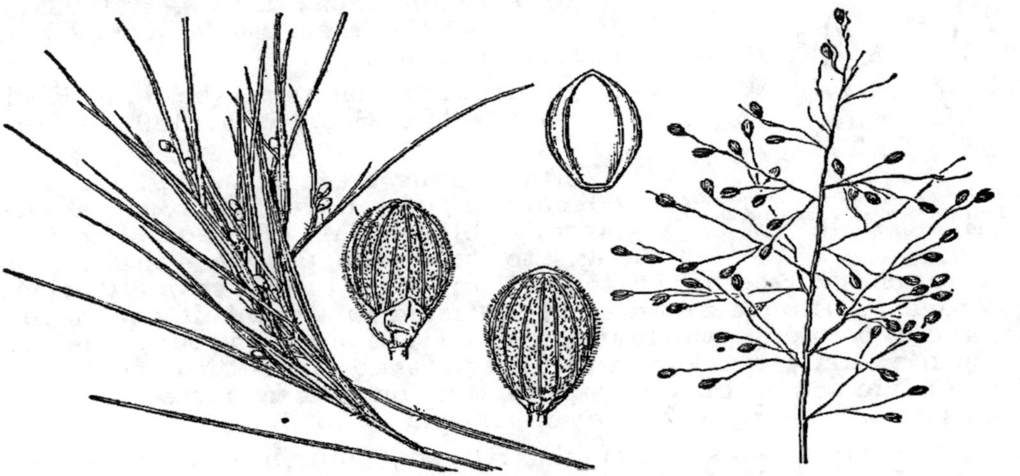

FIGURE 259.—*Panicum aciculare.* Plant, × 1; two views of spikelet, and floret, × 10 (vernal phase, Chase 7148; autumnal phase, Hitchcock 317).

CUBA: Pinar del Río, *Hitchcock* 23253, 23298; *Ekman* 12794, 17891; *Britton and Gager* 7064. Remates, *Ekman* 11374; *Léon* 15355. Laguna Jovero, *Shafer* 10733, 10823. Mordazo, *Léon* 9236, 9576. Sierra de Nipe, *Ekman* 1847, 1848, 2212, 6030, 9066; *Shafer* 2968. Guaro, *Hitchcock* 23428. Without locality, *Wright* 3454, 3461. Isla de Pinos, *Ekman* 11946, 11996, 12189.

JAMAICA: Peckham, *Harris* 12812.

HAITI: Pétionville, *Ekman* H 1312.

DOMINICAN REPUBLIC: Cuenca, *Ekman* H 11056, H 11430.

PUERTO RICO: Mayaguez, *Holm* 47, 47a, 47b; *Chase* 6273. Campo Alegre, *Chase* 6624. Sierra de Naguabo, *Shafer* 3531.

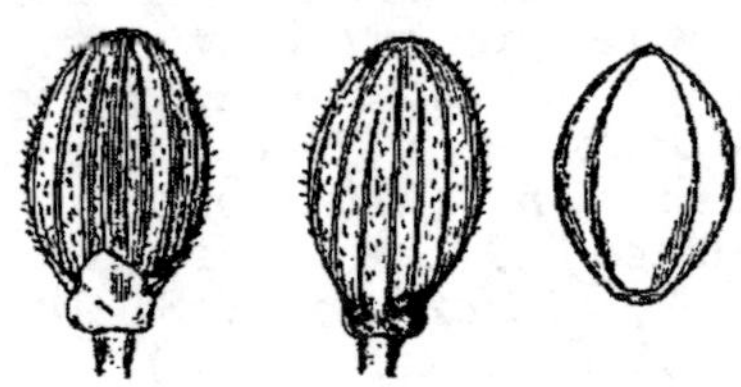

FIGURE 260.—*Panicum nitidum.* Two views of spikelet, and floret, × 10 (type).

68. Panicum nitidum Lam., Tabl. Encycl. 1: 172. 1791. Carolina.

Vernal culms erect or nearly so, 30 to 60 cm tall, the nodes bearded; sheaths glabrous or the lower pubescent, more or less mottled or glandular; blades glabrous, 5 to 12 cm long, 5 to 10 mm wide, the upper often reflexed; panicles ovoid, 5 to 8 cm long, the branches ascending; spikelets elliptic, pubescent, 2 mm long. Autumnal phase with large clusters of branches from the nodes, the reduced blades numerous (fig. 260).

Low moist or marshy ground, southeastern United States; Bahamas; Greater Antilles.

BAHAMAS: Great Bahama, *Britton and Millspaugh* 2736.

CUBA: Remates, *Ekman* 11169. Manacas, *Léon* 5898. San Marcos, *Léon* 9203. Banao Mountains, *Léon* 7938. La Guanaja, *Léon* 16208. Sierra de Nipe, *Shafer* 2999, 3001; *Ekman* 2647. Guara, *Hitchcock* 23404, 23415. Isla de Pinos, *Britton and Wilson* 15184.

JAMAICA: Bull Head Mountain, *Hitchcock* 9532.

DOMINICAN REPUBLIC: Monción, *Ekman* H 12697. Constanza, *Ekman* H 13932, H 14011, H 14123. San José de Ocoa, *Ekman* H 11895, H 11942.

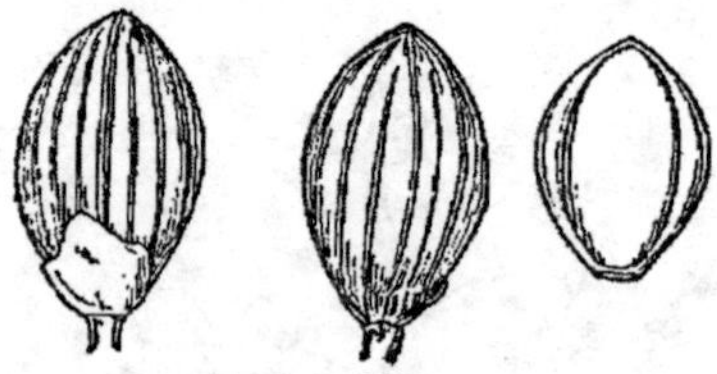

FIGURE 261.—*Panicum roanokense.* Two views of spikelet, and floret. × 10 (Ashe).

69. Panicum roanokense Ashe, Jour. Elisha Mitchell Sci. Soc. 15: 44. 1898. North Carolina.

Vernal culms erect or ascending, 50 to 100 cm tall, the nodes glabrous; sheaths glabrous; blades flat, glabrous, 6 to 9 cm long, 3 to 8 mm wide; panicles 4 to 8 cm long, the branches spreading; spikelets 2 mm long, turgid, strongly nerved, glabrous. Autumnal phase erect or decumbent, branching at the middle and upper nodes, the branches numerous but not in tufts (fig. 261).

Open swampy woods or wet peaty meadows, southeastern United States; Jamaica, in open clay ground among other grasses.

JAMAICA: Bull Head Mountain, *Hitchcock* 9530.

70. Panicum caerulescens Hack.; Hitchc., Contrib. U. S. Natl. Herb. 12: 219. 1909. Florida.

Vernal culms slender, 30 to 75 cm tall; blades commonly purplish beneath, 5 to 8 cm long, 4 to 7 mm wide; panicles 3 to 7 cm long, half as wide or less, the branches narrowly ascending; spikelets glabrous, turgid, 1.5 mm long. Autumnal phase erect or leaning, producing densely fascicled branches at the middle and upper nodes, the reduced blades more or less involute, the reduced panicles with a few long-pediceled spikelets (fig. 262).

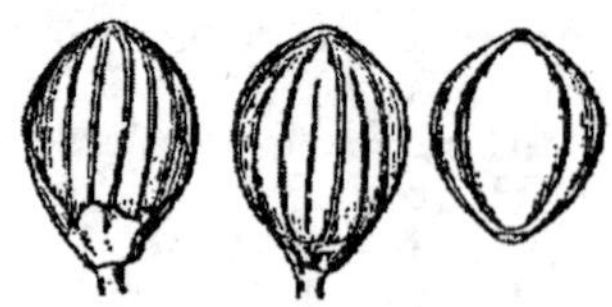

FIGURE 262.—*Panicum caerulescens.* Two views of spikelet, and floret, × 10 (type).

Marshes and swampy woods, southeastern United States and Mexico; Bahamas, Cuba.

BAHAMAS: Great Bahama, *Bruce* 3524; *Britton and Millspaugh* 2506, 2668. Andros, *Brace* 7015. New Providence, *Britton and Brace* 597; *Millspaugh* 2182; *Northrup* 248 (all in Field Mus. Herb.); *Eggers* 4305 (Hackel Herb.).

CUBA: Cajáo, *Léon* 14386. Ciénaga de Zapata, *Ekman* 18376; *Léon* 2206, 2213. Mordazo, *Ekman* 17035; *Léon* 9262; Caibarién, *Léon* 489. Batabanó, *Léon* 6152. Without locality, *Wright* 3463.

71. Panicum leucothrix Nash, Bull. Torrey Bot. Club 24: 41. 1897. Florida.

Vernal culms erect or ascending, appressed papillose-pilose, 25 to 45 cm tall, the nodes pubescent; sheaths papillose-pubescent; ligule pilose, 3 mm long; blades rather firm, puberulent beneath, usually glabrous on the upper surface, 3 to 7 cm long, 3 to 7 mm wide; panicles 3 to 8 cm long, rather densely flowered, the axis appressed-pubescent;

spikelets about 1.3 mm long, pubescent. Autumnal phase ascending, usually decumbent at base, finally with more or less fascicled branchlets, the blades not greatly reduced (fig. 263).

Low pinelands, southeastern United States; Cuba, Hispaniola, and Puerto Rico.

CUBA: Herradura, *Hitchcock* 554, 560, 23438. Guane, *Léon* 6903. San Julián, *Ekman* 11138. Western Cuba, *Wright* 3460, 3463.

PUERTO RICO: San Juan, *Chase* 6770. Sierra de Naguabo, *Shafer* 3530.

DOMINICAN REPUBLIC: Matanzas, *Ekman* H 15886. Sabana de la Mar, *Ekman* H 15636.

72. Panicum wrightianum Scribn., U. S. Dept. Agr., Div. Agrost. Bull: 11: 44. f. 4. 1898. Cuba, *Wright* 3463.

Vernal culms weak and slender, ascending from a decumbent base, minutely puberulent; sheaths glabrous or puberulent; blades spreading, glabrous or puberulent; 2 to 4 cm long, 3 to 5 mm wide; panicles 3 to 6 cm long; spikelets 1 mm long, pubescent. Autumnal phase decumbent-spreading, becoming bushy-branched, the flat or subinvolute blades not much reduced (fig. 264).

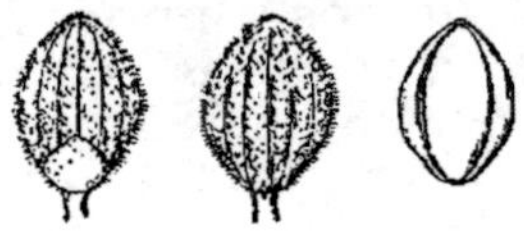

FIGURE 263.—*Panicum leucothrix*. Two views of spikelet, and floret, × 10 (type).

FIGURE 264.—*Panicum wrightianum*. Two views of spikelet, and floret, × 10 (type).

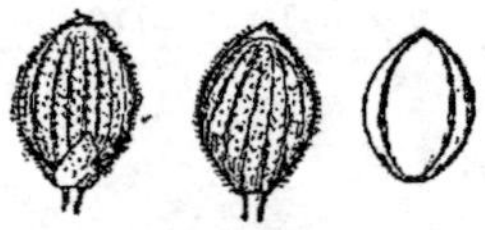

FIGURE 265.—*Panicum longiligulatum*. Two views of spikelet, and floret, × 10 (type).

Margins of streams and ponds, southeastern United States and British Honduras; Cuba.

CUBA: Damují, *Ekman* 10937. Pinar del Río, *Britton and Gager* 6952. Vuelto Abajo, *Wright* 3463. Remates de Guane, *Léon* 15428. Remates, *Ekman* 11215, 11360. La Grifa, *Ekman* 11266. Sábalo, *Ekman* 11438. Herradura, *Ekman* 11586. Laguna Santa María, *Ekman* 17239.

73. Panicum longiligulatum Nash, Bull. Torrey Bot. Club 26: 574. 1899. Florida.

Vernal culms erect or ascending at base, glabrous, relatively stout, 30 to 70 cm tall; sheaths glabrous; ligule 2 to 3 mm long; blades rather thick and firm, glabrous on the upper surface, puberulent beneath, 4 to 8 cm long, 4 to 8 mm wide; panicles 3 to 8 cm long; spikelets a little exceeding 1 mm long, pubescent. Autumnal phase more or less reclining, the branchlets crowded, the reduced blades subinvolute (fig. 265).

Pine barrens and swamps, southeastern United States and British Honduras; Hispaniola.

DOMINICAN REPUBLIC: Cuenca, *Ekman* H 11058. Bayaguana, *Ekman* H 11099.

74. Panicum acuminatum Swartz, Prodr. Veg. Ind. Occ. 23. 1788. Jamaica.

Panicum ornatum Desv.; Hamilt., Prodr. Pl. Ind. Occ. 11. 1825. Puerto Rico.

Panicum dichotomum var. *acuminatum* Swartz; Griseb., Fl. Brit. W. Ind. 553. 1864.

Panicum comophyllum Nash, Bull. Torrey Bot. Club 30: 380. 1903. Puerto Rico, *Heller* 12.

Vernal culms ascending from a geniculate base, densely villous with soft-spreading hairs, 20 to 70 cm tall, the nodes more or less bearded, sheaths velvety papillose-villous or the upper glabrate; ligule 2 to 3 mm long; blades lanceolate, slightly cordate at base, sharply acuminate, usually ciliate, 4 to 8 cm long, 6 to 13 mm wide, the upper surface more or less villous, velvety beneath; panicles 3 to 10 cm long, the axis usually villous, the branches flexuous, the lower sometimes reflexed; spikelets slightly less than 2 mm long (fig. 266).

Sandy pine woods, moist banks, and open ground, Greater Antilles; Colombia.

CUBA: Herradura, *Hitchcock* 140, 23436; *Tracy* 9078; *Britton, Earle, and Gager* 6505. Sumidero, *Léon* 3472; *Shafer and Léon* 13544, 13615. Río Guao, *Britton and Cowell* 9673. San Sebastián, *Léon and Shafer* 13719. Pinar del Río, *Palmer and Riley* 447; *Hitchcock* 23271, 23295; *Léon, Bailey, and Roig* 14821. Viñales, *Léon* 14711. Guane, *Léon* 6902. Cajálbana, *Léon* 4833, 4841. San Diego de los Baños, *Léon* 4371, 4558. San Cristóbal, *Wright* 3874. Isla de Pinos, *Curtiss*, 307, 328; *Palmer and Riley* 989, 1083; *Taylor* in 1901; *Britton and Wilson* 14224, 14228, 14320, 15674.

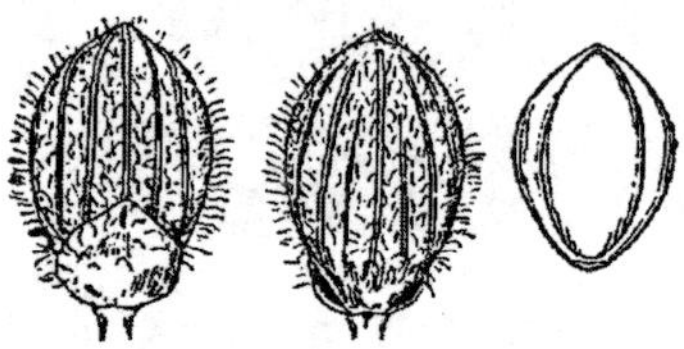

FIGURE 266.—*Panicum acuminatum*. Two views of spikelet, and floret, × 10 (type).

JAMAICA: Abbey Green, *Hitchcock* 9355 (*Amer. Gr. Nat. Herb.* 133). Cinchona, *Harris* 11315, 11371; *Hitchcock* 9697, 9722; *Maxon and Killip* 917. St. Helens Gap, *Harris* 11494; *Maxon and Killip* 594. Claverty Cottage, *Perkins* 1083. Morces Gap, *Maxon and Killip* 1072a. James Hill Savanna, *Harris* 12848. Catherines Peak, *Harris* 11554; *Hitchcock* 9738. Barican, *Hitchcock* 9564. Below Sir Johns Peak, *Harris* 11597. Clyde River, *Harris* 11444. Monkey Hill, *Harris* 11435. Upper Clarendon, *Harris* 11109. Bull Head Mountain, *Hitchcock* 9538. Arntully, *Orcutt* 5181, 5744, 6776. Without locality, *Hart* 736; *Hort. Bot. Jamaica* 736.

HAITI: Marmelade, *Leonard* 8199. Caille la Croix, *Leonard* 7838. Furcy, *Leonard* 4328, 4402, 4701; *Ekman* H 1216; *Cook, Scofield, and Doyle* 37; *Buch* 497, 1541. Grand-Gosier, *Ekman* H 6856. Pétionville, *Ekman* H 1216. Morne de la Selle, *Christ* 1850. Mission, *Leonard* 3821, 3851, 3972.

DOMINICAN REPUBLIC: La Cumbre, *Ekman* H 11547. San José de Ocoa, *Ekman* H 11685.

PUERTO RICO: Maricao, *Britton and Cowell* 4090; *Chase* 6249; *Sintenis* 355. San Juan, *Chase* 6378, 6647, 6765. Adjuntas, *Chase* 6475. Sierra de Loquillo, *Chase* 6719. Cayey, *Chase* 6752. Mayaguez, *Holm* 59b. Santurce, *Heller* in 1903. Lares, *Sintenis* 5908. Fajardo, *Sintenis* 1224.

75. Panicum albemarlense Ashe, Jour. Elisha Mitchell Sci. Soc. 16: 84. 1900. North Carolina.

Vernal phase olivaceous, grayish-villous; culms slender, at first erect, soon geniculate, 25 to 45 cm long; ligule pilose, 1 to 2 mm long;

blades 4 to 7 cm long, 3 to 6 mm wide, the upper surface puberulent as well as villous; panicles 2 to 4 cm long; spikelets about 1.4 mm long, pubescent. Autumnal phase widely decumbent-spreading, the blades reduced, flat (fig. 267).

Sandy woods, eastern United States; Hispaniola.

DOMINICAN REPUBLIC: Monción, *Ekman* H 12798. San José de Ocoa, *Ekman* H 12011.

76. Panicum auburne Ashe, N. C. Agr. Expt. Sta. Bull. 175: 115. 1900. Alabama.

Vernal phase grayish, velvety-villous throughout, the culms geniculate at base, widely spreading, rather slender, 20 to 50 cm tall; ligule 3 to 4 mm long; blades rather thin, 3 to 7 cm long, 3 to 5 mm wide, the upper surface long-pilose, the lower velvety; panicle 3 to 5 cm long, the axis villous; spikelets about 1.4 mm long, pubescent. Autumnal phase early becoming diffusely branched at all the nodes, prostrate spreading, forming large mats (fig. 268).

FIGURE 267.—*Panicum albemarlense*. Two views of spikelet, and floret, × 10 (type).

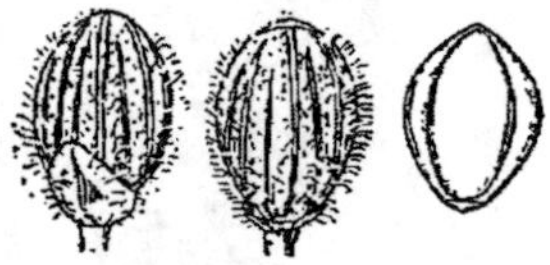

FIGURE 268.—*Panicum auburne*. Two views of spikelet, and floret, × 10 (type).

Sandy woods, southeastern United States; Cuba.

CUBA: Motembo, *Ekman* 16841.

77. Panicum wilmingtonense Ashe, Jour. Elisha Mitchell Sci. Soc. 16: 86. 1900. North Carolina.

Panicum alabamense Ashe, N. C. Agr. Expt. Sta. Bull. 175: 116. 1900. Not *P. alabamense* Trin., 1854. Alabama.

Vernal phase bluish green; culms erect from an ascending base, pilose with soft ascending hairs, 20 to 40 cm tall, the nodes pubescent with soft reflexed hairs; sheaths pubescent like the culms, densely villous-ciliate at the summit; ligule pilose, less than 1 mm long; blades rather stiff, ascending, 4 to 9 cm long, 3 to 7 mm wide, glabrous on the upper surface, softly pubescent to nearly glabrous beneath, strongly ciliate on the margin near the base, the thick cartilaginous margin white at least when dry; panicles 5 to 8 cm long; spikelets 2 mm long, pubescent. Autumnal form branching from the middle and upper nodes, the branches rather crowded, the blades reduced, flat (fig. 269).

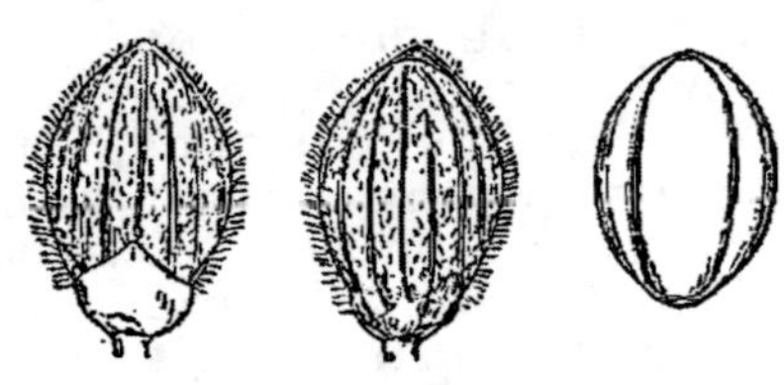

FIGURE 269.—*Panicum wilmingtonense*. Two views of spikelet, and floret; × 10 (type).

Sandy woods, southeastern United States; Cuba.

CUBA: Woodfred, *Ekman* 9099.

78. Panicum sphaerocarpon Ell., Bot. S. C. and Ga. 1: 125. 1816. Georgia.

Vernal phase light green; culms radiate-spreading, 20 to 50 cm long, the nodes pubescent; sheaths glabrous; ligule obsolete; blades firm, 6 to 10 cm long, 7 to 14 mm wide, subcordate, rough on upper surface, smooth beneath, ciliate toward base; panicles 5 to 10 cm long, the axis with viscid spots; spikelets nearly spherical, about 1.7 mm long, puberulent. Autumnal phase prostrate-spreading, rather sparingly branching (fig. 270).

Sandy soil and gravelly banks at low and medium altitudes, eastern United States and Mexico to Venezuela; Cuba.

CUBA: Isla de Pinos, *Ekman* 11820.

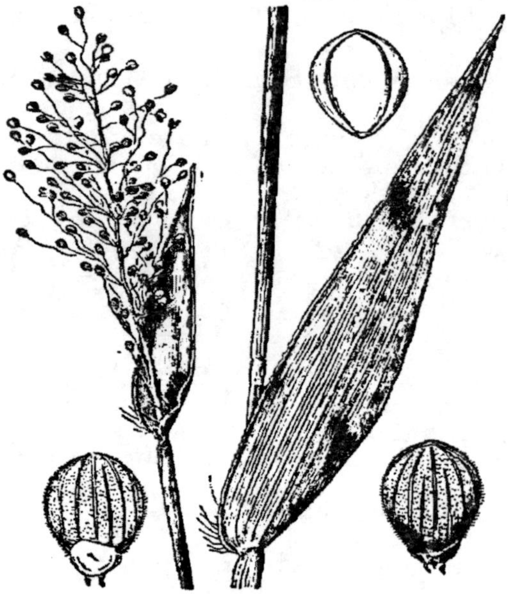

FIGURE 270.—*Panicum sphaerocarpon*. Plant, × 1 two views of spikelet, and floret, × 10 (Deam).

79. Panicum erectifolium Nash, Bull. Torrey Bot. Club 23: 148. 1896. Based on *P. sphaerocarpon* var. *floridanum* Vasey.

Panicum sphaerocarpon var. *floridanum* Vasey, U. S. Dept. Agr., Div. Bot. Bull. 8: 33. 1889. Not *P. floridanum* Trin., 1834. Florida.

Panicum floridanum Chapm., Fl. South. U. S. ed. 3. 585. 1897.

Vernal culms erect or ascending usually stout, glabrous, 30 to 70 cm tall; sheaths glabrous except the ciliate margin; ligule about 0.3 mm long; blades thick, firm, ascending or erect, 7 to 13 cm long, 6 to 12 mm wide, the crowded lower ones usually much longer than the others, tapering from the cordate base to the acuminate apex, smooth on both surfaces, ciliate toward the base; panicles 6 to 12 cm long, half as wide, densely flowered; spikelets about 1 mm long, subspherical, densely puberulent. Autumnal phase remaining erect and simple, finally producing a few erect branches (fig. 271).

Moist pine barrens, swamps, and borders of ponds, southeastern United States; Cuba.

CUBA: Remates, *Ekman* 11188. Vuelto abajo, *Wright* 3462. Laguna del Bufeo, *Shafer* 11021. Laguna Santa Maria, *Britton and Gager* 7170. Motembo, *Léon* 8615. Isla de Pinos, *Britton and Wilson* 14150, 14705, 15706.

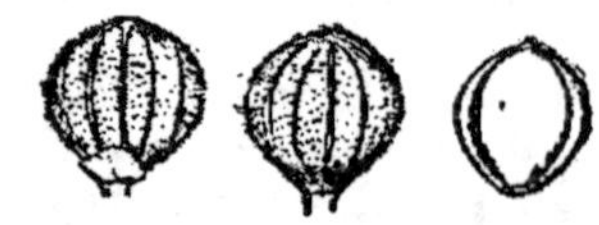

FIGURE 271.—*Panicum erectifolium*. Two views of spikelet, and floret, × 10 (type).

80. Panicum albomarginatum Nash, Bull. Torrey Bot. Club 24: 40. 1897. Florida.

Vernal phase usually grayish green, often purplish; culms densely tufted, slender but firm, ascending or spreading, glabrous, 15 to 40 cm tall; leaves crowded at the base, distant above; blades thick and firm, those of the midculm 4 to 6 cm long, 4 to 6 mm wide, glabrous, the margin (when dry) prominent, white, cartilaginous, the crowded basal blades as much as 11 cm long, the uppermost usually much reduced; panicles 3 to 6 cm long; spikelets about 1.5 mm long, pubescent. Autumnal phase spreading, the primary culms branching from the base and lower nodes, forming bushy tufts (fig. 272).

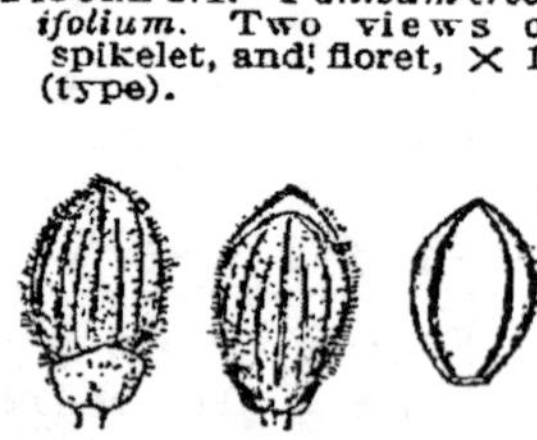

FIGURE 272.—*Panicum albomarginatum*. Two views of spikelet, and floret, × 10 (type).

Sandy woods, southeastern United States; Cuba; Central America; Florida.

CUBA: Herradura, *Ekman* 10687; *Hitchcock* 555, 23433. Guane, *Léon* 7009, 15395. Sumidero, *Léon* 3466, 7006. Isla de Pinos, *Taylor* 32; *Britton and Wilson* 14283, 15383.

81. Panicum trifolium Nash, Bull. Torrey Bot. Club 26: 580. 1899. Georgia.

Similar to *P. albomarginatum*, differing chiefly in the following: Culms in smaller tufts, more slender, erect; leaves less conspicuously crowded at the base, not so stiff, and the basal proportionately not so much longer than those of the midculm; sheaths much shorter than the elongate internodes; blades 3 to 5 cm long, 4 to 5 mm wide, less thick and firm, the uppermost blade not reduced. Autumnal phase erect or leaning, sparingly branched from the middle and upper nodes (fig. 273).

FIGURE 274.—*Panicum chamaelonche.* Two views of spikelet, and floret, × 10 (type).

Sandy woods, southeastern United States; Cuba.

CUBA: Pinar del Río, *Hitchcock* 23270, 23300. Herradura, *Hitchcock* 23437. San Diego de los Baños, *Léon* 4454. Guane, *Léon* 6943. Banao Mountains, *Léon* 2749.

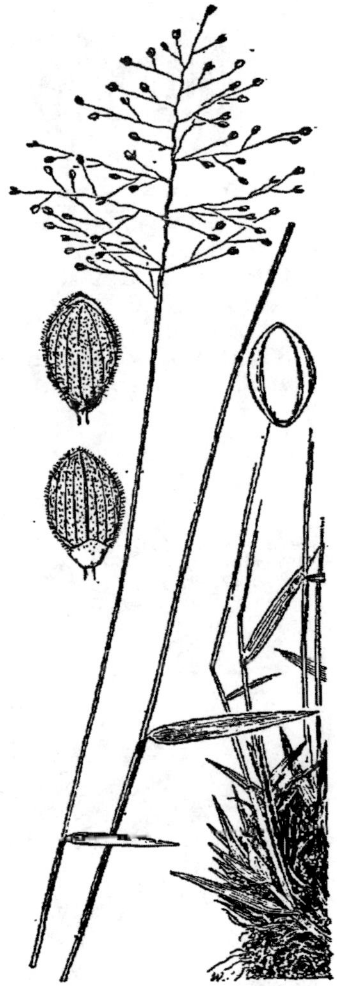

FIGURE 273.—*Panicum trifolium.* Two views of spikelet, and floret, × 10 (type).

82. Panicum chamaelonche Trin., Gram. Pan. 242. 1826. North America.

Vernal culms densely tufted, glabrous, ascending or erect, 10 to 20 cm tall; sheaths glabrous; ligule 0.2 mm long; blades firm, ascending, 1.5 to 4 cm long, 2 to 3 mm wide, more or less involute-pointed, glabrous; panicles 2.5 to 5 cm long; spikelets a little more than 1 mm long, glabrous. Autumnal phase freely branching from the base and lower nodes, forming dense cushions, the scarcely reduced blades drying involute (fig. 274).

Open sandy soil and low pine barrens, southeastern United States and British Honduras; Cuba, found in "white sand."

CUBA: Damují, *Ekman* 11047. Pinar del Río, *Ekman* 11465. Isla de Pinos, *Britton and Wilson* 14218, 14221; *Ekman* 12098, 12152.

83. Panicum portoricense Desv.; Hamilt., Prodr. Pl. Ind. Occ. 11. 1825. Puerto Rico.

Vernal culms erect or geniculate at base, slender, stiff and wiry, crisp-puberulent to nearly glabrous, 15 to 30 cm tall; sheaths much shorter than the internodes, glabrous or crisp-puberulent; blades firm, 2 to 5 cm long, 3 to 6 mm wide, glabrous to puberulent; panicles 2 to

4 cm long, the lower branches often reflexed; spikelets 1.5 mm long, puberulent. Autumnal phase much branched at all except the uppermost nodes forming a bushy mass (fig. 275).

Sandy woods, southeastern United States; Cuba, Puerto Rico.

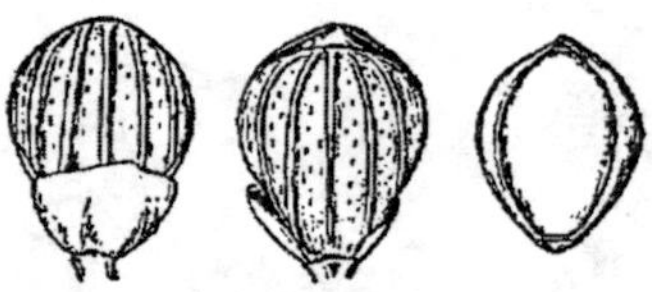

FIGURE 275.—*Panicum portoricense.* Two views of spikelet, and floret, × 10 (Ashe).

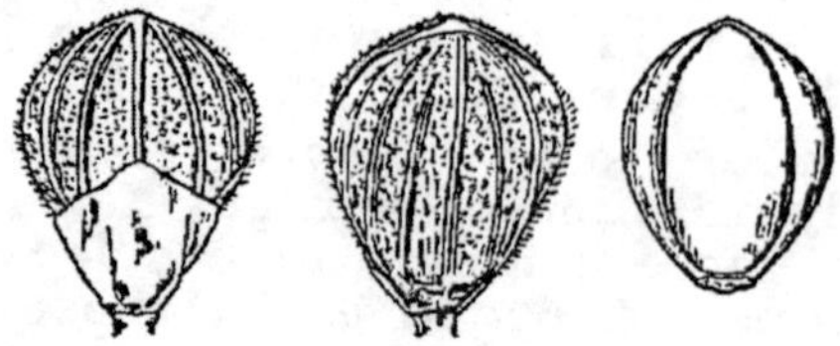

FIGURE 276.—*Panicum patulum.* Two views of spikelet, and floret, × 10 (type).

CUBA: Loma Pelada, *Wright* 3876. Isla de Pinos, *Britton and Wilson* 14216.

PUERTO RICO: Sardinera, *Britton* 8701. San Juan, *Chase* 6357, 6631, 6783. Carolina, *Britton and Brown* 5718. Laguna Tortuguero, *Britton, Cowell, and Brown* 3836; *Britton and Chardon* 6831. Campo Alegre, *Chase* 6434. Dorado, *Britton and Brown* 6651, 6740. Vega Baja, *Heller* 639; *Underwood and Griggs* 955. Santurce, *Heller* 982b, 6442. Sabana Llana, *Stevenson* 2783.

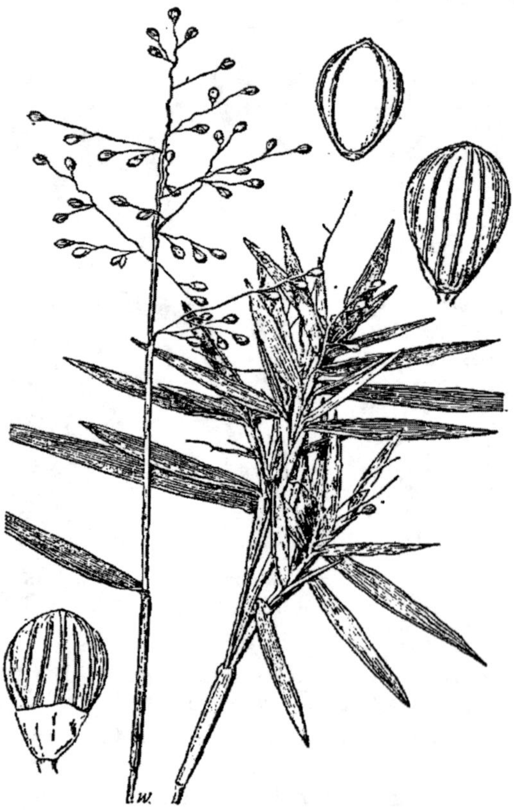

FIGURE 277.—*Panicum lancearium.* Plant, × 1; two views of spikelet, and floret, × 10 (Chase 4545).

84. Panicum patulum (Scribn. and Merr.) Hitchc., Rhodora 8: 209. 1906.

Panicum nashianum patulum Scribn. and Merr., U. S. Dept. Agr., Div. Agrost. Circ. 27: 9. 1900. Florida.

Differing from *P. lancearium* chiefly in the decumbent vernal habit and the lax blades pubescent on both surfaces; spikelets densely pubescent, more globular-pyriform. Autumnal phase more freely branching, forming large mats (fig. 276).

Low woods, southeastern United States; Hispaniola.

DOMINICAN REPUBLIC: Monción, *Ekman* 12705.

85. Panicum lancearium Trin., Gram. Pan. 223. 1826. North America.

Vernal phase usually purplish; culms wiry, 20 to 50 cm tall, minutely crisp-puberulent; blades 2 to 6 cm long, 3 to 7 mm wide, usually glabrous on the upper surface and puberulent beneath; panicles 3 to 6 cm long; spikelets 2 mm long, glabrous or puberulent. Autumnal phase geniculate-spreading, with fascicles of short branches (fig. 277).

Sandy pine woods, southeastern United States and British Honduras; Cuba, Hispaniola.

CUBA: La Grifa, *Ekman* 11261. Lagunillas, *Ekman* 13808. Sábalo, *Ekman* 11427; *Perez and Léon* 15094. Damují, *Ekman* 10952, 11022. San Claudio, *Ekman* 10543. Banao Mountains, *Léon* 5406. Sierra Maestra, *Ekman* 1634, 14674, 15290, 16111. Bayamo, *Ekman* 5064. Eastern Cuba, *Wright* 3460. Isla de Pinos, *Britton and Wilson* 14226, 14747, 15379; *Ekman* 12026, 12161.

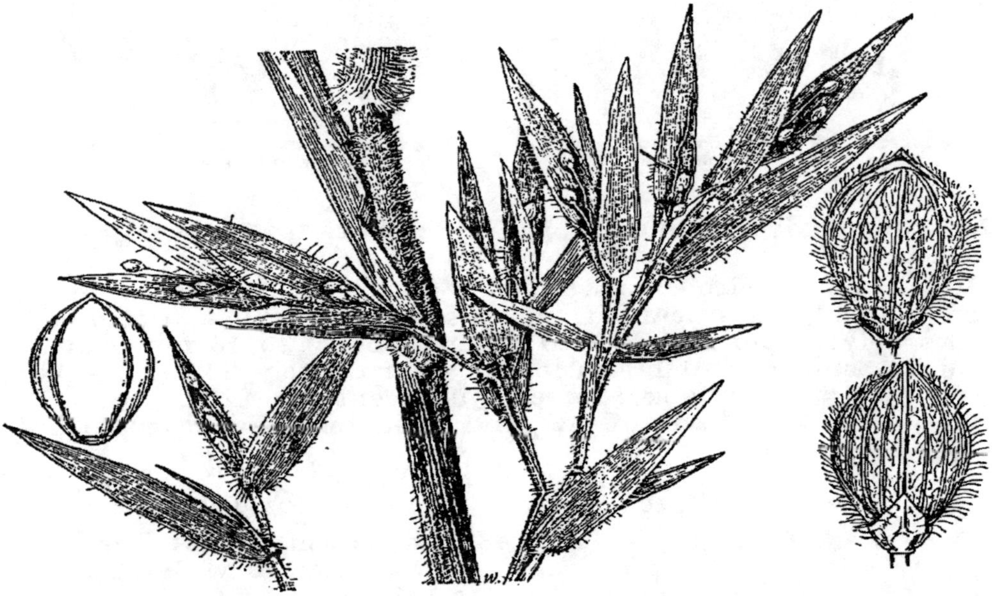

FIGURE 278.—*Panicum scoparium.* Plant, × 1; two views of spikelet, and floret, × 10 (McGregor 212).

DOMINICAN REPUBLIC: Lagunas de Cenobí, *Valeur* 4. Constanza, *Tuerckheim* 3321; *Ekman* H 14094. Monción, *Ekman* H 12704.

86. Panicum scoparium Lam., Encycl. 4: 744. 1798. Carolina.

Vernal phase grayish olive-green, velvety pubescent throughout except as noted; culms erect or ascending, usually geniculate at base, 80 to 130 cm tall, the nodes villous with reflexed hairs, a glabrous viscid ring below; sheaths glabrous on the back toward the summit, the surface here viscid when fresh; ligule 1 mm long; blades 12 to 20 cm long, 10 to 18 mm wide; panicles 8 to 15 cm long, the branches with viscid blotches; spikelets about 2.5 mm long, papillose-pubescent. Autumnal phase leaning or spreading, branches from the middle nodes, finally forming flabellate fascicles with much reduced blades (fig. 278).

Wet or damp soil, southeastern United States; Cuba to Puerto Rico.

CUBA: Pinal Mayarí, *Wright* 3467. Woodfred, *Shafer* 2997, 3018; *Ekman* 9101a. Sierra de Nipe, *Ekman* 2118, 2207, 3201; *Hitchcock* 23414. Pinar de Micara, *Ekman* 15896.

HAITI: Pérodin, *Ekman* H 3431. Carmillan, *Ekman* H 5688.

DOMINICAN REPUBLIC: Monción, *Ekman* H 12943. La Cumbre, *Ekman* H 11432.

PUERTO RICO: Sierra de Naguabo, *Shafer* 3481.

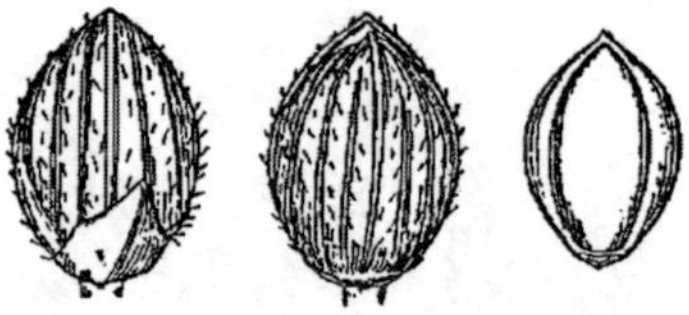

FIGURE 279.—*Panicum viscidellum.* Two views of spikelet, and floret, × 10 (type).

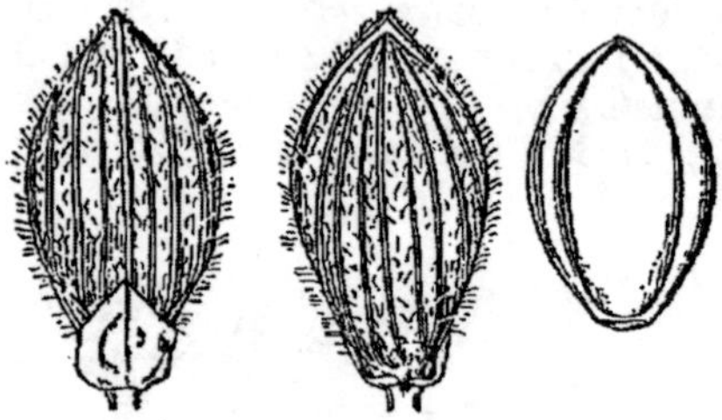

FIGURE 280.—*Panicum joorii.* Two views of spikelet, and floret, × 10 (type).

87. Panicum viscidellum Scribn., U. S. Dept. Agr., Div. Agrost. Circ. 19: 2. 1900. Mexico.

Vernal phase with culms ascending from a spreading or creeping base, villous; nodes bearded; sheaths villous; ligule 2 to 4 mm long; blades velvety-pubescent, 5 to 13 cm long, 9 to 13 mm wide, subcordate; panicles 4 to 11 cm long, rather densely flowered; spikelets about 2 mm long, sparsely pubescent (fig. 279).

Gravelly banks, fields, and open forests, Mexico to Colombia; Cuba.

CUBA: Isla de Pinos, *Ekman* 11651, 11712, 12128, 12406; *Britton and Wilson* 14357; *Palmer and Riley* 1065.

FIGURE 281.—*Panicum chapmani.* Panicle, × 1; two views of spikelet, and floret, × 10 (type).

88. Panicum joorii Vasey, U. S. Dept. Agr., Div. Bot. Bull. 8: 31. 1889. Louisiana.

Vernal culms spreading or ascending from a decumbent base, glabrous, 20 to 50 cm long; blades mostly 10 to 15 cm long and 10 to 15 mm wide, often somewhat falcate, glabrous; panicle 5 to 8 cm long; spikelets about 3 mm long, elliptic, pubescent. Autumnal phase widely spreading, branching, the ultimate branches in short dense fascicles (fig. 280).

Low swampy or sandy woods, southeastern United States; eastern Mexico; Nicaragua; Greater Antilles.

CUBA: Batabanó, *Ekman* 12596; *Léon* 14201. Sancti Spíritus Mountains, *Léon* 6457, 6595. Ciénaga de Zapata, *Roig* 2205. Guantánamo, *Ekman* 10297.

HAITI: Lomielle, *Ekman* H 6189.

89. Panicum chapmani Vasey, Bull. Torrey Bot. Club 11: 61. 1884. Florida.

Culms ascending or spreading, 40 to 100 cm tall; blades erect, linear, 15 to 40 cm long, 2 to 5 mm wide, flat to subinvolute when dry; panicles elongate, sometimes as much as 30 cm long, the appressed distant branches bearing few to several spikelets, the bristle 3 to 6 mm long; spikelets about 2 mm long, obovate; first glume about one-third the length of the spikelet, obtuse or truncate; second glume nearly as long as the fruit (fig. 281).

Coral sand, southern Florida, the Bahamas, and Cuba.

BAHAMAS: New Providence, *Britton and Brace* 401. Rose Island, *Britton and Millspaugh* 2137. Great Exuma, *Britton and Millspaugh* 3076 (all in Field Mus. Herb.).

CUBA: Batabanó, *Ekman* 12615. Cayo Sabinal, *Ekman* 15521.

90. Panicum ophiticola Hitchc. and Ekman, sp. nov.[66]

Culms densely cespitose, very slender, erect or spreading, 30 to 50 cm tall, the nodes mostly glabrous; sheaths scarcely compressed, villous around the summit; ligule a dense line of short hairs; blades flat or usually folded, especially those of the dense basal tuft, often pilose on the upper surface, mostly less than 10 cm long, commonly much shorter, 1 to 2 mm wide, rarely to 3.5 mm wide, the culm blades several, commonly flat; panicles terminal and axillary from the upper sheaths, slender, 2 to 7 cm long, few-flowered, the branches short and appressed; spikelets 2 to 2.8 mm long, the bristle minute (fig. 282).

FIGURE 282.—*Panicum ophiticola*. Plant × 1; spikelet and floret, × 10 (type).

Type in the United States National Herbarium no. 1387464, collected in "cuabales", on serpentine, Loma Cajálbana, prov. Pinar del Río, Cuba, January 2, 1921, by E. L. Ekman (no. 12712).

Rocky slopes, mostly on serpentine, Cuba.

CUBA: Loma de Coca (prov. Habana), *Ekman* 1220. San Miguel de Casanova, *Léon* 12481. Madruga, *Léon* 6372. Minas, *Léon* 4784; *Ekman* in 1921. Canasí (prov. Matanzas), *Léon* 13117. Holguín, *Ekman* 15722.

91. Panicum distantiflorum A. Rich., in Sagra, Hist. Cuba 11: 304. 1850. Cuba.

Culms cespitose, 30 to 50 cm tall, slender, wiry, sometimes geniculate at the lower nodes, producing slender, sometimes fascicled

[66] A *P. utowanaeo* differt foliis brevibus planis 1-3 mm latis, in pagina superiore sparse villosis; spiculis 2–2.8 mm longis.

branches from all the nodes; blades 3 to 12 cm long, 1 to 3 mm wide, flat to strongly involute; panicles numerous, 2 to 8 cm long, very narrow, the branches appressed; branchlets bearing 1 to 3 subsessile spikelets, 1.4 to 1.5 mm long, the bristle shorter than the spikelet (fig. 283).

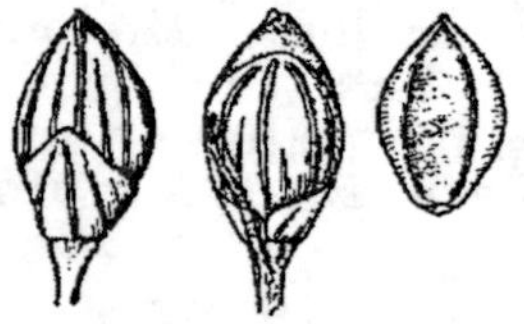
FIGURE 283.—*Panicum distantiflorum*. Two views of spikelet, and floret, × 10 (type).

Limestone hills at low altitudes, Bahamas and Cuba.

BAHAMAS: Inagua, *Hitchcock* in 1890; *Nash and Taylor* 893 (both in Field Mus. Herb.).

CUBA: Yayales, *Ekman* 11191. Mariel, *Ekman* in 1921. Hanábana, *Wright* 3452. Marianao, *Ekman* 434; *Léon* in 1909. Cojimar, *Baker* 2670; *Hitchcock* 144. Río Almendares, *Ekman* 951; *Léon* 2382, 12468. Habana, *Léon* 6299. Cayo de los Patos, *Léon* 9489. Cayo Romano, *Shafer* 2512. Santiago de Cuba, *Léon* 912, 917. Baracoa, *Léon* 12307. Guantánamo, *Ekman* 2894, 10167. Isla de Pinos, *Britton, Wilson, and Léon* 15272.

92. Panicum pradanum Léon, sp. nov.[67]

Culms cespitose, ascending, 50 to 90 cm long, slender, wiry; sheaths shorter than the internodes, ciliate at the auriculate summit; ligule a ring of short hairs; blades flexuous to curled, strongly involute from base to apex, much narrower at base than the summit of the sheath, finally often becoming flat from the middle towards the apex, 15 to 30 cm long, not more than 2 mm wide, often sparsely pubescent with short hairs on the upper surface, slightly scabrous on the margin; panicles 15 to 35 cm long, the branches remote, appressed, the lower not more than 2 cm long, bearing few to several spikelets, the bristle from nearly obsolete to as long as the spikelet or longer; spikelets spreading, 1.8 to 2 mm long, somewhat beaked; first glume about two-fifths the length of the spikelet, acute, 3-nerved; second glume about two-thirds the length of the spikelet, 5-nerved, rarely 7-nerved; sterile lemma 5-nerved, pointed; fruit 1.8 mm long, minutely rugose, slightly beaked at the acute apex (fig. 284).

FIGURE 284.—*Panicum pradanum*. Panicle × 1; spikelet and floret, × 10 (type).

Type in the United States National Herbarium no. 1258962, collected in open thickets on slope of Mesa de Prada, Lower Jauco Valley, Jauco, Province Oriente, Cuba, July 17 to August 4, 1924, by Brother Léon (no. 11710).

Open thickets and rocky slopes, eastern Cuba to Puerto Rico.

CUBA: Jauco, *Léon* 11710. Santiago de Cuba, *Ekman* 8952.

HAITI: Port-au-Prince, *Ekman* H 2020. Morne à Cabrits, *Ekman* H 1027. Port-de-Pai, *Ekman* H 5108; *Leonard* 11032, 11078. Caba-

[67] A *P. utowanaeo* differt foliis longioribus, involutis, vaginis vix compressis, paniculis longioribus (usque ad 30 cm), ramis remotis appressis; spiculis 1.8–2 mm longis.

ret, *Leonard* 11837. Gonaïve Island, *Leonard* 3348; *Eyerdam* 45. Tortuga Island, *Ekman* 4054.

DOMINICAN REPUBLIC: Guayabín, *Abbott* 1006. Navarette, *Abbott* 1085. Los Charcos, *Fuertes* 1427. Rincón, *Fuertes* 1284. Valverde, *Ekman* H 13102.

PUERTO RICO: Cayo Muertos, *Britton, Cowell, and Brown* 5012. Mona Island, *Hess* 455.

93. Panicum utowanaeum Scribn., in Millsp., Field Mus. Bot. 2: 25. 1900. Puerto Rico, *Pl. Utow.* 702.

Panicum sintenisii Nash, Bull. Torrey Bot. Club 30: 382. 1903. Puerto Rico, *Sintenis* 3463.

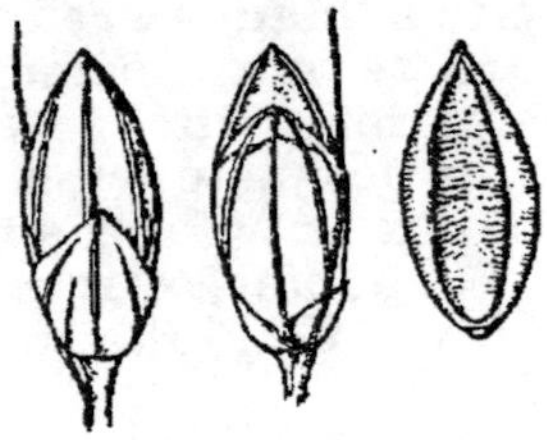

FIGURE 285.—*Panicum utowanaeum*. Two views of spikelet, and floret, × 10 (type).

Culms cespitose, ascending or somewhat spreading, 30 to 70 cm tall, the nodes glabrous; blades ascending, 8 to 20 cm long, 1 to 3 mm wide, flat to involute, often laxly flexuous; panicles very slender, 4 to 10 cm long, the erect branches 1 to 3 cm long, the bristle equaling or exceeding the spikelet; spikelets about 2 mm long, glabrous (fig. 285).

Open rocky soil, mostly near the coast, Cuba and Puerto Rico to Guadeloupe.

CUBA: San Miguel de Casanova, *Léon* 11569. Santa Clara City, *Ekman* 14040. Sabana de Motembo, *Léon* 9363. (The Cuban specimens scarcely characteristic.)

PUERTO RICO: Guanica Bay, *Chase* 6520 (*Amer. Gr. Nat. Herb.* 201), 6533, 6535; *Sintenis* 3365, 3416, 3463. Boqueron, *Britton, Cowell, and Brown* 4617. Playa Sucia Bay, *Britton, Cowell, and Brown* 4754. Desecheo Island, *Hess* 422; *Britton, Cowell, and Brown* 1601. Mona Island, *Britton, Cowell, and Hess* 1698, 1734; *Hess* 431, 457.

VIRGIN ISLANDS: Anegada, *Fishlock* 45.

LEEWARD ISLANDS: Barbuda, *Danforth* 10. Antigua, *Box* 45. Guadeloupe, *Duss* 3177.

94. Panicum leonis Ekman, sp. nov.[68]

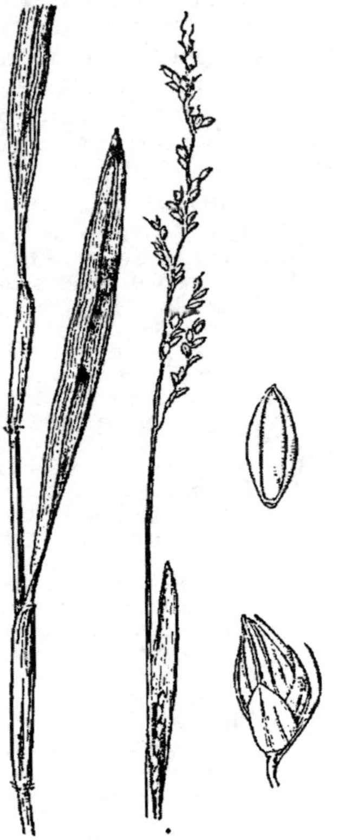

FIGURE 286.—*Panicum leonis*. Plant, × 1; spikelet and floret, × 10 (type).

Loosely cespitose, the slender rhizome better developed than in the other species, the culms slender, erect, or spreading, freely branching, 30 to 60 cm tall, the nodes, at least the lowermost, pubescent, sometimes obscurely so; sheaths somewhat compressed, the lower rarely pubescent, a pubescent line across the collar, short-pilose along the margin at summit; ligule a dense line of short hairs; blades 5 to 15 cm long, 4 to 7 mm wide (rarely but 3 mm wide), flat, narrower than the sheath at base; panicles from all the upper nodes, usually 2 to 5 cm long, relatively dense; spikelets 1.7 to 2 mm long, the bristle from minute to longer than the spikelet (fig. 286).

[68] A *P. utowanaeo* differt laminis planis latioribus (usque ad 7 mm); nodis inferioribus pubescentibus paniculis brevioribus densiusculis; spiculis 1.7–2 mm longis.

Type in the United States National Herbarium, no. 1502160, collected "in fruticetis littoralibus", Cojimar, near Habana, Cuba, September 9, 1921, by E. L. Ekman (no. 13155).

The type specimen and other collections with broad flat rather thick blades are strikingly different from any other species, but there are several specimens with blades only about 4 mm wide and more slender panicles which approach *P. utowanaeum*.

Rocky slopes and clearings, Cuba and Hispaniola.

CUBA: Cojimar, *Ekman* 13155, *Wilson* 9497; *Léon* 305 in part, 567, 5603, 7504; *Hitchcock* 141; *Tracy* 9089. Pastellilo, *Ekman* 15408; Cayo Guajaba, *Shafer* 2830. Antilla, *Ekman* 7308. Jauco, *Léon* 11709.

HAITI: Môle-St.-Nicolas, *Leonard* 13305. Port-de-Pai, *Ekman* H 3974.

DOMINICAN REPUBLIC: Valverde, *Ekman* H 13103.

81. ICHNANTHUS Beauv., Ess. Agrost. 56. pl. 12. f. 1. 1812

Inflorescence and spikelets as in *Panicum* (but more or less laterally compressed), the first glume often nearly as long as the spikelet, the fruit acute or subacute, the margins of the lemma usually flat, the rachilla produced below the lemma into a minute stipe, this bearing on either side membranaceous appendages adnate to the base of the lemma and free above, the appendages often wanting and indicated by minute excavations only; spikelets mostly short-pedicellate along the subsimple branches of a panicle. Mostly perennial, often decumbent at base or straggling.

Appendages of fertile lemma well developed wings.
- Sheaths densely long-villous ---------- 8. I. LEIOCARPUS.
- Sheaths more or less pubescent but not long-villous.
  - Blades lanceolate-elliptic, not more than 6 times longer than wide; spikelets short-pediceled ---------- 7. I. NEMORALIS.
  - Blades lanceolate-linear, many times longer than wide; spikelets long-pediceled ---------- 9. I. ICHNODES.

Appendages of fertile lemma reduced to scars.
- Blades petiolate, usually less than 5 mm wide, the petiole 1 to 15 mm long. ---------- 1. I. MAYARENSIS.
- Blades more or less clasping, usually more than 10 mm wide (4 to 10 mm in *I. tenuis*).
  - Glumes, at least the first, with attenuate tips, usually exceeding the sterile lemma and floret; blades thin, more or less pilose.
    - Spikelets with a few long stiff hairs near the margin toward the summit of both glumes; plants delicate; blades rarely more than 4 cm long and 1 cm wide ---------- 3. I. TENUIS.
    - Spikelets glabrous or scabrous on the midnerves only; blades up to 7 cm long and 2 cm wide ---------- 4. I. NEMOROSUS.
  - Glumes acute or acuminate but not attenuate, the first shorter than the spikelet.
    - Plants delicate, the fertile culms 3 to 8 cm tall; blades thin, 5 to 18 mm long ---------- 2. I. CONJUNCTUS.
    - Plants stouter and taller; blades mostly more than 10 cm long.
      - Blades lanceolate, 1 to 2 cm wide, glabrous ---------- 5. I. PALLENS.
      - Blades oval to ovate-lanceolate, 1.5 to 3.5 cm wide, often pubescent beneath ---------- 6. I. AXILLARIS.

1. Ichnanthus mayarensis (Wright) Hitchc., Contrib. U. S. Natl. Herb. 12: 228. 1909.

Panicum mayarense Wright, An. Acad. Cien. Habana 8: 206. 1871. Cuba, *Wright* 3468.

Ichnanthus wrightii Hitchc., Contrib. U. S. Natl. Herb. 12: 229. 1909. Cuba, *Wright* 3880.

Culms slender, straggling or spreading, 20 to 40 cm long; blades lanceolate to narrowly elliptic, 2 to 5 cm long, 3 to 6 mm wide, glabrous, abruptly narrowed into a petiole 1 to 5 mm long or on sterile shoots as much as 15 mm long; panicles 2 to 10 cm long, the few main branches rather stiffly spreading or ascending, as much as 3 cm long; spikelets about 3 mm long, lanceolate, nearly terete, acute, glabrous, the pedicels 0.5 to 2 mm long.

Dry pine woods and palm barrens, Cuba.

CUBA: Arroyo Hondo, *Wright* 3880. Río Santa Cruz, *Ekman* 17647. Sierra de las Guacamayas, *Ekman* 17992. Madruga, *Léon* 6373. Campo Florido, *Léon* 3450, 4143; *Ekman* 13246. Minas, *Ekman* 13139. San Miguel de los Baños, *Léon* 8885. Banao Mountains, *Léon* 8045, 8045½. Soledad, *Hitchcock* 23331. Sierra de Nipe, *Ekman* 2166, 2243, 3327, 9990; *Shafer* 2966, 3058. Guara, *Hitchcock* 23406, 23421. Jauco River, *Léon* 12322. Baracoa, *Ekman* 3569, 4325. Guantánamo, *Ekman* 10289. Isla de Pinos, *Ekman* 12294, 12304, 12447.

2. Ichnanthus conjunctus Hitchc. and Ekman, sp. nov.[69]

Culms branching and creeping, rooting at the nodes, slender, glabrous except for a

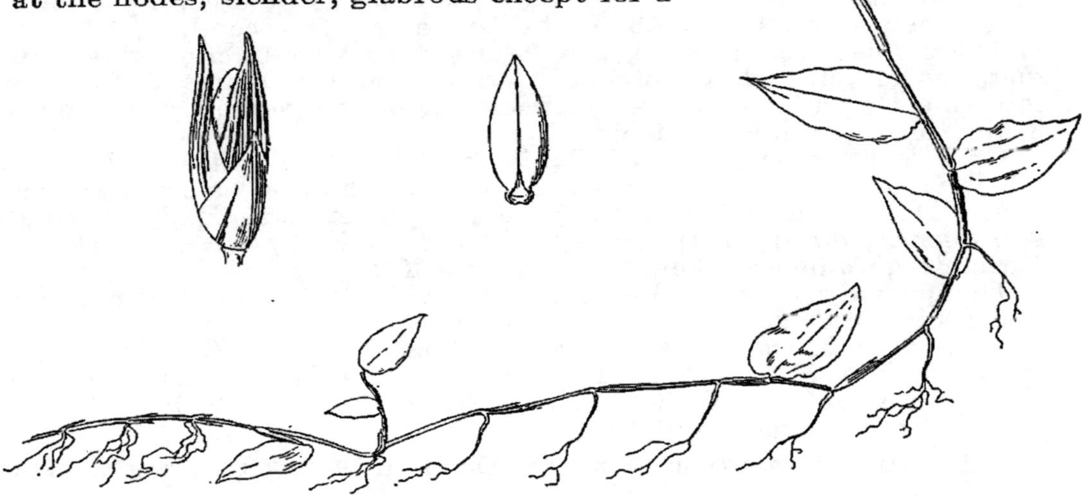

FIGURE 287.—*Ichnanthus conjunctus*. Plant, × 1; spikelet and floret, × 10 (type).

rather indistinct pubescent line, sulcate, the node sparsely and minutely pubescent, the fertile branches ascending, 3 to 8 cm long; sheaths half as long as the nodes or less, sulcate, glabrous except the ciliate margin and throat; ligule a ciliate membrane about 0.5 mm long; blades ovate to ovate-lanceolate, thin, 5 to 18 mm long, as

[69] Culmi ramosi repentes graciles, ramis fertilibus adscendentibus 3–8 cm longis; laminae ovatae vel ovato-lanceolatae tenues 5–18 mm longae glabrae; paniculae angustae pauciflorae 2 cm longae, ramis appressis 5–10 mm longis; spiculae lanceolatae acutae glabrae 3 mm longae; gluma prima 1.5 mm longa acuta 3-nervis; lemma fertile non alatum.

much as 9 mm wide, rounded or somewhat cordate at base with a petiole about 0.5 mm long, minutely scaberulous on the nerves on the upper surface, glabrous beneath except for a little pubescence near the base; panicles narrow, few-flowered, 2 to 2.5 cm long, the few branches narrowly ascending or appressed, 5 to 15 mm long, the lateral pedicels 0.3 mm long; spikelets lanceolate, nearly terete, acute or acuminate, glabrous, strongly nerved, 3 mm long; first glume half as long as the spikelet, 3-nerved; second glume and sterile lemma equal, 5-nerved, acuminate; fertile lemma pale, a little shorter than the spikelet, acute, the wings wanting (fig. 287).

Type in the United States National Herbarium no. 1387342, collected on moist logs in forest, Sabanos, prov. Oriente, Cuba, by E. L. Ekman (no. 6536). Known only from the type collection.

3. **Ichnanthus tenuis** (Presl) Hitchc. and Chase, Contrib. U. S. Natl. Herb. 18: 334. 1917.

Oplismenus tenuis Presl, Rel. Haenk. 1: 319. 1830. Mexico, Panama.

Panicum exile Steud., Nom. Bot. ed. 2. 2: 256. 1841. Based on *Oplismenus tenuis* Presl.

Panicum alsinoides Griseb., Fl. Brit. W. Ind. 550. 1864. Trinidad.

Ichnanthus alsinoides Munro; Hemsl., Biol. Centr. Amer. Bot. 3: 500. 1885.

Apparently annual; culms slender, spreading or creeping, rooting at the nodes, much branched, the fertile shoots ascending, 10 to 20 cm high; blades lanceolate, 2 to 5 cm long, 4 to 10 mm wide, thin, glabrous or puberulent; panicles terminal and axillary, 2 to 4 cm long, mostly on long slender peduncles; spikelets narrowly lanceolate, 3 mm long, acuminate, hispid.

Grisebach's description of *Panicum alsinoides* applies to *I. tenuis* which is not known from Jamaica. Grisebach gives as original localities, "Hab. Jamaica!, March; St. Kitts!; Trinidad!, Pd." March's specimen (sterile) in the Gray Herbarium is *Oplismenus setarius*. Purdie's specimen at Kew Herbarium is *I. tenuis*.

Damp shady places, at low and medium altitudes, Central America, Colombia, and Trinidad.

TRINIDAD: Maracas, *Broadway* in 1925. Maraval, *Broadway* 4912, 4913. Arima, *Hitchcock* 10313. St. Joseph, *Hitchcock* 10174 (*Amer. Gr. Nat. Herb.* 580). Port-of-Spain, *Hitchcock* 10052, 10199. Blanchisseuse Road, *Broadway* 5539.

4. **Ichnanthus nemorosus** (Swartz) Doell, in Mart., Fl. Bras. 2^2: 289. 1877.

Panicum nemorosum Swartz, Prodr. Veg. Ind. Occ. 22. 1788. Jamaica.

Milium nemorosum Moench, Meth. Sup. 67. 1802.

Echinolaena nemorosa Kunth, Rév. Gram. 1: 54. 1829.

Differing from *I. pallens* in the more prostrate habit, thinner, usually proportionately broader, sparsely pilose blades and the blunter spikelets.

Shady banks and rich woods, West Indies, Mexico, and Central America.

CUBA: Retiro, *Wright* 3881. Arroyo Hondo, *Wright* 3858. Mogote de Mono, *Wright* 3882. San Blas, *Jack* 6766. Cabañas, *Ekman* 12967. Mogote de la Bandera, *Roig* 3271. Sierra de Anafe, *Léon* 2873; *Wilson and Léon* 11538. Mendoza, *Léon* 3635. Banao Mountains, *Léon* 3997, 7866. La Perla, *Léon* 3908. Bayote, *Ekman* 2383. Sierra Maestra, *Léon* 10078, 10153; *Ekman* 1569, 8299, 8815. Sierra de Nipe, *Ekman* 9872.

JAMAICA: Gordon Town, *Harris* 11476; *Hart* 923. Claremont, *Hitchcock* 9523 (*Amer. Gr. Nat. Herb.* 582). Catherines Peak, *Hitchcock* 9741. Castleton, *Harris* 11296. Clyde River, *Harris* 11447. Troy, *Hitchcock* 9798; *Harris* 12595. Windsor, *Miller* 1516.

HAITI: Mission, *Leonard* 3975. Pétionville, *Leonard* 4858, 5052. Port-au-Prince, *Ekman* H 9105, H 9505. Morne Cabaio, *Ekman* H 1680.

DOMINICAN REPUBLIC: Old Heart River, *Abbott* 1366. Sánchez, *Abbott* 172.

PUERTO RICO: Cayey, *Sintenis* 2406.

LEEWARD ISLANDS: St. Kitts, *Box* 139, 141, 144, 145; *Britton and Cowell* 632. Nevis, *Box* 168.

WINDWARD ISLANDS: Grenada, *Broadway* 177.

TRINIDAD: Mount Tucuche, *Britton, Hazen, and Mendelson* 1328. Blanchisseuse Road, *Broadway* 6004. Balandra Bay, *Britton and Hazen* 432. Caparo, *Broadway* 4931. Port-of-Spain, *Hitchcock* 10041.

5. Ichnanthus pallens (Swartz) Munro; Benth., Fl. Hongk. 414. 1861.

Panicum pallens Swartz, Prodr. Veg. Ind. Occ. 23. 1788. Jamaica.

Culms much branched, spreading, creeping at the base, rooting at the nodes, the fertile culms ascending, 30 to 80 cm long, puberulent; blades lanceolate, often somewhat falcate, 5 to 10 cm long, 1 to 2 cm wide, somewhat clasping at the asymmetric narrowed base, glabrous or nearly so, but more or less scaberulous on the upper surface; panicles terminal and from several of the upper axils, 5 to 10 cm long, the spikelets appressed along the ascending branches; spikelets 3 to 3.5 mm, glabrous, the glumes and sterile lemma acuminate or more or less attenuate-pointed; appendages of fertile lemma reduced to scars (fig. 288).

Shady banks and rich woods, tropical regions of America in low and medium altitudes. To be found on probably all the West Indian islands from the Greater Antilles to Trinidad.

6. Ichnanthus axillaris (Nees) Hitchc. and Chase, Contrib. U. S. Natl. Herb. 18: 334. 1917.

Panicum axillare Nees, Agrost. Bras. 141. 1829. Brazil.

Differing from *I. pallens* in the firmer broader blades (ovate or ovate-lanceolate), often very scabrous on the upper surface, cordate-clasping at base, larger panicles, and often sparsely pilose spikelets.

Moist more or less shaded slopes in the uplands, Central America to Brazil; Hispaniola, Puerto Rico; Trinidad, Tobago.

HAITI: Plaisance, *Leonard* 9190.

DOMINICAN REPUBLIC: Los Haitises, *Ekman* H 15512. La Cumbre *Ekman* H 14215. Bayaguana, *Ekman* H 11096. Altagracia, *Ekman* H 11256, H 11257.

PUERTO RICO: Adjuntas, *Chase* 6472; *Sintenis* 4610; *Britton and Shafer* 2018. Aybonito, *Sintenis* 2869. Utuado, *Britton and Cowell* 1008. Cayey, *Chase* 6735. Mayaguez, *Heller* 4479.

TRINIDAD: Tabaquite, *Hitchcock* 10125, 10129 (*Amer. Gr. Nat. Herb.* 585), 10133. Maraval, *Bot. Gard. Herb.* 5425; *Britton, Freeman, and Nowell* 2607. Maracas Waterfall, *Britton, Hazen, and Mendelson* 1647. Maracas Bay, *Broadway* 8950.

TOBAGO: *Hitchcock* 10263.

FIGURE 288.—*Ichnanthus pallens.* Plant, × ⅔; spikelet and floret, × 10 (Ekman 9504).

7. Ichnanthus nemoralis (Schrad.) Hitchc. and Chase, Contrib. U. S. Natl. Herb. 18: 334. 1917.

Panicum nemorale Schrad.; Schult., Mant. 2: 255. 1824. Brazil.

Culms as much as 1 m tall, more or less decumbent at base, pubescent or glabrous; sheaths more or less pubescent, villous on the collar; ligule a ciliate membrane about 1 mm long; blades elliptic or narrowly lanceolate, up to about 10 or 15 cm long, as much as 3 cm wide, narrowed into a petiole 1 to 2 mm long, many-nerved, pubescent on both surfaces or glabrous above; panicle 10 to 15 cm long, the few stout branches stiffly ascending, pubescent at base; spikelets about 4.5 mm long, glabrous, or the glumes slightly roughened on the internerves toward the apex; fruit 3.5 mm long, the appendages 1.5 mm long.

Among shrubs, Trinidad to Brazil. This species was described under *Panicum lagotis* Trin., by Grisebach.[70]

TRINIDAD: Without locality, *Bot. Gard. Herb.* 2278; *Crueger* 78, 82.

TOBAGO: *Broadway* 4472.

[70] Fl. Brit. W. Ind. 550. 1864.

8. Ichnanthus leiocarpus (Spreng.) Kunth, Rév. Gram. 1: Sup. X. 1830.

Panicum leiocarpon Spreng., Neu. Entd. 1: 243. 1820. Brazil.

Culms 1 to 2 m tall, pubescent; sheaths villous or lanate; ligule a ciliate membrane, the hairs 1 to 2 mm long; blades narrowly lanceolate, 10 to 20 cm long, 1 to 3 cm wide, pilose on both surfaces; panicle large and open, about 30 cm long, obovoid, the axis villous below, scabrous above, the branches spreading, pubescent at base, these and the branchlets somewhat flexuous; spikelets about 4 mm long, glabrous; first glume about half as long as spikelet; fruit narrow, brownish, 3 mm long, the appendages about 1 mm long (fig. 289).

Wooded slopes, Trinidad to Brazil.

TRINIDAD: Without locality, *Bot. Gard. Herb.* 3318.

9. Ichnanthus ichnodes (Griseb.) Hitchc. and Chase, Contrib. U. S. Natl. Herb. 18: 335. 1917.

Panicum ichnodes Griseb., Fl. Brit. W. Ind. 551. 1864. Trinidad.

Ichnanthus trinitensis Mez, Repert. Sp. Nov. Fedde 15: 130. 1918. Trinidad.

FIGURE 289.—*Ichnanthus leiocarpus.* Spikelet and floret, × 10 (type).

Erect from a somewhat decumbent base, bearing short knotty, rhizomes and forming colonies; culms 1 to 2 m tall, glabrous, or sparingly villous below; sheaths keeled, the lower overlapping, glabrous or sparsely villous, densely villous on the margin and on the collar; ligule about 1 mm long; blades narrowly lanceolate to linear, the lower as much as 30 cm long, 1 to 2 cm wide, narrowed below, scabrous, sometimes sparsely villous, densely villous above near base; panicle oblong, as much as 30 cm long, the branches fascicled or branched at base, finally spreading; spikelets blunt, about 2.5 mm long; first glume more than half as long as spikelet, often sparsely villous; second glume roughened toward apex; sterile floret often staminate; fruit 2 mm long, the appendages 0.5 mm long.

The elongate blades and the large, much-branched, many-flowered panicles of blunt spikelets give this species the aspect of a species of *Panicum*, but the appendages at the base of the fertile lemma show that the species belongs to *Ichnanthus*.

Wood borders in partial shade, Trinidad to Brazil.

TRINIDAD: St. Joseph, *Hitchcock* 10178, 10179, 10191. Port-of-Spain, *Hitchcock* 9999 (*Amer. Gr. Nat. Herb.* 586), 10003 (*Amer. Gr. Nat. Herb.* 587); *Bot. Gard. Herb.* 3182; *Broadway* 5060. Piarco Savanna, *Hitchcock* 10357. Pitch Lake, *Bot. Gard. Herb.* 2299. Without locality, *Crueger* 77.

82. LASIACIS (Griesb.) Hitchc., Contrib. U. S. Natl. Herb. 15: 16. 1910. Tibisee

(*Panicum* section *Lasiacis* Griseb., Fl. Brit. W. Ind. 551. 1864)

Spikelets subglobose, placed obliquely on their pedicels; first glume broad, somewhat inflated-ventricose, usually not more than one-third the length of the spikelet; second glume and sterile lemma about equal, broad, abruptly apiculate, papery-chartaceous, shining, many-nerved, glabrous, or lanose at the apex only, the lemma enclosing a membranaceous palea and sometimes a staminate flower; fertile lemma white, bony-indurate, obovoid, obtuse, this and the palea of the same texture bearing at the apex in a slight crateriform depression a tuft of woolly hairs, the palea concave below, gibbous above, the apex often free at maturity. Large branching perennials with woody culms, often clambering, mostly firm blades narrowed into a minute petiole, and open or slightly compact panicles.

Main culm prostrate, the fertile shoots prostrate, ascending, or erect.
  Blades lanceolate, mostly less than 5 cm long; fertile shoots strongly dorsiventral mostly prostrate ---------- 1. L. RUGELII.
  Blades linear-lanceolate, mostly 10 to 12 cm long; fertile shoots ascending or erect from a decumbent base, not dorsiventral ---------- 2. L. GRISEBACHII.
Main culm clambering or much branched and forming a tangled mass.
  Ligule noticeable, brownish, about 2 mm long.
    Blades glabrous beneath, scabrous on both surfaces, elongate, more than 10 times as long as wide; plants not forming a strong central clambering cane ---------- 3. L. OAXACENSIS.
    Blades puberulent beneath, glabrous or scabrous on the upper surface, less than 10 times as long as wide; plants forming a strong central clambering cane ---------- 4. L. LIGULATA.
  Ligule inconspicuous, hidden within the mouth of the sheath, rarely as much as 1 mm long.
    Plants not high-climbing, decumbent and rooting at base, forming a tangled mass, with no strong central cane; spikelets clustered toward the ends of the branches ---------- 5. L. RHIZOPHORA.
    Plants high-climbing, forming a strong central cane; spikelets not clustered toward the ends of the branches.
      Blades glabrous on both surfaces, often more or less scabrous.
        Blades narrow, usually 3 to 4 mm, sometimes 5 mm, wide, 8 to 10 cm long ---------- 6. L. HARRISII.
        Blades more than 5 mm wide, if as much as 10 cm long.
          Panicles few-flowered, 5 to 10 cm long; branches strongly zigzag, the branchlets strongly divaricate or reflexed; blades narrowly lanceolate, firm, mostly less than 1 cm wide (sometimes wider on vigorous shoots) ---------- 7. L. DIVARICATA.
          Panicles many-flowered, usually 15 to 25 cm long or more on the primary branches; branches straight or arcuate, not zigzag; blades mostly more than 1.5 cm wide.
            Spikelets 4.5 to 5 mm long, on short stiff appressed pedicels; blades oblong-ovate or elliptic-lanceolate ---------- 8. L. SLOANEI.
            Spikelets 3.5 to 4 mm long on flexuous spreading pedicels, blades lanceolate or narrowly lanceolate ---------- 9. L. PATENTIFLORA.
      Blades pubescent on one or both surfaces (rarely nearly glabrous in *L. ruscifolia*).
        Blades narrowly lanceolate, averaging 8 to 10 times as long as wide; panicle large and open; spikelets 4 to 5 mm long. 10. L. SORGHOIDEA.
        Blades ovate-lanceolate or elliptic, sometimes lanceolate, often more or less cordate-clasping; panicle often compact, or at least the branches commonly compactly flowered; spikelets 3 to 4 mm long.
          Sterile lemma 1 ---------- 11. L. RUSCIFOLIA.
          Sterile lemmas 2 ---------- 12. L. ANOMALA.

1. Lasiacis rugelii (Griseb.) Hitchc., Bot. Gaz. 51: 302. 1911.

Panicum rugelii Griseb., Cat. Pl. Cub. 233. 1866. Cuba, *Rugel* 188.

Culms much branched, prostrate, the main culms slender, mostly about 2 mm, sometimes 2.5 mm, thick, appressed-hispidulous, the sterile shoots prostrate, dorsiventral, the leaves strongly distichous, approximate, the fertile shoots sometimes ascending toward the end; sheaths overlapping, hispidulous, villous on the margin and around the summit; ligule inconspicuous; blades lanceolate or oblong-lanceolate, 2 to 5 cm long, 4 to 12 mm wide, hispidulous or puberulent on both surfaces; panicles few-flowered, usually not more than 5 cm long, the few branches spreading, the axes pubescent, scabrous on the angles; spikelets 5 mm long.

Rich thickets, Cuba and Hispaniola.

CUBA: Valestina, *Wright* 3465. Sierra de Anafe, *Wilson* 11449. San Antonio, *Hitchcock* 176. Boco de Canasí, *Léon* 13698. Canasí, *Ekman* 16489. Camoa, *Ekman* 13516. San Miguel de Casanova, *Léon* 12458, 12459, 12460, 12461, 12462. Guantánamo, *Ekman* 10306. Niquero, *Ekman* 16151. Santiago de Cuba, *Ekman* 7699. Sierra de Nipe, *Ekman* 15242. Isla dè Pinos, *Britton and Wilson* 14860; *Ekman* 12446.

HAITI: Tortuga Island, *Ekman* H 4254.

DOMINICAN REPUBLIC: Sosúa, *Ekman* H 14531.

2. Lasiacis grisebachii (Nash) Hitchc., Bot. Gaz. 51: 302. 1911.

Panicum grisebachii Nash, Bull. Torrey Bot. Club 35: 301. 1908. Cuba, *Britton and Shafer* 758.

Plants much branched, the main culms creeping and rooting at the nodes, as much as 2 mm in diameter, the fertile shoots erect or ascending, 20 to 40 cm tall; ligule inconspicuous; blades narrowly lanceolate, 6 to 12 cm long, 5 to 10 mm wide, puberulent beneath, glabrous above; panicles ovate, mostly 5 to 6 cm long, the few branches rather stiffly ascending, few-flowered; spikelets 4 mm long.

Rich woods and shady banks, carpeting the floor of dark thickets, Cuba; eastern Mexico and Central America.

CUBA: Sierra del Brujo, *Léon* 12916. Viñales, *Hitchcock* 23315; *Killip* 13528. Valestina, *Wright* 3457. Sierra de Anafe, *Wilson and Léon* 2874, 11467; *Wilson* 11309. Cabanas, *Ekman* 10506. Bahia Honda, *Shafer* 12006. Taco Taco, *Baker* 3817. Buenaventura, *Wilson* 9238, 9332. Matanzas, *Rugel* 187. Madruga, *Britton and Shafer* 758. Guanajay, *Baker and Van Hermann* 4269. San Antonio, *Hitchcock* 131. Manatí, *Léon* 5685. Peninsula de Zapata, *Ekman* 18340. Boca de Canasí, *Léon* 15106. Lomas de Camoa, *Léon* 1972; *Ekman* 13462, 13531. Gerardo, *Ekman* 12646.

3. Lasiacis oaxacensis (Steud.) Hitchc., Biol. Soc. Wash. Proc. 24: 145. 1911.

Panicum oaxacense Steud., Syn. Pl. Glum. 1: 73. 1854. Mexico.

Straggling and branching, but not high-climbing nor with a strong central cane; culms decumbent and geniculate at base, rooting at the lower nodes, the ascending branches 1 to 2 m long, glabrous; sheaths glabrous or rarely appressed-pubescent, the margin villous; ligule prominent, 2 to 5 mm long, brownish; blades narrowly lanceolate, 10 to 25 cm long, 1 to 2 cm wide, abruptly narrowed at base, long-tapering at apex, scabrous on both surfaces; panicles open, as much as 30 cm long and nearly as wide, the slender scabrous branches and branchlets ascending or the lower finally spreading, naked below, the spikelets clustered toward the tips, no smaller secondary panicles developed; spikelets 4 mm long, elliptic, often purple.

Edges of woods, thickets, and copses, Mexico to Ecuador; Jamaica, Hispaniola.

Jamaica: Peckham, *Harris* 12828. Troy, *Hitchcock* 9800. Lindos Hill, *Harris* 11832. Ipswich, *Hitchcock* 9608. Mount Diablo, *Ridley* 27.

Haiti: Buttet, *Ekman* H 7153. Port-Margot, *Ekman* H 2841. Caille la Croix, *Leonard* 7997. Marmelade, *Leonard* 8192. Dondou, *Leonard* 8572. Plaisance, *Leonard* 9391.

Dominican Republic: Sanchéz, *Abbott* 180.

4. **Lasiacis ligulata** Hitchc. and Chase, Contrib. U. S. Natl. Herb. 18: 337. 1917. Trinidad, *Hitchcock* 10007.

Panicum divaricatum var. *puberulum* Griseb., Fl. Brit. W. Ind. 551. 1864. Trinidad, *Crueger*.

Clambering to a height of 5 to 10 m, the robust glabrous central cane as much as 1 cm in diameter, the wide-spreading main branches and the arcuate secondary ones not in fascicles, not zigzag; sheaths ciliate on the overlapping margin, otherwise glabrous; ligule a ciliate membrane, brown, 1 to 2 mm long; blades flat, firm, 6 to 12 cm long, 0.8 to 1.5 cm wide, lanceolate, acuminate, narrowed to the base, glabrous on the upper surface, puberulent beneath, the margins scabrous; panicles terminating the numerous branches, exserted or partly included, oval in outline, rather open, 5 to 10 cm long, usually half to three-fourths as wide, the branches few, spreading, finally reflexed, branching or flowering from near the base, usually bearing 5 to 10 short-pedicled spikelets; spikelets about 4 mm long, obovoid and purplish black at maturity, the glumes and sterile lemma as well as the fruit with a lanate tuft at the tips.

Copses and edges of woods, Central America and the West Indies to Ecuador and Brazil.

Dominican Republic: Río San Juan, *Miller* 1184. Sanchéz, *Abbott* 121.

Puerto Rico: Lares, *Sintenis* 5918. Cayey, *Chase* 6734, 6747. Maricao, *Sintenis* 215. Loquillo Mountains, *Wilson* 350. Arecibo, *Chase* 6454. Mayaguez, *Britton and Marble* 678.

Virgin Islands: Tortola, *Shafer* 1147. St. Thomas, *Britton and Marble* 1230.

Trinidad: Port-of-Spain, *Hitchcock* 9962. St. Joseph, *Hitchcock* 10020. Morne Bleu, *Britton, Freeman, and Bailey* 2266. Aripo, *Broadway* 9929. Diego Martin, *Bot. Gard. Herb.* 7717. Caparo, *Broadway* 4923. Tamana, *Broadway* 4952, 4959. Tabaquite, *Hitchcock* 10120. Moruga, *Broadway* 7915. Cedros, *Hitchcock* 10151.

Tobago: *Hitchcock* 10261, 10262, 10269, 10275; *Broadway* 3551, 4038.

5. Lasiacis rhizophora (Fourn.) Hitchc., Biol. Soc. Wash. Proc. 24: 145. 1911.

Panicum rhizophorum Fourn., Mex. Pl. 2: 31. 1886. Mexico.

Branching and straggling, not forming a strong central cane, decumbent at base and rooting at the lower nodes, the fertile culms ascending, 30 to 100 cm long, glabrous or pubescent; sheaths appressed-hispidulous or glabrescent, villous on the margin; ligule inconspicuous; blades lanceolate to ovate-lanceolate, 7 to 14 cm long, 1.5 to 3 cm wide, somewhat cordate at base, rather abruptly narrowed above to an acuminate point, scabrous above, pubescent or scabrous beneath; panicles 8 to 15 cm long, the branches stiffly ascending, naked below, the spikelets clustered toward their tips, the axes scabrous; spikelets 3 to 4 mm long, ovoid.

Copses and moist forest, Mexico and Central America; Cuba; Hispaniola.

CUBA: Lomas de Camoa (prov. Habana), *Ekman* 13511, 13530. Sierra de los Órganos, *Ekman* 17542. Mariel, *Ekman* 13046. Pan de Matanzas, *Ekman* 16464.

DOMINICAN REPUBLIC: Santiago, *Ekman* H 13200 (sterile specimen which appears to be this species).

6. Lasiacis harrisii Nash, Torreya 13: 274. 1913. Jamaica, *Marble* 222.

Plants bright green, clambering among bushes to the height of 5 m or more, the main canes slender but strong, the very slender branches pendent, the young twigs commonly rosy purple; sheaths slender, glabrous except the margin and throat, or rarely the young ones sparsely hispid; ligule inconspicuous; blades linear-lanceolate, 5 to 10 cm long, 2 to 6 mm wide, gradually narrowed to an acuminate apex, thin and lax, glabrous, the margins scabrous; panicles narrow, mostly less than 5 cm long, often partially included in the uppermost sheath, the branches short and appressed, the longer usually not more than 1 cm long, and bearing not more than 4 spikelets; spikelets similar to those of *L. divaricata* but less turgid.

This species is easily recognized by its long narrow blades and pendent branches.

Shaded slopes at higher altitudes, West Indies and Colombia.

JAMAICA: Catherines Peak, *Hitchcock* 9726, 9730; *Harris* 11552. Cold Spring Gap, *Harris* 11354. Strawberry Hill, *Harris* 11487. Abbey Green, *Harris* 11587; *Hitchcock* 9363 (*Amer. Gr. Nat. Herb.* 588). Farm Hill, *Orcutt* 3544.

DOMINICAN REPUBLIC: Polo (prov. Barahona), *Abbott* 1876. Jarabaco, *Ekman* H 14176.

PUERTO RICO: Maricao, *Chase* 6224, 6228; *Stevens and Hess* 4882. Cayey, *Chase* 6742. Quebradillas, *Chase* 6578.

VIRGIN ISLANDS: St. John, *Eggers* 3121.

7. Lasiacis divaricata (L.) Hitchc., Contrib. U. S. Natl. Herb. 15: 16. 1910.

Panicum divaricatum L., Syst. Nat. ed. 10. 2: 871. 1759. Jamaica.

Panicum bambusioides Desv.; Hamilt., Prodr. Pl. Ind. Occ. 10. 1825. Puerto Rico.

Panicum chauvinii Steud., Syn. Pl. Glum. 1: 68. 1854. Guadeloupe.

Panicum divaricatum var. *stenostachyum* Griseb., Fl. Brit. W. Ind. 551. 1864. Jamaica.

Usually glabrous throughout except the margin of the sheaths; culms woody, much branched, clambering over shrubs to the height of 3 to 4 m, the main culm strong, as much as 6 mm in diameter, the main branches often fascicled, the vigorous secondary sterile shoots usually strongly divaricate or zigzag; sheaths sometimes hispid on the collar; ligule inconspicuous; blades narrowly lanceolate, 5 to 12 cm long, 5 to 15 mm wide, or on the vigorous sterile shoots much larger, narrowed at the base, gradually acuminate, scabrous on the margin and sometimes slightly on the surface, the older ones deciduous from the sheaths, the basal portion of the fertile shoots bearing the old sheaths but otherwise naked; panicles terminating the main culm and the fertile branches, ovate or oblong, 5 to 20 cm long, loosely flowered, the branches distant, spreading, or often reflexed, the axes angled, scabrous, flexuous, the lower usually 2 to 4 cm (sometimes as much as 10 cm) long, the main branches ordinarily 5 to 10 flowered; spikelets ovoid, about 4 mm long (fig. 290).

Among shrubs at low altitudes, southern Florida to Central and South America; throughout the West Indies. *Panicum divaricatum* and *P. sloanei* were included by Richard[71] under the name *P. glutinosum*. In Cuba called "pito de bejuco."

The commonest West Indian species of the genus, growing on all the islands, especially near the coast.

8. **Lasiacis sloanei** (Griseb.) Hitchc., Bot. Gaz. 51: 302. 1911.

Panicum latifolium Hamilt., Prodr. Pl. Ind. Occ. 10. 1825. Not *P. latifolium* L., 1753. Antilles.

Panicum sloanei Griseb., Fl. Brit. W. Ind. 551. 1864. Jamaica.

Climbing to a height of 3 or 4 m, forming a strong central cane; branches solitary or 2 or 3 together, elongate; blades parchmentlike in texture at maturity, commonly 12 to 15 cm long and 2 to 3 cm wide, narrowed into a very short pubescent petiole; panicles commonly as much as 20 cm long, nearly as wide, the branches rather rigid. The spikelets are larger in this species than in any other of the genus in the region.

Climbing among bushes and small trees, West Indies to Central and South America.

CUBA: Sierra Mendoza, *Shafer* 11147. Sierra de Anafe, *Wilson* 11421. Valestina, *Wright* 3878. Santiago de los Baños, *Léon* 4563, 5148. Mariel, *Ekman* 12853. Las Pozas, *Ekman* 12743. Guanajay, *Ekman* 13035; *Baker* 4587. Camoa Hills, *Léon* 766. Jamaica, *Léon* 1969. Cojimar, *Léon* 1973. San Antonio, *Hitchcock* 128. Ariguanabo, *Léon* 9751. Almendares River, *Léon* 12463. Malanga, *Rugel* 872. Boca de Canasí, *Léon* 13171. Loma Descada, *Ekman* 15319. Soledad, *Jack* 5187. Amaro, *Léon* 9435. Mayarí Arriba, *Ekman* 15851. Isla de Pinos, *Britton and Wilson* 15134.

JAMAICA: Montego Bay, *Ridley* 35; *Maxon and Killip* 1673. Troy, *Hitchcock* 9801; *Harris* 12614, 12615. Ipswich, *Hitchcock* 9606. Ewarton, *Hitchcock* 9413. Bog Walk, *Maxon* 10502; *Hitchcock* 9305 (*Amer. Gr. Nat. Herb.* 591). Ferry River, *Harris* 11325. Halls

[71] Richard, in Sagra, Hist. Cuba 11: 307. 1850

Delight, *Harris* 11260. Gordon Town, *Harris* 11454. Bryans Hill, *Harris* 11531. Kingston, *Hitchcock* 9267 (*Amer. Gr. Nat. Herb.* 590), 9280.

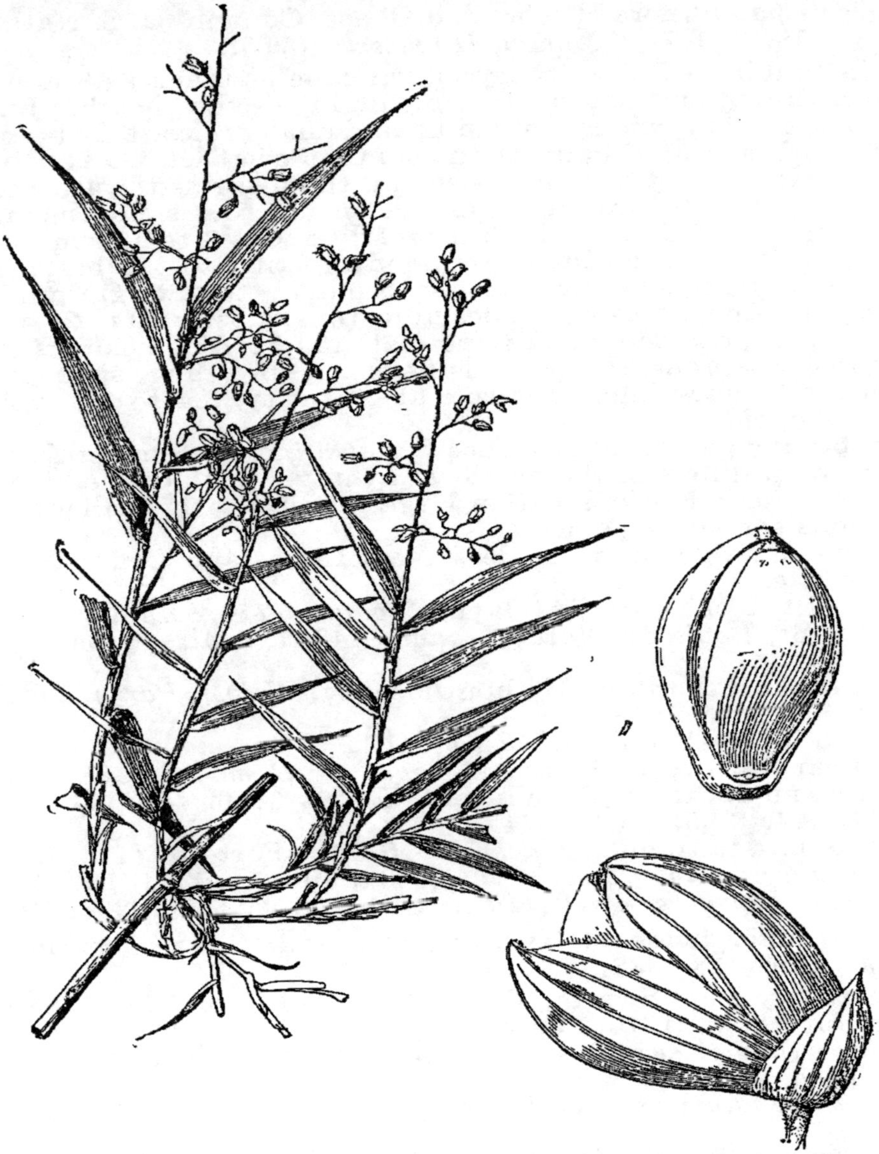

FIGURE 290.—*Lasiacis divaricata.* Plant, × ½; spikelet and floret, × 10 (Curtiss 5530).

HAITI: Pétionville, *Leonard* 4883, 5024, 5054; *Ekman* H 2190. Port-de-Pai, *Ekman* H 4438. St. Raphael, *Leonard* 7650. Ennery, *Leonard* 9466. Gonaïve Island, *Leonard* 3105, 3290, 5121. Anse-à-Foleur, *Ekman* H 4330.

DOMINICAN REPUBLIC: La Romana, *Ekman* H 12094.

PUERTO RICO: Vieques Island, *Shafer* 2549. Mayaguez, *Chase* 6824, 6825.

LEEWARD ISLANDS: Antigua, *Box* 119.

9. Lasiacis patentiflora Hitchc. and Chase, Contrib. U. S. Natl. Herb. 18: 338. 1917. Tobago, *Hitchcock* 10268.

High-climbing with a strong central cane as much as 8 mm thick, glabrous throughout except at the summit of the sheaths; branches numerous, solitary, widely spreading and finally repeatedly branching; sheaths with a ring of hairs at the summit or at least a tuft of hairs on either side, sometimes pubescent on the margins toward the summit; ligule about 0.5 mm long; blades on vigorous shoots as much as 14 cm long, and 2.5 cm wide, but mostly about 8 to 12 cm long and 1.5 to 2 cm wide, acuminate, rounded-tapering to the base, usually somewhat asymmetric, glabrous, scabrous on the margin and somewhat so on both surfaces; panicles numerous, mostly 12 to 20 cm long, nearly as wide, the slender axis and distant spreading flexuous branchlets angled, scabrous, the pedicels flexuous, spreading; spikelets pale, blotched with dark blue or purple at maturity, 3.4 to 3.8 mm long, globose-obovoid.

In habit and general appearance *L. patentiflora* resembles *P. sloanei*, from which it differs in the narrower average width of the blades and the more loosely flowered, rather large panicles with smaller spikelets on flexuous spreading pedicels.

Borders of woods and jungles, West Indies and Central America to Venezuela.

HAITI: St. Michel de l'Atalaye, *Leonard* 7776. Thibaud, *Ekman* H 2624. St. Louis du Nord, *Leonard* 14292. Miragoane, *Eyerdam* 594.

DOMINICAN REPUBLIC: Without locality, *Wright, Parry, and Brummel* 614.

PUERTO RICO: San Juan, *Chase* 6412.

LEEWARD ISLANDS: Dominica, *Jones* 49; *Ramage* in 1889.

WINDWARD ISLANDS: St. Vincent, *Eggers* 6546. Grenada, *Broadway* 227, 947, 1385, 4666, 4674a.

TRINIDAD: Manzanilla, *Hitchcock* 10374. Port-of-Spain, *Hitchcock* 9990 (*Amer. Gr. Nat. Herb.* 592), 10034, 10037, 10323, 10324.

TOBAGO: *Broadway* 4841; *Hitchcock* 10255, 10257, 10268, 10270.

10. Lasiacis sorghoidea (Desv.) Hitchc. and Chase, Contrib. U. S. Nat. Herb. 18: 338. 1917.

Panicum lanatum Swartz, Prodr. Veg. Ind. Occ. 24. 1788. Not *P. lanatum* Rottb., 1776. Jamaica.

Panicum sorghoideum Desv.; Hamilt., Prodr. Pl. Ind. Occ. 10. 1825. Puerto Rico.

Panicum lanatum var. *sorghoideum* Griseb., Fl. Brit. W. Ind. 551. 1864.

Panicum martinicense Griseb., Fl. Brit. W. Ind. 552. 1864. Martinique.

Panicum swartzianum Hitchc., Contrib. U. S. Natl. Herb. 12: 140. 1908. Based on *P. lanatum* Swartz.

Lasiacis swartziana Hitchc., Bot. Gaz. 51: 302. 1911.

Culms much branched, erect or clambering to a height of 5 to 7 m, the strong central cane as much as 1 cm thick, glabrous or pubescent, the main branches sometimes 1 m long or more, bearing slender branchlets toward the pendent ends, or the branchlets fascicled on the main culm; young shoots usually pubescent; sheaths pubescent, especially on the margin and collar, the surface sometimes glabrate; ligule inconspicuous; blades lanceolate or elliptic-lanceolate, those of the main culm or of vigorous shoots as much as 20 cm long and 3 cm wide, those of the fertile branches usually 8 to 12 cm long and 1.5 cm wide, on the fascicled branchlets smaller, often falcate, velvety on both surfaces or puberulent to glabrate above; panicles on the main culm and larger branches usually 10 to 20 cm long, at maturity as wide or wider, rather compactly many-flowered; spikelets 4 to 5 mm long.

Ravines, wood borders, and hedges, Mexico and West Indies to Argentina and Bolivia. Rather infrequent in Cuba, but there are numerous collections from the Greater Antilles, and the other islands except Trinidad, and at least one collection from Virgin Gorda, St. John, St. Croix, St. Thomas, St. Kitts, Antigua, Guadeloupe, Dominica, Montserrat, Martinique, St. Lucia, Grenada, and Tobago.

CUBA: Soledad, *Hitchcock* 23325. Rincón to Banao, *Shafer* 12323. Sierra de Nipe, *Ekman* 10095, 10108. Papayo, *Ekman* 10318. Pinar de Bayamita, Sierra Maestra, *Ekman* 10324. San Blas, *Jack* 6443. El Rosario, *Léon* 14118. Lomas de Siguanca, *Ekman* 13878.

Urban [72] takes up *Panicum maculatum* Aubl. for this species. Aublet's meager description [73] does not identify the plant. The synonym cited refers to an unpublished plate at Berlin which Urban states probably represents *Lasiacis sorghoidea.* The plate was based on a plant from Martinique. Aublet's flora treats of the plants of French Guiana.

11. **Lasiacis ruscifolia** (H. B. K.) Hitchc., Biol. Soc. Wash. Proc. 24: 145. 1911.

Panicum ruscifolium H. B. K., Nov. Gen. et Sp. 1: 101. 1815. Mexico.

Panicum compactum Swartz, Adnot. Bot. 14. 1829. Jamaica.

Lasiacis compacta Hitchc., Bot. Gaz. 51: 302. 1911.

More robust than any other species, freely branching, the shoots usually strongly dorsiventral; culms becoming several meters long, glabrous or rarely puberulent; sheaths sometimes hispidulous toward the apex, glabrous to villous on the margin, especially near the summit, the collar glabrous or villous; ligule inconspicuous; blades ovate-lanceolate or elliptic, sometimes lanceolate, the primary ones 10 to 15 cm long, 3 to 6 cm wide, narrowed or often cordate-clasping at the asymmetric base, rather abruptly narrowed to an acuminate but not attenuate apex, puberulent or glabrous beneath, glabrous or scabrous above, the secondary blades similar or reduced; panicles 5 to 20 cm long, narrow and compact, rarely somewhat open, with spreading, implicate but rather closely flowered branches; spikelets 3 to 4 mm long, nearly globose at maturity. This species is variable as to pubescence.

Climbing over bushes at low altitudes, Mexico to Peru; Cuba.

CUBA: Sabanaso, *Ekman* 6535. Palo Seco, *Ekman* 15318. Sancti Spíritus, *Léon* 905. Guantánamo, *Léon* 3778. Ensenada de Mora, *Britton, Cowell, and Shafer* 12979. Rioja, *Ekman* 4903. Santiago de

[72] Repert. Sp. Nov. Fedde 16: 149. 1919.
[73] Pl. Guian. 1: 51. 1775.

Cuba, *Ekman* 7681. Isla de Pinos, *Curtiss* 520; *Palmer and Riley* 904; *Britton and Wilson* 14659, 15065; *Ekman* 11721.

12. Lasiacis anomala Hitchc., Jour. Wash. Acad. Sci. 9: 37. 1919. Trinidad, *Amer. Gr. Nat. Herb.* 595.

Differing from *L. ruscifolia* in having a second sterile lemma.

This species has been confused with *L. ruscifolia* and was included under that name in Grasses of the West Indies, in which the following statement appears: "In all the Trinidad specimens the spikelets contain a second sterile lemma, a character not found in any other species known to us. This second sterile lemma equals the first, contains a hyaline palea, and infolds the fruit rather more closely than the sterile lemma commonly does in other species. The fruit borne one joint higher on the rachilla consequently faces in the direction opposite to the one usual in Paniceae; that is, the palea side of the fruit faces the second instead of the first glume." A reconsideration [74] of the group led the writer to the conclusion that, "we have here a distinct species, for not only is there this unusual character of a second sterile lemma but also a distinct geographical range. Of the group to which it had been referred, all the specimens from Trinidad, the lower Orinoco, and eastern Brazil have a second sterile lemma; outside of this range, that is, north and west, there is but one sterile lemma in all the specimens examined. In other respects, such as shape of blades and panicle, pubescence, and shape and size of spikelets, this species does not differ from *L. ruscifolia.* The specimens of *L. anomala* agree closely among themselves in all these characters, but also agree with many specimens referred to the more variable species, *L. ruscifolia.*"

Copses and edges of forests, Trinidad and Venezuela to eastern Brazil.

TRINIDAD: Moros, *Broadway* 7447. Chaguaramus, *Broadway* 6739, 7721. Lopinot Road, *Broadway* 6736. Chacachacare, *Hitchcock* 10063. Port-of-Spain, *Hitchcock* 9977 (*Amer. Gr. Nat. Herb.* 595), 10001. St. Joseph, *Hitchcock* 10021. San Fernando, *Hitchcock* 10117. Brighton, *Britton* 2905. Cedros, *Bot. Gard. Herb.* 7297; *Hitchcock* 10136. Moruga, *Broadway* 2504. Mayaro, *Broadway* 2627. Tetron Bay, *Broadway* 6775. Point Gourde, *Broadway* 8081, 8083. Without locality, *Eggers* 13480; *Broadway* 2564; *Bot. Gard. Herb.* 2303.

83. SACCIOLEPIS Nash, in Britton, Man. 89. 1901

Spikelets oblong-conic; first glume small, much shorter than the spikelet; second glume broad, inflated-saccate, strongly many-nerved; sterile lemma narrower, flat, fewer nerved, its palea nearly as long, often subtending a staminate flower; fertile lemma stipitate, elliptic, chartaceous-indurate, the margins inrolled, the palea not enclosed at the summit. Aquatic or subaquatic perennials or annuals, with dense narrow panicles.

Spikelets 4 mm long on slender pedicels .... 1. S. STRIATA.
Spikelets 2 to 3 mm long, subsessile.
  Spikelets 3 mm long; panicle often interrupted .... 2. S. VILVOIDES.
  Spikelets 2 mm long; panicle dense .... 3. S. MYUROS.

[74] Jour. Wash. Acad. Sci. 9: 37. 1919.

1. **Sacciolepis striata** (L.) Nash, Bull. Torrey Bot. Club 30: 383. 1903.

Holcus striatus L., Sp. Pl. 1048. 1753. Virginia.
Panicum striatum Lam., Tabl. Encycl. 1: 172. 1791.
Hymenachne striata Griseb., Fl. Brit. W. Ind. 554. 1864.

Aquatic or semiaquatic perennial, glabrous or the sheaths sometimes pubescent; culms 1 to 2 m tall, rooting at the geniculate lower nodes, bearing a few erect flowering shoots; blades flat, linear-lanceolate, 8 to 15 cm long, 5 to 10 mm wide; panicles 10 to 15 cm long, the branches appressed, or the lower somewhat spreading, as much as 5 cm long; spikelets glabrous, about 3.5 mm long, the pedicels slender, flexuous or curved (fig. 291, *A*).

Swamps and ditches, southeastern United States and the West Indies.

CUBA: Pinar del Río, *Wright* 3885. Herradura, *Ekman* 10747. San Fran-

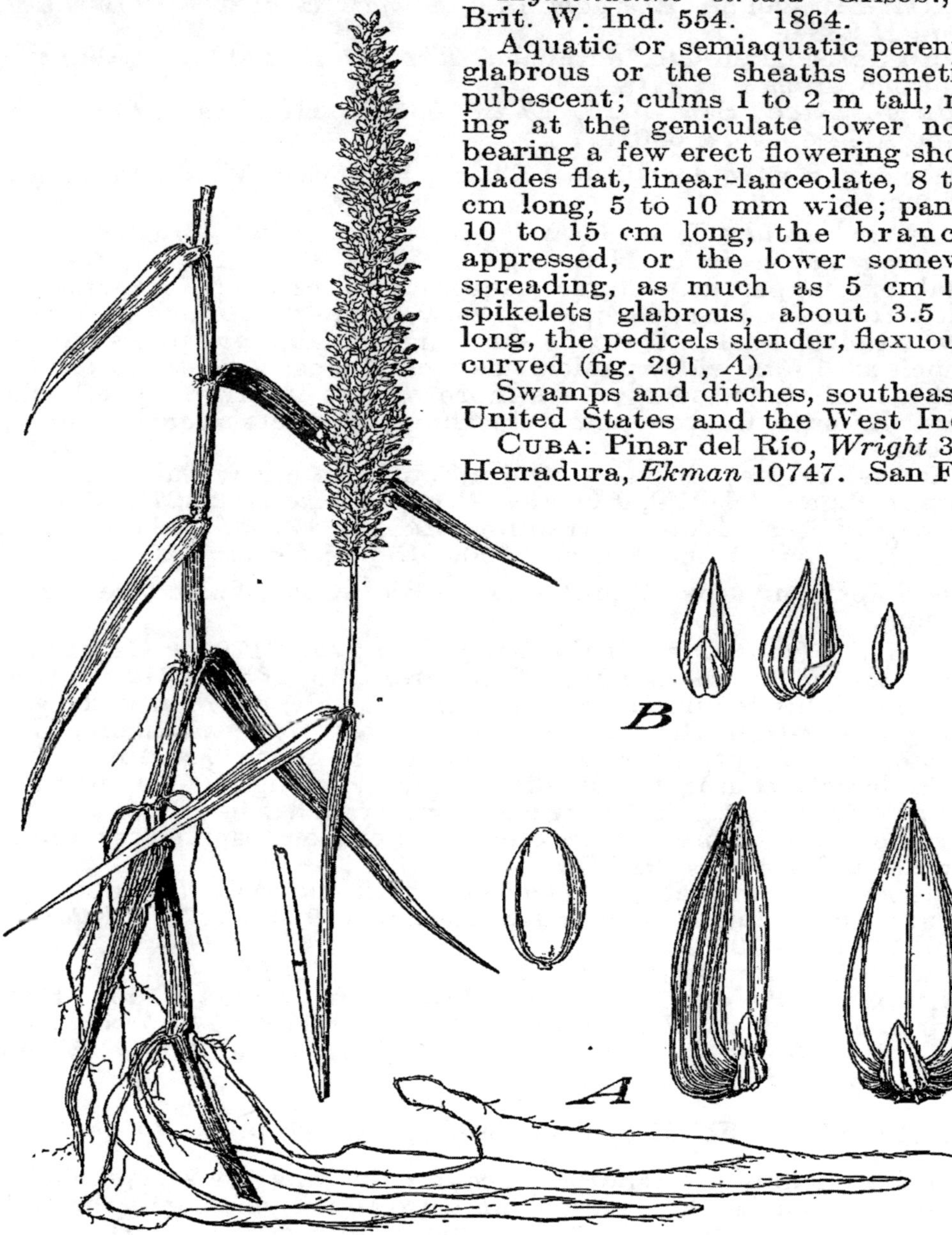

FIGURE 291.—*A*, *Sacciolepis striata*. Plant, × ½; two views of spikelet and floret, × 10 (Chase 4240). *B*, *S. myuros*, × 10 (type).

cisco, *Ekman* 10984. Remates, *Ekman* 11173. Laguna de Ariguanabo, *Ekman* 11512. Habana, *Léon* 5750. Cayo La Rosa, *Ekman* in 1921 (*Amer. Gr. Nat. Herb.* 993). Ciénaga de Zapata, *Léon* 9520. Isla de Pinos, *Ekman* 12426.

JAMAICA: Grasmond Marsh, *Harris* 11749.

HAITI: Miragoane, *Eyerdam* 168; *Ekman* H 6527. Port-Margot, *Ekman* H 2884.

DOMINICAN REPUBLIC: Jarabaco, *Ekman* H 14141. Sabana del Guabatico, *Ekman* H 11049.

PUERTO RICO: San Juan, *Chase* 6353. Humacao, *Eggers* 666. Campo Alegre, *Chase* 6801.

2. **Sacciolepis vilvoides** (Trin.) Chase, Biol. Soc. Wash. Proc. 21: 7. 1908.

Panicum vilvoides Trin., Gram. Pan. 171. 1826. Brazil.

Hymenachne fluviatilis Nees, Agrost. Bras. 273. 1829. Brazil.

Glabrous, apparently annual; aquatic; culms erect, branched only slightly from the base, succulent below, usually as much as 1 m tall or even taller; blades 15 to 20 cm long, usually narrow, sometimes as much as 5 mm wide; panicles elongate, mostly 20 to 40 cm long, about 8 mm thick, compact or more or less interrupted, especially toward the base, the branches very short; spikelets about 3 mm long, glabrous.

Marshes and wet places, northern South America; Cuba.

CUBA: Pinar del Río, *Ekman* 17917; *Hitchcock* 23276. Los Almacigos, *Wright* 3470. Herradura, *Ekman* 17793. Isla de Pinos, *Curtiss* 304; *Britton and Wilson* 15009, 15679; *Ekman* 12210.

3. **Sacciolepis myuros** (Lam.) Chase, Biol. Soc. Wash. Proc. 21: 7. 1908.

Panicum myuros Lam., Tabl. Encycl. 1: 172. 1791. Cayenne.

Hymenachne myuros Beauv., Ess. Agrost. 49, 165. 1812.

Slender glabrous annual as much as 1 m tall; culms usually erect, branched only from the base, the lower part often succulent; blades elongate, erect, flat, narrow, sometimes as much as 7 mm wide; panicles erect, compact, spikelike, usually elongate, sometimes as much as 40 cm long, 3 to 5 mm wide, the branches usually very short, rarely the lower (appressed) as much as 3 cm long; spikelets glabrous, 1.5 to 2 mm long (fig. 291, *B*).

Marshes and wet places, Mexico to Brazil and Bolivia; Cuba.

CUBA: Isla de Pinos, *Curtiss* 428; *Ekman* 11980, 12176; *Britton and Wilson* 14155, 14709.

DOMINICAN REPUBLIC: Cuenca, *Ekman* H 10971.

TRINIDAD: O'Meara Savanna, *Britton and Hazen* 1566. Piarco Savanna, *Britton and Hazen* 712; *Broadway* 2142; *Hitchcock* 10356. Pitch Lake, *Hitchcock* 10085 (*Amer. Gr. Nat. Herb.* 303). Without locality, *Bot. Gard. Herb.* 3354.

84. HYMENACHNE Beauv., Ess. Agrost. 48. pl. 10. f. 8. 1812

Spikelets acuminate, short-pedicellate in long dense spikelike or interrupted panicles; first glume one-third to half as long as the spikelet, remote, a distinct stipe below the second glume; sterile lemma 5-nerved, acuminate, exceeding the lanceolate stramineous fruit; lemma and palea membranaceous, the margins of the lemma thin (not broad and hyaline), not inrolled; palea not enclosed above. Aquatic perennials with succulent sparingly branching culms, flat blades, and soft dense panicles.

Inflorescence dense, spikelike .... 1. H. AMPLEXICAULIS.
Inflorescence long and narrow with ascending branches, not spikelike.
2. H. DONACIFOLIA.

1. **Hymenachne amplexicaulis** (Rudge) Nees, Agrost. Bras. 276. 1829.

Panicum amplexicaule Rudge, Pl. Guian. 1: 21. pl. 27. 1805. British Guiana.

Agrostis monostachya Poir., in Lam., Encycl. Sup. 1: 256. 1810. Puerto Rico.

Panicum hymenachne Desv., Opusc. 82. 1831. Puerto Rico.

Culms commonly 1 m or more tall; blades 20 to 35 cm long, 2 to 3 cm wide, cordate-clasping; panicles about 8 mm thick and 20 to 50 cm long; spikelets acuminate, 3 to 4 mm long (fig. 292).

Marshes and shallow water, often forming pure colonies, Tropics of both hemispheres. Common on all the Greater Antilles and Trinidad. Specimens have been seen also from Guadeloupe, Dominica, Martinique, and St. Lucia. Grisebach[75] misapplies the name *Hymenachne myurus* to this species.

2. **Hymenachne donacifolia** (Raddi) Chase, Jour. Wash. Acad. Sci. 13: 177. 1923.

Panicum donacifolium Raddi, Agrost. Bras. 44. 1823. Brazil.

Panicum auriculatum Willd., in Spreng., Syst. Veg. 1: 322. 1825. Tropical America.

Hymenachne patula Fourn., Mex. Pl. 2: 37. 1886. Cuba, *Liebmann* 402.

Hymenachne auriculata Chase, Biol. Soc. Wash. Proc. 21: 5. 1908.

Similar to *H. amplexicaulis*, olivaceous throughout (at least when dry); panicles of numerous ascending, densely flowered branches, the lower distant; spikelets about 3 mm long.

Marshes and shallow water, Panama to Brazil; Cuba.

CUBA: Mendoza, *Ekman* 11481, 11492. Habana, *Léon* 808. Between La Mulata and Las Posas, *Ekman* 17368.

TRINIDAD: St. Francique, *Broadway* 4978. Oropuche Lagoon, *Britton, Hazen, and Freeman* 1149. Without locality, *Bot. Gard. Herb.* 3355.

85. SCUTACHNE Hitchc. and Chase, Biol. Soc. Wash. Proc. 24: 148. 1911

Inflorescence paniculate, the spikelets short-pediceled along the slender, simple or nearly simple branches; spikelets fusiform, acuminate, the base attenuate, the internodes of the rachilla elongate, the lowermost forming a stipe, the first glume adnate to it; first glume membranaceous, about half the length of the spikelet, broad, the margins connate below; second glume and sterile lemma subequal, a manifest internode of the rachilla between them, leathery-indurate, brown or brownish, 5-nerved, the lemma enclosing a palea of similar texture (and in *S. dura* a staminate flower); fruit but slightly more indurate than the second glume and sterile lemma, elliptic in outline,

[75] Fl. Brit. W. Ind. 553. 1864.

FIGURE 292.—*Hymenachne amplexicaulis*, × ½ (Chase 6317).

the lemma abruptly acuminate into a slender, densely pubescent tip, the margins slightly inrolled below, membranaceous, flat and pubescent above, the summit of the palea not enclosed, densely pubescent on the margin. Tufted wiry perennials with firm blades.

Culms leafy, the blades elongate; panicles terminal only, of several branches.
1. S. DURA.

Culms nearly naked, the leaves reduced to the sheaths or nearly so, the basal leaves with blades; panicles terminal and axillary, simple.
2. S. AMPHISTEMON.

1. Scutachne dura (Griseb.) Hitchc. and Chase, Biol. Soc. Wash. Proc. 24: 149. 1911.

Panicum durum Griseb., Mem. Amer. Acad. (n. s.) 8: 533. 1862. Cuba, *Wright* 1539.

Alloteropsis dura Hitchc., Contrib. U. S. Natl. Herb. 12: 211. 1909.

Culms erect, 40 to 70 cm tall, the nodes glabrous or puberulent; blades flat or more or less involute, rather stiff, sharply acuminate, elongate, usually 4 to 6 mm wide, sometimes as much as 10 mm wide; panicles 6 to 10 cm long, the branches ascending; spikelets elliptic, attenuate at base, acute, about 5 mm long, the glabrous first glume a lighter color than the brown pubescent second glume and sterile lemma (fig. 293).

Rocky hills, Cuba, Jamaica, and Hispaniola.

Cuba: Río Taco Taco, *Ekman* 17624. Pastelillo, *Ekman* 15406, 15433, in 1922 (*Amer. Gr. Nat. Herb.* 995). "Farallones, N. Sophie", *Wright* 1539. Valestina, *Wright* 3868. Baconao, *Ekman* 8229. Guantánamo, *Ekman* in 1922 (*Amer. Gr. Nat. Herb.* 996), 2893, 15770.

Jamaica: Albion Mountain, St. Thomas, *Harris* 12163.

Haiti: St. Marc, *Leonard* 2923. Môle-St.-Nicolas, *Leonard* 13187. Port-á-Piment, *Ekman* H 322. Morne-à-Cabrits, *Ekman* H 898.

Dominican Republic: Barahona, *Fuertes* 1423, 1426. San Juan, *Ekman* H 13478.

2. Scutachne amphistemon (Wright) Hitchc. and Chase, Biol. Soc. Wash. Proc. 24: 149. 1911.

Panicum amphistemon Wright, An. Acad. Cien. Habana 8: 207. 1871. Cuba, *Wright* 3464.

Alloteropsis amphistemon Hitchc., Contrib. U. S. Natl. Herb. 12: 211. 1909.

Culms tufted, slender, 25 to 40 cm tall; leaves clustered at the base; blades glabrous, thick, erect, flat or folded, 10 to 20 cm long, 2 to 4 mm wide; panicles narrow, few-flowered, 3 to 8 cm long; spikelets nearly glabrous, 7 to 8 mm long.

Rocky slopes, Cuba.

Cuba: San Miguel de los Baños, *Léon* 8855. Canasí, *Ekman* 17103. Ponce, *Ekman* 17168. Tiffin, *Ekman* 15381. Pastelillo, *Ekman* 15434. Mayarí Abajo, *Wright* 3464. Sierra de Nipe, *Ekman* in 1922 (*Amer. Gr. Nat. Herb.* 994), 15162. Holguín, *Ekman* 15727. Jauco, *Léon* 12300.

86. ISACHNE R. Br., Prodr. Fl. Nov. Holl. 196. 1810

Spikelets obovoid to subglobose; glumes membranaceous, about equal and as long as the fruits or at maturity exceeded by them; lower floret perfect or staminate, its lemma and palea indurate and similar in form and texture to those of the upper floret; both florets (or fruits) plano-convex, obtuse, equal in size or the upper shorter, the pair usually remaining attached by the minute rachilla joint between them. Mostly perennials with firm blades and open or contracted panicles. *Isachne polygonoides* is exceptional in that the lower floret is unlike the upper. In all the species the lower floret of some of the spikelets may fail to perfect a grain. When sterile the

FIGURE 293.—*Scutachne dura*. Plant, × ½; spikelet and floret, × 10 (Fuertes 1423).

floret is often longer and the lemma less convex than when fertile, the spikelets on the same panicle thus having a somewhat diverse appearance.

Florets appressed-pubescent.
  Blades ovate-clasping ---------------------------------- 1. I. POLYGONOIDES.
  Blades linear -- 2. I. LEERSIOIDES.
Florets glabrous, or the palea minutely hispidulous.
  Panicle contracted, spikelike, not more than 3 cm long, the branches appressed or the lower sometimes ascending; plants low and spreading -- 3. I. PYGMAEA.
  Panicle open, the branches spreading or ascending.
    Blades about 3 mm wide, thick, rigid, pungent, with conspicuously thickened midrib -- 4. I. RIGIDIFOLIA.
    Blades mostly 5 to 20 mm wide, firm but not pungent nor with thickened midrib.
      Plants trailing; blades rarely more than 5 cm long -------- 5. I. RIGENS.
      Plants clambering; blades mostly more than 5 cm long.
        Glumes pubescent; blades firm, not more than 12 cm long and 1 cm wide ---------------------------------- 6. I. ANGUSTIFOLIA.
        Glumes glabrous (rarely obscurely pubescent at the tips); blades mostly more than 15 cm long and 1.5 cm wide.
          Spikelets aggregate toward the ends of the branches and branchlets. 7. I. ARUNDINACEA.
          Spikelets not aggregate; panicle loosely flowered ---- 8. I. DISPERMA.

1. Isachne polygonoides (Lam.) Doell, in Mart., Fl. Bras. 2^2: 273. 1877.

Panicum polygonoides Lam., Encycl. 4: 742. 1798. Cayenne.

Apparently annual; flowering shoots 20 to 30 cm tall, erect from a long creeping, freely branching culm, rooting at the nodes, the whole plant often a meter in length, the erect shoots finally bearing fascicled branchlets; sheaths hispid; blades spreading, lanceolate-ovate, very scabrous; panicles included at base, about 5 cm long and as broad, loosely many-flowered.

This is distinguished from all others of the West Indies by the ovate clasping blades and by the dissimilarity of the two florets.

Moist ground, often in water, British Honduras and Guatemala to Trinidad and Brazil; Cuba, Hispaniola.

CUBA: Isla de Pinos, *Ekman* 11702.

DOMINICAN REPUBLIC: Cotuy, *Abbott* 748. Jarabaco, *Ekman* H 14139. Villa Altagracia, *Ekman* H 11222. Sánchez, *Ekman* H 14718. Tomas, *Ekman* H 13020.

TRINIDAD: Piarco Savanna, *Britton and Hazen* 704; *Hitchcock* 10362 (*Amer. Gr. Nat. Herb.* 598).

In the Florence Herbarium there is a specimen of this species said to be collected by LeDru in Puerto Rico. No other specimen from that island has been seen.

2. Isachne leersioides Griseb., Mem. Amer. Acad. (n. s.) 8: 533. 1862. Cuba, *Wright* 755.

Culms slender, branched, trailing, glabrous, striate, 1 to 2 m long; sheaths on the main culms much shorter than the elongate internodes, overlapping on the flowering branches, appressed papillose-hispid or nearly glabrous; ligule a very short membrane, ciliate with stiff hairs about 1 mm long; blades linear, ascending, rather firm, 5 to 15 cm long, 0.5 to 4 mm wide, long-acuminate, cartilaginous-margined, scabrous or hispidulous on both surfaces; panicles terminating the branches, ovoid or oblong, 5 to 15 cm long, as much as 7 cm wide, the branches mostly single, rather stiffly ascending or spreading, bearing from near the base stiffly spreading branchlets, the spreading pedicels 2 to 3 mm long; spikelets about 1 mm long; glumes hispidulous; florets appressed-pubescent.

Dry cliffs, slopes, and pine barrens, Cuba.

CUBA: Cajálbana, *Léon* 4843. San Diego de los Baños, *Léon* 5078. Bahía Honda, *Ekman* 12678. Zaza de Tunas, *Léon* 6730. Sancti Spíritus Mountains, *Léon* 6520. La Perla, *Shafer* 3013, 8561. Sierra Maestra, *Ekman* 1633. Baracoa, *Ekman* 3981. Guara, *Hitchcock* 23403, 23413. Eastern Cuba, *Wright* 755.

3. **Isachne pygmaea** Griseb., Fl. Brit. W. Ind. 553. 1864. Jamaica, *Macfayden*.

Plants low, the slender branches spreading, glabrous, the flowering shoots usually less than 15 cm tall, rarely as much as 30 cm long; sheaths glabrous, ciliate on the margins; ligule a very short hispidulous ring; blades narrowly oblong-lanceolate, 0.5 to 2 cm, or rarely 3 cm, long, rarely more than 2 mm wide, spreading, glabrous or puberulent, the white cartilaginous margin somewhat scabrous; panicles long-exserted, narrow, compact and spikelike, usually less than 2 cm long, the lower branches short and somewhat distant, appressed or rarely ascending; spikelets about 1.3 mm long, nearly sessile; glumes glabrous, about two-thirds as long as the spikelet; florets glabrous.

Grassy banks. This grass has a very limited distribution, being known only from a small area in the Blue Mountains of Jamaica between Newcastle and Cinchona, at about 1,500 m altitude.

JAMAICA: Vinegar Hill, *Perkins* 1085. Cold Spring Gap, *Hitchcock* 9742 (*Amer. Gr. Nat. Herb.* 419); *Harris* 11314, 12490. Moodys Gap, *Britton* 3375. Arntully, *Orcutt* 5756.

4. **Isachne rigidifolia** (Poir.) Urban, Symb. Antill. 4: 85. 1903.

Agrostis rigidifolia Poir., in Lam., Encycl. Sup. 1: 257. 1810. Santo Domingo.

Milium rigidifolium Roem. and Schult., Syst. Veg. 2: 319. 1817.

Panicum rigidifolium Kunth, Rév. Gram. 1: 37. 1829.

Culms spreading and branching, the flowering shoots firm and rigid, 15 to 40 cm tall; sheaths glabrous, stiffly ciliate on the margin, overlapping on the flowering shoots; ligule a very short, lacerate or ciliate membrane; blades oblong, 2 to 4 cm long, 2 to 4 mm wide, firm, rigidly spreading, pungently pointed, glabrous, the cartilaginous margin and thick midrib whitish; panicles long-exserted, open, oblong, rather narrow, 2 to 5 cm long, the branches ascending or spreading, bearing the branchlets mostly on the lower side, the pedicels rigid, 1 to 2 mm long; spikelets about 2 mm long, purplish, borne obliquely upon the pedicels; glumes glabrous or sparsely appressed-hispidulous near apex; florets smooth.

The species is easily recognized by its smooth, rigid, spreading, pungently pointed, conspicuously distichous blades.

Mountain bogs and limestone ridges, West Indies.

CUBA: Sierra del Cristal, *Ekman* 6839.

HAITI: Mission, *Leonard* 3829, 3890. Furcy, *Leonard* 4324, 4569. Pérodin, *Ekman* H 3473. Pétionville, *Ekman* H 1437. Petite Goave, *Ekman* H 7311.

DOMINICAN REPUBLIC: Río Yague, *Fuertes* 1729. Lagunas de Cenobí, *Valeur* 29. Loma Diego de Ocampo, *Ekman* H 16326. San José de Ocoa, *Ekman* H 11872.

LEEWARD ISLANDS: Guadeloupe *Duss* 3190. St. Kitts, *Box* 313.
WINDWARD ISLANDS: Martinique, *Hahn* 1435; *Duss* 1312.

5. Isachne rigens (Swartz) Trin., Gram. Pan. 252. 1826.

Panicum rigens Swartz, Prodr. Veg. Ind. Occ. 23. 1788. Jamaica.

Culms tufted, glabrous, slender, wiry, trailing, 1 to 2 m long, as much as 2 mm thick, the numerous flowering shoots curving upward, 10 to 30 cm long; sheaths glabrous or puberulent, ciliate on the margin; ligule a ring of stiff hairs about 0.5 mm long; blades narrowly oblong-lanceolate 2 to 5 cm long, 2 to 5 mm wide, spreading, moderately, firm but not stiff and rigid, scabrous on both surfaces and on the cartilaginous margin; panicles ovoid or oblong, 2 to 5 cm long, the branches and branchlets stiffly ascending or spreading, the pedicels 1 to 2 mm long; spikelets 1.8 to 2 mm long; glumes minutely hispidulous; rachilla between the two florets minutely villous; palea of upper floret sparsely appressed-hispidulous.

Damp shady banks, Blue Mountains, Jamaica, at 1,000 to 2,000 m altitude; Venezuela to Ecuador.

JAMAICA: St. Helens Gap, *Maxon and Killip* 614. Catherines Peak, *Hitchcock* 9732. Abbey Green, *Hitchcock* 9362; *Harris* 11585. Cinchona, *Harris* 11316, 11333, 11417, 11432, 12480; *Hitchcock* 9706 (*Amer. Gr. Nat. Herb.* 420), Sir Johns Peak, *Harris* 11595. Hardware Gap, *Harris* 11543. Clyde River, *Harris* 11445. Cold Spring Gap, *Harris* 11336, 12489.

6. Isachne angustifolia Nash, Bull. Torrey Bot. Club 30: 377. 1903. Puerto Rico, *Wilson* 160.

Culms clambering, as much as 2 m long and 2 mm thick, hard and wiry, with a long naked base, branching from the upper nodes, the branches long, leafy, nearly parallel, bearing secondary branches toward the ends, the whole forming a wide, flabellate or loosely corymbose mass, in its most characteristic development pushing through the jungle of stream bank or trail side and hanging over bushes; sheaths appressed papillose-pilose or roughened with papillae, or glabrous, the margin ciliate; ligule a ring of very short stiff hairs less than 0.5 mm long; blades narrowly lanceolate, 3 to 15 cm long, but mostly more than 5 cm long, 5 to 12 mm wide, rather firm and stiffly spreading, scaberulous or glabrate, papillose-ciliate at base or papillose only; panicles ellipsoid or oblong, as much as 15 cm long, the branches stiffly ascending or finally spreading, the branchlets and pedicels finally divaricate, these and the main axis scabrous; spikelets about 1.5 mm long; glumes minutely hispidulous toward the tip; florets and rachilla glabrous.

Rocky slopes among brush, Puerto Rico and Leeward Islands.

PUERTO RICO: El Yunque, *Wilson* 160; *Sintenis* 1355. Sierra Loquillo, *Hioram* 369. Adjuntas, *Sintenis* 4045. Rio Icaco, *Shafer* 3477. Utuado, *Sintenis* 6421. Monte Torrecilla, *Britton, Cowell, and Brown* 5595. Cayey, *Chase* 6750. Maricao, *Britton and Cowell* 4271; *Britton, Stevens, and Hess* 2566; *Chase* 6222.

LEEWARD ISLANDS: Guadeloupe, *Duss* 2705. St. Kitts, *Box* 146, 314.

7. Isachne arundinacea (Swartz) Griseb., Fl. Brit. W. Ind. 553. 1864.

Panicum arundinaceum Swartz, Prodr. Veg. Ind. Occ. 24. 1788. Jamaica.

Culms climbing among shrubs or small trees to a height of as much as 6 m, as much as 5 mm thick at base, with strong canes and elongate branches; sheaths glabrous, or rarely slightly scabrous, ciliate on the margin, sometimes a little papillose near the summit, overlapping on the flowering shoots; ligule of stiff hairs as much as 5 mm long; blades narrowly lanceolate, as much as 20 cm long and 2 cm wide, long-acuminate, scabrous, sometimes becoming smoothish, often papillose on the margin at base; panicles ovoid or ellipsoid, as much as 12 cm long and 10 cm wide, rounded at summit, the branches ascending or the lower finally spreading, branched from about the middle, the spikelets somewhat aggregate on the branchlets, the panicle thus rather compactly flowered at the periphery, the pedicels 0.5 to 2 mm long; spikelets about 1.5 mm long; glumes glabrous or with a few short stiff hairs at the summit; florets glabrous (fig. 294).

Wooded hillsides, Jamaica, at 1,000 to 2,000 m altitude; Mexico to Bolivia and Trinidad.

JAMAICA: Catherines Peak, *Hitchcock* 9728 (*Amer. Gr. Nat. Herb.* 418); *Eggers* 3583. Hardware Gap, *Ridley* 14. Track to Mabess River, *Perkins* 1089. Mount Lebanon, *Harris* 12487. Bryans Hill, *Harris* 11529. Content Gap, *Harris* 11517. Wallenford, *Harris* 11551, 11567. Cuna Cuna Gap, *Maxon* 9160. Morces Gap, *Maxon and Killip* 745. Abbey Green, *Hitchcock* 9386. Cold Spring Gap, *Harris* 11337, 12491. Flamstead, *Harris* 11468, 11581. Whitfield Hall, *Harris* 11583. Farm Hill, *Orcutt* 3679. Gordon Town, *Hart* 708.

LEEWARD ISLANDS: St. Kitts, *Box* 152. Nevis, *Box* 169.

TRINIDAD: Blanchisseuse Road, *Broadway* 6746.

8. Isachne disperma (Lam.) Doell, in Mart., Fl. Bras. 2²: 274. 1877.

Panicum dispermum Lam., Tabl. Encycl. 1: 173. 1791. Tropical America.

Panicum multinerve Desv.; Poir., in Lam., Encycl. Sup. 4: 279. 1816. Antilles.

Panicum confertum Desv.; Poir., in Lam., Encycl. Sup. 4: 279. 1816. Antilles.

Aspect of plant as in *I. arundinacea;* sheaths glabrous or rarely papillose-hispidulous; ligule hairs as much as 2 mm long; blades on the average larger than in *I. arundinacea,* glabrous, scabrous toward the apex; panicles as much as 20 cm long, the branches and branchlets spreading, the spikelets in twos or threes at the ends of the branchlets, the panicle thus more open and flowered more equally throughout than in *I. arundinacea,* the spikelets not strongly aggregate toward the periphery; spikelets slightly over 1 mm long; glumes and florets glabrous.

Mountain woods, Lesser Antilles.

LEEWARD ISLANDS: St. Kitts, *Britton and Cowell* 395. Guadeloupe, *Duss* 3189. Dominica, *Jones* 38; *Eggers* 1056.

WINDWARD ISLANDS: Martinique, *Duss* 1311. Grenada, *Broadway* 76.

TOBAGO: *Hitchcock* 10279 (*Amer. Gr. Nat. Herb.* 597).

87. OPLISMENUS Beauv., Fl. Owar. 2: 14. pl. 68. f. 1. 1809

Spikelets terete or somewhat laterally compressed, subsessile, solitary or in pairs, in two rows, crowded or approximate on one side of a narrow scabrous or hairy rachis; glumes about equal, emarginate or 2-lobed, awned from between the lobes; sterile lemma exceeding the glumes and fruit, mucronate or short-awned, enclosing a hyaline palea; fertile lemma elliptic, acute, convex or boat-shaped, the firm margins clasping the palea, not inrolled. Freely branching, creeping,

FIGURE 294.—*Isachne arundinacea*, × ½ (Hitchcock 9728, Amer. Gr. Nat. Herb. 418).

shade-loving annuals or perennials, with erect flowering shoots, flat, thin, lanceolate or ovate acuminate blades, and several one-sided, thickish, short racemes rather distant on a main axis.

Awns antrorsely scabrous; racemes villous with long hairs; plants annual.
1. O. BURMANNI.
Awns smooth or obscurely roughened; racemes not villous or with a few long hairs only; plants perennial.
Rachis of racemes mostly 2 to 3 mm long, bearing usually not more than 5 spikelets; blades 1 to 3 cm long, 4 to 10 mm wide------2. O. SETARIUS.
Rachis of lower racemes more than 1 cm long, bearing usually more than 8 spikelets; blades mostly more than 4 cm long, 1 to 2 cm wide.
3. O. HIRTELLUS.

1. Oplismenus burmanni (Retz.) Beauv., Ess. Agrost. 54. 1812.

Panicum burmanni Retz., Obs. Bot. 3: 10. 1783. India.

Orthopogon burmanni Trin., Fund. Agrost. 181. 1820.

Low, creeping, freely branching annual; sheaths pilose; blades broadly lanceolate-elliptic; racemes 3 to 5, pale villous, ascending, approximate along a flexuous axis; awns slender, about 1 cm long.

Waste places, open ground, and partial shade, a common weed at low altitudes in the Tropics of both hemispheres, introduced in North America. Cuba and Hispaniola.

CUBA: Papayo, *Ekman* 10335.

HAITI: Pétionville, *Ekman* H 2346. St. Michel de l'Atalaye, *Leonard* 7224, 7542. Furcy, *Leonard* 4343, 4645.

DOMINICAN REPUBLIC: Ocoa, *Tuerckheim* 3610. Constanza, *Tuerckheim* 2883. Majagüitas, *Ekman* H 13626.

2. Oplismenus setarius (Lam.) Roem. and Schult., Syst. Veg. 2: 481. 1817.

Panicum setarium Lam., Tabl. Encycl. 1: 170. 1791. Tropical America.

Orthopogon setarius Spreng., Syst. Veg. 1: 306. 1825.

Slender creeping branching perennial, the ascending flowering culms 20 to 30 cm high; blades 1 to 3 cm long, 4 to 10 mm wide, conspicuously undulate-margined; racemes distant, very short, the spikelets appearing to be in clusters on the rather strict axis; awns 4 to 8 mm long (fig. 295).

Shady places, southern United States, Mexico, and the West Indies to Paraguay.

BERMUDA: *Brown and Britton* 13; *Harris* 424; *Collins* 150.

BAHAMAS: *Britton* 3200.

CUBA: Pinar del Río, *Hitchcock* 23311, 23316. Cojimar River, *Léon* 4720. Campo Florido, *Léon* 4139. Caibarién, *Fernando* 141. Sierra Maestra, *Léon* 10380. Bayate, *Ekman* 3411. Guara, *Hitchcock* 23401. Prov. Santa Clara, *Jack* 6351. Eastern Cuba, *Wright* 1543.

JAMAICA: Troy, *Hitchcock* 9783; *Maxon* 2951; *Harris* 12577. Clyde River, *Harris* 11446. Bryans Hill, *Harris* 6826. Hardware Gap, *Harris* 11843. Stony Hill, *Harris* 11339. Mount Hybla, *Harris* 11307. Kingston, *Hitchcock* 9468. Claremont, *Hitchcock* 9521. Abbey Green, *Hitchcock* 9358. Castleton, *Harris* 11342; *Hitchcock* 9388 (*Amer. Gr. Nat. Herb.* 600). Savanna-la-Mar, *Hitchcock* 9871. Barican, *Hitchcock* 9568. Montego Bay, *Hitchcock* 9681. Ipswich, *Hitchcock* 9621. Newcastle, *Hitchcock* 9337. Ewarton, *Hitchcock* 9415. Catherines Peak, *Hitchcock* 9731, 9737. Blue Hole, *Fredholm* 3196. Ferry, *Ridley* 56. Roaring River Falls, *Ridley* 54. Farm Hill, *Orcutt* 3701. Content Gap, *Harris* 11364. Gordon Town, *Hart* 578.

HAITI: St. Michel de l'Atalaye, *Leonard* 7010, 7265, 7808. Marmelade, *Leonard* 8414. Plaisance, *Leonard* 9238. Port-au-Prince, *Ekman* H 9106. St. Louis du Nord, *Leonard* 14130. Port-de-Pai,

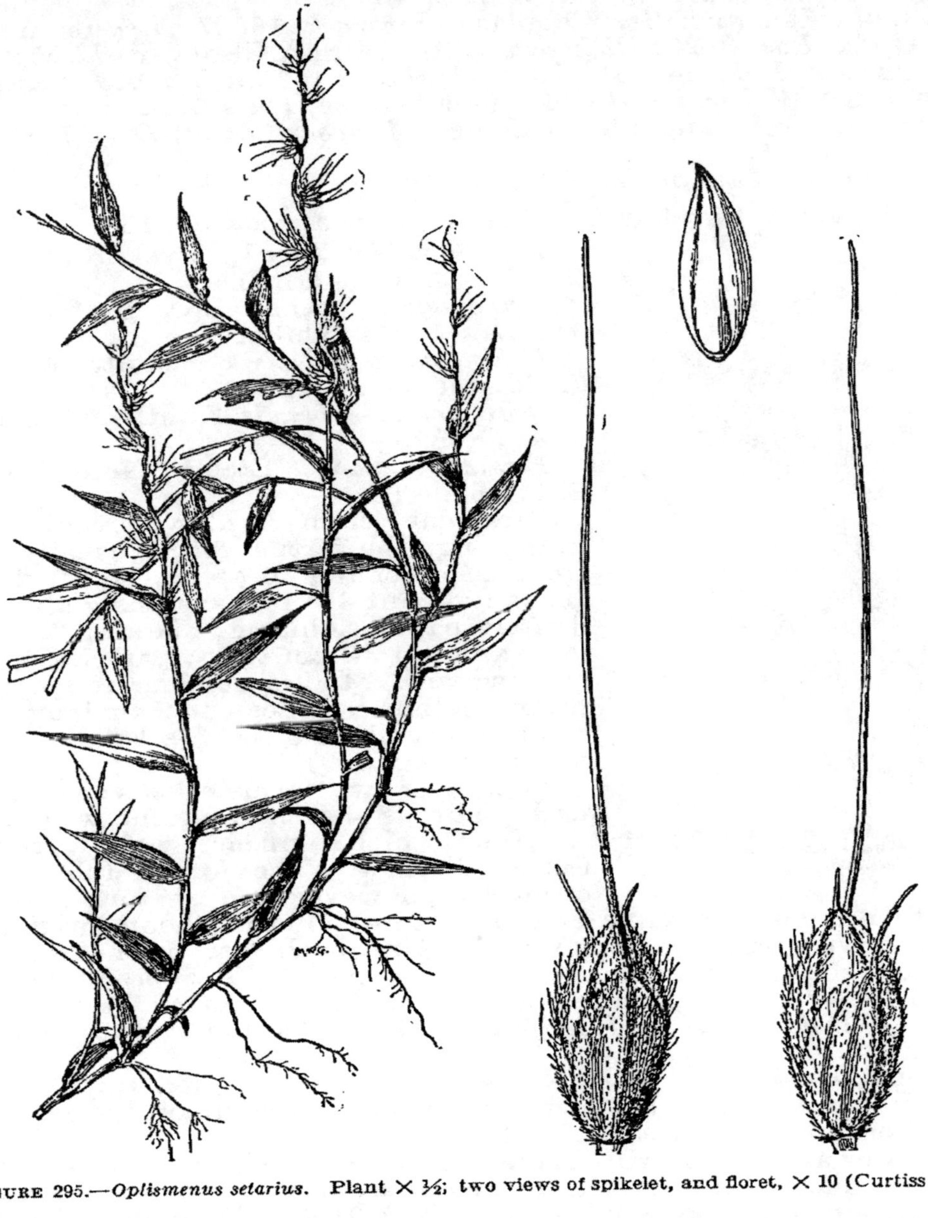

FIGURE 295.—*Oplismenus setarius.* Plant × ½; two views of spikelet, and floret, × 10 (Curtiss 5553).

Leonard 12132. Fond Parisien, *Leonard* 4217. Tortue Island, *Leonard* 11458. Gonaïve Island, *Leonard* 3038.

DOMINICAN REPUBLIC: Rincón, *Fuertes* 1282. Las Lagunas, *Ekman* H 16209. Sabaneta, *Valeur* 482.

PUERTO RICO: Mayaguez, *Holm* 124; *Sintenis* 72b. Cayey, *Sintenis* 2225, 2286. Rio Grande, *Chase* 6721. Vega Baja, *Chase* 6413. Arecibo, *Chase* 6556. Vieques Island, *Chase* 6682; *Shafer* 2626. Culebra, *Britton and Wheeler* 106.

VIRGIN ISLANDS: St. Thomas, *Hitchcock* 16307; *Eggers* in 1881. St. Croix, *Rose* 3625; *Ricksecker* 250. Virgin Gorda, *Fishlock* 116.

LEEWARD ISLANDS: St. Kitts, *Hitchcock* 16355; *Box* 143. Antigua, *Rose* 3485; *Wullschlaegel* 626. Guadeloupe, *Duss* 2714.

WINDWARD ISLANDS: Martinique, *Hitchcock* 16450; *Duss* 7786. St. Lucia, *Kemp* 55.

TRINIDAD: Tabaquite, *Hitchcock* 10126.

3. Oplismenus hirtellus (L.) Beauv., Ess. Agrost. 54, 168. 1812.

Panicum hirtellum L., Syst. Nat. ed. 10. 2: 870. 1759. Jamaica.

Orthopogon cubensis Spreng., Syst. Veg. 1: 307. 1825. Cuba.

Echinochloa cubensis Schult., Mant. 3 (Add. 1): 596. [1827.]

Oplismenus cubensis Kunth, Rév. Gram. 1: 45. 1829.

Panicum cubense Steud., Nom. Bot. ed. 2. 2: 255. 1841.

FIGURE 296.—*Oplismenus hirtellus*, × 1 (Hitchcock 10005, Amer. Gr. Nat. Herb. 602).

Perennial; culms widely creeping and branching, the fertile culms usually erect from an ascending base, 20 to 70 cm tall (usually about 30 cm); sheaths glabrous to densely papillose-hispid; blades 5 to 10 cm long and 1 to 2 cm wide; panicles 5 to 10 cm long with 3 to 7 ascending or spreading rather distant racemes 1 to 2 cm long; awns smooth, usually purple, the longer 5 to 10 mm long (fig. 296).

There are two forms of this species, one with glabrous sheaths and one with hispid sheaths, which appear, when growing, rather distinct. The forms differ in no other way, however, and are found growing together under the same conditions, but all the shoots originating from a given plant are of one form. Grisebach [76] refers the form with glabrous sheaths to *Orthopogon loliaceus* Spreng. (*Oplismenus loliaceus* (Lam.) Beauv.), an Asiatic species. Richard [77] refers the pubescent form to *Oplismenus undulatifolius*. In Cuba the species is called "pitillo."

Moist woods and shady banks at low and medium altitudes, Mexico and the West Indies to Argentina. A common species to be found on probably all the islands.

A variegated form, with blades striped with white, is cultivated as a basket plant. It is naturalized in a few places in the Lesser Antilles.

LEEWARD ISLANDS: Guadeloupe, *Duss* 3155. Dominica, *Jones* 37.

WINDWARD ISLANDS: Martinique, *Duss* 1325. Grenada, *Hitchcock* 17674. St. Lucia, *Box* 194.

---

[76] Fl. Brit. W. Ind. 545. 1864.

[77] Richard, in Sagra, Hist. Cuba 11: 308. 1850.

88. ECHINOCHLOA Beauv., Ess. Agrost. 53. pl. 11. f. 2. 1812

Spikelets plano-convex, often stiffly hispid, subsessile, solitary or in irregular clusters on one side of the panicle branches; first glume about half the length of the spikelet, pointed; second glume and sterile lemma equal, pointed, mucronate, or the glume short-awned and the lemma long-awned, sometimes conspicuously so, enclosing a membranaceous palea and sometimes a staminate flower; fertile lemma plano-convex, smooth and shining, acuminate-pointed, the margins inrolled below, flat above, the apex of the palea not enclosed. Coarse, often succulent, annuals or perennials with compressed sheaths, linear flat blades, and rather compact panicles composed of short, densely flowered racemes along a main axis.

Ligule a dense line of stiff yellowish hairs; plants perennial.
- Fruit about 2.5 mm long; awn of sterile lemma less than two mm long. 1. E. PYRAMIDALIS.
- Fruit about 4 mm long; awn of sterile lemma usually 5 to 10 mm long. 2. E. POLYSTACHYA.

Ligule wanting, the ligular area sometimes pubescent; plants annual.
- Racemes simple, rather distant, 1 to 2 cm long; spikelets crowded in about 4 rows, the awn of the sterile lemma reduced to a short point; blades 3 to 6 mm wide ---------- 3. E. COLONUM.
- Racemes more or less branched, usually more than 2 cm long; spikelets irregularly crowded and fascicled, usually not arranged in rows, the awn of the sterile lemma variable; blades usually more than 5 mm wide.
  - Sheaths, at least the lower, papillose-hispid; panicle dense (small in depauperate specimens), the spikelets long-awned ---------- 4. E. WALTERI.
  - Sheaths smooth; awns variable, but the panicle not a dense mass of long-awned spikelets.
    - Panicles soft and nodding; spikelets inconspicuously hispid. 5. E. CRUS-PAVONIS.
    - Panicles erect and rather stiff; spikelets conspicuously hispid. 6. E. CRUSGALLI.

1. Echinochloa pyramidalis (Lam.) Hitchc. and Chase, Contrib. U. S. Natl. Herb. 18: 345. 1917.

Panicum pyramidale Lam., Tabl. Encycl. 1: 171. 1791. Senegal.

Panicum spectabile var. *guadeloupense* Hack., Notizbl. Bot. Gart. Berlin 1: 328. 1897. Guadeloupe, *Duss* 3176.

Echinochloa guadeloupensis Wieg., Rhodora 23: 63. 1921.

Perennial; culms erect, rather fleshy, 1.5 to 2.5 m tall, glabrous; sheaths glabrous; ligule a dense row of stiff yellowish hairs 1 to 2 mm long; blades 40 to 60 cm long, 5 to 10 mm wide, glabrous above, scabrous on the margins and on the nerves beneath; panicle 20 to 40 cm long, the axis scabrous; racemes numerous, ascending, 2 to 7 cm long, single or somewhat fascicled, distant below but overlapping, stiffly pilose at base and sparsely so along the scabrous or hispidulous rachis; spikelets about 3 mm long, rather loosely arranged along the rachis, scabrous or slightly hispidulous on the nerves, glabrous or nearly so on the internerves; sterile lemma mucronate or with an awn 1 to 2 mm long; fruit about 2.5 cm long, mucronate (fig. 297).

Brackish marshes and ditches, Guadeloupe. Common in tropical Africa; introduced in Guadeloupe.[78]

[78] In 1919 the author observed this species on the island of Guadeloupe, where it is abundant in one locality. Later he had the opportunity of examining *Echinochloa pyramidalis* in tropical Africa where it is common, and he is of the opinion that the Guadeloupe plant is the same as the African species. Wiegand (Rhodora 23: 63. 1921) described the Guadeloupe plant as a distinct species.

LEEWARD ISLANDS: Guadeloupe, *Duss* 3175, 3176, 3920; *Hitchcock* 16412 (*Amer. Gr. Nat. Herb.* 711); *L'Herminier* 61.

FIGURE 297.—*Echinochloa pyramidalis*, × 1 (Duss 3175).

2. Echinochloa polystachya (H. B. K.) Hitchc., Contrib. U. S. Natl. Herb. 22: 135. 1920.

Oplismenus polystachyus H. B. K., Nov. Gen. et Sp. 1: 107. 1815. Colombia.

Panicum spectabile Nees, in Trin., Gram. Pan. 138. 1826. Brazil.

Echinochloa spectabilis Link, Hort. Berol. 2: 209. 1833.

Perennial, usually in colonies; culms coarse, 1 to 2 m tall, from a long creeping rooting base, glabrous; nodes densely hispid with appressed yellowish hairs; sheaths glabrous or papillose-hispid; ligule a dense line of stiff yellowish hairs as much as 4 mm long; blades as much as 2.5 cm wide, scabrous on the margins and upper surface; panicle 10 to 30 cm long, rather dense; racemes ascending, the lower mostly 3 to 6 cm long, densely hispid at base, the rachis very scabrous and more or less papillose-hispid; spikelets rather closely set, nearly sessile, about 5 mm long; sterile floret staminate, the awn 2 to 10 mm long; fruit rather soft, about 4 mm long, extending into a point about 0.5 mm long (fig. 298).

Marshes and ditches near the coast, Mexico, and the West Indies to Argentina.

CUBA: Habana, *Léon* 4168; *Ekman* 13524. Almendares, *Ekman* in 1921. Sierra de Imías, *Léon* 12451 (cultivated). Habana, *Ekman* 13405.

JAMAICA: Savanna-la-Mar, *Hitchcock* 9868.

HAITI: Dessalines, *Ekman* H 8532. Port-Margot, *Ekman* H 4798.

DOMINICAN REPUBLIC: San Francisco de Macoris, *Ekman* H

FIGURE 298.—*Echinochloa polystachya*, × 1 (Pittier 4383).

12318. Sánchez, *Taylor* 66. Rincón, *Fuertes* 1419. Jaina, *Ekman* 12473; *Faris* 100, 400. Santiago, *Ekman* H 16392.

PUERTO RICO: Mayaguez, *Chase* 6290, 6319. Bayamon, *Hioram* 324 in part. Caguas, *Sintenis* 2543. Lares, *Chase* 6583.

LEEWARD ISLANDS: Antigua, *Wullschlaegel* 635; *Box* 110.

WINDWARD ISLANDS: Martinique, *Duss* 542. St. Lucia, *Box* 198.

TOBAGO: *Broadway* 4896; *Hitchcock* 10284.

3. Echinochloa colonum (L.) Link, Hort. Berol. 2: 209. 1833.
JUNGLE-RICE.

Panicum colonum L., Syst. Nat. ed. 10. 2: 870. 1759. Jamaica.

Milium colonum Moench, Meth. Pl. 202. 1794.

Oplismenus colonus H. B. K., Nov. Gen. et Sp. 1: 108. 1815.

Panicum zonale Guss., Fl. Sic. Prodr. 1: 62. 1827. Sicily.

Panicum colonum var. *zonale* L. H. Dewey, Contrib. U. S. Nat. Herb. 2: 502. 1894.

Echinochloa colonum var. *zonalis* Woot. and Standl., N. Mex. Coll. Agr. Bull. 81: 45. 1912.

FIGURE 299.—*Echinochloa colonum*, × 1 (Bentley).

Annual, usually much branched at base; culms prostrate-spreading, ascending or erect, usually 20 to 40 cm long, glabrous; sheaths glabrous; blades rather lax, 5 to 10 cm long, rarely longer, 3 to 6 rarely 10 mm wide, somewhat scabrous on the margin, occasionally bearing transverse purple bands (zonate); panicles 5 to 10 or even 15 cm long; racemes several, 1 to 2 cm long, rarely longer, appressed or ascending, the lower usually distant as much as 1 cm; spikelets about 3 mm long, crowded, nearly sessile, in about 4 rows; awn reduced to a short point (fig. 299).

Ditches and moist places, a common weed in the warmer parts of both hemispheres; introduced in the Americas where it is found from Virginia and Missouri to Argentina; originally described from India, the type being, however, from Jamaica, collected by Patrick Browne. The word "colonum" appears to be a genitive plural. To be found on probably all the islands.[79]

[79] See Hitchcock, Contrib. U. S. Natl. Herb. 17: 256. 1913.

4. Echinochloa walteri (Pursh) Heller, Cat. N. Amer. Pl. ed. 2. 21. 1900.

Panicum hirtellum Walt., Fl. Carol. 72. 1788. Not *P. hirtellum* L., 1759. South Carolina.

Panicum walteri Pursh, Fl. Amer. Sept. 66. 1814. Based on *P. hirtellum* Walt.

Annual; erect, often succulent and rooting at the lower nodes when growing in mud or water, 1 to 2 m high, as much as 2.5 cm thick at base; sheaths papillose-hispid, or papillose only, rarely glabrous, the collar more or less pubescent; ligule wanting, the ligular area often pubescent; blades usually 10 to 15 mm wide sometimes as much as 3 cm wide, mostly scabrous on both surfaces; panicle dense, as much as 30 cm long, erect or nodding; racemes appressed or ascending, approximate or the lower somewhat distant, as much as 10 cm long; spikelets closely arranged, mostly long-awned, often purple, about 3 mm long; sterile lemma with an awn usually 1 to 2 cm long, sometimes longer, rarely reduced to a short point (fig. 300).

FIGURE 300.—*Echinochloa walteri*, × 1 (Chase 1426).

Marshes, lagoons, and wet places, eastern United States; Cuba, Hispaniola.

CUBA: Ciénaga de Zapata, *Ekman* 16947. Los Coyuelos, *Roig* 3231. Hanábana, *Wright* 3879 in part.

JAMAICA: Black River, *Hitchcock* 9650.

HAITI: Étang de l'Abovane, *Ekman* H 375. Solon, *Ekman* H 826. Aux Cayes, *Ekman* H 758. Dame-Marie, *Ekman* H 10450.

5. Echinochloa crus-pavonis (H. B. K.) Schult., Mant. 2: 269. 1824.

Oplismenus crus-pavonis H. B. K., Nov. Gen. et Sp. 1: 108. 1815. Venezuela.

Panicum sabulicola Nees, Agost. Bras. 258. 1829. Brazil.

Panicum crus-pavonis Nees, Agrost. Bras. 259. 1829.

Panicum aristatum Macfad., Bot. Misc. Hook. 2: 115. 1831. Not *P. aristatum* Retz., 1786. Jamaica.

Oplismenus jamaicensis Kunth, Enum. Pl. 1: 147. 1833. Based on *Panicum aristatum* Macfad.

Panicum jamaicense Steud., Nom. Bot. ed. 2. 2: 257. 1841.

Echinochloa sabulicola Hitchc., Contrib. U. S. Natl. Herb. 17: 257. 1913.

Echinochloa crusgalli var. *crus-pavonis* Hitchc., Contrib. U. S. Natl. Herb. 22: 148. 1920.

Annual; culms erect or sometimes decumbent at base, as much as 1 m or even 1.5 m tall, glabrous; sheaths glabrous; ligule wanting, the ligular area sometimes slightly pubescent; blades 5 to 15 mm wide, scabrous on the margins, sometimes on the upper surface; panicles 10 to 20 cm long, more or less nodding; racemes mostly ascending or appressed, the lower somewhat distant, the upper approximate; spikelets crowded, excluding the awns about 3 mm long, hispid on the nerves, hispidulous on the intervenes; sterile lemma with an awn 1 to 10 mm long (fig. 301).

Marshes and wet places, often in the water, at low and medium altitudes, Mexico and the West Indies to Argentina.

BERMUDA: *Collins* 343.

CUBA: Habana, *Léon* 747, 2588, 2785, 7646, 11467; *Ekman* 241. *Liebmann* 378; *Rugel* 889. Yumuri Mountains, *Rugel* 884. Caibarién, *Ekman* 16308. Gamboa, *Ekman* 14977. Without locality, *Wright* in 1865, *Ekman* 13130.

JAMAICA: Grosmond Marsh, *Harris* 11751. Meylersfield, *Harris* 11824. Savanna-la-Mar, *Hitchcock* 9862.

HAITI: Miragoane, *Eyerdam* 493; *Ekman* H 6523. Dessalines, *Ekman* H 3518, 8533. Port-Margot, *Ekman* H 2681.

DOMINICAN REPUBLIC: Santo Domingo, *Ekman* H 12254. Jarabaco, *Ekman* H 14135.

PUERTO RICO: Loiza Road, *Britton* 9235. Humacao, *Sintenis* 1889. Canovanas, *Stevenson* 5388. San Juan, *Chase* 6352, 6396. Lares, *Chase* 6596. Rio Piedras, *Stevenson and Rose* 6428. Trujillo Alto, *Britton and Matz* 7049. Vega Baja, *Britton* 7960. Without locality, *Eggers* 685.

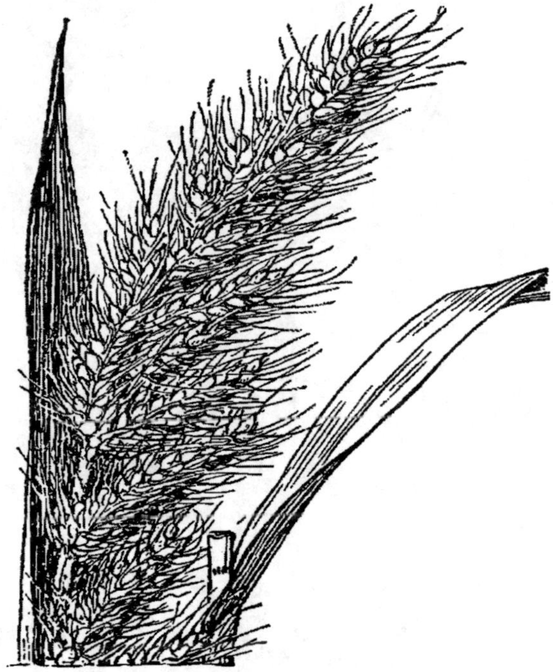

FIGURE 301.—*Echinochloa crus-pavonis*, × 1 (Sintenis 1889).

LEEWARD ISLANDS: Guadeloupe, *Duss* 3161.

TRINIDAD: Oropuche Lagoon, *Britton, Hazen, and Freeman* 1143. Without locality, *Bot. Gard. Herb.* 1678.

6. Echinochloa crusgalli (L.) Beauv., Ess. Agrost. 53, 161, 169. 1812.
BARNYARD GRASS.

Panicum crusgalli L., Sp. Pl. 56. 1753. Europe and Virginia.

Resembling *E. crus-pavonis;* differing in the stiffer panicle, erect or nodding only when large and heavy, the somewhat larger spikelets, and especially in the strongly hispid or papillose-hispid nerves of the second glume and sterile lemma (fig. 302).

The species is common in the United States and Mexico but rare in the West Indies. It is not always easy to distinguish it from *E. crus-pavonis*, especially in small or depauperate specimens, for which reason the latter has often been considered to be a variety of the former. The awn is variable in length in *E. crusgalli*, whereas in

FIGURE 302.—*Echinochloa crusgalli*. Plant, × ½; two views of spikelet, and floret, × 10 (Somes 3725).

E. crus-pavonis it is usually short, not more than 1 cm in length. The most noticeable difference is the soft nodding panicle of *E. crus-pavonis* as compared with the stiffer erect panicle (unless large and heavy) of *E. crusgalli*. The spikelets of *E. crusgalli* are usually conspicuously papillose-hispid. In *E. crus-pavonis* the spikelets are more or less hispid but the strong hairs on the nerves are less conspicuous. The following specimens have been referred to *E. crusgalli*.

BERMUDA: *Brown, Britton, and Bisset* 1961.

CUBA: Batabanó, *Léon* 13447.

HAITI: Manneville, *Ekman* H 3061.

89. CHAETIUM Nees, Agrost. Bras. 269. 1829

Spikelets short-pediceled, dorsally compressed, lanceolate, the joint of the rachilla between the glumes elongate, the bearded base of the first glume adnate to it, forming a long slender callus; glumes bearing awns 3 to 4 times the length of the body of the spikelet, the first reduced to the awn or the pair broadened and enclosing the rest of the spikelet; sterile lemma bearing a shorter awn or awn-tipped only; fruit subindurate, lanceolate, the lemma acuminate into a scabrous awn or point, the thin margins flat, the summit of the palea not enclosed. Perennials with long narrow blades and dense narrow panicles.

1. Chaetium cubanum (Wright) Hitchc., Contrib. U. S. Natl. Herb. 12: 232. 1909.

Perotis? cubana Wright, Ann. Acad. Cien. Habana 8: 288. 1871. Cuba, *Wright* 735.

Culms tufted, stiffly erect, 40 to 60 cm tall; blades flat or loosely involute, 5 to 10 cm long, 1 to 4 mm wide, puberulent on the upper surface; panicles narrow, few-flowered, 4 to 7 cm long, the branches appressed; spikelets about 6 mm long, the fertile lemma about 4.5 mm long (fig. 303).

Dry hills, Cuba.

CUBA: Canasí, *Léon* 13074; *Ekman* 16474. El Cobre, *Ekman* 15699, in 1922 (*Amer. Gr. Nat. Herb.* 796). Eastern Cuba, *Wright* 735. Motembo, *Ekman* 16827.

90. TRICHOLAENA Schrad.; Schult., Mant. 2: 163. 1824

Spikelets on short capillary pedicels; first glume minute; second glume and sterile lemma equal, raised on a stipe above the first glume, emarginate or slightly lobed, short-awned, covered, except toward the apex, with long silky hairs, the palea of the sterile lemma well developed, fertile lemma shorter than the spikelet, cartilaginous, smooth, boat-shaped, obtuse, the margins thin, not inrolled, the palea not enclosed. Perennials or annuals with rather open panicles of silky spikelets.

1. Tricholaena repens (Willd.) Hitchc. NATAL GRASS.

Saccharum repens Willd., Sp. Pl. 1: 322. 1797. "Guinea."

Tricholaena rosea Nees, "Cat. Sem. Hort. Vratisl. a. 1836"; Fl. Afr. Austr. 1: 17. 1841. South Africa.

Rhynchelytrum roseum Stapf and Hubb.; Bews, World's Grasses 223. 1929.

Rhynchelytrum repens C. E. Hubb., Kew Bull. Misc. Inf. 1934: 110. 1934.

FIGURE 303.—*Chaetium cubanum.* Plant, × ½; spikelet and floret, × 5 (Ekman 15699).

Annual or short-lived perennial; culms tufted, slender, often decumbent at base, about 1 m tall; sheaths sparsely papillose-hirsute; blades flat, 5 to 15 cm long, 2 to 7 mm wide; panicles beautifully silky, rosy-purple or sometimes pale, 10 to 15 cm long; spikelets about 5 mm long, the hairs extending 4 to 5 mm beyond (fig. 304).

Waste ground, becoming rather common in the warmer regions of North America; introduced from South Africa. This species has some value for forage and can be utilized on poor sandy soil.

CUBA: Santiago de las Vegas, *Juzepczuk* 1987. Habana, *Léon* 817, 6361; *Ekman* 29. Campo Florido, *Léon* 4146. Matanzas, *Britton and Wilson* 13996; *Cowell* 13334. Cienfuegos, *Grey* in 1919. Santiago de Cuba, *Ekman* 7999. San Miguel de los Baños, *Killip* 13937.

JAMAICA: Botanical Garden, *Cousins* in 1925 (grown from seed from Colombia; will probably escape).

HAITI: Fond-Blanc, *Ekman* H 9889.

DOMINICAN REPUBLIC: Monción, *Ekman* H 12691; *Valeur* 162. Jaina, *Ekman* H 5801; *Faris* 5. Constanza, *Ekman* H 14087.

PUERTO RICO: Rio Piedras, *Britton and Matz* 7056. Sardinera, *Britton* 8703.

LEEWARD ISLANDS: Antigua, *Box* 25. Guadeloupe, *Franceschi* in 1892; *Stehlé* 41.

WINDWARD ISLANDS: Barbados, *Hitchcock* 16511.

TRINIDAD: Port-of-Spain, *Broadway* 4962 (cultivated).

91. SETARIA Beauv., Ess. Agrost. 51. pl. 13. f. 3. 1812

(*Chaetochloa* Scribn., U.S.Dept.Agr., Div. Agrost. Bull. 4: 38. 1897)

Spikelets subtended by one to several bristles (sterile branchlets) falling free from the bristles, awnless; first glume broad, usually less

FIGURE 304.—*Tricholaena repens*. Plant, × ½; spikelet and floret, × 10 (Tracy 9365).

than half the length of the spikelet, 3- to 5-nerved; second glume and sterile lemma equal, or the glume shorter, several-nerved; fertile lemma coriaceous-indurate, smooth or rugose. Annuals or perennials with narrow terminal panicles.

Blades narrowly elliptic, plaited; bristles below only a part of the spikelets (Subgenus *Ptychophyllum*).
  Plant annual; blades usually less than 2 cm wide ____________ 1. S. BARBATA.
  Plants perennial; blades usually more than 3 cm wide.
    Panicle of numerous approximate, more or less 1-sided racemes, spikelet-bearing to the base, 2 to 5 cm long, rarely the lower much longer. 2. S. POIRETIANA.
    Panicle of more or less fascicled branches, not or scarcely 1-sided, some of them elongate and naked at base.
      Branches of panicle as much as 10 cm long; bristles usually not more than twice as long as the spikelets, inconspicuous; blades as much as 6 cm wide ________________ 3. S. PALMIFOLIA.
      Branches of panicle slender, finally spreading, as much as 20 cm long; bristles as much as 15 mm long; blades as much as 10 cm wide. 4. S. PANICULIFERA.
Blades linear-lanceolate, narrow; bristles below all the spikelets.
  Bristles below each spikelet numerous, at least more than five. Panicles dense, cylindric, spikelike.
    Plants annual; spikelets 3 mm long ____________ 5. S. LUTESCENS.
    Plants perennial; spikelets 2 to 2.5 mm long ____________ 6. S. GENICULATA.
  Bristles below each spikelet 1 or by abortion of the spikelets, 2 or 3.
    Bristles more or less retrorsely scabrous.
      Plants perennial; spikelets globose or nearly so ____________ 7. S. TENAX.
      Plants annual; spikelets not globose.
        Spikelets about 2 mm long ____________ 8. S. VERTICILLATA.
        Spikelets about 1.5 mm long.
          Panicles usually green, rarely as much as 8 cm long, less than 5 mm thick, the bristles 2 to 3 mm long ________ 9. S. SCANDENS.
          Panicles usually purple, as much as 15 cm long and 1 cm thick, the bristles about 1 cm long ____________ 10. S. TENACISSIMA.
    Bristles antrorsely scabrous only.
      Plants annual.
        Fertile lemma at maturity finely cross-veined or nearly smooth.
          Plants as much as 3 m tall ____________ 11. S. MAGNA.
          Plants less than 1 m tall ____________ 12. S. VIRIDIS.
        Fertile lemma coarsely transversely rugose ______ 13. S. CORRUGATA.
      Plants perennial.
        Spikelets 3 mm long. Panicle large, rather loose. 18. S. MACROSPERMA.
        Spikelets 2 to 2.5 mm long.
          Panicle narrowed somewhat at summit but not attenuate.
            Primary panicle large and dense, as much as 25 cm long, yellowish or brownish, the bristles 1 to 2 cm long; blades as much as 2 cm wide ____________ 19. S. VULPISETA.
            Primary panicle 5 to 10 cm long, green, the bristles 5 to 10 mm long; blades 3 to 5 mm wide _______ 14. S. MACROSTACHYA.
          Panicle attenuate at apex.
            Fertile lemma acuminate, not turgid; obscurely cross-lined. 20. S. SUBTRANSIENS.
            Fertile lemma acute, turgid, sharply cross-ridged.
              Blades linear-lanceolate, more than 5 mm wide; panicle interrupted or branched, the branches 1 to 3 cm long.
                Blades usually pubescent on one or both surfaces, thickish, usually less than 1 cm wide ____________ 15. S. SETOSA.
                Blades glabrous, thin, usually 1 to 2 cm wide. 16. S. LEIOPHYLLA.
              Blades slender, mostly less than 5 mm wide; panicle slender, very narrow ____________ 17. S. RARIFLORA.

1. Setaria barbata (Lam.) Kunth, Rév. Gram. 1: 47. 1829.

Panicum barbatum Lam., Tabl. Encycl. 1: 171. 1791. Mauritius.

Chaetochloa barbata Hitchc. and Chase, Contrib. U. S. Natl. Herb. 18: 348. 1917.

Branching annual; culms decumbent, spreading, often rooting at the lower nodes, glabrous, scabrous, or villous near the pubescent nodes, as much as 2 m long, but often much less; blades narrowly elliptic, flat and rather thin, as much as 30 cm long and 2.5 cm wide, distinctly plicate in large specimens, obscurely so in dwarf ones; panicles green, as much as 20 cm long, the branches ascending or spreading, as much as 4 cm long; spikelets oblong-elliptic, glabrous, about 2.5 mm long, tending to be in two rows along the branches, at least along the upper part, often clustered on branchlets on the lower part of the branches, the bristles flexuous, 5 to 10 mm long, usually rather numerous (fig. 305).

Thickets and waste places, tropical Asia; introduced in the Americas, West Indies to Brazil. Grisebach [80] and Hooker [81] described this species under *Panicum flavescens* Swartz.

Common in the Lesser Antilles and in Jamaica. No specimens have been seen from Cuba. Called "Mary grass" in Tobago.

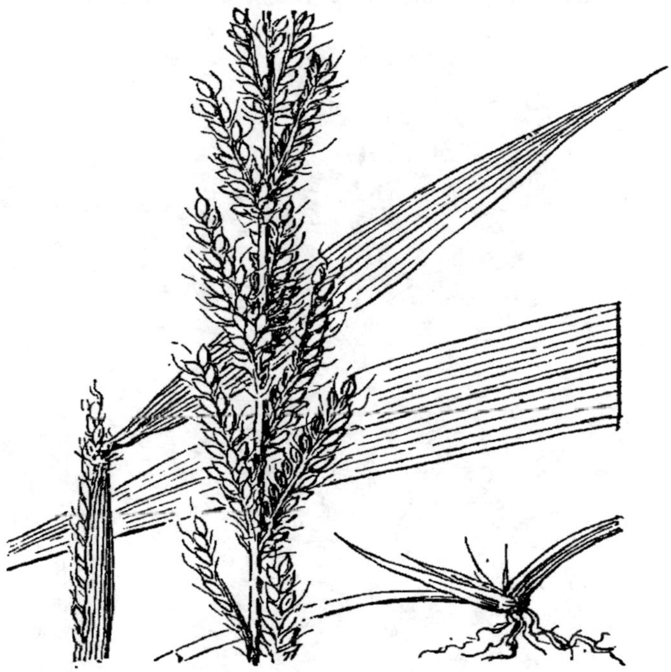

FIGURE 305.—*Setaria barbata*, × 1 (Hitchcock 9391, Amer. Gr. Nat. Herb. 603).

JAMAICA: Castleton, *Hitchcock* 9391 (*Amer. Gr. Nat. Herb.* 603). Moneague, *Maxon and Killip* 367. Ferry, *Ridley* 43; *Harris* 11782. Bog Walk, *Hitchcock* 9308; *Ridley* 59. Troy, *Harris* 12587; *Hitchcock* 9793. Kingston, *Cockerell* in 1892; *Hitchcock* 9270, 9277, 9473. Ipswich, *Hitchcock* 9604. Alligator Pond, *Hitchcock* 9834. Buff Bay, *Hitchcock* 9768. Montego Bay, *Hitchcock* 9694. Mavis Bank, *Harris* 11602. Temple Hall, *Harris* 11360. Gordon Town, *Harris* 11511. Claremont, *Hitchcock* 9515. Ewarton, *Hitchcock* 9412.

DOMINICAN REPUBLIC: Río San Juan, *Miller* 1143. Sosúa, *Ekman* H 14521. Los Haitises, *Ekman* H 15494. Samaná, *Ekman* H 14889, H 14931, H 14989.

[80] Fl. Brit. W. Ind. 547. 1864.
[81] Fl. Brit. Ind. 7: 56. 1896.

60256—36——22

PUERTO RICO: Mayaguez, *Heller* 4373, 4488; *Chase* 6159; *Holm* in 1915.

LEEWARD ISLANDS: Antigua, *Hitchcock* 16381; *Box* 66; *Rose* 3391; *Wullschlaegel* 618. Guadeloupe, *Duss* 3175; *Hitchcock* 16399. Dominica, *Jones* 43; *Hitchcock* 16429.

WINDWARD ISLANDS: Martinique, *Duss* 544; *Hitchcock* 16463. Barbados, *Eggers* 7128; *Hitchcock* 16498. St. Lucia, *Glasgow* 10; *Hitchcock* 16495; *Kemp* 39. Grenada, *Broadway* in 1904; *Hitchcock* 17680.

TRINIDAD: Port-of-Spain, *Britton and Hazen* 1690; *Hitchcock* 9965. St. Anns, *Broadway* 7783. San Fernando, *Broadway* 7950.

TOBAGO: *Broadway* 4335, 4737; *Hitchcock* 10225, 10251.

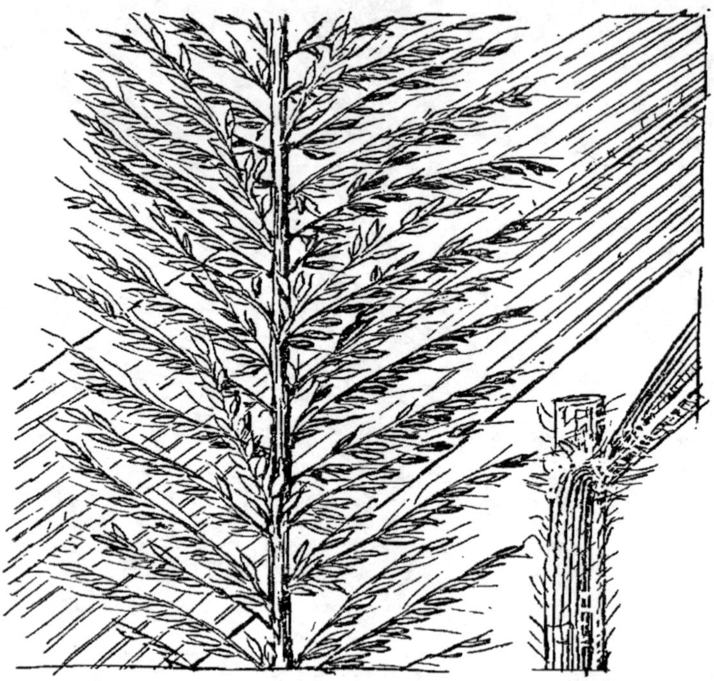

FIGURE 306.—*Setaria poiretiana*, × 1 (Pringle 3921).

2. Setaria poiretiana (Schult.) Kunth, Rév. Gram. 1: 47. 1829.

Panicum elongatum Poir., in Lam., Encycl. Sup. 4: 278. 1816. Not *P. elongatum* Salisb., 1796. Brazil.

Panicum sulcatum Bertol., Opusc. Sci. 4: 230. 1820; Excerpt. 14. 1820. Not *P. sulcatum* Aubl., 1775. Brazil.

Setaria sulcata Raddi, Agrost. Bras. 50. 1823. Based on *Panicum sulcatum* Bertol.

Panicum poiretianum Schult., Mant. 2: 229. 1824. Based on *P. elongatum* Poir.

Chaetochloa poiretiana Hitchc., Contrib. U. S. Natl. Herb. 22: 159. 1920.

Tufted perennial; culms erect, 1 to 1.5 m tall; sheaths papillose-hispid; blades strongly plicate, flat, as much as 1 m long and 10 cm wide, narrowed toward each end, the base resembling a petiole; panicles erect, densely flowered, commonly purple, long-exserted, as much as 60 cm long and 10 cm wide, the branches ascending, irregularly clustered, approximate, usually somewhat falcate, the lower usually 3 to 5 cm long; spikelets secund on the branches, narrowly ellipsoid, about 3 mm long (fig. 306).

Moist woods, Mexico to Brazil; Trinidad and Tobago. Called gamalote in Trinidad, where it is a troublesome weed in cocao groves.

TRINIDAD: Port-of-Spain, *Hitchcock* 9978, 10043 (*Amer. Gr. Nat. Herb.* 604), 10171.

TOBAGO: *Hitchcock* 10282.

3. Setaria palmifolia (Willd.) Stapf, Jour. Linn. Soc. Bot. 42: 186. 1914. PALMGRASS.

Panicum plicatum Willd., Enum. Pl. 1033. 1809. Not *P. plicatum* Lam., 1791. India.

Panicum palmifolium Willd.; Poir., in Lam., Encycl. Sup. 4: 282. 1816. Probably India.

Panicum plicatum var. *haitiense* Kunth; Griseb., Fl. Brit. W. Ind. 547. 1864. Haiti.

Chamaeraphis palmifolia Kuntze, Rev. Gen. Pl. 2: 771. 1891.

Chaetochloa palmifolia Hitchc. and Chase, Contrib. U. S. Natl. Herb. 18: 348. 1917.

FIGURE 307.—*Setaria palmifolia*, × 1 (Hitchcock 9727).

Perennial; culms 1 to 1.5 m tall; sheaths papillose-hispid or glabrate; blades strongly plicate, flat, pubescent or glabrate, elliptic, narrowed to a petiolelike base, as much as 50 cm long and 6 cm wide; panicles loose and open, as much as 40 cm long, the branches ascending or spreading, scattered, somewhat distant, especially below, 5 to 10 cm long, compound; spikelets lanceolate, acute, about 3 mm long, closely arranged on short branchlets appressed along the main branches, forming interrupted compound racemes, the bristles inconspicuous, usually not more than twice as long as the spikelets, often short and imperfectly developed; sterile floret with a palea but without stamens (fig. 307).

Rocky woods and shady banks, often growing in large colonies, a native of southeastern Asia; introduced in Jamaica. The varietal name ascribed by Grisebach to Kunth was probably a herbarium name. It is not found in any of Kunth's works so far as we know. The name *Panicum plicatum* Lam. has been applied to this species by many authors, *P. palmifolium* Willd. being based upon *P. plicatum* as described by Willdenow.[82] *Panicum palmaefolium* Koen.,[83] an earlier nomen nudum, is probably the same species.

JAMAICA: Hardware Gap, *Ridley* in 1916; *Harris* 10911. St. Helens Gap, *Maxon and Killip* 586. Catherines Peak, *Hitchcock* 9727. Buff Bay, *Hitchcock* 9762. Buff River, *Orcutt* 3786. Gordon Town,

[82] Enum. Pl. 1033. 1809.
[83] Naturf. 23: 208. 1788.

Hitchcock 9320 (*Amer. Gr. Nat. Herb.* 605); *Hart* 815. Mount Hybla, *Harris* 11535. Cinchona, *Hitchcock* 9719; *Harris and Lawrence* 15232. Castleton, *Harris* 11286. Morces Gap, *Nichols* 37.

4. Setaria paniculifera (Steud.) Fourn.; Hemsl., Biol. Centr. Amer. Bot. 3: 505. 1885.

Panicum sulcatum Aubl., Pl. Guian. 1: 50. 1775. Not *Setaria sulcata* Raddi, 1823, based on *Panicum sulcatum* Bertol., 1820, which is *Setaria poiretiana*. French Guiana.

Panicum paniculiferum Steud., Syn. Pl. Glum. 1: 54. 1854. Mexico.

Chamaeraphis paniculifera Kuntze, Rev. Gen. Pl. 2: 770. 1891.

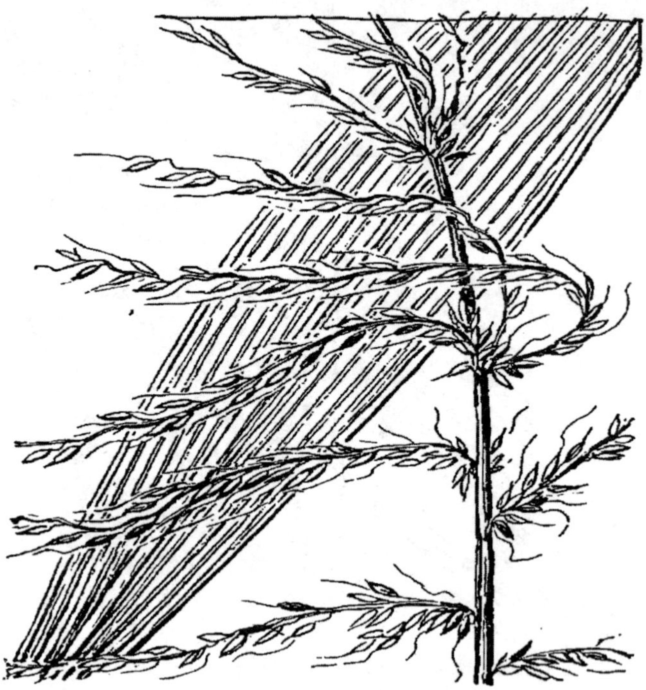

FIGURE 308.—*Setaria paniculifera*, × 1 (Collins and Goll 09).

Chamaeraphis sulcata Kuntze, Rev. Gen. Pl. 2: 770. 1891.

Chaetochloa sulcata Hitchc., Contrib. U. S. Natl. Herb. 17: 260. 1913.

Setaria sulcata A. Camus, Bull. Mus. Hist. Nat. 30: 108. 1924. Based on *Panicum sulcatum* Aubl. Not *S. sulcata* Raddi, 1823.

Robust perennial; culms as much as 4 m tall, glabrous; sheaths papillose-hispid all over or only at the margin and on the collar; blades flat, strongly plicate, somewhat scabrous, as much as 1 m long and 10 cm wide at the middle, tapering toward each end, the lower into a long petiole-like base; panicles green or purplish, often very large, as much as 70 cm long, the branches ascending, finally spreading, as much as 20 cm long, these branching and rebranching, the panicle often becoming loose and open; spikelets usually loosely arranged, elliptic-lanceolate, about 3 mm long, obscurely nerved, scabrous-pubescent, the flexuous bristles as much as 15 mm long (fig. 308).

Moist ground and shady banks, southern Mexico and Guadeloupe to Colombia. Often called palmgrass; in Tobago called gamalote (not the gamalote of Trinidad, which is *S. poiretiana*).

LEEWARD ISLANDS: Guadeloupe, *Duss* 3185. Dominica, *Jones* 3.

WINDWARD ISLANDS: Martinque, *Duss* 4656. Grenada, *Broadway* 123; *Buckmire* 1382.

TOBAGO: *Eggers* 5682; *Hitchcock* 10276.

5. Setaria lutescens (Weigel) F. T. Hubb., Rhodora 18: 232. 1916.
YELLOW BRISTLEGRASS.

Panicum lutescens Weigel, Obs. Bot. 20. 1772. Germany.

Chaetochloa lutescens Stuntz, U. S. Dept. Agr., Bur. Plant Indus. Inventory Seeds 31: 36, 86. 1914.

This species has been commonly known as *Panicum glaucum*, *Setaria glauca*, and *Chaetochloa glauca*. However, *Panicum glaucum* of Linnaeus should apply to the species usually known as *Pennisetum typhoideum* L. Rich. or *Penicillaria spicata* Willd., commonly called in the United States pearl millet.[84] The following synonyms are based on *Panicum glaucum* L. as to name but refer to *Setaria lutescens* as to plant.

Setaria glauca Beauv., Ess. Agrost. 51, 169, 178. 1812.

Chamaeraphis glauca Kuntze, Rev. Gen. Pl. 2: 767. 1891.

Ixophorus glaucus Nash, Bull. Torrey Bot. Club 22: 423. 1895.

Chaetochloa glauca Scribn., U. S. Dept. Agr., Div. Agrost. Bull. 4: 39. 1897.

Erect annual, often much branched at base, the culms becoming geniculate below or in open ground spreading or even prostrate-spreading; culms rather succulent below, 25 to 50 cm tall (in the West Indies); sheaths smooth, compressed-keeled; blades flat, 5 to 20 cm long, 4 to 7 mm wide, scabrous on the upper surface, glabrous beneath; panicles dense, nearly cylindric, spikelike, yellow at maturity, mostly 2 to 8 cm long, almost 1 cm thick (including the bristles); bristles antrorsely scabrous, yellow, the longer ones 2 to 3 times as long as the spikelet; spikelets about 3 mm long, strongly convex on one side; fertile floret marked with numerous transverse ridges (fig. 309).

A common weed in cultivated soil and waste places in the eastern United States, rare in the Tropics; introduced from Europe.

JAMAICA: Cinchona, *Hart* 740; *Hitchcock* 9702; *Harris* 11272, 11457. Resource, *Perkins* 1141.

HAITI: Pétionville, *Ekman* H 3233, H 10027. Kenskoff Mountain, *Buch* 1452. Furcy, *Leonard* 4388, 4394, 4424, 4452.

6. Setaria geniculata (Lam.) Beauv., Ess. Agrost. 51, 178. 1812.
KNOTROOT BRISTLEGRASS.

Panicum geniculatum Lam., Encycl. 4: 727 (err. typ. 737). 1798. Guadeloupe.

Cenchrus parviflorus Poir., in Lam., Encycl. 6: 52. 1804. Puerto Rico.

Panicum imberbe Poir., in Lam., Encycl. Sup. 4: 272. 1816. North America and Brazil.

Setaria berteroniana Schult., Mant. 2: 276. 1824. Santo Domingo.

Setaria ventenatii Kunth, Rév. Gram. 1: 251. pl. 37. 1830. Puerto Rico.

Setaria glauca var. *imberbis* Griseb., Fl. Brit. W. Ind. 554. 1864.

Chaetochloa geniculata Millsp. and Chase, Field Mus. Bot. 3: 37. 1903.

These names have been referred to *Panicum*, *Setaria*, *Chaetochloa*, and *Chamaeraphis*.[85]

---

[84] For further discussion see Chase, Amer. Jour. Bot. 8: 41. 1921; and Contrib. U. S. Natl. Herb. 22: 216. 1921.

[85] For full synonymy see Hitchcock, U. S. Dept. Agr., Misc. Pub. 200: 943. 1935.

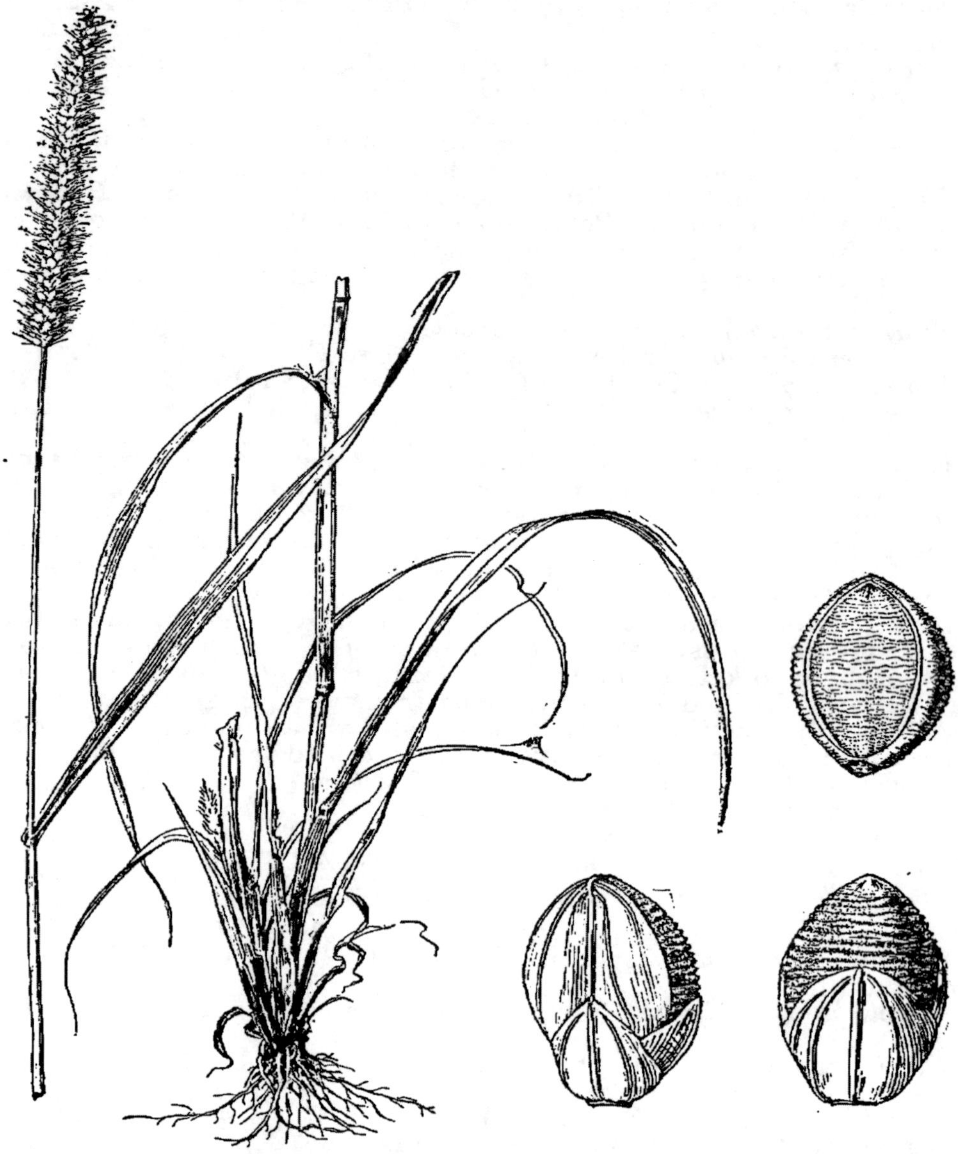

FIGURE 309.—*Setaria lutescens*. Plant, × ½; two views of spikelet, and floret, × 10 (Chase 2986).

Perennial, producing short knotty branching rhizomes as much as 4 cm long; culms erect to nearly prostrate, as much as 1 m tall, sometimes dwarfed, the base usually hard and wiry, often more slender than the upper part; blades flat, scabrous, often more or less villous toward the base on the upper surface, commonly 10 to 20 cm long and 4 to 8 mm wide; panicle erect, cylindric, densely flowered, rounded or truncate (not narrowed), at summit, 1 to 10 cm long or in robust specimens longer, 4 to 8 mm thick (excluding the bristles), yellow, purple, tawny, or greenish; bristles mostly 8 to 12, yellow or purple, 1 to 3 times as long as the spikelets, sometimes longer; spikelets 2 to 2.5 or even 3 mm long, ovoid, planoconvex; fertile lemma transversely rugose with close narrow ridges (fig. 310).

This species is exceedingly variable in general appearance, due to the variation in the color and length of the bristles, which are long early in the season and in cultivated soil and short in plants in dry situations.

Open ground pastures, cultivated soil, and moist ground, United States to Argentina; common at low and medium altitudes. To be found on all the West Indian islands.

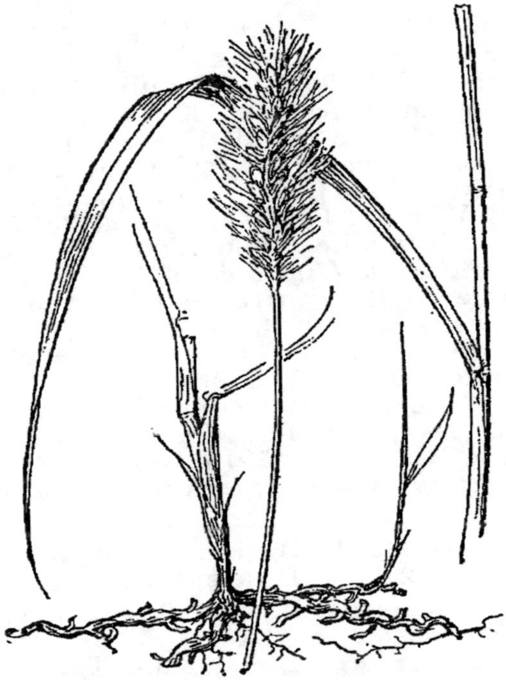

FIGURE 310.—*Setaria geniculata*, × 1 (Chase 2981).

FIGURE 311.—*Setaria tenax*, × 1 (Tracy 9090).

7. Setaria tenax (L. Rich.) Desv., Opusc. 78. 1831.

Panicum tenax L. Rich., Act. Soc. Hist. Nat. Paris 1: 106. 1792. Cayenne.

Setaria biconvexa Griseb., Fl. Brit. W. Ind. 555. 1864. Trinidad.

Chaetochloa tenax Hitchc., Contrib. U. S. Natl. Herb. 22: 176. 1920.

Perennial; culms scabrous below the panicle, 1 to 1.5 m tall, often geniculate at base; sheaths villous on the margin, densely hispid on the collar; ligule densely pilose, 2 to 3 mm long; blades flat, as much as 35 cm long and 2 cm wide, narrowed at base, acuminate; panicles rather densely flowered, narrowed toward summit but not attenuate, 15 to 30 cm long, 2 to 3 cm wide, the branches ascending, the lower about 2 cm long; bristles 1 or 2 below each spikelet, 1 to 2 cm long, flexuous, retrorsely scabrous and often also antrorsely toward the base, sometimes barblets directed both ways intermixed, pale or tawny, becoming implicate and somewhat one-sided with age; spikelets subspheric, about 2 mm long, very turgid on one side and somewhat convex on the other; fertile lemma rather indistinctly cross-wrinkled (fig. 311).

Savannas, rocky banks, and open woods, Mexico and the West Indies to Brazil.

This was described by Grisebach [86] as *Setaria onurus* and by Hitchcock and Chase [87] as *Chaetochloa onurus*, but a reconsideration of the type leads to the conclusion that the original *Panicum onurus* Willd. in Trin.,[88] from Montevideo, collected by Sello, is a different species, later described as *Setaria caespitosa* Hack. and Arech., not known from North America.

CUBA: Las Mangas, *Ekman* 13069. Bahía Honda, *Wilson* 9411, Triscornia, *Tracy* 9090. Campo Florido, *Léon* 4145. Madruga. *Léon* 3456. San Miguel de los Baños, *Léon* 8911. Yumuri, *Rugel* 880. Guanabacoa, *Wright* 3474. Soledad, *Hitchcock* 23327. Sancti Spíritus, *Léon* 828. Baraguá, *Hitchcock* 23349; *Walker* in 1925. Zaza del Sur, *Sergius* 2712. Manati, *Léon* 5684. Woodfred, *Shafer* 3020. Guara, *Hitchcock* 23392. Without locality, *Wright* 3887.

JAMAICA: Two-Mile-Wood Pen, *Harris* 12065. New Forest, *Hitchcock* 9891 (*Amer. Gr. Nat. Herb.* 608). Lititz, *Harris* 11657. Yardley Chase, *Harris* 9673.

HAITI: Cap-à-Faux, *Ekman* H 10848. Tortuga Island, *Ekman* H 4136.

WINDWARD ISLANDS: Barbados, *Dash* 603.

TRINIDAD: Port-of-Spain, *Hitchcock* 9991, 10000 (*Amer. Gr. Nat. Herb.* 609). St. Joseph, *Hitchcock* 10180. St. Anns, *Broadway* 7368.

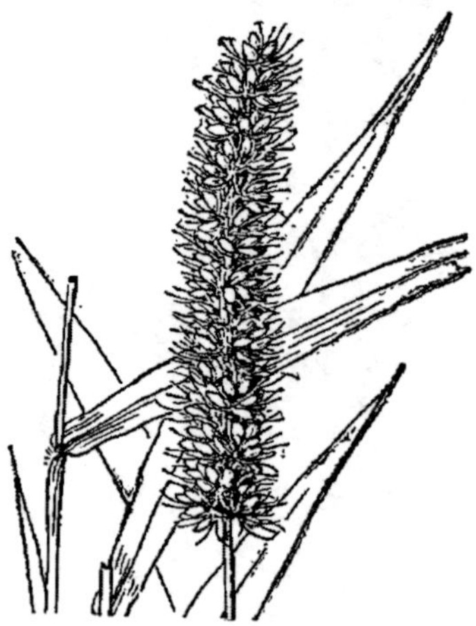

FIGURE 312.—*Setaria verticillata*, × 1 (Steele).

8. Setaria verticillata (L.) Beauv., Ess. Agrost. 51, 178. 1812. BUR BRISTLEGRASS.

Panicum verticillatum L., Sp. Pl. ed. 2. 1: 82. 1762. Europe.

Ixophorus verticillatus Nash, Bull. Torrey Bot. Club 22: 422. 1895.

Chaetochloa verticillata Scribn., U. S. Dept. Agr., Div. Agrost. Bull. 4: 39. 1897.

Annual, often much branched at base and geniculate-spreading; blades flat, rather thin, usually 10 to 20 cm long and 5 to 10 mm wide; scabrous on both surfaces, often more or less pilose; panicles erect but not stiff, subcylindric, more or less lobate or interrupted, especially toward base, mostly 5 to 15 cm long, 7 to 15 mm wide; bristles 1 to 3 times as long as the spikelets, somewhat flexuous, retrorsely scabrous to base; spikelets about 2 mm long, oblong-elliptic, not very turgid on the convex side; fertile lemma finely cross-wrinkled (fig. 312).

Fields and waste places, temperate and warm regions of both hemispheres, introduced in America. Called in Cuba "pega-pega" and "amor seco."

BERMUDA: *Collins* 161; *Brown and Britton* 116, 302; *Harshberger* in 1905; *Millspaugh* 99, 127; *Brown* 676.

[86] Fl. Brit. W. Ind. 555. 1864.

[87] Contrib. U. S. Natl. Herb. 18: 349. 1917. First published by Scribn. and Merrill, U. S. Dept. Agr., Div. Agrost. Bull. 21: 27. 1900.

[88] Mém. Acad. St. Pétersb. VI. Sci. Nat. 1: 226. 1834.

Cuba: Habana, *Curtiss* 693; *Hitchcock* 491; *Léon* 555; *Liebmann* 346, 347, 348; *Ekman* 110, 13120.

9. Setaria scandens Schrad.; Schult., Mant. 2: 279. 1824.

Panicum scandens Trin., Gram. Pan. 166. 1826.

Chaetochloa scandens Scribn., in Donn. Smith, Enum. Pl. Guat. 5: 91. 1899.

Slender annual, much branched below, erect or soon geniculate-spreading; culms sometimes rooting at the lower nodes, as much as 80 cm long; blades flat, linear-lanceolate, as much as 10 cm long and 1 cm wide, scabrous, especially on upper surface, usually sparsely, sometimes densely, pilose on both surfaces; panicles slender, erect, cylindric, densely flowered, sometimes interrupted, especially at base, often purplish, as much as 8 cm long, mostly less than 5 mm thick, the axis softly pubescent and also long-villous, the scattered hairs often longer than the spikelets; bristles somewhat flexuous but not becoming implicate, 1 to 2 times as long as the spikelets, antrorsely scabrous except near the tip, there more or less retrorsely scabrous; spikelets about 1.5 mm long, ovoid, turgid on the convex side; fertile lemma transversely striate or weakly rugose (fig. 313).

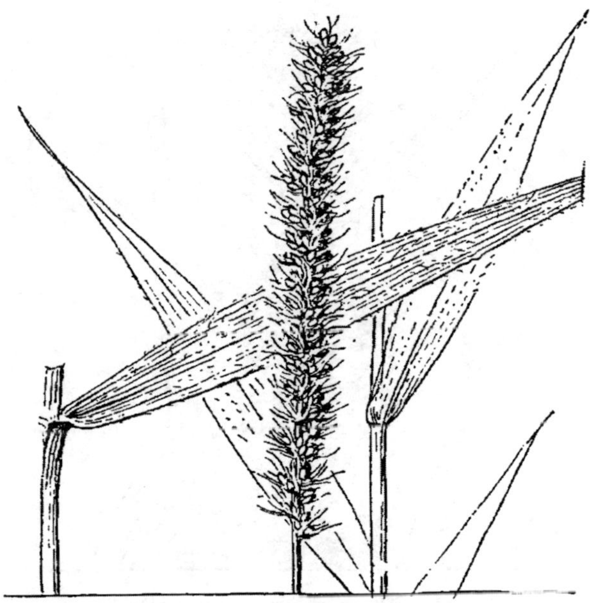

Figure 313.—*Setaria scandens*, × 1 (Hitchcock 9723).

Open ground, Guatemala to Paraguay; Cuba, Jamaica, Hispaniola. Originally described from a garden specimen in Vienna, the native country unknown. A weed in fields and waste places in Jamaica where it appears to be introduced.

Cuba: Sierra de Nipe, *Ekman* 9798.

Jamaica: Cinchona, *Hitchcock* 9718, 9723. Portland Gap, *Orcutt* 5419. Killits, *Harris* 11157. Mount Hybla, *Harris* 11380. Chapelton, *Ridley* 58. Malvern, *Harris* 9739. Troy, *Hitchcock* 9812. Ewarton, *Hitchcock* 9408. Davids Hill, *Harris* 12668. Resource, *Perkins* 1140. Arntully, *Orcutt* 2732, 3063. Gordon Town, *Hart* 796, 1487.

Haiti: Marmelade, *Nash* 693; *Leonard* 8112, 8257. Port-au-Prince, *Cook, Scofield, and Doyle* 62, 67; *Ekman* H 6633; *Buch* 1682, 1738. Caille la Croix, *Leonard* 7964. Dondou, *Leonard* 8565. Ennery, *Leonard* 8853, 9498. Furcy, *Leonard* 4555. Mission, *Leonard* 3705. Pétionville, *Ekman* H 1354. Morne Basil, *Ekman* H 2487. Bombardopolis, *Leonard* 13475.

Dominican Republic: Lagunas de Cenobí, *Valeur* 10. San José de Ocoa, *Ekman* H 12029.

10. Setaria tenacissima Schrad.; Schult., Mant. 2: 279. 1824. Brazil.

Panicum tenacissimum Nees, Agrost. Bras. 238. 1829.

Chaetochloa tenacissima Hitchc. and Chase, Contrib. U. S. Natl. Herb. 18: 352. 1917.

Slender annual, mostly simple or little branched; culms erect, 1 to 2 m tall, leaning on or clambering over other vegetation; blades flat, very scabrous on both surfaces and more or less pubescent, especially beneath, mostly 10 to 15 cm, sometimes as much as 20 cm long, mostly not more than 8 mm wide, tapering to a long-acuminate apex, rather abruptly narrowed at base; panicles somewhat nodding or flexuous, rather densely flowered and tapering toward the summit, somewhat interrupted toward the base, as much as 15 cm long and 1 cm thick (excluding bristles), the axis densely pubescent and sparsely villous with long weak hairs; bristles flexuous, becoming implicate, about 1 cm long, scabrous, antrorsely below, retrorsely above; spikelets about 1.5 mm long, often dark purple; fertile lemma transversely rugose with numerous fine ridges (fig. 314).

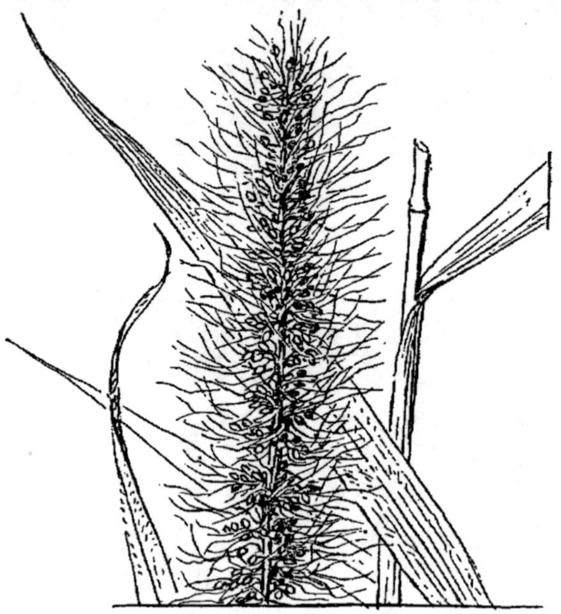

FIGURE 314.—*Setaria tenacissima*, × 1 (Hitchcock 10002, Amer. Gr. Nat. Herb. 610).

Brushy hillsides, Central America and West Indies to Brazil.

HAITI: St. Michel de l'Atalaye, *Leonard* 8053.

DOMINICAN REPUBLIC: Lagunas de Cenobí, *Valeur* 12; *Ekman* H 12768. Bonao, *Ekman* H 11481.

PUERTO RICO: Utuado, *Sintenis* 6498.

TRINIDAD: Port-of-Spain, *Hitchcock* 10002 (*Amer. Gr. Nat. Herb.* 610).

11. Setaria magna Griseb., Fl. Brit. W. Ind. 554. 1864. Jamaica, *Purdie*. GIANT BRISTLEGRASS.

Chamaeraphis magna Beal, Grasses N. Amer. 2: 152. 1896.

Chaetochloa magna Scribn., U. S. Dept. Agr., Div. Agrost. Bull. 4: 39. 1897.

Robust erect annual, usually not branched at base, sparingly branched above, the branches erect; culms as much as 4 m tall, rarely taller, and 2 cm thick at base; blades flat, scabrous, as much as 50 cm long and 3.5 cm wide; panicles densely flowered, nodding, often interrupted at base, tapering at each end, as much as 40 cm long and 3 cm thick, those of the branches much smaller; bristles somewhat flexuous, 1 or 2 below each spikelet, 1 to 2 cm long; spikelets about 2 mm long; fertile lemma smooth (fig. 315).

Marshes and wet places along the coast, eastern United States, West Indies, Costa Rica.

BERMUDA: *Munro* in 1864. The species is not known to grow in Bermuda now.

JAMAICA: Black River, *Hitchcock* 9646.

PUERTO RICO: Campo Alegre, *Chase* 6800. Without locality, *Eggers* 709.

WINDWARD ISLANDS: Martinique, *Duss* 3918.

12. Setaria viridis (L.) Beauv., Ess. Agrost. 51, 178. 1812.
GREEN BRISTLEGRASS.

Panicum viride L., Syst. Nat. ed. 10. 2: 870. 1759. Europe.
Chamaeraphis viridis Millsp., Fl. W. Va. 466. 1892.
Ixophorus viridis Nash, Bull. Torrey Bot. Club 22: 423. 1895.
Chaetochloa viridis Scribn., U. S. Dept. Agr., Div. Agrost. Bull. 4: 39. 1897.

Annual, sometimes geniculate-spreading; culms 20 to 50 cm tall; blades flat, usually less than 15 cm long, commonly less than 1 cm wide; panicle densely flowered, green or purple, tapering a little at the summit (the smaller ones ovate), 5 to 10 cm long, commonly 5 to 8 mm thick (excluding bristles); bristles 1 to 3 below each spikelet, mostly three to four times as long as the spikelet; spikelets 2 to 2.5 mm long, elliptic, not much turgid on the convex side; fertile lemma finely transversely wrinkled.

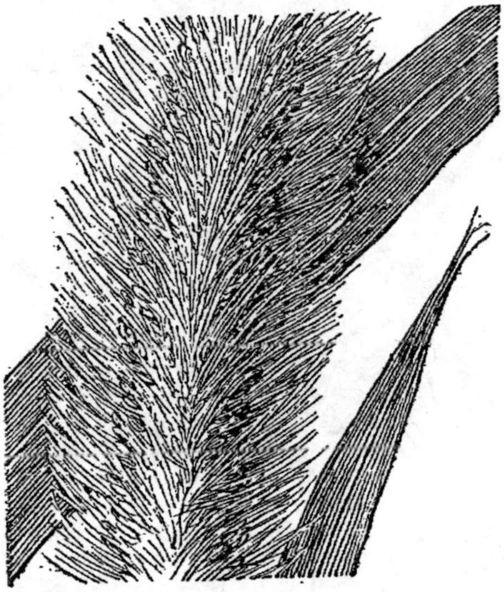

FIGURE 315.—*Setaria magna*, × 1 (Nash 1279).

Cultivated soil and waste ground, temperate regions of both hemispheres, rare in the Tropics; introduced in America.

BERMUDA: *Collins* 159, 160.

SETARIA ITALICA (L.) Beauv., Ess. Agrost. 51, 170, 178. 1812. The common millet, differing from *S. viridis* in the larger size, the panicle often lobed or interrupted, is said by Grisebach [89] to be naturalized in Jamaica. In the herbarium of the New York Botanical Garden is a specimen from Martinique (*Duss* 1315).

13. Setaria corrugata Schult., Mant. 2: 276. 1824.

Panicum corrugatum Ell., Bot. S. C. and Ga. 1: 113. 1816. Georgia.
Chamaeraphis corrugata Kuntze, Rev. Gen. Pl. 2: 770. 1891.
Chaetochloa corrugata Scribn., U. S. Dept. Agr., Div. Agrost. Bull. 4: 39. 1897.
Chaetochloa hispida Scribn. and Merr., U. S. Dept. Agr., Div. Agrost. Bull. 21: 25. f. 13. 1900. Cuba, *Wright* in 1865.
Setaria hispida Schum., Just's Bot. Jahresber. 28 [1]: 417. 1902.

[89] Fl. Brit. W. Ind. 554. 1864.

Annual, branched at base, erect or geniculate-spreading; culms scabrous or the lower part smooth, 50 to 100 cm tall; sheaths compressed-keeled, scabrous at least toward the summit, sometimes appressed-pilose; blades flat, scabrous, usually 15 to 25 cm long and 3 to 5 mm wide; panicles cylindric, densely flowered, usually 3 to 5 cm long, the axis densely hispid-scabrous and also rather densely villous; spikelets about 2 mm long, the bristles about 5 to 6 mm long; fertile lemma coarsely transversely rugose (fig. 316).

Sandy woods, southeastern United States; Cuba.

CUBA: La Grifa, *Wright* in 1865. Laguna Santa Bárbara, *Ekman* 18118. Isla de Pinos, *Britton and Wilson* 14817.

FIGURE 316.—*Setaria corrugata*, × 1 (Pollard and Collins 253).

FIGURE 317.—*Setaria macrostachya*, × 1 (Hitchcock 13605).

14. Setaria macrostachya H. B. K., Nov. Gen. et Sp. 1: 110. 1815. Mexico. PRAIRIE BRISTLEGRASS.

Chaetochloa macrostachya Scribn. and Merr., U. S. Dept. Agr., Div. Agrost. Bull. 21: 29. f. 16. 1900.

Perennial, tufted, usually pale or glaucous; culms erect or geniculate at base, scabrous below the panicle, 40 to 120 cm tall; sheaths more or less compressed-keeled; blades flat or folded, 15 to 40 cm long, 3 to 5 mm wide; panicles erect, spikelike, mostly 5 to 10 cm long, slightly tapering above but not attenuate, densely flowered, or somewhat interrupted or lobed below; spikelets about 2 mm long, the bristles 5 to 10 mm long; fertile lemma rather sharply but finely marked with cross-wrinkles (fig. 317).

Open dry ground and dry woods, southwestern United States to Oaxaca; Hispaniola.

HAITI: Fond Parisien, *Leonard* 4155, 4155a. Cabaret, *Leonard* 12038.

DOMINICAN REPUBLIC: Jarabaco, *Ekman* H 14161.

15. Setaria setosa (Swartz) Beauv., Ess. Agrost. 51, 171, 178. 1812.

Panicum setosum Swartz, Prodr. Veg. Ind. Occ. 22. 1788. Jamaica.

Panicum caudatum Lam., Tabl. Encycl. 1: 171. 1791. "E Brasilio, Commerson, * * * Cayenna, Richard." The type, bearing the name in Lamarck's script, is from Richard.

Panicum brachiatum Poir., in Lam., Encycl. Sup. 4: 282. 1816. Antilles.

Setaria caudata Roem. and Schult., Syst. Veg. 2: 495. 1817.

Setaria elongata Spreng.; Schult., Mant. 2: 280. 1824. Santo Domingo.

Setaria brachiata Kunth, Rév. Gram. 1: 47. 1829.

Panicum paractaenoides Trin., Mém. Acad. St. Pétersb. VI. Sci. Nat. 1: 219. 1834. Crab Island [Vieques].

Panicum dumetorum A. Rich.; Steud., Syn. Pl. Glum. 1: 49. 1854. "Antilles" (the type specimen from St. Croix).

Panicum restitutum Steud., Syn. Pl. Glum. 1: 53. 1854. Based on *Setaria elongata* Spreng.

Setaria setosa var. *caudata* Griseb., Fl. Brit. W. Ind. 555. 1864.

Chamaeraphis setosa Kuntze, Rev. Gen. Pl. 2: 768. 1891.

Chamaeraphis caudata Britton, Ann. N. Y. Acad. 7: 264. 1893.

Chaetochloa setosa Scribn., U. S. Dept. Agr., Div. Agrost. Bull. 4: 39. 1897.

Chaetochloa caudata Scribn., Mo. Bot. Gard. Rept. 10: 52. 1899.

Setaria paractaenoides Urban, Repert. Sp. Nov. Fedde 15: 98. 1917.

Perennial; culms erect, often wiry, finally branching, sometimes becoming decumbent or even prostrate and woody at base, with upright branches, mostly not more than 1 m tall; sheaths often overlapping below; blades flat or folded, rather firm and stiffly spreading, usually pubescent, commonly 15 to 25 cm long and 6 to 10 mm wide; panicles mostly narrow, from loosely spikelike to rather open, attenuate at summit, usually 10 to 20 cm long, the branches short and crowded or ascending and 1 to 2 cm long, approximate or, especially the lower, 1 to 3 cm distant, these rarely to 5 cm long and spreading or reflexed; spikelets about 2 mm long, the bristles 5 to 10 mm long, sometimes scarcely exceeding the spikelets; fertile lemma acutish, finely but strongly cross-ridged (fig. 318).

This species is exceedingly variable. On dry slopes the culms are sometimes rigid, decumbent, and rooting at the nodes with erect flowering branches. The panicles in such plants may be subspikelike or open with spreading distant branches, 1 to 4 cm long. In *Chase* 6519 both forms of panicle were borne on the same individual. Open-panicled plants were described as *Panicum brachiatum, P. paractaenoides,* and *P. dumetorum.* Numerous intermediate specimens connect this form with typical *Setaria setosa* (fig. 319).

Dry or rocky woods, West Indies to Brazil.

BAHAMAS: Water Cay, *Geogr. Soc. Baltimore* 522.

CUBA: Mendoza, *Ekman* 11484. Cayo Paloma, *Shafer* 2565. Jauco, *Léon* 11939, 12385. Santiago de Cuba, *Léon* 118, 829, 830,

831, 3946. Guantánamo, *Ekman* 10233; *Léon* 3775, 3776; *Britton* 1930, 2105. Isla de Pinos, *Palmer and Riley* 1000.

JAMAICA: Kingston, *Maxon and Killip* 310; *Hitchcock* 9315, 9316 (*Amer. Gr. Nat. Herb.* 606), 9745; *Ridley* 61, 62; *Alexander Prior* in 1853. Long Mountain Road, *Harris* 11301, 11303. Gordon Town, *Harris* 11348; 11458; *Hitchcock* 9325. Musgrave Road, *Harris* 11479. Spanish Town Road, *Harris* 9297, 12477. Inverness, *Harris* 12745. New Forest, *Hitchcock* 9846. Hope, *Harris* 11292. Without locality, *Hart* 826, 829.

HAITI: Port-à-l'Ecu, *Leonard* 13881. Tortuga Island, *Leonard* 11325, 11721, 15298; *Ekman* H 4161. Gonaïve Island, *Leonard* 3136,

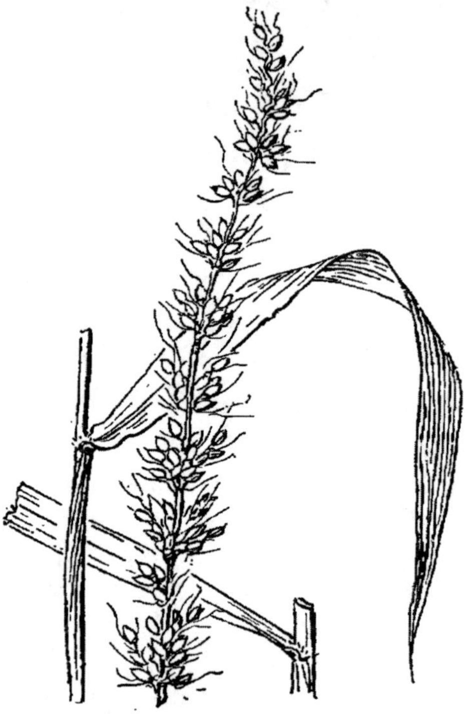

FIGURE 318.—*Setaria setosa*, × 1 (Hitchcock 9846).

FIGURE 319.—*Setaria setosa*, open panicled form, × 1 (Chase 6519).

5150, 5200, 5226. Jean Ravel, *Leonard* 13033. St. Marc, *Leonard* 2889, 2984. Pétionville, *Leonard* 4945. St. Michel de l'Atalaye, *Leonard* 7475a, 7743. Ennery, *Leonard* 8838. Port-de-Pai, *Ekman* 3598, 3939. Port-au-Prince, *Leonard* 15849; *Buch* 1986. Port-à-Piment, *Ekman* H 691.

DOMINICAN REPUBLIC: Guayubín, *Abbott* 939, 951, 954, 1023. Mao, *Abbott* 1044. Rincón, *Fuertes* 1378. Santiago, *Eggers* 2378; *Ekman* H 15973, H 16520.

PUERTO RICO: Coamo, *Sintenis* 2987, 3197; *Chase* 6541. Guanica, *Sintenis* 3577; *Britton and Shafer* 1901; *Johnston* 1027; *Chase* 6518 (*Amer. Gr. Nat. Herb.* 607), 6519, 6536. Boqueron, *Chase* 6505. Cabo Rojo, *Sintenis* 853. Mona Island, *Hess* 447. Desecheo Island,

Britton, Cowell, and Hess 1604; *Hess* 424. Culebra Island, *Britton and Wheeler* 18, 233.

VIRGIN ISLANDS: St. Croix, *Thompson* 343, 446, 488; *Ricksecker* 407. St. Thomas, *Eggers* in 1882; *Hitchcock* 16303, 16312. Virgin Gorda, *Fishlock* 57. St. John, *Britton and Shafer* 631.

LEEWARD ISLANDS: Antigua, *Box* 109. Guadeloupe, *Duss* 2698, 3188; *Stehlé* 289. Nevis, *Box* 174. Dominica, *Jones* 34.

TRINIDAD: Chacachacare, *Hitchcock* 10059.

16. Setaria leiophylla (Nees) Kunth, Rév. Gram. 1: Sup. XII. 1830.

Panicum leiophyllum Nees, Agrost. Bras. 249. 1829. Brazil.

Differing from *Setaria setosa* in the thinner broader flat, glabrous blades as much as 2 cm wide; panicle as much as 30 cm long, the branches ascending or spreading, as much as 3.5 cm long, overlapping or the lower distant.

Shady places, in damp or rather dry soil, West Indies, rare; Brazil.

HAITI: St. Marc, mountain slopes, common, *Leonard* 2992.

PUERTO RICO: Ponce, dry brushy limestone hillside, *Chase* 6488. Desecheo, shade of mixed forest, *Hess* 426.

LEEWARD ISLANDS: Antigua, shady wooded places, *Box* 16, rocky damp ground by roadside in woodland, *Box* 83; woods on dry limestone hill, *Box* 88.

FIGURE 320.—*Setaria rariflora*, × 1 (Ricksecker 67).

17. Setaria rariflora Mikan; Trin., in Spreng., Neu. Entd. 2: 78. 1821. Brazil.

Setaria vaginata Spreng., Syst. Veg. 4: Cur. Post. 33. 1827. Brazil.

Chaetochloa rariflora Hitchc. and Chase, Contrib. U. S. Natl. Herb. 18: 349. 1917.

Perennial; culms erect or decumbent at base, 30 to 60 cm tall; sheaths pubescent or glabrate, keeled, mostly overlapping; blades elongate, pubescent on both surfaces, narrow at base, usually 2 to 3 mm wide; panicles narrow, tapering above, 10 to 15 cm long, often less, the branches ascending, the lower 5 to 10 mm long, often shorter; spikelets about 2 mm long, the bristles 4 to 7 mm long; fertile lemma finely and sharply cross-ridged (fig. 320).

This species differs from *S. setosa* chiefly in the long narrow blades and the usually narrower and less bristly panicle. The second glume is shorter and usually 7-nerved. The two forms are given specific rank because the specimens from Brazil agree in having slender, rather lax blades and narrow, few-flowered, interruptedly spikelike panicles like the type of *S. rariflora*. *Setaria setosa* is confined to the West Indies and adjacent parts of South America.

Dry hills, West Indies to Brazil.

CUBA: Isla de Pinos, *Ekman* 11728.

PUERTO RICO: Boqueron, *Chase* 6502.

VIRGIN ISLANDS: St. Croix, *Ricksecker* 67. St. Thomas, *Orsted.*

LEEWARD ISLANDS: Antigua, *Wullschlaegel* 629.

18. Setaria macrosperma (Scribn. and Merr.) Schum., Just's Bot. Jahresber. 28[1]: 417. 1902.

Chaetochloa macrosperma Scribn. and Merr., U. S. Dept. Agr., Div. Agrost. Bull. 21: 33. f. 18. 1900. Florida.

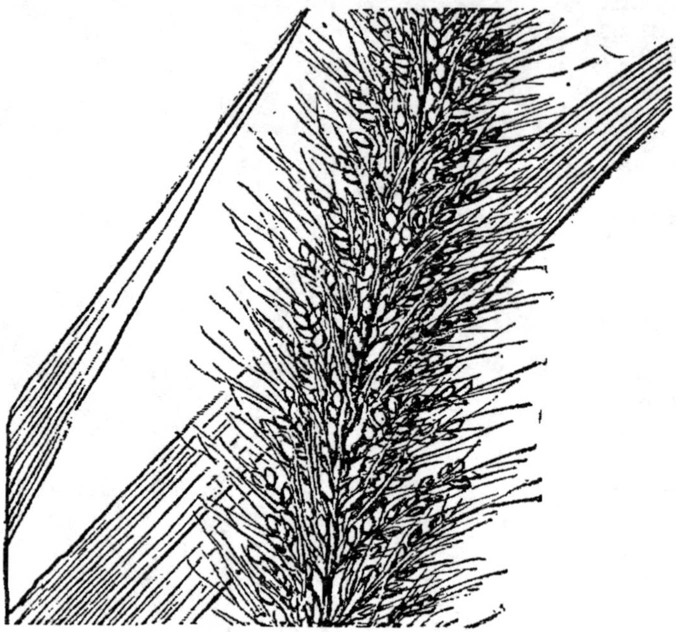

FIGURE 321.—*Setaria macrosperma*, × 1 (Curtiss 3617).

Plant perennial, often in large tufts; culms usually more or less geniculate at base and often rooting at the lower nodes, smooth, scabrous below the panicle, rather stout, 1 to 1.5 m tall; blades flat, very scabrous on the upper surface, smooth or scaberulous beneath, as much as 50 cm long and 2 cm wide; panicle rather loose, tapering above, as much as 25 cm long (the secondary panicles much smaller and more compact), the branches ascending, as much as 2 cm long, about equally distributed, the panicle thus not interrupted or lobed; spikelets about 3 mm long, lanceolate-ovate, the bristles 1.5 to 3 cm long; fertile lemma acute, finely and not very distinctly cross-wrinkled (fig. 321).

Open ground, mostly on coral rock or coral sand, Florida and the Bahamas.

BAHAMAS: Frozen Cay, Berry Islands, *Britton and Millspaugh* 2203 (N. Y. Bot. Gard. Herb.).

19. Setaria vulpiseta (Lam.) Roem. and Schult., Syst. Veg. 2: 495. 1817.

Panicum vulpisetum Lam., Encycl. 4: 735 (err. typ. 745). 1798. Santo Domingo.

Chaetochloa vulpiseta Hitchc. and Chase, Contrib. U. S. Natl. Herb. 18: 350. 1917.

Perennial, branching at base, often in large tufts; culms stout, often decumbent at base, as much as 2 m tall; blades flat, gradually narrowed from the middle toward both ends, the larger somewhat plaited, scabrous, especially beneath, as much as 50 cm long and 3 cm wide; panicles rather densely and evenly flowered, tapering toward the apex and often somewhat tapering at base, as much as 30 cm long and 4 or 5 cm wide (secondary panicles much smaller, sometimes only 5 cm long), the branches stiffly ascending or spreading, as much as 2 or 3 cm long and of about equal length except toward the summit, the axis densely villous; bristles 1 or 2 at the base of each spikelet, slightly flexuous, brownish, antrorsely scabrous, mostly 1 to 2 cm long, appearing secund on the branches after the fall of the spikelets; spikelets ovoid, 2 to 2.5 mm long, pale; fertile lemma strongly and rather coarsely cross-wrinkled (fig. 322).

Open ground and brushy slopes at low and medium altitudes, West Indies and Central America to Peru and Argentina.

Puerto Rico: Rio Piedras, *Stevenson* 3024; *Chase* 6371. Humacao, *Eggers* in 1881. Joyuya, *Sintenis* 6335 ("cult.").

Trinidad: Without locality, *Bot. Gard. Herb.* 3304; *Crueger*.

Tobago: *Broadway* 4898.

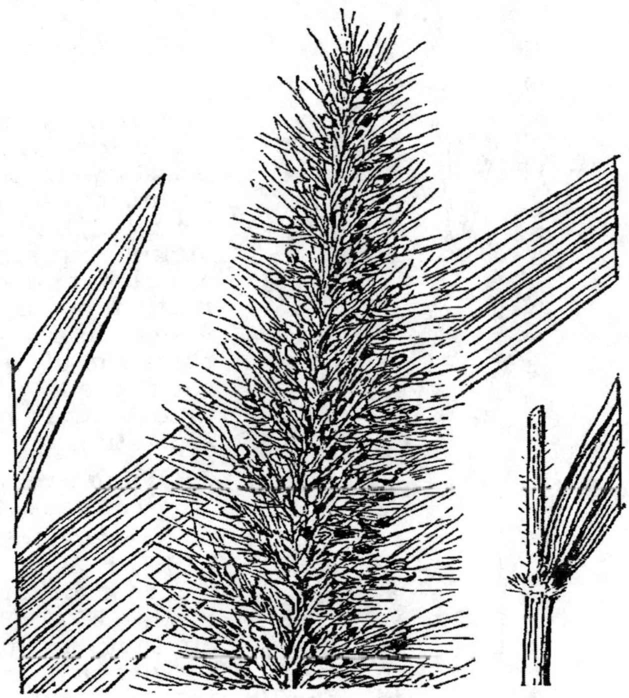

Figure 322.—*Setaria vulpiseta*, × 1 (Stevenson 3024).

20. Setaria subtransiens Hitchc. and Ekman, sp. nov.[90]

Perennial; culms tufted, erect, slender, glabrous, 60 to 100 cm tall, the nodes glabrous, or the lower pubescent; sheaths glabrous, keeled, somewhat auricled at summit (the auricle on one side sometimes conspicuous); ligule less than 1 mm long, membranaceous below, densely ciliate above; blades mostly erect, flat or involute, scabrous or puberulent on the upper surface, glabrous beneath, 10 to 20 cm long, 1 to 3 mm wide, gradually narrowed toward the base; panicles slender, interrupted, especially below, attenuate at summit, 5 to 15 cm long, the branches appressed, short, the lower sometimes as much as 2 cm long, the axis scabrous; bristles mostly single below each spikelet, sometimes wanting below some of the spikelets, appressed, about 5 mm long or some of them shorter; spikelets 2 to 2.5 mm long, somewhat oblique upon the short pedicel, lanceolate, acute, glabrous; first glume 3-nerved, about one-third as long as the spikelet; second glume 5-nerved, about

[90] Planta perennis; culmi caespitosi erecti graciles 60–100 cm alti; nodis glabris vel infimis pubescentibus; laminae erectae planae vel involutae, supra scabrae vel puberulentae, 10–20 cm longae 1–3 mm latae, a basi sensim angustatae; paniculae angustae, superne attenuatae, 5–15 cm longae, axi scabro; setae infra spiculas solitariae, circa 5 mm longae; spiculae lanceolatae acutae glabrae 2 mm longae; lemma fertile acuminatum obscure transversim striatum.

60256—36——23

half as long as the spikelet; sterile lemma 5- to 7-nerved, about as long as the fertile lemma, without stamens but with a palea as long as the lemma; fertile floret acuminate, not strongly turgid on the convex side, obscurely cross-lined (fig. 323).

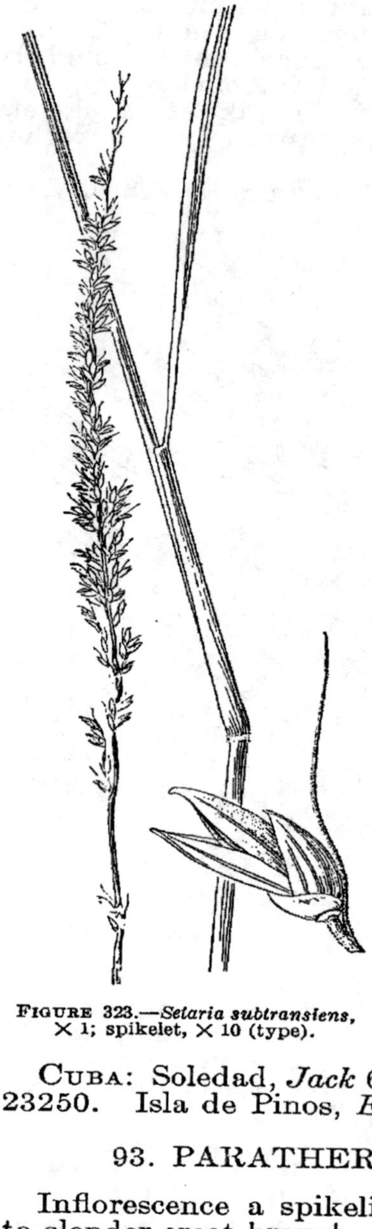

FIGURE 323.—*Setaria subtransiens*, × 1; spikelet, × 10 (type).

Type in the United States National Herbarium, no. 1161839, collected in thickets on serpentine, "cuabales", Motembo, prov. Santa Clara, Cuba, June 27, 1923, by Erik L. Ekman (no. 16828).

Also collected by Dr. Ekman in the Province of Oriente: Holguín, *Ekman* 3267, 7572; Sierra de Nipe, *Ekman* 2510.

92. IXOPHORUS Schlecht., Linnaea 31: 420. 1862

Spikelets lanceolate, glabrous, short-pediceled, the pedicel bearing a flexuous bristle just below the spikelet; first glume about one-fourth as long as the spikelet, rounded, 3-nerved; second glume and sterile lemma equal, pointed, the latter enclosing a palea and staminate flower, the palea at maturity cartilaginous and winged, much wider than the spikelet; fertile floret shorter than the sterile lemma, indurate, minutely roughened. A succulent annual with flat blades and narrow panicles of numerous ascending 1-sided racemes along a main axis.

1. Ixophorus unisetus (Presl) Schlecht., Linnaea 31: 420, 747. 1862.

Urochloa uniseta Presl, Rel. Haenk. 1: 319. 1830. Mexico.

Erect or spreading, 50 to 150 cm tall; blades 15 to 30 cm or even as much as 60 cm long, as much as 4 cm wide; panicles 10 to 20 cm long, the racemes approximate, 3 to 6 cm long; spikelets about 4 mm long, the bristles 3 to 10 mm long (fig. 324).

Low thickets, ditches, and wet places, at low altitudes, Mexico to Colombia; Cuba, introduced or escaped from cultivation. Said to have some forage value.

CUBA: Soledad, *Jack* 6265, 8318. Santiago de las Vegas, *Hitchcock* 23250. Isla de Pinos, *Ekman* 12173.

93. PARATHERIA Griseb., Cat. Pl. Cub. 236. 1866

Inflorescence a spikelike panicle, the solitary spikelets appressed to slender erect branches, the ends of the branches produced beyond the spikelets as slender bristles, the articulation at the base of the branch, this forming a sharp callus below the attached acuminate spikelet; glumes minute or obsolete; sterile lemma equaling the sub-

FIGURE 324.—*Ixophorus unisetus*, × ½ (Pringle 8493).

indurate fruit, 3-nerved; fertile lemma 3-nerved; palea similar to the lemma but a little shorter, 2-nerved. Decumbent-spreading leafy perennial with flat blades and slender panicles.

1. **Paratheria prostrata** Griseb., Cat. Pl. Cub. 236. 1866. Cuba, *Wright* in 1865.

Chamaeraphis parvigluma Munro; Wright and Sauv., An. Acad. Cien. Habana 8: 208. 1871, nomen nudum.

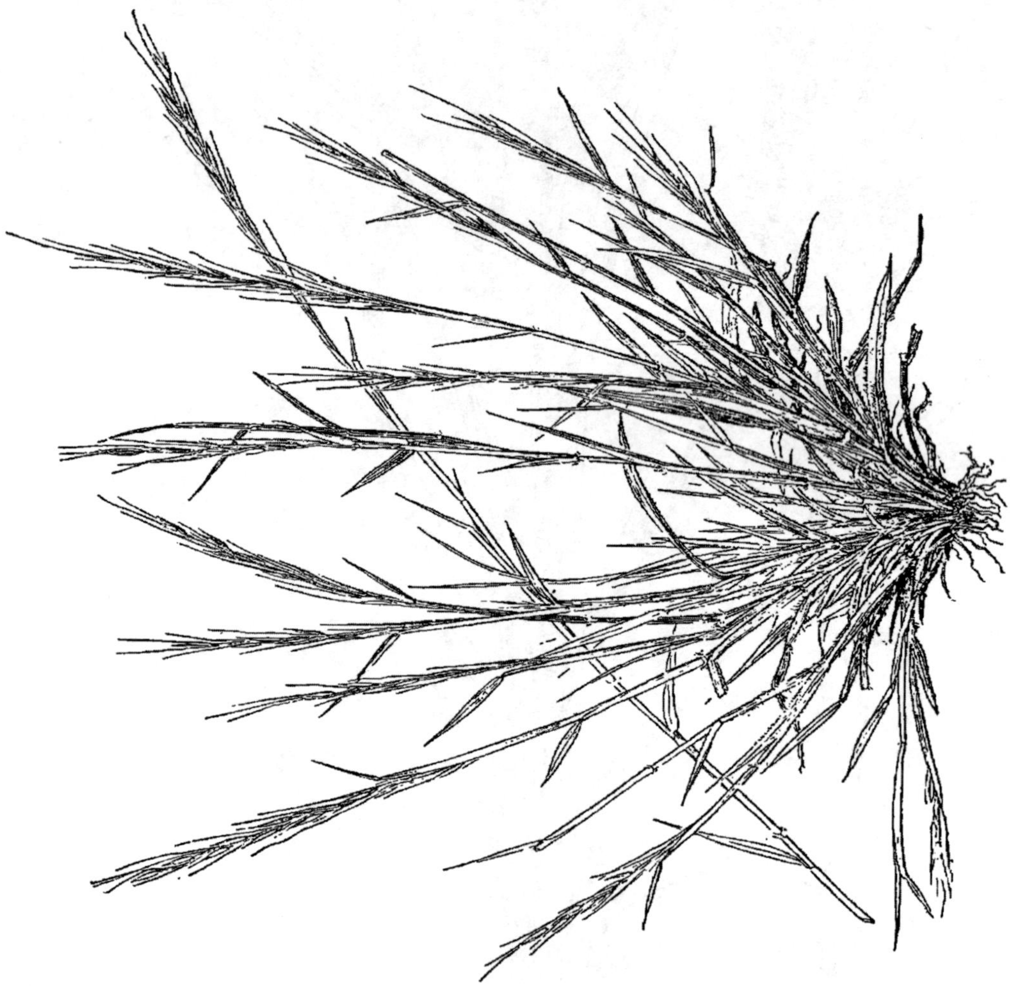

FIGURE 325.—*Paratheria prostrata.* Plant, X ½ (Wright 3908).

Culms tufted, several-noded, sparingly branching, 20 to 60 cm long, the nodes pubescent; blades pubescent, mostly 3 to 5 cm long, sometimes longer, 2 to 3 mm wide; panicles 5 to 15 cm long, more or less included in the uppermost sheath, the bristles appressed; spikelets about 7 mm long, a few slender hairs at the base (fig. 325).

Low moist ground, Cuba and Hispaniola; Brazil.

CUBA: Río Feo (Pinar del Río), *Ekman* 17248 (*Amer. Gr. Nat. Herb.* 798). Without locality, *Wright* 3906, in 1865. Isla de Pinos, *Curtiss* 461.

DOMINICAN REPUBLIC: Cuenca, *Ekman* H 13303.

94. PENNISETUM L. Rich., in Pers., Syn. Pl. 1: 72. 1805

Spikelets solitary or in groups of 2 or 3, surrounded by an involucre of bristles, these not united except at the very base, often plumose, falling attached to the spikelets; first glume shorter than the spikelet, sometimes minute or wanting; second glume shorter than or equaling the sterile lemma; fertile lemma chartaceous, smooth, the margin thin, enclosing the palea. Annuals or perennials with usually flat blades and dense spikelike panicles.

Bristles about 4 cm long; panicles oval, feathery; spikelets 10 to 12 mm long. 1. P. VILLOSUM.
Bristles rarely over 2 cm long, most of them shorter; panicles cylindric or nearly so; spikelets not more than 7 mm long.
  Grain at maturity subglobose, bursting through the lemma and palea; panicle solidly dense, 2 cm or more thick; plants annual ---------- 4. P. GLAUCUM.
  Grain permanently enclosed in the lemma and palea; panicles less than 2 cm thick, not solid; plants perennial.
    Culms 2 to 4 m tall, robust; panicles mostly more than 15 cm long, very dense. Blades flat ---------- 5. P. PURPUREUM.
    Culms mostly less than 2 m tall or if taller, slender and branching.
      Bristles naked. Spike not more than 5 cm long, loose; spikelets about 4 mm long ---------- 7. P. DOMINGENSE.
      Bristles or some of them plumose.
        Culms low and spreading; involucre with a turbinate naked base. 3. P. CILIARE.
        Culms erect, tall and rather stout; involucre with no naked base.
          Spikelets about 3 mm long, solitary in the sessile involucre. 6. P. SETOSUM.
          Spikelets about 5 mm long, 2 or more in the peduncled involucre. 2. P. ORIENTALE var. TRIFLORUM.

1. Pennisetum villosum R. Br., in Fres. Mus. Senckenb. Abh. 2: 134. 1837. Abyssinia. FEATHERTOP.

Plant perennial; culms densely tufted from a knotted crown, 15 to 50 cm tall; blades elongate, 3 to 6 mm wide; panicles tawny, very dense, oval, 3 to 15 cm long, 3 to 5 cm wide including the bristles; fascicles short-peduncled; bristles slender, spreading, the longest 4 to 5 cm long, the inner plumose below; spikelets 1 to 4 in a fascicle, 10 to 12 mm long (fig. 326).

A native of East Africa; cultivated for ornament in America and occasionally escaped.

JAMAICA: Resource, *Harris* 12402 (probably cultivated or escaped from cultivation).

2. Pennisetum orientale var. **triflorum** (Nees) Stapf, in Hook. Fl. Brit. Ind. 7: 86. 1896.

Pennisetum triflorum Nees, in Steud., Syn. Pl. Glum. 1: 107. 1854. India.

Plant perennial, forming tough clumps from knotted crowns, culm erect from an ascending base, usually 1 m or more tall, rather robust, simple or sparingly branched, pubescent or scabrous below the panicle; blades flat, lax, 5 to 10 mm wide, elongate; panicles 12 to 20 cm long, 15 to 20 mm thick, purplish, rather loose at least toward the base, nodding; fascicles peduncled, spreading or reflexed; bristles slender, flexuous, unequal, the outer shorter, scabrous only, the inner mostly 1 to 1.5 cm long, plumose below, the innermost one a little stronger and 2 to 2.5 cm long; spikelets 1 to several in a fascicle, 5 to 7 mm long (fig. 327).

Native of India, introduced in the West Indies, where it is called Himalaya grass and is said to be a good forage grass; escaped from cultivation and found along trails in open grassland.

CUBA: Habana, *Ekman* 12820; *Léon* 10613.

JAMAICA: Cinchona, *Hitchcock* 9700, 9725 (*Amer. Gr. Nat. Herb.* 613); *Harris* 11300, 11433.

TRINIDAD: Port-of-Spain, *Hitchcock* 10169.

3. Pennisetum ciliare (L.) Link, Hort. Berol. 1: 213. 1827.

Cenchrus ciliaris L., Mant. Pl. 302. 1771. South Africa.

Pennisetum cenchroides L. Rich., in Pers., Syn. Pl. 1: 72. 1805. Based on *Cenchrus ciliaris* L.

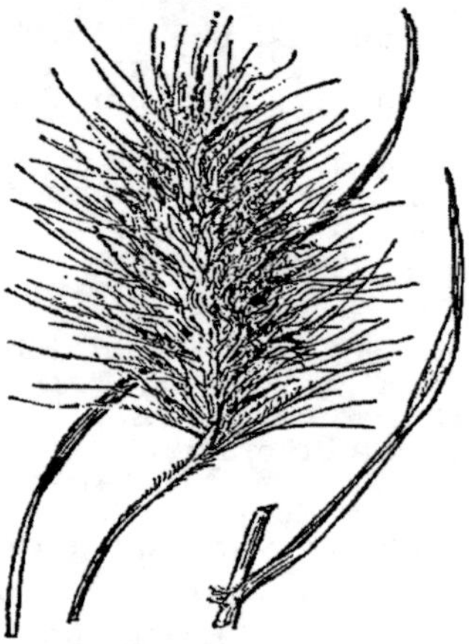

FIGURE 326.—*Pennisetum villosum*, × ½ (Eastwood 172).

FIGURE 327.—*Pennisetum orientale* var. *triflorum*, × ⅔ (Hitchcock 9725, Amer. Gr. Nat. Herb. 613).

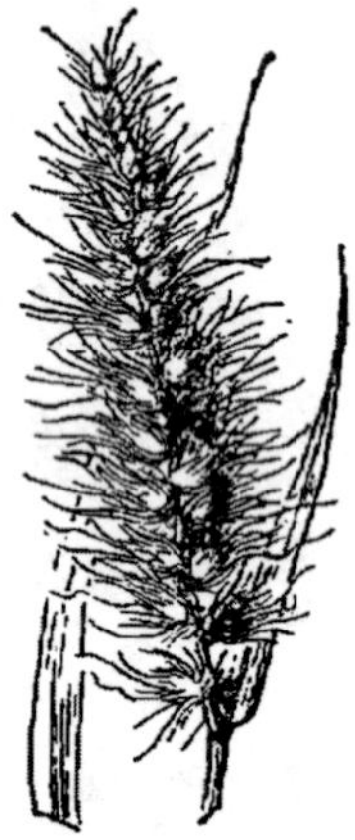

FIGURE 328.—*Pennisetum ciliare*, × ⅔ (Drummond).

Perennial, tufted from a knotted crown; culms geniculate, 10 to 50 cm tall, sometimes taller, sparingly branching; blades flat or folded; panicle 1.5 to 10 cm long, not dense, purplish, mostly flexuous; the fascicles spreading; bristles united at the very base, flexuous, unequal, the outer short, slender, scabrous only, the inner thicker, about twice the length of the spikelet, ciliate, the innermost one a little longer than the rest; spikelets 1 to 5 in a fascicle (fig. 328).

Arid open ground, Eastern Hemisphere, introduced in Central America and Puerto Rico.

PUERTO RICO: Ponce, *Britton, Cowell, and Brown* 5380.

4. Pennisetum glaucum (L.) R. Br., Prodr. Fl. Nov. Holl. 1: 195. 1810. PEARL MILLET.

Panicum glaucum L., Sp. Pl. 56. 1753.[91]

Holcus spicatus L., Syst. Nat. ed. 10. 2: 1305. 1759.

Pennisetum typhoideum L. Rich., in Pers., Syn. Pl. 1: 72. 1805.

[91] For the nomenclatural history of the species see CHASE, Contrib. U. S. Natl. Herb. 22: 216. 1921; Amer. Jour. Bot. 8: 41–49. 1921.

Penicillaria spicata Willd., Enum. Pl. 1037. 1809.

Plant annual; culms robust, as much as 2 m or more tall (depauperate escaped plants much smaller), densely villous below the panicle; blades flat, cordate at base, as much as 1 m long and 5 cm wide; panicles cylindric, stiff, very dense, as much as 40 to 50 cm long and 2 to 2.5 cm thick, pale, bluish or tawny; bristles about as long as the spikelets.

Known only in cultivation. Common in Africa and occasional in the southern United States and other American countries. Not grown in the West Indies, but depauperate specimens have been collected along the roadsides in Haiti.

HAITI: Port-au-Prince, *Ekman* H 3014. Ennery, *Leonard* 8830.

5. **Pennisetum purpureum** Schumach., Beskr. Guin. Pl. 64. 1827. Guinea. NAPIER GRASS.

This tropical African species is being introduced as fodder in various parts of tropical America under the name of Napier grass and elephant grass. It is a robust leafy tufted branching perennial, 2 to 4 m tall, with elongate blades 2 to 3 cm wide, and dense stiff, tawny or purplish panicles, the fascicles sessile, the sparsely plumose bristles exceeding the 2 or 3 unequally pediceled spikelets. The plants escape occasionally from cultivation.

CUBA: Aspiro, *Léon* 15555. Experiment Station, Santiago de las Vegas, *Hitchcock* 23247, 23251. Cruz de Piedra, *Léon* 14247.

HAITI: Port-au-Prince, *Ekman* H 9127.

DOMINICAN REPUBLIC: Jaina, *Faris* 92.

PUERTO RICO: Joyuya, *Perkins* in 1928.

VIRGIN ISLANDS: St. Croix, *Thompson* 466.

LEEWARD ISLANDS: Antigua, *Box* 101.

6. **Pennisetum setosum** (Swartz) L. Rich., in Pers., Syn. Pl. 1: 72. 1805.

Cenchrus setosus Swartz, Prodr. Veg. Ind. Occ. 26. 1788. West Indies.

Pennisetum alopecuroides Desv.; Hamilt., Prodr. Pl. Ind. Occ. 11. 1825. Not *P. alopecuroides* Spreng., 1825. West Indies.

Pennisetum erubescens Desv.; Hamilt. Prodr. Pl. Ind. Occ. 11. 1825. St. Thomas.

Pennisetum hamiltonii Steud., Nom. Bot. ed. 2. 2: 297. 1841. Based on *P. alopecuroides* Hamilt.

Perennial, in loose clumps, sometimes of 30 or more culms; culms usually 1 to 2 m tall, slender to robust, subcompressed, ascending or suberect from the more or less geniculate, sometimes rooting lower nodes, bearing one to several flowering branches from the lower and middle nodes, scabrous below the panicle, otherwise glabrous; blades mostly rather firm, 10 to 40 cm long, 4 to 18 mm wide; panicles terminating the primary culm and branches, occasionally one or two axillary panicles borne in the upper sheaths, 10 to 25 cm long, 8 to 10 mm thick, excluding the elongate bristles, rather dense, usually somewhat nodding, from pale yellow to dusky purple or brown; fascicles sessile, at first ascending, spreading or reflexed in age; bristles unequal, the outer delicate, most of them shorter than the spikelet, the inner densely silky-plumose below, the hairs directed inward, those of the erect lower part of adjoining bristles matted and beautifully crimped; spikelets solitary (fig. 329).

FIGURE 329.—*Pennisetum setosum*. Plant, × ½; two views of spikelet, and fertile floret, × 10 (Garber).

Open slopes and savannas, southern Florida and Mexico to Bolivia and Brazil.

CUBA: San Juan de Buenavista, *Wright* 3471. Río San Juan, *Ekman* 18069.

JAMAICA: There is a specimen in the Trinius Herbarium sent from Jamaica by Swartz, but it may not have been collected there. The species is not known to occur in Jamaica.

HAITI: Mirebalais, *Ekman* H 5508. La Source, *Ekman* H 3386. St. Michel de l'Atalaye, *Leonard* 7411, 8059. Caille la Croix, *Leonard* 7888. Ennery, *Leonard* 8975.

LEEWARD ISLANDS: St. Kitts, *Fairchild* 2662; *Hitchcock* 16349; *Thompson* 559; *Box* 136. Guadeloupe, *Duss* 4152. Dominica, *Jones* 5; *Hitchcock* 16436.

WINDWARD ISLANDS: Martinique, *Duss* 1136, 4017; *Hahn* 1012. Barbados, *Hitchcock* 16504; *Dash* 346.

TRINIDAD: St. Joseph, *Hitchcock* 10176 (*Amer. Gr. Nat. Herb.* 612). Icacos, *Broadway* 4964; *Hitchcock* 10153 (*Amer. Gr. Nat. Herb.* 611).

TOBAGO: *Broadway* 4683; *Hitchcock* 10235.

7. Pennisetum domingense (Spreng.) Spreng., Syst. Veg. 1: 302. 1825.

Gymnothrix domingensis Spreng.; Schult., Mant. 2: 284. 1824. Santo Domingo.

Perennial, glabrous; culms slender, rigid, glaucous, as much as 7 m tall, branching, the branches borne singly or in fascicles of 2 to 4, about equaling the main culm, stiffly spreading at an angle of about 30°; nodes mostly swollen; blades 0.5 to 4 cm long, 1 to 2 mm wide, involute, divergent, firm, finally falling from the sheaths; panicles 2 to 5 cm long, terminal only, loosely flowered; bristles unequal, most of them 4 to 10 mm long, the innermost less slender and 15 to 20 mm long; spikelets 4.2 to 4.5 mm long (fig. 330).

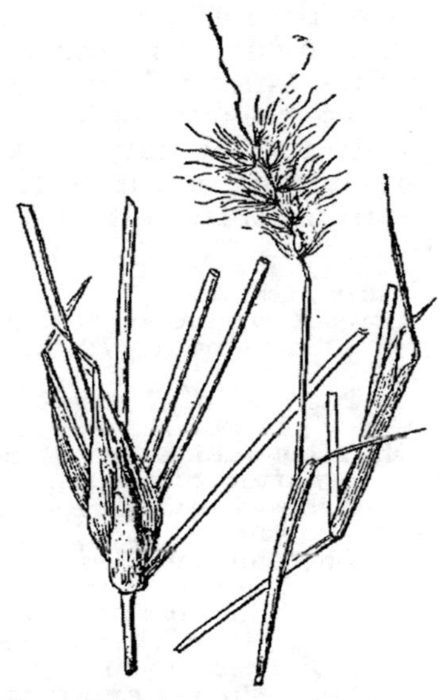

FIGURE 330.—*Pennisetum domingense*, × 1 (Tuerckheim 3669).

On dry shrubby hillsides, Cuba and Hispaniola.

CUBA: Eastern Cuba, *Wright* 1547.

DOMINICAN REPUBLIC: Los Furnios, *Ekman* H 9859. Maniel de Ocoa, *Tuerckheim* 3669. San José de Ocoa, *Ekman* H 11673. Monción, *Ekman* H 13087.

In Grasses of the West Indies [92] *Pennisetum antillarum* (Poir.) Desv. is included, the type, marked "Antilles", having been examined in the herbarium of the Botanical Garden at Florence and a fragment deposited in the United States National Herbarium. In 1932 C. E. Hubbard, of Kew Herbarium, sent us specimens of *Pennisetum hordeoides* (Lam.) Steud., from West Africa, for comparison with the fragment. As Mr. Hubbard suggested, the two proved to belong to

[92] Contrib. U. S. Natl. Herb. 18: 353. 1917.

the same species. "Antilles" is probably an error, though possibly the species may have been introduced in the slave trade, but failed to persist.

95. CENCHRUS L., Sp. Pl. 1049. 1753

Spikelets sessile, 1 to several together, permanently enclosed in a bristly or spiny involucre or bur, composed of more or less coalesced sterile branchlets; burs sessile or nearly so on a slender, compressed, or angled axis, its apex produced into a short point beyond the uppermost bur, the burs falling entire, the grains germinating within them; involucre (especially in our species) somewhat oblique, its body irregularly cleft, the lobes rigid, in most species resembling the spines, the cleft on the side of the bur next to the axis reaching to the tapering, abruptly narrowed or truncate base, the bristles or spines barbed, at least toward the summit; spikelets mostly glabrous or nearly so; first glume 1-nerved, usually narrow, sometimes wanting; second glume and sterile lemma 3- to 5-nerved, the lemma enclosing a well-developed palea and usually a staminate flower; fruit usually turgid, indurate, the lemma acuminate, the nerves visible toward the summit, the margins thin, flat. Annuals or perennials, with terminal racemes of burs.

Plants perennial.
  Bristles and lobes of the involucre slender and terete or nearly so.
    Burs about 5 mm high; involucral lobes united at base only. 1. C. MYOSUROIDES.
    Burs about 7 mm high; involucral lobes united a short distance above the base ---------- 2. C. EKMANIANUS.
  Bristles unlike, the outer slender, terete, the inner, or the lobes of the involucre, flattened at base.
    Lobes of involucre as long as spikelet; thick base of bur nearly as broad as the bur ---------- 7. C. MICROCEPHALUS.
    Lobes of involucre longer than the spikelets; base of bur triangular, narrower than the bur.
      Blades involute, squarrose, conspicuously distichous, not more than 2.5 cm long, about 1 cm apart ---------- 3. C. DISTICHOPHYLLUS.
      Blades not involute and squarrose, nor conspicuously distichous, much longer and further apart ---------- 6. C. GRACILLIMUS.
Plants annual.
  Involucre with a ring of slender bristles at base.
    Burs, excluding the bristles, not more than 4 mm wide, numerous, crowded in a long spike; lobes of involucre interlocking, not spinelike. 4. C. BROWNII.
    Burs, excluding bristles, about 5.5 mm wide, not densely crowded; lobes of the involucre erect or nearly so or rarely one or two lobes loosely interlocking, the tips spinelike ---------- 5. C. ECHINATUS.
  Involucre with flattened spreading spines, no ring of slender bristles at base.
    Burs, including spines, 7 to 8 mm wide, finely pubescent. 8. C. PAUCIFLORUS.
    Burs, including spines, 10 to 12 mm wide, usually densely woolly. 9. C. TRIBULOIDES.

1. Cenchrus myosuroides H. B. K., Nov. Gen. et Sp. 1: 115. pl. 35. 1815. Cuba. Flamingo Key (near Batabanó), *Humboldt and Bonpland.*

Pennisetum myosuroides Spreng., Syst. Veg. 1: 303. 1825.
Cenchropsis myosuroides Nash, in Small, Fl. Southeast. U. S. 109, 1327. 1903.

Plants perennial; culms solitary or in small clumps, usually 1 to 2 m tall, glabrous, rather robust and woody, commonly glaucous, often branching; blades firm, 15 to 40 cm long, 5 to 12 mm wide, tapering from the rounded flat base to an attenuate, often involute tip; spike 10 to 25 cm long, strict, dense; burs 1-flowered, about 5 mm high, the bristles united at the base only, the lowest row shorter, the inner slender about equaling the spikelet (fig. 331).

Moist, sandy open ground or scrubland near the coast, southern Georgia to Texas, south through Mexico to Argentina; Greater Antilles.

CUBA: Santiago de Cuba, *Léon* 835. Guantánamo, *Ekman* 2858.

HAITI: Miragoane, *Eyerdam* 216. Peninsula de Barahona, *Ekman* H 7059. Môle-St.-Nicolas, *Ekman* H 4493. Tortuga Island, *Ekman* H 4143.

DOMINICAN REPUBLIC: Monte Chico, *Ekman* H 13171.

PUERTO RICO: Cabo Rojo, *Hess* 118. Mona Island, *Hess* 443; *Britton, Cowell, and Hess* 1674.

2. Cenchrus ekmanianus Hitchc., sp. nov.[93]

Perennial; culms erect, branched, glabrous, 80 to 100 cm tall; sheaths loose, overlapping; ligule about 2 mm long, membranaceous below, ciliate above; blades folded, glabrous, 15 to 20 cm long, 3 to 5 mm wide, attenuate to a fine involute point; spikes short-exserted or partially included, 8 to 12 cm long, the burs crowded, the axis angled, flexuous, rather stout, pubescent; burs about 7 mm high (including the bristles), the broad turbinate base puberulent; bristles united for a short distance above the base, the outer 2 to 3 mm long, scabrous, the inner erect or somewhat spreading, puberulent at base; spikelets 1 or 2, about 5 mm long, about as long as the inner spines; first glume half as long as the spikelet; second glume a little shorter than the sterile and fertile lemmas, these 7-nerved.

FIGURE 331.—*Cenchrus myosuroides*. Bur, two views of spikelet, and floret, × 5 (Léon 835).

Type in the United States National Herbarium, no. 1502107, collected in sandy open soil, Monte Chico, Los Siete Hermanos, prov. Monte Cristi, Dominican Republic, July 14, 1929, by E. L. Ekman (no. H 13172).

This species is related to *C. myosuroides* from which it differs in the larger burs, the bristles more united at base, and in the stouter, more flexuous axis of the spike. Known only from the type collection.

3. Cenchrus distichophyllus Griseb., Cat. Pl. Cub. 234. 1866. Cuba, *Wright* 3475.

Plants perennial; culms tufted, rigid, erect or ascending from a curved base, the numerous internodes very short, the long leafless upper part of the culm appressed-pubescent; blades 1.5 to 2.5 cm long, about 1.5 mm wide, conspicuously distichous, stiffly spreading at a uniform angle and usually about 1 cm apart, involute, sharp-pointed; spike 2 to 3 cm long, bearing usually 5 to 7 spreading yellow burs; burs, including the spines, 5 to 6 mm long, the body puberulent;

[93] Perennis: culmi glabri ramosi 80–100 cm alti; laminae glabrae 15–20 cm longae 3–5 mm latae plicatae longe-attenuatae; spicae 8–12 cm longae: involucrum circa 7 mm altum; spiculae una vel duae in quoque involucro; setae longitudine spicularum, exteriores breviores; gluma prima dimidiam spiculam aequans.

outer spines shorter, subterete, the lobes of the involucre about 10; spikelet solitary, about 3.3 mm long (fig. 332).

Dry, sandy pine barrens, Province of Pinar del Río, Cuba.

CUBA: La Grifa, *Ekman* 11250. Pinar del Río, *Ekman* 17845. Laguna Santa Bárbara, *Ekman* 18102. Guane, *Léon* 7475 (*Amer. Gr. Nat. Herb.* 434). San Julián, *Léon* 6941. Laguna Jovero, *Shafer* 10717. Western Cuba, *Wright* 3475.

4. **Cenchrus brownii** Roem. and Schult., Syst. Veg. 2: 258. 1817. Based on *C. inflexus* R. Br.

Cenchrus inflexus R. Br., Prodr. Fl. Nov. Holl. 1: 195. 1810. Not *C. inflexus* Poir., 1804. Australia.

Cenchrus viridis Spreng., Syst. Veg. 1: 301. 1825. Guadeloupe.

Cenchrus echinatus var. *viridis* Spreng.; Griseb., Fl. Brit. W. Ind. 556. 1864.

Culms often rather robust, 30 to 100 cm tall or more, erect from a more or less geniculate base, sparingly branching from the base or

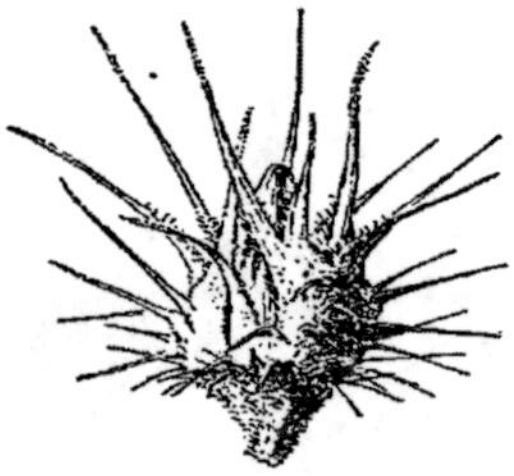

FIGURE 332.—*Cenchrus distichophyllus.* Bur, spikelet, and floret, × 5 (type).

FIGURE 333.—*Cenchrus brownii.* Bur, two views of spikelet, and floret, × 5 (type).

lower nodes; blades thin, flat, lax, mostly 10 to 30 cm long, 6 to 12 mm wide; spike usually short-exserted, 4 to 10 cm long, rarely longer, dense; burs depressed-globose, the body about 4 mm high, as broad or broader, villous, tawny, the outer bristles numerous, very slender, crowded toward the base, the inner usually exceeding the body and the spikelets, erect or spreading, the lobes of the body usually 6 to 8, interlocking at maturity; spikelets usually 3 (fig. 333).

Open ground and waste spaces, often a weed in cultivated fields, southern Florida and Mexico to Brazil.

BAHAMAS: Andros Island, *Small and Carter* 8711.

CUBA: Sierra Mendoza, *Shafer* 11152. Habana, *Léon* 5618. Sancti Spíritus, *Léon* 837; *Clemente* 3442. Camaguey, *Léon* 3963. Cayo Ballenato Grande, *Shafer* 1022. Manatí, *Léon* 5683, 6007. El Cuero, *Britton and Cowell* 12798. Santiago de Cuba, *Pollard, Palmer, and Palmer* 284. Woodfred, *Shafer* 3172. Without locality, *Wright* 3889. Isla de Pinos, *Britton, Wilson, and Léon* 15296.

JAMAICA: Tyre, *Harris* 12617. Hope Gardens, *Harris* 11237; *Hitchcock* 9314; *Maxon* 1640. Spanish Town, *Harris* 12479. Bog Walk, *Hitchcock* 9300. Ipswich, *Hitchcock* 9588. Ewarton, *Hitchcock* 9440. New Forest, *Hitchcock* 9841. Gordon Town, *Hart* 783. Grand Cayman, *Millspaugh* 1268.

HAITI: Port-au-Prince, *Hitchcock* 19870, 19877; *Leonard* 2762. Fond Parisien, *Leonard* 4215. Gonaïve Island, *Leonard* 3084, 5156.

St. Marc, *Leonard* 2969. Pétionville, *Ekman* H 2337. Miragoane, *Eyerdam* 568. Tortuga Island, *Leonard* 11519, 15579. St. Michel de l'Atalaye, *Leonard* 7461. Ennery, *Leonard* 8855.

DOMINICAN REPUBLIC: Santo Domingo, *Millspaugh* 808. Azua, *Rose* 3948. Jaina, *Faris* 12, 108. San Juan, *Ekman* H 13617. Guayubín, *Abbott* 888. Without locality, *Parry and Brummel* 621.

PUERTO RICO: Juana Diaz, *Sintenis* 2904. Guanica Bay, *Chase* 6517. Cayo Muertos, *Britton, Cowell, and Brown* 4986. Vieques Island, *Chase* 6667; *Shafer* 2653. Culebra Island, *Millspaugh* 619; *Britton and Wheeler* 122.

VIRGIN ISLANDS: St. Thomas, *Hitchcock* 16294.

LEEWARD ISLANDS: Guadeloupe, *Duss* 2718.

WINDWARD ISLANDS: Martinique, *Duss* 790.

TRINIDAD: Port-of-Spain, *Hitchcock* 9995. Palo Seco, *Britton and Hazen* 1164. Jawuba Ridge, *Bot. Gard. Herb.* 579. San Juan, *Broadway* 2609. Cedros, *Broadway* 4916.

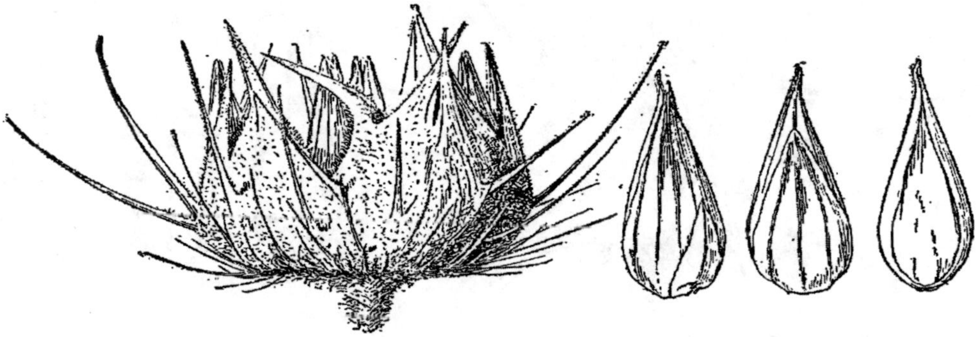

FIGURE 334.—*Cenchrus echinatus*. Bur, two views of spikelet, and floret, × 5 (Hitchcock 9379).

5. Cenchrus echinatus L., Sp. Pl. 1050. 1753. Jamaica and Curaçao.

Culms ascending from a geniculate or decumbent base, often rooting at the lower nodes, branching from the base and usually from the lower nodes, commonly 25 to 60 cm long, sometimes as much as 1 m long; blades commonly 6 to 20 cm long and 3 to 8 mm wide; spikes finally rather long-exserted, 3 to 10 cm long (commonly not more than 7 cm long), not very dense; burs truncate at base, the body 4 to 7 mm high, as broad or broader, pubescent, tawny or plumbeous, the outer bristles slender, the inner stout, broadened at base, the longest of them usually about equaling the lobes of the body, ascending or spreading, the lobes of the body commonly 10, erect or bent inward, the tips hard and spinelike, retrorsely barbed; spikelets about 4 (fig. 334).

Open ground and waste places, a common weed throughout the American Tropics at low and medium altitudes. To be found on probably all the West Indian islands.

6. Cenchrus gracillimus Nash, Bull. Torrey Bot. Club 22: 299. 1895. Florida.

Plants perennial, at length forming dense clumps, glabrous as a whole; culms 20 to 80 cm tall, slender, wiry, erect or ascending; blades usually folded and stiffly flexuous, 5 to 20 cm long, usually 2 to 3 mm wide; spikes 2 to 6 cm long, the burs not crowded; burs 3.5 to 5 mm wide (excluding the spines), somewhat tapering at the base, glabrous; spines spreading or reflexed, all glabrous and flat, broadened at the base, the lowest shorter, the upper 5 to 6 mm long; spikelets 2 or 3, 5.5 to 7 mm long (fig. 335).

Sandy open ground, Florida, Cuba, Jamaica, and Hispaniola.

CUBA: Morillo, *Ekman* 17402. Isla de Pinos, *Britton and Wilson* 14934.

JAMAICA: Southern Manchester, *Harris* 12690; *Hitchcock* 9851 (New Forest).

HAITI: Tortuga Island, *Ekman* H 9760.

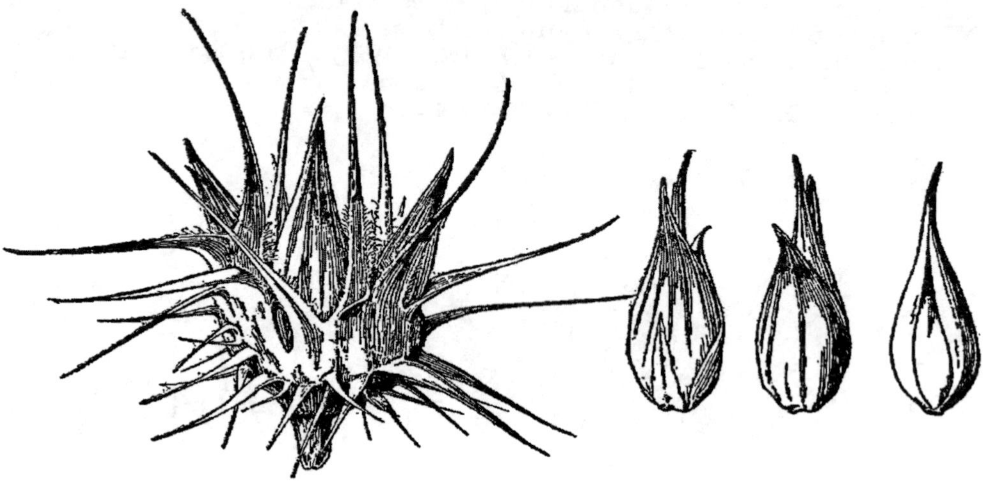

FIGURE 335.—*Cenchrus gracillimus*. Bur, two views of spikelet, and floret, × 5 (type collection).

DOMINICAN REPUBLIC: Matanzas, *Ekman* H 15909. Punto Icacos, *Ekman* H 15786.

7. Cenchrus microcephalus Nash, Contrib. U. S. Natl. Herb. 18: 356. 1917. Bahamas, *Britton and Millspaugh* 2249.

Plants probably perennial, tufted, with numerous leafy sterile shoots at the base, glabrous as a whole; culms 30 to 70 cm tall, slender, scabrous below the spike, ascending from a decumbent base, branching from the middle and upper nodes; blades folded at base, often flat above, rather thin, 10 to 20 cm long, 2 to 3 mm wide, pilose on the upper surface; spikes 3 to 5 cm long; burs (including the bristles) about 6 mm long and 5 mm wide, the body scarcely wider than the thick base; spines flat, broadened at the base, the lowest short and spreading, the upper stout, ciliate at base, shorter than the 5 or 6 lobes of the involucre, these erect or ascending, ciliate nearly to the summit, spikelets usually 2, 4 to 4.5 mm long (fig. 336).

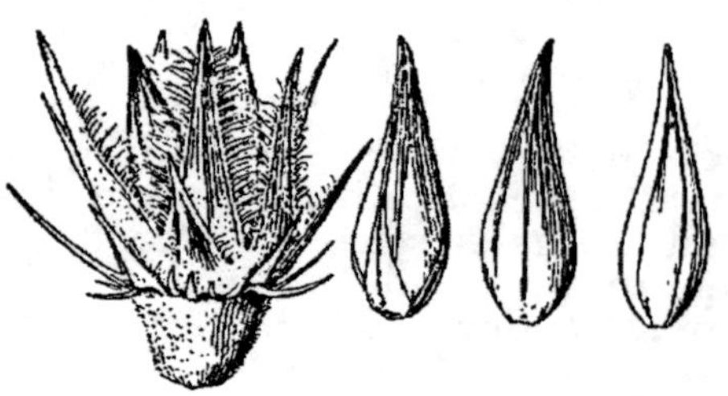

FIGURE 336.—*Cenchrus microcephalus*. Bur, two views of spikelet, and floret, × 5 (type).

Known only from the Berry Islands.

BAHAMAS: Berry Islands, *Britton and Millspaugh* 2211, 2249.

8. Cenchrus pauciflorus Benth., Bot. Voy. Sulph. 56. 1840. Baja California. FIELD SANDBUR.

Sometimes forming large mats; culms 20 to 90 cm long, rather stout, spreading to ascending from a decumbent base, usually freely branching; blades from flat to subinvolute or folded, 3 to 15 cm long, 2 to 7 mm wide; spikes numerous, short-exserted or partly included, 3 to 10 cm long; burs rather crowded (excluding the spines), 3 to 7 mm wide (commonly 4 to 6 mm), pubescent, often densely so, rarely nearly glabrous; spines numerous, spreading or reflexed, flat, broadened at base, the lowermost shorter and relatively slender, some of the upper ones commonly 4 to 5 mm long, usually villous at the base; body of the bur often with one deep cleft on the outer face, the lobes commonly about 8, usually villous at the base, rigid and spinelike; spikelets usually 2 (fig. 337).

This is the species to which the name *Cenchrus tribuloides* was commonly applied until 1908 when it was shown [94] that this name should apply to the large-burred coastal plant which had been distinguished as *C. macrocephalus*. The name *C. carolinianus* Walt. was then applied to this species, but Walter's diagnosis does not agree with its characters and it has not been found in Walter's region.

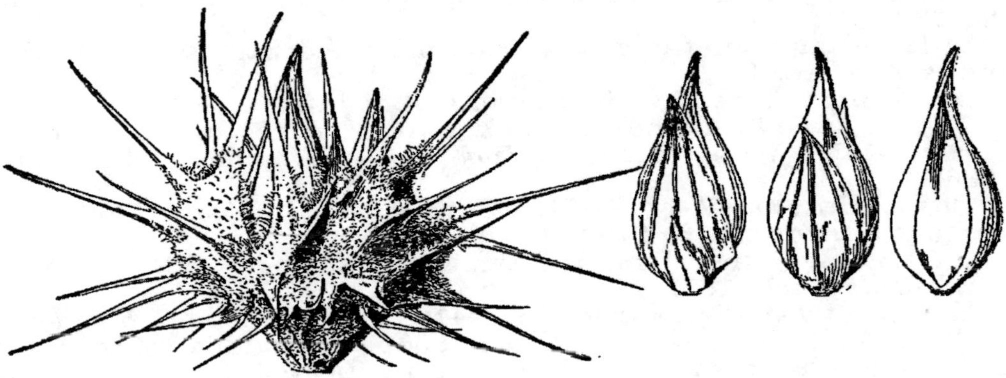

FIGURE 337.—*Cenchrus pauciflorus*. Bur, two views of spikelet, and floret, × 5 (Hitchcock 13582).

Sandy open ground, United States, Mexico, and the West Indies to Argentina.

BAHAMAS: Nassau, *Geogr. Soc. Baltimore* 101.

CUBA: Laguna Santa Bárbara, *Ekman* 18102a, Sábbalo, *Ekman* 11446. Vicinity of Habana, *Hitchcock* 492, 493, 23445; *Léon* 188½, 836, 2391, 3445, 3453; *Ekman* 799; *Palmer and Riley* 1146. Bahía de Manatí, *Léon* 15755, 16026. Without locality, *Wright* 3476.

JAMAICA: Black River, *Hitchcock* 9637. Pigeon Island, *Maxon and Killip* 1569.

HAITI: Gonaîve Island, *Leonard* 3050. Tortuga Island, *Leonard* 13898, 15330; *Ekman* H 4160.

DOMINICAN REPUBLIC: Higüey, *Ekman* H 12228. Los Siete Hermanos, *Ekman* H 13167.

PUERTO RICO: Santurce, *Chase* 6345½.

[94] Contrib. U. S. Natl. Herb. 12: 127. 1908.

VIRGIN ISLANDS: St. Thomas, *Raunkiaer* 634.
LEEWARD ISLANDS: Antigua, *Wullschlaegel* 634; *Box* 104. Barbuda, *Danforth* 7. Guadeloupe, *Stehlé* 197.

9. Cenchrus tribuloides L., Sp. Pl. 1050. 1753. Virginia.

DUNE SANDBUR.

Plants annual, very leafy; culms stout, at first erect, soon branching and becoming radiate-decumbent, 15 to 60 cm long, the ends ascending, rooting at the nodes and with numerous ascending branches 10 to 30 cm tall; sheaths usually overlapping, sharply keeled, those below the spikes inflated; spikes numerous, 3 to 9 cm long, the burs crowded; burs 5 to 6 mm wide, 8 to 9 mm high (excluding the spines), usually conspicuously villous, but sometimes short-pubescent only, the base puberulent; spines finally spreading, flat, the lowermost relatively short and slender, the upper broadened at the base, sometimes as much as 3 mm broad, some of these 5 to 8 mm long, long-villous on the inner face and margins of the broad base; spikelets usually 2, 7 to 8 mm long (fig. 338).

In loose sands of the coast, eastern United States and the West Indies, and Brazil.

BERMUDA: *Collins* 143; *Brown and Britton* 128.

BAHAMAS: Nassau, collector unknown. Andros Island, *Small and Carter* 8972. Water Key, *Wilson* 8151. Anguilla Isles, *Wilson* 7936.

CUBA: Habana, *Léon* 5634. Cayo Sabinal, *Shafer* 700. Cayo Paredon Grande, *Shafer* 2737.

CAYMAN ISLANDS: Grand Cayman, *Millspaugh* 1249. Cayman Brac, *Millspaugh* 1162.

HAITI: Port-de-Pai, *Ekman* H 3941. Gonaïve Island, *Eyerdam* 88.

PUERTO RICO: Arecibo, *Chase* 6561. Aguadilla, *Chase* 6604. Cabo Rojo, *Sintenis* 29b. Cayo Muertos, *Britton, Cowell, and Brown* 5046. Mona Island, *Hess* 440. Vieques Island, *Chase* 6696.

96. OLYRA L., Syst. Nat. ed. 10. 2: 1261. 1759

Plants monoecious; inflorescence paniculate; pistillate spikelets borne on the upper branches and on the ends of the lower branches of loose terminal panicles, the smaller staminate spikelets pedicellate along the lower branches; pistillate spikelets rather large; first glume wanting; second glume and sterile lemma herbaceous, caudate-acuminate; fruit bony-indurate; staminate spikelets readily deciduous; glumes and sterile lemma wanting, the lemma and palea membranaceous. Erect or clambering often woody perennials with broad blades.

Fruit smooth and shining; plants usually more than 3 m tall. ---- 1. O. LATIFOLIA.
Fruit clothed with thick silky hairs at base and summit; plants less than 1 m tall ---- 2. O. CILIATIFOLIA.

1. Olyra latifolia L., Syst. Nat. ed. 10. 2: 1261. 1759. Jamaica.

Olyra paniculata Swartz, Prodr. Veg. Ind. Occ. 21. 1788. Jamaica.

Olyra arundinacea H. B. K., Nov. Gen. et Sp. 1: 197. 1816. Colombia.

Olyra latifolia var. *arundinacea* Griseb., Fl. Brit. W. Ind. 535. 1864.

FIGURE 338.—*Cenchrus tribuloides*. Plant, × ½; two views of spikelet, and floret, × 10 (Kearney).

Glabrous perennial, bamboolike in aspect, commonly 5 m tall, the strong hollow culms sometimes 1 cm thick, erect and unsupported, the summit only arching (or weaker culms leaning among brush), the lower half to two-thirds simple and naked, the short sheaths bladeless or nearly so, the elongate internodes blotched with dull purple, branching from the upper nodes, the branches commonly fascicled, divaricate, often 1 m long, sometimes again branching; blades convolute in the bud, spreading, flat, firm, unsymmetrically lanceolate-oblong, abruptly acuminate, commonly 20 cm long and 5 cm wide, those of the ultimate branches smaller, the lowermost on both primary culm and branches rudimentary; panicles 10 to 15 cm long, about two-thirds as wide, those of the secondary branches reduced, the branches stiffly ascending or spreading, each bearing a single large long-acuminate pistillate spikelet at the thickened summit and several small slender-pediceled staminate spikelets along the rachis (fig. 339).

The form described as *Olyra arundinacea*, has glabrous sheaths and more loosely flowered green panicles. It is found in the West Indies chiefly from Puerto Rico to Trinidad and extends to Brazil. The typical form of *O. latifolia*, with hispid sheaths and denser purple panicle, is found chiefly in Cuba and Jamaica, but extends from Mexico to Brazil. The differences mentioned above are best seen in the primary culms and panicles.

Copses and shady banks, Mexico and West Indies to South America. In Cuba this is one of the grasses called "tibisi." The species is to be found on probably all the West Indian islands. It has not been observed in Bermuda or in the Bahamas.

2. Olyra ciliatifolia Raddi, Agrost. Bras. 19. 1823. Brazil.

Culms erect, mostly simple, in small clumps but gregarious, glabrous, mostly 40 to 80 cm tall; sheaths hispidulous or the lower glabrate; blades flat, glabrous, oblong-elliptic, 8 to 15 cm long, 2 to 4 cm wide, asymmetric at base, one side rounded, the other side straight for 1.5 to 4 cm at an angle of 30° to 45°, the tip acuminate; panicles 10 to 15 cm long, the lower half or two-thirds staminate, the pistillate spikelets in the upper part of the panicle and at the ends of the upper branches; staminate spikelets narrow, about 5 mm long, short-awned; pistillate spikelets elliptic on thickened pedicels, glabrous, acuminate, about 1 cm long, the first glume bearing an awn 1 to 2 cm long; fruit loosely clothed with silky hairs.

Shade of trees, Trinidad to Brazil. Referred by Grisebach[95] to *O. semiovata* Trin.

TRINIDAD: Port-of-Spain, *Hitchcock* 10133; *Broadway* 9194. Without locality, *Broadway* in 1918; *Purdie* 26.

97. LITHACHNE Beauv., Ess. Agrost. 135. pl. 24. f. 2. 1812

Plants monoecious; spikelets in small axillary panicles, these with a single pistillate spikelet at the summit and 1 to several staminate spikelets below; terminal panicle if present wholly staminate; first glume of pistillate spikelet wanting; second glume and sterile lemma herbaceous, long-acuminate; fruit bony-indurate, laterally subcom-

[95] Fl. Brit. W. Ind. 535. 1864.

FIGURE 339.—*Olyra latifolia.* Plant, × ½; pistillate and staminate spikelets, and fertile floret, × 5 (Chase 6416).

pressed, the lemma greatly swollen or gibbous on the back, the narrow palea slightly convex; staminate spikelets reduced to the lemma and palea. Slender perennials with wiry culms and flat blades.

Blades 1.5 to 3 cm wide .... 1. L. PAUCIFLORA.
Blades less than 5 mm wide .... 2. L. PINETI.

1. Lithachne pauciflora (Swartz) Beauv.; Poir., Dict. Sci. Nat. 27: 60. 1823.

Olyra pauciflora Swartz, Prodr. Veg. Ind. Occ. 21. 1788. Jamaica.

Tufted perennial; culms slender, hard, geniculate and naked below, ascending and leafy above, commonly 30 to 50 cm tall; blades flat, usually 5 to 8 cm long, asymmetric, rhombic-lanceolate, acuminate, spreading, crowded toward the summit, the small axillary panicles produced from the upper sheaths; fruit 4 to 5 mm long, white (fig. 340).

Moist woods up to about 2,000 m, Mexico and the West Indies to Argentina. In Cuba called "pito enano."

CUBA: Pinar del Río, *Hitchcock* 23313. Herradura, *Hitchcock* 265. Sumidero, *Shafer and Léon* 13533. Sierra Guane, *Shafer* 10553. El Guama, *Palmer and Riley* 105. Loma Esperon, *Ekman* 644. Madruga, *Curtiss* 661. Laguno de Castellano, *Wilson* 9560. Habana, *Léon* 584. Santiago de las Vegas, *Hitchcock* 264. Cumbre Hermosa, *Wilson and Léon* 11620. San Antonio, *Hitchcock* 266. Cienfuegos, *Pringle* 54; *Jack* 6159. Pozo Azul, *Eggers* 5356. San Blas, *Bailey* 12426; *Jack* 7836. La Gloria, *Shafer* 53. Bayate, *Ekman* 5842. Guara, *Hitchcock* 23399. Isla de Pinos, *Britton and Wilson* 15549. Eastern Cuba, *Wright* 732.

JAMAICA: Chapleton, *Ridley* 69. Roaring River Falls, *Ridley* 73. Kingston, *Hitchcock* 9263. Castleton, *Hitchcock* 9402; *Harris* 11279. Flamstead, *Harris* 11467. Sir Johns Peak, *Harris* 11593. Buff Bay, *Hitchcock* 9770. Savanna-la-Mar, *Hitchcock* 9872. Troy, *Hitchcock* 9815; *Harris* 12575. Ewarton, *Hitchcock* 9424. Ipswich, *Hitchcock* 9613. Claremont, *Hitchcock* 9522. Blue Hole, *Fredholm* 3193. Johns Hall, *Harris* 12834.

HAITI: Port-au-Prince, *Leonard* 5266; *Ekman* H 2178. Cap Haitien, *Leonard* 5283. Pétionville, *Leonard* 4879. St. Louis du Nord, *Leonard* 14188. Port-de-Pai, *Leonard* 12278. Bombardopolis, *Leonard* 13553. Caille la Croix, *Leonard* 7998. Marmelade, *Leonard* 8176. Dondou, *Leonard* 8573. Ennery, *Leonard* 8952. Plaisance, *Leonard* 9379. Pilate, *Leonard* 9597.

DOMINICAN REPUBLIC: Higüey, *Ekman* H 12136.

PUERTO RICO: Mayaguez, *Chase* 6265, 6311. Quebradillas, *Chase* 6569. Arecibo, *Chase* 6456. Bayamon, *Chase* 6410. Cayey, *Sintenis* 2396.

VIRGIN ISLANDS: St. Croix, *Thompson* 372.

LEEWARD ISLANDS: Antigua, *Box* 76; *Rose* 3486. Guadeloupe, *Duss* 3178.

WINDWARD ISLANDS: Martinique, *Duss* 733.

2. Lithachne pineti (Wright) Chase, Biol. Soc. Wash. Proc. 21: 182. 1908.

Olyra pineti Wright; Griseb., Mem. Amer. Acad. (n. s.) 8: 532. 1862. Eastern Cuba, *Wright* 1536.

Perennial; culms tufted, filiform, lax, spreading, 10 to 20 cm long; blades ovate to lanceolate, soon reflexed, 10 to 15 mm long, 3 to 7 mm

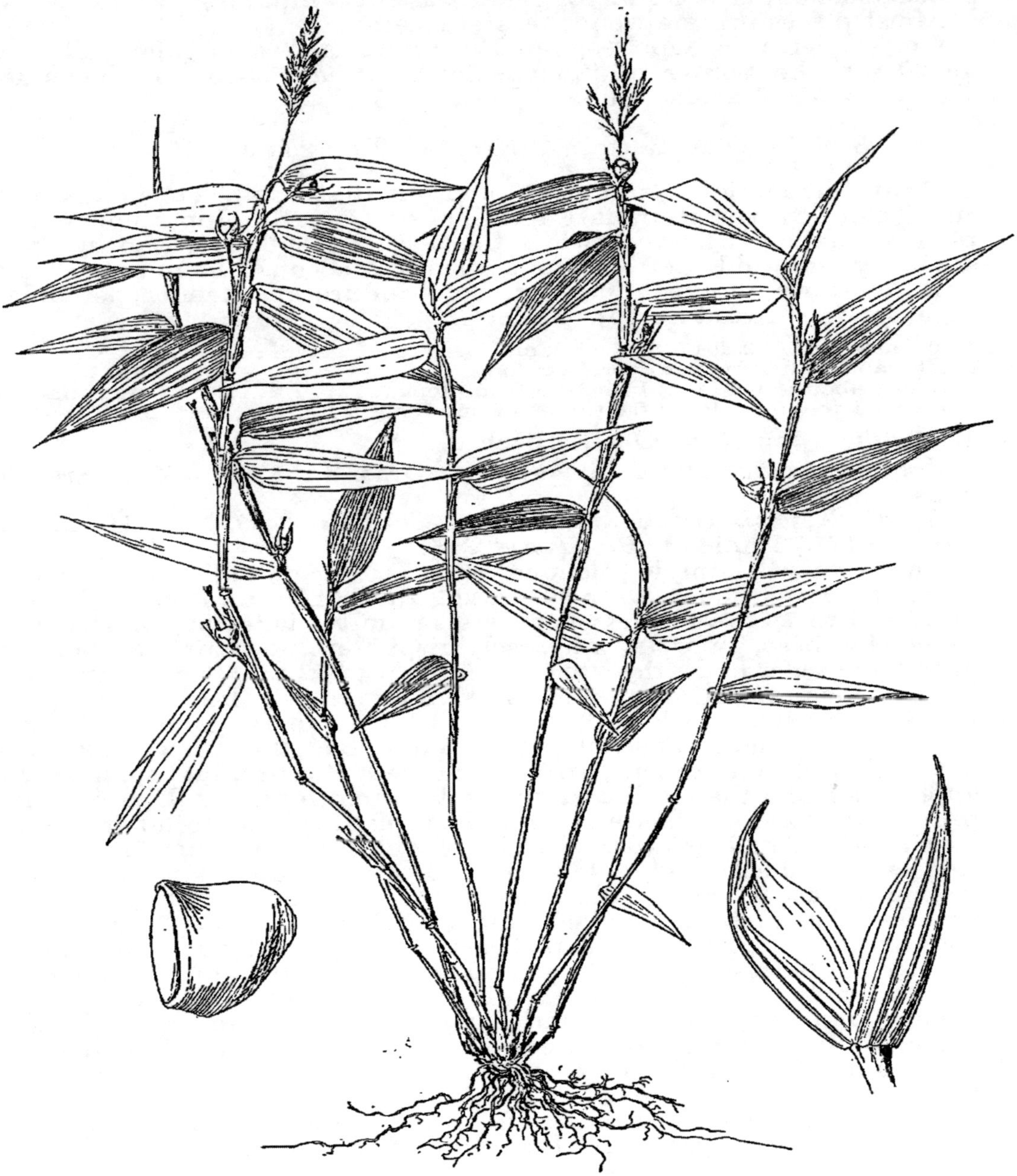

FIGURE 340.—*Lithachne pauciflora*. Plant, × ½; glumes and floret of pistillate spikelet, × 5 (Shafer 53).

wide; staminate spikelets narrow, 3 to 4 mm long; glumes of pistillate spikelets acuminate, 5 mm long; fruit about 3 mm long.

Moist places in pine woods, eastern Cuba.

CUBA: Sierra de Nipe, edge of Río Piloto, in "carrascales", *Ekman* 19160; on the border of "manacales", *Ekman* 2560; in pinelands, *Ekman* 2287. Eastern Cuba, *Wright* 1536.

98. RADDIA Bertol., Opusc. Sci. Bologna 3: 410. 1819

Plants monoecious; staminate and pistillate spikelets in distinct small panicles, the staminate terminal or from the upper nodes, the pistillate axillary; first glume of the pistillate spikelets wanting, the second glume and sterile lemma membranaceous, acuminate; fruit dorsally subcompressed, narrow, bony-indurate. Slender perennial with flat blades and narrow panicles.

Fruit pubescent; blades 5 to 7 cm long .... 1. R. SYMPODICA.
Fruit glabrous; blades not over 4 cm long.
  Blades about 3 cm long; fruit 6 to 7 mm long .... 2. R. GUIANENSIS.
  Blades 1 to 1.5 cm long; fruit about 2 mm long .... 3. R. NANA.

1. **Raddia sympodica** (Doell) Hitchc.

Olyra sympodica Doell, in Mart., Fl. Bras. 2^2: 322. 1877. French Guiana.

Raddia biformis Hitchc. and Chase, Contrib. U. S. Natl. Herb. 18: 358. 1917. Trinidad, *Broadway* 2375.

Culms tufted, simple, slender, erect, or ascending from strongly geniculate lower nodes, 15 to 30 cm tall, the sterile culms naked below, bearing 5 to 7 crowded leaves at the summit; blades flat, lanceolate, rounded at base, glabrous or sparsely hispid on upper surface, sparsely hispid and paler beneath, 3 to 7 cm long, 6 to 12 mm wide; staminate inflorescence consisting of small spikelike panicles of 2 to 5 spikelets borne in the upper axils and at the ends of the leafy culms the lateral spikelets staminate, subsessile, about 3 mm long, 0.8 mm wide, acuminate, minutely puberulent, strongly nerved, the terminal spikelets in appearance like the pistillate ones, 7 to 8 mm long, on short obconic pedicels, neutral or with a rudimentary pistil; pistillate inflorescence consisting of small spikelike panicles of 2 or 3 fertile spikelets on short thickened pedicels and a few more or less rudimentary subsessile staminate ones borne at the ends and in the upper slightly inflated sheaths of low slender naked culms arising from the base; fertile spikelets on short thickened pedicels, 7 to 8 mm long, 2 mm wide, subterete, oblong-elliptic; glume and sterile lemma subequal, puberulent, strongly nerved, acuminate into short setaceous scabrous tips about 1 mm long; fruit 6.5 mm long, about 1.5 mm wide, elliptic, apiculate, becoming lead-colored at maturity, clothed with soft silky appressed hairs, a glabrous stripe down the back, the margins of the lemma nearly meeting over the palea.

Shady forest floors, Trinidad and French Guiana. "A dwarf grass in sandy soil on slopes under the shade of large forest trees" (Broadway).

TRINIDAD: Tabaquite, *Hitchcock* 10127. Ortoire River, Guayaguayari Road, *Britton, Freeman, and Nowell* 2530. Caparo, *Broadway* 2375.

2. Raddia guianensis (Brongn.) Hitchc.

Strephium guianense Brongn., Bull. Soc. Bot. France 7: 471. 1860. French Guiana.

Raddia urbaniana Hitchc. and Chase, Contrib. U. S. Natl. Herb. 18: 359. 1917. Tobago, *Hitchcock* 10267.

Olyra urbaniana Mez, Notizbl. Bot. Gart. Berlin 7: 47. 1917. Tobago, *Eggers* 5841.

Culms tufted, slender, ascending from more or less geniculate lower nodes, 20 to 45 cm tall, naked below, toward the summit bearing 12 to 24 approximate leaves with overlapping sheaths and distichous spreading blades; blades flat, glabrous, oblong-lanceolate, rounded at both ends, mucronate, 2 to 3.5 cm long, 4 to 8 mm wide; staminate panicles several to many from the axils of the upper sheaths, narrow, few-flowered, the axis and pedicels angled, scabrous, the spikelets 5 to 6 mm long, acuminate-pointed; pistillate panicles 1 or 2 from the middle nodes, bearing 2 to 5 spikelets on short clavate pedicels; spikelets lanceolate, the glume 8 mm long, much exceeding the fruit, the sterile lemma 5 mm long, both acuminate-setaceous; fruit 4 mm long, about 1 mm wide, bluntly acuminate, whitish, glabrous (fig. 341).

Shady banks and floor of forest, Tobago to Brazil.

TOBAGO: *Hitchcock* 10267 (*Amer. Gr. Nat. Herb.* 626); *Broadway* 3004, 4360; *Eggers* 5841.

FIGURE 341.—*Raddia guianensis*. Plant, × ½; staminate and pistillate spikelets and pistillate floret, × 5 (Hitchcock 10267, Amer. Gr. Nat. Herb. 626).

3. Raddia nana (Doell) Chase, Biol. Soc. Wash. Proc. 21: 185. 1908.

Olyra nana Doell, in Mart., Fl. Bras. 2^2: 329. 1877. Brazil.

Culms tufted, delicate, lax or straggling, nearly simple, 10 to 30 cm long, naked below; blades flat, oblong- to ovate-triangular, spreading or reflexed, 10 to 12 mm long, 5 to 7 mm wide, mucronate at the rounded apex; racemes small and few-flowered, axillary, scarcely exserted from the upper sheaths; pistillate spikelets ovoid, 2 mm long, the glumes puberulent.

Wet sandy savannas, Trinidad to Brazil.

TRINIDAD: Aripo Savanna, *Hitchcock* 10079; *Broadway* 7685. *Bot. Gard. Herb.* 6671.

99. MNIOCHLOA Chase, Biol. Soc. Wash. Proc. 21: 185. 1908

Plants monoecious; inflorescence a pair of slender racemes, one pistillate, the other staminate, at the summit of a naked culm; pistillate spikelets subsessile; first glume wanting; second glume and sterile lemma subequal, obtuse, or subacute; fruit white, cartilaginous, subindurate; staminate spikelets smaller, reduced to the lemma and palea. Slender perennials with flat firm subpetiolate blades.

Flowering culms much exceeding the sterile ones; fruit glabrous. 1. M. PULCHELLA.

Flowering culms mostly shorter than the sterile culms; fruit pubescent. 2. M. STREPHIOIDES.

1. Mniochloa pulchella (Griseb.) Chase, Biol. Soc. Wash. Proc. 21: 186. pl. 4. 1908.

Digitaria pulchella Griseb., Cat. Pl. Cub. 231. 1866. Cuba, *Wright* 3448.

Strephium? pulchellum Wright, An. Acad. Cienc. Habana 8: 202. 1871.

Culms tufted, filiform, lax and spreading, the sterile 5 to 10 cm long, the flowering culm erect or ascending, 10 to 20 cm tall, bearing a single sheath about the middle and another near the base; blades lanceolate-oblong, flat, sparsely hispidulous on the upper surface, scabrous beneath, 10 to 18 mm long, 4 to 7 mm wide; racemes 2 to 3 cm long; pistillate spikelets about 2.7 mm long; staminate spikelets about 1.4 mm long (fig. 342).

On shady limestone rocks, rare, eastern Cuba.

CUBA: El Yunque de Baracoa, *Wright* 3448; *Ekman* 3916.

2. Mniochloa strephioides (Griseb.) Chase, Biol. Soc. Wash. Proc. 21: 186. 1908.

Olyra strephioides Griseb., Cat. Pl. Cub. 229. 1866. Cuba, *Wright* 3435.

Culms lax, erect or more or less spreading, the sterile usually 10 to 15 cm tall, the fertile 4 to 7 cm tall, bearing a single sheath about the middle; blades oblong to ovate-triangular, flat, finely puberulent or scabrous, truncate at base, 5 to 15 mm long, 3 to 8 mm wide; racemes 1.5 to 2 cm long; pistillate spikelets about 4.5 mm long; staminate spikelets 1.5 mm long.

Shady banks and ravines, western Cuba.

CUBA: Cayabos, *Ekman* 12945. Cabanas, *Ekman* in 1921. San Diego de los Baños, *Léon* 4391, 4572, 4593; *Caldwell and Baker* 7011. Pinar del Río, *Hitchcock* 23310. Habana, *Ekman* 1238. Campo Florido, *Léon* 4140. Western Cuba, *Wright* 3435.

100. EKMANOCHLOA Hitchc., gen. nov.[96]

Plants monoecious; inflorescence a pair of slender racemes, one pistillate, the other staminate, at the summit of leafy culms; pistillate spikelets short-pediceled along a slender rachis; first glume wanting;

[96] Planta monoica; racemi bini, uno masculo, uno femineo; spiculae femineae: Gluma prima nulla; gluma secunda et lemma sterile subaequalia, 3-5-nervia; lemma fertile subteres, cartilagineum, versus apicem angustatum, aristatum; arista tenui; palea in lemmate inclusa; spiculae masculae: Lemma et palea subaequalia acuta lemmate 3-nervio.

second glume and sterile lemma somewhat unequal, 3- to 5-nerved; fertile lemma subterete, cartilaginous, gradually narrowed into a slender awn; palea as long as the body of the lemma and enclosed within it; staminate spikelets smaller, reduced to subequal lemma and palea. Slender tufted perennials with flat narrowly lanceolate blades, often reduced. The genus is named for the late Dr. Erik L. Ekman, indefatigable botanical explorer.

Type species, *E. subaphylla* Hitchc.

Glume and sterile lemma much shorter than the floret.
1. E. SUBAPHYLLA.
Glume and sterile lemma about as long as the body of the floret...2. E. ARISTATA.

1. Ekmanochloa subaphylla Hitchc., sp. nov.[97]

Perennial; culms cespitose, slender, erect, rather wiry, glabrous, 50 to 100 cm tall; sheaths shorter than the internodes, glabrous; ligule very minute; blades from minute to well developed, flat, 1 to 3.5 cm long, 1 to 4 mm wide, narrowly lanceolate, rather distinctly nerved, scaberulous or puberulent, with a puberulent petiole 1 mm long or less; racemes conjugate, erect, appressed or approximate, the pistillate one 3 to 4 cm long, the staminate about half as long, the rachis slender, terete or somewhat angular, glabrous; pistillate spikelets appressed, distant (4 to 6 mm), about 6 mm long excluding the awn, the pedicel 1 mm long or a little less, rather thick; second glume 1.5 to 2 mm long, 3-nerved, glabrous, the sterile lemma similar but a little longer; fertile lemma glabrous, broadest about 2 mm above the base (about 0.7 mm thick), gradually narrowed above, the awn somewhat flexuous, slightly scaberulous, 1

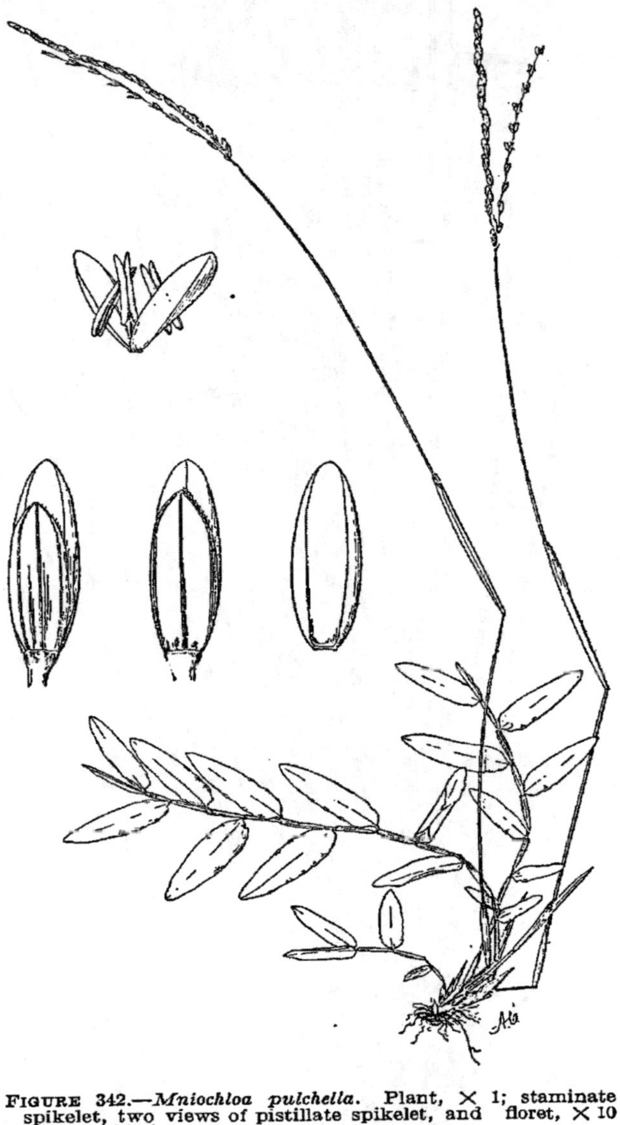

FIGURE 342.—*Mniochloa pulchella*. Plant, × 1; staminate spikelet, two views of pistillate spikelet, and floret, × 10 (Wright 3448).

[97] Perennis culmi caespitosi tenues erecti glabri 50–100 cm alti; vaginae plerumque sine laminis; laminae perfectae planae anguste lanceolatae, minute scaberulae, usque ad 3 cm longae 1–4 mm latae; racemi appressi erecti, feminei 3–4 cm longi, masculi breviores; spiculae femineae arista exclusa 6 mm longae; gluma 1.5–2 mm longa; spiculae masculae 2 mm longae.

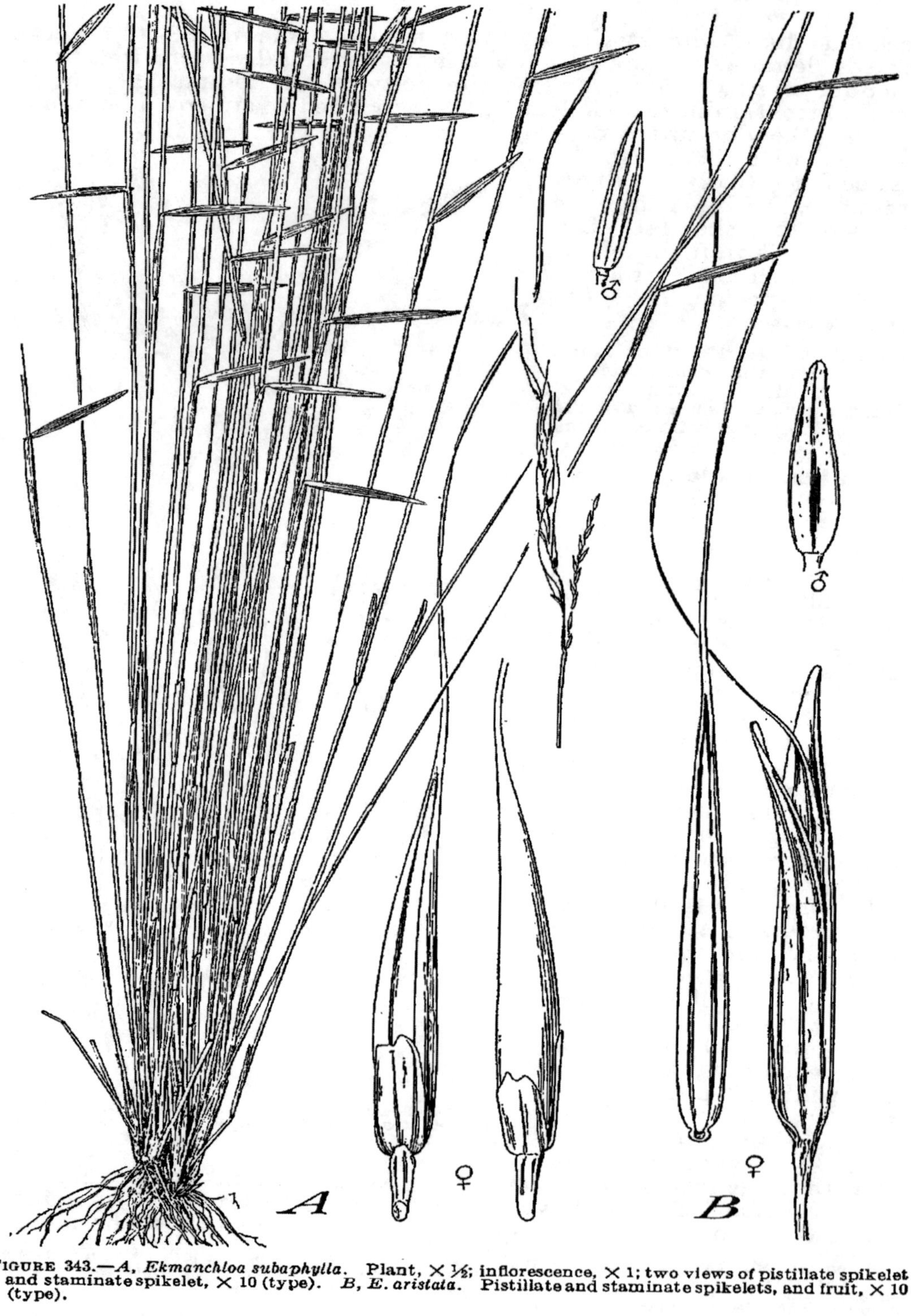

FIGURE 343.—*A*, *Ekmanchloa subaphylla*. Plant, × ½; inflorescence, × 1; two views of pistillate spikelet and staminate spikelet, × 10 (type). *B*, *E. aristata*. Pistillate and staminate spikelets, and fruit, × 10 (type).

to 1.5 cm long; staminate spikelets about 2 mm apart, appressed, about 2 mm long, the lemma and palea subequal, acute, the lemma 3-nerved, the pedicel less than 1 mm long (fig. 343, *A*).

Type in the United States National Herbarium, no. 1259999, collected on overhanging limestone rocks of Loma Picote, Sierra de Nipe, prov. Oriente, Cuba, altitude 500 m, November 2, 1922, by E. L. Ekman.

Only known from province of Oriente, Cuba, the other specimen seen being from Sierra de Nipe, in limestone hills at Río Jimbambay, *Ekman* 9870.

2. Ekmanochloa aristata Ekman, sp. nov.[98]

Similar to *E. subaphylla*, about 50 cm tall; sheaths shorter, with a few long hairs at the summit; blades, except the lower, developed, 1 to 3.7 cm long, 1.5 to 4 mm wide; inflorescence few-flowered, the staminate and pistillate spikelets each 4 or 5; pistillate spikelets 8 to 9 mm long excluding the awn, the glume and sterile lemma equaling the body of the fertile floret, 3 and 5 nerved, obscurely pubescent between the nerves; awn of the fertile floret about 15 mm long; staminate spikelets 3 to 3.2 mm long, obscurely pubescent (fig. 343, *B*).

Type in the United States National Herbarium no. 1385553, collected "in carrascales-pinales, between Taco and Nibujon, prov. Oriente, very rare", December 4, 1914, by E. L. Ekman (no. 3729). Only known from the type collection.

TRIBE 13. ANDROPOGONEAE

101. IMPERATA Cyrillo, Pl. Rar. Neap. 2: 26. 1792

Spikelets all alike, awnless, in pairs, unequally pedicellate on a slender continuous rachis, surrounded by long silky hairs; glumes about equal, membranaceous; sterile lemma, fertile lemma, and palea thin and hyaline. Slender erect perennials with terminal narrow silky panicles.

Panicle rarely more than 15 cm long; spikelets 4 mm long. 1. I. BRASILIENSIS.
Panicle as much as 40 cm long; spikelets 3 mm long. 2. I. CONTRACTA.

1. Imperata brasiliensis Trin., Mém. Acad. St. Pétersb. VI. Math. Phys. Nat. 2: 331. 1832. Brazil.

Perennial, erect, tufted, with scaly rhizomes; culm slender, simple, 0.5 to 1 m tall; leaves mostly clustered toward the base, the blades flat, 5 to 10 mm wide; panicle pale, narrow (fig. 344).

Open rather dry ground at low altitudes, Bahamas and southern Mexico to Brazil.

BAHAMAS: Andros Island, *Small and Carter* 8910. Eleuthera, *E. Britton* 6506.

CUBA: Sierra de los Órganos, *Ekman* 10678. Herradura, *Van Hermann* 575. Consolación del Sur, *Palmer and Riley* 472. Paso Real, *Léon* 4262. Calvario, *Léon* 1582. Loma Menqura, *Shafer* 3856. Riverside, *Shafer* 1145. Without locality, *Wright* 3486. Isla de Pinos, *Jennings* 296; *Britton and Wilson* 14397, 14399.

JAMAICA: Lititz, *Harris* 11660, 11742, 12880.

[98] Ab *E. subaphylla* differt vaginis brevioribus, spicula femina 8–9 mm longa; gluma et lemmate sterili lemma fertile aequantibus.

FIGURE 344.—*Imperata brasiliensis*. Plant, × ½; spikelet, × 5 (Chapman)

HAITI: Mission, *Leonard* 3830. Massif du Nord, Gros-Morne, *Ekman* H 5020.

DOMINICAN REPUBLIC: Monción, *Ekman* H 12894.

TRINIDAD: O'Meara Savanna, *Britton and Hazen* 1577. Pitch Lake, *Hitchcock* 10095 (*Amer. Gr. Nat. Herb.* 232). Jerningham Junction, *Broadway* 4787.

2. Imperata contracta (H. B. K.) Hitchc., Rep. Mo. Bot. Gard. 4: 146. 1893.

Saccharum contractum H. B. K., Nov. Gen. et Sp. 1: 182. 1816. Colombia.

Saccharum caudatum Meyer, Prim. Fl. Esseq. 68. 1818. British Guiana.

Anatherum caudatum Schult., Mant. 2: 445. 1824.

Anatherum portoricense Spreng., Syst. Veg. 1: 290. 1825. Puerto Rico.

Imperata caudata Trin., Mém. Acad. St. Pétersb. VI. Math. Phys. Nat. 2: 331. 1832.

Taller than the preceding, the culms leafy, the panicle as much as 40 cm long.

Swamps and moist open ground, southern Mexico and the West Indies to Brazil.

CUBA: Colonia San Rafael, *Léon* 5682. La Prenda, *Hioram* 2408. Bayate, *Ekman* 5877.

JAMAICA: Berwick, *Harris* 11532. Westphalia, *Harris* 11569. Troy, *Hitchcock* 9804; *Harris* 12619. Resource, *Harris* 12416. Without locality, *Wilson*. Grand Cayman, *Hitchcock* in 1891.

HAITI: Morne Basil, *Ekman* H 2488. Massif de la Hotte, *Ekman* H 7341. Aux Cayes, *Ekman* H 255.

DOMINICAN REPUBLIC: Valle del Cibao, *Ekman* H 13284. Jarabaco, *Ekman* H 14127.

PUERTO RICO: Hato Grande, *Sintenis* 2720. Cayey, *Chase* 6746. Arecibo, *Chase* 6438. Without locality, *Eggers* 602.

LEEWARD ISLANDS: Guadeloupe, *Duss* 3886.

WINDWARD ISLANDS: Martinique, *Duss* 1306.

TRINIDAD: Icacos, *Broadway* 4963. Cedros, *Hitchcock* 10142. St. Joseph, *Hitchcock* 10027. California, *Hitchcock* 10119. Without locality, *Bot. Gard. Herb.* 3379.

TOBAGO: *Hitchcock* 10273.

MISCANTHUS SINENSIS Anderss., Ofv. Svensk. Vet. Akad. Forh. 12: 166. 1856. EULALIA.

Tall reed growing in large bunches, 1 to 3 m tall, with flat mostly basal blades, about 1 m long and 1 cm wide, gradually narrowed to a slender point; panicle fan-shaped, consisting of numerous silky racemes 10 to 20 cm long, aggregate at the summit of the culm. Occasionally cultivated for ornament. Native of Asia.

CUBA: Habana, *Léon* 2012.

102. SACCHARUM L., Sp. Pl. 54. 1753

Spikelets in pairs, one sessile, the other pedicellate, both perfect, awnless, arranged in panicled racemes, the axis disarticulating below the spikelets; glumes somewhat indurate, sterile lemma similar but hyaline; fertile lemma hyaline, sometimes wanting. Tall perennials with feathery panicles.

1. Saccharum officinarum L., Sp. Pl. 54. 1753. India. SUGARCANE.

Saccharum violaceum Tussac, Fl. Antill. 1: 160. pl. 25. 1808. Jamaica.

Gigantic perennial with broad leaves, the overlapping sheaths falling from the short-jointed lower part of the culms, the great plumy panicles pinkish silvery; forming seed sparingly (fig. 345).

Cultivated in Tropics and Subtropics of both hemispheres. The West Indian specimens in herbaria are probably all from cultivated plants. The Spanish name is "caña de azúcar." Called in Haiti "canne à sucre."

SACCHARUM CILIARE Anderss., Öfv. Svensk. Vet. Akad. Förh. 12: 155. 1855. An Asiatic species with elongate blades and long narrow feathery panicles, sparingly cultivated for ornament, escaped in St. Kitts (*Box* 162.)

103. ERIOCHRYSIS Beauv., Ess. Agrost. 8. pl. 4 f. 11. 1812

Spikelets awnless, the sessile spikelets perfect, the pedicellate spikelets pistillate, smaller but fruitful, readily falling, the rachis rather tardily disjointing; racemes short, crowded in a narrow, dense, silky interrupted spikelike panicle. Erect perennials with yellow or brown compact woolly inflorescence.

1. Eriochrysis cayennensis Beauv., Ess. Agrost. 8. pl. 4 f. 11. 1812. (Beauvois spells the name "Cayanensis.") Cayenne.

Saccharum cayennense Benth., Jour. Linn. Soc. Bot. 19: 66. 1881.

Erect perennial 1 to 2 m or more tall, the long narrow blades densely velvety, the compact silky golden brown panicle 10 to 12 cm long (fig. 346).

Moist slopes and savannas, southern Mexico and the West Indies to Uruguay. The type locality is presumably Cayenne, though no locality is mentioned in the original description.

HAITI: Marmelade, *Leonard* 8242a, 8243. Ridge between Morne Darras and Morne Beaubrun, *Ekman* H 4787. Pérodin, *Ekman* H 3410. Mount Organisé, *Ekman* H 6224.

DOMINICAN REPUBLIC: Lagunas de Cenobí, *Valeur* 21. Valle del Cibao, *Ekman* H 13281. Sabana del Guabatico, *Ekman* H 11050. San Juan, *Ekman* H 13613. Monción, *Ekman* H 12993. Sánchez, *Ekman* H 14734. El Valle, *Ekman* H 15662.

PUERTO RICO: Maricao, *Hioram* 818; *Britton and Cowell* 4265. San Juan, *Chase* 6762.

TRINIDAD: Arima, O'Meara Savanna, *Broadway* 2374.

104. ERIANTHUS Michx., Fl. Bor. Amer. 1: 54. 1803

Spikelets all alike, in pairs along a slender axis, one sessile, the other pedicellate, the rachis disarticulating below the spikelets, the rachis joint and pedicel falling attached to the sessile spikelet; glumes coriaceous, equal, usually copiously clothed, at least at the base, with long silky spreading hairs; sterile lemma thin and hyaline; fertile lemma hyaline, the midnerve extending into a slender awn; palea small and hyaline. Robust reedlike perennials, with flat blades and terminal oblong, usually dense silky panicles.

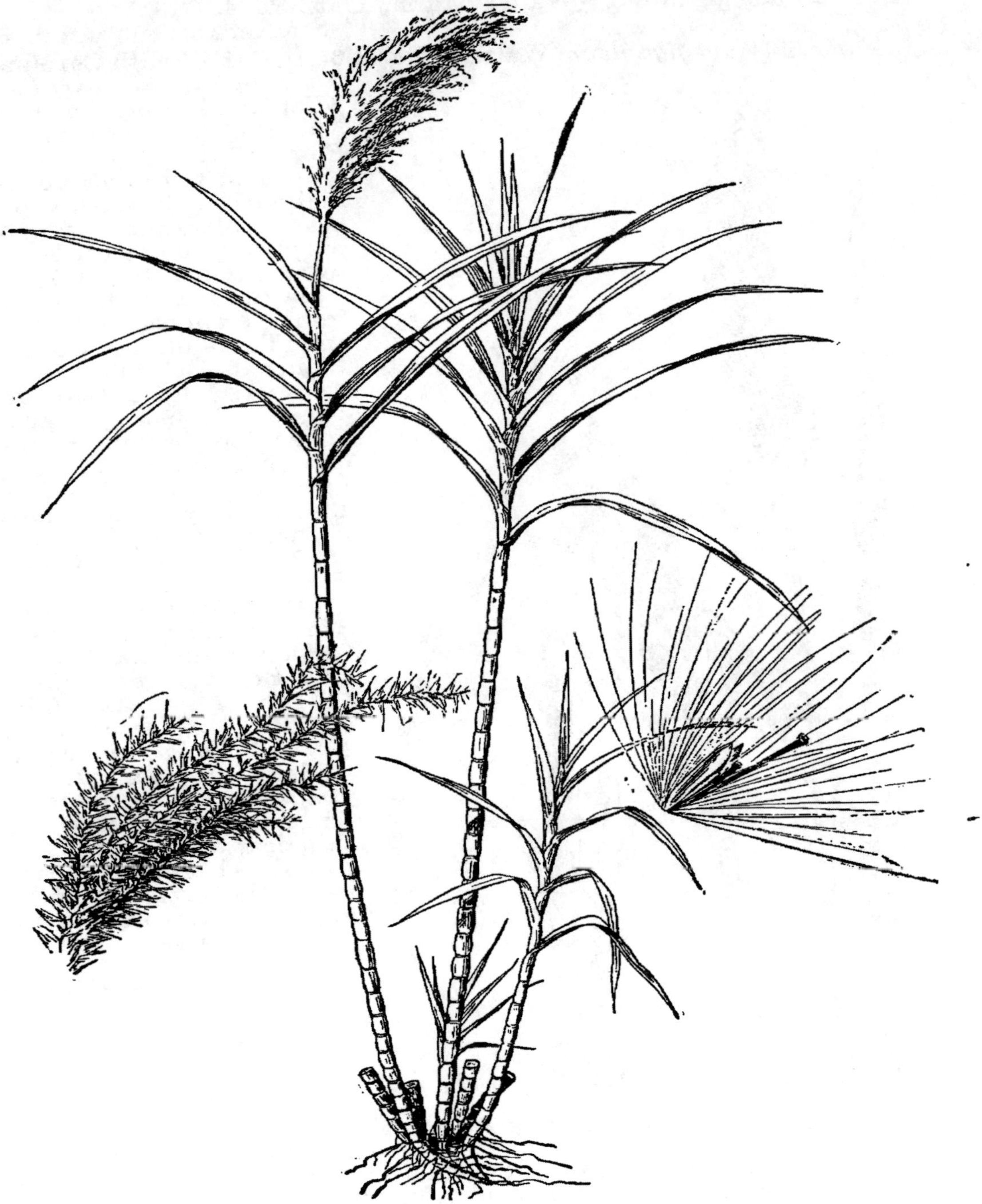

FIGURE 345.—*Saccharum officinarum*. Plant, much reduced; racemes, × ½; spikelet with pedicel and rachis joint, × 5 (Pringle).

1. Erianthus giganteus (Walt.) Muhl., Cat. Pl. 4. 1813. SUGARCANE PLUMEGRASS.

Anthoxanthum giganteum Walt., Fl. Carol. 65. 1788. South Carolina. *Erianthus saccharoides* Michx., Fl. Bor. Amer. 1: 55. 1803. Carolina to Florida.

Robust tall erect perennial with long harshly pubescent blades and tawny or purplish plumy panicles up to 40 cm long (fig. 347).

Swamps and moist soil from New Jersey to Florida and Texas on the Coastal Plain; also in Cuba.

CUBA: Laguna San Mateo, *Wright* 3903. Laguna Jovero to Laguna Herradura, *Shafer* 10934. Batabanó, *Ekman* 12586; *Léon* 13443. Cayo de los Pavos, Ciénaga de Zapata, *Léon* 9529. Sabana del Guaní, *Fernando* 434.

DOMINICAN REPUBLIC: Sánchez, *Ekman* H 15937.

ERIANTHUS RAVENNAE (L.) Beauv., Ess. Agrost. 14, 162, 177. 1812. (*Saccharum jamaicense* Trin., *Erianthus jamaicensis* Anderss.; *E. ravennae* var. *jamaicensis* Hack.) was described by Trinius from Jamaica, but his specimen was doubtless a cultivated plant, the species being grown for ornament in warm climates.

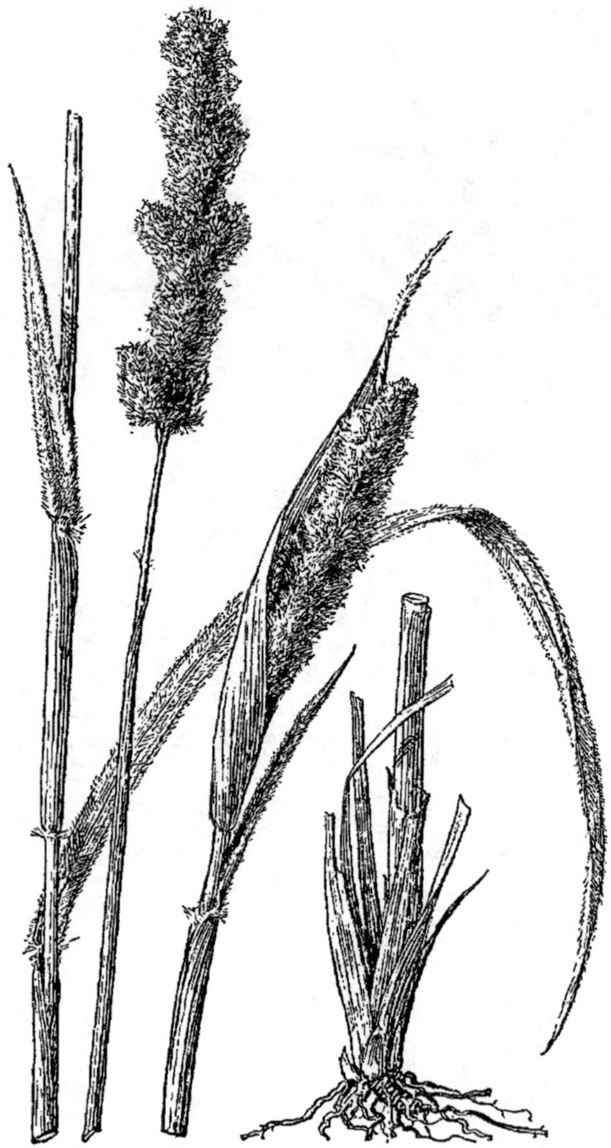

FIGURE 346.—*Eriochrysis cayennensis*, × ½ (Hioram 818).

105. ARTHRAXON Beauv., Ess. Agrost. 111. pl. 11. f. 6. 1812

Perfect spikelets awned, sessile, the secondary spikelet and its pedicel wanting or present only at the lower joints of the filiform articulate rachis; racemes terminating the branches of a dichotomously forking panicle, in appearance subdigitate or fascicled. Branching annuals with broad blades and slender racemes.

FIGURE 347.—*Erianthus giganteus.* Plant, × ½; spikelet with pedicel and rachis joint, × 5 (Langlois 96).

60256—36——25

1. Arthraxon quartinianus (A. Rich.) Nash, N. Amer. Fl. 17: 99. 1912.

Alectoridia quartiniana A. Rich., Tent. Fl. Abyss. 2: 448. 1852. Abyssinia.

Arthraxon ciliaris subsp. *quartinianus* Hack., in DC. Monogr. Phan. 6: 356. 1889.

FIGURE 348.—*Arthraxon quartinianus*, × ½ (Duss 2712).

Weak-stemmed, laxly branching creeping annual, with ascending flowering branches, bearing flat thin ovate blades cordate at base, and flabellate fascicles of slender racemes (fig. 348).

Shady banks, Jamaica and Guadeloupe, introduced from the Tropics of the Old World.

JAMAICA: Hardware Gap, *Ridley* 105; *Harris* 10910. Wallingford, *Perkins* 1484; *Harris* 11550. St. Helens Gap, *Maxon and Killip* 589. Whitefield, *Harris* 11563. Halls Delight, *Harris* 11536. Cold Spring Gap, *Harris* 11708. Cinchona, *Harris* 11309, 11416.

LEEWARD ISLANDS: Guadeloupe, *Duss* 2712, 3136.

106. ANDROPOGON L., Sp. Pl. 1045. 1753. Beardgrass

Spikelets in pairs at each node of an articulate rachis, one sessile and perfect, the other pedicellate and either staminate, neuter, or reduced to the pedicel, the rachis and the pedicels of the sterile spikelets often villous, sometimes conspicuously so; glumes of the fertile spikelet coriaceous, narrow, awnless, the first rounded, flat, or concave on the back, several-nerved, the median nerve weak or wanting; sterile lemma hyaline; fertile lemma hyaline, narrow, usually bearing a bent and twisted awn from the apex or from between apical lobes; pedicellate spikelet usually awnless, sometimes staminate and about as large as the sessile spikelet, sometimes consisting of one or more reduced glumes, sometimes wanting, only the pedicel present. Usually coarse perennials, with solid culms, the spikelets arranged in racemes, these numerous, aggregate on an exserted peduncle, or single, in pairs, or sometimes in threes or fours, the common peduncle usually enclosed by a spathelike sheath, these sheaths often numerous, forming a compound inflorescence, usually narrow, but sometimes in dense subcorymbose masses.

Lower 1 or 2 pairs of spikelets of the raceme differing from those above in consisting of two similar staminate spikelets. Racemes 1 to several, digitate or aggregate; sessile and pediceled spikelets alike in size and shape, the former (when fertile) awned, the latter awnless. (Section Dichanthium).
  Racemes several, on slender flexuous peduncles ------ 1. A. condylotrichus.
  Racemes, if more than 1, on short straight peduncles.
    Racemes usually 3 to 6; spikelets slightly overlapping, the pedicels usually in part visible ---------- 2. A. annulatus.
    Racemes usually 1, sometimes 2, rarely more; spikelets closely overlapping, the pedicels hidden.
      Culms glabrous below racemes ---------- 3. A. caricosus.
      Culms pubescent below racemes ---------- 4. A. nodosus.
Lower pairs like the others, the sessile spikelet fertile, usually awned, the pediceled spikelet staminate or neuter, usually smaller than the sessile one, often much reduced.
  Racemes solitary at the ends of the culms and branches, from bladeless sheaths or spathes. (Section Schizachyrium, except *A. virgatus* of section Hypogynium.)
    Plants annual.
      Culms weak, decumbent, trailing or vinelike; blades obtuse, mostly 1 to 3 cm long; peduncles capillary ---------- 5. A. brevifolius.
      Culms erect, relatively stout; blades acute, mostly 5 to 10 cm long; peduncles slender but not capillary -------- 6. A. malacostachyus.
    Plants perennial.
      Rachis slender, nearly straight or usually conspicuously zigzag, the spikelets spreading.
        Blades flat; racemes very numerous in a corymbose panicle; plants robust ---------- 7. A. condensatus.
        Blades folded or involute; racemes few; plants slender (tall in *A. reedii*). (See also *A. urbanianus*.)
          Racemes densely white-villous with long hairs; awns 1 to 2 cm long. 8. A. gracilis.
          Racemes sparsely or moderately villous; awns mostly less than 1 cm long.
            Pedicellate spikelet about as long as the sessile; racemes moderately villous ---------- 9. A. reedii.
            Pedicellate spikelet much reduced; racemes sparsely villous. 10. A. cubensis.
      Rachis straight, more or less thickened, the spikelets appressed or narrowly ascending.
        Spikelets awnless.
          Racemes about 1 cm long, partly enclosed in the subtending spathe, numerous, aggregate in a narrow panicle ----- 17. A. virgatus.

Racemes 3 to 8 cm long, few, exserted.
Culm blades 10 to 20 cm long ---------------- 11. A. SALZMANNI.
Culm blades 2 to 5 cm long ---------------- 12. A. PARVIFOLIUS.
Spikelets awned.
First glume of sessile spikelet villous ------------ 13. A. HIRTIFLORUS.
First glume of sessile spikelet glabrous or nearly so.
Blades terete, filiform; sessile spikelet 1.5 mm broad.
16. A. MULTINERVOSUS.
Blades flat or folded or sometimes involute toward the apex.
Sessile spikelet about 4 mm long, 1 mm wide; blades not more than 1.5 mm wide ------------------------ 15. A. TENER.
Sessile spikelet about 5 mm long; blades 2 to 5 mm wide.
14. A. SEMIBERBIS.
Racemes more than one at the summit of the culms and branches (one of the pair occasionally abortive in *A. urbanianus*).
Racemes several or numerous in an exserted panicle.
Pedicellate spikelet about as large as the sessile.
First glume of sessile spikelet pitted on the back ---- 30. A. PERTUSUS.
First glume of sessile spikelet not pitted ---------- 31. A. ISCHAEMUM.
Pedicellate spikelet much smaller than the sessile --- 29. A. SACCHAROIDES.
Racemes 2 to 4 (sometimes more in *A. selloanus*), fascicled, subtended by a bladeless sheath (spathe), exserted or partly included.
Spikelets awnless.
Plants robust, 1.25 to 2 m tall; spathes aggregate in a corymbose, usually dense inflorescence ------------------------ 18. A. BICORNIS.
Plants slender, usually less than 1 m tall; spathes not aggregate.
Sessile spikelets about 3 mm long; blades usually not more than 2 mm wide, the apex acuminate ------------ 19. A. LEUCOSTACHYUS.
Sessile spikelets about 4 mm long; blades 3 to 5 mm wide, the apex boat-shaped ---------------------------- 20. A. SELLOANUS.
Spikelets awned.
Pedicellate spikelet as large as the sessile ---------- 21. A. LATERALIS.
Pedicellate spikelet reduced.
Racemes densely white-woolly, the hairs almost hiding the spikelets ---------------------------------- 22. A. NASHIANUS.
Racemes more or less villous, but the hairs not hiding the spikelets.
Blades involute, firm ---------------------- 23. A. URBANIANUS.
Blades flat or folded, comparatively soft.
Sheaths, especially the upper, long and inflated, more or less aggregate, the spathes inconspicuous ----- 24. A. ELLIOTTII.
Sheaths not conspicuously inflated.
Spathes aggregate in a compound flabellate or club-shaped inflorescence --------------------- 25. A. GLOMERATUS.
Spathes sometimes numerous but not aggregate in a compound club-shaped inflorescence.
Peduncle of the 2 racemes 3 to 5 cm long.
Pedicellate spikelet wanting or nearly so.
27. A. REINOLDII.
Pedicellate spikelet prominent but the awn reduced.
28. A. ANGUSTATUS.
Peduncle of racemes less than 1 cm long.
26. A. VIRGINICUS.

1. **Andropogon condylotrichus** Hochst.; Steud., Syn. Pl. Glum. 1:377. 1854. Abyssinia.

Andropogon piptatherus Hack., in Mart., Fl. Bras. 2^3: 293. 1883. Brazil.

Sorghum piptatherum Kuntze, Rev. Gen. Pl. 2: 792. 1891.

Amphilophis piptatherus Nash, N. Amer. Fl. 17: 127. 1912.

Euclasta condylotricha Stapf, in Prain, Fl. Trop. Afr. 9: 181. 1917.

Weak-stemmed branching annual; culms 1 to 2 m long, the nodes villous; blades 15 to 20 cm long, 4 to 8 mm wide, setaceous-pointed; racemes several, fascicled, 2 to 5 cm long, on slender flexuous peduncles; pediceled spikelets about 5 mm long; spikelets, rachis joints, and pedicels loosely pilose.

Moist cliffs and shady banks, Mexico and Cuba to Brazil; also in tropical Africa.

CUBA: Holguín, *Ekman* 15732.

JAMAICA: Halls Delight, *Harris* 12460. Barican, *Hitchcock* 9565. Mount Charles, *Harris* 11558. Flamstead, *Harris* 11471. Narbrook, *Harris* 12712.

HAITI: St. Michel de l'Atalaye, *Leonard* 7383. Ennery, *Ekman* H 2472. Port-au-Prince, *Ekman* H 2184; *Leonard* 15838; *Buch* 1777, 1899.

DOMINICAN REPUBLIC: Constanza, *Ekman* H 13964.

2. **Andropogon annulatus** Forsk., Fl. Aegypt. Arab. 173. 1775. Egypt.

Andropogon bladhii Retz., Obs. Bot. 2: 27. 1781. China.

Andropogon annulatus var. *bladhii* Hack., in DC., Monogr. Phan. 6: 572. 1889.

Dichanthium annulatum Stapf, in Prain, Fl. Trop. Afr. 9: 178. 1917.

Culms ascending from a decumbent base, 50 to 100 cm long, the nodes pubescent; blades flat, 5 to 20 cm long, tapering to a fine point; racemes usually 3 to 6, sometimes more (var. *bladhii* (Retz.) Hack.), 3 to 7 cm long; sessile and pedicellate spikelets alike, the first glumes imbricate, oblong, rounded at summit.

Ditches, roadsides, and open ground, sparingly introduced; a native of the Old World.

CUBA: Paso Real to San Diego, *Léon* 5077. Jibacoa, *Léon* 14215. Corral Nuevo, *Léon* 15463.

HAITI: Port-au-Prince, *Ekman* H 9126 (var. *bladhii*).

PUERTO RICO: Aguirre, *Britton and Earle* 6494.

3. **Andropogon caricosus** L., Sp. Pl. ed. 2. 1840. 1763. India.

Andropogon annulatus var. *subrepens* Hack., Notizbl. Bot. Gart. Berlin 1: 327. 1897. Guadeloupe, *Duss* 3678.

Decumbent, freely branched low perennial with flat blades 2 to 8 cm long and solitary or paired racemes, the sterile spikelets as conspicuous as the fertile ones, giving the appearance of a flat 2-ranked scaly spike; awns slender, twisted, and bent.

Waste places; introduced in a few places in the West Indies from southern Asia.

CUBA: Habana, *Ekman* 1263, 18300; *Léon* 2389. Santiago de las Vegas, *Juzepczuk* 4055. Guanabacoa, *Wilson* 9163; *Hitchcock* 23228, 23235; *Léon* 2013, 2574, 15111, 15112.

LEEWARD ISLANDS: Guadeloupe, *Duss* 3678; *Hitchcock* 16413.

WINDWARD ISLANDS: St. Lucia, *Watts* in 1909.

4. **Andropogon nodosus** (Willem.) Nash, N. Amer. Fl. 17: 122. 1912.

Dichanthium nodosum Willem., Ann. Bot. Usteri 18: 11. 1796. Mauritius.

Similar to *A. caricosus* (possibly only a variety of that species), somewhat larger, the blades and racemes longer; culm pubescent below the inflorescence.

Waste places; introduced in a few places in the West Indies from the Tropics of the Old World.

CUBA: Jibacoa, *Léon* 13854.

LEEWARD ISLANDS: Antigua, *Rose* 3382, 3415; *Box* 37, 112, 123. Guadeloupe, *Duss* 3678.

WINDWARD ISLANDS: Barbados, *Bot. Sta. Herb.* 443. Grenada, *Hitchcock* 17679; *Meyers* 4590.

5. **Andropogon brevifolius** Swartz, Prodr. Veg. Ind. Occ. 26. 1788. Jamaica.

Andropogon obtusifolius Poir., in Lam., Encycl. Sup. 1: 583. 1810. Puerto Rico.

Pollinia brevifolia Spreng., Pl. Pugill. 2: 13. 1815.

Schizachyrium brevifolium Nees; Kunth, Enum. Pl. 1: 488. 1833.

Sorghum brevifolium Kuntze, Rev. Gen. Pl. 2: 791. 1891.

Slender trailing or reclining glabrous branching annual; culms from 15 cm to as much as 1 m long; blades flat, obtuse; racemes delicate, 1 to 2 cm long; spikelets about 3 mm long; awns 4 to 8 mm long.

Moist banks, tropical regions of both hemispheres. To be found in probably all of the West Indian islands from Cuba to Trinidad. Not represented in collections from Bermuda and the Bahamas.

6. **Andropogon malacostachyus** Presl, Rel. Haenk. 1: 337. 1830. Mexico.

Schizachyrium malacostachyum Nash, N. Amer. Fl. 17: 102. 1912.

Rather slender erect or spreading, glabrous, pale or reddish brown annual; culms 30 to 100 cm long; blades flat, 1 to 4 mm wide; racemes slender, 2 to 3 cm long, more or less enclosed in the spathes on the erect branches along the upper part of the culm; sterile pedicels and joints of the rachis villous; sessile spikelet 7 mm long, the awn about 1 cm.

Dry slopes and rocky hills, southern Mexico to Colombia; Cuba.

CUBA: Habana (Vibora), *Léon* 1956. Guanabacoa, *Hitchcock* 479, 23225; *Léon* 1529. Without locality, *Ekman* 13559.

7. **Andropogon condensatus** H. B. K., Nov. Gen. et Sp. 1: 188. 1816. Colombia.

Andropogon microstachyus Desv.; Hamilt., Prodr. Pl. Ind. Occ. 8. 1825. Antilles.

Schizachyrium condensatum Nees, Agrost. Bras. 333. 1829.

Pollinia microstachya Desv., Opusc. 70. 1831.

Robust tufted erect glabrous perennial, 1 to 1.5 m tall; culm repeatedly branching toward the summit, forming a large corymbose compound inflorescence; blades 10 to 20 cm long, 5 to 10 mm wide, usually stiffly spreading; racemes 2 to 3 cm long, the slender rachis very flexuous, the pedicels and rachilla joints long-villous; awns delicate, about 12 mm long.

Open, rather dry ground, eastern Mexico and the southern West Indies to Argentina.

LEEWARD ISLANDS: Guadeloupe, *Duss* 3817. Dominica, *Hitchcock* 16432; *Jones* 8.

WINDWARD ISLANDS: Martinique, *Hitchcock* 16464; *Duss* 1297, 4026; *Hahn* 690. St. Lucia, *Hitchcock* 16472; *Brooks* 30; *Kemp* 6; *Box* 192. St. Vincent, *Eggers* 6577. Grenada, *Broadway* 1783.

TRINIDAD: Port-of-Spain, *Hitchcock* 9998, 10038. Point-á-Pierre, *Broadway* 4945. Cedros, *Broadway* 4949. Burkes Pasture, *Bot. Gard. Herb.* 3383.

TOBAGO: *Broadway* 4799; *Hitchcock* 10206.

8. **Andropogon gracilis** Spreng., Syst. Veg. 1: 284. 1825. Hispaniola.

Andropogon juncifolius Desv.; Hamilt., Prodr. Pl. Ind. Occ. 9. 1825.[99] St. Croix.

Sorghum gracile Kuntze, Rev. Gen. Pl. 2: 791. 1891.

Schizachyrium gracile Nash, in Small, Fl. Southeast. U. S. 60. 1903.

Densely tufted slender erect wiry glabrous perennial with filiform blades and delicate pale feathery racemes 2 to 5 cm long, the delicate awns 1 to 1.5 cm long; culms 20 to 60 cm tall; racemes silvery, long-exserted, the rachis slender, very villous; sessile spikelet about 5 mm long; pedicellate spikelet reduced to an awned or awnless glume, the pedicel very villous (fig. 349).

Rocky hills and banks, southern Florida and the West Indies.

BAHAMAS: New Providence, *Curtiss* 152; *Eggers* 4444.

CUBA: Sumidero, *Shafer* 13529; *Shafer and Léon* 13715, 13720. San Diego de los Baños, *Léon* 5085, 5168. La Grifa, *Ekman* 18167. Cajálbana, *Wright* 204. Pinar del Río, *Hitchcock* 23314. Herradura, *Tracy* 9067. Candelaria, *Earle and Wilson* 1637. Habana, *Ekman* 850, 1005; *Léon* 562. Santiago de las Vegas, *Juzepczuk* 4052. Sancti Spiritus, *Léon* 820, 825, 826. Gavilanes, *Léon* 6652. Baraguá, *Hitchcock* 23362. Guara, *Hitchcock* 23390, 23432. Sierra de Nipe, *Shafer* 2988. Loma Menqura, *Shafer* 3855. Sabinilla, *Shafer* 8397. Eastern Cuba, *Wright* 1557. Without locality, *Wright* 3484. Isla de Pinos, *Curtiss* 380; *Jennings* 58.

FIGURE 349.—*Andropogon gracilis*, × 1 (Hitchcock 682).

JAMAICA: Cascade River, *Maxon* 10571. Ipswich, *Maxon and Killip* 1492a; *Hitchcock* 9616. Bog Walk, *Hitchcock* 9296 (*Amer. Gr. Nat. Herb.* 257). New Forest, *Hitchcock* 9844. Cinchona, *Hitchcock* 9707; *Hart* 689, 754; *Harris* 9503, 11265, 11332, 11412. Abbey Green, *Hitchcock* 9384. Barican, *Hitchcock* 9576. New Castle, *Hitchcock* 9342. Narbrook, *Harris* 12710. Lititz, *Harris* 11656, 11720. Flamstead, *Harris* 11578. Cane River Valley, *Harris* 9622, 11370. Guava Ridge, *Harris* 11318, 11338.

HAITI: Bassin Bleu, *Leonard* 15002. Port-au-Prince, *Ekman* H 1648, H 7121; *Buch* 1213. St. Michel de l'Atalaye, *Leonard* 7405a, 7423; *Buch* 1071. Marmelade, *Leonard* 8226. Ennery, *Leonard* 9010. Plaisance, *Leonard* 9419. Fond Parisien, *Leonard* 4204.

DOMINICAN REPUBLIC: Jarabaco, *Eggers* 2321 (in part). Valle Nuevo, *Ekman* H 13852.

PUERTO RICO: Mayaguez, *Chase* 6816. Lares, *Chase* 6589. Arecibo, *Chase* 6558.

LEEWARD ISLANDS: Guadeloupe, *Duss* 2719.

ANDROPOGON GRACILIS var. FIRMIOR Hitchc., var. nov.[1]

Differing from *A. gracilis* in having erect or somewhat spreading or leaning, firm, hard, branching culms, 60 to 100 cm tall.

Type in the United States National Herbarium, no. 1296100, collected near Morne Fort Jacques, Pétionville, Massif de la Selle,

[99] It is uncertain which of these names is the earlier.

[1] A *A. gracile* culmis patulis, firmis, duris, ramosis, 60–100 cm altis, foliis firmioribus et crassioribus differt.

Haiti, 1,200 m altitude, September 18, 1924, by E. L. Ekman (no. H 1944).

Dry slopes and sterile pinelands, Hispaniola.

HAITI: Port-au-Prince, *Ekman* H 7120. Ennery, *Leonard* 8832. Pétionville, *Ekman* H 1944, H 2329.

DOMINICAN REPUBLIC: San José de Ocoa, *Ekman* H 11885. Valle Nuevo, *Ekman* H 13853, H 13854, H 13862.

9. Andropogon reedii Hitchc. and Ekman, sp. nov.[2]

Culms erect, cespitose, slender, glabrous, about 1 m tall; sheaths glabrous, keeled but not much compressed; ligule a membrane about 0.5 mm long; blades rarely flat, usually folded or involute, erect, firm, as much as 30 cm long, 0.5 to 1.5 mm wide, scaberulous on the upper surface and sparsely pilose near the base, glabrous beneath, the midrib prominent beneath, the margins scabrous and also papillose-pilose toward the base; inflorescence about one-third the entire height of the culm, branched, the branches several or numerous, appressed; racemes solitary, 2 to 4 cm long, finally exserted from the spathes, the rachis slender, somewhat flexuous or nearly straight, the internodes about 3 mm long, pilose with hairs 3 to 5 mm long; sessile spikelet 4 mm long, the first glume concave on the back but not channeled, hispidulous on the angles toward the tip; awn about 1 cm long, geniculate, twisted below; pedicellate spikelet prominent, mostly 4 to 5 mm long, sometimes less, awnless, the pedicel 3 to 4 mm long, pilose like the internode.

Type in the United States National Herbarium, no. 1161264, collected in savannas at Minas, prov. Camagüey, Cuba, October 5, 1922, by E. L. Ekman.

At Dr. Ekman's suggestion the species is named for A. C. Reed, general manager of the Cuba Railroad, who had extended courtesies to him.

Savannas and serpentine hills, Cuba, only known from the province of Camagüey.

CUBA: Minas, *Ekman* in 1922. Canasí, *Ekman* 17186; *Léon* 13121.

10. Andropogon cubensis Hack., Flora 68: 121. 1885. Cuba, *Wright* 3898.

Sorghum cubense Kuntze, Rev. Gen. Pl. 2: 791. 1891.

Schizachyrium cubense Nash, N. Amer. Fl. 17: 109. 1912.

Culms slender, erect from a loose rhizomatous base, 50 to 70 cm tall; blades involute, very slender, rather soft, the lowermost culm blade about 5 cm long, the upper successively shorter; peduncles long-exserted, 1 terminal and 1 or 2 from the upper sheaths; racemes erect or nodding, inconspicuously silky, 4 to 6 cm long, loosely flowered, the rachis slender, flexuous, pilose, the joints 3 to 10 mm long; sessile spikelet about 4 mm long, the awn 4 to 8 mm long; pedicellate spikelet much reduced, the pedicel slender, usually becoming recurved-spreading.

Sandy soil, Cuba.

CUBA: Damují (Pinar del Río), *Ekman* 11049; Laguna del Perro, *Ekman* 18122. Without locality, *Wright* 3898. Isla de Pinos, *Britton and Wilson* 14291.

[2] Culmi erecti caespitosi graciles, circa 1 m alti; laminae plerumque complicatae vel involutae; racemi solitarii 2–4 cm longi, rachide saepius leviter undulata longe pilosa; spiculae sessiles 4 mm longae, arista gracili 1 cm longa; spiculae pedicellatae 4–5 mm longae; pedicelli longe pilosi.

11. Andropogon salzmanni (Trin.) Hack., in Repert. Sp. Nov. Fedde 6: 341. 1909.

Rottboellia salzmanni Trin.; Steud., Syn. Pl. Glum. 1: 361. 1854. Brazil.

Andropogon imberbis var. *muticus* Hack., in DC., Monogr. Phan. 6: 380. 1889.

Culms ascending, about 50 cm tall; sheaths compressed; blades long, linear, curled or flexuous, 2 to 3 mm wide; racemes yellow, nearly glabrous, 5 to 7 cm long; sessile spikelets appressed, awnless, about 6 mm long.

Sandy hills, southern Mexico to Brazil; Lesser Antilles.

LEEWARD ISLANDS: Guadeloupe, *Duss* 3171.

WINDWARD ISLANDS: Martinique, *Duss* 784, 4022.

12. Andropogon parvifolius Hitchc., sp. nov.[3]

Culms in small tufts, slender, erect or somewhat spreading at base, glabrous, mostly 4- or 5-noded, 15 to 30 cm tall; sheaths glabrous, striate, shorter than the internodes; ligule less than 0.5 mm long; blades flat, smooth beneath, scabrous on the upper surface, 2 to 5 cm long, the uppermost about 1 cm long, 1 mm or less wide; racemes solitary, slender, terminating the main culms, glabrous throughout, 3 to 5 cm long, the rachis rather thick; sessile spikelet oblong-lanceolate, acute, weakly several-nerved, awnless, about 5 mm long, the internodes of the rachis about 3 mm long; pedicellate spikelet reduced, 2 to 3 mm long.

Type in the United States National Herbarium, no. 1387467, collected in moist pinelands south of railroad, Herradura, Cuba, June 22, 1922, by E. L. Ekman (no. 14094).

Known only from the type collection. Related to *Andropogon salzmanni*, but differing in the smaller size of the culms, leaves, and racemes.

13. Andropogon hirtiflorus (Nees) Kunth, Rév. Gram. 1: Sup. XXXIX. 1830.

Streptachne domingensis Spreng.; Schult., Mant. 2: 188. 1824. Not *Andropogon domingensis* Steud. 1821. Santo Domingo.

Schizachyrium hirtiflorum Nees, Agrost. Bras. 334. 1829. Brazil.

Aristida? domingensis Kunth, Rév. Gram. 1: 62. 1829.

Andropogon semiberbis var. *incertus* Hack., in DC., Monogr. Phan. 6: 370. 1889. Cuba, *Wright* 1558.

Schizachyrium domingense Nash, N. Amer. Fl. 17: 103. 1912.

Andropogon domingensis F. T. Hubb., Amer. Acad. Sci. Proc. 49: 493. 1913. Not *A. domingensis* Steud. 1821.

Slender erect tufted perennial; culms compressed, 0.5 to 1.5 m tall; blades flat, 2 to 4 mm wide; racemes mostly 4 to 8 cm long; rachis joints and pedicels villous; sessile spikelet 5 to 6 mm long, its first glume more or less villous on the rounded back; awn about 1 cm long (fig. 350).

Rocky or gravelly hills or flats, Florida, through the West Indies to Paraguay.

CUBA: Sancti Spíritus, *Léon* 4094. Eastern Cuba, *Wright* 1558.

JAMAICA: New Forest, *Hitchcock* 9855 (*Amer. Gr. Nat. Herb.* 260). Lititz, *Harris* 12704.

---

[3] Culmi graciles 15–30 cm alti; laminae planae 2–5 cm longae, 0.5–1 mm latae glabrae, supra scabrae; racemi solitarii graciles 3–5 cm longi; spicula sessilis, plurinervia, oblongo-lanceolata, acuta, mutica 5 mm longa; spicula pedicellata reducta 2–3 mm longa.

HAITI: Las Cahobas, *Cook, Scofield, and Doyle* 99. Ennery, *Leonard* 8937, 8958, 9492. Pétionville, *Ekman* H 1733. Port-au-Prince, *Buch* 1811, 1856; *Ekman* H 7122. Aux Cayes, *Ekman* H 251.

DOMINICAN REPUBLIC: Jarabaco, *Ekman* H 14157.

PUERTO RICO: Maricao, *Chase* 6202.

TRINIDAD: St. Joseph, *Hitchcock* 10194 (*Amer. Gr. Nat. Herb.* 550. This is labeled *A. semiberbis.* It is better referred to *A. hirtiflorus*, though it is an intermediate specimen).

14. Andropogon semiberbis (Nees) Kunth, Rév. Gram. Sup. 1: XXXIX. 1830.

Schizachyrium semiberbis Nees, Agrost. Bras. 336. 1829. Brazil.

Closely resembling *A. hirtiflorus*, which may be a variety of this; usually stouter and taller, often glaucous, blades averaging wider; first glume of sessile spikelet smooth on the back; rachis joints and pedicels sparingly villous, the racemes appearing nearly smooth (those of *A. hirtiflorus* appearing whitish-villous) (fig. 351).

FIGURE 350.—*Andropogon hirtiflorus*, × 1 (Chase 1943).

FIGURE 351.—*Andropogon semiberbis*, × 1 (C. H. Baker 327).

Grassy hills and savannas, Florida, through the West Indies and eastern Mexico to Argentina and Ecuador; also in tropical Asia and Africa.

BAHAMAS: New Providence, *Britton and Brace* 432; *Geogr. Soc. Baltimore* 542.

CUBA: Pinar del Río, *Hitchcock* 23301. Herradura, *Baker and Abarca* 4179. Guanabacoa, *Léon* 2877, 12452, 12465; *Hitchcock* 23225½, 23246. Manacas, *Léon* 5994, 9295. Mordazo, *Ekman* 17097. Baraguá, *Hitchcock* 23364. Sancti Spíritus, *Léon* 854, 855; *Sergius* 2791. Bayate, *Ekman* 2816. Holguín, *Shafer* 2936; *Ekman* 15733. Guara, *Hitchcock* 23393. Nagua, *Ekman* 11339. Without locality, *Wright* 3891. Isla de Pinos, *Britton and Wilson* 14420, 14792.

HAITI: Port-au-Prince, *Christ* 2158. Los Angeles, *Ekman* H 382. Étang Ténété, *Ekman* H 332. Pétionville, *Ekman* H 1725. St. Michel de l'Atalaye, *Leonard* 7159, 8055.

DOMINICAN REPUBLIC: Azua, *Fuertes* 1886. Polo, *Abbott* 1865. Monción, *Ekman* H 12656.

PUERTO RICO: Las Marias, *Sintenis* 5988. Mayaguez, *Holm* 178; *Chase* 6161, 6818. Campo Alegre, *Chase* 6623, 6807. San Juan, *Chase* 6771.

VIRGIN ISLANDS: St. Croix, *Thompson* 257.

15. Andropogon tener (Nees) Kunth, Rév. Gram. 1: Sup. XXXIX. 1830.

Schizachyrium tenerum Nees, Agrost. Bras. 336. 1829. Brazil.

Densely tufted bunch grass; culms slender, reclining, 30 to 100 cm long; blades subinvolute, 1 to 3 mm wide; racemes slender, 2 to 5 cm long, nearly glabrous; lower half of first glume of sessile spikelet light colored, giving the raceme a somewhat zonate appearance; awn about 1 cm long (fig. 352).

Grassy hills and rocky cliffs, southern United States to Argentina.

CUBA: Herradura, *Tracy* 9068. Pinar del Río, *Ekman* 17287; *Hitchcock* 23306. Sumidero, *Léon* 3397. Madruga, *Léon* 6326. Placetas del Sur, *Léon* 6432. Manacas, *Léon* 5818. Almacigos, *Wright* 3482.

JAMAICA: Jacks Hill, *Harris* 12865. Hope, *Harris* 12686. Newcastle, *Hitchcock* 9343. Barican, *Hitchcock* 9575. Without locality, *Harris* 11439.

HAITI: Nouvelle Touraine, *Buch* 1686. Corail, *Ekman* H 10763. Furcy, *Ekman* H 1744.

DOMINICAN REPUBLIC: Rincón, *Ekman* H 13289.

16. Andropogon multinervosus (Nash) Hitchc. and Chase, Contrib. U. S. Natl. Herb. 18: 280. 1917.

Schizachyrium multinervosum Nash, N. Amer. Fl. 17: 109. 1912. Cuba, *Britton and Shafer* 608.

Wiry, sparingly branching perennial with filiform blades and few racemes; culms 20 to 40 cm tall; racemes 3 to 6 cm long; sessile spikelet 4 to 5 mm long, glabrous, minutely bearded at base, the awn about 1 cm long; pedicellate spikelet much reduced, the pedicel ciliate above on one side.

Rocky hills and palm barrens, Cuba.

CUBA: Canasí, *Ekman* 17187; *Léon* 13058, 13120. Santayana, *Ekman* 19038; *Britton* 2414. Madruga, *Léon* 6326; *Britton and Shafer* 608. Santa Clara City, *Léon* 14960, 15610.

FIGURE 352.—*Andropogon tener*, × 1 (Rolfs 986).

17. Andropogon virgatus Desv.; Hamilt., Prodr. Pl. Ind. Occ. 9. 1825. Antilles.

Hypogynium spathiflorum Nees, Agrost. Bras. 366. 1829. Brazil.

Anatherum virgatum Desv., Opusc. 71. 1831.

Andropogon spathiflorus Kunth, Rév. Gram. 1: Sup. XL. 1830.

Andropogon inermis Steud., Syn. Pl. Glum. 1: 390. 1854. Colombia.

Anatherum spathiflorum Griseb., Cat. Pl. Cub. 236. 1866.

Anatherum inerme Griseb., Cat. Pl. Cub. 236. 1866.

Glabrous tufted perennial; culms compressed, rigid, about 1 m tall; blades 2 to 4 mm wide; inflorescence elongate, of numerous glabrous racemes about 1 cm long, partly enclosed in rufous or purplish spathes; spikelets 3 to 4 mm long, awnless.

Wet, sandy open swamps or savannas, West Indies and Central America to Brazil.

CUBA: Laguna Santa María, *Ekman* 17258. Pinar del Río, *Hitchcock* 23274. Herradura, *Baker and Dimmock* 4814. Guane, *Léon* 6988. Los Almacigos, *Wright* 3480, 3481. Isla de Pinos, *Taylor* 23; *Curtiss* 460; *Britton and Wilson* 14310.

DOMINICAN REPUBLIC: Cotuy, *Abbott* 812, 846, 2805a, 2814. Cuenca, *Ekman* H 11010. Without locality, *Wright, Parry, and Brummel* 625.

PUERTO RICO: San Juan, *Chase* 6633, 6768. Campo Alegre, *Chase* 6620. Lares, *Sintenis* 5902.

TRINIDAD: Arima, *Broadway* 2373. Arouca, *Hitchcock* 10348. Comuto Station, *Hitchcock* 10070.

18. Andropogon bicornis L., Sp. Pl. 1046. 1753. Brazil, Jamaica.

Anatherum bicorne Beauv., Ess. Agrost. 128. 1812.

Saccharum bicorne Griseb., Abh. Ges. Wiss. Göttingen 7: 266. 1857.

Sorghum bicorne Kuntze, Rev. Gen. Pl. 2: 791. 1891.

Robust tufted perennial; culms mostly 1 to 2 m tall; blades 2 to 5 mm wide, scabrous on the margin; inflorescence large, corymbose, of delicate flexuous racemes 2 to 3 cm long, whitish or tawny, feathery with hairs as much as 5 mm long; 1, sometimes 2, of the uppermost pedicellate spikelets larger than the fertile ones, the other pedicellate spikelets rudimentary.

Grassy hills and banks, southern Mexico to Brazil and widely distributed in the West Indies. Probably to be found on all the islands from Greater Antilles southward. In West Indies called foxtail and sometimes "ridging grass."

19. Andropogon leucostachyus H. B. K., Nov. Gen. et Sp. 1: 187. 1816. Venezuela.

Anatherum domingense Roem. and Schult., Syst. Veg. 2: 809. 1817. Santo Domingo.

Andropogon domingensis Steud., Nom. Bot. 45. 1821.

Andropogon leucostachyus subvar. *subvillosus* Hack., in DC., Monogr. Phan. 6: 420. 1889. Brazil.

Sorghum leucostachyum Kuntze, Rev. Gen. Pl. 2: 792. 1891.

Slender, densely tufted erect perennial; culms 30 to 50 cm tall; blades 1 to 3 mm wide, with a deeply impressed midvein; ligule about 2 mm long; racemes 2 or 3, whitish, 1.5 to 3 cm long, on slender exserted peduncles, the spikelets obscured by the copious long silky hairs. Foliage villous in some of the Trinidad specimens, the subvar. *subvillosus* Hack.

Cliffs and grassy slopes, West Indies and southern Mexico to Brazil.

Cuba: Sumidero, *Shafer and Léon* 13613, 13717. Herradura, *Tracy* 9046. Consolación del Sur, *Palmer and Riley* 480. Madruga, *Léon* 3459. Minas, *Léon* 6222. Banao Mountains, *Léon* 5407. Placetas del Sur, *Léon* 6428, 6431. Sancti Spíritus, *Léon* 827. Sancti Spíritus Mountains, *Léon* 6529. Pasto Estancia, *Shafer* 1639, 1681. Loma del Gato, *Léon* 10324. Isla de Pinos, *Britton and Wilson* 15110; *Ekman* 12203.

Jamaica: Port Antonio, *Fredholm* 3334. Bull Head Mountain, *Hitchcock* 9546. Barican, *Hitchcock* 9577. Mount Hybla, *Harris* 12458. Hollis Savanna, *Harris* 12244. Below Content Gap, *Harris* 11349.

Haiti: Aux Cayes, *Ekman* H 230. Furcy, *Leonard* 4312; *Buch* 1573. Marmelade, *Leonard* 8242, 8258. Plaisance, *Leonard* 9348. Caille la Croix, *Leonard* 7883. Pétionville, *Ekman* H 1746. San Michel, *Miller* 301; *Sweet* in 1925.

Dominican Republic: Jarabaco, *Eggers* H 2321 (in part). Monción, *Ekman* H 12769.

Puerto Rico: Adjuntas, *Sintenis* 4481. Mayaguez, *Heller* 4396; *Britton and Marble* 654; *Britton and Hess* 2813; *Chase* 6163, 6819. *Holm* 76. San Juan, *Chase* 6366, 6383, 6636, 6776; *Sein* 322. Cayey, *Chase* 6733. Maricao, *Chase* 6216; *Britton and Cowell* 4267; *Britton*,

Cowell, and Brown 4477. Rio Piedras, *Hioram* 214; *Cowgill* 686. Without locality, *Heller* 933, 984.

TRINIDAD: Brighton, *Hitchcock* 10097. O'Meara Savanna, *Britton and Hazen* 1579. Port-of-Spain, *Broadway* 5040. Piarco Savanna, *Hitchcock* 10345. Aripo Savanna, *Hitchcock* 10072. Without locality, *Bot. Gard. Herb.* 3382.

20. Andropogon selloanus (Hack.) Hack., Bull. Herb. Boiss. (II) 4: 266. 1904.

Euklastaxon tenuifolius Steud., Syn. Pl. Glum. 1: 412. 1855. Not *Andropogon tenuifolius* Steud. Brazil.

Andropogon leucostachyus subsp. *selloanus* Hack., in DC., Monogr. Phan. 6: 420. 1889. Brazil.

Similar to *A. leucostachyus*, differing in the somewhat stouter culms, shorter and broader blades with a boat-shaped tip, shorter ligule (less than 1 mm long); racemes often 3 to 5, more densely villous, tawny rather than white.

Savannas and open ground, West Indies to Paraguay.

CUBA: Santa Cruz de los Pinos, *Léon* 7435. Hanábana, *Wright* 3900. Prov. Santa Clara, *Léon* 6424, 9159. Isla de Pinos, *Ekman* 12103; *Curtiss* 314; *Taylor* 16.

TRINIDAD: St. Joseph, *Hitchcock* 10188. La Brea, *Broadway* 3258, 4981.

TOBAGO: *Broadway* 2982, 4044.

21. Andropogon lateralis Nees, Agrost. Bras. 329. 1829. Brazil.

Andropogon incanus Hack., in DC., Monogr. Phan. 6: 431. 1889. Uruguay.

Andropogon lateralis var. *incanus* Henr., Med. Rijks Herb. Leiden 40: 42. 1921.

Culms stout, erect, about 1.5 m tall; blades elongate, folded or involute; racemes in pairs, often of unequal length, 2 to 5 cm long, the rachis slender, straight or somewhat flexuous, rather sparsely long-pilose; sessile spikelet about 4 mm long, the awn weak, about 5 mm long; pedicellate spikelet prominent, larger than the sessile, about 5 mm long, the pedicel long-pilose like the rachis.

Grassy hills, Brazil to Ecuador and Peru; Cuba.

CUBA: Laguna Santa María, Pinar del Río, *Ekman* 17264,17271. Remates (Pinar del Río), *Ekman* 11362; *Léon* 15357.

These specimens belong to the form described as var. *incanus* (Hack.) Henr., in which the racemes are usually two.

22. Andropogon nashianus Hitchc., Contrib. U. S. Natl. Herb. 12: 193. 1909. Cuba, *Wright* 3899.

Culms solitary or few in a cluster, slender, erect, 30 to 45 cm tall from short branching rhizomes; blades narrow, folded, glabrous, those of the upper culm much reduced; racemes in pairs, 3 to 4 cm long, very villous with tawny hairs 5 to 7 mm long; sessile spikelet 3 to 4 mm long; pedicellate spikelet much reduced.

Sandy barrens, Cuba.

CUBA: Pinar del Río, *Wright* 3899; *Hitchcock* 23265. Laguna Jovero to Mendoza, *Shafer* 10850. Herradura, *Tracy* 9069; *Hitchcock* 481; *Ekman* in 1922. San Diego de los Baños, *Léon* 4453, 4560. Loma del Gato, *Ekman* 15652. Isla de Pinos, *Britton and Wilson* 14804; *Taylor* 17.

23. Andropogon urbanianus Hitchc., Bot. Gaz. 54: 424. 1912. Dominican Republic, *Fuertes* 1420.

Culms erect or ascending, 75 to 150 cm tall; blades 10 to 30 cm long, involute, firm, rather stiff, appressed; racemes numerous along the upper third of the plant, the terminal mostly in pairs, the axillary in pairs or sometimes solitary, 2 to 4 cm long, partly enclosed in the spathe or exserted, the slender rachis and pedicels long-pilose; sessile spikelet 5 mm long, the awn 1 to 2 cm long; pedicellate spikelets narrow, 2 to 4 mm long or sometimes rather prominent.

Dry slopes and rocky hills, Hispaniola.

HAITI: St. Michel de l'Atalayé, *Leonard* 7374, 7392, 7830, 8061a. Port-au-Prince, *Ekman* H 2087. Torbeek, *Ekman* H 5358. Ennery, *Leonard* 8976. Pétionville, *Ekman* H 1434, H 1936. Mission, *Leonard* 3716, 3826, 3853. Furcy, *Buch* 961. St. Michel ad l'Amache, *Buch* 1074, 1077.

DOMINICAN REPUBLIC: Las Salinas, *Fuertes* 1420. Constanza, *Ekman* H 14092. San José de Ocoa, *Ekman* H 11920.

FIGURE 353.—*Andropogon elliottii*, × 1 (Commons 115).

24. Andropogon elliottii Chapm., Fl. South U. S. 581. 1860. Florida.

ELLIOTT BEARDGRASS.

Sorghum elliottii Kuntze, Rev. Gen. Pl. 2: 791. 1891.

Culms erect, 30 to 80 cm tall; sheaths more or less villous, the upper inflated and aggregate; racemes in pairs (rarely 3 or 4), 3 to 4 cm long, some of the peduncles exserted from the appressed spathe and from the inflated sheath; sessile spikelet 4 to 5 mm long, the awn 10 to 15 mm long, geniculate, twisted (fig. 353).

Open ground and old fields, Coastal Plain of the eastern United States; Cuba.

CUBA: Bayamo (prov. Oriente), *Ekman* 5067.

25. Andropogon glomeratus (Walt.) B. S. P., Prel. Cat. N. Y. 67. 1888.

BUSHY BEARDGRASS.

Cinna glomerata Walt., Fl. Carol. 59. 1788. South Carolina.

Andropogon macrourus Michx., Fl. Bor. Amer. 1: 56. 1803. Virginia or Carolina.

Andropogon densus Desv.; Hamilt., Prodr. Pl. Ind. Occ. 8. 1825. Antilles.

Anatherum macrourum Griseb., Mem. Amer. Acad. (n.s.) 8: 534. 1863.

Andropogon tenuispatheus Nash, N. Amer. Fl. 17: 113. 1912. Florida.

Rather robust, densely tufted perennial; culms compressed, 1 to 1.5 m tall; lower sheaths crowded, keeled; blades flat or folded, mostly 3 to 5 mm wide; inflorescence dense, feathery, club-shaped; racemes in pairs, 1.5 to 3 cm long, villous with whitish or tawny hairs; rachis slender, flexuous; sessile spikelet 3 to 4 mm long, the awn about 1.5 cm long (fig. 354).

Moist or open ground, southeastern United States through Mexico and the West Indies to northern South America.

BAHAMAS: Eleuthera, *Hitchcock* in 1890. Andros Island, *Brace* 4951. New Providence, *Wilson* 8267; *Hitchcock* in 1890.

CUBA: Guane, *Shafer* 10385. Habana, *Léon* 572, 821, 821b; *Schott* 103. Batabanó, *Ekman* 902. Santiago de las Vegas, *Wilson* 2207. Guanabacoa, *Léon* 193, 565, 8838. Cayo Ramano, *Shafer* 2614. San Miguel de los Baños, *Léon* 8391. Manacas, *Léon* 5821. Manajanabo, *Léon* 5302. Baraguá, *Hitchcock* 23372. Guara, *Hitchcock* 23389. Sierra de Nipe, *Ekman* 9807; *Shafer* 3007. Orientes Grandes, *Léon* 823. Isla de Pinos, *Jennings* 283. Without locality, *Wright* 1555.

JAMAICA: Rockport, *Ridley* 80. Port Antonio, *Fredholm* 3291; *Maxon and Killip* 288. Black River, *Harris* 12545; *Hitchcock* 9647. Troy, *Hitchcock* 9806; *Maxon* 2811, 2945; *Harris* 12586, 12592. Cinchona, *Harris* 12483, 13399; *Hart* 682 in part. Claremont, *Hitchcock* 9486. Ewarton, *Hitchcock* 9446. Castleton, *Hitchcock* 9406. Newcastle, *Hitchcock* 9348. Bog Walk, *Hitchcock* 9291. Mouth of Cockpit River, *Harris* 12465. Kingston, *Cockerell* in 1892. Arntully, *Orcutt* 2621. Gordon Town, *Hart* 869. Ipswich, *Hitchcock* 9620. Buff Bay, *Hitchcock* 9763. Montego Bay, *Hitchcock* 9677.

FIGURE 354.—*Andropogon glomeratus*, × 1 (Hitchcock 437).

HAITI: Port-au-Prince, *Buch* 2048; *Cook, Scofield, and Doyle* 58. Gonaïve Island, *Leonard* 3253, 3333; *Eyerdam* 107a. St. Michel de l'Atalaye, *Leonard* 7284, 7373. Tortuga Island, *Leonard* 13923; *Ekman* H 4263. Aux Cayes, *Ekman* H 72. Morne la Selle, *Buch* 1352.

DOMINICAN REPUBLIC: Prov Barahona, *Fuertes* 1281. Jaina, *Faris* 402. Punta Icacos, *Ekman* H 15787.

PUERTO RICO: Maricao, *Hioram* 816; *Chase* 6203. Mayaguez, *Chase* 6165. San Juan, *Chase* 6355. Ponce, *Chase* 6480. Arecibo, *Chase* 6555. Lares, *Chase* 6586.

LEEWARD ISLANDS: St. Kitts, *Hitchcock* 16361. Antigua, *Box* 54, 128. Nevis, *Box* 170. Guadeloupe, *Duss* 3548, 3937.

WINDWARD ISLANDS: Martinique, *Duss* 1301.

26. Andropogon virginicus L., Sp. Pl. 1046. 1753. Virginia. BROOMSEDGE.

Densely tufted, with a mass of long leaves at the base; culms 1 to 1.5 m tall; sheaths compressed-keeled, glabrous or somewhat appressed villous; blades 2 to 4 mm wide; inflorescence slender, one-third to one-half the length of the plant; racemes 1.5 to 3 cm long, more or less included in the spathes; rachis slender, flexuous, this and the pedicels villous with white hairs 3 to 5 mm long; awn delicate, straight, 10 to 15 mm long (fig. 355).

Sterile hills and open woods, eastern United States to the West Indies and Panama. Virginia.

BERMUDA: *Brown and Britton* 225.

FIGURE 355.—*Andropogon virginicus*. Plant, × ½; spikelet with rachis joint and pedicel, × 5 (Earle 4).

BAHAMAS: New Providence, *Wilson* 8285. Elbow Cay, *Geogr. Soc. Baltimore* 569.

CUBA: Cajálbana, *Léon* 4851. Pinar del Río, *Hitchcock* 23294. Viñales, *Léon* 15862. Laguna de Ariguanabo, *Ekman* 11520. Santiago de las Vegas, *Baker and Wilson* 599. San Miguel de los Baños, *Léon* 8853. Loma del Gato, *Hioram* 7609. Prov. Santa Clara, *Léon* 824, 5400, 5972, 6656, 7924. Without locality, *Wright* 3901.

JAMAICA: Upper Clarendon, *Harris* 12851. Lititz, *Harris* 12682. Lower Clarendon, *Harris* 12732. Cinchona, *Hitchcock* 9704; *Harris* 11263, 11268. Appleton, *Hitchcock* 9656½. Montego Bay, *Hitchcock* 9680. Bull Head Mountain, *Hitchcock* 9542. Ewarton, *Hitchcock* 9460. Newcastle, *Hitchcock* 9338. Abbey Green, *Hitchcock* 9361, 9385. Castleton, *Harris* 11295. Salt Hill, *Harris* 11362. Cold Spring Gap, *Harris* 11378. Ramble, *Hitchcock* 9481, 9488 (*Amer. Gr. Nat. Herb.* 275). Port Antonio, *Fredholm* 3333. Gordon Town, *Hart* 692, 734, 831.

HAITI: Pétionville, *Ekman* H 1846. Dondou, *Leonard* 8622. Ennery, *Leonard* 9077. Furcy, *Leonard* 4576, 4576a. Godet, *Buch* 1666.

DOMINICAN REPUBLIC: Monción, *Ekman* H 12771. Pimentel, *Ekman* H 13254.

26a. Andropogon virginicus var. **graciliformis** Léon, in Britton, Bull. Torrey Bot. Club 53: 457. 1926. Cuba, *Léon* 11343.

Culms slender, usually less than 50 cm tall; basal sheaths not compressed-keeled; blades, especially of the innovations, very slender, folded, becoming flat and flexuous with age, usually not more than 1 to 2 mm wide when flat; spathes few. Distinguished from the species by the more delicate culms, terete rather than compressed sheaths, more slender blades, and fewer pairs of racemes.

Sandy savannas, Cuba.

CUBA: Pinar del Río, *Hitchcock* 23283, 23288. Chirigota, *Léon* 7437. Sabana de Motembo, *Léon* 11343.

27. Andropogon reinoldii Léon, Mem. Soc. Cub. Hist. Nat. Poey 5. 1922. Cuba, *Léon* 9932.

Culms tufted, erect, 50 to 80 cm tall; sheaths glabrous, the basal ones somewhat compressed but not so strongly as in *A. virginicus;* ligule visible from the side view of the sheath, about 1 mm long; blades flat or, especially at the base, folded, glabrous, somewhat scabrous, 10 to 35 cm long, 2.5 to 5 mm wide; racemes in pairs, the pairs several along the upper part of the culm; racemes 2 to 4 cm long, villous but the spikelets not hidden by the hairs, the peduncle enclosed in the spathe, 3 to 5 cm long, the racemes partly enclosed in the spathe or barely exserted; sessile spikelet 3 mm long, the awn nearly straight, about 7 or 8 mm long; pedicellate spikelet wanting or nearly so. Differs from *A. virginicus* in the long peduncles, the smaller spikelets, and the less compressed basal sheaths.

Gravelly soil and pastures, open slopes, Cuba.

CUBA: Loma del Gato, Sierra Maestra, Cobre, *Léon* 9832, 9932; *Ekman* in 1922. Herradura, *Ekman* 14081.

60256—36——26

28. Andropogon angustatus (Presl) Steud., Syn. Pl. Glum. 1: 370. 1854.

Diectomis laxa Nees, Agrost. Bras. 340. 1829. Not *Andropogon laxus* Willd., 1806. Brazil.

Diectomis angustata Presl, Rel. Haenk. 1: 333. 1830. Mexico.

Andropogon apricus Trin., Mém. Acad. St. Pétersb. VI. Sci. Nat. 2^1: 83. 1836. Brazil.

Erect slender perennial about 1 m tall; blades flat, elongate, 1 to 2 mm wide; racemes in pairs, 2 to 3 cm long, the pairs on slender branches from several of the upper leaves, forming a loose inflorescence, each branch at first enclosed in a spathe but finally exserted 5 to 10 cm; pedicels and joints of rachis stiffly ciliate with whitish hairs; fertile (sessile) spikelet about 6 mm long, laterally compressed, nearly glabrous, the callus sharp, barbate, 1 mm long; first glume narrow, deeply sulcate on the back; second glume compressed, keeled, bearing from the apex a slender divergent awn 1 cm long; awn of fertile floret geniculate, twisted, brown, scabrous-hispidulous, 3 to 4 cm long.

Dry savannas, Mexico to Brazil; Cuba.

Cuba: Manacas, *Léon* 5841. Holguín, *Ekman* in 1922. Isla de Pinos, *Ekman* 12520.

29. Andropogon saccharoides Swartz, Prodr. Veg. Ind. Occ. 26. 1788. Jamaica. Silver beardgrass.

Andropogon saccharoides subsp. *leucopogon* subvar. *paucirameus* Hack., in DC., Monogr. Phan. 6: 497. 1889. Cuba, *Wright* 1556.

Sorghum saccharoides Kuntze, Rev. Gen. Pl. 2: 792. 1891.

Holcus saccharoides Kuntze, in Stuckert, An. Mus. Nac. Buenos Aires 11: 48. 1904.

Amphilophis saccharoides Nash, N. Amer. Fl. 17: 125. 1912.

Andropogon saccharoides var. *surius* Krause, Bot. Centbl. Beihefte 32: 334. 1914. Barbados, *Wiegand* 2085.

Erect perennial; culms simple, brittle, 60 to 150 cm tall; nodes white-hispid; blades flat, glabrous or nearly so, 2 to 8 mm wide; panicles exserted, 5 to 15 cm long, oblong, pale, silky, of numerous crowded, ascending racemes; awns 1.5 to 2 cm long (fig. 356).

Rocky hills and grassy slopes, southwestern United States to South America and the West Indies. The Cuban specimens were referred by Hitchcock[4] to *A. leucopogon* Nees. Several of them and a few from other islands are the form with fewer racemes described as subvar. *paucirameus*. This is one of the grasses called "rabo de zorra" in Cuba.

Cuba: Viñales, *Léon* 15346. Habana, *Léon* 2557, 4716. Sancti Spíritus, *Léon* 893, 955, 4097, 4101, 5357; *Shafer* 12073. Manajanabo, *Léon* 5277, 5301. Manatí, *Léon* 6008. Isla de Pinos, *Curtiss* 382; *Ekman* 12195.

Jamaica: Liguanea Ridge, *Harris* 12213. Mavis Bank, *Harris* 11449. Newcastle, *Harris* 11396; *Hitchcock* 9345. Halls Delight, *Harris* 11293. Ashley Hall, *Harris* 12736. Lititz, *Harris* 11655, 11781, 12698. Ipswich, *Harris* 12501. Gordon Town, *Hart* 570; *Hitchcock* 9377. New Forest, *Hitchcock* 9848. Barican, *Hitchcock* 9578 (*Amer. Gr. Nat. Herb.* 267).

[4] Contrib. U. S. Natl. Herb. 12: 193. 1909.

Haiti: St. Michel de l'Atalaye, *Leonard* 7156, 8447. Dondou, *Leonard* 8756. Ennery, *Leonard* 8883, 8938, 8977. Bombardopolis, *Leonard* 13478. Port-au-Prince, *Ekman* H 7128; *Buch* 1806, 1855. Furcy, *Leonard* 4824. Mission, *Leonard* 3849. Étang Ténéllé, *Ekman* H 331. Grand-Gosier, *Ekman* H 6866. Hinche, *Ekman* H 6132.

Dominican Republic: Constanza, *Tuerckheim* 2882. Monción, *Ekman* H 12679. Without locality, *Wright, Parry, and Brummel* 631.

Puerto Rico: Mayaguez, *Chase* 6270, 6817. Mariaco, *Chase* 6226.

Leeward Islands: St. Kitts, *Box* 155. Antigua, *Box* 95, 98, 316.

Figure 356.—*Andropogon saccharoides*, × 1 (Hitchcock 5370).

30. Andropogon pertusus (L.) Willd., Sp. Pl. 4: 922. 1806.

Holcus pertusus L., Mant. Pl. 2: 301. 1771. India.

Andropogon panormitanus Parl., "in Diar. Congr. Venezia 1847"; Fl. Ital. 1: 140. 1848. Italy.

Andropogon pertusus var. *panormitanus* Hack., in DC., Monogr. Phan. 6: 481. 1889.

Amphilophis pertusa Stapf, in Prain, Fl. Trop. Afr. 9: 175. 1917.

Culms ascending, branching, 20 to 100 cm tall, the nodes bearded or (in var. *panormitanus*) glabrous; blades 10 to 20 cm long, 1 to 4 mm wide, pubescent or nearly glabrous; racemes flabellately aggregate on a short axis, few to several, 2 to 6 cm long, villous; first glume with a pit or pinhole in the middle of the back; awn of sessile spikelet twice-geniculate, brown, about 15 mm long. The var. *panormitanus* differs only in the glabrous nodes, less pubescent blades, and often more numerous racemes.

Roadsides and open grassy places, Tropics of the Old World; introduced in the West Indies.

Called "sourgrass" in Tobago and "Barbados sourgrass" in many of the islands. A somewhat more slender form with, on the average, fewer racemes, is called in the Virgin Islands "hurricane grass." This form is said to be relished by stock and makes more satisfactory forage than does Barbados sourgrass.

Cuba: Habana, *Léon* 11388, 12466. Santiago de las Vegas, *Léon* 9757. Sancti Spíritus, *Léon* 7826. Gamboa, *Ekman* 14941. Marianao, *Léon* 15093.

Jamaica: Constant Spring, *Hitchcock* 9387 (*Amer. Gr. Nat. Herb.* 265); *Harris* 11262. Gordon Town, *Harris* 11514. Kingston, *Ridley* 77; *Hitchcock* 9472. Hope Gardens, *Harris* 12517. Musgrave Road, *Harris* 11478. Alligator Pond, *Harris* 12694.

Dominican Republic: Between Nizao and Baní, *Ekman* H 13358.

VIRGIN ISLANDS: St. Croix, *Rose* 3523, 3533; *Thompson* 9; *Baker* in 1929; *Ricksecker* 209; *Hitchcock* 16330. St. Thomas, *Hitchcock* 16317.

LEEWARD ISLANDS: Antigua, *Box* 3, 181. Nevis, *Box* 173. Dominica, *Bot. Gard.* 1.

WINDWARD ISLANDS: Barbados, *Hitchcock* 16518. Grenada, *Hitchcock* 17683.

TRINIDAD: *Bot. Gard. Herb.* 5064.

TOBAGO: *Eggers* 5654; *Broadway* 4727; *Hitchcock* 10220, 10234.

31. Andropogon ischaemum L., Sp. Pl. 1047. 1753. Europe.

Andropogon ischaemum var. *americanus* Hack., in DC., Monogr. Phan. 6: 476. 1889. Venezuela and Antigua.

Sorghum ischaemum Kuntze, Rev. Gen. Pl. 2: 792. 1891.

Amphilophis ischaemum Nash, N. Amer. Fl. 17: 124. 1912.

Differing from *A. pertusus* in the absence of a pit on the back of the first glume of the sessile spikelet.

Introduced; open ground, Leeward Islands; Tropics of the Old World.

LEEWARD ISLANDS: Antigua, *Wullschlaegel.*

107. DIECTOMIS H. B. K. Nov. Gen. et Sp. 1: 193. pl. 64. 1816[5]

Spikelets arranged as in *Andropogon;* raceme solitary, subtended by a spathe; first glume of pediceled spikelet large, flat, herbaceous, many-nerved, awned from between 2 slender teeth; first glume of fertile (sessile) spikelet narrow, 2-keeled; second glume laterally compressed, the midnerve wing-keeled, awned; fertile lemma with a bent awn more than twice as long as those of the glumes. Erect annual with flat blades.

1. Diectomis fastigiata (Swartz) H. B. K., Nov. Gen. et Sp. 1: 193. pl. 64. 1816.

Andropogon fastigiatus Swartz, Prodr. Veg. Ind. Occ. 26. 1788. Jamaica.

Slender, glabrous; culms 0.5 to 1.5 m tall, freely branching above; ligules firm, up to 2 cm long; blades 1 to 4 mm wide; racemes 2 to 6 cm long; joint of rachis and sterile pedicel winged at the summit, long-villous, the white hairs as much as 7 mm long; the conspicuous pediceled spikelet 8 mm long; awn of fertile lemma geniculate, 4 to 5 cm long (fig. 357).

Dry open ground, southern Mexico and the West Indies to Brazil.

CUBA: Asiento Viejo de San Julián, *Léon* 6911; *Wright* 3485. San Cristótal, *Wright* 3483. Guane, *Shafer* 10384, 10413, 11218. San Juan y Martínez, *Ekman* 18074. Guanabacoa, *Hitchcock* 23230; *Léon* 3451, 4719; *Wilson and Léon* 2876.

JAMAICA: Bellevue, *Harris* 11288. Content Gap, *Harris* 11344. Temple Hall, *Harris* 11358. Flamstead, *Harris* 11464. Mavis Bank, *Harris* 11507. Barican, *Hitchcock* 9572. Lititz, *Harris* 12700. Southern Manchester, *Harris* 12692.

HAITI: St. Michel de l'Atalaye, *Leonard* 7154, 7290, 7525. Marmelade, *Leonard* 8201. Ennery, *Leonard* 8801, 9068. Plaisance, *Leonard* 9414. Montagne du Trou d'Eau, *Ekman* H 2317. Pétionville, *Ekman* H 2331. Petite Rivière, *Sweet* in 1924. Morne Castilleur, *Ekman* H 6420.

[5] For discussion of the nomenclature, see Contrib. U. S. Natl. Herb. 24: 206, 1925; 692, 1930.

PUERTO RICO: Coamo, *Sintenis* 3247. Rincón, *Sintenis* 5516. Maricao, *Sintenis* 353. Mayaguez, *Holm* 82; *Chase* 6808. Campo Alegre, *Chase* 6622. Lares, *Chase* 6593. Santa Ana, *Britton and Cowell* 4026.

WINDWARD ISLANDS: Grenada, *Broadway* 253.

108. CYMBOPOGON Spreng., Pl. Pugill. 2: 14. 1815.

OIL GRASS.

Racemes in pairs subtended by spathes, these collected in a decompound inflorescence; spikelets in pairs as in *Andropogon*, but the lowermost pair of one or both racemes sterile and similar to the pedicled spikelets above; fertile (sessile) spikelets dorsally compressed, flat or dorsally grooved, sharply 2-keeled at the edges; fertile lemma narrow, the awn from between 2 teeth or lobes. Perennial densely tufted usually aromatic grasses. The two species mentioned below are cultivated occasionally in the West Indies. These and other species are used in perfumery.[6]

First glume of sessile spikelet flat on the back ---------- 1. C. CITRATUS.
First glume of sessile spikelet concave on the back ---------- 2. C. NARDUS.

1. **Cymbopogon citratus** (DC.) Stapf, Kew Bull. Misc. Inf. 1906: 322. 1906.

LEMON GRASS.

Andropogon citratus DC., Cat. Hort. Monsp. 78. 1813 (name only); Nees, Allgem. Gartenzeit. 3: 267. 1835. Described from a garden specimen.

Stout perennial with leafy sterile shoots from a short rhizome; culms erect, 2 m or more tall; blades long-attenuate toward the base and tapering upward to a setaceous point, as much as 1 m long, 5 to 15 mm wide, glabrous, scabrous on the margins and above

[6] A detailed account of these grasses is given by Stapf, Kew Bull. Misc. Inf. 1906: 297–363. 1906.

FIGURE 357.—*Diectomis fastigiata*, × ½ (Swallen 4187).

toward the tip, the midrib rather stout below, whitish on the upper side; inflorescence 30 to 60 cm long, nodding (fig. 358).

Sparingly escaped from cultivation. Called "hierba de limon" in Cuba.

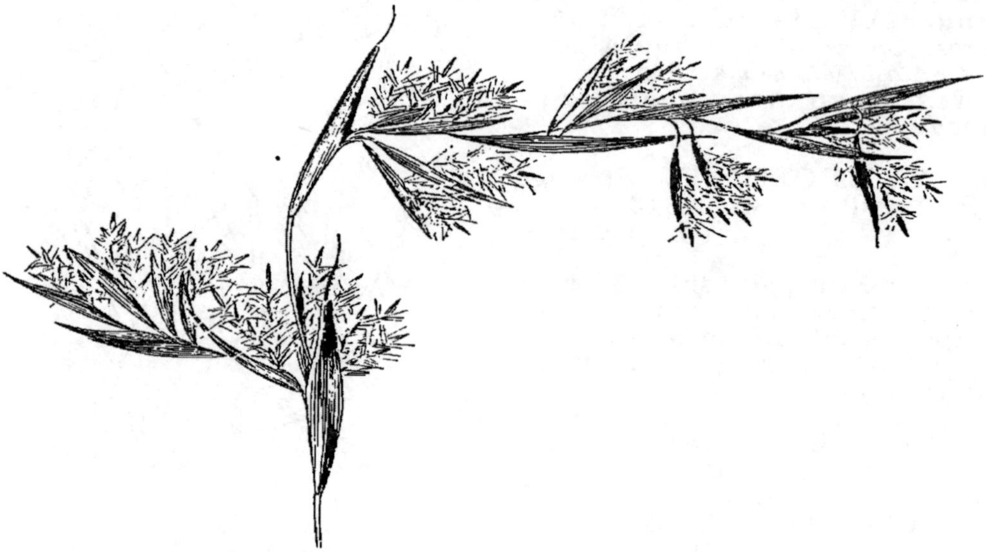

FIGURE 358.—*Cymbopogon citratus.* Branchlet, × 1 (Sintenis 5295).

2. **Cymbopogon nardus** (L.) Rendle, Cat. Afr. Pl. Welw. 2: 155. 1899. CITRONELLA GRASS.

Andropogon nardus L., Sp. Pl. 1046. 1753. India.

Similar to *C. citratus* in habit, differing in the concave glumes of the sessile spikelet. In Puerto Rico the fibrous rootstock is used as a toothbrush by the poorer people.

109. HYPARRHENIA Anderss.; Stapf, in Prain, Fl. Trop. Africa 9: 291. 1918

Spikelets in pairs, as in *Andropogon*, but spikelets of the lower pairs alike, sterile, and awnless; fertile spikelets 1 to few in each raceme, terete or flattened on the back, the margins of the first glume rounded, not sharply inflexed nor keeled (keeled toward the summit in *H. rufa*), the base usually elongate into a sharp callus, the fertile lemma with a strong geniculate awn; sterile spikelets awnless; racemes in pairs, on slender peduncles, and subtended by a spathe. Tall perennials, the pairs of racemes and their spathes more or less crowded, forming a rather large inflorescence at the upper part of the plant.

Spikelets nearly glabrous or rather sparsely hirsute; pubescence usually rufous. 1. H. RUFA.
Spikelets densely villous; pubescence whitish ---------- 2. H. HIRTA.

1. **Hyparrhenia rufa** (Nees) Stapf, in Prain, Fl. Trop. Afr. 9: 304. 1918.

Trachypogon rufus Nees, Agrost. Bras. 345. 1829. Brazil.
Andropogon rufus Kunth, Rév. Gram. 1: Sup. XXXIX. 1830.
Cymbopogon rufus Rendle, Cat. Afr. Pl. Welw. 2: 155. 1899.

Perennial; culms erect, rather stout, 1 to 2.5 m tall; blades mostly 2 to 8 mm wide, sometimes more than 1 cm; inflorescence 20 to 40 cm long, the pairs of racemes toward the ends of the numerous branches on long slender flexuous peduncles; racemes about 2 cm long, reddish brown; fertile spikelets mostly 5 to 7 in each raceme, 3 to 4 mm long, flattened from the back, pubescent with dark-red hairs, the pedicels and rachis-joints ciliate with red hairs; awn 15 to 20 mm long, twice geniculate, twisted, red-brown, hispidulous (fig. 359).

Moist, open ground, Venezuela to Brazil; Tropics of the Old World. Sometimes cultivated under the name "jaragua." Has some forage value.

CUBA: Baragua, *Hitchcock* 23380 (*Amer. Gr. Nat. Herb.* 1000). Santiago de las Vegas, escaped from experiment station plots, *Hitchcock* 23249. Manacas, *Léon* 5841, 5870.

PUERTO RICO: Mayaguez, *Britton* 7443, cultivated under the name "canophora."

LEEWARD ISLANDS: St. Kitts, *Box* 131.

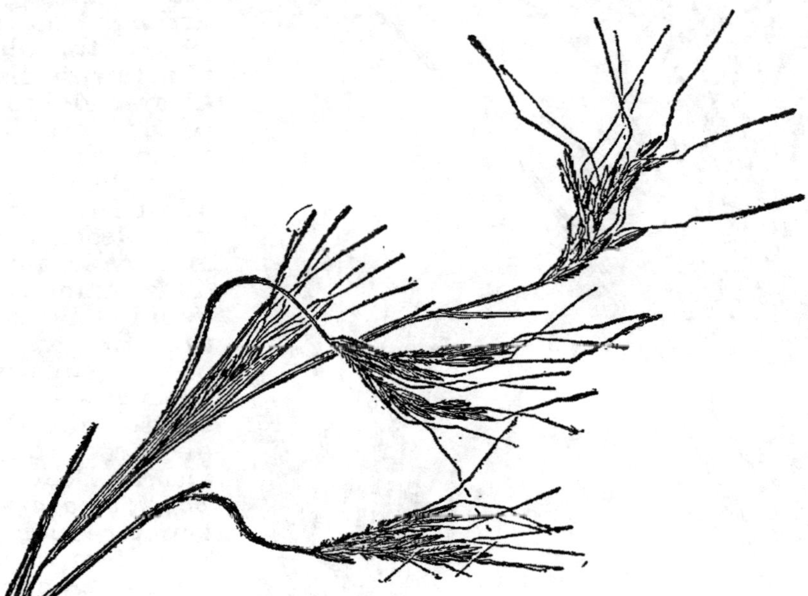

FIGURE 359.—*Hyparrhenia rufa*, × 1 (Moldenke 243).

2. Hyparrhenia hirta (L.) Stapf, in Prain, Fl. Trop. Afr. 9: 315. 1918.

Andropogon hirtus L., Sp. Pl. 1046. 1753. Mediterranean region.

Cymbopogon hirtus Stapf; Burtt-Davy, Ann. Transv. Mus. 3: 121. 1912.

Differing from *H. rufa* in the usually longer racemes (4 to 5 cm) and in the denser and more silky whitish pubescence of the inflorescence.

Waste places, introduced in a few localities in tropical America; Mediterranean region to South Africa.

CUBA: Habana, *Ekman* 13195 (*Amer. Gr. Nat. Herb.* 999); *Léon* 2788, 3492.

DOMINICAN REPUBLIC: Province of Santo Domingo, *Ekman* H 11419. Monción, *Ekman* H 13052. Santo Domingo City, *Ekman* H 13292. Cuesta Piedras, *Ekman* H 14298. Without locality, *Wright, Parry, and Brummel* 616.

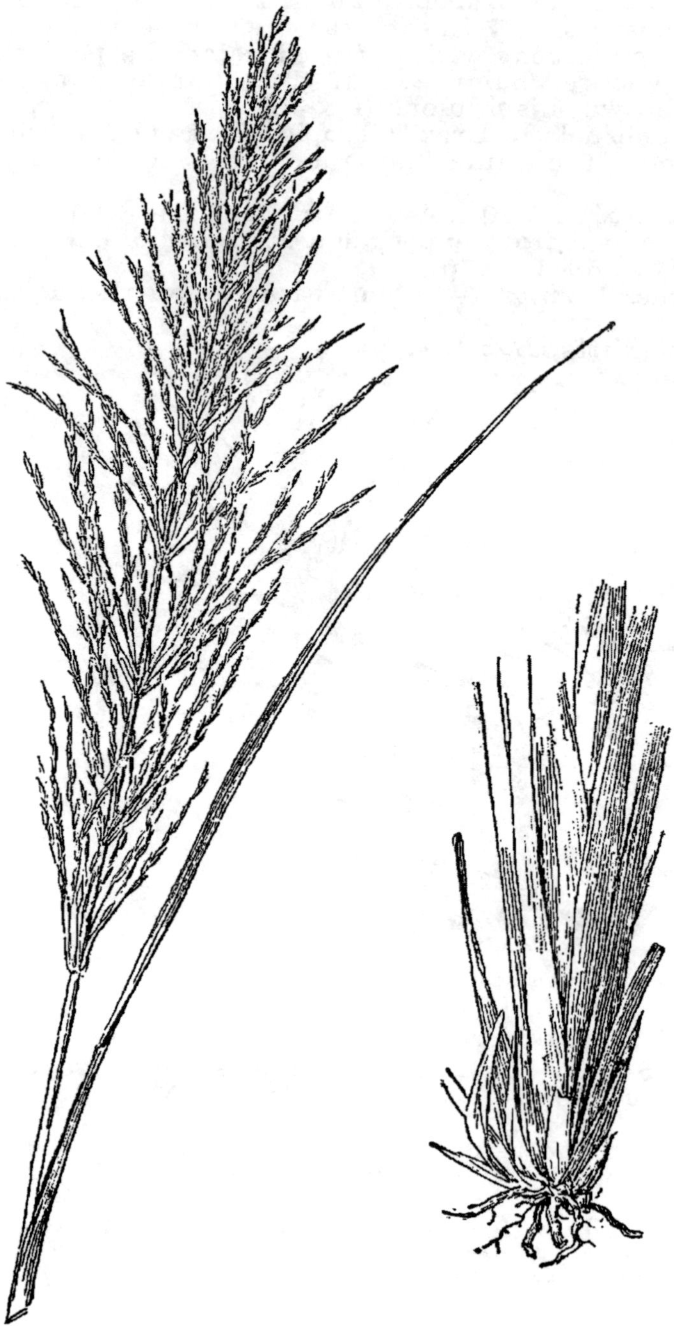

FIGURE 360.—*Vetiveria zizanioides*, × ½ (Hitchcock 9435).

110. VETIVERIA Bory, in Lem., Bull. Soc. Philom. 1822: 43. 1822

Racemes long, slender, solitary, on long filiform peduncles borne in whorls on an elongate axis, forming a large panicle; spikelets awnless (in ours), arranged as in *Andropogon*, the filiform rachis tardily disjointing. Coarse glabrous perennials with stout rhizomes.

In the Grasses of the West Indies this genus was described under *Anatherum* Beauv. This name was there typified by *A. muricatum* Beauv., the first of two equally eligible species. It seems better to take the second of these species, *A. bicorne* Beauv. (*Andropogon bicornis* L.) as the type, reducing *Antherum* Beauv. to a synonym of *Andropogon* and leaving *Vetiveria* for the aromatic grass commonly known under that name.

1. Vetiveria zizanioides (L.) Nash, in Small, Fl. Southeast. U. S. 67. 1903. KHUS-KHUS.

Phalaris zizanioides L., Mant. Pl. 183. 1771. India.

Andropogon muricatus Retz., Obs. Bot. 3: 43. 1783. India.

Anatherum muricatum Beauv., Ess. Agrost. 128, 150. pl. 22, f. 10. 1812.

Vetiveria arundinacea Griseb., Fl. Brit. W. Ind. 559. 1864. Jamaica, Trinidad.

Vetiveria muricata Griseb., Fl. Brit. W. Ind. 560. 1864.

Sorghum zizanioides Kuntze, Rev. Gen. Pl. 2: 791. 1891.

Andropogon zizanioides Urban, Symb. Antill. 4: 79. 1903.

Anatherum zizanioides Hitchc. and Chase, Contrib. U. S. Natl. Herb. 18: 285. 1917.

Robust, densely tufted, erect, branching perennial; culms 1 to 2 m tall, blades glabrous, firm or rigid, 30 to 100 cm long, 4 to 10 mm wide, scabrous on the margin; panicle elongate-pyramidal, 20 to 30 cm long, the branches in 6 to 10 whorls of as many as 20 rays, the lower naked part as much as 5 cm; racemes as much as 5 cm long (fig. 360).

A native of Asia, cultivated in the Tropics of both hemispheres. Commonly cultivated in the West Indies as a hedge plant and for its aromatic roots. Sometimes escaped along roadsides. It is called "vetiver"[7] in Cuba. The roots are packed with articles of clothing to preserve them from moths. This is the grass that produces the aromatic roots called in Puerto Rico "pacholi"[8] or "pachuli." The Indian name "khus-khus" is used in the English islands. The aromatic roots are sometimes woven into screens which, when wet, are used to perfume living quarters. Also sometimes called "cockroach grass" and "khas-khas."

111. SORGHUM Moench, Meth. Pl. 207. 1794[9]

Spikelets in pairs, one sessile and fertile, the other pedicellate, sterile but well developed, usually staminate, the terminal sessile spikelet with two pedicellate spikelets. Annual or perennial, tall or moderately tall grasses, with flat blades and terminal panicles of 1- to 5-jointed tardily disarticulating racemes. The numerous varieties of the cultivated *Sorghum* are considered species by some.

Plants perennial, with creeping rhizomes .... 1. S. HALEPENSE.
Plants annual .... 2. S. VULGARE.

1. Sorghum halepense (L.) Pers., Syn. Pl. 1: 101. 1805. JOHNSON GRASS.

Holcus halepensis L., Sp. Pl. 1047. 1753. Syria.

Andropogon halepensis Brot., Fl. Lusit. 1: 89. 1804.

Robust perennial with numerous stout rhizomes; culms mostly 1 to 1.5 m tall; blades mostly less than 1.5 cm wide, the midrib prominent, the white margins scabrous; panicle 15 to 25 cm long; fertile spikelets plump, 5 mm long, the awn when present 7 to 10 mm long, deciduous; staminate spikelets 4 mm long, the pedicel 3 mm long (fig. 361).

A weed in fields and waste places in the warmer parts of North America; introduced from the Old World. Found in all the large islands and probably in most of the smaller ones.

[7] Est. Expt. Agron. Bol. 22: 108. 1914.
[8] Contrib. U. S. Natl. Herb. 8: 208. 1903.
[9] *Holcus* L. was used for this genus in Grasses of the West Indies. The historic type of that genus is *Holcus sorghum* L., but a standard species, *H. lanatus* L., has been adopted instead, in order to conserve *Holcus* for the velvet grass and to make *Sorghum* Moench available for the economically important sorghums.

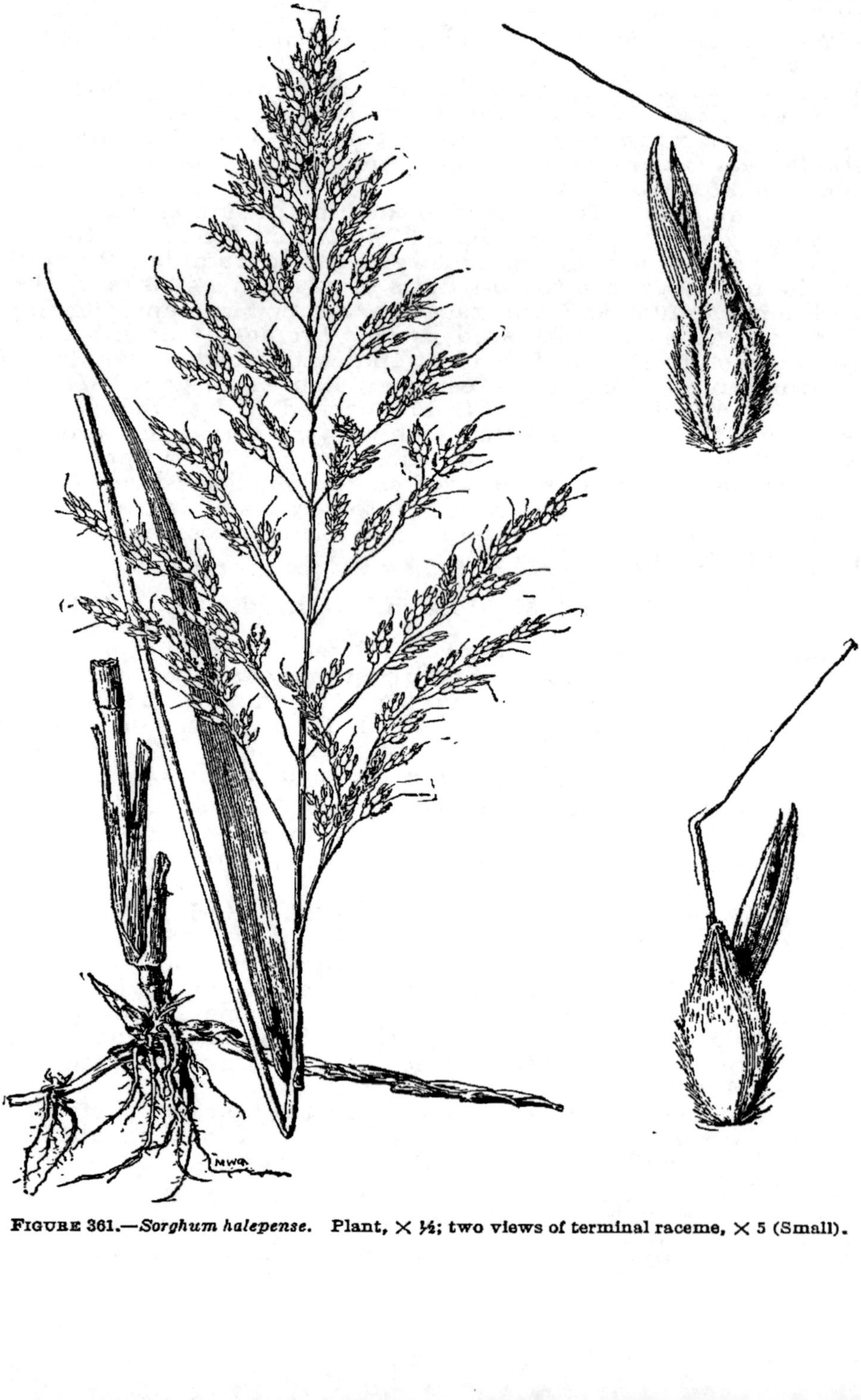

FIGURE 361.—*Sorghum halepense.* Plant, × ½; two views of terminal raceme, × 5 (Small).

This species is described by Humboldt, Bonpland, and Kunth,[10] with Habana, Cuba, given as locality, under the name "*Andropogon avenaceus* Schrad." This is evidently a misprint for *A. arundinaceus* Willd., as described by Schrader.[11] In Cuba this is called "cañuela" and "hierba de Don Carlos."

2. Sorghum vulgare (L.) Pers., Syn. Pl. 1: 101. 1805.
SORGHUM OR SORGO.

Holcus sorghum L., Sp. Pl. 1047. 1753. India.
Andropogon sorghum Brot., Fl. Lusit. 1: 88. 1804.
Sorghum dura Griseb., Fl. Brit. W. Ind. 560. 1864.

Large broad-leaved annual, with a compact panicle of turgid persistent spikelets.

Occasionally cultivated in the West Indies and sometimes spontaneous in waste places or near fields. Widely cultivated in other parts of North America and in the Old World. In the English Islands it is often called "Guinea corn"; in Cuba it is called "millo."

There are numerous varieties. One variety, Sudan grass (*S. vulgare* var. *sudanense* (Piper) Hitchc.), is a comparatively slender form 1 to 2 m tall, with a large open panicle, used for forage. Another variety, broomcorn, has a large erect or fan-shaped panicle with long naked branches, the spikelets crowded near the ends.

112. SORGHASTRUM Nash, in Britton, Man. 71. 1901

Spikelets in pairs, one nearly terete, sessile and fertile, the other wanting, only the hairy pedicel being present; glumes coriaceous, brown or yellowish, the first hirsute, the edges inflexed over the second; sterile and fertile lemmas thin and hyaline, the latter extending into a usually well-developed bent and twisted awn. Perennial, erect, rather tall grasses, with narrow flat blades and narrow terminal panicles of one- to few-jointed racemes.

Awn straight or slightly bent, not strongly spirally twisted at base, shorter than the spikelet or sometimes a little longer ---------------- 1. S. SETOSUM.
Awn geniculate, strongly spirally twisted at base, about 3 times as long as the spikelet -- 2. S. STIPOIDES.

1. Sorghastrum setosum (Griseb.) Hitchc., Contrib. U. S. Natl. Herb. 12: 195. 1909.

Sorghum parviflorum Desv.; Hamilt., Prodr. Pl. Ind. Occ. 12. 1825. Not *S. parviflorum* Beauv., 1812. Hispaniola.

Andropogon setosus Griseb., Cat. Pl. Cub. 235. 1866. Cuba, *Wright* 3897.

Andropogon francavillanus Fourn., Mex. Pl. 2: 56. 1886. Mexico.

Sorghastrum francavillanum Hitchc., Contrib. U.S. Natl. Herb. 12: 195. 1909.

Sorghastrum parviflorum Hitchc. and Chase, Contrib. U. S. Natl. Herb. 18: 287. 1917.

Tall erect tufted glabrous perennial with long, flat, or subinvolute blades and long lanceolate panicles with slender or subcapillary branchlets and peduncles and golden brown spikelets, the ultimate

[10] Nov. Gen. et Sp. 1: 189. 1816.
[11] Fl. Germ. 1: 237. 1806.

peduncles, the sterile pedicels, and the base of the spikelet clothed with white hairs; awn variable in length.

Grassy hillsides, southern Mexico and the West Indies to Argentina. Grisebach cites *Piptatherum setosum* A. Rich., "ex descr.", but Richard's description does not apply to this species. *Andropogon setosus* is taken to be a new species based on *Wright* 3897, rather than a change of name (see p. 182) (fig. 362).

CUBA: Sancti Spíritus, *Léon* 894, 895, 5365. Nagua, *Ekman* 14903a.

JAMAICA: Hardware Gap, *Harris* 11437. Flamstead, *Harris* 11463. Bermuda Mountain, *Harris* 11635. Gorden Town, *Hart* 812. Newcastle, *Hitchcock* 9346. Halls Delight *Harris* 12934.

HAITI: Port-au-Prince, *Ekman* H 419. Las Cahobas, *Cook, Scofield, and Doyle* 98. Petite Rivière de l'Artibonite, *Picarda* 1634. Morne Robin, *Buch* 1475. Lamarque, *Buch* 1652.

DOMINICAN REPUBLIC: Pimentel, *Ekman* H 13257. Monción, *Ekman* H 12687. Sabana de la Mar, *Ekman* H 15615.

PUERTO RICO: Trujillo Alto, *Sein* 318; *Chase* 6370, 6773. San Juan, *Chase* 6638. Vega Baja, *Chase* 6421. Rio Piedras, *Cowgill* 687, 696.

TRINIDAD: Icacos, *Broadway* 9290.

2. Sorghastrum stipoides (H. B. K.) Nash, N. Amer. Fl. 17: 129. 1912.

Andropogon stipoides H. B. K., Nov. Gen. et Sp. 1: 189. 1816. Colombia.

Andropogon domingensis Spreng.; Steud., Nom. Bot. ed. 2. 1: 91. 1840, as synonym of *A. stipoides*, but the specimen is *Sorghastrum setosum*.

More slender than the preceding, the narrower blades convolute, the spikelets slightly larger, and the awns well developed.

Palm barrens, Cuba; Colombia to Brazil. This is the species referred by Hitchcock [12] to *S. francavillanum*.

CUBA: Mangas, *Ekman* 17592. Pinar del Río, *Hitchcock* 23252, 23303. Santa Cruz de los Pinos, *Ekman* 17680 (*Amer. Gr. Nat. Herb.* 998). Guane, *Shafer* 10353. Hanábana, *Wright* 3897. Viñales, *Léon* 15864.

113. RHAPHIS Lour.[13] Fl. Cochinch. 552. 1790

Inflorescence a few-flowered panicle, the racemes reduced to a single joint of the rachis with a sessile perfect spikelet and 2 pedicellate sterile spikelets (the latter sometimes obsolete) borne at the ends of slender naked peduncles, these disjointing obliquely near the summit, forming a sharp callus below the long-awned spikelets. Perennials or rarely annuals, with narrow blades and terminal panicles.

1. Rhaphis pauciflora (Chapm.) Nash, in Small, Fl. Southeast. U. S. 67. 1903.

Andropogon wrightii Munro; Wright, An. Acad. Cienc. Habana 8: 288. 1871 (name only). Cuba, *Wright* 3895.

Sorghum pauciflorum Chapm., Bot. Gaz. 3: 20. 1878. Florida.

Chrysopogon pauciflorus Benth.; Vasey, Grasses U. S. 20. 1883.

[12] Contrib. U. S. Natl. Herb. 12: 195. 1909.

[13] The name Rhapis L. f.; Ait., Hort. Kew. 3: 473. 1789, having a different derivation and pronunciation should not invalidate Rhaphis Lour. The latter name should replace Chrysopogon Trin., Fund. Agrost. 187. 1820.

FIGURE 362.—*Sorghastrum setosum.* Plant × ½ ; two views of spikelet, × 10 (Léon 5365).

FIGURE 363.—*Rhaphis pauciflora*. Plant, × ½; fruiting spikelet, × 5 (Combs 1359).

A slender branching annual with flat or folded ciliate blades and a few-flowered panicle with capillary branchlets, the brown spikelets raised on a hairy callus of nearly equal length, the twisted bent awns up to 15 cm long (fig. 363).

Sandy pine barrens, Florida and Cuba.

CUBA: Pinar del Río, *Wright* 3895. Baraguá, *Hitchcock* 23383. Isla de Pinos, *Ekman* 11628; *Taylor* 46.

114. HETEROPOGON Pers., Syn. Pl. 2: 533. 1807

Spikelets in pairs, one sessile, the other pedicellate, both of the lower few to several pairs staminate or neuter, the remainder of the sessile spikelets perfect, terete, long-awned, the pedicellate spikelets, like the lower staminate, flat, conspicuous, awnless; glumes of the fertile spikelet equal, coriaceous, the first brown-hirsute, infolding the second; lemmas thin and hyaline, the fertile one narrow, extending into a strong bent and twisted brown awn; glumes of the staminate spikelet membranaceous, the first green, faintly many-nerved, asymmetric, one submarginal keel rather broadly winged, the other wingless, the margins inflexed, the second glume narrower, symmetric. Annual or perennial grasses, with flat blades and mostly solitary racemes terminal on the culms and branches; rachis slender, the lower part, bearing the pairs of staminate spikelets, continuous, the remainder disarticulating obliquely at the base of each joint, the joint forming a sharp barbed callus below the fertile spikelet, the pedicellate spikelet readily falling.

Plants perennial, 60 to 100 cm tall; first glume of staminate spikelet pilose. 1. H. CONTORTUS.

Plants annual, usually more than 1 m tall; first glume of staminate spikelet beset with a row of glands along the back, not pilose__2. H. MELANOCARPUS.

1. Heteropogon contortus (L.) Beauv.; Roem. and Schult., Syst. Veg. 2: 836. 1817. TANGLEHEAD.

Andropogon contortus L., Sp. Pl. 1045. 1753. India.

Andropogon secundus Willd.; Nees, Agrost. Bras. 364. 1829. Brazil.

Branching perennial; culms compressed, 40 to 100 cm tall; blades 2 to 4 mm wide, scabrous; racemes solitary, excluding awns 3 to 8 cm long, somewhat curved; spikelets imbricate, the lower awnless, the upper with brown bent awns, 5 to 8 cm long, red-brown. Lemon-scented when fresh (fig. 364).

Rocky slopes and cliffs. Southwestern United States and the West Indies to Argentina and Bolivia; warmer parts of the Old World.

CUBA: Arroyo Arenas, *Léon* 16423. Sancti Spíritus, *Léon* 897, 4095, 5356; *Sergius* 2792. Guantánamo, *Ekman* 10179. Eastern Cuba, *Wright* 1559.

JAMAICA: Halls Delight, *Harris* 11259. Grants Pen, *Harris* 11540. Guava Ridge, *Harris* 11290. Gordon Town, *Hitchcock* 9324. Healthshire Hills, *Harris* 11351, 11610; *Hitchcock* 9756. Lititz, *Harris* 11738. New Forest, *Hitchcock* 9839.

HAITI: Monte Cabrete, *Cook, Scofield, and Doyle* 71, 102. Port-au-Prince, *Ekman* H 2028; *Leonard* 15862. Pétionville, *Leonard* 4942; *Ekman* H 3244. St. Marc, *Leonard* 3419. Les Anglais, *Ekman* H 383.

FIGURE 364.—*Heteropogon contortus*. Plant, × ½; fruiting spikelet, × 5 (Griffiths 1844).

DOMINICAN REPUBLIC: Monción, *Ekman* H 12686. Azua, *Rose* 3826. Barahona, *Fuertes* 1455b. Los Charcos, *Fuertes* 1418. Santiago, *Ekman* H 16225.

VIRGIN ISLANDS: Virgin Gorda, *Fishlock* 208.

LEEWARD ISLANDS: St. Kitts, *Box* 154. Antigua, *Wullschlagel; Box* 71. Guadeloupe, *Duss* 3137; *Stehlé* 286.

2. **Heteropogon melanocarpus** (Ell.) Benth., Jour. Linn. Soc. Bot. 19: 71. 1882. SWEET TANGLEHEAD.

Andropogon melanocarpus Ell., Bot. S. C. and Ga. 1: 146. 1816. Georgia.

Culms stout, often glaucous, the lower nodes often producing stilt-roots; blades as much as 1 cm wide; racemes several, combined with the spathes and upper leaves forming a rather dense inflorescence 20 to 30 cm long; first glume of staminate spikelet 15 mm long; mature fertile spikelet terete, dark brown, 6 to 7 mm long with a sharp bearded callus about 2 mm long; awn hispidulous, 6 to 10 cm long (fig. 365).

FIGURE 365.—*Heteropogon melanocarpus*, × 1 (Fredholm 6405).

Grassy slopes and open ground, southern United States to Brazil and Bolivia; Haiti; also Tropics of the Old World.

HAITI: Pétionville, *Ekman* H 1909.

115. TRACHYPOGON Nees, Agrost. Bras. 341. 1829

Spikelets in pairs, along a slender continuous rachis, one nearly sessile, staminate, awnless, the other pedicellate, perfect, long-awned; the pedicel of the perfect spikelet obliquely disarticulating near the base, forming a sharp barbed callus below the spikelet; first glume firm-membranaceous, rounded on the back, several-nerved, obtuse; second glume firm, obscurely nerved; fertile lemma narrow, extending into a stout twisted and bent or flexuous awn; sessile spikelet persistent, as large as the fertile spikelet and similar but awnless. Perennial, moderately tall grasses, with terminal spikelike racemes, these single or clustered.

Awn 10 to 12 cm long, conspicuously plumose .... 1. T. GOUINII.
Awn mostly not more than 5 cm long, appressed-plumose on the lower part, scabrous above.
  Blades flat; racemes usually 2 or 3, sometimes solitary .. 2. T. LIGULARIS.
  Blades involute; racemes usually solitary .... 3. T. FILIFOLIUS.

1. **Trachypogon gouinii** Fourn., Mex. Pl. 2: 66. 1886. Vera Cruz, Mexico.

Tall slender glabrous perennial, sparingly producing scaly rhizomes; culms simple, usually geniculate below; blades involute; raceme narrow, pale, feathery, 15 to 30 cm long.

Open ground in the vicinity of Habana, Cuba, introduced from eastern Mexico.

CUBA: Vicinity of Habana, *Léon* 209, 300; *Tracy* 9086; *Juzepczuk* 17. Minas, *Ekman* 15376.

2. Trachypogon ligularis Nees, Agrost. Bras. 345. 1829. Brazil.

Culms erect, 1 to 1.5 m tall, often sparingly branching below, the sheaths overlapping; ligule 5 to 18 mm long, firm; blades mostly reflexed, flat, 3 to 7 mm wide, scabrous, long-attenuate; racemes 2 or 3, sometimes solitary, 10 to 20 cm long; awns 4 to 7 cm long, pilose.

In the Grasses of the West Indies this species was referred to *T. plumosus* Humb. and Bonpl. The type of that in the Paris Herbarium was examined in 1935 and is found to be a species confined to South America.

Wet savannas, Trinidad to Colombia, south to central Brazil.

TRINIDAD: Mount St. Benedict, *Broadway* 5061. St. Joseph, *Hitchcock* 10185. Piarco Savanna, *Hitchcock* 10342. Arima, *Eggers* 1379.

FIGURE 366.—*Trachypogon filifolius*. Inflorescence, × 1; fertile spikelet, × 5 (Ekman 11571).

3. Trachypogon filifolius (Hack.) Hitchc., Contrib. U. S. Natl. Herb. 12: 191. 1909.

Trachypogon polymorphus var. *filifolius* Hack., in Mart., Fl. Bras. 2³: 642. 1883. Brazil.

Slender, wiry, tufted, 1 to 1.3 m tall; ligule 2 to 4 mm long; blades erect, involute, slender, elongate, smooth; racemes solitary, 8 to 12 cm long, mostly more slender; awns mostly not more than 5 cm long, sparsely pilose (fig. 366).

Sandy pine woods, western Cuba; Brazil.

CUBA: Herradura, *Ekman* 11571; *Ekman* in 1923. Pinar del Río, *Hitchcock* 23308; *Wright* 3892, 3893; *Léon* 3398. Viñales, *Léon* 15863.

116. ISCHAEMUM L., Sp. Pl. 1049. 1753

Sessile spikelets perfect, awned; pedicellate spikelets perfect but not always fruitful; rachis disjointing; racemes 2 to several, digitate or aggregate on a short axis. Culms branching, with flat blades and digitate or flabellate inflorescence with slender awns.

Racemes 2, conjugate; first glume strongly rugose across the back..1. I. RUGOSUM.
Racemes several in a cluster; first glume not rugose..........2. I. LATIFOLIUM.

1. Ischaemum rugosum Salisb., Icon. Stirp. Rar. 1. pl. 1. 1791. India.

Annual; culms 0.5 to 1 m tall; geniculate below; nodes bearded; blades 8 to 12 mm wide, sparsely pilose; racemes 5 to 10 cm long, erect, so closely appressed to each other as often to appear like a single spike; spikelets 3 to 4 mm long, obtuse, the awn about 1.5 cm long.

Waste places in Cuba and Jamaica; introduced from the Old World.

CUBA: Madruga, *Curtiss* 533. Manacas, *Léon* 5886. Bayate, *Ekman* 10063. Camp la Gloria, south of Sierra Moa, *Shafer* 8104.

JAMAICA: Savanna-la-Mar, *Hitchcock* 9858.

TRINIDAD: Rio Claro, *Bot. Gard. Herb.* 12075.

2. Ischaemum latifolium (Spreng.) Kunth, Rév. Gram. 1: 168. 1829.

Andropogon latifolius Spreng., Syst. Veg. 1: 286. 1825.

Ischaemopogon latifolius Griseb., Fl. Brit. W. Ind. 560. 1864. Guadeloupe and Martinique.

Perennial, spreading and straggling, decumbent, rooting at the lower nodes; blades oblong-lanceolate, as much as 20 cm long and 3 cm wide; racemes 5 to 15, 4 to 8 cm long (fig. 367).

Moist, shady places, southern Mexico and the Lesser Antilles to Brazil and Ecuador.

LEEWARD ISLANDS: Guadeloupe, *Duss* 2696; *Stehlé* 111. Dominica, *Jones* 17, 41.

WINDWARD ISLANDS: Martinique, *Hitchcock* 16459; *Hahn* in 1867–1870. St. Vincent, *Eggers* 6710.

TRINIDAD: *Bot. Gard. Herb.* 3380.

ISCHAEMUM ANGUSTIFOLIUM (Trin.) Hack., in Hook., Icon. Pl. 18: pl. 1773. 1888. In the herbarium of the Botanical Department, Trinidad, is a specimen of this collected in 1895 by J. H. Hart, and said to be introduced. It is distinguished by its elongate narrow blades.

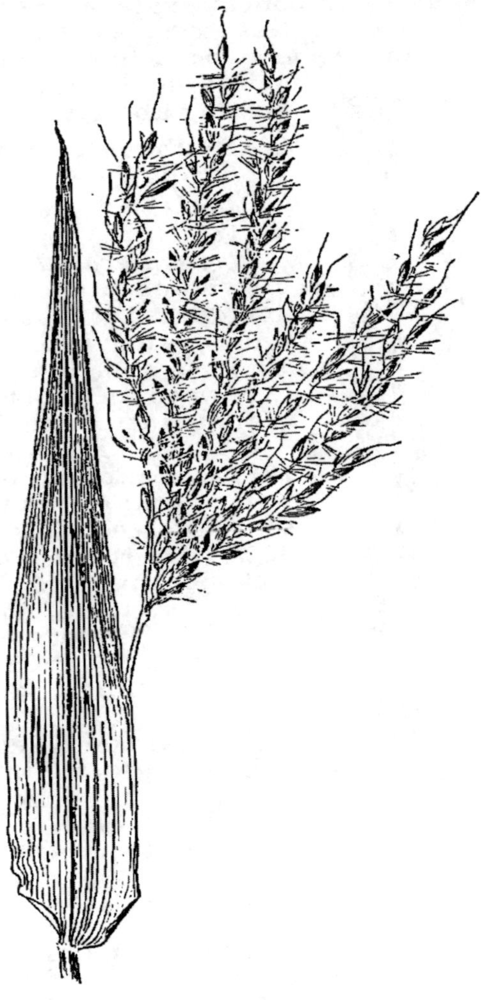

FIGURE 367.—*Ischaemum latifolium.* Inflorescence, × 1 (Duss 2696).

RHYTACHNE ROTTBOELLIOIDES Desv.; Hamilt., Prodr. Pl. Ind. Occ. 11. 1825. Described from a specimen purporting to be from the "Antilles" in the Desvaux Herbarium. The genus is an African one and the locality given is probably an error, as with many other Desvaux specimens. The specimen could not be found in the Paris Herbarium.

117. ROTTBOELLIA L. f., Nov. Gram. Gen. 22. pl. 1. 1779; Amoen. Acad. 10: 22. 1790

Spikelets awnless, in pairs at the nodes of a thickened articulate rachis, one sessile and perfect, the other pedicellate, sterile; rachis-joints hollow above, the thickened pedicel adnate to it, the pedicellate spikelet appearing to be sessile; sessile spikelet fitting closely against the concave side of the rachis-joint, the first glume coriaceous, the second less coriaceous; sterile and fertile lemmas and palea hyaline. Coarse branching annual with broad flat blades and subcylindric racemes, dwindling toward the summit and bearing abortive spikelets only.

FIGURE 368.—*Rottboellia exaltata*, × 1 (Ridley).

1. **Rottboellia exaltata** L. f., Sup. Pl. 114. 1781. India.

Manisuris exaltata Kuntze, Rev. Gen. Pl. 2: 779. 1891.

Stegosia exaltata Nash, N. Amer. Fl. 17: 84. 1909.

A stout branching leafy annual with hispid sheaths, long flat scabrous blades, and numerous axillary racemes, the summit of these dwindling and bearing abortive spikelets only (fig. 368).

A weed in moist soil, in several of the West Indian islands, introduced from southern Asia.

CUBA: Habana, *Léon* 2683. Soledad, *Hitchcock* 23323. Sancti Spiritus, *Léon* 847. El Cristo, *Ekman* 9000.

JAMAICA: Castleton, *Ridley* 125; *Harris* 11387. Kingston, *Hitchcock* 9257. Bog Walk, *Ridley* 108; *Hitchcock* 9283 (*Amer. Gr. Nat. Herb.* 238). Hope Gardens, *Harris* 11256. Ipswich, *Hitchcock* 9605. Barican, *Hitchcock* 9567. Ewarton, *Hitchcock* 9462. Gordon Town, *Hart* 809.

HAITI: Ennery, *Ekman* H 2447; *Leonard* 8822. St. Michel de l'Atalaye, *Leonard* 7362, 7834. Plaisance, *Leonard* 9270. San Rafael, *Cook, Scofield, and Doyle* 152, 153.

DOMINICAN REPUBLIC: Azua, *Ekman* H 13618.

LEEWARD ISLANDS: St. Kitts, *Box* 135.

TRINIDAD: Icacos, *Broadway* 4965. Point-à-Pierre, *Broadway*, 4943. Port-of-Spain, *Hitchcock* 9944. Without locality, *Bot. Gard. Herb.* 3221.

118. MANISURIS L., Mant. Pl. 164. 1771

Spikelets awnless, in pairs at the nodes of a thickened articulate rachis, one sessile and perfect, the other pedicellate rudimentary (developed but sterile in *M. altissima*), the pedicel thickened and appressed to the rachis, the sessile spikelet fitting closely against the rachis (sometimes partly adnate in *M. altissima*), forming a cylindric or flattened raceme; glumes mostly obtuse, the first coriaceous, fitting over the hollow containing the spikelet, the keels winged at the summit, the second less coriaceous than the first; sterile lemma, fertile lemma, and palea thin and hyaline. Perennial slender, moderately tall, or tall grasses, with usually numerous glabrous cylindric or flattened solitary racemes.

Racemes compressed, tardily disarticulating .... 1. M. ALTISSIMA.
Racemes cylindric or nearly so, readily disarticulating.
First glume emarginate and winged above .... 2. M. AURITA.
First glume not winged.
Blades flat; sheaths compressed-keeled. First glume roughened or wrinkled crosswise or nearly smooth .... 3. M. TUBERCULOSA.
Blades involute; sheaths cylindric, not keeled.
First glume strongly transverse-rugose .... 4. M. LORICATA.
First glume not rugose .... 5. M. IMPRESSA.

1. **Manisuris altissima** (Poir.) Hitchc., Jour. Wash. Acad. Sci. 24: 292. 1934.

Rottboellia altissima Poir., Voy. Barb. 2: 105. 1789. Barbary.
Rottboellia fasciculata Lam., Tabl. Encycl. 1: 204. 1791. Barbary.
Hemarthria fasciculata Kunth, Rév. Gram. 1: 153. 1829.
Rottboellia compressa var. *fasciculata* Hack., in DC., Monogr. Phan. 6: 286. 1889.
Manisuris fasciculata Hitchc., Amer. Jour. Bot. 2: 299. 1915.
Hemarthria altissima Stapf and Hubbard, Kew Bull. Misc. Inf. 1934: 109. 1934.

Culms erect or spreading, compressed, slender, glabrous, 50 to 100 cm tall; blades flat or folded, 2 to 5 mm wide; racemes 5 to 10 cm long, falcate, from several of the upper sheaths (fig. 369).

Shallow water, ditches, and moist ground. An Old World species introduced into the American Tropics. Mexico and Jamaica to Argentina.

JAMAICA: Black River, *Harris* 12550, 12874.

FIGURE 369.—*Manisuris altissima*, × 1 (Hitchcock).

FIGURE 370.—*Manisuris tuberculosa*, × 1 (Nash 1074).

2. **Manisuris aurita** (Steud.) Hitchc. and Chase, Contrib. U. S. Natl. Herb. 18: 276. 1917.

Rottboellia aurita Steud., Syn. Pl. Glum. 1: 361. 1854. Brazil.

Culms erect, glabrous, 1 to 1.5 m tall; blades flat or folded, 4 to 8 mm wide; racemes mostly 5 to 10 cm long, included at base in the upper sheaths or exserted; sessile spikelets 4 mm long, the first glume smooth or indistinctly pitted.

Grassy hillsides, Brazil to Trinidad; in the latter known from a specimen in the Gray Herbarium collected by Finlay (*Bot. Gard. Herb.* 2304).

3. **Manisuris tuberculosa** Nash, Bull. N. Y. Bot. Gard. 1: 430. 1900. Florida.

Coelorachis tuberculosa Nash, N. Amer. Fl. 17: 86. 1909.

Culms erect, 1 to 1.5 m tall; sheaths compressed-keeled; blades flat; racemes several, slender, 2 to 5 cm long; joints about 5 mm long (fig. 370).

Swampy places, Florida and Cuba.

CUBA: Laguna Santa María, *Ekman* 17260.

4. **Manisuris loricata** (Trin.) Kuntze, Rev. Gen. Pl. 2: 780. 1891.

Rottboellia loricata Trin., Mém. Acad. St. Pétersb. VI. Math. Phys. Nat. 2: 250. 1832. Brazil.

Rottboellia filifolia Wright, An. Acad. Cien. Habana 8: 209. 1871. Cuba, *Wright* 3905.

Coelorachis loricata Nash, N. Amer. Fl. 17: 85. 1909.

A slender erect unbranched tufted perennial with narrow involute blades, the solitary terminal raceme up to 25 cm long.

Pine barren swamps, western Cuba and Brazil.

CUBA: Herradura, *Baker and Abarca* 4181; *Tracy* 9059; *Hitchcock* 476; Pinar de Cajálbana, *Ekman* 17339. Mordazo, *Ekman* 17106. Dayaniguas, *Wright* 3905. Isla de Pinos, *Ekman* 11959.

5. **Manisuris impressa** (Griseb.) Kuntze, Rev. Gen. Pl. 2: 780. 1891.

Rottboellia impressa Griseb., Cat. Pl. Cub. 235. 1866. Cuba, *Wright* 3904.

Coelorachis impressa Nash, N. Amer. Fl. 17: 85. 1909.

Manisuris leonina Hitchc. and Chase, Contrib. U. S. Natl. Herb. 18: 275. 1917. Cuba, *Léon* 6981.

Stouter than the preceding, 1 m or more tall, the culm branching, bearing terminal and axillary racemes 10 to 15 cm long.

Pine barrens, Cuba.

CUBA: Remates, *Ekman* 11320. Damují, *Ekman* 11048. San Julián, south of Guane, *Léon* 6981. El Salado, *Wright* 3904. Motembo, *Léon* 8206, 9367; *Ekman* 16818. San Cristobal, *Ekman* 13752. Santayana, *Ekman* 15360. Isla de Pinos, *Ekman* 11645.

119. HACKELOCHLOA Kuntze, Rev. Gen. Pl. 2: 776. 1891

(*Rytilix* Raf., Bull. Bot. Seringe 1: 219. 1830. No generic description)

Spikelets awnless, in pairs, the rachis joint and pedicel grown together, the two clasped between the edges of the globose alveolate first glume of the sessile spikelet; pedicellate spikelet conspicuous, staminate. Freely branching annual with flat blades and numerous short racemes.

1. **Hackelochloa granularis** (L.) Kuntze, Rev. Gen. Pl. 2: 776. 1891.

Cenchrus granularis L., Mant. Pl. 2: 575. 1771. East Indies.

Manisuris granularis Swartz, Prodr. Veg. Ind. Occ. 25. 1788.

Rytilix granularis Skeels, U. S. Dept. Agr., Bur. Plant Indus. Bull. 282: 20. 1913.

Coarsely hispid; culms 30 to 100 cm tall; blades mostly less than 10 cm long, 5 to 10 mm wide; racemes terminal and axillary, 1 to 2.5 cm long (fig. 371).

A common weed throughout tropical America, introduced from the Old World. In the West Indies found in Cuba, Jamaica, Haiti, Dominican Republic, Puerto Rico, Guadeloupe, and Martinique, and probably to be found on other islands.

120. THEMEDA Forsk., Fl. Aegypt. Arab. 178. 1775

Inflorescence a flabellate cluster of several racemes, each subtended by a leaflike spathe, the entire cluster (or panicle) subtended or partly enclosed by a larger spathe; racemes consisting of 2 approximate pairs of sessile awnless staminate or neuter spikelets and a single fertile awned spikelet with a pair of sterile pedicellate ones, the rachis disjointing above the pairs of sessile staminate spikelets and forming a pointed callus below the fertile one. Perennial or annual, often robust grasses, with leafy compound panicles.

Perfect spikelets villous; glumes of sessile neuter spikelets not strongly papillose ---------- 1. T. ARGUENS.
Perfect spikelets not villous; glumes of sessile neuter spikelets strongly papillose, the papillae bearing long stiff hairs ---------- 2. T. QUADRIVALVIS.

FIGURE 371.—*Hackelochloa granularis.* Plant, × ½; single raceme, × 2; two views of spikelets with rachis joint, × 5 (Pringle).

1. Themeda arguens (L.) Hack., in DC., Monogr. Phan. 6: 657. 1889. CHRISTMAS GRASS.

Stipa arguens L., Sp. Pl. ed. 2. 117. 1762. India.

An ascending annual with compressed branching culms, flat scabrous blades, and V-shaped clusters of long-awned spikelets; fruit dark brown, the awn 5 to 7 cm long (fig. 372).

FIGURE 372.—*Themeda arguens*, × ½ (Harris 12461).

Introduced in Jamaica and Barbados; native of Asia.

JAMAICA: Troy, *Harris* 12702; *Hitchcock* 9805. Hope Gardens, *Harris* 12461. Prospect, *Harris* 11538.

WINDWARD ISLANDS: Barbados, *Ballou* in 1927.

2. Themeda quadrivalvis (L.) Kuntze, Rev. Gen. Pl. 2: 794. 1891.
KANGAROO GRASS.

Andropogon quadrivalvis L., Syst. Veg. ed. 13. 758. 1774. India.
Anthistiria ciliata L. f., Sup. 113. 1781. Based on the preceding.
Themeda ciliata Hack., in DC., Monogr. Phan. 6: 664. 1889.

Usually taller than the preceding with an elongate inflorescence of more numerous and smaller clusters of spikelets; fruit pale, the awn mostly less than 5 cm long.

Introduced in the West Indies; native of the East Indies. In Haiti called Madame Michel grass.

CUBA: Isla le Pinos, *Ekman* 12261.

HAITI: St. Michel, *Baker* 13. St. Michel de l'Atalaye, *Leonard* 7000, 8513. Restauración, *Ekman* H 6260. Petite Rivière, *Sweet* in 1925. Mirebalais, *Cook, Scofield, and Doyle* 82. Port-au-Prince, *Buch* 1807. Pétionville, *Ekman* H 1728.

DOMINICAN REPUBLIC: San Juan, *Ekman* H 13400.

WINDWARD ISLANDS: Martinique, *Duss* 533, 4723. Barbados, *Botanic Station* 585.

TRIBE 14. TRIPSACEAE

121. COIX L., Sp. Pl. 972. 1753

Spikelets unisexual; pistillate spikelets 2 or 3 together, 1 fertile and 1 or 2 rudimentary, enclosed in a bony beadlike involucre (morphologically a subtending leaf sheath); staminate spikelets approximate in threes (the third sometimes obsolete) on a slender rachis forming a short raceme, the rachis protruding from the orifice of the involucre, these ultimate inflorescences borne on the ends of numerous branches. Broad-leaved annual.

1. Coix lacryma-jobi L., Sp. Pl. 972. 1753. East Indies.
JOBS-TEARS.

Freely branching, 1 m or more tall, the cordate clasping blades 2 to 3 cm broad, the "beads" 8 to 10 mm long (fig. 373).

Moist ground and waste places, especially near dwellings, throughout tropical America, cultivated as an ornamental and for the ivory or grayish beads; often escaped. Called also "Christs tears," "camandula," "lágrimas de Job," and "graine maldioc" (Haiti).

Common in the West Indies and to be found on probably all of the islands.

122. TRIPSACUM L., Syst. Nat. ed. 10. 2: 1261. 1759

Spikelets unisexual; staminate spikelets 2-flowered, in pairs on one side of a continuous rachis, one sessile, the other sessile or pedicellate, similar to those of *Zea*, the glumes firmer; pistillate spikelets single and on opposite sides at each joint of the thick, hard articulate lower part of the same rachis, sunken in hollows in the joints, consisting of one perfect floret and a sterile lemma; first glume coriaceous, nearly infolding the spikelet, fitting into and closing the hollow of the rachis; second glume similar to the first but smaller, infolding the remainder of the spikelet; sterile lemma, fertile lemma, and palea very thin and hyaline, these progressively smaller. Robust perennial grasses, with usually broad flat blades and monoecious terminal and axillary inflorescences of 1 to several racemes, the pistillate part below, breaking up into bony, seedlike joints, the staminate above on the same rachis, deciduous as a whole.

Spikes 2 to 4 in the terminal inflorescence; blades 1 to 2 cm wide. 1. T. DACTYLOIDES.
Spikes solitary; blades usually 2.5 to 5 cm wide............2. T. LATIFOLIUM.

FIGURE 373.—*Coix lacryma-jobi*, × 1 (cult.).

1. Tripsacum dactyloides (L.) L., Syst. Nat. ed. 10. 2: 1261. 1759. GAMA GRASS.

Coix dactyloides L., Sp. Pl. 972. 1753. America, no definite locality given.

In large clumps with thick knotty rhizomes; culms 2 to 3 m tall; blades usually 1 to 2 cm wide; spikes 2 to 4 in the terminal inflorescence, usually solitary on the branches, 15 to 25 cm long, the pistillate part not more than one-fourth the entire length (fig. 374).

In the Cuban specimens the blades are only 4 to 7 mm wide and the terminal spike is solitary, suggesting an approach to *Tripsacum floridanum* Porter, of southern Florida, but the blades are flat or folded and have prominent midrib as in *T. dactyloides*, those of *T. floridanum* being 1 to 4 mm wide and subinvolute.

Moist ground at low altitudes, eastern United States and the West Indies to Brazil.

CUBA: Road to Nagua Yara (Province of Oriente), *Ekman* 14152; *Léon* 11332.

HAITI: Port-au-Prince, *Cook, Scofield, and Doyle* 65; *Ekman* H 8170. Pétionville, *Leonard* 4846, 5064. Mission, *Leonard* 3945. Puilboreau Mountain, *Baker* 9. St. Michel de l'Atalaye, *Leonard* 7157. Ennery, *Leonard* 8936. Bassin Bleu, *Leonard* 14997.

DOMINICAN REPUBLIC: Barahona, *Fuertes* 1424.

2. Tripsacum latifolium Hitchc., Bot. Gaz. 41: 294. 1906. Guatemala.

Differs from the preceding chiefly in the longer broader blades, as much as 70 cm long and 5 to 6 cm wide, rarely less than 2 cm, narrowed to a slender base; sheaths commonly purple; spikes all solitary,

FIGURE 374.—*Tripsacum dactyloides*. Plant, × ½; pistillate spikelets with rachis joint and pair of staminate spikelets with rachis joint, × 5 (Amer. Gr. Nat. Herb. 229).

more slender than usual in *T. dactyloides*, the joints of the pistillate part often slightly roughened.

Moist slopes in the higher foothills, Hispaniola and Trinidad; Mexico and Central America. Cultivated for fodder in Antigua (*Box* 126).

HAITI: Port-à-Piment, *Ekman* 338.

DOMINICAN REPUBLIC: Villa Altagracia, "forming vast colonies, steep slope of Loma Marián, Chicle, near the top," *Ekman* H 14253. Santiago, *Ekman* H 16229.

TRINIDAD: St. Joseph, *Hitchcock* 10017. La Brea, *Broadway* 4982. Without locality, *Bot. Gard. Herb.* 3303.

TRIPSACUM LAXUM Nash, N. Amer. Fl. 17: 81. 1909, a stout species with fascicled spikes and blades as much as 8 or 9 cm wide, not narrowed at base, is sparingly cultivated for forage, under the name Guatemala grass, in Cuba, Puerto Rico, and St. Croix. Mexico and Central America.

ZOYSIA MATRELLA (L.) Merr., Manila grass, a low perennial with slender rhizomes, fine foilage and slender spikes, about 2 cm long, has recently been introduced as a lawn grass in Puerto Rico. It is said to form a good turf. Native of the Philippine Islands.

EREMOCHLOA OPHIUROIDES (Munro) Hack., Centipede grass, a low perennial with thick leafy stolons, spreading narrow blades, and subcylindric spikelike racemes, was recently found near Mayaguez, Puerto Rico, forming an excellent turf in partly shaded ground. It has been recommended as a lawn grass in the southern United States. Native of southeastern Asia.

LIST OF NEW GENERA AND SPECIES AND NEW NAMES

	Page
Andropogon gracilis var. *firmior* Hitchc., var. nov	389
Andropogon parvifolius Hitchc., sp. nov	391
Andropogon reedii Hitchc. and Ekman, sp. nov	390
Arthrostylidium ekmanii Hitchc., sp. nov	16
Arthrostylidium reflexum Hitchc. and Ekman, sp. nov	19
Axonopus anceps (Mez) Hitchc	190
Paspalum anceps Mez.	
Cenchrus ekmanianus Hitchc., sp. nov	361
Chloris arenaria Hitchc. and Ekman, sp. nov	131
Chloris cubensis Hitchc. and Ekman, sp. nov	131
Chloris ekmanii Hitchc., sp. nov	129
Chloris rupestris (Ridley) Hitchc	126
Gymnopogon rupestris Ridley.	
Danthonia obtorta Chase, sp. nov	70
Deschampsia domingensis Hitchc. and Ekman, sp. nov	67
Digitaria ekmanii Hitchc., sp. nov	176
Digitaria pinetorum Hitchc., sp. nov	176
Ekmanochloa Hitchc., gen. nov	374
Ekmanochloa aristata Ekman, sp. nov	377
Ekmanochloa subaphylla Hitchc., sp. nov	375
Eragrostis ekmanii Hitchc., sp. nov	43
Eriochloa ekmanii Hitchc., sp. nov	183
Eriochloa setosa (A. Rich.) Hitchc	182
Piptatherum setosum A. Rich.	
Ichnanthus conjunctus Hitchc. and Ekman, sp. nov	297
Lepturidium Hitchc. and Ekman, gen. nov	111
Lepturidium insulare Hitchc. and Ekman, sp. nov	111
Panicum beyeri Hitchc. and Ekman, sp. nov	265
Panicum lacustre Hitchc. and Ekman, sp. nov	253
Panicum leonis Ekman, sp. nov	295
Panicum ophiticola Hitchc. and Ekman, sp. nov	293
Panicum petersonii Hitchc. and Ekman, sp. nov	263
Panicum pradanum Léon, sp. nov	294
Paspalum urbanianum Ekman, sp. nov	237
Raddia guianensis (Brongn.) Hitchc	373
Strephium guianense Brongn.	
Raddia sympodica (Doell) Hitchc	372
Olyra sympodica Doell.	
Saugetia pleiostachya Hitchc. and Ekman, sp. nov	123
Setaria subtransiens Hitchc. and Ekman, sp. nov	351
Sporobolus pyramidatus (Lam.) Hitchc	84
Agrostis pyramidata Lam.	
Trichachne laxa (Reichenb.) Hitchc	165
Reimaria laxa Reichenb.	
Tricholaena repens (Willd.) Hitchc	331
Saccharum repens Willd.	

INDEX

[Synonyms are in *italic* type. Where more than one entry is given, the main entry is set in heavy-face type]

Page

- Achlaena ... 157
  - piptostachya ... 157
- *Acroceras oryzoides* ... 278
- *Agrosticula muralis* ... 81
- Agrostideae ... 8, 71
- Agrostis ... 72
  - alba ... 73
  - *brasiliensis* ... 191
  - canina ... 73
  - *compressa* ... 82, 188
  - *cruciata* ... 129
  - *domingensis* ... 85
  - *elongata* ... 82
  - hiemalis ... 73, 75
  - *indica* ... 82
  - *jamaicensis* ... 174
  - *laxiflora* var. *montana* ... 75
  - *littoralis* ... 77, 87
  - *lutosa* ... 77
  - *monostachya* ... 313
  - *oreophila* ... 75
  - *punctata* ... 184
  - *purpurascens* ... 86
  - *pyramidalis* ... 84
  - *pyramidata* ... 84
  - *radiata* ... 126
  - *rigidifolia* ... 318
  - *scabra* ... 73
  - *tenuissima* ... 82
  - *torreyi* ... 75
  - verticillata ... 73
  - *virginica* ... 87
- Aira *brasiliensis* ... 81
  - *gigantea* ... 51
  - *laxa* ... 55
  - *obtusata* ... 64
  - *spicata* ... 64
- *Alectoridia quartiniana* ... 384
- Alloteropsis *amphistemon* ... 315
  - *dura* ... 315
- Alopecurus *monspeliensis* ... 75
- Amor seco ... 342
- *Amphilophis ischaemum* ... 402
  - *pertusa* ... 401
  - *piptatherus* ... 386
  - *saccharoides* ... 400
- *Anastrophus capillaris* ... 188
  - *compressus* ... 188
  - *furcatus* ... 189
  - *platycaulis* ... 188
- *Anatherum* ... 406
  - *bicorne* ... 394, 406
  - *caudatum* ... 379
  - *domingense* ... 394
  - *inerme* ... 393
  - *macrourum* ... 396
  - *muricatum* ... 406, 407
  - *portoricense* ... 379
  - *spathiflorum* ... 393
  - *virgatum* ... 393
  - *zizanioides* ... 407
- Andropogon ... 165, 385, 403, 406
  - *ambiguus* ... 119
  - angustatus ... 400
  - annulatus ... 387
    - *bladhii* ... 387
    - *subrepens* ... 387
  - *apricus* ... 400
  - *arundinaceus* ... 409
  - *arenaceus* ... 409
  - *barbatum* ... 133, 134
  - *barbatus* ... 132
  - bicornis ... 394, 406
  - *bladhii* ... 387

Andropogon—Continued. Page

  - brevifolius ... 388
  - caricosus ... 387
  - *citratus* ... 403
  - condensatus ... 388
  - condylotrichus ... 386
  - *contortus* ... 413
  - cubensis ... 390
  - *densus* ... 396
  - *domingensis* ... 391, 394, 410
  - elliottii ... 396
  - *fastigiatus* ... 402
  - *francavillanus* ... 409
  - glomeratus ... 396
  - gracilis ... 389
    - firmior ... 389
  - *halepensis* ... 407
  - hirtiflorus ... 391, 392
  - *hirtus* ... 405
  - *imberis* var. *muticus* ... 391
  - *incanus* ... 395
  - *inermis* ... 393
  - *insularis* ... 165
  - ischaemum ... 402
    - *americanus* ... 402
  - *juncifolius* ... 389
  - lateralis ... 395
    - *incanus* ... 395
  - *latifolius* ... 417
  - *laxus* ... 400
  - leucopogon ... 400
  - leucostachyus ... 394, 395
    - *selloanus* ... 395
    - *subvillosus* ... 394
  - *macrourus* ... 396
  - malacostachyus ... 388
  - *melanocarpus* ... 415
  - *microstachyus* ... 388
  - multinervosus ... 393
  - *muricatus* ... 406
  - *nardus* ... 404
  - nashianus ... 395
  - nodosus ... 387
  - *obtusifolius* ... 388
  - *panormitanus* ... 401
  - parvifolius ... 391
  - pertusus ... 401
    - *panormitanus* ... 401
  - *piptatherus* ... 386
  - *polydactylon* ... 132
  - *quadrivalvis* ... 423
  - reedii ... 390
  - reinoldii ... 399
  - *rufus* ... 401
  - saccharoides ... 400
    - *leucopogon* subvar. *paucirameus* ... 400
    - *surius* ... 400
  - salzmanni ... 391
  - *secundus* ... 413
  - selloanus ... 395
  - semiberbis ... 392
    - *incertus* ... 391
  - *setosus* ... 182, 409, 410
  - *sorghum* ... 409
  - *spathiflorus* ... 393
  - *stipoides* ... 410
  - tener ... 392
  - *tenuispatheus* ... 396
  - urbanianus ... 396
  - virgatus ... 393
  - virginicus ... 397, 399
    - graciliformis ... 399
  - wrightii ... 410
  - *zizanioides* ... 407
- Andropogoneae ... 12, 377

Page

Annual bluegrass 29
Anthaenantia *lanata* 163
Anthephora 98
  elegans 98
  hermaphrodita 98
  villosa 100
Anthistiria ciliata 423
Anthoxanthum 142
  giganteum 382
  odoratum 142
Apluda *zeugites* 58
Arana 48
Aristida 87
  adscensionis 89
    americana 138
  affinis 96
  americana 138
  antillarum 138
  brittonorum 96
  calcicola 97
  chaseae 94
  cognata 96
  curtifolia 93
  debilis 89
  divaricata 91
  domingensis 391
  eggersii 92
  erecta 93
  fragilis 91
  gyrans 93
  laevigata 90
  maritima 89
  neglecta 92
  palustris 96
  pansa 91
  portoricensis 94
  purpurascens 93
  pradana 91
  refracta 97
  rosei 97
  scabra 88
  spiciformis 90
  stricta 89
  subbiflora 138
  swartziana 94
  ternipes 88, 91
  vilfifolia 93
  virgata var. *palustris* 96
Aromatic grass 406
Arthraxon 382
  ciliaris subsp. *quartinianus* 384
  quartinianus 384
Arthropogon *stipitatus* 157
Arthrostylidium 15
  angustifolium 20
  capillifolium 15, 123
  cubense 21
  distichum 19
  ekmanii 16
  excelsum 21
  fimbriatum 19
  haitiense 16
  multispicatum 17
  obtusatum 21
  prestoei 20
  pubescens 20
  reflexum 19
  sarmentosum 18
  urbanii 21
Arundinaria *capillifolia* 15
  cubensis 21
  excelsa 21
  haitiensis 16
  microclada 22
  multispicata 17
  obtusata 21
  pubescens 20
  urbanii 21
Arundinella 155
  berteroniana 156
  confinis 155
  cubensis 156
  deppeana 156
  martinicensis 155
  phragmitoides 156
Arundo 51
  donax 4, 51
  occidentalis 54
  phragmites 54

Page

Atheropogon domingensis 138
Avena 68
  fatua 68
  sativa 68
Aveneae 8, 62
Axonopus 2, 187
  anceps 190
  appendiculatus 187
  aureus 188
  capillaris 188
  compressus 3, 188
  digitatus 169
  equitans 190
  furcatus 189
  leptostachyus 190
  macrostachyus 190
  paniceus 174
  pellitus 191
  poiretii 82
Bahama grass 3, 116
Bahia grass 3, 203
Bamboo, common 4, 14
Bambos 14
Bambusa 14
  latifolia 14
  nana 14
  sieberi 14
  vulgaris 4, 14
Bambuseae 6, 14
Barba de indio 165
Barbados sourgrass 401
Barley 4, 61
  little 61
Barnyard grass 329
Beardgrass 385
  bushy 396
  Elliott 396
  silver 400
Bentgrass 72
Bermuda grass 2, 3, 116
Biatherium foliosum 119
Big quaking grass 30
Bluegrass 29
  annual 29
  Canada 29
  Kentucky 30
Bouteloua 137
  americana 138
  disticha 140
  elatior 138
  heterostega 139
  humboldtiana 139
  juncea 138
  litigiosa 138
  porphyrantha 139
  vaneedeni 137
Brachiaria 185
  erucaeformis 186
  extensa 185
  isachne 186
  platyphylla 185
  prostrata 247
Brazilian grass 4
Bristlegrass, bur 342
  giant 344
  green 345
  knotroot 339
  prairie 346
  yellow 339
Briza 30
  maxima 30
  minor 30
Bromegrass 24
Bromus 24
  catharticus 25
  dertonensis 26
  maximus 25
  rigidus 25
  spicatus 111
  sterilis 24
  unioloides 25
  villosus 25
  virgatus 108
Broomcorn 409
  millet 257
Broomsedge 397
Browntop millet 250
Bull paspalum 239
Bur bristlegrass 342

Page

- Bushy beardgrass 396
- Cabrera, section of Axonopus 187
- Caguazo 232
- Calamagrostis 71
  - leonardii 72
- Calyptrogyne occidentalis 266
- Camalote 177
- Camandula 423
- Cambute 177
- Caña brava 4, 14
  - de azucar 380
  - de Castillo 4, 51
- Canada bluegrass 29
- Cañamazo amargo 177
  - de sabana 189
  - dulce 189
  - macho 189
- Canary grass 142
- Canne à sucre 380
- Canophora 405
- Cañuela 409
- Capim jaraguá 4
- *Capriola* 116
  - *dactylon* 3, 116
- Carib grass 2
- Carpet grass 3
- Carrizo 51
- *Caryochloa bahiensis* 149
- Catingueiro 4
- *Cenchropsis myosuroides* 360
- Cenchrus 360
  - brownii 362
  - *carolinianus* 365
  - *ciliaris* 356
  - distichophyllus 112, 361
  - echinatus 363
    - *viridis* 362
  - ekmanianus 361
  - gracillimus 363
  - *granularis* 420
  - *inflexus* 362
  - *macrocephalus* 365
  - microcephalus 364
  - myosuroides 360
  - *parviflorus* 339
  - pauciflorus 365
  - *setosus* 357
  - tribuloides 365, 366
  - *villosus* 100
  - *viridis* 362
- *Chaetaria affinis* 96
  - *antillarum* 138
- Chaetium 331
  - cubanum 331
- *Chaetochloa* 332, 339
  - *barbata* 335
  - *caudata* 347
  - *corrugata* 345
  - *geniculata* 339
  - *glauca* 339
  - *hispida* 345
  - *lutescens* 330
  - *macrosperma* 350
  - *macrostachya* 346
  - *magna* 344
  - *onurus* 342
  - *palmifolia* 337
  - *poiretiana* 336
  - *rariflora* 349
  - *scandens* 343
  - *setosa* 347
  - *sulcata* 338
  - *tenacissima* 344
  - *tenax* 341
  - *verticillata* 342
  - *viridis* 345
  - *vulpiseta* 350
- Chamaeraphis 339
  - *caudata* 347
  - *corrugata* 345
  - *glauca* 339
  - *magna* 344
  - *palmifolia* 337
  - *paniculifera* 338
  - *parvigluma* 354
  - *setosa* 347

Chamaeraphis—Continued.

  - *sulcata* 338
  - *viridis* 345
- Chiendent 3, 116
- Chlorideae 9, 102
- Chloris 124
  - *angustiflora* 126
  - arenaria 131
  - *barbata* 132, 134
  - *brevigluma* 129
  - ciliata 133
  - cruciata 129
  - cubensis 130, 131
  - *durandiana* 126
  - ekmanii 129, 130
  - *elegans* 134
  - *eleusinoides* 130
    - *vestita* 131
  - *foliosa* 119
  - gayana 3, 125
  - *glaucescens* 126
  - *gracilis* 106, 126
  - *humboldtiana* 129
  - inflata 133
  - *leptantha* 126
  - *luetzelburgii* 126
  - *morales-coelloi* 130
  - orthonoton 131
  - paraguaiensis 134
  - petraea 124
  - polydactyla 132
  - *propinqua* 133
  - radiata 126
  - rupestris 126
  - sagraeana 130, 131, 132
  - *swartziana* 125
  - *swartzii* 124
  - virgata 134
- Christmas grass 421
- Christs tears 423
- *Chrysopogon pauciflorus* 410
- Chusquea 22
  - abietifolia 22
- Cinna *glomerata* 396
- Citronella grass 4, 404
- Cockroach grass 407
- *Coelorachis impressa* 420
  - *loricata* 420
  - *tuberculosa* 419
- Coix 423
  - *dactyloides* 424
  - lacryma-jobi 423
- Common reed 54
- Cordgrass 116
  - saltmeadow 117
- Corn 2
- Cornucopiae *hiemalis* 73
- Cortadero 229, 232
- Crabgrass 167
  - smooth 171
- Crowfoot grass 113
- Cupgrass 182
- Cymbopogon 403
  - citratus 4, 403
  - *hirtus* 405
  - nardus 4, 404
  - *rufus* 404
- Cynodon 116
  - dactylon 116
- Cynosurus *aegyptius* 113
  - *domingensis* 106
  - *indicus* 113
  - *scoparius* 126
  - *virgatus* 106
- *Cyrtococcum trigonum* 277
- Dactylis 49
  - glomerata 49
  - *patens* 117
- Dactyloctenium 113
  - aegyptium 113
- Dallis grass 3, 229
- Danthonia 70
  - domingensis 70
  - obtorta 70
  - *shrerei* 70
- Darnel 61
- Dendrocalamus strictus 4

Page

- Deschampsia, 64
  - caespitosa, 67
  - domingensis, 67
- Devil's grass, 116
- *Dichanthium annulatum*, 387
  - *nodosum*, 387
- Diectomis, 402
  - *angustata*, 400
  - fastigiata, 402
  - *laxa*, 400
- Digitaria, 167
  - argillacea, 175
  - argyrostachya, 170
  - *chinensis*, 170
  - curvinervis, 175
  - *digitata*, 169
  - *domingensis*, 188
  - *eggersii*, 165
  - ekmanii, 176
  - filiformis, 175
  - *fimbriata*, 169
  - *foliosa*, 200
  - *glabra*, 171
  - horizontalis, 169
  - *humifusa*, 171
  - *insularis*, 165
  - ischaemum, 171
  - *jamaicensis*, 169
  - *laxa*, 167
  - *leucocoma*, 173
  - *leucophaea*, 165
  - longiflora, 171
  - *marginata*, 169
  - panicea, 174, 175
  - pinetorum, 176
  - *platicaulis*, 188
  - *pulchella*, 374
  - sanguinalis, 169
  - serotina, 170
  - *setigera*, 169
  - *setosa*, 169
  - villosa, 171
  - violascens, 170
- *Dimorphostachys ciliifera*, 210
  - *langei*, 210
  - *pilosa*, 209
- *Diplachne virgata*, 110
- Distichlis, 47
  - spicata, 47
- Ditch polypogon, 77
- Dropseed, 80
- Dune sandbur, 366
- Durra, 2
- Dutch grass, 2, 247
- *Eatonia obtusata*, 64
- Echinochloa, 325
  - colonum, 327
    - *zonalis*, 327
  - crusgalli, 329, 331
    - *crus-pavonis*, 328
  - crus-pavonis, 328, 329, 331
  - *cubensis*, 324
  - *guadeloupensis*, 325
  - polystachya, 326
  - pyramidalis, 325
  - *sabulicola*, 328
  - *spectabilis*, 326
  - walteri, 328
- Echinolaena *nemorosa*, 298
- Ekmanochloa, 374
  - aristata, 377
  - subaphylla, 375
- Elephant grass, 3, 357
- Eleusine, 113
  - *aegyptiaca*, 113
  - indica, 113
  - *mucronata*, 102
  - *verticillata*, 113
  - *virgata*, 106
- Elliott beardgrass, 396
- Espartillo, 82
  - fino, 82
- Eragrostis, 33
  - acutiflora, 43
  - *airoides*, 81
  - amabilis, 34
  - *arabica*, 36
  - bahamensis, 41

Eragrostis—Continued.

  - bahiensis, 42
  - barrelieri, 41
  - berteroniana, 40
  - cilianensis, 39
  - ciliaris, 34
    - brachystachya, 36
    - laxa, 34
  - *conferta*, 39
  - cubensis, 41
  - domingensis, 45
  - ekmanii, 43
  - elliottii, 42
  - excelsa, 44
  - *gigantea*, 45
  - glomerata, 39
  - glutinosa, 36
  - hypnoides, 36
  - *leonina*, 36
  - *macropoda*, 42
  - *major*, 39
  - *megastachya*, 39
  - pilosa, 39
  - *plumosa*, 34
  - poaeoides, 41
  - prolifera, 44
  - purpurascens, 44
  - *purshii*, 40
  - salzmannii, 44
  - *sudans*, 36
  - tephrosanthos, 40
  - urbaniana, 36
- Eremochloa ophiuroides, 426
- Erianthus, 380
  - giganteus, 382
  - *jamaicensis*, 382
  - ravennae, 382
    - *jamaicensis*, 382
  - *saccharoides*, 382
- Eriochloa, 182
  - boxiana, 183
  - ekmanii, 183
  - *filifolia*, 182
  - polystachya, 2, 185, 247
  - punctata, 184
    - *subglabra*, 185
  - ramosa, 183
  - setosa, 182, 183
  - *subglabra*, 185
- Eriochrysis, 380
  - cayennensis, 380
- *Euclasta condylotricha*, 386
- *Euklastaxon tenuifolius*, 395
- Eulalia, 379
- *Eustachys petraea*, 124
- *Eutriana antillarum*, 138
  - *heterostega*, 139
  - *juncea*, 138
  - *ledebouri*, 138
- Feathertop, 355
- Fescue, 26
  - meadow, 28
- Festuca, 26
  - *bromoides*, 26
  - dertonensis, 26
  - elatior, 28
  - *fascicularis*, 104
  - *filiformis*, 102
  - *laxiflora*, 108
  - myuros, 26
  - *phleoides*, 62
  - *polystachya*, 104
  - *thouini*, 104
- Festuceae, 7, 24
- Festucoideae, 5
- Field sandbur, 365
- Fingergrass, 124
  - feather, 134
- Forage grasses, 2, 4, 126, 169, 185, 189, 203, 229, 247, 259, 332, 356, 357, 401, 405, 409
- Foxtail, 394
- Gama grass, 424
- Gamalote, 336, 338
- Giant bristlegrass, 344
  - reed, 4, 51
- Goosegrass, 113
- Gordura, 4

	Page
Gouinia	108
gracilis	108
virgata	108
Grama	3, 116, 137
de caballo	113
Gramon de costa	177
Graine maldioc	423
Green bristlegrass	345
Guadua	14
latifolia	14
Guatemala grass	426
Gü'n	4, 51
Guinea cimarrona	148
corn	409
grass	2, 259
Gymnopogon	118
ambiguus	119
filiformis	119
foliosus	119
rupestris	126
spicatus	119
Gymnothrix domingensis	359
Gynerium	49
saccharoides	51
sagittatum	4, 51
Hackelochloa	420
granularis	420
Hairgrass	64
Helopus punctatus	184
Hemarthria altissima	419
fasciculata	419
Heteropogon	413
contortus	413
melanocarpus	415
Heterosteca juncifolia	139
rhadina	139
Hierba bruja	2, 247
de Don Carlos	409
de limon	404
de venado	148
del Paral	247
del Prado	3, 116
fina	3, 116
Guinea	2, 259
Paral	2
Himalaya grass	356
Hog millet	257
Holcus	68, 407
halepensis	407
lanatus	68, 407
pertusus	401
saccharoides	400
sorghum	407, 409
spicatus	356
striatus	311
Homalocenchrus	147
grandiflorus	149
hexandrus	147
monandrus	148
Honey grass	4
Hordeae	8, 61
Hordeum	61
pusillum	61
Hurricane grass	401
Hymenachne	161, 312
amplexicaulis	313
auriculata	313
donacifolia	313
fluviatilis	312
frondescens	271
myuros	312
myurus	313
patula	313
striata	311
Hyparrhenia	404
hirta	405
rufa	4, 404
Hypogynium spathiflorum	393
Ichnanthus	161, 296
alsinoides	298
axillaris	299
conjunctus	297
ichnodes	301
leiocarpus	301
mayarensis	296
nemoralis	300
nemorosus	298
pallens	299

Ichnanthus—Continued.	Page
tenuis	298
trinitensis	301
wrightii	296
Ilusión	41
Imperata	377
brasiliensis	377
caudata	379
contracta	379
India lovegrass	39
Indian corn	4
Isachne	315
angustifolia	319
arundinacea	319, 320
disperma	320
leersioides	317
polygonoides	315, 317
pygmaea	318
rigens	319
rigidifolia	318
Ischaemopogon latifolius	417
Ischaemum	416
angustifolium	417
latifolium	417
rugosum	416
secundatum	177
Ixophorus	352
glaucus	339
unisetus	352
verticillatus	342
viridis	345
Jaraguá	4, 405
Jobs-tears	423
Johnson grass	407
Jungle-rice	327
Kafir	2
Kangaroo grass	423
Kentucky bluegrass	30
Khas-khas	407
Khus-khus	406, 407
Knotgrass	201
Knotroot bristlegrass	339
Koeleria	62
phleoides	62
Lagrimas de Job	423
Lappago aliena	102
Lasiacis	302
anomala	310
compacta	309
divaricata	305
grisebachii	303
harricii	305
ligulata	304
oaxacensis	303
patentiflora	308
rhizophora	305
rugelii	303
ruscifolia	309, 310
sloanei	306
sorghoidea	308
swartziana	308
Leersia	147
grandiflora	148
hexandra	147
monandra	148
Lemon grass	4, 403
Lepideilema lancifolium	24
Leptochloa	102
brachiata	102
domingensis	106
fascicularis	104
filiformis	102
imbricata	104
longa	107
monticola	107
mucronata	102
multiflora	104
nealleyi	105
perennis	106
scabra	105
spicata	111
uninervia	104
virgata	106
domingensis	106
gracilis	106
Leptocoryphium	163
lanatum	163
Leptostachys virgata	106

Page
Leptothrium 98
  rigidum 98
Lepturidium 111
  insulare 111
Lithachne 368
  pauciflora 370
  pineti 370
Little quaking grass 30
Lolium 61
  italicum 62
  maximum 61
  multiflorum 62
  temulentum 61
    leptochaeton 61, 62
Long grass 165
Longtom 202
Lovegrass 33
  India 39
Luziola 149
  alabamensis 149
  bahiensis 149
  longivalvula 149
  peruviana 149
  spruceana 151
Maize 4
Malojilla 2, 185, 247
Manisuris 418
  altissima 418, 419
  aurita 419
  exaltata 418
  fasciculata 419
  granularis 420
  impressa 420
  leonina 420
  loricata 419
  tuberculosa 419
Mary grass 335
Meadow fescue 28
Megastachya berteroniana 40
  uninervia 104
Melinideae 10, 155
Melinis 160
  minutiflora 3, 161
Mesosetum 180
  loliiforme 180
  wrightii 180
Milium *colonum* 327
  compressum 188
  digitatum 169
  lanatum 163
  nemorosum 298
  paniceum 174, 175
  punctatum 184
  rigidifolium 318
  villosum 165
Millet, broomcorn 257
  browntop 250
  common 345
  hog 257
Millo 409
Miscanthus sinensis 379
Mniochloa 374
  pulchella 374
  strephioides 374
Molasses grass 3, 161
Monachne punctata 184
  subglabra 185
Monanthochloë 45
  littoralis 45
Muhlenbergia 77
  berteroniana 156
  capillaris 78
  parviglumis 78
  spicata 123
Napier grass 2, 357
Natal grass 4, 331
  redtop 4
Nazia 101
  aliena 102
Neurolepis 23
  virgata 23
Notholcus lanatus 68
Oat 4, 68
  wild 68
Oatgrass 70
Oedipachne punctata 184
Oil grasses 4, 403

Page
Olyra 366
  arundinacea 366, 368
  ciliatifolia 368
  latifolia 366, 368
    arundinacea 366
  nana 373
  paniculata 366
  pauciflora 370
  pineti 370
  semiovata 368
  strephioides 374
  sympodica 372
  urbaniana 373
Opizia 140
  stolonifera 141
Oplismenus 320
  burmanni 322
  colonus 327
  crus-pavonis 328
  cubensis 324
  hirtellus 324
  jamaicensis 328
  loliaceus 324
  polystachyus 326
  setarius 298, 322
  tenuis 298
  undulatifolius 324
Orthoclada 55
  laxa 55
  rariflora 55
Orthopogon burmanni 322
  cubensis 324
  loliaceus 324
  setarius 322
Oryza 144
  hexandra 147
  latifolia 145
  monandra 148
    grandiflora 148
  perennis 145
  sativa 4, 145
    latifolia 145
Oryzeae 9, 144
Oxydenia virgata 106
Pacholi 407
Pachuli 407
Palmgrass 337, 338
Paniceae 10, 161
Panicoideae 6
Panicum 160, 161, 242, 339
  aciculare 283
  acuminatum 285
  adspersum 251
  alabamense 287
  albemarlense 286
  albomarginatum 288, 289
  alsinoides 298
  altissimum 276
  altum 262
  amarulum 263
  amphistemon 315
  amplexicaule 313
  angustifolium 281, 282, 283
  aquaticum 254
  arenicoloides 282
  argyrostachyum 170
  aristatum 328
  arundinaceum 319
  asperifolium 277
  auburne 287
  auriculatum 313
  axillare 299
  bambusioides 305
  barbatum 335
  barbinode 247
  bartowense 253
  berteronianum 274
  beyeri 265
  boliviense 268
  brachiatum 347
  brevifolium 272
  burmanni 322
  caerulescens 284
  caespitosum 247
  capillaceum 272
  capillare 255
  caricoides 264

Panicum—Continued. Page
caudatum 347
cayennense 257
chamaelonche 289
chapmani 293
chartaginense 250, 251
chauvinii 306
chrysopsidifolium 280
colonum 327
 zonale 327
comophyllum 286
compactum 309
condensum 266
confertum 320
corrugatum 345
crusgalli 329
crus-pavonis 328
cubense 324
curvinerve 175
cyanescens 273
dactylon 116
decumbens 207
diandrum 269
dichotomiflorum 252, 254
dichotomum var. *acuminatum* 286
diffusum 257
discrepans 278
dispermum 320
dissectum 198
distantiflorum 266, 293
distichum 267
 lancifolium 267
divaricatum 305
 puberulum 304
 stenostachyum 306
domingense 171
donacifolium 313
duchaissingii 165
dumetorum 347
durum 315
echinulatum 251
eggersii 165
elephantipes 255
elongatum 336
erectifolium 288
erucaeforme 186
exiguiflorum 269
exile 298
falsum 165
fasciculatum 250, 251
 flavescens 250
 fuscum 250
fastigiatum 250
flavescens 250, 335
floridanum 288
frondescens 271
fusco-rubens 250
fuscum 250
 fasciculatum 250
fusiforme 281
geminatum 247
geniculatum 339
ghiesbreghtii 258
glaucum 339, 356
glutinosum 275, 306
gouini 262
grande 277
grisebachii 303
grossarium 247
guadaloupense 247
hamiltoni 169
hirsutum 259
hirtellum 324, 328
hirticaule 255
hirtivaginum 258
hirtum 279
horizontale 169
hymenachne 313
ichnodes 301
illinoniense 250
imberbe 339
ineptum 273
insulare 165
insularum 247
isachne 186
ischaemum 171
jamaicense 328

Panicum—Continued. Page
joorii 292
jumentorum 259
keyense 251
lacustre 253
laeve 259
lagotis 300
lanatum 165, 308
 sorghoideum 308
lancearium 290
latifolium 306
laxum 269
 variegatum 270
leiocarpon 301
leiophyllum 349
leonis 295
leucocomum 173
leucophaeum 165
leucothrix 284
lindeni 275
loliiforme 180
longiflorum 171
longiligulatum 285
lutescens 339
maculatum 309
martinicense 308
maximum 2, 259
mayarense 296
megiston 276
mertensii 276
miliaceum 257
milleflorum 267
millegrana 275
minutiflorum 269
molle 251
multinerve 320
muticum 247
myrianthum 277
myuros 312
nashianum patulum 290
nemorale 300
nemorosum 298
nervosum 273
neuranthum 282
 ramosum 281
nitidum 283
nudiculme 161
numidianum 247
oaxacense 303
obtusiflorum 275
onurus 342
ophiticola 293
oplismenoides 272
ornatum 285
orthophyllum 282
oryzoides 278
oxyanthum 191
pallens 299
palmaefolium 337
palmifolium 337
paniculatum 211
paniculiferum 338
paractenoides 347
parvifolium 272
paspalodes 247
patentissimum 275
patulum 290
petersonii 263
pilosum 267
platyphyllum 185
plicatulum 236
plicatum 337
 haitiense 337
poiretianum 336
polycaulon 280
polygamum 259
polygonatum 267
polygonoides 317
portoricense 289
potamium 267
pradanum 294
proliferum var. *strictum* 254
prostratum 247
 pilosum 250
pulchellum 271
purpurascens 2, 247
pyramidale 325

Panicum—Continued. Page
ramosum 281
rariflorum 55
repens 259
reptans 247
restitutum 347
reticulatum 250
rhizophorum 305
rigens 319
rigidifolium 318
roanokense 284
rudgei 276
rugelii 303
rugulosum var. *hirtiglume* 274
ruscifolium 309
sabulicola 328
saccharoides 165, 241
sanguinale 169
scandens 343
schiffneri 271
scoparium Lam 291
scoparium 276
sellowii 274
setaceum 283
setarium 322
setosum 347
sintenisii 295
sloanei 306
sorghoideum 308
spectabile 326
guadeloupense 325
sphaerocarpon 287
floridanum 288
stenodes 265
stenodoides 265
stevensianum 269
stoloniferum 270
streptostachys 277
striatum 311
strigosum 280
sulcatum 336, 338
swartzianum 308
tenacissimum 344
tenax 341
tenerum 264
tenuissimum 81
thomasianum 251
thrasya 178
trichanthum 272
trichocondylum 259
trichoides 272
tricolor 270
trifolium 289
trigonum 277
unispicatum 209
utowanaeum 295, 296
valenzuelanum 274
venezuelae 273
verticillatum 342
vilvoides 312
violascens 170
virgatum var. cubense 262
var. *scorteum* 262
viride 345
viscidellum 292
vulpisetum 350
walteri 328
wilmingtonense 287
wrightianum 285
xalapense 279, 280
zizanioides 278
zonale 327
Pappophorum 59
alopecuroideum 60
laguroideum 60
pappiferium 60
Pará grass 2, 185, 247
Parana 2, 247
Paratheria 352
prostrata 354
Pariana sylvestris 61
Paspalidium geminatum 247
Paspalum 2, 3, 165, 193, 229
acutifolium 214
affine 211
alterniflorum 217
amphicarpum 225
anceps 190, 191

Paspalum—Continued. Page
antillense 236
appendiculatum 187
arundinaceum 233
aureum 188
bakeri 214
blodgettii 212
boscianum 239
brachiatum 200
breve 224
bull 239
caespitosum 213, 222
capillare 188
capillifolium 222
caudicatum 220
chinensis 170
ciliatifolium 206
ciliiferum 210
clavuliferum 223
compressum 188
conjugatum 226
pubescens 226
convexum 238
coryphaeum 235
cubense 148
debile 205
decumbens 207, 208
densum 234
denticulatum 203
digitatum 169
dilatatum 3, 229
dispar 208
dissectum 198
distachyon 201
distichum 201
vaginatum 200
distortum 219
dolichophyllum 217
edmondi 224
elegans 239
fasciculatum 229
filiforme 218
filostachyum 188
fimbriatum 241
floribundum 215
foliosum 200
furcatum 189
glabrum 215
gracile 213
grass 3, 229
helleri 215
hemicryptum 238
hemisphericum 211
heterophyllum 213
heterotrichon 197
paucispicatum 197
inflatum 200
insulare 220
koleopodum 215
lanatum 163
langei 210
larrañagai 229
laticulmum 188
laxum 215
lenormandi 224
leoninum 221, 222
leptocaulon 218
leptostachyum 190
leucocheilum 231
lindenianum 219
lineare 205
lividum 202
lloydii 208
longiflorum 171
longifolium 219
maritimum 212
megaphyllum 219
melanospermun 238, 239
miliare 215
milioideum 215
millegrana 233
minus 204
minutiflorum 170
molle 214
motembense 237
multicaule 223
nanum 220
neesii 205

	Page
Paspalum—Continued.	
nesiotes	210
notatum	3, 203, 204
nutans	208
oligostachyum	211
olivaceum	238
orbiculatum	224
paniceum	234
paniculatum	211
minor	211
parviflorum	223
pellitum	191
pilosum	209
platicaulon	188
platyphyllum	185
pleostachyum	217
plicatulum	236
poiretii	213, 222
polystachyum	241
portoricense	214
propinquum	206
pubiflorum	202
pulchellum	239
pulchrum	188
pumilum	204
pusillum	224
racemosum	199
raunkiaerii	188
repens	198
reptatum	225
rhizomatosum	215
richardii	215
rocanum	217
rottboellioides	218
rupestre	221, 222
saccharoides	241
saugetii	221
secans	232
serpentinum	205
serratum	198
setaceum	206
simpsoni	212
sinuosum	215
sour	226
stellatum	197
strictum	211
swartzianus	218
taphrophyllum	203
tenacissimum	215
underwoodii	233
undulatum	236
unispicatum	209
urbanianum	237
urvillei	3, 229
vaginatum	200
nanum	200
vaseyanum	3, 229
violascens	235
virgatum	229
jacquinianus	229
stramineum	231
wrightii	236
Pata de gallina	3, 113, 116, 169
Pata de gallina fina	170
Pearl millet	3, 339, 356
Pega-pega	342
Penicillaria spicata	339, 357
Pennisetum	355
alopecuroides	357
antillarum	359
cenchroides	356
ciliare	356
domingense	359
erubescens	357
glaucum	3, 356
hamiltonii	357
hordeoides	359
myosuroides	360
orientale var. triflorum	355
purpureum	2, 357
setosum	357
triflorum	355
typhoideum	3, 339, 356
villosum	355
Perotis *cubana*	331
Phalarideae	9, 142
Phalaris	142
canariensis	142
Phalaris—Continued.	
zizanioides	406
Pharus	151
brasiliensis	152
glaber	152
lancifolius	152
lappulaceus	152
latifolius	152
ovalifolius	152
parvifolius	152
Phleum	77
pratense	77
Phragmites	51
communis	54
martinicensis	54
phragmites	54
Piptatherum confine	155
setosum	182, 410
Pitillo	324
Pito de bejuco	306
enano	370
Planotia	23
virgata	23
Platonia	23
virgata	23
Poa	29
acutiflora	43
amabilis	34
annua	29
carinata	36
berteroniana	40
cilianensis	39
ciliaris	34
compressa	29
conferta	39
domingensis	45
elegans	34
glomerata	39
glutinosa	36
hypnoides	36
nitida	42
pilosa	39
plumosa	34
pratensis	30
prolifera	44
purpurascens	44
rigida	29
trivialis	30
virgata	48
Pollinia brevifolia	388
microstachya	388
Polyodon disticha	140
Polypogon	75
cubensis	160
ditch	77
littoralis	77
lutosus	77
monspeliensis	75
spicatus	119
Prairie bristlegrass	346
Quaking grass	30
Rabbitfoot grass	75
Rabdochloa domingensis	106
mucronata	102
Rabo de zorra	165, 400
Raddia	372
biformis	372
guianensis	373
nana	373
sympodica	372
urbaniana	373
Red sprangletop	102
Redtop	73
Reed, common	54
Reimaria brasiliensis	191
elegans	239
laxa	165
oligostachya	191
Reimarochloa	191
brasiliensis	191
oligostachya	191
Rescue grass	25
Reynaudia	159
filiformis	160
Rhaphis	410
pauciflora	410
Rhapis	410
Rhodes grass	3, 125

Page

Rhynchelytrum repens 331
  roseum 331
Rhytachne rottboellioides 417
Rice 4, 145
Ridging grass 394
Ripgut grass 25
Rottboellia 418
  altissima 419
  aurita 419
  compressa var. *fasciculata* 419
  exaltata 418
  fasciculata 419
  filifolia 419
  impressa 420
  loricata 419
  salzmanni 391
  stolonifera 177
Rye 4, 61
Ryegrass 61
  Italian 62
Rytilix 420
  granularis 420
Saccharum 379
  bicorne 394
  caudatum 379
  cayennense 380
  ciliare 380
  contractum 379
  jamaicense 382
  officinarum 4, 380
  pappiferum 60
  polystachyum 165, 241
  repens 331
  sagittatum 51
  violaceum 380
Sacciolepis 310
  myuros 312
  striata 311
  vilvoides 312
St. Augustine grass 177
Saltgrass 47
Saltmeadow cordgrass 117
San Juan de Castillo 250
Sandbur, dune 366
  field 365
Saugetia 121
  fasciculata 121
  pleiostachya 123
Schizachyrium brevifolium 388
  condensatum 388
  cubense 390
  domingense 391
  gracile 389
  hirtiflorum 391
  malacostachyum 388
  multinervosum 393
  semiberbis 392
  tenerum 392
Schultesia petraea 124
Scleropoa 28
  rigida 29
Scotch grass 2, 247
Scutachne 313
  amphistemon 315
  dura 315
Sea-oats 48
Seashore saltgrass 47
Secale cereale 61
Senites 58
  haitiensis 58
  zeugites 58
Setaria 332, 339
  barbata 335
  berteroniana 339
  biconvexa 341
  brachiata 347
  caespitosa 342
  caudata 347
  corrugata 345
  elongata 347
  geniculata 339
  glauca 339
    imberbis 339
  hispida 345
  italica 345
  leiophylla 349
  lutescens 339

Setaria—Continued. Page
  macrosperma 350
  macrostachya 346
  magna 344
  onurus 342
  palmifolia 337
  paniculifera 338
  paractaenoides 347
  poiretiana 336
  rariflora 349, 350
  scandens 343
  setosa 347, 349, 350
    caudata 347
  subtransiens 351
  sulcata 336, 338
  tenacissima 344
  tenax 341
  vaginata 349
  ventenatii 339
  verticillata 342
  viridis 345
  vulpiseta 350
Silver beardgrass 400
Smutgrass 82
Sorghastrum 409
  francavillanum 409, 410
  parviflorum 409
  setosum 182, 409, 410
  stipoides 410
Sorghum 407, 409
  bicorne 394
  brevifolium 388
  cubense 390
  dura 409
  elliottii 396
  gracile 389
  halepense 407
  ischaemum 402
  leucostachyum 394
  parviflorum 409
  pauciflorum 410
  piptatherum 386
  saccharoides 400
  vulgare 2, 409
    sudanense 2, 409
  zizanioides 407
Sorghums 2
Sorgo 2, 409
Sour paspalum 226
Sourgrass 165, 401
  Barbados 401
Spartina 116
  brasiliensis 118
  cynosuroides 118
  juncea 117
  patens 117
    juncea 117
Sphenopholis 62
  obtusata 64
Spider grass 88
Spike trisetum 64
Sporobolus 80
  argutus 84
  atrovirens 81
  bahamensis 81
  berteroanus 82
  brasiliensis 81
  cubensis 85
  domingensis 85
  indicus 82, 84
  inordinatus 85
  jacquemontii 82, 84
  lamarckii 82
  littoralis 87
  muralis 81
  poiretii 82
  purpurascens 86
  pyramidatus 84, 85
  tenuissimus 81, 82
  virginicus 87
Sprangletop 102
Stegosia exaltata 418
Stenotaphrum 177
  americanum 177
  dimidiatum var. *americanum* 177
  glabrum var. *americanum* 177
  secundatum 177

	Page
Stinkgrass	39
Stipa *arguens*	421
capillaris	78
Strephium guianense	373
pulchellum	374
Streptachne *cubensis*	88
domingensis	391
scabra	88
Streptochaeta	23
spicata	24
Streptogyne	55
crinita	55
Streptostaschis asperifolia	277
Streptostachys aspera	277
Sudan grass	2, 409
Sugarcane	4, 380
plumegrass	382
Súrbana	251
Sweet vernalgrass	142
Syntherisma	167
argillacea	175
argyrostachya	170
chinensis	170
curvinervis	175
digitata	169
fimbriata	169
glabrum	171
helleri	170
insularis	165
ischaemum	171
leucocoma	173
longiflora	171
paniceum	174
sanguinalis	169
serotina	170
setosa	169
simpsoni	177
villosa	171
violascens	170
Tanglehead	413
sweet	415
Themeda	420
arguens	421
ciliata	423
quadrivalvis	423
Thrasya	177
hirsuta	180
paspaloides	178
robusta	180
trinitensis	178
Three-awn	87
Tibisee	302
Tibisi	15, 368
Tickle grass	73
Timothy	77
Trachynotia juncea	117
Trachypogon	415
filifolius	416
gouinii	415
ligularis	416
plumosus	416
polymorphus var. *filifolius*	416
rufus	404
Tragus	101
alienus	102
berteronianus	101
Triaena juncea	138
Triathera juncea	138
Trichachne	163
eggersii	165
insularis	165
laxa	165
Trichloris	134
pluriflora	136
Trichochloa berteroniana	156
Trichodium montanum	75
Tricholaena	331
insularis	165
repens	4, 331
rosea	4, 331
saccharoides	165, 241
Tricuspis simplex	111
Triodia	54
eragrostoides	54
Tripogon	110
spicatus	111
Tripsaceae	13, 423
Tripsacum	423
dactyloides	424
floridanum	424
hermaphroditum	98
latifolium	424
laxum	426
Triscenia	161
ovina	161
Trisetum	64
spicatum	64
Triticum aestivum	61
spinulosum	61
Uniola	48
paniculata	48
racemiflora	48
sparta	48
spicata	47
virgata	48
Urochloa reptans	250
uniseta	352
Valota	163
eggersii	165
insularis	165
laxa	165
Vasey grass	3, 229
Velvet bent	73
grass	68, 407
Vernalgrass, sweet	142
Vetiver	4, 407
Vetiveria	406
arundinacea	407
muricata	407
zizanioides	4, 406
Vilfa arguta	84
berteroana	82
domingensis	85
indica	82
jacquemontii	82
richardi	84
virginica	87
Water-grass	3
paspalum	3
Wedgegrass	62
prairie	64
Wheat	4, 61
Wild cane	4, 51
Wild oat	31, 152
Wine grass	4
Witchgrass	255
Wynne grass	4
Yaragua	4
Yellow bristlegrass	339
Zacate gordura	161
Zeugites	58
americana	58
haitiensis	58
haitiensis	58
jamaicensis	58
Zizanieae	10, 149
Zoysia matrella	426
Zoysieae	8, 98